analyzing social data
a statistical orientation

analyzing
social data

a statistical orientation

Karl Schuessler *Indiana University*

Houghton Mifflin Company · Boston

New York · Atlanta · Geneva, Illinois · Dallas · Palo Alto

Library of Congress Catalog Card Number: 70-130657

ISBN: 0-395-05384-6

To Lucille, my wife

Contents

9 Transformation of Statistical Data

Preface

Our complete title was chosen to reflect the concerns of this book as well as its contents. Our concern with data analysis is reflected in the main title. Lately, the attention of statistically-minded sociologists has shifted somewhat from data analysis to causal analysis. But in many investigations there is little or no warrant for causal analysis, and data analysis alone may be justified. Much social research is undertaken to isolate factors of relevance in a given effect which is considered to be problematic. In such work, the aim is to establish empirical regularities without regard to the causal mechanisms producing them, although these mechanisms may be considered subsequently. The 1965 survey of educational opportunity and achievement, carried out under the auspices of the U.S. Office of Education, has been criticized* on the grounds that no causal model was stated and tested. But that criticism may be countered, and has been,** by the point that knowledge about educational opportunity and achievement is too meager at the moment to permit the formulation of a causal scheme. An emphasis on data analysis is warranted by the continuing need in sociology for reliable empirical knowledge.

The subtitle, "A Statistical Orientation," reflects our concern with orientation as well as with methods and techniques. The orientation which this volume seeks to foster will probably survive long after the technical details have been forgotten. This orientation is essentially a habit of planning to the end that factors in a given effect be disentangled and measured, and that spurious relations be detected and exposed. The subtitle also serves to underline our goal of directing the student to a body of useful technical knowledge which will contribute to his research prowess. Some of this knowledge is embodied in the references at the end of each chapter. These references cover not only methods and techniques, but also applications of those methods in sociology.

Much of this book's content had its inception in questions arising regularly in the intermediate course in social statistics (for first-year graduate students in sociology) for which published answers are overly technical or unhandy,

---

* Cain, Glen G. and Harold W. Watts. "Problems in making policy inferences from the Coleman Report." *American Sociological Review* 35 (1970): 228–241.
** Coleman, James S. "Reply to Cain and Watts." *American Sociological Review* 35 (1970): 242–248.

or both. Examples of such questions are: "How does one factor a matrix?" "What are communalities?" "What is a rotation?" "When are classifications in a two-way table orthogonal?" "Why are results for cluster samples less precise than those for simple random samples?" "What is the difference between a scalogram and a latent structure?" "Is it true that a measure's validity can be no greater than its reliability?" "What is meant by rectifying a plotted relationship?" Although authoritative answers to these questions appear in many places, they are seldom framed with the sociologist in mind. Furthermore, they seldom appear in sociological writing and are usually unhandy for those who must (of necessity) limit themselves to that literature. Our aim is to make available materials which are technically manageable and which may be profitably used either collaterally in the course in intermediate social statistics or perhaps as a base in a seminar on sociological methodology.

From the above paragraph, it is clear that the book was written with the student in mind rather than his mentor. Consistent with this objective, our discourse is restricted to the level of elementary algebra. No one would deny the advantages of more advanced mathematics for purposes of compact expression, but the employment of these methods would restrict the range of potential users. For the same reason we give no strict statistical proofs; in fact, we are basically unqualified to do that. Here and there, we give statistical arguments in support of a particular conclusion or result, but none of these would be construed as a rigorous proof. We anticipate that these formulations may induce the more quantitatively-minded student to examine the technical literature on which they are based.

In any event, one cannot become proficient from the narrative alone. For more than a superficial understanding of methods, it will be necessary to carry out the numerical exercises by hand. Such calculations take on added significance with the accessibility of the computer. With the computer to do the work, there is a tendency to forego manual operations entirely, even at the instructional stage, and to rely altogether on electrically powered machinery. This natural tendency to save time and energy may have perverse consequences: (1) methods may be mindlessly applied without regard for their assumptions, and (2) researchers may be unable to carry out necessary checks by hand. These considerations underline the value of hand operations, especially during the period of professional training. To lessen the drudgery of such operations, we have scaled down the exercises to unrealistic proportions and given answers to most of the numerical problems.

The matter of statistical notation, always troublesome, is even more so with a volume covering various and sundry topics. In statistical writing, notation varies not only from one topic to another, but also within the same topic. Consequently, notation will be lacking in uniformity, unless we adhere to a standard system, such as that recommended by the Committee of Presidents of Statistical Societies' Committee on Notation and Symbols.* But the

---

* Halpern, Max, H. O. Hartley and P. G. Hoel. "Recommended standards for statistical symbols and notation." *The American Statistician* 19 (1965): 12–14.

adoption of that system would militate against the use of our primary sources, which we wish to encourage.

Statistical notation has been curtailed to the point that some expressions will appear as incomplete to the statistically-trained eye. These omissions reflect our judgment that the cost of losing students is greater than the cost of a little ambiguity. One typographical feature requires special mention: to represent "i" as an ordinal number, we have attached "th" to that letter as a superscript. Although it is more conventional to attach "th" as a suffix, we believe that our somewhat unorthodox style leaves less room for possible misunderstanding. To reduce clutter we have numbered only those formulas to which reference is made in the narrative. Numbers may be assigned to unnumbered formulas by the reader; these could be "interpolated" by means of an additional period.

The book is not statistically self-contained, and at least a beginning course in statistics or its equivalent is a prerequisite to its study and use. Some familiarity with correlation, sampling, the analysis of variance, significance testing, statistical expectations, and the like is presupposed. Although basic methods could be covered concurrently with special topics, that schedule would make unrealistically heavy demands on the students' time. To make it more self-sufficient, we have covered a few topics which are usually taken up in the first course in social statistics. Notwithstanding these "reviews," which presumably will yield fresh insights, the book cannot be very profitably pursued by one without some training in statistical methods.

Nor is the book self-contained in a topical sense. The selection of topics was not by abstract scheme, but rather pragmatically in response to questions raised by students. One commentator wondered whether the general linear model might not be employed as a unifying theme and whether topics such as path analysis might not be included as special cases of that model. There is merit in this suggestion, but this suggestion is at odds with our concept of a book of questions and answers rather than a formal system of axioms and deductions. It should also be noted that the priorities of sociological methodologists are subject to flux, and that specific methods wax and wane in their popularity. Just now, as previously noted, causal equations and their like are under exploration in sociology, and some readers would doubtless have preferred a discussion of that topic. But the day of the self-sufficient course book is past, and we have increasingly come to rely on a panel of several or more books.

With the many numbers in this book, mistakes will occur—mistakes in calculating, in transcribing, in linotyping, etc. Although we have made a diligent effort to catch these, we admit to their probable existence. As a counter to this gloomy prospect, a friendly student remarked that many readers get much pleasure in finding mistakes. By this psychology, we turn vice into virtue.

Karl Schuessler

Acknowledgments

Since it is practically impossible to list all contributing to this book, it seems proper to issue a note of blanket appreciation at the start. By this device, we discharge our total indebtedness and, incidentally, affirm that a book is the product of many minds and many hands. However, if we were to stop with this and say no more, we would forego the pleasure of thanking those whose help was expressly solicited. Although these persons are not legion in number, they are more than a small group.

We are in debt to the following publishers for permission to reproduce materials on which they hold copyright: The American Public Health Association, Inc.; The Biometric Society and Professor M. S. Bartlett; The British Psychological Society; Cambridge University Press; Iowa State University Press; The Macmillan Company and The Free Press; Princeton University Press; The University of Chicago Press; and the Wayne State University Press. Also, I am indebted to the Literary Executor of the late Sir Ronald A. Fisher, F.R.S., and to Oliver & Boyd, Edinburgh, for their permission to reprint Tables 4 and 5 from their book *Statistical Methods for Research Workers*. Moreover, I am indebted to the Literary Executor of the late Sir Ronald A. Fisher, F.R.S.; to Dr. Frank Yates, F.R.S.; and to Oliver & Boyd, Edinburgh, for permission to reprint Tables III, IV, and V from their book *Statistical Tables for Biological, Agricultural and Medical Research*.

A number of persons read longer or shorter parts of the manuscript and indicated respects in which it might be wanting and ways in which it might be refined. The materials on correlation and factor analysis were critically reviewed by Duncan McRae, Jr.; those on sampling and the analysis of variance and covariance by Kalton Graham; the materials on measurement and transformation by David R. Heise. Since the changes they prompted carry no special markings, it is necessary to make this public declaration of their worth. This holds equally true for changes suggested by persons reading lesser portions of the manuscript: Roland J. Chilton, Dean Harper, Neil W. Henry, Richard J. Hill, Elton F. Jackson, Gerald Slatin, and Joseph L. Zinnes. For many improvements, credit is theirs; but they do not share in the responsibility for needed improvements.

The persons on whose writings I mainly drew may be discerned from the name index; hence, it is unnecessary to list them here. I would like to make one exception: in my excursions into the field of statistics, I came to rely in particular on the writings of William G. Cochran. I mention this not only to express admiration, but also to guide fellow sociologists wishing to explore some of the primary sources on which this volume rests. As statistical laymen, they would surely appreciate Cochran's instinct for clear and plain writing.

The numerous examples and exercises reflect the endeavors of graduate students in sociology, past or present, who assisted in the course for which these materials were developed. Phyllis N. Greenfield and Philip R. Weinberger collected problems for Chapters 1–3; Charles E. Starnes for Chapters 4–6; James Kretz for Chapter 7. Albert S. Gates did the calculations for Table 9.2.3 and also prepared some of the exercises for Chapter 9. Lois Downey not only contributed exercises here and there, but also checked the computations in the text and independently calculated the answers in the key. Ann Springfield worked out many numerical examples, only a fraction of which could be practically included in the published text. I am grateful to the aforementioned students who helped me so conscientiously in these matters.

In the difficult typing of the manuscript, Jane Wellman persevered with civility and good humor, even as corrections were added to corrections. I am indeed grateful to her. Also, to Anita L. Reynolds who graciously helped in the final stages and who was unperturbed by the call for last-minute changes. In preparing the manuscript for the publisher, I was materially assisted by Lena Dunn Lo, whose discerning eye caught not only mistakes in spelling, arithmetic, and the like, but also inelegancies in language, which she removed. Also, my thanks to Margaret Connors of Houghton Mifflin for her helpful suggestions and for expeditiously moving the manuscript from the publisher's desk to the print shop.

One last word: I would be remiss in not noting the favorable conditions at Indiana University for research and writing. I am particularly indebted to Byrum Carter, who, as Dean of the College of Arts and Sciences in 1968, created a special dispensation for me which enormously facilitated the completion of this project.

K.S.

1

Correlation

PART 1
Simple Correlation

Foreword. The current interest in factor analysis among sociologists is naturally related to its increased use in sociological research. Practically every issue of the major professional sociological journals contains one or more articles in which there are references to the results of factor analysis. This upward trend in the use of factor analysis has led students in sociology to be concerned about the details of its scope and method. The common questions include: What is it? Is it applicable to sociological data? When is its use appropriate? Is a strong background in mathematics necessary to understand it?

Our object in this and the next two chapters is to provide answers to some of these questions. The materials in these chapters, together with the exercises, will enable the student to "read the literature" and to assess, at least in a preliminary way, the suitability of factor analysis for a given research problem. Those who wish to become specialists in factor analysis would have to master all or most of the contents of several of the standard treatises on the subject (Harman 1967; Horst 1965; Thurstone 1947) and some of the journal literature.

Since factor analysis begins with simple correlations, and since it is closely linked to multiple and partial correlation, we begin in this chapter with a consideration of these procedures. In developing these methods, we regard correlation as the proportion of variance in the dependent variable that is attributable to one or more independent variables. From this standpoint, correlation is a technique for partitioning the variance, belonging to the general family of methods whose common goal is the analysis of variance into its several parts. It goes without saying that multiple and partial correlation are extremely versatile procedures whose utility is not limited to factor analysis, but rather extends over a wide range of problems. For example, the study of causal inferences from nonexperimental data (Simon 1957; Blalock 1964) leans on the manipulation of partial correlations; similarly, the prediction of one social characteristic from two or more related characteristics (Duncan 1961) is usually undertaken within the framework of multiple correlation.

Correlation Defined. On an abstract level, it is useful to define correlation as the degree to which one variable may be predicted from another variable. If we can predict X_0 from X_1 without error, the correlation between them is said to be perfect; if our prediction of X_0 is no better with the aid of X_1 than without it, the two variables are said to be perfectly uncorrelated. When correlation is thus defined, each dependent value may be regarded as the algebraic sum of two terms: (1) the value of X_0 predicted from X_1, symbolized $\hat{X}_{0.1}$, and (2) the deviation (algebraic) of the observed value from the predicted value, symbolized $X_{0.1}$. As an equation:

$$X_0 = \hat{X}_{0.1} + (X_0 - \hat{X}_{0.1})$$
$$= \hat{X}_{0.1} + X_{0.1},$$

where $X_{0.1} = X_0 - \hat{X}_{0.1}$. Table 1.1.1 is designed to clarify this conception of X_0 as the sum of its components. Subtracting predicted values (Column 3) from corresponding observed values (Column 2), we get residuals (Column 4); adding residuals to predicted values, we get observed

Table 1.1.1 *Observed Value as Sum of Predicted Value and Error*

	(1)	(2)	(3)	(4)
Case No.	X_1	X_0	$\hat{X}_{0.1}$	$X_0 - \hat{X}_{0.1} = X_{0.1}$
1	19	15	13.3	1.7
2	16	11	10.8	.2
3	15	10	10.0	.0
4	11	7	6.7	.3
5	17	8	11.7	−3.7
6	14	9	9.2	− .2
7	18	13	12.5	.5
8	13	12	8.3	3.7
9	12	5	7.5	−2.5
Sum	135	90	90.0	0.0
Mean	15	10	10.0	0.0

values. Our prediction is perfect for No. 3, but in error by 3.7 for No. 5. Clearly, the more nearly $\hat{X}_{0.1}$ resembles X_0 in a series of measures, the higher the correlation between the two variables.

If we lay down the restriction that predicted values be statistically independent of residual values, we may write the variance of X_0 as the sum of its component variances: (1) the variance of the predicted values, and (2) the variance of the residuals (by the rule that the variance of a sum of statistically independent variables is the sum of their variances). In symbols:

$$\sigma_0^2 = \hat{\sigma}_{0.1}^2 + \sigma_{0.1}^2.$$

Expressing the explained variance as a proportion of the total variance, we get the ratio,

(1.1.1) $$\hat{\sigma}_{0.1}^2/\sigma_0^2.$$

The numerical value of this ratio gives the proportion of variance in X_0 attributable to X_1. It is thus a measure of correlation between X_0 and X_1. Since $0 < \hat{\sigma}_{0.1}^2 < \sigma_0^2$, this ratio (1.1.1) will take values only on the interval from 0 to 1. At one extreme, when X_0 is perfectly predictable from X_1, $\hat{\sigma}_{0.1}^2$ is equal to σ_0^2, and the correlation ratio $\hat{\sigma}_{0.1}^2/\sigma_0^2$ is equal to 1; at the other extreme, when $\hat{\sigma}_{0.1}^2$ is equal to zero, the ratio $\hat{\sigma}_{0.1}^2/\sigma_0^2$ will likewise be equal to zero, signifying the absence of correlation between the two variables.

Simple and Multiple Correlation Compared. We expect that a combination of two or more variables may yield a more accurate prediction than one alone. In such cases, our correlation is between a dependent variable X_0 and a composite variable which itself is a function of $X_1, X_2, \ldots, X_n$, (where $n =$ the number of predictor variables). We may correlate occupational prestige X_0 with a composite of income X_1 and education X_2.

The variables which have been combined are identified in the secondary subscript on the predicted value. For example, in the expression

$$X_0 = \hat{X}_{0.12} + (X_0 - \hat{X}_{0.12}),$$

the subscript "0.12" signifies that variables X_1 and X_2 have been pooled for purposes of predicting X_0.

Since $\hat{\sigma}_{0.12\ldots n}^2$ denotes that part of the total variance σ_0^2 attributable to the pool of n independent variables, the ratio, $\hat{\sigma}_{0.12\ldots n}^2/\sigma_0^2$, is a measure of multiple correlation. It registers the joint influence of n independent variables on the dependent variable X_0. When the ratio of explained to total variance registers the influence of a simple rather than a compound variable, it is a measure of simple correlation. In this section we restrict ourselves to simple correlation.

Figure 1.1.1 *Linear Scatter,* $\hat{X}_{0.1} = -2.5 + .83X_1$

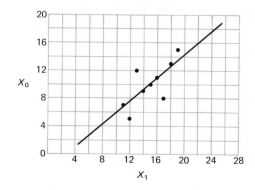

Predicting the Dependent Variable X_0 from X_1. Our discussion, up to this point, has been on an abstract level, without reference to operating procedures which would endow $\hat{\sigma}^2_{0.1}$ with statistical meaning. Ideally, we would determine $\hat{\sigma}^2_{0.1}$ in such a manner that none of the potentially reproducible variation in X_0 is excluded. Our goal is to predict as much of the variation in X_0 as possible and thereby to maximize $\hat{\sigma}^2_{0.1}$, or equivalently to minimize the unexplained variance, $\sigma^2_{0.1}$.

Now, to predict X_0 from X_1, we must assume that X_0 changes on X_1 in some systematic manner; in other words, we assume that X_0 is a mathematical function of X_1. Our problem then is to select that function (curve) which will maximize $\hat{\sigma}^2_{0.1}$. Technically speaking, we choose that curve which best fits the plot of observed data, since that curve will permit us to predict the dependent variable with the least error. In the last analysis, the explained variance rests on such an empirically fitted curve (equation).

When the change in X_0 per unit change of X_1 is approximately uniform over the range of X_1, as in Figure 1.1.1, a linear equation of the form

(1.1.2) $$\hat{X}_{0.1} = a + bX_1$$

may do very well (where a is the value of $\hat{X}_{0.1}$ when $X_1 = 0$, and b is the constant change in $\hat{X}_{0.1}$ per unit change of X_1). Obviously, if we fit a straight line to a compact swarm whose trend is linear, the observed values will not diverge greatly from those predicted and, correspondingly, the error variance ($\sigma^2_{0.1}$) will be small. By the same token, the predicted, or explained, variance ($\hat{\sigma}^2_{0.1}$) will be large, as will be the ratio of the explained to total variance.

In other cases, where the relationship between X_0 and X_1 is curvilinear, we may select a higher degree equation for purposes of predicting X_0. Thus, if the plot of X_0 on X_1 resembles a parabola (Figure 1.1.2), we might adopt a second degree equation of the form $a + bX_1 + cX_1^2$. If the plot is marked by two peaks, we might have recourse to an equation of the third degree, $a + bX_1 + cX_1^2 + dX_1^3$. Since we are free to choose a curve of any form,

Figure 1.1.2   *Curvilinear Scatter,* $\hat{X}_{0.1} = 8.5 + .17X_1$

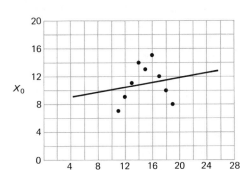

it would seem logical at first blush to select that curve (equation) which gives the best prediction and, in consequence, the largest possible value of the explained variance. But in practice we seldom choose the best-fitting curve; rather, we pragmatically select the simplest model yielding results of requisite accuracy. We sacrifice goodness of fit for simplicity of representation.

Prediction by Straight Line. As a rule, we base our prediction on a straight line, which will fit very well when the plot of X_0 and X_1 is actually linear (Figure 1.1.1), but will be a poor fit when the plot is curvilinear (Figure 1.1.2). But why use a straight line in instances when a curve would fit better? One answer, possibly platitudinous, is this: "Whenever that procedure will satisfy the requirements of our research." If we wish to express the relationship between two variables in the most economical fashion, we would use a straight line, since a curve with one or more bends will produce more complex results. Or, if we are required only to place a lower limit on the degree of correlation, we would likewise use a straight line, since generally a curve will produce a larger correlation coefficient. We may be confident that a straight line will never exaggerate the degree of correlation, although it may fail to do it justice. Since a straight line cannot pick up the curvilinear components in a relationship, it will yield a conservative measure of relationship.

A second answer, reflecting an altogether different principle, is this: "Whenever it is possible to change a curvilinear scatter into a linear one." It is often possible to rectify (straighten out) a curvilinear plot by suitably transforming one or both variables, after which transformation we may use the straight line as a basis for measuring correlation (see Chapter 9). Instead of fitting our line to the curvature in the scatter, we adjust the scatter so that its shape is approximately linear and amenable to accurate description by a straight line. Or we may achieve linearity by ignoring the outliers in a linear swarm, if we have reason to believe that such exceptions to the main trend are attributable to extraneous and accidental factors. We redress our scatter, so to speak, by removing the deviant cases.

Principle of Least Squares. Although the decision to employ a straight line in the form, $a + bX_1$, may be questionable in a given problem, there usually can be little question about the choice of the constants, a and b, once that decision has been made. For, given that decision, we wish to solve for a and b in such a manner as to yield the best fit of line to the plotted swarm. If we agree that the fit is best when the sum of the squared residuals is least, then we must find those constants which will minimize the sum of the squared errors. This test of best fit is termed the "least squares criterion," and requires that we minimize the quantity $\sum(X_0 - \hat{X}_{0.1})^2$, where $\hat{X}_{0.1} = a + bX_1$. (We note in passing that predicted values and residuals will be independent when the criterion of least squares is met.)

Standard Measures. It is in the solution of this problem that the convenience of standard measures becomes quite evident. To convert a set of values into standard measures, we take the mean from each value and divide that algebraic deviation by the standard deviation. In common notation: $x' = \dfrac{X - \bar{X}}{\sigma}$. Technically speaking, we shift the origin of our scale to the mean and adopt the standard deviation as our scale unit. Such measures, here symbolized x', have properties which make them especially amenable to manipulation. In particular, for a complete set of standard measures:

(1)
$$\sum_{1}^{N} x' = 0,$$

(2)
$$\sum(x' - \bar{x}')^2 = \sum(x')^2,$$

(3)
$$\frac{1}{N}\sum x'^2 = \frac{1}{N}\sum\left(\frac{x}{\sigma}\right)^2 = \frac{\sum x^2}{N\sigma^2} = 1,$$

(4)
$$\sum x'^2 = N.$$

Since these results will be used with some regularity, it will not be amiss to put them in words for emphasis and reference: (1) the sum of a complete set of standard measures is zero; hence, their mean is zero; (2) the sum of the squared standard measures is equal to the sum of the squared deviations around the mean; (3) the variance (σ^2) of a complete set of standard measures is 1; hence, the standard deviation is 1; (4) the sum of the squared standard measures is equal to their number, N.

With all measures in standard form, $\sigma^2 = 1$, and in consequence $\hat{\sigma}_{0.1}^2 + \sigma_{0.1}^2 = 1$. The ratio of predicted to total variance then simplifies to $\hat{\sigma}_{0.1}^2$, conventionally symbolized r_{01}^2; the ratio of the error variance to the total variance simplifies to $\sigma_{0.1}^2 = 1 - r_{01}^2$.

Formulas for Constants. With raw measures in standard form, we seek those values of a and b which will minimize the sum of the squared errors as defined above. As a reminder that we are in standard form, and in the absence of overriding convention, we shall substitute the Greek letters α and β in Equation (1.1.4) for italicized letters a and b. Our problem, subject to the restriction that predicted values and errors be statistically independent, is to determine the constants α and β simultaneously, so that $\hat{\sigma}_{0.1}^2$ will be as large as possible, or, equivalently, $\sigma_{0.1}^2$, as small as possible. It is of interest, as well as practically convenient, that there is a general solution to this problem which permits these constants to be readily calculated by formula.

It may be proved by mathematical methods that the sum of the squared errors will be least when

$$\alpha = 0,$$

(1.1.3)
$$\beta_{01} = \frac{\sum x_0' x_1'}{\sum x_1'^2}.$$

Our straight line equation, $a + bX_1$, then takes the form:

$$\hat{x}_{0.1} = \beta_{01} x_1'.$$

Without further ado, we may now express the component variances in terms of predicted and residual values:

(1.1.4)
$$\hat{\sigma}_{0.1}^2 = \frac{1}{N} \sum (\beta_{01} x_1')^2,$$

(1.1.5)
$$\sigma_{0.1}^2 = \frac{1}{N} \sum (x_0 - \beta_{01} x_1')^2.$$

The mean of the squared regression values has come to be known as *the explained variance*, and its complement—the mean of the squared residuals— as *the unexplained variance*.

Before we proceed to multiple correlation, it may be profitable to examine the structure of β_{01}, since higher-order regression coefficients are of the same general form. Dividing both terms on the right (1.1.3) by the number of cases N, we get

$$\beta_{01} = \frac{\dfrac{\sum x_0' x_1'}{N}}{\dfrac{\sum x_1'^2}{N}}$$

$$= \sigma_{01}/\sigma_1^2.$$

The denominator is the variance of the independent variable in standard form; the numerator is the mean product of paired deviations, each in standard form, or the covariance of X_0 and X_1 in standard form, which is here symbolized σ_{01}. It is pertinent that any linear regression coefficient, whatever its order (p. 25), may be expressed as the ratio of a covariance to a variance, so that we may readily get a required regression coefficient when the corresponding covariance and variance are known.

Lastly, we note that the standardized regression coefficient (β_{01}) and the correlation coefficient (r_{01}), defined as the covariance of X_0 and X_1 in standard form, are algebraically identical:

$$r_{01} = \frac{1}{N} \sum x_0' x_1'$$
$$= \beta_{01} \frac{1}{N} \sum x_1'^2$$
$$= \beta_{01}(1)$$
$$= \beta_{01}.$$

However, the unstandardized covariance of X and Y is not equal to the unstandardized regression coefficient of Y on X: $\frac{1}{N} \sum xy \neq \frac{\sum xy}{\sum x^2}$. If our problem calls for these coefficients, as in some kinds of causal analysis (Blalock 1968), we must carry out our calculations on the raw measures.

EXERCISES

1. Given the following series: 2, 8, 11, 13, 13, 13,
   (a) Calculate the mean and the standard deviation, and convert each raw measure into a standard measure.
   (b) Verify that
   $$\sum x' = 0,$$
   $$\bar{x}' = 0,$$
   $$\sum (x' - \bar{x}')^2 = \sum (x')^2,$$
   $$\sigma_{x'}^2 = 1,$$
   $$\sum x'^2 = N.$$

2. Given:

X_0	X_1
1	2
3	8
5	11
7	13
9	13
11	13

(a) Convert X_0 and X_1 to standard form and find r_{01}^2.

(b) Verify that $r_{01} = \beta_{01}$.

3. Given the following hypothetical figures on suicide (X_0) and income (X_1):

X_0	X_1
18	47
16	47
15	55
14	57
14	57
11	98
13	100
12	90
13	78

(a) Compute $r_{01} = \dfrac{\sum x_0 x_1}{\sqrt{\sum x_0^2 \sum x_1^2}}$.

(b) Convert X_0 and X_1 to standard form and verify that $r_{01} = \dfrac{1}{N}\sum x_0' x_1'$.

(c) Compute $\hat{x}_{0.1} = \beta_{01} x_1'$ and

$\qquad x_{0.1} = x_0' - \beta_{01} x_1'$.

(d) Verify that $\sum \hat{x}_{0.1} x_{0.1} = 0$.

(e) Verify that $\dfrac{1}{N}\sum \hat{x}_{0.1}^2 = r_{01}^2$.

(f) What proportion of the variance in suicide (X_0) is attributable to income (X_1)?

4. Plot X_0 and X_1 (Exercise 3) as a scatter diagram:

(a) Draw what appears to be the best-fitting straight line through the scatter of points.

(b) From your freehand line, estimate the change in X_0 per unit increase in X_1.

(c) Could the fit be improved by allowing the line to "bend" in one or more places?

5. Plot the following time series on arithmetic graph paper:

X_0	X_1
16	1890
18	1900
40	1910
74	1920
148	1930
203	1940
334	1950

(a) Make a freehand drawing of the best-fitting straight line.

(b) Could the fit be improved by allowing the line to "bend" as a growth curve?
(c) Take the common logarithm of X_0 and plot these logs on X_1.
(d) Draw a straight line through this scatter of points. Has the fit been improved? Explain why it has or has not.

6. Given: $\hat{x}_{0.1} = \beta_{01}x_1'$ and
$$x_{0.1} = x_0' - \beta_{01}x_1'.$$
Show: $\dfrac{1}{N}\sum \hat{x}_{0.1}^2 + \dfrac{1}{N}\sum x_{0.1}^2 = 1.$

7. Show that $\beta_{01} = \beta_{10}$. (Hint: express β_{01} as a covariance divided by a variance.)

8. Show that $\hat{\sigma}_{0.1}^2 = \hat{\sigma}_{1.0}^2$. What principle is suggested by this identity?

PART 2
Multiple Correlation

Multiple Correlation Defined. Multiple correlation may be defined broadly as the correlation between a single variable and a combination of two or more predictor variables. The correlation between delinquency and a composite of income and education is a multiple correlation. More restrictively, and as used here, it is the correlation between the dependent variable, X_0, and the sum of n independent variables (regressors), each weighted so as to minimize the sum of the squared deviations between X_0 and that sum.

As in simple correlation, we regard each observed value as the sum of two parts: its predicted value and its deviation from that predicted value. In symbols:
$$X_0 = \hat{X}_{0.12...n} + (X_0 - \hat{X}_{0.12...n}),$$
where the secondary subscript (to the right of the period) designates by numerals 1 through n the variables which have been pooled for purposes of prediction. On the assumption that component terms are statistically independent, we may write the total variance as the sum of its component variances:
$$\sigma_0^2 = \hat{\sigma}_{0.12...n}^2 + \sigma_{0.12...n}^2.$$

Expressing the explained variance as a fraction of the total variance, we get the squared multiple correlation (*SMC*), conventionally symbolized $R_{0.12...n}^2$. Thus:
$$R_{0.12...n}^2 = \frac{\hat{\sigma}_{0.12...n}^2}{\sigma_0^2}.$$

Since R^2 is a measure of the influence of two or more predictor variables, it is called "coefficient of multiple determination."

As in simple correlation, we proceed as if X_0 changed in a determinate manner on the set consisting of X_1 and X_2 and ... X_n. Again, our problem is to choose whichever equation (curve) fits best in the sense of minimizing the sum of the squared deviations between X_0 and that equation. Nevertheless, as in simple correlation, we start ordinarily with the simplest model, which we either retain intact or modify for a better fit as the analysis unfolds. The simplest model combining two or more predictor variables is an equation of the form:

(1.2.1) $$\hat{X}_{0.12...n} = a + b_1 X_1 + b_2 X_2 + \cdots + b_n X_n.$$

Equation (1.2.1), it will be recognized, is an extension of (1.1.2) which is the basis of simple linear correlation. Equation (1.2.1) specializes to (1.1.2) when $n = 1$. Since all variables in Equation (1.2.1) are of degree 1, and since variables are added up but not multiplied together, the expression on the right side is sometimes referred to as a linear, additive model.

Statement of the Problem. The fundamental problem in multiple linear correlation is to find those weights (b_i's) which will minimize the unexplained (partial) variance $\sigma^2_{0.12...n}$. However, our limited goal is to supply a simplified procedure for computing that variance from the zero-order correlations among the $n + 1$ variables. With the unexplained variance in hand, we need only to subtract it from the total variance to get the explained variance, which in turn may be expressed as a fraction of the total variance for the squared multiple correlation, R^2. In its essentials, this procedure entails removing the influence of n independent variables in sequence 1 through n, until the influence of all n of them has been removed from the dependent variable, X_0. Since the unexplained variance is cumulatively reduced in a sequence consisting of $n + 1$ stages, the entire process has come to be known as "reducing the criterion variance."

Remark. Although the order in which the n variables are removed has no effect on the value of R^2, we may remove at each stage (except the first which is preparatory) whichever variable will reduce as much as possible the unexplained variance. In the second stage, we eliminate whichever variable will reduce as much as possible the total variance; in the third stage, we remove whichever variable will reduce as much as possible the variance left standing at the end of the second stage. Since only one variable will remain after n stages, we necessarily eliminate that variable in the $(n + 1)^{\text{th}}$ stage. Variables are thus removed according to the magnitude of their effect on the unresolved variance; statistically speaking, we choose for elimination whichever variable will yield the smallest unexplained variance. The term "stepwise regression" is sometimes applied to those procedures in which variables (regressors) are removed according to a well-defined statistical criterion. Such methods are not without their difficulties. For a discussion and evaluation, see Draper and Smith (1966).

Reducing the Criterion Variance. As an exemplification of this process, we consider in detail the manageable case of two independent variables, X_1 and X_2, which we shall correlate with the dependent variable X_0. Our analysis will culminate in a second-order partial (unexplained) variance expressible as a difference between first-order terms as follows:

(1.2.2) $$\sigma^2_{0.12} = \sigma^2_{0.2} - \beta_{01.2}\sigma_{01.2}.$$

To give meaning to this expression, we set forth the procedure for obtaining first-order terms on the right side from zero-order terms which we take as given.* Once these first-order terms have been gotten, they may be substituted in (1.2.2) to get the sought-for second-order partial variance, which may be subtracted from 1.00 for $R^2_{0.12}$. Throughout, it is to be understood that each measure will have been reduced by its mean and that remainder divided by its standard deviation before we begin this operation. In brief, all measures will be in standard form.

Partial Variance, $\sigma^2_{i.j}$. We are familiar with the procedure for finding a first-order partial variance from zero-order terms: subtract the explained variance r^2_{01} from the total variance which is equal to 1. In symbols:

(1.2.3) $$\sigma^2_{0.1} = 1 - r^2_{01}.$$

The variance remaining in X_0, after the influence of X_1 has been statistically removed, is equal to the total variance minus the explained variance. This procedure rests on the general principle that a partial (unexplained) variance of order n may be obtained from terms of order $n - 1$, and, conversely, that terms of order $n - 1$ may be manipulated to yield a partial variance of order n. An implication is that, starting with zero-order terms, we may eventually get an nth order partial variance.

Partial Covariance, $\sigma_{ij.k}$. The procedure for finding the first-order partial covariance $\sigma_{ij.k}$ is possibly less familiar to the student. To unfold that procedure, we start with the definition of the covariance of two variables, X and

---

* The order of a term is equal to the number of variables whose influence has been statistically removed. Those variables are listed in the secondary subscript. For example, r_{01} represents a zero-order correlation; $r_{01.2}$ represents a first-order partial correlation; $r_{01.23}$ represents a second-order partial correlation; etc.

Y, as the mean of the products:

$$\sigma_{xy} = \frac{1}{N} \sum (X - \bar{X})(Y - \bar{Y}).$$

Our immediate object is the covariance of the paired residuals, $x_{i.k}$ and $x_{j.k}$, or the covariance between i and j after each has been adjusted for the effect of k. To get that covariance, we express each residual as a deviation from its mean, form products, sum, and divide by N. But the mean of a complete set of residuals is zero;* hence, the covariance is the mean product of the residuals themselves:

(1.2.4) $$\sigma_{ij.k} = \frac{1}{N} \sum (x_i' - \beta_{ik}x_k')(x_j' - \beta_{jk}x_k').$$

Because this result is based on partial values, it is termed a *partial covariance*; it is a *first-order* partial covariance because partial values are rid of the influence of one variable, as indicated by the secondary subscript. The expression on the right (1.2.4) is subject to considerable simplification. Multiplying binomials, summing, and dividing by N, we get

$$\frac{1}{N} \sum x_i'x_j' - \beta_{ik} \frac{1}{N} \sum x_j'x_k' - \beta_{jk} \frac{1}{N} \sum x_i'x_k' + \beta_{ik}\beta_{jk} \frac{1}{N} \sum x_k'x_k'.$$

Relabeling, we get

$$\sigma_{ij} - \beta_{ik}\sigma_{jk} - \beta_{jk}\sigma_{ik} + \beta_{ik}\sigma_{jk},$$

which reduces to

(1.2.5) $$\sigma_{ij} - \beta_{ik}\sigma_{jk} = \sigma_{ij.k}.$$

This formula is an instance of the generalization that a partial covariance of order n is equal to a partial covariance of order $n - 1$ minus the product of a regression coefficient and partial covariance of order $n - 1$. Substituting our numbers for letters in (1.2.5), we get

$$\sigma_{01.2} = \sigma_{01} - \beta_{02}\sigma_{12}.$$

---

* Explanation:
$$\sum (x_i' - \beta_{ij}x_j') = \sum x_i' - \beta_{ij}\sum x_j'$$
$$= 0 - \beta_{ij}(0)$$
$$= 0.$$

Standardized Partial Regression Coefficient, $\beta_{ij.k}$. As previously noted, the fundamental problem in multiple correlation is to choose the regression coefficients so as to minimize the unexplained variance (or maximize the explained variance). In particular, when $n = 2$ and

$$\hat{x}_{i.jk} = \alpha + \beta_{ij.k}x'_j + \beta_{ik.j}x'_k,$$

where

$$\alpha = \text{value of } \hat{x}_{i.jk} \text{ with } x'_i \text{ and } x'_j \text{ zero,}$$
$$\beta_{ij.k} = \text{coefficient of } x'_j, \text{ and}$$
$$\beta_{ik.j} = \text{coefficient of } x'_k,$$

our problem is to choose α, $\beta_{ij.k}$, and $\beta_{ik.j}$ so as to minimize the sum of the squared residuals. It may be shown by standard mathematical methods that this sum will be least when

$$\alpha = 0,$$

(1.2.6)
$$\beta_{ij.k} = \sigma_{ij.k}/\sigma^2_{j.k}$$
$$= (\sigma_{ij} - \beta_{ik}\sigma_{jk})/(1 - \sigma^2_{jk}),$$

and

$$\beta_{ik.j} = \sigma_{ik.j}/\sigma^2_{k.j}$$
$$= (\sigma_{ik} - \beta_{ij}\sigma_{jk})(1 - \sigma^2_{kj}),$$

which serves to verify that first-order regression coefficients may be obtained from zero-order terms. In our example,

$$\beta_{01.2} = (\sigma_{01} - \beta_{02}\sigma_{12})/(1 - \sigma^2_{12}).$$

Partial Variance, $\sigma^2_{0.12}$. We now reverse ourselves and move in successive stages from zero-order terms to the sought-for partial variance, $\sigma^2_{0.12}$ (1.2.2), which we subtract from 1 for $R^2_{0.12}$. In this demonstration, it will be convenient to refer to a numerical example. Let us suppose that we are given intercorrelations among occupational prestige scores X_0, income X_1, and education X_2, as follows:

$$r_{01} = .80,$$
$$r_{02} = .70,$$
$$r_{12} = .30,$$

and that we wish to calculate the multiple correlation ($R_{0.12}$) between occupational prestige, income, and education. As a reference, we set down

$R_{0.12}^2$ in first-order terms:

$$R_{0.12}^2 = 1 - \sigma_{0.12}^2$$
$$= 1 - [\sigma_{0.2}^2 - \beta_{01.2}\sigma_{01.2}].$$

Using this formula as a guide, we get in succession:

$$\hat{\sigma}_{0.1}^2 = .64$$
$$\hat{\sigma}_{0.2}^2 = .49$$
$$\hat{\sigma}_{1.2}^2 = .09$$
$$\sigma_{0.2}^2 = 1.00 - .49 = .51$$
$$\sigma_{1.2}^2 = 1.00 - .09 = .91$$
$$\sigma_{01.2} = .80 - (.30)(.70) = .59$$
$$\beta_{01.2} = .59/.91.$$

Substituting these results, we get in a second round of calculations:

$$\sigma_{0.12}^2 = .51 - \frac{(.59)^2}{.91} = .11$$
$$R_{0.12}^2 = 1.00 - .11 = .89.$$

We interpret this to mean that 89 percent of the variance in prestige scores may be attributed to the combined influence of income and education.

Computation of R^2. We may regard the foregoing procedure as consisting of three stages, with zero-order terms occupying the first stage; first-order terms, the second stage; and second-order terms, the third and final stage. Generalizing from this example, we may state that a partial variance of order n may be gotten through a progression of $n + 1$ stages, each consisting of terms whose order is lower by one than the terms of the next succeeding stage, or higher by one than the terms of the immediately preceding stage. The burden of our discussion will be to illustrate this conclusion and to demonstrate the relative ease with which the squared multiple correlation, R^2, may be obtained by manual methods, when zero-order correlations are given.

Layout for One Independent Variable. We begin with the simplest case of all: that of a single independent variable (regressor). In the simplest case, where $n = 1$, multiple correlation is identical with simple correlation, since $\hat{\sigma}_{0.1}^2 = r_{01}^2$ by definition. Our procedure, anticipating the general procedure of which this is a special case, will be to compute the error variance $\sigma_{0.1}^2$ and subtract that result from the total variance σ_0^2 to obtain $R_{0.1}^2$. (If we are required to convert this result into r_{01}, we simply take its square root and attach the sign of the covariance, σ_{01}.)

For purposes of computing the partial (unexplained) variance, we set up a 2×2 table, reserving the first row and first column for the independent variable X_1 (in standard form) and the second row and second column for the dependent or criterion variable X_0. Rows and columns are labeled appropriately to show these assignments as follows:

	x_1'	x_0'
x_1'	σ_1^2	σ_{01}
x_0'	β_{01}	σ_0^2

	$x_{0.1}$	
$x_{0.1}$	$\sigma_{0.1}^2$	$1 - \sigma_{0.1}^2 = \hat{\sigma}_{0.1}^2$

At the same time, we prepare a 1×1 table, conveniently aligning it with the right-hand column of the 2×2 table which will stand immediately above it. In this single cell, we will enter $\sigma_{0.1}^2$, or the variance of x_0', with the effects of x_1' removed. Since $\sigma_{0.1}^2$ is a description of the partial variable $x_{0.1}$, we designate its row and column by the caption "$x_{0.1}$". (Since we do not transform partial measures into standard form, we attach no prime to the letter representing them.) Alongside this cell, we draw an answer box in which will be recorded the explained variance, $\hat{\sigma}_{0.1}^2$, or the squared multiple correlation, $R_{0.1}^2$.

With empty tables constructed in the aforesaid manner before us, we put σ_1^2 in the first row and first column, and σ_0^2 in the second row and second column. The total variances thus appear on the diagonally arranged cells, running from upper left to lower right—sometimes designated the major diagonal. Since measures were put in standard form at the start, each of these variances is necessarily equal to 1; hence, we may enter that numerical value in each of the cells on the major diagonal.

We may now calculate σ_{01}, the covariance of X_0 and X_1 in standard form, and record that result in the first row and second column. (It may be mentioned that covariances in this layout will always lie to the right of the major diagonal.) This result may be obtained by the computing formula with which the student is probably familiar:

$$\sigma_{01} = \frac{\sum x_0 x_1}{\sqrt{\sum x_0^2 \sum x_1^2}}.$$

We utilize this result, σ_{01}, together with the total variance σ_1^2, to find

$$\beta_{01} = \frac{\sigma_{01}}{\sigma_1^2},$$

which result is last to be recorded in the 2 × 2 table. Reduced to a routine: to get β_{01}, divide the entry in the first row, second column by the entry in the first row, first column, recording the answer in the second row, first colum. Given the placement of variances and covariances, the regression coefficients will necessarily be to the left of the major diagonal.

All numerical quantities for the solution of $\sigma_{0.1}^2 = \sigma_0^2 - \beta_{01}\sigma_{01}$ are now in hand. Accordingly, we multiply β_{01} and σ_{01}, which are located symmetrically on opposite sides of the diagonal, and subtract their product from σ_0^2. This result is recorded in the 1 × 1 table, which corresponds, as previously noted, to the second row and second column of the 2 × 2 table. The 1 × 1 table may be regarded as the 2 × 2 table stripped of the first row and first column. More strictly, it provides us with a record of the variation in X_0 after the influence of X_1 has been removed according to the prescribed procedure. It is this result, $\sigma_{0.1}^2$, which we use to calculate the squared multiple correlation, or $R_{0.1}^2$, the latter being equal to $1 - \sigma_{0.1}^2$.

Numerical Example. To calculate $R_{0.1}^2$ by this method, we set up a 2 × 2

	x_1'	x_2'
x_1'	1.00	.59
x_2'	.59	1.00

	$x_{0.1}$	
$x_{0.1}$	.65	$1.00 - .65 = .35$

table with values of 1 in cells of the major diagonal. Next, we calculate $\sigma_{01} = r_{01} = .59$ and enter this result to the right of the diagonal. Dividing .59 by 1.00, we obtain $\beta_{01} = .59$, which we enter to the left of the diagonal. To get $\sigma_{0.1}^2$, we subtract the product of β_{01} and σ_{01} from 1.00: $1.00 - (.59)(.59) = .65$. We enter this result in the 1 × 1 table, which we will have aligned on the 2 × 2 table. As our last step, we subtract the unexplained variance from 1.00 to get the squared multiple correlation of .35. The square root of $R_{0.1}^2$ returns us to the zero-order correlation coefficient with which we began the analysis.

Layout for Two Independent Variables. When $n = 2$, we begin by constructing a 3 × 3 table, arranging predictor variables in columns from right to left (or rows from top to bottom), according to the order of their elimination, and putting the dependent variable in the third column (row), since it is not eliminated at all.

	x_2'	x_1'	x_0'
x_2'	σ_2^2	σ_{12}	σ_{02}
x_1'	β_{12}	σ_1^2	σ_{01}
x_0'	β_{02}		σ_0^2

	$x_{1.2}$	$x_{0.2}$
$x_{1.2}$	$\sigma_{1.2}^2$	$\sigma_{01.2}$
$x_{0.2}$	$\beta_{01.2}$	$\sigma_{0.2}^2$

	$x_{0.12}$	
$x_{0.12}$	$\sigma_{0.12}^2$	$1 - \sigma_{0.12}^2 = R_{0.12}^2$

Next we draw a 2 × 2 table, aligning its rows on the second and third rows of the 3 × 3 table as a visual reminder that its entries characterize X_0 and X_1, with X_2 constant. To signify the conditional nature of the entries in this table, headings are written "$x_{1.2}$" and "$x_{0.2}$," respectively. Lastly, we construct a 1 × 1 table to accommodate X_0 after the effects of X_2 and X_1 have been removed. Accordingly, its single row carries the caption "$x_{0.12}$." Inside the answer box adjacent to this cell, we show the computation of $R_{0.12}^2$. Note that partial measures are not standard measures, although all measures were in standard form at the start of our analysis.

Required Computations. In principle, we first calculate the total variances σ_0^2, σ_1^2, σ_2^2, which quantities are entered in the cells comprising the major diagonal. In practice, however, we simply write "1" in each cell, since the total variance of a variable in standard form is 1.

All possible covariances (in standard form), in this case σ_{01}, σ_{02}, and σ_{12}, are next computed and entered to the right of the major diagonal. (In general, there will be $[n(n + 1)]/2$ possible covariances for n independent variables and one dependent variable, which the reader will recognize as an adaptation of the procedure for finding the number of ways of taking things two at a time from a total of n things.)

The required regression coefficients β_{12} and β_{02} are now calculated from entries in the 3 × 3 table by the formula, $\beta_{ij} = \sigma_{ij}/\sigma_j^2$, and duly recorded in the first column of that table. As a computing routine, this entails the division of each entry in the first row by the first entry in that same row. It is of some practical interest that we do not compute β_{01} (third row, second column), as that result is not required for the solution of $\sigma_{0.12}^2$. For reasons of economy, we compute only the minimum number of terms required to get the explained variance, $\hat{\sigma}_{0.12}^2$. In a later section, we give a procedure for determining the value of that minimum number.

We are now ready to move to the reduced 2×2 table in which we will enter first-order results after these have been computed. Variances are again recorded on the major diagonal, except that $\sigma_{2.2}^2 = 0$ is necessarily omitted. Each variance is now a partial variance in that it represents only that fraction of the total variance which cannot be linearly attributed to X_2. The procedure for computing such a variance is by now familiar to the reader. To compute $\sigma_{1.2}^2$, we subtract the product of β_{12} and σ_{12} from σ_1^2; likewise, to compute $\sigma_{0.2}^2$, we subtract the product of β_{02} and σ_{02} from σ_2^2. The mechanics of this operation are as follows: after locating σ_i^2, move left in that row to β_{i2} and upwards in that column to σ_{i2}; multiply σ_{i2} by β_{i2} and subtract from σ_i^2. For example, from σ_0^2 we move laterally to β_{02} and vertically to σ_{02}. Their product subtracted from σ_0^2 gives $\sigma_{0.2}^2$.

To find the partial covariance $\sigma_{01.2}$, we have recourse to the previously given general formula (1.2.5):

$$\sigma_{ij.k} = \sigma_{ij} - \beta_{jk}\sigma_{ik}.$$

Thus, to get $\sigma_{01.2}$, we multiply β_{12} by σ_{02} and subtract from σ_{01}. We take these quantities from the 3×3 table, with which we started our analysis, and manipulate them as required to obtain the first-order covariances. Again, antecedent terms are conveniently arranged to facilitate subsequent calculations. In this instance, the location of σ_{01} fixes the position of β_{12} and σ_{02}, which lie, respectively, to the left in the same row and above in the same column. With these quantities in hand, we multiply them together and take that product from σ_{01} to get $\sigma_{01.2}$.

To get $\beta_{01.2}$, we avail ourselves of $\sigma_{01.2}$ and $\sigma_{1.2}^2$, dividing the former by the latter, according to the prescribed general formula (1.2.6):

$$\beta_{ij.k} = \frac{\sigma_{ij.k}}{\sigma_{j.k}^2}.$$

In passing, we note that $\beta_{ij.k}$ is the weight to be attached to the jth predictor variable in order to minimize the sum of the squared residuals.

It is now an easy step to $\sigma_{0.12}^2$, which is calculated according to the formula: $\sigma_{0.12}^2 = \sigma_{0.1}^2 - \beta_{01.2}\sigma_{01.2}$. All quantities on the right are present in the foregoing 2×2 table, and need only to be appropriately substituted and manipulated by formula.

Lastly, we subtract $\sigma_{0.12}^2$ from 1, to reach our goal of the explained variance, or $R_{0.12}^2$.

Numerical Example. To calculate $R_{0.12}^2$, we set up a 3×3 table and enter 1 in each cell of the major diagonal. Next, we calculate $\sigma_{12} = .19, \sigma_{02} = .30$, and $\sigma_{01} = .59$, and enter these results to the right of the major diagonal. Dividing .19 and .30 by 1, we get $\beta_{12} = .19$ and $\beta_{02} = .30$, which results are entered in the first column. Since β_{01} is not used in our solution, we do not enter that value in the table. With all required entries in the 3 × 3 table, we are ready to reduce the criterion variance in successive stages. Our operations culminate in a second-order partial variance of .62, which we deduct from 1.00 for the explained variance, or squared multiple correlation, of .38.

	x_2'	x_1'	x_0'
x_2'	1.00	.19	.30
x_1'	.19	1.00	.59
x_0'	.30		1.00

	$x_{1.2}$	$x_{0.2}$
$x_{1.2}$	.96	.53
$x_{0.2}$	.55	.91

	$x_{0.12}$
$x_{0.12}$	.62	$1.00 - .62 = .38$

Three Independent Variables, $n = 3$. Since some purpose will be served by repetition, we set forth, although in less detail, the layout and procedure for calculating $\hat{\sigma}_{0.123}^2$, or the coefficient of multiple determination when $n = 3$.

(a) We first prepare a set of square tables of diminishing order 4 through 1:

	x_3'	x_2'	x_1'	x_0'
x_3'	σ_3^2	σ_{23}	σ_{13}	σ_{03}
x_2'	β_{23}	σ_2^2	σ_{12}	σ_{02}
x_1'	β_{13}		σ_1^2	σ_{01}
x_0'	β_{03}			σ_0^2

	$x_{2.3}$	$x_{1.3}$	$x_{0.3}$
$x_{2.3}$	$\sigma_{2.3}^2$	$\sigma_{12.3}$	$\sigma_{02.3}$
$x_{1.3}$	$\beta_{12.3}$	$\sigma_{1.3}^2$	$\sigma_{01.3}$
$x_{0.3}$	$\beta_{02.3}$		$\sigma_{0.3}^2$

	$x_{1.23}$	$x_{0.23}$
$x_{1.23}$	$\sigma_{1.23}^2$	$\sigma_{01.23}$
$x_{0.23}$	$\beta_{01.23}$	$\sigma_{0.23}^2$

	$x_{0.123}$
$x_{0.123}$	$\sigma_{0.123}^2$	$1 - \sigma_{0.123}^2 = R_{0.123}^2$

(b) Again variables are arranged, right to left (top to bottom), according to the order of their elimination. Row and column captions identify variables which have been eliminated at each stage. Thus, the heading "$x_{i.23}$" designates the ith variable, with the effects of X_2 and X_3 removed.

(c) Our chain of operations begins by entering $\sigma_i^2 = 1$ in each cell along the major diagonal. Since we have $3 + 1$ variables, there will be four such entries.

(d) Covariances in standard form σ_{ij} are next entered in the block of cells to the right of the major diagonal. There will be $[(n + 1)n]/2 = 6$ such values.

(e) Next, we obtain all regression coefficients appearing in the first column by dividing each covariance in the first row by the single variance in that same row and recording these values in the first column. There will be $n - 0$ such entries.

(f) We are now ready to move to the 3×3 table, the composition of which will be analogous to that of the 4×4 table which we have just described. We calculate partial variances by the formula,*

(1.2.7)
$$\sigma_{i.j}^2 = \sigma_i^2 - \beta_{ij}\sigma_{ij},$$

and enter these values on the major diagonal; covariances are then obtained by Formula (1.2.5):

$$\sigma_{ij.k} = \sigma_{ij} - \beta_{ik}\sigma_{jk},$$

and appropriately entered in the cells above the major diagonal. Lastly, we divide each partial covariance in the first row by the partial variance recorded in the first cell of that row to get the required first-order standardized regression coefficients, which will be $n - 1 = 2$ in number.

Since the sequence of operations is identical for each succeeding but reduced table, it will suffice to set forth the identities which underlie these operations. For the 2×2 table, these identities are:

$$\sigma_{1.23}^2 = \sigma_{1.3}^2 - \beta_{12.3}\sigma_{12.3}$$

$$\sigma_{0.23}^2 = \sigma_{0.3}^2 - \beta_{02.3}\sigma_{02.3}$$

$$\sigma_{01.23} = \sigma_{01.3} - \beta_{12.3}\sigma_{02.3}$$

$$\beta_{01.23} = \sigma_{01.23}/\sigma_{1.23}^2.$$

---

* Equivalent to Formulas (1.1.5) and (1.2.3).

For the 1×1 table, we have the single identity:

$$\sigma^2_{0.123} = \sigma^2_{0.23} - \beta_{01.23}\sigma_{01.23}.$$

Finally, in what is now a familiar step, we must subtract the partial variance from 1 to get the explained variance, or $R^2_{0.123}$.

Numerical Example. To calculate $R^2_{0.123}$, we set up a 4×4 table, entering 1 in each cell along the major diagonal. Next, we calculate zero-order covariances, which we enter to the right of the diagonal. Dividing these zero-order covariances by 1, we get the required zero-order standardized regression coefficients: $\beta_{23} = .10$, $\beta_{13} = -.18$, and $\beta_{03} = -.37$. With these entries in place, we are ready to move through progressively smaller tables, eventually to obtain our unexplained variance of .53, and its complement of .47, which is the squared multiple correlation.

	x'_3	x'_2	x'_1	x'_0
x'_3	1.00	.10	−.18	−.37
x'_2	.10	1.00	.19	.30
x'_1	−.18		1.00	.59
x'_0	−.37			1.00

	$x_{2.3}$	$x_{1.3}$	$x_{0.3}$
$x_{2.3}$	.99	.21	.34
$x_{1.3}$	.21	.97	.52
$x_{0.3}$	.34		.86

	$x_{1.23}$	$x_{0.23}$
$x_{1.23}$	.92	.45
$x_{0.23}$	.49	.75

	$x_{0.123}$	
$x_{0.123}$	.53	$1.00 - .53 = .47$

Minimum Quantities. When there are n predictor variables, or $n + 1$ variables in all, the calculation of the squared multiple correlation, as described above, will necessarily pass through $n + 1$ stages, each corresponding to a prescribed schedule of computations. The reader may have observed that the last, or $(n + 1)^{th}$, stage consists of a single partial variance of order n.

Possibly he will also have noticed that the next-to-the-last, or n^{th}, stage consists of four results of order $n - 1$, arranged in a fourfold table. However, at the next preceding, or the $(n - 1)^{th}$, stage, the 3×3 table remains incomplete; there is no entry in the last row, middle column, which is reserved for a regression coefficient of order $n - 2$. Since complete tables are required at only the last and next-to-the-last stages, it is natural to wonder about the number of determinations required at the ith stage, where i takes all values 1 through $n + 1$. From a general solution for the ith stage, we could, by addition over all $n + 1$ stages, find the minimum number of quantities needed to get the multiple correlation by the procedure of "reducing the criterion variable."

For the ith stage, the required number of quantities, given here without proof, is as follows:

Term	Required Number
Variance	$n - i + 2$
Covariance	$\dfrac{(n - i + 2)(n - i + 1)}{2}$
Regression Coefficient	$n - i + 1$

To illustrate these formulas, consider the following: when $i = n + 1$, we get a total of 1; when $i = n$, we get a total of four quantities; when $i = n - 1$, we get a total of eight determinations, which results necessarily agree with those based on our examples. By means of these formulas, we may obtain the number of quantities required at each particular stage and hence the required total for all $n + 1$ stages. To illustrate, we have computed these totals for $n = 1, 2, 3, 4, 5$:

n	Number of Terms	First Difference	Second Difference
1	5		
2	13	8	
3	26	13	5
4	45	19	6
5	71	26	7

Since the total number of required terms progresses in a regular manner, as shown by the first- and second-order differences, we anticipate that it may be expressed as a formula. This is:

$$\text{Minimum Number} = \frac{(n + 1)(n^2 + 8n + 6)}{6}.$$

Thus, in the case of three independent variables, we have

$$\frac{(3 + 1)[3^2 + (8 \times 3) + 6]}{6} = 26,$$

which result could be verified by counting all entries in the succession of four tables, beginning with the 4×4 table. Given all zero-order quantities, the minimum number of calculations for R^2 is $n(n^2 + 6n - 1)/6$ (Dubois 1957: 20).

Remark. To an increasing extent, statistical calculations are carried out electronically without being touched by the human hand. Accordingly, it is not anticipated that research workers will often avail themselves of the simple hand routine for "reducing the criterion variance." It was included here with the idea that the student will have a better grasp of the multiple correlation coefficient for having produced a few himself. It is important, or at least it is the author's conviction, that limited exercises be carried out by the student during his period of university training. Even when he has a computer at his disposal, he may need to check the accuracy of outputs by trial numerical examples; moreover, the understanding acquired through numerical exercises must be transmitted to the next generation of students.

Standardized Partial Regression Coefficient (β) Defined. The weights which are attached to the independent variables in standard form and which satisfy the criterion of least squares are conventionally denoted by the Greek letter "β" with an identifying subscript. Such weights are more than mere auxiliary constants; each is an important statistical result in its own right, carrying a quite simple meaning. As a statistical quantity, a beta is the average change in the criterion variable per unit change in the independent variable with the influence of $n - 1$ variables statistically removed. Thus, we would interpret $\beta_{01.2} = .25$ as follows: the expected change in x_0' per unit change in x_1' is .25, with the x_2' constant. A beta is therefore a measure of slope. We note in passing that the path coefficients in a recursive system (no reciprocal causation or looping) are reducible to standardized partial regression coefficients (betas) and that therefore they may be construed as slopes. Path coefficients purport to measure the effect of one variable on another after the effects of the other causal variables in the system have been taken into account (Duncan 1966: 7). (Caution: standardized partial regression coefficients and corresponding partial correlation coefficients are not equal, e.g., $\beta_{01.2} \neq r_{01.2}$; $\beta_{01.23} \neq r_{01.23}$. However, the standardized zero-order regression coefficient is equal to its corresponding zero-order correlation coefficient, e.g., $\beta_{01} = r_{01}$.)

Composition of Beta. The student is already familiar with the statistical process of removing the influence of one or more independent variables from a specific criterion variable. Thus, to eliminate the contribution of X_2 from X_0, we compute

$$x_{0.2} = x_0' - \beta_{02}x_2'.$$

Since $\beta_{02}x_2'$ reflects the influence of x_2 on x_0, by removing it from x_0 we obtain a reduced variable which is free of the influence of x_2; hence, we designate it $x_{0.2}$. Similarly, we may deduct the influence of x_2 from x_1 as follows:

$$x_{1.2} = x_1' - \beta_{12}x_2'.$$

Now the coefficient of linear regression of one variable on another is the sum of the products divided by the sum of the squares of the independent variable. Applying this formula to our reduced measures $x_{0.2}$ and $x_{1.2}$, we get

$$\beta_{01.2} = \frac{\sum x_{0.2}x_{1.2}}{\sum x_{1.2}^2}.$$

Dividing both numerator and denominator by N and relabeling, we get

$$\beta_{01.2} = \frac{\sigma_{01.2}}{\sigma_{1.2}^2},$$

which the student will recognize as an instance of the general formula for obtaining a beta: a covariance divided by a variance—in this instance a first-order covariance divided by a first-order variance.

From this quite brief analysis, we see that a beta is a measure of the regression of one set of residuals on another set of residuals. Since the n betas are attached as weights to variables whose means and standard deviations have been equalized at zero and 1, respectively, we may utilize them to gauge the relative importance of each variable in predicting the criterion variable. The variable with the largest beta will make the largest contribution; the variable with the smallest beta will make the smallest contribution, etc. However, authorities warn that one should not attempt to judge the substantive importance of a variable from its beta weight. The magnitude of a variable's beta will be affected by the relation of that variable to every other variable in the set. Other things being equal, highly correlated (redundant) variables will have lower betas than weakly correlated independent variables, and many highly correlated variables will have lower betas than a few highly correlated variables. These matters have been explored recently by Gordon (1968) for sociological readers. The limitations of regression coefficients for purposes of guiding social and educational policy are discussed by Cain and Watts in a current paper (1970).

Computing Procedure. As previously shown, we are not required to calculate a full set of betas in order to find the multiple correlation ratio, $\hat{\sigma}_{0.12...n}^2$. Indeed, we are required to calculate only $\beta_{01.23...n}$, when variables are removed in sequence n through 1. However, if all n betas are required, as in the prediction of individual values, they may be gotten from results appearing in the solution of $\sigma_{0.12...n}^2$, in a reverse operation. Owing to the interrelationships among the n betas, it is possible to set up a simple procedure for finding all n of them from the quantities required to compute $R_{0.12...n}^2$. Beginning with the simplest case of $n = 2$, we move toward a somewhat general statement.

When $n = 2$, and variables are taken out in order n through 1, our procedure for finding $\sigma_{0.12}^2$ yields $\beta_{01.2}$, but not $\beta_{02.1}$. To find $\beta_{02.1}$, we take advantage of the identity, $\beta_{02.1} = \beta_{02} - \beta_{01.2}\beta_{12}$, the proof of which is simple but cumbersome (DuBois 1957: 136). It may be undertaken as an exercise by the algebraically minded student. Since all terms on the right side appear in the solution of $\sigma_{0.12}^2$, we get $\beta_{02.1}$ by substituting these known quantities in the foregoing equation. As a rule, then, to get $\beta_{02.1}$, multiply $\beta_{01.2}$ by β_{12} and subtract that product from β_{02}:

(1.2.8) $$\beta_{02.1} = \beta_{02} - \beta_{01.2}\beta_{12}.$$

When $n = 3$, and variables are removed in sequence n through 1, our solution of $\sigma_{0.123}^2$ yields $\beta_{01.23}$, but neither $\beta_{02.13}$ nor $\beta_{03.12}$. In this case, we may take advantage of the identity:

(1.2.9) $$\beta_{02.13} = \beta_{02.3} - \beta_{01.23}\beta_{12.3},$$

the right side of which, it will be observed, is identical in form to (1.2.8), except that terms are higher in order by one. Since all terms on the right side appear in the solution of $\sigma_{0.123}^2$, we may readily obtain $\beta_{02.13}$ by substituting known quantities in Formula (1.2.9).

However, this method is not feasible for finding $\beta_{03.12}$. Although

$$\beta_{03.12} = \beta_{03.2} - \beta_{01.23}\beta_{13.2},$$

we cannot avail ourselves of this identity, since $\beta_{03.2}$ and $\beta_{13.2}$ do not appear in our solution. Consequently, we have recourse to an alternative identity, here taken as given, which permits us to take advantage of known results to obtain a solution of $\beta_{03.12}$. This will be

(1.2.10) $$\beta_{03.12} = \beta_{03} - (\beta_{01.23}\beta_{13} + \beta_{02.13}\beta_{23}),$$

proof of which may be furnished by the student. Thus, to get the third and last beta, we subtract the sum of two terms, each the product of a beta of order $n - 1$ and a beta of $n - n$, and each coming from quantities obtained in the solution of $R_{0.123}^2$, from a beta of order $n - n = 0$.

Although this procedure is somewhat cumbersome, it does enable us to utilize known results in the solution of $R_{0.123}^2$, to obtain a complete set of betas. Thus all terms on the right side of (1.2.10) appear in the solution of $\sigma_{0.123}^2$, except $\beta_{02.13}$, which may be obtained directly from results appearing in that solution. When $n = 3$, our three betas may be computed in sequence as follows:

$$\beta_{01.23} = \sigma_{01.23}/\sigma_{1.23}^2$$

$$\beta_{02.13} = \beta_{02.3} - \beta_{01.23}\beta_{12.3}$$

$$\beta_{03.12} = \beta_{03} - (\beta_{01.23}\beta_{13} + \beta_{02.13}\beta_{23}).$$

Generalization of Rule. These formulas are an instance of the more general rule: to get a complete set of betas of order $n - 1$, operate in sequence on betas of diminishing order, $n - 2, n - 3$, through $n - n$, given the solution of $\sigma_{0.12...n}^2$. From a beta of order $n - 2$, we subtract a single term; from a beta of order $n - 3$, we take the sum of two terms; and from a beta of order $n - i$, we take the sum of $i - 1$ terms. Thus, when $i = n$, we subtract the sum of $n - 1$ terms from a beta of order $n - n$. These conclusions may be put in the form of a chart for convenient reference:

Order of Reduced Beta	Number of Terms in Sum
$n - 2$	$2 - 1$
$n - 3$	$3 - 1$
$n - i$	$i - 1$
$n - n$	$n - 1$

It may be noted that each term in the sum on the right side of (1.2.10) is the product of a beta of order $3 - 1 = 2$, and a beta of order $3 - 3 = 0$. Generalizing from this, we may state that any beta of order $n - 1$ may be written as the difference between a beta of order $n - n = 0$, and a sum composed of $n - 1$ terms, each of these terms being the product of a beta of order $n - 1$, and a beta of order $n - n$.

For $n = 4$, the equations in order of their solution will read

$$\beta_{01.234} = \sigma_{01.234}/\sigma_{1.234}^2$$

$$\beta_{02.134} = \beta_{02.34} - \beta_{01.234}\beta_{12.34}$$

$$\beta_{03.124} = \beta_{03.4} - (\beta_{01.234}\beta_{13.4} + \beta_{02.134}\beta_{23.4})$$

$$\beta_{04.123} = \beta_{04} - (\beta_{01.234}\beta_{14} + \beta_{02.134}\beta_{24} + \beta_{03.124}\beta_{34}).$$

Numerical Example. We give a numerical example of these computations, given the solution of $\sigma^2_{0.1234}$.

		Solution of $\sigma^2_{0.1234}$				Computing the Betas, $n = 4$

Solution of $\sigma^2_{0.1234}$

	4	3	2	1	0
4	1.00	.90	.60	.50	.70
3	.90	1.00	.60	.50	.80
2	.60		1.00	.80	.50
1	.50			1.00	.60
0	.70				1.00

Zero-Order Terms

First-Order Terms

	3.4	2.4	1.4	0.4
3.4	.19	.06	.05	.17
2.4	.32	.64	.50	.08
1.4	.26		.75	.25
0.4	.89			.51

Second-Order Terms

	2.34	1.34	0.34
2.34	.62	.48	.03
1.34	.77	.74	.21
0.34	.05		.36

Third-Order Terms

	1.234	0.234
1.234	.37	.19
0.234	.51	.36

Computing the Betas, $n = 4$

$\sigma_{01.234} = .19$
$\sigma^2_{1.234} = .37$
$\beta_{01.234} = .19/.37$
$= .51$

$\beta_{02.34} = .05$
$\beta_{12.34} = .77$
$\beta_{02.134} = .05 - (.51)(.77)$
$= .05 - .39$
$= -.34$

$\beta_{03.4} = .89$
$\beta_{13.4} = .26$
$\beta_{23.4} = .32$
$\beta_{03.124} = .89 - [(.51)(.26) + (-.34)(.32)]$
$= .89 - (.13 - 11)$
$= .89 - .02$
$= .87$

$\beta_{04} = .70$
$\beta_{14} = .50$
$\beta_{24} = .60$
$\beta_{34} = .90$
$\beta_{04.123} = .70 - [(.51)(.50) + (-.34)(.60) + (.87)(.90)]$
$= .70 - [.26 + (-.20) + .78]$
$= .70 - .84$
$= -.14$

Remark. It will be recalled that the n partial regression coefficients in any given problem are to be chosen so that the sum of the squared deviations of the observed from the expected values will be least. The solution of this problem by mathematical methods yields a set of n simultaneous equations, with as many unknowns as there are equations. These equations have come to be known in statistics as the "normal equations." There are several alternative ways of solving these equations, including the method in which we work forward to the solution of $\beta_{01.23...n}$, and backward to the remaining $n - 1$ betas of the same order. This "forward-backward" procedure for finding the betas, it is to be understood, has no special theoretical significance; it is simply a convenient device for computing the betas. When n is relatively small, the "forward-backward" solution may be performed handily, and from such manipulation the student may obtain some additional insight into the nature of partial regression coefficients. But such routine calculations should not be permitted to blur the fundamental nature of these coefficients, each as the average change of one variable on another, with the effects of $n - 1$ variables under statistical control.

EXERCISES

1. Hypothetical correlations between income (X_0) and occupation (X_1) and education (X_2) are as follows:

$$r_{01} = .85$$

$$r_{02} = .75$$

$$r_{12} = .80$$

Find the squared multiple correlation, $R^2_{0.12}$.

2. Given the following correlations (adapted from Sewell and Shah 1968b), find $R^2_{0.123}$.

	X_3	X_2	X_1	X_0
X_3 parental encouragement		.25	.50	.40
X_2 college plans			.80	.60
X_1 college attendance				.60
X_0 college graduate				

3. Correlations (hypothetical) between political preference and four independent variables are as follows:

	X_4	X_3	X_2	X_1	X_0
X_4 attitude on foreign policy		.90	.60	.50	.70
X_3 attitude on domestic policy			.60	.50	.80
X_2 education				.80	.50
X_1 father's political preference					.60
X_0 political preference					

Find $R^2_{0.1234}$.

4. Find $R^2_{5.4321}$ from the following correlations:

	X_1	X_2	X_3	X_4	X_5
X_1					
X_2	.60				
X_3	−.33	−.06			
X_4	−.64	−.48	.25		
X_5	−.58	−.60	.12	.46	

5. The following table gives intercorrelations for 133 U.S. cities, 100,000 population or more, 1960:

	X_3	X_2	X_1	X_0
X_3 percent families, 1 or more child under age 6		.10	−.18	−.37
X_2 median monthly rent			.19	.30
X_1 percent males divorced, age 14 and over				.59
X_0 suicides per 100,000 total population				

Find $R^2_{0.123}$.

6. From the results obtained in Exercise 5, find:

$$\beta_{02.13}$$

$$\beta_{03.12}$$

Give a verbal interpretation of these standardized regression coefficients.

7. A partial variance of order k is equal to a partial variance of order $(k-1)$ minus a reduction term of the form $\beta\sigma_{ij}$, with both β and σ_{ij} of order $(k-1)$. Satisfy yourself that $\sigma^2_{0.1} = 1 - r^2_{01}$ is an instance of this rule.

8. Satisfy yourself that $\sigma_{01.2} = r_{01} - r_{02}r_{12}$ is covered by the rule that a kth order covariance is equal to a $(k-1)^{\text{th}}$ order covariance minus a reduction term of the form $\beta\sigma_{ij}$, β and σ_{ij}, both being of order $(k-1)$.

9. From the following coefficients, compute the correlation between undergraduate grade point average and law school admission tests for both Indiana undergraduates and others.

Predictor variable(s)	Indiana undergraduates ($N = 462$)	Other university undergraduates ($N = 423$)
Undergraduate GPA	0.55	0.44
Law School Admission Test	0.40	0.57
UGPA and LSAT	0.59	0.64

PART 3

Partial Correlation Coefficient

Introduction. In this section we focus on the partial correlation coefficient, momentarily disregarding its place in the general system of multiple correlation which we have described. By this emphasis, we will be prepared better to utilize the partial correlation coefficient in factor analysis and possibly, for that matter, in those analytical schemes in which it plays an integral part. Thus, we will be better able to understand its role in those methods which seek to interpret the relation between two variables on the basis of their dependence on one or more presumably causal variables (see Simon 1957; Blalock 1964).

Nature of Partial Correlation. We may conceive of partial correlation as the relation between two variables X_0 and X_1 after each has been statistically freed of the influence of one or more disturbing variables. Corresponding to this conception, our problem is to rid X_0 and X_1 of specific unwanted effects before measuring the correlation between them. Except in this regard, the measurement of partial correlation is identical to that of simple correlation, as is therefore the interpretation to be attached to the partial correlation coefficient. Thus, the coefficient of partial determination $r_{yx.z}^2$ is the proportion of variation in Y which may be attributed to X after both have been adjusted for their dependence on Z.

Process Illustrated. To illustrate the process of partial correlation and, in particular, the procedure of adjusting values, we get a value of X_0 which is free of the influence of X_2; likewise, a value of X_1 which is free of X_2. To complete our problem, we obtain the product-moment correlation between these once-adjusted values, using the symbol $r_{01.2}$ to signify that we have removed the influence of X_2 from both X_0 and X_1, before finding the correlation between them. From this simple example, we move to the more general case of n control variables, or to the correlation between two variables that have been adjusted n times.

First-Order Residuals. To remove the influence of X_2 from X_0, we simply subtract the expected value $\beta_{02}x_2'$ from the observed value x_0':

$$x_{0.2} = x_0' - \beta_{02}x_2'.$$

The following argument provides a justification for this procedure: if we remove from X_0 what is attributable to its linear regression on X_2, the remainder necessarily will be independent of X_2. Hence, the partial variable $x_{0.2}$ may be taken as free of the influence of the observed variable x_2'.

In exactly the same way, we rid X_1 of the influence of X_2:

$$x_{1.2} = x_1' - \beta_{12}x_2'.$$

Once residuals or partial variables, as they are sometimes called, have been computed, we need only to find their covariance and put that result in standard form for the coefficient of partial correlation, $r_{01.2}$. This conversion requires division of the covariance by the product of the respective standard deviations of the two sets of residuals on which the covariance rests. Since the mean of a complete set of residuals is equal to 0,* the covariance may be written:

$$\text{Covariance} = \frac{1}{N} \sum (x_0' - \beta_{02}x_2')(x_1' - \beta_{12}x_2').$$

The standard deviation of a complete set of residuals will be the square root of the sum of the squared residuals divided by N. In symbols:

$$SD = \sqrt{\frac{1}{N} \sum (x_0' - \beta_{02}x_2')^2}.$$

Expanding the binomial, summing and collecting terms, we get

$$SD = \sqrt{\frac{1}{N} \sum x_0'^2 - \frac{1}{N} \sum x_0'x_2' \frac{1}{N} \sum x_0'x_2'},$$

which we relabel

$$\sigma_{0.2} = \sqrt{\sigma_0^2 - \beta_{02}\sigma_{02}}.$$

It is clear that the variance of $x_0' - \beta_{02}x_2'$, which by definition is X_0 rid of the influence of X_2, is the residual variance, $\sigma_{0.2}^2$, as defined in the foregoing analysis of multiple correlation (p. 21). Analogously,

$$\sigma_{1.2} = \sqrt{\frac{1}{N} \sum (x_1' - \beta_{12}x_2')^2}.$$

By definition,

$$r_{01.2} = \frac{\sum (x_0' - \beta_{02}x_2')(x_1' - \beta_{12}x_2')}{N\sigma_{0.2}\sigma_{1.2}}.$$

If we expand the numerator and divide each term by N, we get

$$\sigma_{01} - \beta_{12}\sigma_{02} = \sigma_{01.2}.$$

---

* Explanation:

$$\sum (x_0' - \beta_{02}x_2') = \sum x_0' - \beta_{02}\sum x_2'$$
$$= 0 - \beta_{02}(0)$$
$$= 0.$$

Hence,

$$r_{01.2} = \frac{\sigma_{01.2}}{\sigma_{0.2}\sigma_{1.2}}.$$

From this expression, it is evident that the partial correlation coefficient, $r_{01.2}$, may be obtained from terms occurring in the solution of the multiple correlation ratio, $R_{0.12}^2$, by the method of "reducing the criterion variance."

Numerical Example. Let us suppose that we are given the intercorrelations among three variables as follows:

$$r_{01} = .80,$$
$$r_{02} = .50,$$
$$r_{12} = .70,$$

and that we are required to find all possible partial correlations:

$$r_{01.2}, \quad r_{02.1}, \quad r_{12.0}.$$

Substituting in Formula (1.2.7)

$$\sigma_{i.j}^2 = \sigma_i^2 - \beta_{ij}\sigma_{ij},$$

we first calculate:

$$\sigma_{0.1}^2 = 1.00 - (.80)(.80) = .36$$
$$\sigma_{0.2}^2 = 1.00 - (.50)(.50) = .75$$
$$\sigma_{1.2}^2 = 1.00 - (.70)(.70) = .51.$$

Substituting in Formula (1.2.5)

$$\sigma_{ij.k} = \sigma_{ij} - \beta_{jk}\sigma_{ik},$$

we next obtain:

$$\sigma_{01.2} = .80 - (.70)(.50) = .45$$
$$\sigma_{02.1} = .50 - (.70)(.80) = -.06$$
$$\sigma_{12.0} = .70 - (.50)(.80) = .30.$$

Finally, we divide each partial covariance by the product of its corresponding standard deviations to obtain the required partial correlations:

$r_{01.2}$	$r_{02.1}$	$r_{12.0}$
$\dfrac{.45}{\sqrt{(.75)(.51)}}$	$\dfrac{-.06}{\sqrt{(.36)(.51)}}$	$\dfrac{.30}{\sqrt{(.36)(.75)}}$
.73	−.14	.58

Two Variables Held Constant. We move now to the procedure for removing the influence of two variables, so that our correlation will be based on variables which have been rid of the effects of two variables instead of one. To accomplish this objective, as one would suppose, we adjust our variates twice instead of once. In sequence, we (1) remove the influence of X_2 from X_0 and X_1 and from those remainders (2) take whatever influence may be ascribed to X_3. This succession of steps may profitably be put in literal form:

Step 1	Step 2
$(x_0' - \beta_{02}x_2') = x_{0.2}$	$x_{0.2} - (\beta_{03.2}x_{3.2}) = x_{0.23}$

where $\beta_{03.2}$ = the expected change in X_0 per unit change in X_3 after both
have been adjusted for the effect of X_2, and
$x_{0.23}$ = value of X_0 adjusted for X_2 and X_3 (all measures in standard
form at the start).

We attain $x_{1.23}$ in identical fashion:

$$(x_1' - \beta_{12}x_2') - (\beta_{13.2}x_{3.2}) = x_{1.23}.$$

With these twice-adjusted variates in hand, we find their covariance and reduce that result to standard form for the partial correlation coefficient $r_{01.23}$. The order of variables in the secondary subscript is immaterial, since $r_{01.23} = r_{01.32}$.

By methods similar to those of the preceding section, we may show that the variance of a complete set of second-order residuals is equal to $\sigma_{i.jk}^2$ as previously defined. Consequently,

$$r_{01.23} = \frac{\sigma_{01.23}}{\sigma_{0.23}\sigma_{1.23}}.$$

Numerical Example.

Zero-Order Terms

3	2	1	0
1.00	.10	−.18	−.37
.10	1.00	.19	.30
−.18		1.00	.59
−.37			1.00

$$\sigma_{01.23} = .45$$
$$\sigma_{1.23} = \sqrt{.92}$$
$$= .96$$

First-Order Terms

2.3	1.3	0.3
.99	.21	.34
.21	.97	.52
.34		.86

$$\sigma_{0.23} = \sqrt{.75}$$
$$= .87$$

$$r_{01.23} = \frac{.48}{(.96)(.87)}$$
$$= .54$$

Second-Order Terms

1.23	0.23
.92	.45
.49	.75

The General Case of *n* Control Variables. From the foregoing examples, we may formulate the general pattern of partial correlation, where the number of variables to be controlled is *n*. As a routine, we get the covariance between residuals which have been adjusted *n* times and divide that result by the product of their standard deviations. The covariance of variables which have been adjusted *n* times may be written:

$$\sigma_{ij.12...n},$$

where *n* is the number of control variables. In analogous manner we may write the variance of a variable which has been adjusted *n* times:

$$\sigma^2_{i.12...n}.$$

Hence, the general formula for the partial correlation coefficient with n variables held constant is:

$$r_{ij.12...n} = \frac{\sigma_{ij.12...n}}{\sigma_{i.12...n}\sigma_{j.12...n}}.$$

Thus when $n = 1$, we get

$$r_{ij.1} = \frac{\sigma_{ij.1}}{\sigma_{i.1}\sigma_{j.1}},$$

as in the first example. When $n = 2$, we get $r_{ij.12}$, as in the second example. Continuing, when n is four, we would be holding four variables constant, and our expression would read,

$$r_{ij.1234}.$$

All of the foregoing quantities may be obtained by an adaptation of the computing routine for R^2, as will be clear from the exercises.

Concluding Remark. The nature of partial correlation may be clarified by noting that: (a) a simple correlation, by definition, expresses the relation between two variables which are treated as irreducible elements; (b) a multiple correlation (R) measures the relation between a criterion variable and the sum of two or more independent variables weighted so as to maximize the correlation between the criterion and that sum; and (c) a partial correlation similarly expresses the relation between two variables, except that each will have been adjusted in advance to be uncorrelated with the n control variables. In simple correlation, we correlate two variables without regard for their composition; in multiple correlation, we correlate a dependent variable with a composite variable which may be broken down into its parts; in partial correlation, we correlate two variables, each of which will have been identically adjusted before the correlation is measured.

EXERCISES

1. Given the following matrix of zero-order correlations:

	X_1	X_2	X_3	X_4	X_5
X_1		.90	.80	.70	.60
X_2			.72	.63	.54
X_3				.56	.48
X_4					.42
X_5					

(a) Find the reduced covariance table:

	$x_{2.1}$	$x_{3.1}$	$x_{4.1}$	$x_{5.1}$
$x_{2.1}$		$\sigma_{23.1}$	$\sigma_{24.1}$	$\sigma_{25.1}$
$x_{3.1}$			$\sigma_{34.1}$	$\sigma_{35.1}$
$x_{4.1}$				$\sigma_{45.1}$
$x_{5.1}$				

(b) Convert partial covariances to partial correlations by the formula:

$$r_{ij.1} = \frac{\sigma_{ij.1}}{\sigma_{i.1}\sigma_{j.1}}.$$

(c) Describe the influence of X_1 on the other four variables.

2. Given the following variables:

No.	X_0	X_1	X_2
1	1	5	2
2	3	1	8
3	5	3	11
4	7	7	13
5	9	11	13
6	11	9	13

(a) Compute the values of the partial variables for each pair:

$$x_{0.2} = x_0' - \beta_{02}x_2'$$

$$x_{1.2} = x_1' - \beta_{12}x_2'.$$

(b) Compute crossproducts between $x_{0.2}$ and $x_{1.2}$, sum and divide by N.

(c) Contrast this result with $r_{(0.2)(1.2)} = \dfrac{\sigma_{01.2}}{\sigma_{0.2}\sigma_{1.2}}$. Explain the difference between the partial correlation and the covariance of partial measures.

3. Satisfy yourself that:

$$\frac{1}{N}\sum(x_0' - \beta_{02}x_2')(x_1' - \beta_{12}x_2') = \sigma_{01.2}.$$

4. Given the following hypothetical intercorrelations between the crime rate (X_0), socioeconomic status (X_1) and race (X_2):

$$r_{01} = .60$$

$$r_{02} = .60$$

$$r_{12} = .90$$

Find $r_{01.2}$, compare with r_{01}, and comment.

5. Correlations based on data from the 1960 Census for U.S. cities with a population of 100,000 or more are as follows:

	X_1	X_2	X_3	X_0
X_1 percent non-white		$-.48$	.54	.78
X_2 median family income			$-.56$	$-.55$
X_3 percent dwelling units with more than 1.5 persons/room				.69
X_0 murders per 100,000 total population				

Compute $r_{01.2}$, $r_{01.3}$, and $r_{01.23}$ and interpret.

6. Using the data and your computations from Exercise 3, Part 2, Chapter 1, find $r_{01.234}$ and $r_{02.134}$. Interpret these partial correlations.

7. Given that W and Y have only X in common, and that X and Z have only Y in common, we would predict the following (Blalock 1964: 73):

$$r_{wy.x} = 0,$$

$$r_{xz.y} = 0,$$

$$r_{wz.xy} = 0.$$

(a) Do the following intercorrelations for matricentered traits of North American Indians support the predictions?

	W	X	Y	Z
Matridominant division of labor W		.49	.53	.39
Matrilocal residence X			.61	.51
Matricentered land tenure Y				.80
Matrilineal descent Z				

(b) What changes in the predictions are suggested by the partial r's?

8. Duncan (1961: 124) gives zero-order correlation coefficients among occupational prestige (X_1), age-adjusted income (X_2), and age-adjusted education (X_3) as follows:

	X_3	X_2	X_1
X_3		.72	.85
X_2			.84
X_1			

Compute $r_{12.3}$ and $r_{13.2}$. Also, compute $R^2_{1.23}$. Compute standardized partial regression coefficients: $\beta_{12.3}$ and $\beta_{13.2}$.

PART 4
Statistical Significance

The student may have wondered at our disregard of statistical inference in this chapter. This omission reflects no more than our decision to focus on the measurement of correlation rather than on the sampling aspects of the measures themselves—in particular, to concentrate on the structure of r^2 and R^2 rather than on the distribution of these coefficients in repeated samples. It is to be anticipated that sample correlation coefficients will be more or less routinely tested for significance when the conditions for such testing have been met. Since the satisfaction of these conditions may be uncertain in sociological research, the use of significance tests in these investigations is likely to be problematic. In sampling studies of social and economic characteristics, little or nothing may be known about the population distribution; moreover, crude scaling techniques may yield measures of unknown reliability and validity. Under these circumstances, it may be sensible to forego the use of significance tests and to be content with a mere description of the data. It may be mentioned that the application of significance tests to survey data is a matter of debate among specialists in sociological methodology, and that these issues remain unresolved at the moment (Gold 1969; Kruskal 1968).

Primarily as a reminder to the student that statistical inferences may be drawn from sample correlation coefficients, we attach Table 1.4.1, which enables one to test by sight the hypothesis that the correlation in the population is zero. This table (a fragment of a larger table) is based on the formulas:

$$F = \frac{r^2(N-2)}{1-r^2}, \quad df_1 = n, \quad df_2 = N-2,$$

$$F = \frac{R^2}{1-R^2}\frac{(N-n-1)}{n}, \quad df_1 = n, \quad df_2 = N-n-1,$$

where N = number of cases in sample

n = number of predictor variables.

Selected values of df_2 are given in the stub column, and values of $df_1 = 1, 2, 3, 4$ are given in the boxhead at the top of the table. To test the significance of a simple r, we match our sample value against the entry in the $(N-2)^{th}$ row and first column. To test the significance of the multiple correlation, R, we compare our sample value with the entry in the $(N-n-1)^{th}$ row and n^{th} column. We treat a partial correlation like a simple correlation, except that $df_2 = N-n-1$ will be smaller by the number of variables held constant. For example, in testing the significance of $r_{01.23}$, we would match

Table 1.4.1   *The 5% and 1% Points* for r and R*

$df_2 = N - n - 1$	$df_1 = n$			
	1	2	3	4
1	.997	.999	.999	.999
	1.000	1.000	1.000	1.000
5	.754	.836	.874	.898
	.874	.917	.937	.949
10	.576	.671	.726	.763
	.708	.776	.814	.840
15	.482	.574	.630	.670
	.606	.677	.721	.752
20	.423	.509	.563	.604
	.537	.608	.652	.685
25	.381	.462	.514	.553
	.487	.555	.600	.633
30	.349	.426	.476	.514
	.449	.514	.558	.591
40	.304	.373	.419	.455
	.393	.454	.494	.526
60	.250	.308	.348	.380
	.325	.377	.414	.442
100	.195	.241	.274	.300
	.254	.297	.327	.351
200	.138	.172	.196	.215
	.181	.212	.234	.253
500	.088	.109	.124	.137
	.115	.135	.150	.162
1000	.062	.077	.088	.097
	.081	.096	.106	.115

* 5% on first line, 1% on second line, for each "degree of freedom" in stub column.

Reprinted by permission from *Statistical Methods*, Fourth Edition, by George W. Snedecor, © 1946 by the Iowa State University Press, Ames, Iowa.

our obtained value against the entry in the $(N - 4)^{th}$ row and first column. To test the significance of a simple or partial correlation, we always refer to the column whose heading is $n = 1$; to test the significance of a multiple correlation, we necessarily refer to a column whose heading is $n = 2$ or higher.

It is instructive to observe the manner in which the decision to reject the null hypothesis is affected by both sample size (N) and the magnitude of the sample correlation coefficient. For example, an r of .45 in a sample of 32 cases is significant at the 1% level, whereas an r of the same magnitude in a sample of 17 cases would not be significant at the 5% level. In the former instance we reject the null hypothesis at the 1% level; in the latter instance, we cannot reject the null hypothesis at the 5% level. In a sample of 100 cases, a coefficient (r) as small as .25 will be significant at the 1% level, but in a sample of 25 cases, the sample r must be no smaller than .51 to be significant at that level. It is of interest that an R of .75 in a sample of 13 is not significant at the 1% level. By this example, we are reminded that a relatively high multiple correlation in a small sample is no guarantee of statistical significance. The student is invited to extend these comparisons in order to explore more thoroughly the link between sample size and statistical significance.

REFERENCES

Blalock, Hubert M., Jr.
    1964   Causal Inferences in Nonexperimental Research. Chapel Hill: University of North Carolina Press.

    1968   "Standardized and unstandardized measures." Pp. 189–192 in Hubert M. Blalock, Jr. and Ann B. Blalock (eds.), Methodology in Social Research. New York: McGraw-Hill.

Boudon, Raymond
    1965   "A method of linear causal analysis: Dependence analysis." American Sociological Review 30: 365–374.

Brewer, Marilynn B., William D. Crano, and Donald T. Campbell
    1970   "The use of partial correlations to test hypotheses." Sociometry 33: 1–11.

Cain, Glen G. and Harold W. Watts
    1970   "Problems in making policy inferences from the Coleman report." American Sociological Review 35: 228–242.

Cooley, William W. and Paul R. Lohnes
    1962   Multivariate Procedures for the Behavioral Sciences. Chapter 3: "Multiple and canonical correlation." New York: John Wiley and Sons.

Costner, Herbert L.
    1965   "Criteria for measures of association." American Sociological Review 30: 341–353.

Draper, Norman and Harry Smith
    1966   Applied Regression Analysis. Chapter 6: "Selecting the 'best' regression equation." New York: John Wiley and Sons.

DuBois, Philip H.
    1957   Multivariate Correlational Analysis. New York: Harper and Brothers.

Duncan, Otis Dudley
    1961   "A socioeconomic index for all occupations." Pp. 109–138 in Albert J. Reiss, Occupations and Social Status. Glencoe, Illinois: Free Press.

1966 "Path analysis: Sociological examples." American Journal of Sociology 72: 1–16.

Ezekiel, Mordecai and Karl A. Fox
1959 Methods of Correlation and Regression Analysis. Third Edition. New York: John Wiley and Sons.

Gold, David
1969 "Statistical tests and substantive significance." The American Sociologist 4: 42–46.

Goldberger, Arthur S.
1968 Topics in Regression Analysis. Chapter 4: "Coefficients of determination." New York: Macmillan.

Gordon, Robert A.
1968 "Issues in multiple regression." American Journal of Sociology 73: 592–616.

Guttman, Louis
1941 "The quantitative prediction of a quantitative variate." Pp. 276–297 in Paul Horst et al., The Prediction of Personal Adjustment. New York: Social Science Research Council.

Harman, Harry H.
1967 Modern Factor Analysis. Second Edition. Chicago: University of Chicago Press.

Horst, Paul
1965 Factor Analysis of Data Matrices. New York: Holt, Rinehart and Winston.

Kruskal, William H.
1968 "Tests of significance." Pp. 238–250 in International Encyclopedia of the Social Sciences, Vol. 14. New York: Crowell, Collier and Macmillan.

Morrison, Donald F.
1967 Multivariate Statistical Methods. New York: McGraw-Hill.

Schuessler, Karl
1968 "Prediction." Pp. 418–425 in International Encyclopedia of the Social Sciences, Vol. 15. New York: Crowell, Collier and Macmillan.

Sewell, William H. and J. Michael Armer
1966 "Neighborhood context and college plans." American Sociological Review 31: 159–168.

Sewell, William H. and Vimal P. Shah
1968a "Social class, parental encouragement, and educational aspirations." American Journal of Sociology 73: 559–572.

1968b "Parents' education and children's educational aspirations and achievements." American Sociological Review 33: 191–209.

Simon, Herbert A.
1957 Models of Man, Social and Rational. Chapter 2: "Spurious correlation: A causal interpretation." New York: John Wiley and Sons.

Snedecor, George
    1946   Statistical Methods. Fourth Edition. Ames, Iowa: Iowa State University Press.

Sterling, Theodor D. and Seymour V. Pollack
    1968   Introduction to Statistical Data Processing. Chapter 10: "Automatic search techniques." Englewood Cliffs: Prentice-Hall.

Thurstone, Louis L.
    1947   Multiple-Factor Analysis. Chicago: University of Chicago Press.

Tryon, Robert C.
    1939   Cluster Analysis: Correlation Profile and Orthometric (Factor) Analysis for the Isolation of Unities in Mind and Personality. Ann Arbor: Edwards Brothers.

Tufte, Edward R.
    1969   "Improving data analysis in political science." World Politics 21: 641–654.

2

Factors to Correlations

PART 1
Introduction

Factor analysis is a procedure for investigating the possibility that a large number of variables have a small number of factors in common which account for their intercorrelations. Our observations often suggest the possibility of common factors and sometimes supply a suggestion regarding their nature. We observe that pupils who score high in reading tend to score high in spelling and arithmetic; pupils who score low in reading tend to score low in spelling and arithmetic. We ascribe this consistency, or correlation, in pupils' marks to the general factor of intelligence. Similarly, we note that families living in fine houses tend to drive fine cars and wear fine clothes; families living in ordinary houses tend to drive ordinary cars and wear ordinary clothes. We attribute this consistency in the material conditions of family life to the general factor of wealth.

However, many of the problems posed by our observations do not yield to such a simple solution. Often, we are faced by a bewildering set of interrelationships which carry no simple surface explanation. The intercorrelations among the social and economic characteristics of cities—wealth, employment, growth, divorce, crime—may appear to us as a meaningless jumble of figures without a coherent pattern. In such cases, if we wish to determine whether the many observed linkages could have arisen from the presence of a small number of common factors, we may have recourse to factor analysis which was invented for that purpose. If that possibility is sustained by the results of our factor analysis, we may direct our attention to the nature of those factors, although, strictly speaking, this step is outside the bounds of factor analysis.

Logic of Factor Analysis. In the essentials of its logic, factor analysis is similar to the method of agreement as formulated by John Stuart Mill. In brief, this principle holds that a circumstance which is common to a succession of categorically identical events, which otherwise have nothing in common, may be regarded as a cause of that event. Therefore, to discover the cause of an event, we search for that lone circumstance which is always present when the event occurs. In analogous manner, by means of factor analysis, we seek to isolate those common elements which are present in two or more variables and to which the intercorrelations among these variables may be attributed. Factor analysis, in its search for a common factor, thus resembles the method of agreement and to that extent is a quite traditional form of analysis. But its continuity with the past should not be permitted to obscure its distinctive properties as a technique for determining whether a set of observed variables are measures of a latent dimension(s) which accounts for the interrelationships among those variables. The method of agreement is more a principle to guide the search for causes; whereas factor analysis is an arithmetical procedure for determining whether the intercorrelations among many variables could be due to a few common factors. The method of agreement has the isolation of a cause as its stated goal; the isolation of common elements is the task of factor analysis. This distinction may be clarified by a simple path diagram:

$$C \begin{matrix} \nearrow X \\ \searrow Y \end{matrix}$$

We may regard C as either a cause of both X and Y or merely an element present in both variables. Factor analysis considers the possibility that X and Y are indicators of the same thing; the method of agreement considers the hypothesis that they are effects of the same cause. From the observed correlation between X and Y, we may draw the inference that they were produced by the same cause or that they are, in varying degrees, aspects of the same thing. Since an observed correlation cannot speak for itself, our interpretation of that correlation will depend on whether our search is for a common cause or an underlying dimension.

Historical Note. Factor analysis originated in 1900 in the work of Spearman (1904), the British psychologist who drew on the statistical theory of Karl Pearson, also British. Spearman sought to determine whether the correlation among different tests of mental ability could be attributed to a single factor of general intelligence which each test registered to a greater or lesser degree. Accordingly, his theory of mental ability came to be known as the two-factor theory, with each ability regarded as a compound of general intelligence and a factor specific to that particular ability. Much of the work in factor analysis during the first quarter of the twentieth century was undertaken within the framework of this "two-factor theory."

However, a shift in emphasis occurred between 1920 and 1925, reflecting in part a dissatisfaction with Spearman's approach which limited itself to the case of one common factor and disregarded the case of two or more common factors. This shift in emphasis culminated in Thurstone's formulation of multiple factor analysis which, as its name implies, placed no restriction on the number of common factors that might be invoked to account for the intercorrelations (except that it be smaller than the number of variables). In line with this development, the work in factor analysis during the period of 1925 to 1950 was devoted largely to elaborating the theory of multiple factors.

It would perhaps not be unfair to characterize the last twenty years (1950–1970) as lacking in innovations comparable in significance to those of Spearman and Thurstone, although this period has not been devoid of considerable technical advance. Perhaps the most important trend from the standpoint of sociological research is the greatly increased feasibility of factor analysis by virtue of developments in electronic data processing. Before the electronic computer, the application of factor analysis to large bodies of data was virtually prohibitive and could require several or more weeks to complete, whereas at present such analyses may be performed economically in a matter of several minutes. For this reason, we may expect within the next few decades a thorough exploration of the utility of factor analysis in social research.

Sequence of Topics. Although in practice we begin with observed correlations and work backwards to the factors which could have given rise to them, here (for didactic reasons) we begin with variables consisting of one or more factors and move forward to the correlations to which they give rise. In other words, we work from common factors to derived correlations, while in practice we work from observed correlations to their possible latent origins. Of course, if the common factors were accessible to direct observation and measurement, we would not need factor analysis. Factor analysis is an expedient to which we have recourse when the respective components of which the observed variable is presumably constituted are hidden from view.

In this chapter, however, we deal with variables in their decomposed form in order to examine the manner in which their intercorrelations are determined by those factors which they hold in common. We begin with the simplest case of n variables with one factor in common; next, we take up the case of n variables sharing two common factors; finally, for greater generality we consider n variables with m factors in common. By this procedure, which is deliberately repetitious, we intend to expose to view those underlying conditions which the research worker seeks to reconstruct by applying the technique of factor analysis to a set of observed correlations. But here we take these conditions as given, in order to examine the pattern of statistical correlations to which they may give rise. Having examined such patterns, we may comprehend more readily the inferences which are drawn from them concerning the factors which produced them.

Terminology. To distinguish the observed variables, which are manipulated, from the common variables, which are hidden components in them, it is customary to speak of the latter as factors rather than variables. Thus, for the simplest case of two variables, Y_1 and Y_2, where each is the sum of two parts, one part common (F) and one part unique (U_i), i.e., where

$$Y_1 = F + U_1,$$

$$Y_2 = F + U_2,$$

we conventionally speak of Y as a variable and F and U as factors. However, to dispel any confusion concerning the nature of these factors, it may be well to emphasize at the start that factors (within the context of factor analysis) are statistical variables in the usual sense of that term: a "factor" has a mean and a variance; it may be symmetrically distributed; it may be correlated with other factors; etc.

But in that case, if a factor is nothing more than a variable, why not employ the latter term without exception and thereby simplify our vocabulary? Our first answer is that the special term "factor" serves to maintain the distinction between the composite variable, which is observed, and its component parts, which are hypothetical. A second reply is that the results of a factor analysis resemble the results obtained by factoring in arithmetic, in that they may be multiplied together to restore the observed "product" from which they were extracted. In the third place, the distinction is so conventional that we would be doing the student a disservice to ignore it completely.

PART 2

One Factor Model

The Case of One Common Factor, F. To develop this case, we begin with a single variable which we regard as the sum of two parts which are by definition statistically independent. In symbols:

$$Y = F + U.$$

We take this as our model.* The mean of the variable is $\sum Y/N$ and the

---

* By attaching the coefficients a and b to F and U, respectively, we get the more general expression, $Y = aF + bU$. Setting $a = 1$, and $b = 1$, we get the simpler model,

$$Y = F + U,$$

which will do for our purposes.

variance is $\sum(Y - \bar{Y})^2/N$. However, for purposes of our analysis, it is necessary that we express both the mean and variance of Y in terms of its component parts, F and U. Applying the rule that the mean of the sum is the sum of the means, we get

$$\bar{Y} = \bar{F} + \bar{U}.$$

Expressing the deviation from the mean in decomposed form, we have

$$\begin{aligned} Y - \bar{Y} &= (F + U) - (\bar{F} + \bar{U}) \\ &= (F - \bar{F}) + (U - \bar{U}) \\ &= f + u, \end{aligned}$$

where $f = F - \bar{F}$; $u = U - \bar{U}$. Squaring the binomial $(f + u)$, summing, and distributing the constant, $\dfrac{1}{N}$, we get

$$\sigma_y^2 = \frac{1}{N} \sum f^2 + \frac{1}{N} \sum u^2 + \frac{1}{N} \sum fu.$$

Dropping the covariance between F and U (the last term on the right), which is zero by reason of their independence, and using conventional expressions, we get

$$\sigma_y^2 = \sigma_f^2 + \sigma_u^2.$$

This result could have been obtained more readily by applying the rule that the variance of the sum is the equal to the sum of the variances when component parts are statistically independent. Since this is the more convenient procedure, we will use it whenever possible.

We next obtain the covariance between Y and each of its constituent parts, results which are also required in our subsequent analysis. By definition,

$$\sigma_{yf} = \frac{1}{N} \sum yf,$$

where $y = Y - \bar{Y}$. Replacing y by $(f + u)$, we have

$$\sigma_{yf} = \frac{1}{N} \sum (f + u)f.$$

Multiplying and separating terms, we have

$$\sigma_{yf} = \frac{1}{N} \sum f^2 + \frac{1}{N} \sum fu.$$

But the covariance of F and U is zero by definition, hence,

$$\sigma_{yf} = \sigma_f^2.$$

In words: the covariance of the part (F) and the whole (Y) is equal to the variance of F, given that component parts are statistically independent. Likewise,

$$\sigma_{yu} = \sigma_u^2.$$

In words, the covariance between Y and U is equal to the variance of U.

Before taking up the case of two variables, we find the correlation between Y and F, and Y and U, results which will be used regularly as we move toward the general case of n variables and m common factors. Since the product-moment correlation coefficient between two variables is simply their covariance in standard form, we need only divide their covariance by the product of their respective standard deviations in order to find the correlation coefficient. In our case,

$$r_{yf} = \frac{\sigma_{yf}}{\sigma_y \sigma_f}.$$

Substituting σ_f^2 for σ_{yf}, we have

$$r_{yf} = \frac{\sigma_f^2}{\sigma_y \sigma_f} = \frac{\sigma_f}{\sigma_y}.$$

Expressing this result verbally: the correlation between $Y = (F + U)$ and F, given that F and U are statistically independent, is the standard deviation of F divided by the standard deviation of Y. We note in passing that the larger σ_f is relative to σ_u, the greater the degree of correlation between F and Y, and vice-versa.

By the same method, it may be shown that

$$r_{yu} = \frac{\sigma_u}{\sigma_y}.$$

As a rule: to get the correlation between a part and the whole, where parts are statistically independent, divide the standard deviation of the whole into the standard deviation of the part. Summarizing results:

$$\overline{Y} = \overline{F} + \overline{U},$$
$$\sigma_y^2 = \sigma_f^2 + \sigma_u^2,$$
$$\sigma_{yf} = \sigma_f^2,$$
$$r_{yf} = \sigma_f / \sigma_y.$$

Two Variables, Y_1 and Y_2. Continuing our development, we next form a second variable, Y_2, retaining F which is present in Y_1, but discarding U_1 for U_2, which is defined as independent of both F and U_1. In brief,

$$Y_2 = F + U_2,$$

where the subscript designates the number of the variable. Since Y_2 is identical in structure to Y_1 and subject to the same restrictions, its statistical characteristics will be identical in form: its variance will be equal to the sum of its component variances; its covariance with F will be equal to the variance of F; its correlation with F will be equal to the standard deviation of F divided by its own standard deviation. In symbols:

$$\sigma_2^2 = \sigma_f^2 + \sigma_{u_2}^2,$$

$$\sigma_{2f} = \sigma_f^2,$$

$$r_{2f} = \sigma_f/\sigma_2,$$

where σ_2 = standard deviation of Y_2, and σ_{2f} = covariance of Y_2 and F.

At this point our primary goal is the correlation between Y_1 and Y_2, which variables by definition have a single factor F in common. As usual, our procedure is to reduce the covariance σ_{12} to standard form for the correlation coefficient r_{12}. The covariance between Y_1 and Y_2 is by definition:

$$\sigma_{12} = \frac{1}{N} \sum y_1 y_2$$

$$= \frac{1}{N} \sum (f + u_1)(f + u_2).$$

Multiplying and distributing the constant, $1/N$, we get

$$\sigma_{12} = \frac{1}{N} \sum f^2 + \frac{1}{N} \sum u_1 f + \frac{1}{N} \sum u_2 f + \frac{1}{N} \sum u_1 u_2.$$

Since the covariance between F and U_2 is zero by definition, and also the covariance between U_1 and U_2, we have, after simplification,

$$\sigma_{12} = \frac{1}{N} \sum f^2$$

$$= \sigma_f^2.$$

Dividing this covariance by the product of the respective standard deviations σ_1 and σ_2, we get

$$r_{12} = \frac{\sigma_f^2}{\sigma_1 \sigma_2}$$

$$= \frac{\sigma_f}{\sigma_1} \cdot \frac{\sigma_f}{\sigma_2}$$

$$= r_{1f} r_{2f},$$

which is the result we sought to establish. This outcome is of sufficient importance to restate in words: the correlation between two variables sharing one common factor, *given that component parts are statistically independent,* is equal to the product of the correlation of Y_1 and the common part (F) and the correlation between Y_2 and the same common part (F).

By transposing the right side to the left, we get the partial covariance (Formula 1.2.5):

$$\sigma_{12.f} = r_{12} - r_{1f} r_{2f}$$

$$= 0,$$

which permits us to restate the foregoing conclusion as follows: if we remove the one factor that two variables hold in common, their partial covariance will be zero.

Three Variables with One Common Factor, $n = 3$. We move now to the case of three variables, each composed of a common factor, F, and a unique factor, U_i ($i = 1, 2, 3$), subject to the condition that unique factors are statistically independent of one another and of the common factor F. When these conditions are met, we may write the intercorrelations among the variables by rule:

$$r_{12} = r_{1f} r_{2f},$$

$$r_{13} = r_{1f} r_{3f},$$

$$r_{23} = r_{2f} r_{3f}.$$

By virtue of these relations among three variables, it is possible to set up the squared correlation between each variable Y_i and the common factor, F. The procedure is (1) to multiply the correlation of Y_i and Y_j by the correlation of Y_i and Y_k, and (2) to divide that product by the correlation between Y_j and Y_k. That result will be r_{if}^2, as in the following demonstration:

(2.2.1)
$$\frac{r_{ij} r_{ik}}{r_{jk}} = \frac{r_{if} r_{jf} r_{if} r_{kf}}{r_{jf} r_{kf}}$$

$$= r_{if}^2.$$

Taking the square root of this result, we get r_{if}. A summary statement is as follows: when three or more variables have only one factor (F) in common, we may find the squared correlation between a given variable (Y_i) and that common factor (F) by dividing the correlation between any two variables, Y_j and Y_k, into the product of the correlations between those two variables and the variable whose factor correlation is sought. Taking the square root, we get the factor correlation.

Four Variables, One Common Factor. Taking the next step in this sequence, we move to the case of four variables sharing one common factor. A set consisting of four variables will give rise to six intercorrelations which may be written by rule:

$$r_{12} = r_{1f}r_{2f} \qquad r_{23} = r_{2f}r_{3f} \qquad r_{34} = r_{3f}r_{4f}$$

$$r_{13} = r_{1f}r_{3f} \qquad r_{24} = r_{2f}r_{4f}$$

$$r_{14} = r_{1f}r_{4f}$$

Upon analyzing these relationships, we observe that the ratio of r_{12} to r_{13} is equal to the ratio of r_{24} to r_{34}; likewise, the ratio of r_{13} to r_{14} is equal to the ratio of r_{23} to r_{24}. In general, such ratios will be equal if there is a common variable within each ratio and a common pair of variables between such ratios. Therefore, the general formula is

(2.2.2)
$$\frac{r_{ig}}{r_{ik}} = \frac{r_{gl}}{r_{kl}},$$

where i and l occur within ratios, and g and k comprise the common pair between ratios. Thus, in the first example cited above, Y_1 is common to r_{12}/r_{13}; Y_4 is common to r_{24}/r_{34}, and the pair Y_2 and Y_3 is common to both ratios. To verify the equality (2.2.2), we write

$$\frac{r_{ij}}{r_{ik}} = \frac{r_{if}r_{jf}}{r_{if}r_{kf}}.$$

Canceling terms on the right side, we get

$$\frac{r_{ij}}{r_{ik}} = \frac{r_{jf}}{r_{kf}}.$$

Similarly,

$$\frac{r_{jl}}{r_{kl}} = \frac{r_{jf}}{r_{kf}}.$$

Therefore,

$$\frac{r_{ij}}{r_{ik}} = \frac{r_{jl}}{r_{kl}}.$$

With four variables, it is possible to set up six such identities, as may be verified by taking variables one at a time in any order and discarding duplicates as we proceed from the first to the last selected variable. Beginning with Y_1, we get

$$\frac{r_{13}}{r_{14}} = \frac{r_{32}}{r_{42}}; \quad \frac{r_{12}}{r_{14}} = \frac{r_{23}}{r_{43}}; \quad \frac{r_{12}}{r_{13}} = \frac{r_{24}}{r_{34}}.$$

Continuing with Y_2, we need write only two of the three identities, since one of them will have been written with Y_1 as our pivot:

$$\frac{r_{21}}{r_{24}} = \frac{r_{13}}{r_{43}}; \quad \frac{r_{21}}{r_{23}} = \frac{r_{14}}{r_{34}}.$$

To get the sixth such identity, we may begin with either Y_3 or Y_4, since the outcome will be the same regardless of which one we select. Taking Y_3 as our point of departure, we get

$$\frac{r_{31}}{r_{32}} = \frac{r_{14}}{r_{24}}.$$

Although we could complete this phase of our analysis in terms of simple fractions, it will be more convenient, as well as conventional, if we clear fractions and continue in terms of the products between correlations. Performing this operation, and at the same time putting numerals in subscripts in their natural order, we get

$$r_{13}r_{24} = r_{23}r_{14}, \qquad r_{12}r_{34} = r_{24}r_{13},$$

$$r_{12}r_{34} = r_{23}r_{14}, \qquad r_{12}r_{34} = r_{23}r_{14},$$

$$r_{12}r_{34} = r_{24}r_{13}, \qquad r_{13}r_{24} = r_{23}r_{14}.$$

Since the three equations on the right duplicate the three on the left, they may be discarded, and only the three on the left remain.

By transposing the right side to the left side for each of the three remaining equations, we get

$$r_{13}r_{24} - r_{23}r_{14} = 0,$$

$$r_{12}r_{34} - r_{23}r_{14} = 0,$$

$$r_{12}r_{34} - r_{24}r_{13} = 0.$$

Each expression on the left is called a *tetrad difference*, or simply a *tetrad*, since it is a difference founded on a tetrad (set of four) of intercorrelations. Although these three tetrads are distinguishable from one another in composition, any two of them will yield the third by simply subtracting one from the other. For example,

$$(r_{12}r_{34} - r_{23}r_{14}) - (r_{12}r_{34} - r_{24}r_{13}) = r_{13}r_{24} - r_{23}r_{14}.$$

Thus, when two are given, the third is fixed. (By reason of this dependence, we state that only two of the three tetrads are *linearly independent*.) Consequently, when any two of the three tetrads equal zero, the third will necessarily equal zero, as required by our one-factor model. A reversal of this logic is the basis of Spearman's renowned one-factor criterion: if linearly independent tetrads are identically zero, the variables may be presumed to share only one common factor.

Table of Intercorrelations. We may attain additional insight into the pattern of intercorrelations of four variables linked by a single common factor by arranging them in a square table, putting variables in any order. In our example (Table 2.2.1), variables are arranged in numerical order: 1, 2, 3, 4.

Table 2.2.1   *Variables in Arbitrary Order*

Variable	1	2	3	4
1		.56	.42	.63
2	.56		.48	.72
3	.42	.48		.54
4	.63	.72	.54	
Sum	1.61	1.76	1.44	1.89
Mean	.54	.59	.48	.63

We sometimes refer to the correlations to the right (or left) of the diagonal as the "side correlations"—they are to the side of the diagonal. Since the side correlations and the $[n(n - 1)]/2$ intercorrelations among the n variables are identical, we may employ the former term to designate the complete set of intercorrelations when that is convenient.

If the variables share one common factor, as in the case before us, the ratio of entries between any two rows within a given column will equal the ratio of entries (if not missing) between the same two rows within any other column. Thus, the entries in Rows 3 and 4, Column 1, will stand in relation to one another as do the entries in Rows 3 and 4 of the second column. In our example, 42:63 :: 48:72, as required by the one-factor model. By thus examining the table of intercorrelations, we may judge the tenability of the hypothesis that variables have only one factor in common.

We perhaps could judge more readily from the table if we arranged variables left to right and top to bottom according to the average magnitude of the intercorrelations of each variable with all of the others. When so arranged, the variable with the highest average will occupy the first row and column, the variable with the next highest average will occupy the second row and column, etc. Table 2.2.2 shows the variables of Table 2.2.1 rearranged to conform to this rule.

Table 2.2.2 *Variables Arrayed by Magnitude of Average Correlation*

Variable	4	2	1	3
4		.72	.63	.54
2	.72		.56	.48
1	.63	.56		.42
3	.54	.48	.42	
Mean	.63	.59	.54	.48

Correlations now appear in order of diminishing magnitude within rows, left to right, and within columns, top to bottom. Such a configuration of numbers was named "hierarchical order" by Spearman. The requirement that hierarchical order be satisfied in order not to reject the hypothesis of a single common factor is equivalent to the requirement that independent tetrads equal zero.

If we frame the table of intercorrelations on adjacent sides by the correlations between every variable (Y_i) and the common factor (F), we may obtain entries for all cells in the interior table by multiplying each coefficient in Column F by every coefficient in Row F. This process is exemplified by Tables 2.2.3 and 2.2.4. Our table, exclusive of Row F and Column F, now includes n diagonal values, flanked on either side by the side correlations. We refer to this interior 4×4 table of numbers as a *correlation matrix.**

Table 2.2.3 *Values as Products of Factor Correlations (r_{if}) Literal Representation*

	F	1	2	3	4
F		r_{1f}	r_{2f}	r_{3f}	r_{4f}
1	r_{1f}	r_{1f}^2	r_{12}	r_{13}	r_{14}
2	r_{2f}	r_{12}	r_{2f}^2	r_{23}	r_{24}
3	r_{3f}	r_{13}	r_{23}	r_{3f}^2	r_{34}
4	r_{4f}	r_{14}	r_{24}	r_{34}	r_{4f}^2

* A matrix by definition is a set of $r \times c$ numbers arranged in an $r \times c$ table with one and only one entry in each cell. It is therefore impossible for fewer than $r \times c$ numbers deployed in an $r \times c$ grid to constitute a matrix, since a matrix by definition requires that each cell be occupied by one and only one number. For that reason, the table of side correlations with missing diagonal values is not a matrix (although it is sometimes loosely called that).

Table 2.2.4   *Values as Products of Factor Correlations* (r_{if})
Numerical Example

	F	4	2	1	3
F		.90	.80	.70	.60
4	.90	.81	.72	.63	.54
2	.80	.72	.64	.56	.48
1	.70	.63	.56	.49	.42
3	.60	.54	.48	.42	.36

For purposes of distinguishing among correlation matrices, we sometimes refer to a correlation matrix whose diagonal values are identically equal to 1 as a *complete correlation matrix*, and a matrix whose diagonal values are smaller than 1 as a *reduced correlation matrix*. Corresponding to this terminology, we would state that we are presently dealing with a reduced correlation matrix, since $r_{if}^2 < 1$.

Giving our attention to the reduced correlation matrix and the marginal values which frame it (Table 2.2.3), if first we multiply the ith entry in Row F by the jth entry in Column F (i not equal to j), we get r_{ij}. Evidently, we may obtain the complete set of intercorrelations from the entries in Row F (or Column F). Second, we may multiply the ith entry in Row F by the corresponding i^{th} entry in Column F to obtain r_{if}^2. This result is entered along the principal diagonal (running from upper left to lower right). Now, r_{if}^2 by definition is the proportion of the variance of Y_i due to the common factor F. That proportion has come to be known as the *communality*, and is generally symbolized by h^2. Then, by definition, $r_{if}^2 = h_i^2$, for our example. If h_i^2 is the proportion of variance of Y_i attributable to a common factor, F, it follows that $1 - h_i^2$ is the proportion of the total variance having its origin in U_i, the unique factor. Usually, however, the quantity $1 - h_i^2$ is interpreted as a residual variance, the exact composition of which is unknown: some part of it may be due to specific factors and some part to measurement and sampling errors. At this point in the argument, we need not be distracted by such matters, as our major concern is with the common factors and their effect on the intercorrelations.

It is pertinent that we could discard everything but Column F (or Row F), since all values in the reduced correlation matrix may be obtained by manipulating the entries in that column. Since this single column with an entry in each row is an $n \times 1$ table of numbers, it may be called an $n \times 1$ matrix. Because it consists of those factor correlations which permit us to reconstruct the side correlations and communalities, we refer to it as a *factor matrix*. Consolidating terminology, we may state that the one-factor model consists of an $n \times 1$ factor matrix from which the $n \times n$ reduced correlation matrix may be derived.

Intermediate Review. Before proceeding to five variables, it may not be amiss to review the relationships among four variables to which a single common factor gives rise. Such relationships, when observed in a sample, render tenable the hypothesis of one common factor. Given four variables, we have two linearly independent tetrads:

$$r_{12}r_{34} = r_{24}r_{13},$$

$$r_{12}r_{34} = r_{23}r_{14}.$$

In order not to reject the hypothesis of one common factor, we must establish that the tetrads are only insignificantly different from zero, i.e., not statistically significant. Although this condition must be satisfied in order not to reject the hypothesis of a single common factor, its satisfaction does not prove that only one factor is common to the n variables. We thus anticipate that the inferences we draw from a matrix of observed intercorrelations to unknown factors will be much less certain than those deductions we make, as in this discussion, from known factors to correlations. The uncertainties surrounding the inferences we draw from correlations is considered in the next chapter.

Five Variables. For five variables, there will be five factor correlations, corresponding to as many variables, and ten intercorrelations among variables, as may be verified by counting them. However, the number of different tetrads will now exceed the number of intercorrelations by five. Although we could set up all different tetrads in order to ascertain their number, such procedure is rendered unnecessary by the general formula for that total, given n variables. This is (Harman 1967: 74):

$$3\binom{n}{4} = \frac{n(n-1)(n-2)(n-3)}{8}.$$

Substituting 5 for n, we get

$$\frac{5(5-1)(5-2)(5-3)}{8} = 15.$$

But these fifteen different tetrads are not linearly independent of one another; in fact, only five of them are, as may be shown by standard mathematical methods. But intricate mathematics is obviated by the formula for counting the number of independent tetrads (Harman 1967: 74):

$$\binom{n-1}{2} - 1 = \frac{n(n-3)}{2}.$$

Substituting 5 for n, we get

$$\frac{5(5 - 3)}{2} = 5.$$

We interpret this result to mean that the correlations among five variables sharing one common factor give rise to five independent tetrads, each having a numerical value of zero. Conversely, the empirical finding that all five independent tetrads are identically zero is consistent with the hypothesis that each variable in a set of five is of the form $F + U_i$.

Lastly, given the one-factor model, ratios of entries between rows within columns of the correlation matrix will be equal, and it will be possible to arrange the intercorrelations as a hierarchy. Note that hierarchical order is more than a configuration of numbers; its essential condition is that entries in adjoining columns be proportional.

Thus, the case of five variables linked by one common factor does not differ in principle from that of four variables. The difference consists in greater detail: ten intercorrelations instead of six; five independent tetrad differences instead of two; six ways to express each h_i instead of three. Because of its greater intricacy, a 5×5 correlation matrix consisting of twenty-five entries does not lend itself so readily to scanning. Consequently, as the correlation matrix grows, we may expect to become more dependent on mechanical methods to evaluate the possibility that n variables have only one factor in common.

Case of n Variables. Since the case of five variables does not differ in its essentials from that of four, we may suppose that the case of six will not differ from that of five, and that in general the case of n variables will not differ from that of $n - 1$, where $n - 1 \geq 4$. Granting this supposition, we may generalize from the case of four variables to the case of n variables sharing one common factor. That generalization will consist of these particulars:

(1) Each of the $[n(n - 1)]/2$ intercorrelations is expressible as

$$r_{ij} = r_{if}r_{jf}.$$

(2) Each of the n communalities h_i^2 may be written

$$h_i^2 = \frac{r_{ij}r_{ik}}{r_{jk}}.$$

(3) Each of the $[n(n - 3)]/2$ independent tetrads will be zero and consequently all $[n(n - 1)(n - 2)(n - 3)]/8$ tetrads will be zero.

(4) And incidentally, ratios of entries between rows within columns of the correlation matrix will be equal.

Component Parts in Standard Form. At this point, we digress in order to demonstrate that we would have reached the same conclusion about r_{ij} with both variables (Y_i and Y_j) in standard form at the start. To put Y_i in standard form, we set up the identity,

$$y_i = f + u_i,$$

and divide both sides by the standard deviation σ_i:

$$\frac{y_i}{\sigma_i} = \frac{f + u_i}{\sigma_i}.$$

Separating terms on the right and multiplying and dividing each component by its own standard deviation, we obtain

$$\frac{y_i}{\sigma_i} = \left(\frac{\sigma_f}{\sigma_f}\right)\left(\frac{f}{\sigma_i}\right) + \left(\frac{\sigma_{u_i}}{\sigma_{u_i}}\right)\left(\frac{u_i}{\sigma_i}\right).$$

Substituting the familiar f' (p. 6) for f/σ_f, and u_i' for u_i/σ_{u_i}, we get

$$\frac{y_i}{\sigma_i} = \frac{\sigma_f}{\sigma_i}(f') + \frac{\sigma_{u_i}}{\sigma_i}(u_i').$$

If we represent the constant σ_f/σ_i by a_i and the constant σ_{u_i}/σ_i by b_i,* our formulation takes the simpler form:

$$y_i' = a_i f' + b_i u_i'.$$

The correlation between Y_i and Y_j is by definition the covariance in standard form:

$$r_{ij} = \frac{1}{N}\sum y_i' y_j'$$

$$= \frac{1}{N}\sum(a_i f' + b_i u_i')(a_j f' + b_j u_j')$$

$$= a_i a_j.$$

But

$$a_i = \sigma_f/\sigma_i$$

$$= r_{if},$$

---

* b_i is also used to symbolize the regression coefficient (p. 11); in statistical writing it is not uncommon for the same letter to stand for two or more different statistical coefficients.

and

$$a_j = \sigma_f/\sigma_j$$
$$= r_{jf}.$$

Hence,

$$a_i a_j = r_{if} r_{jf},$$

which is the conclusion we sought to confirm.

Correlated Factors. The reader may have anticipated that the identity,

$$a_i = r_{if},$$

holds if, and only if, F and U_i are statistically independent. Since we may lift that restriction, it becomes necessary to distinguish between the *factor correlation* r_{if} and the *factor coefficient* a_i. The former is the correlation between a variable (whole) and a factor (part), the latter is the coefficient of a factor (part) in standard form. Since a factor coefficient is the weight of a factor relative to all other factors, it has come to be known as a *factor loading*, which term we shall use interchangeably with factor coefficient. When the variable is the sum of two factors, as in the case just concluded, there are two factor coefficients; when the variable consists of three terms, as in the case next to be considered, there are three coefficients. In general, there are as many factor coefficients for each variable (in standard form) as there are factors in the sum that constitutes the variable. To express the difference between factor correlations and factor loadings, we refer to a complete set of factor correlations as a *factor structure* and a complete set of factor loadings as a *factor pattern*.

PART 3
Two Common Factors

Remark. From n variables composed of one common factor, we move next to the case of n variables with two common factors, and thence to the general case of n variables sharing m common factors. We note in passing that the abstract notion of n variables, each composed of one common factor and one unique factor, will be related only loosely to many sets of sociological data and will therefore be of limited descriptive utility in social research. Nor will the fit necessarily be improved by adding another common factor to the model. Social dimensions are not that simple. Nevertheless, a grasp of these very simple models will enable the student at a later stage of his work to deal with more complex formulations which may fit the empirical data more closely.

Two-Factor Model. Given n variables sharing two common factors, our problem is to determine the composition of the correlation between any two of them and the pattern of intercorrelations among all n of them. We now conceive of each variable as the sum of three mutually independent parts: two common factors and one unique factor. In symbols,

$$Y_i = F_1 + F_2 + U_i.$$

Since the mean of the sum is the sum of the means, we may write

$$\bar{Y} = \bar{F}_1 + \bar{F}_2 + \bar{U}_i.$$

Subtracting the mean, we get the deviation around the mean

$$y_i = f_1 + f_2 + u_i.$$

By the rule that the variance of a sum of independent parts is the sum of the variances, we write

$$\sigma_i^2 = \sigma_{f_1}^2 + \sigma_{f_2}^2 + \sigma_{u_i}^2.$$

To display the composition of the covariance between any two Y_i's, for instance, Y_1 and Y_2, we get the sum of the products of these deviations in expanded form and divide by N:

$$\sigma_{12} = \frac{1}{N} \sum (f_1 + f_2 + u_2)(f_1 + f_2 + u_1)$$

$$= \frac{1}{N} \sum f_1^2 + \frac{1}{N} \sum f_2^2$$

$$= \sigma_{f_1}^2 + \sigma_{f_2}^2.$$

Our conclusion is that the covariance between two variables composed of two *uncorrelated* common factors is the sum of the variances of the respective common factors. We may regard this result as an extension of that holding for one common factor: with $m = 1$ (where m is the number of common factors), the covariance between any two variables is equal to the variance of the common factor; with $m = 2$, the covariance is equal to the sum of the variances of the two common factors.

Since the correlation coefficient is the covariance in standard form, we anticipate that likewise it will take the form of a sum with as many terms as there are factors. The transformation of the covariance into standard form is accomplished by the now familiar technique of dividing it by the product of the respective standard deviations:

$$r_{12} = \frac{\sigma_{12}}{\sigma_1 \sigma_2}.$$

Rewriting the numerator and separating terms, we get

$$r_{12} = \frac{\sigma_{f_1}^2}{\sigma_1 \sigma_2} + \frac{\sigma_{f_2}^2}{\sigma_1 \sigma_2}.$$

Rewriting the variance of each factor as the standard deviation multiplied by itself, we get

$$r_{12} = \frac{\sigma_{f_1}\sigma_{f_1}}{\sigma_1 \sigma_2} + \frac{\sigma_{f_2}\sigma_{f_2}}{\sigma_1 \sigma_2}.$$

But when component parts are mutually independent,

$$\frac{\sigma_{f_j}}{\sigma_i} = r_{if_j}.$$

Hence,

(2.3.1) $$r_{12} = r_{1f_1} r_{2f_1} + r_{1f_2} r_{2f_2}.$$

Our analysis has thus culminated in the following proposition: the correlation between two variables sharing two uncorrelated factors is equal to the sum of the products of correlations between variables and the respective factors.

When there is only a single common factor, the second term of the sum will be equal to zero, and the expression (2.3.1) reduces to $r_{1f_1} r_{2f_1}$, a result previously obtained by direct methods. Anticipating a later generalization, since r_{ij} is the sum of two terms when two common factors are present, we surmise that the correlation coefficient between two variables will be the sum of three terms when there are three common factors; and, in general, the correlation will be the sum of m terms when there are m factors, subject to the condition that factors are statistically independent.

Standard Form. We could have attained the same result by putting all measures in standard form at the start:

$$y_1' = a_{11} f_1' + a_{12} f_2' + b_1 u_1',$$
$$y_2' = a_{21} f_1' + a_{22} f_2' + b_2 u_2',$$

where the first numeral in the double subscript gives the number of the variable; the second, the number of the factor, and where

$$a_{ij} = \frac{\sigma_{f_j}}{\sigma_i},$$
$$b_i = \frac{\sigma_{u_i}}{\sigma_i}.$$

By definition

$$r_{12} = \frac{1}{N} \sum y_1' y_2'$$

$$= \frac{1}{N} \sum (a_{11}f_1' + a_{12}f_2' + b_1u_1')(a_{21}f_1' + a_{22}f_2' + b_2u_2').$$

Multiplying, separating terms, and discarding covariances which are zero by definition, we get

$$r_{12} = \frac{1}{N} \sum (a_{11}a_{12}f_1'f_1') + \frac{1}{N} \sum (a_{21}a_{22}f_2'f_2')$$

$$= a_{11}a_{12} \frac{1}{N} \sum f_1'^2 + a_{21}a_{22} \frac{1}{N} \sum f_1'^2$$

(2.3.2)
$$= a_{11}a_{12} + a_{21}a_{22}.$$

But $a_{ij} = r_{if_j}$; hence,

$$r_{1f_1}r_{2f_1} + r_{1f_2}r_{2f_2} = a_{11}a_{21} + a_{12}a_{22}.$$

From the foregoing demonstration, we conclude that correlations between factors and variables are equal to corresponding factor coefficients (loadings) and therefore are interchangeable (provided that factors are uncorrelated). Although loadings and factor correlations are identical for this model, it is important to maintain the conceptual distinction between them, since they will not be identical when factors are correlated among themselves.

Two-Factor Matrix and Correlation Matrix. To depict the manner in which intercorrelations are related to common factors, we set up the reduced correlation matrix alongside the factor matrix, which will now consist of two columns corresponding to as many factors. For purposes of illustration, we have prepared a 4×4 correlation matrix with literal values (Table 2.3.1).

Table 2.3.1 4×2 Factor Matrix and Corresponding 4×4 Reduced Correlation Matrix.

Y_i	r_{if_1}	r_{if_2}	1	2	3	4
1	r_{1f_1}	r_{1f_2}	h_1^2	r_{12}	r_{13}	r_{14}
2	r_{2f_1}	r_{2f_2}	r_{12}	h_2^2	r_{23}	r_{24}
3	r_{3f_1}	r_{3f_2}	r_{13}	r_{23}	h_3^2	r_{34}
4	r_{4f_1}	r_{4f_2}	r_{14}	r_{24}	r_{34}	h_4^2

The factor matrix accordingly will consist of four rows, since there will necessarily be as many rows as there are variables in that table of values. In the first column of the factor matrix, we record the first-factor correlations;

in the second column, we record the second-factor correlations. (Since factors are uncorrelated, it is immaterial whether we use the notation for factor correlations or the notation for factor loadings.)

Given the restrictions we have imposed on our variables, we may manipulate entries in the factor matrix by rule to obtain the intercorrelations. To obtain r_{ij}, we get the sum of the product of the ith and j^{th} entries in the first column and the product of the same entries in the second column. In symbols:

$$r_{ij} = r_{if_1}r_{jf_1} + r_{if_2}r_{jf_2}$$
$$= a_{i1}a_{j1} + a_{i2}a_{j2}.$$

In mathematical writing, such a sum of row products is designated an *inner product*. For that reason, when correlations are equivalent to such sums, as in the case before us, we may refer to them as inner products. For an explanation of this terminology, see Harman (1967) or a book on matrix algebra.

Squared Entries. If we multiply each entry in the ith row of the factor matrix by itself and sum these squares, we get the communality of the ith variable, or the proportion of its variance due to the common factors. In symbols:

$$h_i^2 = r_{if_2}^2 + r_{if_2}^2$$
$$= a_{i1}^2 + a_{i2}^2.$$

Where before h_i^2 consisted of a single term, it now is a sum of two terms: the proportion of variance in Y_i due to F_1 and the proportion of variance in Y_i due to F_2. This result is in accord with the general definition of communality as the proportion of variance attributable to the common factors.

If we sum squared entries by columns and divide each column sum by n, we obtain the proportion of the aggregate variance which may be ascribed to the factor in that column. The reasoning is as follows: with all variables in standard form, the variance of each will be equal to 1 and the aggregate variance will therefore be equal to $\sum(1) = n \times 1 = n$. In general, the square of the ith entry in the jth column constitutes that part of the variance for Y_i which is due to F_j; consequently, the sum of all squared terms in the jth column will constitute that part of the aggregate variance which has its source in the jth factor. Hence the relative contribution of the jth factor to the total variance will be the sum of the squared entries in the jth column divided by n.

Summarizing: sums of squares by rows measure the contribution of all factors to individual variables; sums of squares by columns measure the contribution of individual factors to all variables.

PART 4

Some Auxiliary Concepts

Before giving the case of m common factors, which is an easy extension of the case of two factors, it will be opportune to introduce several auxiliary concepts which we use freely in all subsequent discussion, namely: *factor product, factor residual, factor pattern, factorial complexity, equivalent set, rotation, correlated factors,* and *factor structure.*

Factor Product. A factor product is simply the product between two co-efficients on the same factor. In convenient notation:

$$_k p_{ij} = a_{ik} a_{jk},$$

where a_{ik} is the loading of the ith variable on the kth factor and a_{jk} is the loading of the jth variable on the kth factor. Summing factor products for Variables i and j, we get the inner product for those two variables; summing factor products (squares) for the ith variable alone, we get the sum of squares for that variable. When there are two factors, as in the case just concluded, each inner product will consist of two terms: $_1 p_{ij} + _2 p_{ij}$; likewise, the sum of squares for each variable will consist of two terms: $_1 p_{ii} + _2 p_{ii}$.

Factor Residual. To define this term operationally, we first set up the identity:

$$r_{ij} = a_{i1} a_{j1} + a_{i2} a_{j2}$$
$$= _1 p_{ij} + _2 p_{ij}.$$

Transposing the first term on the right, we get

$$r_{ij} - _1 p_{ij} = _2 p_{ij}$$
$$= _1 r_{ij},$$

which is by definition the *first-factor residual* for the ith and j^{th} variables. Its complete title, "first-factor residual correlation," draws attention to both its component parts and its derivation: the observed correlation r_{ij} minus the correlation expected from the first factor alone, $a_{i1} a_{j1}$. Computing $_1 r_{ij}$ for every entry in the correlation matrix, including entries on the diagonal, we get a matrix of first-factor residuals. (Since first-factor residuals equal zero when the variables have only one factor in common, they are subject to the same interpretation as vanishing tetrads.)

Let us now define the *second-factor residual* for the ith and j^{th} variables. This will be the first-factor residual minus the correlation between i and j

expected from the second factor alone. In symbols,

$$_2r_{ij} = {}_1r_{ij} - {}_2p_{ij}.$$

We may regard a second-factor residual as the obtained correlation between the ith and j^{th} variables with the influence of the first and second factors statistically removed. If a set of variables have two and only two factors in common, as in the preceding case, then all second-factor residuals will be identically zero (or all tetrads formed from the matrix of first-order residuals will vanish).

We may thus anticipate that from a succession of factor residuals, it will be possible to determine the number of factors which are common to the n variables. If all first-order residuals are identically zero (within the limits of sampling error), we would conclude that the variables are held together by a single common factor; otherwise, we would conclude that a minimum of two factors is required to account for their intercorrelations, since one factor is insufficient.

To illustrate the process of computing first- and second-factor residuals, consider a 6×2 matrix of factor loadings (Table 2.4.1) together with the correlations which they yield (Table 2.4.2). We calculate in sequence all first-factor products (Table 2.4.3) and their corresponding first-factor residuals (Table 2.4.4); and all second-factor products (Table 2.4.5) and their corresponding second-factor residuals. Since second-factor residuals are necessarily zero, they are omitted. The student may wish to verify this result.

Table 2.4.1 *Factor Loadings*

Y_i	a_{i1}	a_{i2}
1	.70	.10
2	.60	.20
3	.50	.30
4	.30	.50
5	.20	.60
6	.10	.70

Table 2.4.2 *Side Correlations and Communalities*

Y_i	1	2	3	4	5	6
1	.50					
2	.44	.40				
3	.38	.36	.34			
4	.26	.28	.30	.34		
5	.20	.24	.28	.36	.40	
6	.14	.20	.26	.38	.44	.50

It is of interest that first-factor residuals (Table 2.4.4) constitute a hierarchical order, permitting the inference that beyond the first factor there is only one other common factor. In principle, although we rarely do so in practice, we may employ the criterion of vanishing tetrads at any stage to determine whether the residuals at that stage may be ascribed to one factor. When the tetrads obtained from the ith-order residuals vanish, we know that the variables have that many (i) factors in common. Since, owing to the accidents of sampling and measurement, tetrads based on actual measures will never be exactly zero, we must decide at each stage whether to regard them as random errors, or as the effects of additional common factors.

Factor Pattern. Broadly speaking, a factor pattern is a set of factor loadings. Since loadings may take any value between -1 and $+1$, we anticipate that no two factor patterns will be exactly alike. To indicate the variety of such

Table 2.4.3 First-Factor Products, $_1p_{ij} = a_{i1}a_{j1}$

Y_i	1	2	3	4	5	6
1	.49					
2	.42	.36				
3	.35	.30	.25			
4	.21	.18	.15	.09		
5	.14	.12	.10	.06	.04	
6	.07	.06	.05	.03	.02	.01

Table 2.4.4 First-Factor Residuals, $_1r_{ij} = r_{ij} - a_{i1}a_{j1}$

Y_i	1	2	3	4	5	6
1	.01					
2	.02	.04				
3	.03	.06	.09			
4	.05	.10	.15	.25		
5	.08	.12	.18	.30	.36	
6	.07	.14	.21	.35	.42	.49

Table 2.4.5 Second-Factor Products, $_2p_{ij} = a_{i2}a_{j2}$

Y_i	1	2	3	4	5	6
1	.01					
2	.02	.04				
3	.03	.06	.09			
4	.05	.10	.15	.25		
5	.06	.12	.18	.30	.36	
6	.07	.14	.21	.37	.42	.49

patterns, it will be convenient to designate factor loadings as either high ($+$) or low (0), without for the moment giving a precise numerical definition to these categories.

In the case of two factors, a variable may have high loadings on both, low on both, or high on one factor and low on the other. Conversely, a given factor may have high loadings in all n variables—a *general factor*—or high loadings in only some of them—a *group factor*. If every variable is highly loaded on both factors, so that our diagram consists of all $+$'s, it will be impossible to distinguish among variables by the pattern of their loadings. On the other hand, if each variable is loaded by one factor but not the other, each row will have one $+$ and one $-$, as follows:

Y_i	a_{i1}	a_{i2}
1	$+$	0
2	$+$	0
3	$+$	0
4	0	$+$
5	0	$+$
6	0	$+$

Factorial Complexity. When a variable is substantially loaded by only one factor and has negligible loadings on all the rest, as in the above table, it is said to have the lowest possible factorial complexity, or the greatest possible factorial simplicity. If all n variables have the lowest possible complexity, the pattern for all variables will likewise be least complex. Such a pattern, which by definition is a special case of Thurstone's "simple structure," is especially amenable to interpretation and is therefore usually preferred in applied work. But do we have a choice? Are we not obliged to accept whatever pattern of loadings (disregarding its extraction) is given to us and to make the most of that pattern? The simple answer is that we need not accept a pattern without alterations, rather we may modify it to suit our purposes.

Equivalent Sets. By way of explanation: only one set of intercorrelations may be obtained from a given set of loadings, but the same set of intercorrelations may be derived from many different but equivalent sets of loadings. By definition, equivalent sets will yield the same correlation matrix when subjected to the same operations. The significance of such equivalent sets in applied work is this: when the hypothetical true loadings are unknown but equivalent sets are available, we may select whichever set, in our judgment, best represents the true set. Although there is no call for such selection among alternatives when true loadings are given, that procedure is regularly employed in applied work where we progress from observed intercorrelations to unknown factor loadings.

Graphic Rotation. To illustrate the manner in which equivalent sets arise, we analyze the process of converting a given set of loadings on two factors into an equivalent set on the same factors. After conversion, we may compare our initial set with the transformed set to ascertain which one lends itself most readily to interpretation. We begin with the loadings of six variables on two factors (Table 2.4.6), and the fifteen intercorrelations and six communalities they produce (Table 2.4.7).

Table 2.4.6 *Factor Loadings*

Y_i	a_{i1}	a_{i2}
1	.70	.40
2	.60	.50
3	.50	.40
4	−.50	.40
5	−.60	.50
6	−.70	.40

Table 2.4.7 *Correlations and Communalities*

1	.65					
2	.62	.61				
3	.51	.50	.41			
4	−.19	−.10	−.09	.41		
5	−.22	−.11	−.10	.50	.61	
6	−.33	−.22	−.19	.51	.62	.65

In transforming our given loadings (Table 2.4.6) into an equivalent set, our first step is to represent each variable as a plotted point on coordinate graph paper, with the first factor plotted on the horizontal axis and the second factor on the vertical axis (Figure 2.4.1). Through this fixed scatter of

Figure 2.4.1 *45° Rotation of Coordinate Axes*

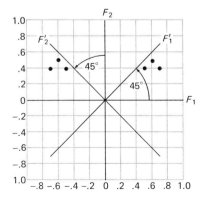

points we now rotate both axes counterclockwise by the same angular distance and determine the projections (coordinates) of the plotted points on the axes in their new positions. The detailed procedure for getting the values of coordinates consists of dropping perpendiculars from plotted points to rotated axes and measuring distances from intersections to origin. Our measurements are given in Table 2.4.8. Note that after rotation the loadings of Nos. 1, 2, and 3 on the second factor are negative, where before these loadings were positive in sign. Furthermore, Nos. 1, 2, and 3 are now relatively high on the first factor and relatively low on the second factor; whereas Nos. 4, 5, and 6 are now relatively low on the first, and relatively high on the second factor. Altogether, these results suggest that we take Nos. 1, 2, and 3 as an index of the first factor, Nos. 4, 5, and 6 as an index of the second factor.

Table 2.4.8   *Transformed Loadings*
Graphic Measures

Y_i	a_{i1}	a_{i2}
1	.78	−.21
2	.78	−.07
3	.64	−.07
4	−.08	.64
5	−.06	.78
6	−.21	.79

To verify that the rotated loadings (Table 2.4.8) are equivalent to the original loadings (Table 2.4.6), we compute sums of the squares by rows and inner products, corresponding respectively to communalities and intercorrelations. These communalities and correlations, as the student should confirm, are identical in value to those based on the original loadings; hence, we may regard the new set as equivalent to the old set by definition. Equivalent sets thus arise from the simple procedure of rotating perpendicular axes and reading the graph for the new values of the loadings. In performing this operation, it is necessary that the 90° separation between axes be maintained, otherwise the constancy of sums of squares and inner products will be disturbed. If we fail to maintain the orthogonality (90° angle) of our axes, we violate the condition of our model that factors be uncorrelated, since statistical independence between factors corresponds (by convention) to the orthogonality of the axes representing them. We may lift the restriction that factors be statistically independent, and correspondingly the requirement that axes be mutually perpendicular, but in that case the relation of loadings to correlations and communalities becomes more complex. Later in this section we consider briefly the model of correlated factors and the principal respects in which it differs from the model of uncorrelated factors.

Formulas of Rotation. To determine by sight the best fit of axes to points, we plot our loadings on coordinate graph paper, taking loadings on one factor as abscissas and loadings on the other factor as ordinates of our n points. If our aim is to reduce the factorial complexity of each variable, we would want our axes to come to rest in a position such that the new loadings (coordinates) altogether had the greatest degree of simplicity. Once we were satisfied, perhaps after many trials, that we had reached that position, we could read the new values from the graph with the help of dividers, parallel rulers, and other drawing instruments. However, at this junction we probably would avail ourselves of the standard "formulas of rotation" (Wilson and Tracey 1937), the results of which ordinarily will be more accurate than those based on graphic readings. For counterclockwise rotation, as in our example, these formulas may be written:

$$a'_{i1} = \quad \cos \theta a_{i1} + \sin \theta a_{i2},$$
$$a'_{i2} = -\sin \theta a_{i1} + \cos \theta a_{i2},$$

where θ = angle of rotation, a'_{i1} = transformed loading. For clockwise rotation, the formulas may be written:

$$a'_{i1} = \cos \theta a_{i1} - \sin \theta a_{i2},$$
$$a'_{i2} = \sin \theta a_{i1} + \cos \theta a_{i2}.$$

To use these formulas, we require both the cosine and sine of the angle between the old and new axes. In our example, the angular separation between axes in their initial and rotated position (Figure 2.4.1) is 45°. To find the cosine and sine of that angle, we refer to a table of angles and their sines and cosines, a fragment of which is reproduced in Table 2.4.9.

Table 2.4.9 *Excerpt from Standard Table of Sines and Cosines*

Degree	Sine	Cosine
0	.0000	1.0000
5	.0872	.9962
10	.1736	.9848
15	.2588	.9659
20	.3420	.9379
25	.4226	.9036
30	.5000	.8660
35	.5736	.8192
40	.6428	.7660
45	.7074	.7074

The cosine of 45° is .707, and the sine of 45° is .707. Substituting these values as constants in the formula for counterclockwise rotation, we obtain

$$a'_{i1} = \quad .707a_{i1} + .707a_{i2},$$

$$a'_{i2} = -.707a_{i1} + .707a_{i2}.$$

To compute the new loadings, we successively substitute all pairs of initial loadings for Variables 1 through 6, and perform the required arithmetical operations as in Table 2.4.10.

Table 2.4.10   *Transformation of Loadings by Rotation Formulas*

No.	$\cos\theta a_{i1} + \sin\theta a_{i2} = a'_{i1}$	$-\sin\theta a_{i1} + \cos\theta a_{i2} = a'_{i2}$
1	.707(.70) + .707(.40) = .78	−.707(.70) + .707(.40) = −.21
2	.707(.60) + .707(.50) = .78	−.707(.60) + .707(.50) = −.07
3	.707(.50) + .707(.40) = .64	−.707(.50) + .707(.40) = −.07
4	.707(−.50) + .707(.40) = −.07	−.707(−.50) + .707(.40) = .64
5	.707(−.60) + .707(.50) = −.07	−.707(−.60) + .707(.50) = .78
6	.707(−.70) + .707(.40) = −.21	−.707(−.70) + .707(.40) = .78

These results correspond closely to those obtained by measuring the coordinates of the plotted points with dividers and ruler. In case of discrepancies, we would retain the computed values and discard the values obtained by sight, since the former are presumably more accurate than the latter.

Criterion of Best Fit. Since axes may come to rest anywhere, we may ask whether there is a best position analogous to the least squares line in a regression problem. A widely employed criterion requires that axes be located to minimize the factorial complexity of the variables. When that criterion is strictly met, each row will have as many zeros as there are columns less one. If we calculate the variance of the squares of these loadings for each column, we will discover that the sum of these variances tends to be larger than comparable sums based on equivalent sets. Consequently, we may employ the sum of the within-column variances of squared loadings as an index of factorial simplicity. We reduce the complexity of the loadings by maximizing the sum of the within-column variances. This criterion has been named the *varimax* by Kaiser (1958) who devised it.

From the foregoing, one should not conclude that rotation is a simple matter. In our example, we stopped after one rotation; usually many trials are required to find the best position. We dealt with only two factors; ordinarily we have to manage several or more factors. Moreover, we maintained the 90° separation between axes (factors), while in practice we often lift this restriction and permit axes to strike an oblique angle. To reiterate: the process of finding the best fit becomes more complicated with more factors and with the removal of the restriction that factors be uncorrelated.

Correlated Factors. The sum of the squared loadings is equal to the communality of a given variable, subject to the condition that factors are uncorrelated. Subject to that same condition, the inner product is equal to the correlation between two variables. If we remove this restriction and permit factors to be correlated, these simple relations no longer hold. However, communalities and intercorrelations still may be expressed in terms of the factor loadings. Anticipating the outcome of this development, we will find that communalities and correlations derived from correlated factors are more complex in their composition than those derived from uncorrelated factors.

We first show the effect of a correlation between F_1 and F_2 on the variance of $Y = F_1 + F_2 + U$. To accomplish this, we write y_i' as the sum of its components, square that expression, sum over all N cases and divide by N. In notation:

$$\sigma_i^2 = \frac{1}{N} \sum (a_{i1}f_1' + a_{i2}f_2' + b_i u_i)^2.$$

Expanding and simplifying, we get

$$\sigma_i^2 = [(a_{i1}^2 + a_{i2}^2) + 2r_{12}a_{i1}a_{i2}] + b_i^2,$$

where r_{12} = the correlation between F_1 and F_2. The total contribution of the correlated common factors to σ_i^2 (in square brackets) thus divides itself into two parts: the *direct* contribution, or the sum of the squared loadings (in parentheses) and the *joint* contribution, or the product of the loadings weighted by two times the correlation between factors, $2r_{12}$. The total variance minus the proportion attributable to the unique factor b_i^2 is no longer equal to the sum of the squared factor loadings, as in the case of uncorrelated factors. Clearly, with correlated factors, the communality is more complex in its composition.

Factor correlations are likewise affected by the correlation between factors, as shown in the next sequence of steps:

$$r_{if_1} = \frac{1}{N} \sum y_i' f_1'$$

$$= \frac{1}{N} \sum (a_{i1}f_1' + a_{i2}f_2' + b_i u_j)(f_1')$$

$$= a_{i1} \frac{1}{N} \sum f_1'^2 + a_{i2} \frac{1}{N} \sum f_1' f_2'$$

$$= a_{i1} + a_{i2}r_{12}.$$

By identical operations, we get

$$r_{if_2} = a_{i2} + a_{i1}r_{12}.$$

From these results it is clear that factor correlations r_{if_j} are not equal to factor loadings a_{ij} when factors are correlated; hence, in these circumstances they are not algebraically interchangeable parts. In particular, when two factors F_1 and F_2 are correlated, the correlation between any variable Y_i and F_1 is equal to the sum of the loading of F_1 in Y_i and the loading of F_2 in Y_i weighted by the correlation between factors r_{12}. In this case, the contribution of F_2 to the correlation between Y_i and F_1 will depend on the strength of F_2 in Y_i and the correlation between factors r_{12}.

In view of the foregoing results, we expect that intercorrelations among variables are affected by the correlation between factors, as well as by the common factors themselves. To verify that general statement, we write the correlation between Y_i and Y_j in expanded form and simplify:

$$r_{ij} = \frac{1}{N} \sum y_2' y_2'$$

$$= \frac{1}{N} \sum (a_{i1}f_1' + a_{i2}f_2' + b_1u_1')(a_{j1}f_1' + a_{j2}f_2' + b_2u_2')$$

(2.4.1) $$= a_{i1}a_{j1} + a_{i2}a_{j2} + r_{12}(a_{i1}a_{j2} + a_{i2}a_{j1}).$$

From (2.4.1) it is clear that correlated factors contribute both directly and jointly to the intercorrelation between variables. The direct contribution consists of products between loadings on the same factor; the joint contribution consists of products between loadings on different factors. It is also clear that if factor loadings are given, together with the value of r_{12}, we may reconstruct the intercorrelation, r_{ij}.

Conversely, if intercorrelations are given, we may obtain the loadings from them, provided that we fix the value of r_{12}. If we make $r_{12} = 0$, our equations take the form of (2.3.2). We thus come to the principle that it is within the discretion of the investigator to fix the value of r_{12}. As in all data fitting, we choose whichever model best suits the purposes of the study.

Factor Structure. From the foregoing analysis, it is patent that factor loadings are equal to factor correlations only when factors themselves are uncorrelated. Since we will not always impose this restriction, we will need regularly to distinguish between factor loadings and factor correlations. To make that distinction, it is conventional to speak of a set of loadings as a *factor pattern*, and a set of factor correlations as a *factor structure*. Hereafter, we shall maintain this distinction and shall refer to a complete set of factor correlations as a factor structure, and to a complete set of factor loadings as a factor pattern. Since each of these will constitute a matrix, we shall occasionally use this more technical term when it is clear from the context whether the elements of the "factor matrix" are loadings or correlations.

PART 5

Multiple Factors

The Case of m Common Factors. We come finally to the case of m factors common to n variables and the intercorrelations to which they give rise. Each variate will now consist of $m + 1$ terms:

$$Y_i = F_1 + F_2 + \cdots + F_m + U_i.$$

Expressing this value as a deviation from the mean, we get

$$y_i = f_1 + f_2 + \cdots + f_m + u_i.$$

Since component parts are mutually independent by definition, the variance of Y_i is equal to the sum of the variances of the component parts, respectively:

$$\sigma_i^2 = \sigma_{f_1}^2 + \sigma_{f_2}^2 + \cdots + \sigma_{f_m}^2 + \sigma_{u_i}^2.$$

The covariance of any two Y's is obtained by dividing their product sum by N:

$$\sigma_{12} = \frac{1}{N} \sum (f_1 + f_2 + \cdots + f_m + u_1)(f_1 + f_2 + \cdots + f_m + u_2),$$

which simplifies by reason of the independence among component parts to

$$\sigma_{12} = \sigma_{f_1}^2 + \sigma_{f_2}^2 + \cdots + \sigma_{f_m}^2.$$

The covariance between any two variables linked by m common factors is thus the sum of the variances of the m common factors.

To obtain the coefficient of correlation between Y_1 and Y_2, we divide the covariance σ_{12} by the product of the respective standard deviations, σ_1 and σ_2.

$$r_{12} = \frac{\sigma_{f_1}^2 + \sigma_{f_2}^2 + \cdots + \sigma_{f_m}^2}{\sigma_1 \sigma_2}.$$

Rewriting this as the sum of m fractions, we get

$$\frac{\sigma_{f_1}^2}{\sigma_1 \sigma_2} + \frac{\sigma_{f_2}^2}{\sigma_1 \sigma_2} + \cdots + \frac{\sigma_{f_m}^2}{\sigma_1 \sigma_2}.$$

Substituting r_{if_j} for $\dfrac{\sigma_{f_j}}{\sigma_i}$, we get finally

$$r_{12} = r_{1f_1}r_{2f_1} + r_{1f_2}r_{2f_2} + \cdots + r_{1f_m}r_{2f_m}.$$

This is expressed verbally as follows: the correlation between two variables sharing m uncorrelated common factors is the sum of m terms, each term being the product of the correlation between the first variable and a given factor and the correlation between the second variable and the same factor.

Standard Form. If we had started with all measures in standard form, the outcome would have been identical. By definition:

$$
\begin{aligned}
r_{12} &= \sum y_1' y_2' \\
&= \frac{1}{N} \sum (a_{11}f_1' + \cdots + a_{1m}f_m' + b_1 u_1') \\
&\qquad\qquad\qquad\qquad \times (a_{21}f_1' + \cdots + a_{2m}f_m' + b_2 u_2'),
\end{aligned}
$$

which, after considerable manipulation, reduces to

$$r_{12} = a_{11}a_{21} + a_{12}a_{22} + \cdots + a_{1m}a_{2m}.$$

When factors are uncorrelated,

$$a_{ij} = r_{if_j},$$

and

$$r_{12} = r_{1f_1}r_{2f_1} + r_{1f_2}r_{2f_2} + \cdots + r_{1f_m}r_{2f_m}.$$

Tabular Display. In a conventional display of factor loadings, variables are placed in rows and factors in columns. Communalities may be recorded in the margin on the right and explained variances at the bottom of the table, as in the accompanying example (Table 2.5.1).

Table 2.5.1   *Factor Loadings and Communalities*

Y_i	a_{i1}	$a_{i2} \ldots a_{im}$	h_i^2
1	a_{11}	$a_{12} \ldots a_{1m}$	$\sum a_{1j}^2$
2	a_{21}	$a_{22} \ldots a_{2m}$	$\sum a_{2j}^2$
$\vdots$	$\vdots$	$\vdots \qquad \vdots$	$\vdots$
n	a_{n1}	$a_{n2} \qquad a_{nm}$	$\sum a_{nj}^2$
	$\sum a_{i1}^2 \quad \sum a_{i2}^2 \ldots \sum a_{im}^2$		$\sum h_i^2$

If we square all elements in the table and sum by rows, we get communalities. If we sum squared entries by columns and divide by $\sum h_i^2$, we obtain the contributions of the respective factors to the common-factor variance; if we divide column sums by n, we get the contributions of the factors
to the total variance.

By multiplying corresponding entries in any two rows and summing for
the inner product, we obtain the coefficient of correlation between the variables in those rows. For example:

$$r_{12} = a_{11}a_{21} + a_{12}a_{22} + \cdots + a_{1m}a_{2m}.$$

Thus, from the table of nm loadings, we may get the communalities of variables, the proportion of common-factor variance and the proportion of
total variance due to each factor, and the intercorrelations among the n
variables. Since each variable is regarded as the sum of $m + 1$ linear factors,
we may speak of our model as linear and additive.

PART 6

Alternative Models

Resumé. A correlation r_{ij} as the sum of m factor products,

(2.6.1) $$r_{ij} = \sum_{1}^{m} a_{ik}a_{jk},$$

holds when each variable is a linear combination of $m + 1$ uncorrelated
factors,

$$y_i' = a_{i1}f_1' + a_{i2}f_2' + \cdots + a_{im}f_m' + b_iu_i'$$

(2.6.2) $$= \sum_{1}^{m} a_{ik}f_k' + b_iu_i'.$$

If we retain the model of each variable as a linear combination of $m + 1$
factors, but remove the restriction that common factors be uncorrelated, the
correlation between two variables will consist of two parts: the sum of the
factor products and a term reflecting the interfactor correlations:

$$r_{ij} = \sum a_{ik}a_{jk} + \sum (a_{ik}a_{jl} + a_{il}a_{jk})r_{kl}, \ k \neq l.$$

The first sum on the right side consists of m terms; the second sum consists
of $\binom{m}{2}$ terms, or the number of interfactor correlations.

Given a set of *mn* loadings, and interfactor correlations all zero, we may obtain the intercorrelations among variables by substituting in (2.6.1); given interfactor correlation all or some not zero, we may find a different set of *mn* loadings which will produce the same intercorrelations. Thus, from the same intercorrelations, we may find loadings consistent with interfactor correlations all zero, or with intercorrelations not all zero. An implication is that we may select whichever interfactor correlations will minimize the complexity of our loadings, or satisfy whatever condition we may wish to impose on them. Although our choice of interfactor correlations may be guided by statistical criteria of best fit, in specific instances it will also be based on theoretical notions and empirical clues which together suggest the range on which the interfactor correlations probably fall.

Thomson's Counter-Example. In lifting the restriction that factors be uncorrelated, we left untouched the definition of the variable as the sum of $m + 1$ linear (first degree) terms, represented by Equation (2.6.2). But this definition is subject to alteration. And having altered it, we may determine the results to which our revised definition gives rise. If those results differ from those produced by Equation (2.6.2), we will have no difficulty in matching results to models. However, if both models give rise to the same pattern of intercorrelations, it will be impossible to infer from that pattern which model produced it. Under these circumstances, the pattern of correlations cannot be taken as crucial evidence, since it cannot rule in favor of one model and against the other.

This possibility was broached by Thomson (1916) who wondered whether variables of the form, $a_i f' + b_i u'_i$, were necessary to produce Spearman's hierarchical order (vanishing tetrads). He granted that such variables were sufficient to produce that order, given the independence between F and U, but he was not convinced that variables formed by a different rule might not give rise to the same hierarchical order. His attack on this problem was to construct $n = 10$ variables by sampling from a pool of $M = 36$ common elements, subject to the restriction that no variable have fewer than 6, or more than 24 common elements, and that each element appear in at least two of the 10 variables. In addition, the number of specific (unshared) factors was made to vary inversely from 0 to 24 as the number of common elements: the variable with the smallest number of common elements had the largest number of specific factors and vice-versa. Each variable thus had either relatively many group (shared) factors and relatively few specific (unshared) factors, or many specific and few group factors. The specific composition of each variable is shown in Thomson's chart, (Table 2.6.1). We may regard each of the ten variables as a merger of r common elements, $6 \leq r \leq 24$, and s specific factors, $0 \leq s \leq 24$.

It was Thomson's expectation that variables constructed in this manner would produce intercorrelations having a hierarchical order, which they did. This result lent support to his conclusion that one-factor variables of the

Table 2.6.1 Composition of Thomson's Ten Variables*

Element	Variable 1	2	3	4	5	6	7	8	9	10
1	×	×	×	×	−	−	−	−	−	−
2	×	×	×	−	×	−	−	−	−	−
3	×	×	−	×	−	×	−	−	−	−
4	×	×	×	−	−	−	×	−	−	−
5	×	×	−	×	×	−	−	−	−	−
6	−	×	×	−	−	−	−	×	−	−
7	×	×	×	−	−	×	−	−	−	−
8	×	×	−	×	−	−	×	−	−	−
9	×	×	−	−	×	−	−	−	×	−
10	×	×	×	−	−	×	−	−	−	−
11	×	×	×	−	−	−	−	−	−	×
12	×	×	−	×	−	−	−	×	−	−
13	×	×	−	−	×	−	×	−	−	−
14	×	×	×	−	−	−	−	−	×	−
15	×	×	−	×	−	−	−	−	−	×
16	−	−	−	×	−	−	−	−	×	−
17	−	−	−	−	×	×	−	×	−	−
18	−	−	−	−	×	−	−	−	−	×
19	−	−	−	−	−	×	×	−	−	−
20	−	−	−	−	−	×	−	−	×	×
21	−	−	−	−	−	−	×	×	×	−
22	−	−	−	−	−	−	×	−	−	×
23	×	−	−	−	−	−	−	×	−	×
24	−	−	×	×	×	−	−	−	−	−
25	−	−	×	×	−	−	−	−	−	−
26	×	−	×	×	−	−	×	−	−	−
27	−	−	−	×	−	×	−	−	−	−
28	×	−	×	×	−	−	−	×	−	−
29	×	−	×	−	×	×	−	−	−	−
30	×	−	×	−	−	−	−	−	×	−
31	−	−	−	−	×	−	×	−	−	−
32	×	×	×	×	×	−	−	−	−	−
33	×	×	×	×	×	−	−	−	−	−
34	×	×	×	×	×	−	−	−	−	−
35	×	×	×	×	−	−	−	−	−	−
36	×	×	×	×	−	−	−	−	−	−
S	0	0	1	3	9	14	16	20	22	24

* Source: Godfrey H. Thomson, "A Hierarchy without a General Factor," *British Journal of Psychology*, 8 (1916), p. 277. Reprinted with permission.

form, $a_i f'_1 + b_i u'_i$, are sufficient but not necessary to produce a hierarchical order. He drew the corollary that vanishing tetrads can attest to the possibility that variables have one factor in common but not demonstrate that

such is actually the case. Thomson's first paper was the beginning of a pro-
longed exchange of views between himself and Spearman, parts of which
are interestingly described in Solomon's (1960) instructive and sophisticated
article on the development of factor analysis. However, our interest is not
in the particulars of this debate, but in Thomson's experimental demonstration that differently constituted variables may give rise to the same pattern
of intercorrelations, and the implication that the mere presence of that pattern cannot be taken as conclusive evidence in favor of one model and
against the other.

Guttman's Counter-Example. Guttman's (1954) work is a variation on the
same theme, except that he was concerned with cumulative variables, which
were unidimensional by definition but whose correlations could not be
arranged in hierarchical order. Two or more such cumulative variables constitute what has come to be known as a Guttman Scale. In his studies he
was able to show that intercorrelations among cumulative variables do not
yield a hierarchy (vanishing tetrads), rather they give rise to a different but
nonetheless systematic pattern which he named "the simplex." By definition, cumulative variables satisfy these interrelated conditions: (1) each variable consists of a larger or smaller part of a general factor (g) and nothing
else; (2) larger variables include smaller variables; (3) variables may be
ranked from least to most inclusive according to their share of the g-factor.
We may represent such variables by a bar diagram (Figure 2.6.1), with the
least inclusive variable as the shortest bar, and the most inclusive variable
as the longest bar. Such variables produce vanishing tetrads, when all four
elements are on one side of the major diagonal; otherwise, they will be
greater than zero. Such a correlation matrix is shown in Table 2.6.2.

The explanation of this result lies in the make-up of the correlations
which are now ratios rather than products of factor correlations, according
to the following argument: If that part of g constituting the ith variable is in
the jth variable as well, the correlation between i and g, with j held constant, will be zero: $r_{ig.j} = 0$. But in that case the correlation between variable i and the general factor (g) will be equal to the product of the correlation

Figure 2.6.1   *Graphic   Representation   of   Cumulative
Variables*

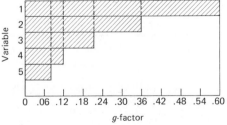

Table 2.6.2 *Factor Correlations (r_{ig}) for Cumulative Variables and Resulting Simplex*

Variable		1	2	3	4	5
	Loading	.07776	.1296	.216	.36	.6
1	.07776	1.0	.6	.36	.216	.1296
2	.1296	.6	1.0	.6	.36	.216
3	.216	.36	.6	1.0	.6	.36
4	.36	.216	.36	.6	1.0	.6
5	.6	.1296	.216	.36	.6	1.0
	Sum	2.3056	2.7760	2.9200	2.7760	2.3056

Reprinted with permission of The Macmillan Company from *Mathematical Thinking in the Measurement of Behavior* by Herbert Solomon (Ed.). © by The Free Press, a Corporation, 1960.

between variables i and j, and the correlation between j and the general factor g (Equation 1.2.5):

$$r_{ig} = r_{ij}r_{gj}.$$

Transposing, we get

$$r_{ij} = \frac{r_{ig}}{r_{jg}}.$$

Each intercorrelation is thus the ratio of a smaller to a larger factor correlation rather than the product between them, as in Spearman's system. A set of such intercorrelations, when variables are arranged from the least to the most inclusive, form a simplex rather than a hierarchy. Our conclusion is that the absence of hierarchy is not inconsistent with the hypothesis that the variables consist of only one factor, since the presence of simplex is also consistent with that hypothetical possibility. The broad principle to be formulated from this brief consideration of Thomson and Guttman is that, on the one hand, differently composed variables may give rise to the same pattern of intercorrelations, and, on the other, different patterns (e.g., both hierarchy and simplex) may be derived from variables which have only one factor in common.

A still broader principle is that our inferences from observed correlations to factor models are drawn with less certainty than our deductions from factor models to hypothetical correlations. The problem of drawing inferences from observed correlations is the topic of the next chapter.

EXERCISES

1. Given three one-factor variables with correlations as follows:

$$r_{12} = .24,$$

$$r_{13} = .32,$$

$$r_{23} = .48,$$

find the communality of each variable by formula, $r_{ij}r_{ik}/r_{jk}$.

2. Set up tetrads for the following table and calculate their values. Are your numerical results consistent with the possibility that variables have only one factor in common?

Intercorrelations and Communalities
for Four Variables

Y_i	1	2	3	4
1	.25	.20	.15	.10
2		.16	.12	.08
3			.09	.06
4				.04

3. Find the number of intercorrelations for ten variables, the total number of tetrads, and the number of linearly independent tetrads by substituting in required formulas (pp. 57–58).

4. Compute intercorrelations among offense rates from factor loadings (Table A) as if these rates had only one factor in common. Compare these correlations with the observed correlations for 1960 (Table B). What conclusion would you draw from this comparison?

Table A *Factor Loadings for Five Offense Rates*

Offense	a_i
Burglary	.76
Auto Theft	.57
Grand Larceny	.56
Robbery	.66
Petty Larceny	.72

Table B *Intercorrelations Among Five Offense Rates,*
Cities 100,000+, United States, 1960

	AT	GL	R	PL
B	.57	.55	.61	.59
AT		.58	.57	.52
GL			.56	.44
R				.40

5. From the loadings in the following table, compute intercorrelations and communalities.

Factor Loadings on Seven Variables

Y_i	a_{i1}	a_{i2}
1	.60	.35
2	.40	.70
3	.80	.15
4	.65	−.10
5	.75	−.25
6	.20	80
7	.05	.70

6. Examine the loadings in the following table and determine:

   (a) Which variable has the highest communality?

   (b) Which variable has the lowest communality?

   (c) What percent of the total variance is attributable to each of the common factors? To both together?

   (d) What percent of the common factor variance is attributable to each of the common factors?

Factor Loadings on Eight Variables

Y_i	a_{i1}	a_{i2}
1	.6	.2
2	.7	.0
3	.6	.0
4	.7	.5
5	.5	.4
6	.4	.0
7	.5	.3
8	.6	.5

7. Write a two-factor matrix of numbers for six variables. Verify that all second-factor residual correlations equal zero.

8. Plot the following loadings as points, taking the horizontal axis as the first factor, the vertical axis as the second factor. Rotate axes 45° clockwise to find equivalent loadings. Note that $\sin (0 - 45)° = \sin (-45)° = -\sin 45°$. Do the transformed loadings have more simplicity than the original loadings?

Factor Loadings on Seven Variables

Y_i	a_{i1}	a_{i2}
1	.74	.04
2	.72	.03
3	.88	.04
4	.65	−.19
5	.10	−.64
6	−.08	−.55
7	−.02	−.53

9. Verify that the transformed loadings in the preceding exercise produce the same communalities as the unrotated loadings.

10. Using the "formulas of rotation," transform loadings in Exercise 8 by rotating axis 30° counterclockwise. Compare the initial and rotated loadings. In your opinion, which set lends itself most readily to interpretation?

11. Examine the loadings in the following table and determine:
    (a) Which variable has the highest communality?
    (b) Which variable has the lowest communality?
    (c) Are there any general (shared-by-all) factors? Which ones?
    (d) Are there any group (shared-by-some-but-not-by-all) factors? Which ones?
    (e) Which variable has the lowest factorial complexity?
    (f) What percent of the total variance may be attributed to the common factors?
    (g) What percent of the total variance may be attributed to each of the common factors?
    (h) What percent of the common factor variance may be attributed to each of the common factors?

Factor Loadings on Eight Variables

Y_i	a_{i1}	a_{i2}	a_{i3}
1	.60	.70	.00
2	.80	.10	−.50
3	.60	.60	−.40
4	.50	.80	.30
5	.70	.00	.00
6	.80	−.10	.20
7	.90	.20	.10
8	.50	.10	−.70

REFERENCES

Cattell, Raymond B.
  1965   "Factor analysis: An introduction to essentials." Biometrics 21:
          190–215; 405–435.

Guttman, Louis
  1954   "A new approach to factor analysis." Pp. 258–348 in Paul F.
          Lazarsfeld (ed.), Mathematical Thinking in the Social Sciences.
          Glencoe, Illinois: Free Press.

Harman, Harry H.
  1967   Modern Factor Analysis. Second Edition. Chicago: University
          of Chicago Press.

Horst, Paul
  1965   Factor Analysis of Data Matrices. New York: Holt, Rinehart
          and Winston.

Kaiser, Henry F.
  1958   "The varimax criterion for analytic rotation in factor analysis."
          Psychometrika 23: 187–200.

MacRae, Duncan, Jr.
  1970   Issues and Parties in Legislative Voting: Methods of Statistical
          Analysis. Chapter 4: "Factor analysis: Introduction." New
          York: Harper and Row.

Rummel, Rudolph J.
  1967   "Understanding factor analysis." Journal of Conflict Resolution
          11: 444–479.

  1970   Applied Factor Analysis. Evanston: Northwestern University
          Press. (Recent applications of factor analysis in political and
          social research are listed in a special chapter.)

Solomon, Herbert
  1960   "A survey of mathematical models in factor analysis." Pp. 269–
          313 in Herbert Solomon (ed.), Mathematical Thinking in the
          Measurement of Behavior. Glencoe, Illinois: Free Press.

Spearman, Charles
  1904   "General intelligence objectively determined and measured."
          American Journal of Psychology 15: 201–293.

Thomson, Godfrey H.
  1916   "A hierarchy without a general factor." British Journal of Psy-
          chology 8: 271–281.

Thurstone, Louis L.
  1947   Multiple-Factor Analysis. Chicago: University of Chicago Press.

Wilson, W. A. and J. I. Tracey
  1937   Analytic Geometry. New York: D.C. Heath and Company

3

Correlations to Factors

PART 1
Introduction

Reasoning from Correlations to Factors. When n variables share m uncorrelated factors whose loadings are given, we may write the intercorrelations among the variables by rule:

$$r_{ij} = \sum_1^m a_{ip} a_{jp}.$$

It is thus a simple matter to move from mn factor loadings to the $[n(n-1)]/2$ intercorrelations among the n variables. However, to find mn unknown loadings from a given correlation matrix is a somewhat more involved task. Where before we started with m common factors and deduced their effects, we now start with n observed variables and infer their common factors. In this inferential process, we test a sequence of hypotheses, beginning with the hypothesis that the n variables share only one common factor. If we accept this opening hypothesis, we forego further testing; if we reject that hypothesis, we set up the hypothesis that there are two common factors and subsequently obtain results which will provide a test of this possibility. If we reject this hypothesis of two common factors, we move to the next hypothesis of three common factors, continuing in this manner until the statistical findings are consistent with the stated hypothesis of m common factors.

The process of factoring a set of intercorrelations may be regarded as a cyclical operation which will be more or less extended, depending on the number of common factors. When the variables have only one factor in common, the process will consist of a single cycle; when the variables have two factors in common, the process will consist of two cycles. In general, there will be at least as many cycles in the factoring process as there are factors held in common by the variables.

Although we may view the factoring process as a series of statistical decisions, in practice we obtain mechanically a succession of higher-order residual correlations, checking each set as it materializes to determine whether the residuals composing it are sufficiently small to justify terminating the factoring process. In still more mechanical fashion, we instruct our computer to extract as many factors as there are variables, discarding at the end those factors whose residuals are deemed to be negligible by a pre-established criterion. If five out of twenty factors based on as many variables will reproduce the correlations with requisite accuracy, we discard the last fifteen and confine our interpretation to the first five factors.

Factor analysis, then, may be regarded as a circular process that starts and finishes with a correlation matrix. From the matrix of observed correlations we get factor loadings, which, after manipulation, yield the fitted correlations which will be very nearly identical with the observed correlations. A flow chart depicts the process:

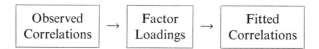

Relevance of Factor Analysis. But not every correlation matrix should be mindlessly factored as a matter of course. We have recourse to factor analysis when the results of that procedure are relevant to the purpose of our inquiry; the use of factor analysis implies a problem whose solution requires the application of that method. Ordinarily, we factor a set of correlations to test the general idea that many different scales are measuring a few underlying characteristics. Factor analysis finds its greatest utility in the realm of measurement and is usually not employed at all in causal analysis, although there are exceptions to this statement. In factor analysis, unlike regression analysis, we do not designate some variables as dependent and others as independent, with the implication that dependent variables are an effect of independent variables. Rather, we treat all variables as dependent in the special sense that all stand in a relation of asymmetrical dependence to the hypothetical common factors.

The Data of Factor Analysis. Factor analysis may fit our problem but, because of the make-up of our variables, it may be inapplicable. Ideally, our correlations should be based on continuous (interval) measures whose respective distributions are normal.* In practice we may be confronted with

---

* Conventional tests of significance in factor analysis are based on this assumption of normality.

correlations resting on ordinal or even nominal scales. In such instances, which are numerous in sociological research, we must satisfy ourselves in advance that the results stemming from an analysis of such numerical coefficients will lend themselves to a meaningful interpretation.

When the goal of the factor analysis is to arrange variables in clusters, the requirement of continuous measures is probably subject to some relaxation. But in any event, we should not blandly factor a matrix of coefficients based on attributes, without noting that attributes are not subject to the same interpretation as continuous measures. It is not possible to decompose an attribute into its common factors, since an attribute by definition is indecomposable. Nevertheless, it is technically possible to factor a matrix of attributes and, from the results of that factoring, to draw inferences about the latent factors which the attributes presumably express (McRae 1970).

Number of Variables. Our variables may be rightly subject to factor analysis but not reducible to a properly small number of factors. Every set of correlations, even correlations which are arbitrary in the sense that they in no way constrain one another, may be resolved into fewer factors than variables. Therefore, the "finding" of fewer factors than variables will be of no consequence unless that number is smaller than the minimum number of factors into which any set of arbitrary correlations may be resolved. To determine that smallest number, or minimum value of $m(mvm)$, we apply the standard formula (Harman 1967: 70),

$$(3.1.1) \qquad mvm = \frac{(2n + 1) - \sqrt{8n + 1}}{2},$$

taking the next higher integer as a solution. Substituting selected values of n in Formula (3.1.1), we get the numerical solutions displayed in Table 3.1.1.

Inspecting this table, we discover that at least four variables are required to test the hypothesis of one factor, since perfectly arbitrary correlations for

Table 3.1.1 *Minimum Value of m for Selected Values of n, Arbitrary Correlations.*

n	mvm
3	1
4	2
5	3
10	6
15	10
25	19
50	41
100	87

three variables always may be resolved into one factor. Similarly, note that at least five variables are needed to test the hypothesis of two factors, since correlations based on four variables always may be resolved into two factors. From the table, we infer that the largest value of m subject to test for n variables is one less than the minimum number of factors into which the arbitrary correlations for n variables may be resolved. By this rule, we are reminded that a "finding" of fewer factors than variables may be no more than a transformation of data and not a piece of scientific evidence. It is always well to keep in mind that the object of factoring is to express many variables in terms of a relatively small number of factors, and that the finding of many factors is somewhat incongruous, if not mathematically inconsistent with the whole notion of factor analysis. We may view the reduction of 100 variables to 25 common factors as a substantial statistical simplification, but the interpretation of that many factors will have complications which would not arise with one or two factors. If we substitute a smaller number of loosely defined hypothetical factors for a larger number of observed variables, we may get results that are statistically more parsimonious but sociologically less meaningful.

PART 2
Communalities

Since communalities are based on hypothetical common factors, we cannot calculate them from the observed data, as we do the correlations among the variables. The observed correlation of a variable with itself is necessarily equal to unity. But communalities must be given at the start of a factor analysis, if we are to find loadings which will restore them at its end.* As is so often the case in statistical work, we must be content with defensible estimates. Ideally, we choose those estimates which will yield, together with the r's, the smallest number of factors. (Technically speaking, we choose diagonal entries which will minimize the rank of the correlation matrix.) In practice, we often begin provisionally with values which fall short of that criterion of best fit.

In selecting even these tentative values, our task is simplified by the requirement that the communality fall within fixed boundaries. In the first place, being a proportion of a total variance which is equal to 1, the communality cannot be larger than 1. Secondly, it may be shown that the communality for a given variable cannot be smaller than the squared multiple

---

* Some methods require that the number of factors (m) rather than communalities be fixed in advance of the factoring. The leading ones are: Harman and Jones's (Harman 1967) method of *minimum residuals* (*minres*) and Lawley's (1963) *maximum-likelihood* method.

correlation (R^2) between that variable and the other $n - 1$ variables. Our range of realistic choices thus has R^2 as a lower limit and 1 as an upper limit. We could choose 1, though we would most certainly overestimate the communality; a more conservative choice of R^2 would underestimate the communality.

Nevertheless, the use of R^2 is favored by some authorities (Guttman 1956) on the technical grounds that (1) the R^2's are equal to the h^2's, if they minimize the rank of the correlation matrix, and (2) R^2 tends to h^2, if the ratio of m to n tends to zero as n tends to infinity. Additionally, there is evidence that the communalities obtained in refactoring tend to stabilize most rapidly with the R^2's as starting values in the diagonal (Harman 1967: 86). For these reasons, the research worker may be confident that in adopting R^2 as the communality he has conformed to sound theoretical principles.

Largest Intercorrelation as Communality. A common procedure of some currency, especially useful when results are to be obtained by hand, as in a pedagogical exercise, is to take a variable's largest correlation as its communality. If intercorrelations have been arranged previously in a square table, we identify the largest absolute value in each column (or row) and enter it as the communality in the empty cell on the diagonal. After making all such entries, we have a correlation matrix which may be factored. Because it requires no computations, this procedure has enjoyed a wide popularity; however, its use will probably disappear as the use of R^2 becomes more practicable.

The employment of the highest intercorrelation as an estimate of communality carries this justification: if r_{ij} is the largest correlation for X_i, and r_{ik}, the next largest, we may assume that r_{jk} will not differ greatly from r_{ik}. If we further assume that these particular variables, X_i, X_j, and X_k are affected by only one common factor, we get the result by Formula (2.2.1):

$$\frac{r_{ij}r_{ik}}{r_{jk}} = r_{ij}^2$$
$$= h_i^2.$$

Although this rough-and-ready procedure does not carry the same strict justification as R^2, it will often yield a close approximation to the best communalities. Moreover, the highest intercorrelation usually will be on the interval extending from R^2 to 1, or on the range of proper values, although within these limits the highest intercorrelation may be too large or too small. In fact, because the largest correlation for variables with low correlations tends to exceed the true communality, and the largest correlation for variables with high correlations tends to be deficient, authorities advise that the largest correlation for variables with low average correlations be lowered a little, and the largest correlation for variables with high average correlations be raised a little. For example, a variable with an average correlation of .20

and a highest correlation of .30 might have its communality set at .25, whereas a variable with an average correlation of .60 and a highest correlation of .80 might have its communality set at .90. In the exercises that follow, such adjustments need not be made, since our interest is in a simple, "quick and dirty" procedure which will permit us to carry out a factor analysis by hand.

Refactoring. Another procedure for getting communalities involves what has come to be known as iteration by refactoring. The factor analysis begins with unity (or any value between 0 and 1) on the diagonal. After a *predetermined* number of factors have been extracted, the obtained communalities for those factors are substituted for unity (or the initial diagonal entries) on the diagonal of the original correlation matrix which is then refactored. Then communalities obtained in this second factoring are inserted in the diagonal of the original correlation matrix, which is factored a third time. This process is repeated until the communalities do not change from one factoring to the next. Because these stable communalities are obtained by a process of iteration, they have come to be known as iterative solutions.

It is clear from the foregoing that the research worker has some leeway in his choice of diagonal values. There is no iron-clad rule to which he must adhere. He may start with R^2, or the highest correlation in each column, or 1. In fact, he may start with 0 and gradually refine his communalities by refactoring. In selecting his diagonal entries, the researcher will be guided by both practical and theoretical considerations. If alternative procedures are equally acceptable, his choice will be based on considerations of cost and convenience. If all procedures are uniformly costly, his choice will be guided altogether by the objectives of the factor analysis. Thus, in any given problem, the choice of communalities will represent a balancing of scientific purposes, on the one hand, against practical costs, on the other. When the research worker is limited to whatever "canned" programs are in his library, he will have to adapt his purposes to those available alternatives.

PART 3
Diagonal Method

With communalities entered along the major diagonal, we are ready to factor the correlation matrix. Of the numerous but related techniques for factoring a matrix of correlations, we have selected three for presentation: the *diagonal* method, the *centroid* or *summation* method, and the *principal-factor* method. Of these three, the principal-factor method is preferred in applied work but impracticable without the aid of an electric computer; the centroid method yields results which closely approximate those produced by the method of principal factors and may be performed readily with a hand calculator;

the diagonal method is ultrasimple, and for that reason we start with it. In each case, we restrict ourselves to the procedure for extracting factors and ignore the procedure(s) for testing the statistical significance of those factors. Although this separation is artificial, it does permit the student to concentrate on one matter at a time. The question of statistical significance is broached in Part 7 of this chapter.

The diagonal method* takes its name from the pivotal role of the entries on the major diagonal of the correlation matrix. It is sometimes called the triangular method after the pattern of factor loadings in which it culminates. When there are as many factors as variables, the loadings may be arranged as a triangle, as shown in Table 3.3.1. When there are fewer factors than variables, we get a truncated triangle, as in Table 3.3.2.

The procedure producing these patterns (Tables 3.3.1 and 3.3.2) requires that the communality and, consequently, the intercorrelations of at least one variable be statistically resolved with the removal of each factor until all n communalities have been resolved. Although variables may be eliminated in any order, a convenient procedure which carries some theoretical justification (Harman 1967: 103) is to select at each stage that variable whose unresolved communality is largest. Conforming to this rule, we begin with the largest communality in the correlation matrix; in the second cycle, we would take whichever residual communality is largest; in the third cycle, we take the largest residual communality appearing at that stage. We continue in this manner until all residual communalities are identically zero. Although this arbitrary rule of procedure is not theoretically required, we shall adhere to it, primarily to simplify our discussion and presentation.

We start with a matrix of numerical correlations (Table 3.3.3) in order to illustrate our steps as we explain them. Our first step is to identify the variable with the largest communality. In our example, this is Y_3, with a communality of .81. We make the loading of the first factor on this variable equal to the square root of its communality,

$$a_{31} = \sqrt{h_3^2}$$
$$= \sqrt{.81}$$
$$= .90,$$

and enter this value in a column set up to accommodate loadings on the first factor:

Y_i	a_{i1}
1	.60
2	.50
3	.90
4	.70

* Also known as the "square root method."

Table 3.3.1 *Factor Loadings by Diagonal Method, m = n.*

Y_i	a_{i1}	a_{i2}	a_{i3}	a_{i4}
1	a_{11}	0	0	0
2	a_{21}	a_{22}	0	0
3	a_{31}	a_{32}	a_{33}	0
4	a_{41}	a_{42}	a_{43}	a_{44}

Table 3.3.2 *Factor Loadings by Diagonal Method, m < n.*

Y_i	a_{i1}	a_{i2}	a_{i3}	a_{i4}
1	a_{11}	0	0	0
2	a_{21}	a_{22}	0	0
3	a_{31}	a_{32}	a_{33}	0
4	a_{41}	a_{42}	a_{43}	0

Table 3.3.3 *4 × 4 Correlation Matrix*

Y_i	1	2	3	4
1	.61	.48	.54	.62
2	.48	.39	.45	.50
3	.54	.45	.81	.63
4	.62	.50	.63	.74

Since the communality of Y_3 is completely determined by F_1, its $n - 1$ intercorrelations all reduce to the general form, $r_{i3} = a_{31}a_{i1}$. On transposing, we get:

$$a_{i1} = \frac{1}{a_{31}} r_{i3},$$

or the loading of the ith variable in the first factor. Substituting given quantities in this formula, we get:

$$a_{11} = .54/.90 = .60$$
$$a_{21} = .45/.90 = .50$$
$$a_{41} = .63/.90 = .70,$$

which numerical solutions we enter in the aforesaid column for first-factor loadings. As a computing routine, the foregoing process entails dividing each entry in the third column (or row) of the correlation matrix by the square root of the diagonal entry in that column.

With loadings on the first factor in hand, we manipulate them as required to obtain first-factor products $_1p_{ij}$ (Table 3.3.4), which we subtract from the observed intercorrelations to get first-factor residual correlations $_1r_{ij}$ (Table 3.3.5). In this operation, we may disregard Y_3, since all residuals for this variable will be identically zero. We include them in Table 3.3.5 to maintain a complete set of first-factor residual correlations.

Table 3.3.4   First-Factor Products, $_1p_{ij}$.

Y_i	1	2	3	4
1	.36	.30	.54	.42
2	.30	.25	.45	.35
3	.54	.45	.81	.63
4	.42	.35	.63	.49

Table 3.3.5   First-Factor Residual
Correlations, $_1r_{ij}$.

Y_i	1	2	3	4
1	.25	.18	.00	.20
2	.18	.14	.00	.15
3	.00	.00	.00	.00
4	.20	.15	.00	.25

Our procedure in the second cycle duplicates that of the first cycle except that we operate on residual correlations instead of the observed correlations. Whenever two or more variables have the largest diagonal value, as in our problem, it is immaterial which variable we select for elimination. We arbitrarily select Y_4. In accordance with the requirement that h_4^2 be completely determined by the first two factors, we get up the relationship:

$$h_4^2 = a_{41}^2 + a_{42}^2.$$

Transposing, we get

$$a_{42}^2 = h_4^2 - a_{41}^2,$$

and

$$a_{42} = \sqrt{_1r_{44}}.$$

As a rule: to get the loading of the second factor on the variable whose communality is to be resolved, take the square root of the residual communality of that variable. For our problem,

$$a_{42} = \sqrt{.25}$$
$$= .50.$$

We enter this value alongside Y_4 in a column set up for second-factor loadings:

Y_i	a_{i2}
1	.40
2	.30
3	.00
4	.50

Since the communality of Y_4 is completely determined by F_1 and F_2, its $n - 1$ intercorrelations all reduce to the general form,

$$r_{i4} = a_{41}a_{i1} + a_{42}a_{i2}.$$

Upon transposing and rewriting, we get:

$$a_{i2} = \frac{r_{i4} - a_{41}a_{i1}}{a_{42}}$$

$$= \frac{1}{a_{42}} \, {}_1r_{i4}.$$

Stated as a rule: to get loadings on the second factor, divide first-factor residuals for Y_4 by a_{42}. In our problem, we divide entries in the fourth column of residual matrix by the square root of the diagonal entry in that column. Carrying out the division, we get

$$a_{12} = .20/.50 = .40,$$

$$a_{22} = .15/.50 = .30,$$

which results are entered in the column for second-factor loadings. Since the communality for Variable 3 is completely accounted for by the first factor, its loading on the second factor is zero. We enter zero alongside Y_3 in the column of second-factor loadings.

We are now ready to calculate second-factor products ${}_2p_{ij}$ and their corresponding residual correlations ${}_2r_{ij}$, keeping in mind that second-factor residuals for Y_4 will be zero and therefore need not be computed. Second-factor products and residuals are shown in Tables 3.3.6 and 3.3.7.

Table 3.3.6 *Second-Factor Products.*

Y_i	1	2	3	4
1	.16	.12	.00	.20
2	.12	.09	.00	.15
3	.00	.00	.00	.00
4	.20	.15	.00	.25

Table 3.3.7   *Second-Factor Residual Correlations.*

Y_i	1	2	3	4
1	.09	.06	.00	.00
2	.06	.05	.00	.00
3	.00	.00	.00	.00
4	.00	.00	.00	.00

Each succeeding cycle is a repetition of the preceding cycle. In the third cycle we find the largest residual communality, which in our case belongs to Y_1. If we make the loading of the third factor on Y_1 equal to the square root of its residual communality, its total communality of .59 will be completely resolved by the first three factors, as required by our method. That is, if we make

$$a_{13} = \sqrt{h_1^2 - (a_{11}^2 + a_{12}^2)}$$
$$= \sqrt{{}_2r_{11}},$$

then

$$h_1^2 = a_{11}^2 + a_{12}^2 + a_{13}^2.$$

For our example:

$$a_{13} = \sqrt{.09}$$
$$= .30.$$

We enter this value in a column for third-factor loadings:

Y_i	a_{i3}
1	.30
2	.20
3	.00
4	.00

Since Y_1 has three common factors by definition, its correlations take the form

$$r_{i1} = a_{11}a_{i1} + a_{12}a_{i2} + a_{13}a_{i3},$$

so that

$$a_{i3} = \frac{1}{a_{13}} {}_2r_{i1}.$$

Substituting known quantities in this formula, we get

$$a_{23} = .06/.30 = .20,$$

which result we enter in the column for third-factor loadings. Since the communalities for Variables 3 and 4 have been resolved by Factors 1 and 2, we enter zeros alongside these variables. As in the preceding cycles, we compute factor products (Table 3.3.8) and deduct these from second-factor residuals for third-factor residuals. Except for the residual communality of Y_2, all third-factor residuals will be identically zero (Table 3.3.9).

Table 3.3.8   *Third-Factor Products.*

Y_i	1	2	3	4
1	.09	.06	.00	.00
2	.06	.04	.00	.00
3	.00	.00	.00	.00
4	.00	.00	.00	.00

Table 3.3.9   *Third-Factor Residual Correlations.*

Y_i	1	2	3	4
1	.00	.00	.00	.00
2	.00	.01	.00	.00
3	.00	.00	.00	.00
4	.00	.00	.00	.00

In the fourth and last cycle, we set the loading of the fourth factor on Y_2 equal to the square root of its residual communality which completes the factoring operation:

$$a_{24} = {}_3r_{22}$$
$$= \sqrt{.01}$$
$$= .10.$$

We enter this result in the column for fourth-factor loadings, together with zeros for the other three variables:

Y_i	a_{i4}
1	.00
2	.10
3	.00
4	.00

Since none of the residuals are affected by this loading—except the communality of Y_2—no further steps are required.

Now, if we arrange variables according to the order of their elimination, and factors according to the order of their extraction, we get the triangular pattern displayed in Table 3.3.10. This pattern is a necessary consequence of our requirement that one communality be completely resolved in each cycle of the factoring process. When factor loadings are so arranged, diagonal entries will be constant divisors for converting correlations to factor loadings. As noted, the diagonal method gets its name from the work load carried by the entries along the diagonal.

Table 3.3.10 *Factor Loadings by Application of Diagonal Method to Table 3.3.3, m = n.*

Y_i	a_{i1}	a_{i2}	a_{i3}	a_{i4}
3	.90	.00	.00	.00
4	.70	.50	.00	.00
1	.60	.40	.30	.00
2	.50	.30	.20	.10

Despite its appealing simplicity, this procedure may encounter technical difficulties in practice (Harman 1967: 42) and therefore is seldom used in applied work. However, in its very simplicity—perhaps deceptive—it does serve as a convenient introduction to the general process of factoring. All factoring is cyclical in nature, and cyclical operations are broadly similar, regardless of the specific method of factoring. In each cycle we get loadings, factor products, and residual correlations. If the residuals obtained at the end of a cycle are negligible within the range of sampling error, we stop the process; otherwise, we continue with the operation. In this respect, the diagonal method is similar to both the centroid method and the method of principal factors which we consider in the ensuing discussion.

PART 4
Centroid or Summation Method

Like the diagonal method, the centroid method is a cyclical process with each cycle culminating in the extraction of one factor. With minor exceptions, we perform essentially the same operation in each cycle, so that our procedure consists of a single operation which is repeated as many times as there are factors to be extracted. Since each factor is made to coincide (in a mathematical sense) with the centroid (center of gravity) of n points representing as many variables, this process of factoring was named by Thurstone the centroid method. But that somewhat technical term will be meaningless to readers unfamiliar with elementary mechanics. For that reason, in a discussion that is limited solely to arithmetical operations, we might reasonably discard the term "centroid" in favor of "summation" as a label for this procedure. Nevertheless, because of its wide currency in writing on factor analysis, we use the term "centroid" as a verbal tag for this factoring method.

In principle, we begin our analysis with the hypothesis of one factor ($H: m = 1$); if we accept this hypothesis (by the criterion that residuals are statistically insignificant), we necessarily terminate the factoring; otherwise, we move to a test of the hypothesis that the second factor, together with the first, will account for the observed correlations ($H: m = 2$). If the observed correlations may be reconstructed with negligible error from two factors, we discontinue the factoring; otherwise, we proceed with a test of the hypothesis that three common factors will account for the observed correlations among the variables ($H: m = 3$). In general, we proceed in this cyclical fashion until we accept the last stated hypothesis of m common factors.

The factoring process thus may be regarded as an instance of fitting a set of expected correlations to a set of observed correlations. In the first cycle, we fit correlations expected from one factor alone. If the fit is not good, we continue through the second cycle, now basing our expected correlations on two factors instead of only one. We continue in this manner until we have achieved a good fit between the observed correlations with which we started the analysis and those yielded by the derived factor loadings. Factor analysis, then, may be construed as an instance of fitting expected to observed values, and testing those expected values for goodness of fit. Such testing will be discussed briefly in Part 7 of this chapter.

The centroid method begins with the provisional hypothesis that all intercorrelations are due to one factor alone. In symbols:

$$r_{ij} = a_{i1}a_{j1}.$$

Upon summing all correlations for the ith variable, we get

$$r_{i1} + r_{i2} + \cdots + r_{in} = a_{i1}a_{11} + a_{i1}a_{21} + \cdots + a_{i1}a_{n1}.$$

Abbreviating the left side, and factoring and simplifying the right side, we get

$$\sum_1^n r_{ij} = a_{i1}(a_{11} + a_{21} + \cdots + a_{i1}a_{n1})$$

$$= a_{i1} \sum_1^n a_{j1}.$$

Rearranging terms and simplifying our notation, we get

(3.4.1) $$a_{i1} = \frac{\sum r_{ij}}{\sum a_{j1}}.$$

Equation (3.4.1) expresses the basic operation of the centroid method, namely: division of the sum of n correlations by the sum of n loadings. By thus expressing the sum of the correlations for each variable as a multiple (fraction) of the sum of the loadings on the first factor, we get a complete set of loadings on that factor.

Computing Procedure. To get the sum of the r's for Y_i, we simply add the entries, including the diagonal entry, in the ith column (or row) of the original correlation matrix. To get the sum of the unknown loadings, $\sum a_{j1}$, from the correlation matrix, we add row sums and take the square root of that sum of sums according to the following logic. By hypothesis,

$$\sum_1^n r_{ij} = a_{i1} \sum_1^n a_{j1},$$

and

$$\sum_1^n \sum_1^n r_{ij} = \sum_1^n \left(a_{i1} \sum_1^n a_{j1} \right).$$

Expanding the right side and simplifying, we obtain

$$\sum_1^n \sum_1^n r_{ij} = a_{11} \sum_1^n a_{j1} + a_{21} \sum_1^n a_{j1} + \cdots + a_{n1} \sum_1^n a_{j1}$$

$$= \sum_1^n a_{j1} \sum_1^n a_{i1}$$

$$= \left(\sum_1^n a_{i1} \right)^2,$$

hence,

(3.4.2)
$$\sum a_{i1} = \sqrt{\sum\sum r_{ij}}$$
$$= \sqrt{T_1},$$

where T_1 is the grand total of all $n \times n$ entries in the correlation matrix.

Expressing this result in words, we say: the square root of the sum of all $n \times n$ entries in the correlation matrix is by hypothesis equal to the sum of the first-factor loadings. But the sum of the first-factor loadings is the constant required to convert the correlation sums into factor loadings. Accordingly, when this sum, $\sqrt{T_1}$, has been computed, we may calculate factor loadings by dividing each column (row) sum by this sum. Our conclusion is that factor loadings are proportional to correlation sums, $\sum_1^n r_{ij}$, with $1/\sqrt{\sum\sum r_{ij}}$ as the constant of proportionality.

To illustrate Formula (3.4.1),' we apply it to five variables composed of two common factors; their communalities and intercorrelations are given in Table 3.4.1.

Table 3.4.1 *Correlations and Communalities for Five Variables.*

Y_i	1	2	3	4	5
1	.82	.60	.33	.64	.58
2	.60	.72	.06	.48	.60
3	.33	.06	.25	.25	.12
4	.64	.48	.25	.50	.46
5	.58	.60	.12	.46	.52

The centroid formula directs us to:
  (1) Sum entries in each row,
  (2) sum these n sums,
  (3) find the square root of the sum of sums,
  (4) take the reciprocal of this square root, and
  (5) multiply each row sum by this reciprocal to get factor loadings.
Carrying out this directive, we get the loadings shown in Table 3.4.2.

From these loadings we compute first-factor products, $_1p_{ij} = a_{i1}a_{j1}$, which we deduct from corresponding correlations to obtain first-factor residual correlations, shown in Table 3.4.3. Since these residuals are significant in a well-defined sense (see p. 129), we reject the hypothesis of a single common factor and consider next the hypothesis of two factors.

Table 3.4.2 *Row Sums and Factor Loadings for Five Variables.*

$\sum r_{ij}$	a_{i1}
2.97	.89
2.46	.74
1.01	.30
2.33	.70
2.28	.69
11.05	3.32

$$.30 = 1/\sqrt{11.05}$$

Table 3.4.3 *First-Factor Residuals*

Y_i	1	2	3	4	5	Sum
1	.02	−.06	.06	.02	−.03	.01
2	−.06	.17	−.16	−.04	.09	−.01
3	.06	−.16	.16	.04	−.09	−.01
3	.02	−.04	.04	.01	−.02	.01
5	−.03	.09	−.09	−.02	.05	.00

Second Cycle. In the second cycle, we begin with the hypothesis that first-factor residual correlations are determined completely by second-factor loadings. In symbols,

$$_1r_{ij} = a_{i2}a_{j2}.$$

(This hypothesis is similar to the hypothesis with which we opened the factoring, namely: $r_{ij} = a_{i1}a_{j1}$.)

Summing first-factor residuals for the ith variable, we get

$$\sum_1^n {}_1r_{ij} = a_{i2}a_{12} + a_{i2}a_{22} + \cdots + a_{i2}a_{n2}$$

$$= a_{i2} \sum_1^n a_{j2}$$

and

(3.4.3) $$a_{i2} = \frac{\sum {}_1r_{ij}}{\sum a_{j2}}.$$

The loading of the second factor on the ith variable is equal to the sum of the first-factor residual correlations for the ith variable divided by the sum of the second-factor loadings.

Since the numerator seemingly may be obtained directly from the matrix of first-factor residuals,* we need only consider a technique for finding the value of the sum of the second-factor loadings. The logic for getting this sum from first-factor residuals will be identical to that for getting the sum of the first-factor loadings from the original correlations. Starting with the relation,

$$_1r_{ij} = a_{i2}a_{j2},$$

we sum for the ith row,

$$\sum_1^n {}_1r_{ij} = a_{i2} \sum_1^n a_{j2},$$

and for all rows,

$$\sum_1^n \sum_1^n {}_1r_{ij} = \sum_1^n \left(a_{i2} \sum_1^n a_{j2} \right).$$

Rewriting, we get

$$\sum_1^n \sum_1^n {}_1r_{ij} = \left(\sum_1^n a_{i2} \right)^2,$$

---

* Residuals on the diagonal are usually replaced by the largest value in each column (row); also, diagonal entries always carry a plus sign

or, equivalently,

(3.4.4)
$$\sum_1^n a_{i2} = \sqrt{\sum_1^n \sum_1^n {}_1r_{ij}}$$
$$= \sqrt{T_2}.$$

We may express this as a rule as follows: to find the sum of the second-factor loadings, take the square root of the sum of all $n \times n$ entries in the first-factor residual correlation matrix. This is the constant which will permit us to convert row (or column) sums into second-factor loadings.

Impasse. Although it would appear that loadings on the second factor may be readily obtained by Formula (3.4.3), when we endeavor to apply that formula we find ourselves at an impasse. All quantities needed to get second-factor loadings are zeros: row sums are identically zero and, hence, the sum of sums is zero. The reason for this outcome will emerge if we retrace our steps in the first cycle and study their consequences. If we write each first-factor residual correlation as the difference between the observed correlation and the inner product based on our derived loadings,

$$_1r_{ij} = r_{ij} - a_{i1}a_{j1},$$

our sum for any row i will be

$$\sum {}_1r_{ij} = \sum r_{ij} - a_{i1}\sum a_{j1}.$$

But

$$\sum r_{ij} = a_{i1}\sum a_{j1};$$

hence,

$$\sum {}_1r_{ij} = \sum r_{ij} - \sum r_{ij}$$
$$= 0,$$

and,

$$\sum_1^n \sum_1^n r_{ij} = 0.$$

At the end of the first cycle, we find ourselves in a predicament similar to that encountered in calculating the mean of the deviations around the mean of a distribution. In that case, since the sum of the algebraic deviations is zero, we ignore signs and take the average of the absolute deviations. In symbols,

$$Mean \; Deviation = \frac{1}{N}|X - \overline{X}|.$$

In the present case, we break the deadlock by changing the signs of all entries in successive rows (columns) until all row sums are greater than zero. When all row sums are positive, we continue with the analysis, dividing each row sum by the square root of the sum of the sums for the loadings on the second factor. While this process is simple enough in the abstract, in practice it is quite tedious and can become, as Cattell (1952: 55) suggests, "as exasperating as trying to hold three footballs in two hands."

The following argument supplies a justification for changing the signs of the correlations for a given variable. If we change the sign of every measure in a distribution (i.e., multiply each value by -1), we reverse the rank order of our original measures: measures which stood high will now stand low; measures standing low will now stand high. Consequently, the meaning of the variable will have reversed itself. If the variable was originally wealth, it will be poverty after the transformation. People high on wealth will necessarily be low on poverty.

A corollary is that if we change the sign of one of the two variables in a product-moment correlation (r), a positive correlation will become negative and a negative correlation will become positive. For example, if wealth was positively correlated with social status in the first place, after reflection to poverty it will be negatively correlated with social status. Inverting this argument: if, for a given variable, we change the signs of all of its correlations, we will, in effect, have changed the signs of its individual values and thereby reversed the meaning of that variable. Conversely, if we reverse the meaning of a given variable, i.e., multiply every value by -1, we must change the signs of all of its correlations. Given an $n \times n$ table of residual correlations whose marginal totals are identically zero, our goal is to obtain marginal totals, each greater than zero, by reflecting one or more variables, i.e., by changing the signs of one or more variables. When all marginal totals are greater than zero, we may apply Formula (3.4.3).

Reflection of Variables. Our immediate problem is this: "Which variables should we reflect?" As a guiding principle, Thurstone suggested that we reflect variables in such manner as "to account for as much as possible of the residual variance." At the end of the first cycle, the residual variance is equal to the total common-factor variance, less that part due to the first factor:

$$\sum h_i^2 - \sum a_{i1}^2.$$

By Thurstone's criterion, we change signs (reflect variables) so as to reduce as much as possible this remainder or to make $\sum a_{i2}^2$ as large as possible.

Although many rules have been devised to facilitate the attainment of this goal, none is free of human judgment, and all have their disadvantages under specific circumstances. For present purposes, we shall consider the problem as solved whenever all row sums are greater than zero. Such a result will permit us to continue with the factoring, although we will not necessarily have met the criterion of reducing as much as possible the residual common-factor variance.

In a purely mechanical fashion, it is possible to reflect variables, one at a time, in any order until every row (column) has a positive sum. However, we may secure this result more quickly by reflecting those variables whose residual correlations are predominantly negative. Thus, if we select on each trial whichever variable has the largest number of negative entries, we will ordinarily have reached our goal of all row sums greater than zero after a relatively small number of trials. For the sake of simplicity, we shall adopt this procedural rule in our work, keeping in mind that alternative procedures will be more efficient in given problems and that our solution, which will enable us to continue factoring, will not necessarily satisfy the criterion of minimizing the residual variance.

To illustrate the process of sign reversal, or reflection, let us return to the table of first-factor residuals. In selecting variables for reflection, we first count the number of negative entries (minus signs) in each row. There are three negative entries for Rows 2 and 5, two negative entries for Rows 1, 3, and 4. Accordingly, we change the signs of all entries in the second row and second column, *except the sign of the diagonal entry which is always positive.* (It is always positive because either the total or residual communality to which it is attached is necessarily greater than zero.) The results of this reflection are given in Table 3.4.4.

Summing entries in Table 3.4.4 by rows, we obtain quantities, all of which are positive except that for the fifth row. Accordingly, we change the signs of all entries in the fifth row and fifth column, noting that by this reflection we will have restored the original sign of the residual correlation between Variables 2 and 5. (An even number of reflections always restores the original sign.) With these changes, sums of all rows are positive (Table 3.4.5) and we are ready to go ahead with factoring according to Formula (3.4.3).

The loadings on second factor are given in the last column of Table 3.4.6. Since reflected variables (2 and 5) are positively correlated with F_2, in their original state they will be negatively correlated with the second factor. Consequently, when factor loadings on the original variables eventually are displayed, we will give these loadings a negative sign, as in Table 3.4.6.

Table 3.4.4 *First-Factor Residuals after Reflecting Variable 2.*

1	2	3	4	5	Sum
.02	.06	.06	.02	−.03	.13
.06	.17	.16	.04	−.09	.34
.06	.16	.16	.04	−.09	.33
.02	.04	.04	.01	−.02	.09
−.03	−.09	−.09	−.02	.05	−.18

Table 3.4.5 *First-Factor Residuals after Reflecting Variables 2 and 5, Second-Factor Loadings.*

	1	2	3	4	5	Sum	a_{i2}
1	.02	.06	.06	.02	.03	.19	.15
2	.06	.17	.16	.04	.09	.52	.41
3	.06	.16	.16	.04	.09	.51	.40
4	.02	.04	.04	.01	.02	.13	.09
5	.03	.09	.09	.02	.05	.28	.22
					Sum	1.63	1.27

$$\frac{1}{\sqrt{T_2}} = \frac{1}{\sqrt{1.63}}$$
$$= 1/1.27$$
$$= .79.$$

Table 3.4.6 *Factor Loadings by Centroid Method.*

Y_i	a_{i1}	a_{i2}	h_i^2
1	.89	.15	.82
2	.74	−.41	.72
3	.30	.40	.25
4	.70	.09	.50
5	.69	−.22	.52

Since all second-factor residuals are identically zero, as the reader may verify, we accept the hypothesis that $m = 2$ and correspondingly discontinue the factoring. On the other hand, if residuals had been significant by a pre-established criterion, we would have manipulated them as necessary to obtain loadings on the third factor. In order of execution, we would have reflected one or more variables, computed T_3, and divided row (column) sums by $\sqrt{T_3}$ for third factor loadings. On the basis of residual correlations derived from these loadings, we would have tested $H: m = 3$.

Generalizations. In each cycle of the centroid process, we sum elements in the correlation matrix by rows (after reflection) and get the sum of these sums. To convert row sums to loadings, we compute the multiplier $1/\sqrt{T_i}$ and apply that coefficient to all row sums. We obtain residuals, $_kr_{ij}$, in each cycle and by these residuals test the hypothesis of k factors. If residual correlations are statistically negligible in the kth cycle, but not in the preceding cycle, we accept the hypothesis of k common factors and discontinue the factoring. To reach a decision, we may examine either the residuals themselves or the relative contribution of the $(k + 1)^{\text{th}}$ factor to the common-factor variance. If the contribution of this factor is negligible, the residuals from which it was derived will be negligible; if residuals are small, they will give rise to a factor which contributes only negligibly to the common-factor variance. The statistical significance of factors is broached in Part 7 of this chapter.

In applying the centroid method, we must reflect variables in each cycle, including the first cycle if necessary, in order that each row sum be positive in sign. To obtain the loadings on each variable as originally constituted, we reverse our reflections at the very end of the factoring process, in accordance with the following rule: when a variable has been reflected in a given cycle, the sign of its loading on the factor extracted in that cycle must be opposite to the sign of its loading on the factor extracted in the preceding cycle. By way of example: let us suppose that a variable (Y_i) was reflected in the second and third cycles but not in the first and fourth of a process consisting of four cycles. Its loadings on the four factors then would carry signs as follows:

	F_1	F_2	F_3	F_4
Y_i	a_{i1}	$-a_{i2}$	a_{i3}	a_{i4}

Concluding Remark. The centroid method was used widely by research workers until 1955, when it was superseded by the method of principal factors, next to be considered. The method of principal factors consists of complex operations which are practicable only on the electronic computer, whereas the centroid method may be readily carried out on the hand calculator. But it should not be concluded that the centroid method is vastly inferior to the method of principal factors and that it is a last resort which would never be used except for practical difficulties. On the contrary, the centroid method, as has been regularly noted, produces results that are closely similar to those yielded by the method of principal components. In any case, since factors are usually rotated after extraction, both methods may culminate in closely similar solutions. For that reason, it is usually all right, particularly for purposes of rough answers, to use the centroid method in factoring a matrix.

PART 5
Method of Principal Factors

The goal of all factoring methods is to produce a set of loadings that will resolve the common-factor variance, or reproduce after manipulation the correlations among the variables. In addition to this general requirement, loadings may be made to satisfy one or more specific conditions which we impose on them. We may, for example, require that the loadings on each succeeding factor reduce as much as possible the common-factor variance left unexplained by all of the previously extracted factors. By this criterion, the first factor would be required to reduce as much as possible the total common-factor variance; the second factor, the common-factor variance left unresolved by the first factor; the third factor, the common-factor variance left unexplained by the first two factors, and so on, until the common-factor variance is completely resolved. This is equivalent to the requirement that we maximize in order

$$\sum a_{i1}^2, \quad \sum a_{i2}^2, \quad \ldots, \quad \sum a_{im}^2,$$

where m is the number of factors required to resolve the common-factor variance.

It is this condition that the method of principal factors is designed to satisfy. Since there is only one set of loadings that will meet this condition, this method necessarily yields only one solution for a given correlation matrix, and in this respect is more restricted than either the diagonal or the centroid method. Both of these methods of factoring may give rise to multiple solutions in a particular application. Since, in applying the method of principal factors, the user is not forced to choose between alternative solutions, it is to that degree more objective than those factoring procedures which require such a choice.

Historical Note. Although the statistical theory underlying this method was formulated around 1900 by Karl Pearson, a working procedure by which a numerical solution might be obtained did not become available until the early 1930s. This procedure, devised by Hotelling (1933), entails extensive computations and is costly to execute without the aid of a high-speed computer—a circumstance explaining its infrequent use before 1960. Since becoming available as a machine program, it has all but replaced the statistically less efficient centroid method which was used almost exclusively from 1935 to 1955. But as previously remarked, it should not be concluded that the centroid method is greatly inferior to that of principal factors. In fact, it will yield results that closely approximate those produced by Hotelling's procedure provided that variables have been reflected so as to maximize T_i at each stage. Thurstone (1947: 178) himself, who was generally regarded as the leading exponent of the centroid method, recognized the statistical advantages of the method of principal factors and commented: "The centroid method of factoring and the centroid solution for the location of the reference axes are to be regarded as a computational compromise, in that they have been found to involve much less labor than the principal-axes solution." Some authorities maintain a stricter attitude. For example, Kendall (1957: 27–28) writes:

Psychological workers have developed numerous methods of component analysis which avoid the arithmetic required by the solution of the characteristic equation. My personal opinion is that they are objectionable and should not be used when they can be avoided. Perhaps they can be justified to some extent as giving approximations to the principal component method, but any discussion of their sampling properties seems almost beyond the range of reasonable possibility.

Principle of Least Squares. Since the method of principal factors is required to maximize the sum of the squared loadings in each cycle, it will necessarily minimize the common-factor variance left standing at the end of each cycle. It is thus consistent with the principle of least squares, and is therefore analogous in character to all methods conforming to that principle.

In this sense the problem of finding the principal factors is no different from the problem of the arithmetic mean. That problem is: find the numerical value such that the sum of the squared deviations around that value is smallest. By mathematical methods, we may demonstrate that the solution to this problem is the arithmetic mean. Analogously, in the case before us, we are required to find the loadings at each stage which will reduce the common-factor variance as much as possible. But there is probably an important practical difference. The computation of the mean, familiar to every school boy, is simple and straightforward: add the values and divide by their number; whereas the computation of the loadings for principal factors is complex and indirect, and is very tedious to perform by hand. Starting with trial values which may be only roughly proportional to loadings, we converge on the loadings through a sequence of quite intricate arithmetical calculations. Although we may carry out these calculations by hand as an exercise, in actual research they are done out of sight by the machine. To gain a better appreciation of principal factors, students are urged to solve a few problems by hand.

Arithmetical Procedures. Like the centroid method, the process of extracting principal factors is cyclical in the sense that successive factors are removed by essentially the same procedure within each cycle. To get factor loadings within each cycle, we perform two distinct operations: (1) obtain by iteration a set of numerical values that are proportional to loadings, and (2) transform these values to loadings by applying to each of them a "coefficient of conversion."

The procedure for obtaining values that are proportional to loadings consists of a sequence of trials (iterations) whose outcomes tend to proportionality. When the working limit of improvement is reached, the iterative process is discontinued. In this operation, we begin with a set of provisional values which are roughly proportional to loadings. These starting values are repeatedly adjusted until they become virtually stationary on successive trials, which stability is a demonstration that proportionality cannot be significantly improved.

First Cycle. For trial values (u_1), we take sums of entries in rows (v_0) of the original correlation matrix, each divided by the largest of these sums $(max\,v_0)^*$. The computation of these first trial values from a matrix of numerical coefficients, shown in Table 3.5.1, is thus quite uncomplicated.

Table 3.5.1 *Correlation Matrix, Row Sums, and First Trial Values.*

Y_i	1	2	3	4	v_0	u_1
1	.58	.53	.71	.67	2.49	.7880
2	.53	.61	.70	.71	2.55	.8070
3	.71	.70	.89	.86	3.16	1.0000
4	.67	.71	.86	.85	3.09	.9778

Source: L. L. Thurstone, Multiple Factor Analysis. Chicago: University of Chicago Press, 1947, p. 481. Copyright 1947 by University of Chicago. Reprinted with permission.

Since row sums are roughly proportional to first-factor loadings, they are more efficient as trial values (i.e., require fewer iterations) than purely arbitrary values. But our procedure will produce principal factors, even though we start with quite arbitrary trial values. A wide variety of trial values will do for our purposes.

The procedure for getting the second trial values is a bit more complicated. We are required to multiply the ith entry in the jth row of the correlation matrix by the ith entry in the column of the first trial values u_1, sum all n products for each row, and divide each of these sums (denoted v_1) by the largest of the lot $(max\,v_1)$. The results of this division will be the second trial values u_2. By way of illustration, the sum of the products for the first row is:

$$(.58)(.7880) + (.53)(.8070) + (.71)(1.0000) + (.67)(.9778) = 2.2499.$$

The sums of products for the second, third, and fourth rows are:

$$(.53)(.7880) + (.61)(.8070) + (.70)(1.0000) + (.71)(.9778) = 2.3041,$$

$$(.71)(.7880) + (.70)(.8070) + (.89)(1.0000) + (.86)(.9778) = 2.8553,$$

$$(.67)(.7880) + (.71)(.8070) + (.86)(1.0000) + (.85)(.9778) = 2.7921.$$

---

* Throughout this discussion, we employ the letter "u" to denote trial values, the letter "v" to denote row sums, and the expression $max\,v$ to denote the largest row sum.

The division of each of these sums by the largest of them yields the second trial values:

v_1	$u_2 = v_1/2.855288$
2.249876	0.787968
2.304148	0.806976
2.855288	1.000000
2.792060	0.977856

When trial values are practically stationary on successive trials, we take them to be proportional to factor loadings. By "stationary" we mean that differences between corresponding entries on adjacent trials are less than a pre-established quantity. If no difference is in excess of the criterion value, we terminate this phase of the analysis; otherwise, we continue to the next set of trial values. For purposes of our example, let us suppose that we have set our criterion value at .00005, signifying that no difference between trial values is to be larger than this value. Upon forming differences between our first and second trial values, we find that one of them (Variable 4) is larger than .00005; consequently, we are obliged to proceed to the third trial values.

u_1	u_2	$u_1 - u_2$
0.788000	0.787968	0.000032
0.807000	0.806976	0.000024
1.000000	1.000000	0.000000
0.977800	0.977856	-0.000056

The procedure for getting the third (and all succeeding) trial values is identical to that for getting the second trial values: multiply the ith entry in the jth row of the original correlation matrix by the ith entry in the column of second trial values, u_2, sum products for each row and divide each sum, v_2, by the largest of them, symbolized $max\,v_2$. These quotients will be the third trial values, u_3. For our problem, the sum of the products for the fourth row is:

$$(.67)(.787968) + (.71)(.806976) + (.86)(1.000000) + (.85)(.977856) = 2.792070$$

The sums for the first three rows are:

$$(.58)(.787968) + (.53)(.806976) + (.71)(1.000000) + (.67)(.977856) = 2.249882$$

$$(.53)(.787968) + (.61)(.806976) + (.70)(1.000000) + (.71)(.977856) = 2.304156$$

$$(.71)(.787968) + (.70)(.806976) + (.89)(1.000000) + (.86)(.977856) = 2.855296$$

The division of these sums by the largest of them yields the third trial values, u_3, recorded alongside the column of v_2-values.

v_2	$u_3 = v_2/2.855296$
2.249882	0.787968
2.304156	0.806976
2.855296	1.000000
2.792070	0.977856

To determine whether trial values are stationary after two iterations, we form the differences between second and third trial values and compare these differences with our criterion value of .00005. Since none of our dif-

u_2	u_3	$u_2 - u_3$
.787968	.787968	0.000000
.806976	.806976	0.000000
1.000000	1.000000	0.000000
.977856	.977856	0.000000

ferences is in excess of this criterion value, we take our third trial values as stationary and by that token proportional to factor loadings. To signify that trial values, u_3, have attained the requisite degree of proportionality and therefore that no more iterations are required, we replace the letter "u" by the Greek letter "α" with an appropriate subscript to denote factor and variable. This completes the first phase of the analysis and permits us to proceed with the conversion of trial values to the factor loadings. In an ordinary problem, the convergence to proportionality will progress much more slowly and entail many more iterations. For this reason, factor analysts usually take advantage of a computational shortcut which enables them to reach the required proportionality (or stability) much more rapidly than would be possible with our long method. We omit this simplification, which goes by the name "acceleration by powering," in order not to increase further the growing complexity of our directions. Interested students should consult Harman (1967).

Conversion Procedure. The arithmetical procedure for converting alpha-values to factor loadings is analogous to those employed in the diagonal and centroid methods, respectively. In the diagonal method, we took loadings on the first factor as proportional to the correlations of the variable with the largest communality, and took the square root of that largest communality as the conversion coefficient. In the centroid method, we made loadings on the first factor proportional to sums of correlations, taking the sum of the loadings on the first factor as our conversion coefficient. In the principal factor method, we take loadings as proportional to alpha-values and convert these alpha-values to loadings in the following sequence of operations:

1. Square each alpha-value and sum these squares:

Y_i	α_{i1}	α_{i1}^2
1	0.787968	0.620894
2	0.806976	0.651210
3	1.000000	1.000000
4	0.977856	0.956300
		Sum 3.228404

2. Divide the largest value in the terminal (t^{th}) set of v's by the sum of the squared alpha-values. In symbols,

$$k^2 = \frac{max\ v_t}{\sum \alpha_{i1}^2}.$$

For our example,

$$k^2 = \frac{2.855296}{3.228404}$$

$$= .884426.$$

3. Take the square root of the k^2. This is the conversion coefficient (k) which permits us to transform our alpha-values to loadings on the first factor. For our example:

$$k = \sqrt{.884426}$$

$$= .940456$$

4. To obtain loadings, multiply each α by k:

Y_i	α_{i1}	$.940456\alpha_{i1} = a_{i1}$
1	0.787968	0.741049
2	0.806976	0.758925
3	1.000000	0.940456
4	0.977856	0.919630

These factor loadings (a_{i1}'s) are unique in the sense that they alone will yield the largest possible value of $\sum a_{i1}^2$, given the restriction that $h_i^2 = \sum a_{ik}^2$ and $r_{ij} = \sum a_{ik} a_{jk}$. They are statistically most efficient in the sense that they remove more of the common-factor variance on the first cycle of factoring than any other set of loadings. They are the loadings on the first principal factor.

Having computed first-factor loadings, we obtain residual correlations according to the now familiar formula,

$$_1 r_{ij} = r_{ij} - {_1 p_{ij}},$$

arranging our results in the form of a 4 × 4 matrix (Table 3.5.2). It is this matrix of first-factor residual correlations from which loadings on the second factor will be derived, unless they are negligible (i.e., within the limits of sampling error), in which case we terminate the factoring process.

Table 3.5.2 *First-Factor Residual Correlation Matrix.*

Y_i	1	2	3	4	Sum
1	.030846	−.032401	.013076	−.011491	.000030
2	−.032401	.034033	−.013736	.012070	−.000034
3	.013076	−.013736	.005543	−.004872	.000011
4	−.011491	.012070	−.004872	.004281	−.000012

Second Principal Factor. The procedure for getting loadings on the second factor is identical to that for obtaining loadings on the first factor, except that we operate on the residual correlations rather than on the original correlations. In performing these operations, we are not required to change signs as in the centroid method; rather we may operate on whatever algebraic values are given in the matrix. In this respect, the method of principal factors is more objective than the centroid method where we arbitrarily reflect one or more variables in order that row sums for residual correlations be greater than zero.

For first trial values on the second factor, we sum residuals (Table 3.5.2) by rows, dividing each of these sums by the largest:

v_0	$u_1 = v_0/(-.000034)$
.000030	−0.882353
−.000034	1.000000
.000011	−0.323529
−.000012	0.352941

These are not necessarily the most efficient trial values (e.g., absolute sums may be better), but their use will obviate the need to introduce new rules and further complicate our procedure.

To obtain our second trial values, we multiply the ith entry in the jth row of the residual correlation matrix by the ith entry in the column of the first

trial values, sum products for each row, and divide each of these sums by the
largest of them. For example, the sum of the products for the first row is:

$$
\begin{array}{r}
-.027217 \\
-.032401 \\
-.004230 \\
-.040556 \\
\hline
-.104404
\end{array}
$$

a result which the student should verify. The sums for the second, third, and
fourth rows are:

(2)	(3)	(4)
.028589	−.011538	.010139
.034033	−.013736	.012070
.004444	−.001793	.001576
.004260	−.001720	.001511
.071326	−.028787	.025296

The division of each of these sums by the largest of them yields the second
set of trial values for the second factor.

v_1	$u_2 = v_1/(-.104404)$
−.104404	1.000000
.071326	−0.683173
−.028787	0.275727
.025296	−0.242290

To determine whether trial values require further adjustment, we form
differences between first and second trial values and compare these differences with our criterion value of .00005:

u_1	u_2	$u_1 - u_2$
−0.882353	1.000000	−1.882353
1.000000	−0.683173	1.683173
−0.323529	0.275727	−0.599256
0.352941	−0.242290	0.595231

Since all of these differences are larger than our criterion value, we continue
to the third trial values by the now familiar process of getting v_2's and converting these to u_3's. Our v_2's are as follows:

(1)	(2)	(3)	(4)
0.030846	−0.032401	0.013076	−0.011491
0.022135	−0.023250	0.009384	−0.008246
0.003605	−0.003787	0.001528	−0.001343
0.002784	−0.002924	0.001180	−0.001037
0.059370	−0.062362	0.025168	−0.002117

Dividing each of these sums by the largest of them yields the third set of trial values for the second factor:

v_2	$u_3 = v_2/(-.062362)$
0.059370	−0.952022
−0.062362	1.000000
0.025168	−0.403579
−0.002117	0.354655

On matching second and third trial values, we get appreciable differences, which result dictates that we proceed to the fourth trial values. We follow the

u_2	u_3	$u_2 - u_3$
1.000000	−0.952022	1.952022
−0.683173	1.000000	−1.683173
0.275727	−0.403579	0.679303
−0.243390	0.354655	−0.598045

familiar procedure of multiplying the ith entry in the jth row of the residual correlation matrix by the ith entry in the set of third trial values, summing resulting products for each row, and dividing each of these sums by the largest of them to get v_3. The sums of products for Rows 1–4 are:

(1)	(2)	(3)	(4)
−0.029366	0.030846	−0.012449	0.010940
−0.032401	0.034033	−0.013736	0.012070
−0.005277	0.005544	−0.002237	0.001966
−0.004075	0.004281	−0.001728	0.001518
−0.071119	0.074704	−0.030150	0.026494

Dividing each of these sums by the largest gives the fourth set of trial values for the second factor:

v_3	$u_4 = v_3/.074704$
−0.071119	−0.952024
0.074704	1.000000
−0.030150	−0.403593
0.026494	0.354653

Upon comparing fourth and third trial values, we get differences, all of which are smaller than our criterion value of .00005:

u_3	u_4	$u_3 - u_4$
−0.952022	−0.952024	.000002
1.000000	1.000000	.000000
−0.403579	−0.403593	.000014
0.354655	0.354653	.000002

It is this result which permits us to convert our last trial values, now designated as alpha-values, to loadings on the second principal factor. In making this conversion, we first square our alpha-values and sum these squares:

α_{i2}	α_{i2}^2
−0.952024	0.906350
1.000000	1.000000
−0.403593	0.162887
0.354653	0.195016
	2.195016

Next, we divide the sum of the squared alpha-values into the largest of the terminal v's for k^2:

$$k^2 = \frac{.074704}{2.195016}$$
$$= .034033.$$

Taking the square root of this result, we get our coefficient of conversion, k:

$$k = \sqrt{.034033}$$
$$= .184482.$$

Multiplying each alpha-value by this conversion coefficient, we get second-factor loadings as follows:

α_{i2}	$a_{i2} = .184482\alpha_{i2}$
-0.952024	-0.175631
1.000000	0.184482
-0.403593	-0.074455
0.354653	0.065427

As with the loadings on the first factor, these second-factor loadings are unique in the sense that they alone yield the largest possible value of $\sum a_{i2}^2$, and therefore remove more of the common-factor variance in the second cycle than any other set of loadings.

On forming inner products from second-factor loadings and subtracting these results from the residual correlations, we get second-factor residual correlations, all of which are very close to zero and which therefore dictate that the factoring process be halted. If these residuals had been appreciable in a well-defined statistical sense, we would have continued with the factoring, performing operations identical to those in the preceding cycle.

Concluding Remark. By means of the foregoing routine, it is possible to compute the numerical loadings of n variables on m principal factors. Such loadings may be compared with those produced by the centroid and diagonal methods, respectively, as a demonstration that different factoring methods produce different sets of loadings. But such differences should not be a source of concern to the researcher who uses factor analysis. They are quite consistent with the aforementioned principle that the same correlation matrix may be reproduced by infinitely many sets of loadings, but a given set of loadings will give rise to only one correlation matrix. In any case, we usually discard those loadings yielded by factoring the matrix, and transform them into loadings more amenable to interpretation. But when are loadings most amenable to interpretation? That is the subject of the ensuing discussion.

Note on Factor Scores. Upon factoring a correlation matrix, by whatever method, one gets the correlation of each factor with each of the n variables. From these results, together with the intercorrelations, it is possible to formulate the linear regression of each factor on all n variables. The measures to which this operation gives rise have come to be known as *factor scores*. A factor score is thus the value obtained on the assumption that a factor is a linear combination of the n variables from which it was derived. It should be emphasized that factor scores do not supply their own validity and must be validated by evidence external to variables composing them. We mention this since there is a tendency among sociologists to use factor scores somewhat uncritically in their research.

PART 6
Rotation

Rotation is a technique for changing the loadings obtained by factoring the matrix into alternative loadings more suitable to the purposes of our study. From an initial solution, we move by successive steps to a preferred solution more amenable to interpretation. Graphically, this process entails the rotation of factors around a fixed origin, like turning the hands of a clock, to a position that best fits the plotted configuration of variables. Although it is not possible to specify the best solution apart from the aims of a particular study, we may indicate those patterns that have predominated in actual research. But before considering these usually preferred methods, we may ask "By what logic may we tinker with loadings as given by the factoring method?" To expand on our previous answer to this question (pp. 68–72), let us return to the simplest factor models.

One-Factor Model. Given that n variables share only one common factor $(y'_i = a_i f' + b_i u'_i)$, the communality of each variable will equal the square of its loading on that factor $(h_i^2 = a_i^2)$. In consequence of this restriction, there can be one and only one numerical factor loading corresponding to each communality. If we factor (by whatever method) a matrix of intercorrelations among such variables, with true communalities along the diagonal, we can get one and only one set of loadings, since only that particular set can reproduce the given correlation matrix. Our conclusion is that loadings derived from correlations based on variables sharing one factor are not subject to adjustment by rotation, (except that we may change all signs by a 180° rotation of our single axis). If we change their numerical values in any way, we destroy their capacity to reproduce the correlations. These loadings are therefore not only sufficient to reproduce the correlations, but they are necessary as well. No other set will do. But this one-to-one correspondence between loadings and intercorrelations does not hold for variables sharing two or more common factors, as will be shown next.

Two-Factor Model: (*a*) **Uncorrelated Factors.** In the case of variables composed of two uncorrelated factors, the communality of each variable will be equal to the sum of its squared loadings $(h_i^2 = a_{i1}^2 + a_{i2}^2)$ and the intercorrelation between any two variables, i and j, will equal their inner product $(r_{ij} = a_{i1}a_{j1} + a_{i2}a_{j2})$. Corresponding to a table of loadings for two factors, there is only one correlation matrix; but corresponding to this same correlation matrix, there are many sets of loadings, each having the capacity to reproduce the correlations among the variables. A given set of loadings will be sufficient but not necessary to produce the intercorrelations, since the same intercorrelations may be produced by many other sets of loadings.

Consider Table 3.6.1: Manipulating the loadings on the left, we get the correlations in the center; factoring this matrix by the centroid method (which the student may wish to duplicate as an exercise), we get the factor pattern on the right. By appropriate operations, we may retrieve the correlation matrix from either solution. Actually, there are an infinite number of such solutions, all equivalent in the sense that from each of them we could get the correlations and communalities.

(*b*) **Correlated Factors.** In the case of two correlated common factors, our results are more complex:

(3.6.1) $$h_i^2 = a_{i1}^2 + a_{i2}^2 + 2r_{12}a_{i1}a_{i2}.$$

(3.6.2) $$r_{ij} = a_{i1}(a_{j1} + a_{j2}r_{12}) + a_{i2}(a_{j2} + a_{j1}r_{12}),$$

where r_{12} is the correlation between factors. But there is no modification of the principle that corresponding to a given correlation matrix, there is an infinite number of interchangeable solutions, each capable of reproducing that matrix. When both loadings and the interfactor correlation, $r_{12} = .38$, are given, as in Table 3.6.2 on the left, we may substitute known values in Formulas (3.6.1) and (3.6.2) to obtain the correlation matrix in the center. But this same matrix may be produced by the alternative loadings on the right, given that $r_{12} = .70$. (The student should verify this.)

If we change the value of the interfactor correlation, as we may at our discretion, we create a new system of solutions, each capable of restoring the original matrix. By thus permitting the interfactor correlation to take any value on its range from -1 to $+1$, we avail ourselves of the widest variety of alternative patterns. Since there appears to be no reason to limit our choice to patterns occurring under the restriction that factors be uncorrelated, most authorities advise that rotation be conducted without that restriction. Cattell (1952: 210), for example, remarks:

> Factors in nature do not function in separate universes, but are likely to have some mutual influence and to be somewhat correlated. Indeed, to object—on grounds of the mathematical convenience of one's calculations— to correlated factors is to object to the complications of any breadth of causal interconnection in any universe of data.

However, this philosophical speculation is incidental to the main point of the present discussion, namely: correlations based on two factors may be produced by infinitely many different patterns of loadings.

Without further ado, this conclusion about two factors may be broadened into a generalization for *m* factors as follows: corresponding to any correlation matrix based on two or more factors, there are infinitely many patterns from which that matrix could be derived. This circumstance is our mandate to "tinker with our original loadings." But such tinkering is not merely permissible, it is an almost essential operation in any factor analysis. For if it

Table 3.6.1 Given Loadings, Correlations, and Factored Loadings.

Y_i	Given Loadings		Intercorrelations, r_{ij}							Factored Loadings	
	a_{i1}	a_{i2}	1	2	3	4	5	6	7	a_{i1}	a_{i2}
1	.80	.30	.73							.68	−.52
2	.50	.70	.61	.74						.86	−.04
3	.70	.30	.65	.56	.58					.63	−.43
4	.40	.75	.55	.73	.51	.72				.85	.07
5	.10	.70	.29	.54	.28	.57	.50			.64	.30
6	−.10	.70	.13	.44	.14	.49	.48	.50		.54	.46
7	.20	.65	.36	.56	.34	.57	.48	.44	.46	.66	.18

Table 3.6.2 Factor Loadings and Correlations, Different Values of r_{12}.

Y_i	Factor Loadings $r_{12} = .38$		Intercorrelations, r_{ij}							Factor Loadings $r_{12} = .70$	
	a_{i1}	a_{i2}	1	2	3	4	5	6	7	a_{i1}	a_{i2}
1	.63	.34	.67							.82	.00
2	−.05	.81	.43	.63						−.06	.83
3	.45	.36	.55	.40	.46					.59	.12
4	.09	.80	.53	.66	.47	.70				.12	.75
5	−.16	.70	.29	.52	.28	.52	.43			−.20	.78
6	−.25	.64	.18	.44	.19	.43	.38	.35		−.32	.77
7	.00	.63	.36	.50	.33	.52	.40	.34	.39	.01	.62

is possible to find a solution that is best for our stated purposes, the investigator is virtually obliged to seek out that result. But the opportunity to search for the best among a multiplicity of alternative patterns is not an unmixed blessing. For, if one man's choice is at odds with the choice of another investigator, how is one to decide which is more faithful to the actual state of affairs? It is a limitation of factor analysis that it cannot differentiate without uncertainty among alternative solutions in respect to their validity. To validate or justify a given solution, it is necessary to have recourse to external evidence or logical argument, or both.

Preferred Solutions. It seems fair to state that the solution most regularly sought in actual research has been simple structure or a variant of that pattern. The concept of simple structure was formulated by Thurstone, who also supplied a set of operational criteria for judging when a table of loadings had a simple structure. Reflecting in part his influence, these criteria, or slight refinements of them, were almost universally applied from their introduction circa 1935 until the development of mathematical indexes during the period of 1950–1960. Although these quantitative indexes have gradually replaced Thurstone's qualitative rules for simple structure, they should not be regarded as rivals of the concept itself, but rather as objective indexes of what Thurstone meant by simple structure.

The criteria of simple structure are explicit enough. They suffer mainly in that they may be met in more than one way when applied by different analysts. Two or more investigators in search of simple structure and guided by Thurstone's rules may obtain different solutions both consistent with those guiding rules. It was this possibility that led Kaiser (1958), a contemporary authority on factor analysis, to characterize these rules as "ambiguous, arbitrary, and mathematically unmanageable." Such dissatisfaction provided the impetus to specialists to develop purely objective criteria of simple structure which have been gaining steadily in favor, since they necessarily produce identical results when applied by different persons. To distinguish these criteria from more flexible guidelines such as those furnished by Thurstone, the term "analytical" is applied to the former and the term "graphical" to the latter, a nomenclature we shall find useful to maintain, as it is quite conventional in the writing on factor analysis.

Simple Structure. The principle underlying simple structure* is that each of the variables will be affected by only some of the m factors, and conversely that each of the factors will contribute to only some of the n variables. Then, given a simple structure, the table of loadings will have one or more

---

* Mathematical note. For Thurstone, simple structure meant the configuration of test vectors in m-space and the best-fitting reference frame onto which the vectors are projected.

zeros in each row and one or more zeros in each column. Taking these minimum consequences as his point of departure, Thurstone (1947: 156) proposed these slightly more conservative rules:

1. Each row of the factor pattern should have at least one entry close to zero.
2. Each column should have at least m entries close to zero (m being the total number of common factors).
3. For every pair of columns there should be at least m variables whose entries are close to zero in one column but not in the other.

Table 3.6.3 *An Example of Simple Structure.*

Y_i	a_{i1}	a_{i2}	a_{i3}
1	.70	.01	.02
2	.60	.03	.00
3	.80	.02	.02
4	.01	.65	.01
5	.01	.85	.01
6	.03	.75	.00
7	.01	.02	.90
8	.03	.02	.80
9	.02	.02	.95

The loadings in Table 3.6.3 are consistent with these rules and supply an illustration. Although no entry is exactly equal to zero, we take each one close to zero as not inconsistent with the hypothesis that its population parameter is zero. When a pattern of loadings, such as that in Table 3.6.3, conforms to the above-mentioned rules, we may regard the loadings as having simple structure. If we plot factors two at a time for a total of $m(m-1)/2$ diagrams, we get many points near the origin, several or more toward the end of each axis, and relatively few between axes in each diagram. It is the appearance of such scatters that factor analysts take as compelling evidence for the presence of simple structure.

If simple structure, as defined by Thurstone's criteria, is the goal of rotation, then we adjust the pattern of loadings repeatedly until we reach an approximation of that pattern. The pursuit of simple structure may thus be regarded as an attempt to reduce as much as possible the complexity of the n variables. Since the lowest complexity for each variable is 1, the ultimate in simple structure would be a pattern in which each variable had one and only one nonvanishing entry. Although such a *uni-factor solution,* as it is called, is of unlikely occurrence in empirical work, it may be regarded as the ideal solution, since all variables are of complexity 1, and all factors are group factors. Such a pattern will serve especially well when the purpose of the analysis is to arrange the n variables into m distinct clusters.

Analytical Methods. These methods are alike in their requirement that either the factor loadings (pattern) or factor correlations (structure) satisfy a mathematical criterion of greatest possible simplicity. The process of imposing a condition on the factor loadings is already familiar to us from our study of the method of principal factors. That method requires that the sum of the squared loadings be a maximum for each successive factor, given the communalities. Instead of that requirement, which is appropriate for factoring the matrix, we lay down for purposes of rotation the requirement that the loadings have the greatest possible simplicity as reflected in their capacity to yield a prescribed numerical limit (maximum or minimum).

Although there were efforts to formulate an analytical procedure from 1935 onward, a practical solution to this problem was not reached until the period 1950 to 1955. That first solution, apparently obtained independently by several statisticians, requires that the complexity of variables (rows) be minimized. An alternative solution, developed by Kaiser during the period 1955 to 1960, requires that the complexity of factors (columns) be minimized. Both of these solutions will be described in a general way, with little or no reference to the lengthy procedures for getting numerical solutions in a given problem.

Quartimax. If we impose the condition that factors be uncorrelated (orthogonal), the communality of each variable will continue to equal the sum of its squared loadings after rotation. In symbols:

$$h_i^2 = \sum_1^m a_{ij}^2.$$

If the sum of the squared loadings for each variable is constant in rotation, the square of that sum will likewise be constant in rotation. That square may be put in expanded form as follows:

$$\left(\sum a_{ij}^2\right)^2 = \sum a_{ij}^4 + 2\sum a_{ij}^2 a_{ik}^2.$$

Summing over all n rows, we get the sum of squared communalities (factors uncorrelated):

$$\sum_1^n \left(\sum_1^m a_{ij}^2\right)^2 = \sum_1^n \sum_1^m a_{ij}^4 + 2 \sum_1^n \sum_1^m a_{ij}^2 a_{ik}^2.$$

Replacing the first term on the right by "Q" and the second term by "$2N$" and representing the left side by "S", we get the simpler expression

$$S = Q + 2N.$$

Since the sum of these terms (Q and $2N$) is necessarily constant in rotation, an increase in one will necessitate a decrease in the other, and vice-versa. The first term on the right will vary inversely as the complexity of the variables, while the second term will vary directly as their complexity; hence, we may take either the maximum value of Q or the minimum value of N as our index of lowest possible complexity in a given problem. Because the first sum consists of fourth powers, the maximum value of that sum was named the *quartimax*, or simply *Q-max*. This maximum value is obtained by repeatedly rotating factors two at a time until it is practically impossible to enlarge the sum of the fourth powers. When loadings have been rotated to yield *Q-max*, we may claim they have the greatest possible simplicity by the criterion of the quartimax. They will not have the greatest possible simplicity by some other criterion. It is to be understood that "greatest possible simplicity" is defined by a set of specific operations. Note that sums of squares for columns are not constant in rotation. For this reason, an interpretation of column sums after rotation is usually not undertaken. When principal factors are extracted, and no rotation is performed, each column sum of squares carries the statistical interpretation that no sum can be larger.

Kurtosis (K). It is of interest that the sum of the loadings to the fourth power, divided by the square of the sum of the squared loadings (not sum of squared communalities) is proportional to the *kurtosis** of the "doubled" distribution consisting of mn loadings and these same mn loadings with signs reversed, with $\dfrac{1}{2mn}$ as the constant of proportionality. In symbols:

$$(3.6.3) \qquad K = \sum\sum a_{ij}^4/(\sum\sum a_{ij}^2)^2.$$

Since the denominator of K is constant in rotation for uncorrelated factors, the requirement that K be maximized is equivalent to the requirement that Q be maximized. It is also equivalent to the requirement that our "doubled" distribution have a sharp peak and relatively long tails, which is a statistical version of simple structure. The reason is this: K becomes larger as the distribution becomes more leptokurtic; hence, the largest possible value of K corresponds to the limit of "leptokurtosis".

Oblimax. It would appear that *K-max* is superfluous, since it carries exactly the same interpretation as the quartimax. Its special utility arises in the case of correlated (oblique) factors. In this case, the sum, $S = Q + 2N$, is not constant in rotation, so that an increase in Q does not necessitate a decrease in $2N$, and hence does not signify a change in the degree of complexity of the variables. Given these circumstances, we must avail ourselves of an index that is independent of the magnitude of the sum of Q and $2N$. The ratio

---

* The ratio of the fourth moment about the mean to the square of the variance is called the *kurtosis* of a distribution, and is sometimes denoted by β_2. Dividing β_2 by the number of cases in the distribution, we get Equation (3.6.3).

(*K*) is such an index. When this ratio reaches its maximum value, with no restriction on the degree of correlation between factors, it is termed the *oblimax*, and written,

$$O\text{-}max = \sum_1^n \sum_1^m r_{ip}^4 \Big/ \left(\sum_1^n \sum_1^m r_{ip}^2 \right)^2,$$

where r_{ip} is the correlation between the ith variable and p^{th} factor*. This maximum, be it noted, is derived from factor correlations rather than factor loadings, a distinction unnecessary for the quartimax, since factor loadings and factor correlations are identical under the condition that factors be uncorrelated. At this juncture, the student should not be distracted by this detail, despite its importance; rather, he should focus on the oblimax as the maximum value of *K*. When *mn* loadings have been transformed to produce this maximum, they may be described as having the greatest possible simplicity as measured by the oblimax. Note that kurtosis (*K*) may attain its maximum value with no correlation between factors. In other words, the best oblique solution may require that factors be orthogonal.

Varimax. The varimax differs from the quartimax in its simplification of columns (factors) rather than rows (variables). By definition, it is the maximum value of the sum of the variances of squared loadings within columns, subject to the restriction that sums of squared loadings by rows (communalities) be maintained in rotation. In statistical notation:

$$(3.6.4) \qquad V = \frac{1}{n} \sum_1^m \sum_1^n a_{ij}^4 - \frac{1}{n^2} \sum_1^m \left(\sum_1^n a_{ij}^2 \right)^2.$$

It thus serves like the quartimax as a criterion of best fit for uncorrelated factors. However, its validity as an index of greatest possible simplicity rests on different but related considerations. A condition of simple structure is that at least *m* elements within each column tend to 0; or, equivalently, that at least *m* elements tend to 1. But the variance of any column (factor) will increase as the elements tend toward 0 and 1. Hence, the variance of the squared elements within each column will vary as the degree of their simplicity. By the same token, the maximum value of the sum of the variances for all columns may be taken as an index of simple structure. That largest value is the varimax.

---

* Strictly speaking, r_{ip} is the correlation between the ith variable and p^{th} reference axis. To obtain loadings on primary factors, whose relations to reference axes are fixed, we apply a standard conversion formula. See Harman (1967: 317) for details.

If we express each loading as a multiple of h_i, and substitute these normalized measures in (3.6.4), we get (after maximization) the so-called *normal varimax*. In symbolic form:

$$V = \frac{1}{n} \sum\sum (a_{ij}/h_i)^4 - \frac{1}{n^2} \sum(\sum a_{ij}/h_i)^2.$$

Since it is this maximum value which is usually sought (because of its equalization of communalities), the general term "varimax" has come to signify this procedure so that we must employ the phrase "raw varimax" if we wish to indicate that loadings were not normalized before rotation.

Covarimin. Instead of maximizing the sum of the variances of columns, we may minimize the sum of the covariances between columns. In symbols:

$$C = \sum \left(n \sum_{1}^{n} r_{ip}^2 r_{iq}^2 - \sum r_{ip}^2 \sum r_{iq}^2 \right).$$

Since the minimization of C entails a simplification of columns, it is comparable to the varimax and was so regarded by Kaiser, who developed it, That the minimum value of C could be reasonable as a measure of simple structure may be clarified by the following argument. The covariance between columns two at a time, and, hence, the sum of all such covariances, will tend to zero, as the fraction of matched zeroes for each pair of columns tends to 1. Therefore, we may take the minimum value of the sum of all possible $\binom{m}{2}$ covariances as an index of least possible complexity. Since the minimum value of this sum of covariances is unaffected by the degree of correlation among factors, it serves as a criterion of best fit for correlated, as well as uncorrelated, factors. It is thus more versatile than the varimax, which is applicable only to uncorrelated factors. Because the covarimin, like the oblimax, is based on factor correlations rather than factor loadings, it reflects the simplicity of a factor structure rather than a factor pattern.

Concluding Remark. It should not be supposed that the inclusion of these analytical methods constitutes a sanction for their use in a given study. They sometimes produce results that are at odds with the very simplification which their application sought to achieve. Therefore, specialists in the field of factor analysis refrain from suggesting an all-purpose criterion that is usable on all occasions and recognize that specific methods may be misleading when used uncritically. They do suggest that the several purposes of a given study be set forth in advance and arranged in order of importance before choosing a particular analytic criterion from among the alternatives that may be available. But the selection of the best technique for the purpose on hand is a requirement of all studies.

PART 7
Statistical Inference in Factor Analysis

Statement of the Problem. In factoring a matrix of sample correlations, we may obtain as many factors as there are variables—if there are ten variables, we may obtain ten factors. But not all of these results will be attributable to common factors in the population; some will be attributable to the accidents of random sampling. On "taking out" n factors, we anticipate that only k of them will be significant, and that $n - k$ will have to be discarded as a form of sampling error.

That a sample correlation (r) and/or its derivative results may be in error will be familiar to the student from his study of sampling from a bivariate population. Owing to the vagaries of random sampling, the sample r will seldom, if ever, be equal to the population coefficient ρ. If $\rho = 0$ in the population, r in the sample will be smaller or larger than 0, but never (except under the most exceptional circumstances) exactly equal to 0. If several or more variables are mutually uncorrelated in a given population, i.e., if every $\rho_{ij} = 0$, the r's based on a sample of N cases will each depart from 0 to a greater or lesser degree. Given a matrix of these sample r's, we may factor it, set up a table of loadings, and even formulate an interpretation of our "final" results. Although that procedure would be a form of negligence, it does represent the possibility that we may mistakenly treat a set of r's as having their basis in one or more common factors, when in fact they are rooted in the accidents of random sampling. It is this possibility that requires us to distinguish between results which could plausibly be ascribed to common factors and those which are very likely the result of the sampling process.

This question has been variously posed as: "When to stop factoring," "On the number of factors," "Goodness of fit between observed and fitted r's," etc. Although this issue is by no means dead, it may have lost some of its urgency since the advent of the computer. When factors were extracted manually, it was a matter of economy not to take out several or even one factor that might be later discarded as statistically insignificant. However, with the machines to do the work, it is practically feasible to take out as many factors as there are variables and to retain only those that are statistically significant by a pre-established criterion.

Some Solutions. The question of when to stop factoring has evoked a wide variety of responses, ranging from somewhat flexible but simple guides to relatively strict but mathematically more complex criteria. A simple but crude technique requires that the standard deviation of the residuals be approximately equal to $1/\sqrt{N}$. If the kth-order residuals have a standard deviation that is appreciably larger than $1/\sqrt{N}$, we reject the hypothesis of k common factors and accept the alternative that the number of common factors is larger than k. If the kth-order residuals are considerably smaller than $1/\sqrt{N}$, we reject the hypothesis of k common factors and accept the alternative that the number is less than k.

A currently favored criterion, due to Kaiser (1960), rests on the arrangement of factors according to the strength of their contribution to the aggregate total variance (which is equal to n with all measures in standard form). This criterion specifies that a factor contribute no less than $1/n$ to the total variance in order to be retained as significant. From sampling distributions produced on the computer (with unities on the diagonal), Kaiser concluded that this rule will lead to the inclusion of factors that are significant, reliable, and meaningful. In the absence of compelling reasons to the contrary, research workers are advised to apply Kaiser's simple test for distinguishing between statistically significant and insignificant factors.

Summary. The object of factor analysis is to determine whether $n(n > 3)$ variables have $m(m < n)$ factors in common which account for their intercorrelations. The results of a factor analysis consist of numerical loadings which reflect the degree to which each variable is affected by each factor. To obtain those numerical coefficients, we perform two distinct operations: (1) factor the correlation matrix to obtain a set of arbitrary loadings, and (2) rotate the factors to calculate transformed loadings which are presumably more amenable to interpretation. Before factoring the matrix, we insert entries on the diagonal which may be arbitrary values such as 0 or 1, or values which in our judgment closely approximate the true communalities. Once these diagonal values have been fixed, the matrix is factored in a purely mechanical fashion. The results of that factoring are then rotated in order to satisfy some objective criterion of simplicity, such as the quartimax or varimax.

The interpretation of factor loadings, be it noted, is not a statistical operation, and two or more analysts may offer differing interpretations of the same set of numerical findings. Such differences may reflect differences in sociological orientation. To adjudicate between possibly rival interpretations, we have recourse to external evidence, very much as we have recourse to external evidence to validate a test of attitudes. Although the question of what the factors represent has been slighted in this writing, that question is of appreciable importance and can hardly be ignored by the research worker in his applied work.

It would be helpful to summarize the stages into which the application of factor analysis falls naturally: (1) a determination that factor analysis is suitable to the research problem; (2) the assurance that the data matrix lends itself to factoring; (3) a factoring of the matrix to obtain arbitrary loadings; (4) the transformation of arbitrary loadings to loadings which lend themselves to interpretation; and (5) the interpretation of those findings within the framework of some theory. From this summary, it is clear that the use of factor analysis requires good judgment as well as proficiency in statistical methods.

EXERCISES

1. List some problems in sociological research which, in your judgment, would require the use of factor analysis.

2. Under what circumstances might the application of factor analysis to qualitative (nominal) data be justified?

3. Consider and discuss exigencies in social research which may limit one's choice of communalities.

4. Factor the following correlation matrix by the diagonal method, communalities given:

Variable	1	2	3	4
1	.85	.84	.62	.61
2	.84	.85	.68	.69
3	.62	.68	.68	.74
4	.61	.69	.74	.82

5. Factor the following correlation matrix by the diagonal method, using as diagonal entries:
   (a) R^2's,
   (b) largest r's,
   (c) unities.

Variable	1	2	3	4
1		.50	.70	.60
2	.50		.40	.80
3	.70	.40		.70
4	.60	.80	.70	

Compare results and comment on the possibility that substantive differences might be ascribed to differences in choice of diagonal entries.

6. Using the following literal values, illustrate schematically the diagonal method. Give expressions for all computations. Assume that four factors are necessary to resolve the communalities.

Y_i	1	2	3	4
1	h_1^2			
2	r_{12}	h_2^2		
3	r_{13}	r_{23}	h_3^2	
4	r_{14}	r_{24}	r_{34}	h_4^2

7. Factor the following correlation matrix by the centroid method:

Variable	1	2	3	4
1	.61	.48	.54	.62
2	.48	.39	.45	.50
3	.54	.45	.81	.63
4	.62	.50	.63	.74

Compare with diagonal solution (p. 98).

8. Factor the following intercorrelations among major crimes by the centroid method. In each cycle use largest column values (signs disregarded) for diagonal entries.

		1	2	3	4	5	6
Burglary	1						
Auto Theft	2	.57					
Grand Larceny	3	.55	.58				
Robbery	4	.61	.57	.56			
Murder	5	.37	.43	.34	.30		
Petty Larceny	6	.59	.52	.44	.40	.10	
Aggravated Assault	7	.41	.34	.24	.42	.52	.15

How many factors have you extracted? Give an interpretation and justify it. If you cannot interpret your solution, explain why. How well can the original correlations be reproduced from your solution?

9. Calculate loadings on first principal factor and verify that they contribute 35% to the total variance.

Variable	1	2	3	4	5	Loading
1	1.000	0.438	−0.137	0.205	−0.178	.737
2	0.438	1.000	0.031	0.180	−0.304	.749
3	−0.137	0.031	1.000	0.161	0.372	−.358
4	0.205	0.180	0.161	1.000	−0.013	.313
5	−0.178	−0.304	0.372	−0.013	1.000	−.654
Sum	1.328	1.345	1.427	1.533	0.877	

10. Verify that following correlation matrix has two principal factors, as shown in the last two columns.

Variable	1	2	3	4	a_{i1}	a_{i2}
1	1.00	.80	.60	.60	.894	.447
2	.80	1.00	.96	.00	.984	−.178
3	.60	.96	1.00	−.28	.894	−.447
4	.60	.00	−.28	1.00	.178	.984
Sum	3.00	2.76	2.28	1.32		

REFERENCES

Abu-Lughod, Janet
    1969   "Testing the theory of social area analysis: The ecology of Cairo, Egypt." American Sociological Review 34: 198–212.

Alker, Hayward, R., Jr.
    1964   "Dimensions of conflict in the general assembly." American Political Science Review 58: 642–657.

Anderson, T. W. and H. Rubin
    1956   "Statistical inference in factor analysis." Proceedings of the Third Berkeley Symposium on Mathematical Statistics and Probability 5: 111–150.

Armstrong, J. Scott
    1967   "Derivation of theory by means of factor analysis or Tom Swift and his electrical analysis machine." The American Statistician 21: 17–21.

Bales, Robert F.
    1970   Personality and Interpersonal Behavior. Appendix 5: "The value profile: A factor-analytic study of value statements." New York: Holt, Rinehart and Winston.

Bell, Wendell
    1955   "Economic, family, and ethnic status: An empirical test." American Sociological Review 20: 45–52.

Blau, Peter
    1962   "Patterns of choice in interpersonal relations." American Sociological Review 27: 41–55.

Boggs, Sarah L.
    1965   "Urban crime patterns." American Sociological Review 30: 899–908.

Borgatta, Edgar F., Leonard S. Cottrell, Jr., and Henry J. Meyer
    1956   "On the dimensions of group behavior." Sociometry 19: 223–240.

Cartwright, Demond S.
  1965 "A misapplication of factor analysis." American Sociological Review 30: 249–252.

Cattell, Raymond B.
  1952 Factor Analysis. New York: Harper and Brothers.

Cattell, Raymond B., H. Bruel, and H. P. Hartman
  1952 "An attempt at more refined definition of the cultural dimensions of syntality in modern nations." American Sociological Review 17: 408–421.

Chilton, Roland J.
  1964 "Delinquency area research in Baltimore, Detroit, and Indianapolis." American Sociological Review 29: 71–83.

Driver, Harold E. and Karl Schuessler
  1967 "Correlational analysis of Murdock's 1957 ethnographic sample." American Anthropologist 69: 332–352.

Educational and Psychological Measurement
  1940 to 1970 (Contents of this journal especially reflect problems and difficulties in applied factor analysis.)

Empey, LaMar T. and Steven G. Lubeck
  1968 "Conformity and deviance in the 'situation of company'." American Sociological Review 33: 760–774.

Farber, Bernard
  1962 "Elements of competence in interpersonal relations: A factor analysis." Sociometry 25: 30–47.

Goldberg, Louis C., Frank Baker and Albert H. Rubenstein
  1965 "Local-cosmopolitan: Unidimensional or multidimensional." American Journal of Sociology 70: 704–710.

Gordon, Robert
  1967 "Issues in the ecological study of delinquency." American Sociological Review 32: 927–944.

  1968 "On the interpretation of oblique factors." American Sociological Review 33: 601–620.

Gouldner, Alvin W. and Richard A. Peterson
  1962 Technology and the Moral Order. Indianapolis: Bobbs-Merrill.

Guttman, Louis
  1956 "'Best possible' systematic estimates of communalities." Psychometrika 21: 273–285.

Harman, Harry H.
  1967 Modern Factor Analysis. Second Edition. Chicago: University of Chicago Press.

Henrysson, Sten
  1957 Applicability of Factor Analysis in the Behavioral Sciences: A Methodological Study. Stockholm: Almquist and Wiksell.

Hotelling, Harold
1933 "Analysis of a complex of statistical variables into principal components." Journal of Educational Psychology 24: 417–441; 498–520.

1936 "Simplified calculation of principal components." Psychometrika 1: 27–35.

Jenkins, C. David
1966 "Group differences in perception: A study of community beliefs and feelings about tuberculosis." American Journal of Sociology 71: 417–429.

Joreskog, K. G.
1963 Statistical Estimation in Factor Analysis. Stockholm: Almquist and Wiksell.

Kahl, Joseph and James Davis
1955 "A comparison of indexes of socioeconomic status." American Sociological Review 20: 317–325.

Kaiser, Henry F.
1958 "The varimax criterion for analytic rotation in factor analysis." Psychometrika 23: 187–200.

1960 "The application of electronic computers to factor analysis." Educational and Psychological Measurement 20: 141–151.

Kaiser, H. and John Caffrey
1965 "Alpha factor analysis." Psychometrika 30: 1–13.

Kendall, M. G.
1957 A Course in Multivariate Analysis. London: Charles Griffin.

Lawley, D. N. and A. E. Maxwell
1963 Factor Analysis as a Statistical Method. London: Butterworth.

MacRae, Duncan, Jr.
1960 "Direct factor analysis of sociometric data." Sociometry 23: 360–371.

1970 Issues and Parties in Legislative Voting: Methods of Statistical Analysis. Chapter 5: "Principal-component analysis and roll-call data." New York: Harper and Row.

Murdie, Robert A.
1969 Factorial Ecology of Metropolitan Toronto, 1951–1961. Chicago: The University of Chicago, Department of Geography.

Neal, Arthur G. and Salomon Rettig
1967 "On the multidimensionality of alienation." American Sociological Review 32: 54–64.

Parkman, Margaret A. and Jack Sawyer
1967 "Dimensions of ethnic intermarriage in Hawaii." American Sociological Review 32: 593–607.

Pettigrew, Thomas and Rosalind Spier
1962 "The ecological structure of Negro homicide." American Journal of Sociology 67: 621–629.

Psychometrika
    1936–1970 (Contents of this journal reflect many important develop-
           ments in factor analysis during the last 35 years.)

Sawyer, Jack
    1967 "Dimensions of nations: Size, wealth, and politics." American
          Journal of Sociology 73: 145–172.

Sawyer, Jack and Robert A. Levine
    1966 "Cultural dimensions: A factor analysis of the world ethno-
          graphic sample." American Anthropologist 68: 708–731.

Schmid, C.
    1960 "Urban crime areas: Part I." American Sociological Review 25:
          527–542.

Schuessler, Karl and Gerald Slatin
    1964 "Sources of variation in city crime 1950 and 1960." Journal of
          Research in Crime and Delinquency 1: 127–148.

Selvin, Hanan C. and Warren O. Hagstrom
    1963 "The empirical classification of formal groups." American
          Sociological Review 28: 399–411.

Sewell, William and A. Haller
    1959 "Factors in the relationship between social status and the person-
          ality adjustment of the child." American Sociological Review 24:
          511–520.

Short, James F., Jr., Ray A. Tennyson, and Kenneth I. Howard
    1963 "Behavior dimensions of gang delinquency." American Socio-
          logical Review 28: 411–428.

Strodtbeck, Fred L. and L. Harmon Hook
    1961 "The social dimensions of a twelve-man jury table." Sociometry
          24: 397–415.

Thurstone, Louis L.
    1947 Multiple-Factor Analysis. Chicago: University of Chicago Press.

Tryon, Robert C.
    1955 Identification of Social Areas by Cluster Analysis: A General
          Method with an Application to the San Francisco Bay Area.
          Berkeley and Los Angeles: University of California Press.

Van Arsdol, Maurice D., Santo F. Camilleri, and Calvin F. Schmid
    1958 "The generality of urban social area indexes." American Socio-
          logical Review 23: 277–284.

Westoff, Charles, Marvin Bressler, and Philip Sagi
    1960 "The concept of social mobility: An empirical inquiry." Ameri-
          can Sociological Review 25: 375–385.

Winch, Robert
    1947 "Heuristic and empirical typologies: A job for factor analysis."
          American Sociological Review 12: 68–75.

Wright, Benjamin and Mary Sue Evitts
    1961 "Direct factor analysis in sociometry." Sociometry 24: 82–98.

4

Analysis of Variance: Disproportionate Data

PART 1
Resolving Sums of Squares

Foreword. Whenever our object is to determine whether there are differences between group means, as well as differences among measures within groups, we may avail ourselves of the analysis of variance (AOV). If we wish to determine whether there are differences between schools in academic achievement, as well as individual differences within schools, we may employ the analysis of variance to answer that question. For example, in their study of educational inequality, Coleman and his associates (1966) sought to determine whether a pupil's academic achievement is affected both by the quality of his school *sui generis* and by such individual traits as intelligence and motivation. Their specific question was: "What proportion of the total variation in pupil achievement is attributable to differences in the quality of schools?" Their findings suggest that achievement (as measured) is more dependent on individual aptitude and motivation, whatever their origin, than on the quality of the school (as measured). They reached this conclusion by dividing the total variation (100%) into two parts, one part (10%) having its source in differences between schools, the other part (90%) having its source in differences among pupils within schools.

If we are required to determine whether part of the total variation in a set of measures is attributable to differences between groups, we may avail ourselves of AOV techniques, provided, as usual, that underlying assumptions (Eisenhart 1947) are met. If we hypothesize that the suicide rates of U.S. cities differ by region, we may employ the techniques of AOV to determine what part of their total variation is assignable to differences among regions.

The AOV is thus a technique for measuring the statistical (but not necessarily causal) effect of a given factor on the dependent variable (e.g., the effect of region on suicide). Leaving aside the question of its practical utility in sociological research, we consider the analysis of variance worthy of study because of the mentality it exemplifies. With its emphasis on comparisons free of confounding factors, it fosters a habit of planning to the end that the effect of a given factor on a given variable may be isolated and measured, and that spurious attributions of causality be avoided. Even if presently the AOV has a quite limited utility in social research, owing to sampling and measurement conditions which cannot readily be met, an examination of its fundamentals should still be worthwhile because of the analytical approach they represent. As a research model, the AOV may be valuable to the sociologist, even though, as a technique, its application cannot always be justified.

Single Classification. When a dependent variable (Y) is classified in terms of a single factor (A), we are necessarily restricted to investigating the statistical dependence of Y on A alone. A grouping of college aptitude scores by race permits us to explore the dependence of college aptitude on the factor of race alone. A classification of measures according to a single criterion is the simplest of all statistical groupings, and correspondingly the procedure for analyzing the variance of measures thus arranged is least complicated. Since we disregard all factors but one in our analysis, we can assess only the effect of that one factor; we cannot disentangle the effects of two or more factors on the dependent variable.

To illustrate the one-way analysis of variance (AOV), as it has come to be known, we take three samples of three items each, having equal means and equal variances:

				T_i
A_1	7	8	9	24
A_2	8	7	9	24
A_3	8	9	7	24

where T_i is sum of values in i^{th} row and A_i is the ith category. It is of interest that the values within each sample of a one-way tabulation may be arranged in any order whatsoever without affecting the results of the analysis.

To analyze the variance of these three samples, we proceed in the usual way, computing first the sum of the squares around the mean of all nine measures:

$$\text{TSS} = \sum_1^{n.} (Y_{ij} - \bar{Y}.)^2,$$

where Y_{ij} is the jth value in the ith class, $n.$ is the total number of cases, and $\bar{Y}.$ is the mean of all values. We symbolize this result TSS and label it the *total sum of squares*. For our problem, $\bar{Y}. = 8$, TSS $= 6$.

Next, we find the sum of the sums of squares within the respective samples. We may calculate this quantity directly by computing the sum of squares within each sample and summing these sums:

$$\text{WSS} = \sum^{r} \sum^{n_i} (Y_{ij} - \bar{Y}_i)^2,$$

where n_i is the number of cases in the ith sample, and r is the number of samples (rows). When n_i's are equal, we may denote that number by n. This result we name the *within sum of squares* and symbolize by the letters WSS. For our problem, WSS = 6. Since WSS = TSS, we state that the variation within samples completely accounts (in a statistical sense) for the total variation.

Now, let us purposefully upset the equality among row means by adding a constant value of 2 to each value in the second row and a constant of 4 to each value in the third row, leaving values in the first row unchanged. We then have:

				T_i
A_1	7	8	9	24
A_2	10	9	11	30
A_3	12	13	11	36

Such an adjustment will not disturb the sums of squares within A_2 and A_3 respectively, since the addition of a constant to each value in a set leaves the original sum of squares unaltered; hence, WSS will remain unchanged.

However, the total sum of squares is now 30, where before it was 6. That is,

$$\text{TSS} = 30,$$

a result which the reader should verify. Obviously, the total sum of squares is no longer exhausted by the within sum of squares; instead, we are left with an appreciable remainder of 24. By disturbing the equality of means, we have increased the total sum of squares from 6 to 30. Of this total, we may attribute 80 percent to the differences among means and 20 percent to the within sum of squares.

To verify that the differences among the sample means do indeed account for the difference between the total and the within sum of squares, we proceed stepwise as follows:

(1) Compute the deviations between the three sample means and the overall mean,
(2) square each such deviation,
(3) weight each squared deviation by the number of items in the sample from which it was derived, and
(4) sum all such weighted squares.

In symbolic form:

$$\text{BSS} = \sum n(\overline{Y}_i - \overline{Y}_{.})^2.$$

Applying this procedure to the revised samples, we obtain:

	$(\overline{Y}_i - \overline{Y}_{.})$	$(\overline{Y}_i - \overline{Y}_{.})^2$	$n(\overline{Y}_i - \overline{Y}_{.})^2$
A_1	$8 - 10$	$(-2)^2$	$3(-2)^2 = 12$
A_2	$10 - 10$	0	0
A_3	$12 - 10$	$(2)^2$	$3(2)^2 = 12$
			$\overline{24}$

thereby verifying that BSS = TSS − WSS. Obviously, the total sum of squares would be exactly equal to the *between sum of squares* if every value was equal to the mean of its set, as if there were no variation within samples, only variation between them.

Significance Testing. Now, in sampling studies, it is natural to wonder whether the magnitude of BSS, which reflects the differences among sample means, is so large as to be inconsistent with the hypothesis that population means are identical. The numerical difference between BSS and WSS will not supply an answer to that question, nor will the ratio of BSS to WSS serve that purpose. Neither quantity may be readily matched to a probability on the basis of which a decision on the null hypothesis could be reached. For an answer, we must convert these raw sums of squares into estimates of the population variance by prescribed methods, which estimates may then be compared in ratio form to test the hypothesis that samples were drawn from populations having a common mean.

To estimate a population variance from a sample sum of squares, we simply divide that sum by its degrees of freedom. Applying this rule, we get

$$s_w^2 = \frac{\text{WSS}}{nr - r},$$

where $r = $ number of samples or rows, and

$$s_b^2 = \frac{\text{BSS}}{r - 1}.$$

But before we compare estimates, we must specify the populations from which the samples were drawn and about which inferences will be made. In particular, it is necessary to specify whether sampled classes are fixed in repeated sampling or whether they themselves are subject to sampling variation. When classes are fixed in repeated sampling, our inferences are limited to those fixed classes; on the other hand, when the classes themselves are subject to random variation, we may extend our generalizations to the sampled population of classes. When classes and, hence, their effects are the same in repeated sampling, we speak of the model to be tested as the "fixed effects model"; when classes and, hence, their effects are subject to random variation in repeated sampling, we speak of the model to be tested as the "random effects model." By expressing both models in symbolic form, we may represent more precisely the distinctive features of each, and the differences between them.

Fixed Effects Model (Model I). In this model we regard each value (Y_{ij}) as the sum of three components:

$$Y_{ij} = \mu_. + \alpha_i + e_{ij}$$

where $\mu_.$ is the overall mean, $\alpha_i = \mu_i - \mu_.$, and $e_{ij} = Y_{ij} - \mu_i$. We assume that Y_{ij} is normally distributed around μ_i with variance σ^2, or that e_{ij} is normally distributed around zero with variance σ^2. In conventional notation: $e_{ij} = N(0, \sigma^2)$. If these conditions hold in the population, and if we have sampled r fixed classes, the mean squares between and within classes have these expectations (Edwards 1964):

$$E(s_w^2) = \sigma^2$$

$$E(s_b^2) = \sigma^2 + \frac{n\sum\alpha_i^2}{r-1},$$

where r is the number of rows. If class means are identical so that $\sum\alpha_i^2 = 0$, the mean square between classes reduces to σ^2 and the ratio of s_b^2 to s_w^2 distributes as F. However, when class means differ so that $\sum\alpha_i^2 > 0$, the ratio of s_b^2 to s_w^2 will not distribute as F, with a consequent greater tendency to reject the null hypothesis of no difference among population means.

Random Effects Model (Model II). In superficial appearance, Model II and Model I are exactly alike:

$$Y_{ij} = \mu_. + \alpha_i + e_{ij},$$

where $\mu_.$ is the overall mean, $\alpha_i = \mu_i - \mu_.$, and $e_{ij} = Y_{ij} - \mu_i$. As in Model I, we assume that Y_{ij} is normally distributed with variance σ^2. However, we diverge from Model I in our assumption that α_i is normally distributed around zero, with variance σ_α^2. If these conditions hold, and if our r samples come from classes which themselves were randomly drawn from infinitely many classes, the mean squares between and within classes have these expectations:

$$E(s_w^2) = \sigma^2$$

$$E(s_b^2) = \sigma^2 + n\sigma_\alpha^2.$$

If all α_i's are identically zero, or if class means are identical, the mean square between classes has σ^2 as its expectation. In that event, the ratio of s_b^2 to s_w^2 distributes as F around a mean value close to 1; otherwise the ratio will tend to exceed 1, with a consequent greater tendency to reject the null hypothesis.

It is of interest that the null hypothesis of Model I, $\sum \alpha_i^2 = 0$, and the null hypothesis of Model II, $\sigma_\alpha^2 = 0$, are tested by the same calculations. Evidently, the difference between Model I and Model II lies not in the arithmetical operations we perform on the sample measures, but rather in the way in which the r classes are defined. In Model I, we define our r classes as fixed, and restrict our inference to those r classes; in Model II, we regard our r classes as a random sample from an infinite population of classes which is the target of our generalization.

Two-Way Classification. A two-way classification differs from a one-way classification in that each value (Y) is classified in two ways instead of one: by A and B, rather than by A alone. Since two-way groupings may be regarded as classes within classes, we sometimes refer to them as subclasses, or subsamples. With values arranged in subclasses, it is possible to divide the total sum of squares into four parts based on these differences: (1) among values within subclasses; (2) among row means; (3) among column means; and (4) among differences among subsample means within columns (or rows). From these results we may test the hypothesis that the means of the populations in rows are identical; the hypothesis that the means of the populations in columns are identical; the hypothesis that differences among subsample means within columns (or rows) are constant, or the equivalent hypothesis of no interaction between A and B.

For example, if measures have been classified by ethnic background and occupation, we may test the hypothesis that the means of the ethnic groups do not differ; the hypothesis that the means of the occupational groups do not differ; the hypothesis that differences among ethnic groups are unaffected by occupation; or that differences among occupations are unaffected by ethnic background. This latter is the hypothesis of no interaction between occupation and ethnic background.

Although it is possible to extract more information from measures grouped into subclasses than into main classes alone, it is not always possible to analyze their variation by simple routine procedures. In fact, unless subclass frequencies are in the same proportion as marginal frequencies, a condition which the data do not always meet, a somewhat elaborate method is required. It is thus the two-classification and the complications which pertain to its analysis in the absence of proportionality which set the problem of this chapter. However, before considering that problem, we may find it profitable to review the two-way analysis of variance for the usual case of proportional subclass frequencies. We begin with nine subsamples whose means and variances are equal:

	B_1	B_2	B_3
A_1	7	7	7
	8	8	8
	9	9	9
A_2	7	7	7
	8	8	8
	9	9	9
A_3	7	7	7
	8	8	8
	9	9	9

To analyze the variance of these nine subsamples, we proceed in the usual manner, computing first the sum of squares for the entire set of $nrc = 3 \times 3 \times 3 = 27$ measures, where n is the number of cases in each subsample. Taking the grand mean from each measure, squaring these deviations and summing, we get

$$\text{TSS} = \sum(Y_{ijk} - \bar{Y}_{..})^2$$
$$= 18,$$

where Y_{ijk} is the kth value in the ith row and j^{th} column, $\bar{Y}_{..}$ is the mean of all nrc measures. For our problem, $\bar{Y}_{..} = 8$, and TSS $= 18$.

Next, we obtain the sum of squares within each subsample, and total these sums for WSS. Since the sum of squares within each subsample is identical in our example, we need only to obtain the sum of squares in any one of them and multiply that result by $rc = 9$, the number of subsamples, to get WSS. Thus:

$$\text{WSS} = 9[(7 - 8)^2 + (8 - 8)^2 + (9 - 8)^2]$$
$$= 9(2)$$
$$= 18.$$

In our example, the total sum of squares is completely exhausted by WSS, thereby proving that subsample means are identical. As a general conclusion: when there are no differences among subsample means, TSS $=$ WSS.

Let us now deliberately disturb the equality among subsample means, while preserving the equality among marginal means and also the equality of sums of squares within subsamples. Of the many ways in which this might be accomplished, we subtract 2 from each measure in A_1B_1 and A_3B_3 and add that quantity to each measure in A_1B_3 and A_3B_1. We then have these once-revised measures:

	B_1	B_2	B_3
A_1	5	7	9
	6	8	10
	7	9	11
A_2	7	7	7
	8	8	8
	9	9	9
A_3	9	7	5
	10	8	6
	11	9	7

and these once-revised subsample and marginal means:

	B_1	B_2	B_3	
A_1	6	8	10	8
A_2	8	8	8	8
A_3	10	8	6	8
	8	8	8	

Such an adjustment does not affect the within sum of squares, by reason that measures in each subsample were revised by the addition of a constant (including zero). Hence, WSS = 18 remains unchanged. However, the total sum of squares (TSS) is larger by 48 than the total sum of squares for the original set:

$$\text{TSS} = \sum(Y_{ijk} - \bar{Y}_{..})^2$$
$$= 66,$$

reflecting the greater variation of the revised measures around the grand mean of 8. Since the marginal means are identical, and since WSS = 18, it is logical to attribute the excess of $66 - 18 = 48$ to the differences among the subsample means. To verify this conclusion, we take the grand mean from each subsample mean, square each deviation and weight by n, and sum all rc weighted squares:

$$\text{BSS} = \sum n(\bar{Y}_{ij} - \bar{Y}_{..})^2$$
$$= 48.$$

Putting results together, we get the foregone conclusion: TSS = BSS + WSS (as in a one-way table). We will attribute this variation among subsample means to the interaction of A and B if it is too large to be regarded as sampling error.

Our next step should be obvious by now: we disturb the equality among row means, maintaining at the same time the equality among column means, as well as differences among values within subsamples. To do this, we add the same value to all values within a given row but a different value to values in different rows. If, adhering to this rule, we reduce each value in the first row by 1, increase each value in the third row by 1, and leave intact the values in the second row, the once-revised values become these twice-revised measures:

	B_1	B_2	B_3
A_1	4	6	8
	5	7	9
	6	8	10
A_2	7	7	7
	8	8	8
	9	9	9
A_3	10	8	6
	11	9	7
	12	10	8

with twice-revised means as follows:

	B_1	B_2	B_3	
A_1	5	7	9	7
A_2	8	8	8	8
A_3	11	9	7	9
	8	8	8	8

Our interest, of course, lies in the effect of this revision on the total sum of squares and its component parts. Taking the grand mean of 8 from each of the 27 values, squaring deviations, and summing, we get

$$\text{TSS} = 84,$$

which is larger by 18 than the total sum of squares (66) for the once-revised measures. From this result, it is evident that the total sum of squares increases as the differences among row means increase, other conditions constant.

As our first step in decomposing this total of 84, we verify that it is equal to the sum of WSS and BSS. Since values within subsamples were increased or decreased by the same amount, WSS will be 18 as before; hence for purposes of verification, we need only to compute BSS. Taking the grand mean from each subsample mean, squaring each deviation, weighting by n, and summing weighted squares, we obtain

$$\text{BSS} = \sum n(\bar{Y}_{ij} - \bar{Y}_{..})^2$$
$$= 66,$$

which together with WSS is equal to TSS.

Upon examining BSS = 66, we find it larger by 18 than BSS with row means equal, as in the once-revised tabulation. It is natural to suppose that this excess is due to the differences among row means, a supposition that may be verified by computing the sum of squares for row means in straight-forward manner:

$$\text{RSS} = \sum n_{i.}(\bar{Y}_{i.} - \bar{Y}_{..})^2$$
$$= 18,$$

where $n_{i.} = nc$ is the number of values in the ith row. Subtracting this result of 18 from 66, we get 48, the value of BSS before the second adjustment of values.

To complete our demonstration, we establish differences among column means where before there were none, adding the same constant to all values within a given column, a different constant in different columns. To provide simple numerical results, we subtract 1 from each value in the first column, add 1 to each value in the third, and leave values in the middle column unchanged. After these revisions, we have these thrice-revised measures:

	B_1	B_2	B_3
A_1	3	6	9
	4	7	10
	5	8	11
A_2	6	7	8
	7	8	9
	8	9	10
A_3	9	8	7
	10	9	8
	11	10	9

and these thrice-revised means:

	B_1	B_2	B_3	
A_1	4	7	10	7
A_2	7	8	9	8
A_3	10	9	8	9
	7	8	9	8

For these thrice-revised measures, TSS = 102, as the student may wish to confirm. Since WSS is unaffected by the arithmetical adjustment, we have

$$\text{BSS} = 102 - 18$$
$$= 84.$$

Comparing this result with the case of no differences among column means, we see that it is larger by 18. Clearly, differences among column means, like those among row means, have an effect: they inflate the sum of squares for subsample means. To determine the magnitude of that inflation, we find, as in the case of row means, the sum of squares for differences among column means. Taking the grand mean from each column mean, squaring each deviation and weighting that square by $n_{.j}$, and summing weighted squares, we get

$$\text{CSS} = \sum n_{.j}(\bar{Y}_{.j} - \bar{Y}_{..})^2$$
$$= 18,$$

where $n_{.j} = nr$, the number of measures in the jth column. Inasmuch as row means were purposely maintained, the sum of squares of 18 based on differences among row means is unchanged. Together the marginal means contribute $18 + 18 = 36$ to the sum of squares of 84 for subsample means. Deducting 36 from 84 we reach 48, or the sum of squares for subsample means with identical row and column means, as in the once-revised tabulation. This operation serves to exemplify the general rule: to obtain the sum of squares expected in the absence of differences among marginal means, subtract the quantity RSS + CSS from BSS.

    This remainder has come to be known, although not too aptly, as the interaction sum of squares (ISS), since an interaction, as defined, between the main classifications, A and B, may contribute to its magnitude. An interaction between A and B is defined as the failure of the pattern of differences among subclass means within a given row (or column) to reproduce the pattern of differences among column (or row) means, rows (or columns) disregarded. For example, if in a 4×2 table the difference between column means is $+10$ and the difference between subclass means within the first row is -10, then A and B may be said to be in interaction. While measures in B_1 are on the average larger by 10 than measures in B_2, this difference is reversed within the first row, thereby demonstrating that the effect of B on Y is contingent on the level of A.

Special Case, $n = 1$. If we have only a single measure in each cell, it is impossible to get a within sum of squares; hence, in this limiting case, TSS = BSS. Under these special circumstances, our analysis necessarily will be limited to decomposing BSS into its component parts: RSS, CSS, and ISS.

To illustrate this procedure, we deal with a set of nine measures, each classified according to A and B, with no two measures in the same subclass:

	B_1	B_2	B_3	$T_{i.}$	$\bar{Y}_{i.}$
A_1	3	9	9	21	7
A_2	5	3	4	12	4
A_3	4	6	20	30	10
$T_{.j}$	12	18	33	63	
$\bar{Y}_{.j}$	4	6	11		7

We first compute the total sum of squares, subtracting the correction factor (C) from the sum of the squared values:

$$(4.1.1) \qquad \begin{aligned} \text{TSS} &= \sum Y_{ij}^2 - C \\ &= 673 - 441 \\ &= 232, \end{aligned}$$

where Y_{ij} = measure in A_i and B_j, and $C = T_{..}^2/n_{..}$. Formula (4.1.1) provides us with an instance of the general result that the sum of the squares around the mean is equal to the sum of the squares around an arbitrary origin, corrected by the weighted distance between the mean and that arbitrary origin.

As our first step in partitioning this total sum of squares, which here is construed as BSS, we obtain the sum of squares for differences among the column means. Applying a convenient and familiar algebraic identity for purposes of hand calculation,

$$\text{CSS} = \sum r(\bar{Y}_{.j} - \bar{Y}_{..})^2$$

$$(4.1.2) \qquad = \frac{\sum T_{.j}^2}{r} - C$$

we calculate,

$$CSS = 519 - 441$$
$$= 78,$$

where CSS = sum of squares based on differences among column means.

Next, in identical manner, we calculate the sum of squares for differences among row means. The formula is:

$$RSS = \sum c(\bar{Y}_{i.} - \bar{Y}_{..})^2$$

(4.1.3)
$$= \frac{\sum T_{i.}^2}{c} - C.$$

Applying (4.1.3) to our data, we get

$$RSS = \frac{(21)^2 + (12)^2 + (30)^2}{3} - \frac{(63)^2}{9}$$
$$= 495 - 441$$
$$= 54.$$

Consolidating 54 and the previous result of 78, we get 132, which falls short of BSS by 100. Obviously, some residual variation remains which can be laid neither to differences among row means nor to differences among column means.

To explore in limited fashion the composition of this remainder, let us determine the values expected in the event of no differences among row means and column means, respectively, with the overall mean unchanged. We need only to adjust values so that differences among marginal means are eliminated. Where before we created differences to discern the effect of that adjustment, we now eliminate differences in order to discern the effect of that correction.

To eliminate differences among column means, we adjust each individual measure by an amount equal to the deviation of its column mean from the overall mean. We lower values, be it noted, when the column mean is larger than the overall mean; we raise them when the column mean is smaller. Thus, we raise values in the first and second columns by 3 and 1, respectively; we lower values in the third column by 4. After this adjustment, we have these once-adjusted values:

	B_1	B_2	B_3	$T_{i.}$	$\bar{Y}_{i.}$
A_1	6	10	5	21	7
A_2	8	4	0	12	4
A_3	7	7	16	30	10
$\bar{Y}_{.j} - \bar{Y}_{..}$	-3	-1	4	63	
$\bar{Y}_{.i}$	7	7	7		7

Since the deviations of the observed column means sum to zero, row means are unaffected by this adjustment, as are the initial differences among them.

To equalize row means, we apply deviations of row means from the overall mean to our once-adjusted values, an operation that will not disturb the now-established equality of column means, since the net increment within each column is necessarily zero. Again, we lower values where row means are in excess of the overall mean; we raise values where row means are below the overall mean. By this adjustment, we obtain a set of measures which still vary among themselves internally but whose row and column totals are now equal:

	B_1	B_2	B_3	$\bar{Y}_{i.} - \bar{Y}_{..}$	$\bar{Y}_{i.}$
A_1	6	10	5	0	7
A_2	11	7	3	-3	7
A_3	4	4	13	3	7
$\bar{Y}_{.j}$	7	7	7		7

Upon calculating the sum of squares for this set, we find it to be 100, the result previously obtained by subtracting row and column sums of squares from the between sum of squares, BSS. Although the interaction sum of squares may be obtained readily by deducting the quantity (RSS + CSS) from BSS, the student should apply the foregoing technique to easy numerical examples in order to heighten his appreciation of its essential nature.

Hypothesis Testing. Needless to say, the decomposition of the total sum of squares into its constituent sums of squares is seldom if ever undertaken for its own sake; rather we do that to determine whether the variation among these component sums (expressed as mean squares) is inconsistent with the null hypothesis that sampled populations have identical means. In particular, we wish to determine whether the differences among row or column means, respectively, might have their source in random sampling, and similarly, whether the observed inconsistency in differences among subsample means within rows or columns could be the result of sampling fluctuations.

To test these possibilities, as with the one-way table, it is necessary to specify the populations from which our samples were drawn and to which our statistical inferences apply. We will stipulate that main classes are either fixed or randomly drawn from a population of classes. However, since we are now required to assess the effects of two factors, A and B, instead of one alone, we must provide for the possibility that classes are fixed on one factor and subject to random variation on the other. This possibility gives rise to what has come to be known as the mixed model. To point up the differences among models, we again have recourse to quite conventional symbolic expressions.

Fixed Effects (Model I). In this model, we regard each value as the sum of four components as follows:

$$(4.1.4) \qquad Y_{ijk} = \mu_{..} + \alpha_i + \beta_j + e_{ijk},$$

where $\mu_{..}$ is the overall mean, $\alpha_i = \mu_{i.} - \mu_{..}$, $\beta_j = \mu_{.j} - \mu_{..}$, and $e_{ijk} = Y_{ijk} - \hat{\mu}_{ij}$. Since the effects of A and B are added to the overall effect $\mu_{..}$, we speak of Equation (4.1.4) as an additive model. We assume that Y_{ijk} is normally distributed around $\hat{\mu}_{ij}$, with variance σ^2. Our analysis will permit us to decide (with a specified degree of confidence) whether or not our data are consistent with this model, and, accordingly, whether to retain it or to discard it in favor of an alternative model.

When the conditions of Model I hold, and when sampling is from fixed subclasses, the mean squares based on the differences within subsamples, differences among row means, differences among column means, and differences among row (column) means within columns (rows) have these expectations respectively:

$$E(s_w^2) = \sigma^2$$

$$E(s_r^2) = \sigma^2 + \frac{nc\sum\alpha_i^2}{r - 1}$$

$$E(s_c^2) = \sigma^2 + \frac{nr\sum\beta_j^2}{c - 1}$$

$$E(s_{rc}^2) = \sigma^2 + \frac{n\sum(\mu_{ij} - \hat{\mu}_{ij})^2}{(r - 1)(c - 1)},$$

where $\mu_{ij} =$ subclass mean. Since s_w^2 is an unbiased estimate of the common variance, σ^2, the ratio of s_r^2 to s_w^2 may be used to test the hypothesis that row means are equal, or that $\sum\alpha_i^2 = 0$. Similarly, the ratio of s_c^2 to s_w^2 may be used to test the hypothesis that column means are identical, or that $\sum\beta_j^2 = 0$. And, thirdly, the ratio of s_{rc}^2 to s_w^2 may be used to test the hypothesis of no interaction, or $\sum(\mu_{ij} - \hat{\mu}_{ij})^2 = 0$.

It may be noted in passing that Model I may not be subject to test, when $n = 1$. Under this restriction, there can be no sum of squares within sub-samples, and no mean square based on differences within subsamples, since at least two entries are required to compute a sum of squares. In this situation it is impossible to test the hypothesis that row (column) means are equal, unless it is reasonable to suppose that there is no interaction between A and B. In the presumed absence of interaction, we may employ s_{rc}^2 as the base of our F-ratio, since under these conditions this mean square has the hypothetical common variance as its statistical expectation; otherwise, its expectation will be greater than the common variance by an amount proportional to $\sum(\mu_{ij} - \hat{\mu}_{ij})^2$ and its use as an error term in the F-ratio will therefore tend to obscure actual differences among population means.

Random Effects (Model II). In Model II, as in I, we regard each value as the sum of four components:

$$Y_{ijk} = \mu_{..} + \alpha_i + \beta_j + e_{ijk},$$

where $e_{ijk} = N(\sigma^2, 0)$. The difference between Models I and II lies not in our conception of Y, but rather in our definition of main factors, A and B. In Model I, we take both A and B as fixed, whereas in Model II we assume that both A and B are random variables. When the conditions of Model II hold, and we have samples from each of rc randomly selected subclasses, the mean squares corresponding to component sums of squares have these expectations:

$$E(s_w^2) = \sigma^2$$

$$E(s_r^2) = \sigma^2 + n\sigma_{\alpha\beta}^2 + nc\sigma_{\alpha}^2$$

$$E(s_c^2) = \sigma^2 + n\sigma_{\alpha\beta}^2 + nr\sigma_{\beta}^2$$

$$E(s_{rc}^2) = \sigma^2 + n\sigma_{\alpha\beta}^2,$$

where $\sigma_{\alpha\beta}^2 = E(\mu_{ij} - \hat{\mu}_{ij})^2$. Since s_w^2 is an unbiased estimate of the population variance, the ratio of s_{rc}^2 to s_w^2 may be used to test the hypothesis that interaction is absent, or that $E(\mu_{ij} - \hat{\mu}_{ij})^2 = 0$. In order to test the hypothesis that row means are equal, we have recourse to the ratio of s_r^2 to s_{rc}^2, which will distribute as F when $\sigma_\alpha^2 = 0$. Similarly, the ratio of s_c^2 to s_{rc}^2 will have an F-distribution when $\sigma_\beta^2 = 0$, and therefore this ratio may be used to test the hypothesis that column means are equal. Notice that in testing the significance of row and column means, we have employed the mean square for interaction as our error term. In general, the appropriate error term for the test of a given factor is the mean square whose expectation contains all components that are in the expectation of the mean square for that factor, except the component directly attributable to that factor (see Edwards 1964: 97).

Mixed Model. As previously noted, one set of effects may be fixed, while the other set was randomly selected from a population of classes. In that case, we speak of our model as a mixed model. If A is fixed and B is random, the mean squares have these expectations:

$$E(s_w^2) = \sigma^2$$

$$E(s_r^2) = \sigma^2 + n\sigma_{\alpha\beta}^2 + \frac{nc\sum \alpha_i^2}{r-1}$$

$$E(s_c^2) = \sigma^2 + nr\sigma_{\beta}^2$$

$$E(s_{rc}^2) = \sigma^2 + n\sigma_{\alpha\beta}^2.$$

From these expectations, we may surmise (correctly) that our procedure for running significance tests will not correspond exactly to the procedure for either Model I or Model II. To test the significance of row means, we set up the ratio of s_r^2 to s_{rc}^2; to test the significance of column means, we set up the ratio of s_c^2 to s_w^2. With the mixed model, we again encounter difficulties when $n = 1$. For in this case, it will be impossible to test the significance of main effects unless we are willing to assume the absence of interaction between A and B.

From all of the foregoing it is clear that populations must be specified before significance tests are run, since procedures differ according to whether classes are fixed or subject to random variation. If we use the wrong procedure, we run the risk of giving ourselves more or less statistical significance than we deserve. We will encounter this same problem in multi-stage sampling (Chapter 6).

PART 2
Disproportionate Frequencies

Statement of the Problem. The foregoing procedure for a two-way table is inapplicable unless subclass frequencies are in the same proportion as the corresponding marginal frequencies, i.e., unless $n_{ij}/n_{i.} = n_{.j}/n_{..}$. For in the absence of such proportionality, the relative weight of B_i will differ from one level of A to another, and likewise the relative weight of A_i will differ from one level of B to another. And in consequence, differences among row means will spuriously reflect differences in the relative weight of B_i, as well as differences in the A-factor whose influence we wish to measure.

By way of example, consider a 2×3 factorial study in which prejudice scores (Y) are cross-tabulated by income (B) and education (A), with subsample and marginal means as follows:

		High	Middle	Low	Mean
		\multicolumn{3}{c}{Income (B)}	
	High	24	21	18	21
Education (A)	Low	20	15	10	15
	Mean	22	18	14	

We may take the difference between row means as a measure of the effect of education, presumably free of the effect of income. But that procedure will be justified only if the relative frequency of cases by columns is the same for each row. Otherwise, row means will be larger or smaller, as will the difference between them, according to the distribution of cases by columns

within rows. Thus, if there are disproportionately few persons of high education with high incomes, the mean for all persons of high education will be
low relative to the mean for all persons of low education. The economic
factor will have thus intruded itself into the comparison of educational
levels. Likewise, if there are relatively few well-to-do persons with high
education, the educational factor will have confounded the comparison
among income levels.

A similar complication arises in the analysis of vital statistics: differences
among crude birth rates may reflect differences in age composition rather
than differences in fertility. For that reason, we standardize birth rates by
age in order to render them more comparable. So, in the two-way analysis
of variance, we may be required to adjust the distribution of cases within
columns before comparing row means, or adjust the distribution of cases
within rows before comparing column means. Before considering alternative
procedures for making such adjustments, let us examine the response of the
marginal means to varying subclass frequencies, with and without the
restriction of no interaction, and especially the complications produced by
departures from proportionality.

No Interaction. In the absence of interaction, differences among marginal
means are unaffected by shifting subclass frequencies provided that proportionality is maintained. As a demonstration, we successively apply the
proportionate subclass frequencies of Table 4.2.1 to a set of hypothetical
subclass means, in each case computing row means and the difference between

Table 4.2.1 *Proportional Subclass Frequencies*

(a)			(b)			(c)		
25	25	50	30	30	60	60	20	80
25	25	50	20	20	40	15	5	20
50	50	100	50	50	100	75	25	100

them. For easy manipulation, we take fictitious birth rates (number of births
per 1,000 population) by social class and color (Table 4.2.2). Since there is
no interaction between color and class, the difference between cell means
within rows (columns) is constant. To get row means, we multiply subclass
means by corresponding subclass frequencies, sum products by rows, and
divide each sum by its marginal frequency. Applying subclass frequencies (a)
from Table 4.2.1, we get these results:

$n_{ij}\overline{Y}_{ij}$		$\sum n_{ij}\overline{Y}_{ij}$	$\overline{Y}_{i.}$
375	500	875	17.5
125	250	375	7.5

$$\overline{Y}_{1.} - \overline{Y}_{2.} = 10.0$$

Table 4.2.2   *Subclass Means, No Interaction*

Color (A)	Social Class (B)	
	Upper	*Lower*
Black	15	20
White	5	10

We take the difference between row means as a measure of the effect of color.

Applying the second set of subclass frequencies (*b*), which are identical within rows but different between them, we obtain these quantities:

$n_{ij}\overline{Y}_{ij}$		$\sum n_{ij}\overline{Y}_{ij}$	$\overline{Y}_{i.}$
450	600	1050	17.5
100	200	300	7.5

$$\overline{Y}_{1.} - \overline{Y}_{2.} = 10.0$$

The pertinent result is that the difference between row means is left undisturbed by the revised frequencies; consequently, our conclusion about the effect of color on fertility remains unchanged.

Nor is the difference between row means affected by substituting subclass frequencies (*c*), where they differ within rows as well as between them.

$n_{ij}\overline{Y}_{ij}$		$\sum n_{ij}\overline{Y}_{ij}$	$\overline{Y}_{i.}$
900	400	1300	16.25
75	50	125	6.25

$$\overline{Y}_{1.} - \overline{Y}_{2.} = 10.0$$

In this case, row means themselves undergo a downward change, but the difference between them remains unaltered. It is thus evident that the effect of color on the birth rate as measured by the difference between row means is unaffected by changing subclass frequencies, provided that proportionality is preserved.

On the other hand, differences among marginal means will be affected by the presence of disproportionality and will vary as the degree of that disproportionality. Hence, we may no longer take these differences as measures of the influence of one condition relative to another.

To discern the manner in which the difference between row means is affected by disproportionality, we successively weight the subclass means of Table 4.2.2 by subclass frequencies which differ in their degree of proportionality (Table 4.2.3). As before, we multiply subclass means by subclass

Table 4.2.3 *Disproportional Subclass Frequencies*

	(a)				(b)				(c)		
	U	L			U	L			U	L	
Black	2	8	10		5	5	10		8	2	10
White	30	60	90		30	60	90		20	70	90
	32	68			35	65			28	72	

frequencies, sum products by rows and divide by corresponding marginal totals for row means. Lastly, we subtract the mean of Row 1 from the mean of Row 2 for the difference between them. Carrying out these operations, we get:

	$n_{ij}\overline{Y}_{ij}$		$\sum n_{ij}\overline{Y}_{ij}$	$\overline{Y}_{i.}$
(a)	30	160	190	19.00
	150	600	750	8.33
				10.67
(b)	75	100	175	17.50
	150	600	750	8.33
				9.17
(c)	120	40	160	16.00
	100	700	800	8.89
				7.11

Comparing these differences with the constant difference of 10.00 for proportional frequencies, we note that the factor of color (A) appears to exert a stronger or weaker influence on the birth rate (Y) according to the relative frequency of social classes within color groupings. For instance, when lower class whites are twice as numerous as upper class whites, and upper and lower class blacks are equally numerous, the difference between row means is 9.17. When lower class whites are twice as numerous as upper class whites, and when lower class blacks are four times as numerous as upper class blacks, the difference between row means is 10.67. In general, the difference will be larger than the difference for proportional frequencies when the lower class is underrepresented among whites; the difference will be smaller than that for proportional frequencies when the lower class is overrepresented among whites.

To correct such discrepancies, we might give equal weight to each subclass mean, as if subclass frequencies were uniform in size. As an alternative procedure, we might weight subclass means within rows by the same set of proportions (relative frequencies), as in direct standardization. But whatever solution we adopt, we cannot mindlessly take the difference between row means as a measure of the effect of color (*A*) on fertility (*Y*), without first having rid that difference of the spurious contribution of social class (*B*). Nor could we take the difference between column means as a measure of the effect of social class on fertility without having made the proper adjustment for the contribution of color.

Algebraic Version. The effect of disproportionality may be demonstrated more strictly by the manipulation of literal values in a 2 × 2 table, with each value regarded as the sum of four components (Goulden 1952: 330):

$$Y_{ijk} = m + a_i + b_i + e_{ijk},$$

where

$$m = \text{factor common to all values}$$

$$a_i = \text{factor specific to values in } A_i$$

$$b_j = \text{factor specific to values in } B_j$$

$$e_{ijk} = \text{random error.}$$

Summing values for any subsample, we get:

$$T_{ij} = n_{ij}(a_i + b_j + m) + \sum e_{ijk},$$

where T_{ij} is sum of values in the ith row and j^{th} column. Upon summing values in the ith row and dropping the error term which has no effect on subsequent results, we get

(4.2.1) $$T_{i.} = n_{i.}(a_i + m) + n_{i1}b_1 + n_{i2}b_2,$$

where $T_{i.}$ is the sum of the values in the ith row. Dividing this quantity (4.2.1) by $n_{i.}$ we get the mean value for the ith row:

$$\overline{Y}_{i.} = m + a_i + \frac{n_{i1}}{n_{i.}}b_1 + \frac{n_{i2}}{n_{i.}}b_2.$$

Subtracting the mean of the second row from the mean of the first row, we obtain the difference,

$$\overline{Y}_{1.} - \overline{Y}_{2.} = (a_1 - a_2) + b_1\left[\frac{n_{11}}{n_{1.}} - \frac{n_{21}}{n_{2.}}\right] + b_2\left[\frac{n_{12}}{n_{1.}} - \frac{n_{22}}{n_{2.}}\right].$$

In the case of proportionality, $\dfrac{n_{1i}}{n_{1.}} - \dfrac{n_{2i}}{n_{2.}} = 0$, and the difference between row means reduces to $a_1 - a_2$. On the other hand, when subclass frequencies are disproportional, i.e., when $n_{1i}/n_{1.} - n_{2i}/n_{2.} \neq 0$, the difference between row means contains the quantity $\dfrac{n_{12}n_{21} - n_{11}n_{22}}{n_{1.}n_{2.}} (b_1 - b_2)$, as one of its components. It is this unwanted intrusion of B into A that must be eliminated by suitable methods.

Interaction Present: Proportional Frequencies. With interaction present, matters are slightly more complicated. In this case, differences among marginal means may be affected by shifting subclass frequencies, even though proportionality is maintained. To corroborate this claim, we set up a 2 × 2 table of subclass means with interaction (Table 4.2.4), and apply the proportional frequencies of Table 4.2.1 to these subclass means. Among blacks (Table 4.2.4), it will be noticed, the lower class has a higher rate than the

Table 4.2.4   Subclass Means, Interaction Present

Color	Social Class	
	U	L
Black	15	20
White	10	5

upper class; among whites the order is reversed—the upper class has a higher rate than the lower class. In short, there is an interaction between color and class.

Applying the subclass frequencies of Table 4.2.1 to Table 4.2.4, we get products, sums of products, and row means and differences between them as follows:

	$n_{ij}\overline{Y}_{ij}$		$\sum n_{ij}\overline{Y}_{ij}$	$\overline{Y}_{i.}$
(a)	375	500	875	17.5
	250	125	375	7.5
			$\overline{Y}_{1.} - \overline{Y}_{2.} =$	10.00
(b)	450	600	1050	17.5
	200	100	300	7.5
			$\overline{Y}_{1.} - \overline{Y}_{2.} =$	10.00

900	400
150	25

(c)

1300   16.25

175   8.75

$$\overline{Y}_{1.} - \overline{Y}_{2.} = \overline{7.50}$$

Note that the second difference (b) is equal to the first (a), but not to the third (c) which is smaller by 2.5. Since all calculations were performed on the same subclass means (Table 4.2.4), and since proportionality was maintained in each case, the change in the difference between row means must be attributed to the change in the ratio of column frequencies. For (a) and (b) the ratio of column frequencies is 50:50; for (c) the ratio is 75:25. From these examples, we surmise that in the presence of interaction the difference between marginal means will change as the marginal weights change, even though subclass frequencies retain their proportionality. Thus, if we give relatively more weight to the upper class than to the lower class, we reduce the difference between the means of the blacks and the whites; if we give relatively more weight to the lower class, we magnify the difference between the means of the color groups. Notwithstanding that the difference between blacks and whites changes in magnitude, that difference remains free of the effect of social class, and no special methods for getting sums of squares and mean squares are required. Our conclusion is that routine methods of analyzing the variance of measures in a two-way table hold, provided that proportionality is maintained. However, our test of the null hypothesis is more complicated, be it noted, when sampling is proportional to subpopulation size and there are unequal numbers in subpopulations. In this case, the procedure for calculating sums of squares and mean squares is unchanged, but the simple ratios between mean squares may no longer be used to test the significance of main effects. For the special methods required in this case, see Bancroft (1968: 13).

Disproportional Frequencies. On the other hand, when subclass frequencies are disproportional, main effects become entangled with one another and with interaction, and special methods for getting sums of squares must be applied. Although it is quite possible to express these entanglements algebraically (as on p. 156), it must suffice for our purposes to illustrate them numerically. We start with three sets of subclass frequencies (Table 4.2.5),

Table 4.2.5 *Disproportional Subclass Frequencies, Identical Marginal Ratios*

	(a) U	(a) L		(b) U	(b) L		(c) U	(c) L	
B	2	8	10	5	5	10	8	2	10
W	30	60	90	27	63	90	24	66	90
	32	68		32	68		32	68	

identical in their marginal ratios but different in their degree of disproportionality. When we apply these frequencies (Table 4.2.5) to the subclass
means with interaction (Table 4.2.4), we obtain marginal means and sums
as follows:

	$n_{ij}\bar{Y}_{ij}$		$\sum n_{ij}\bar{Y}_{ij}$	$\bar{Y}_{i.}$
(a)	30	160	190	19.00
	300	300	600	6.67
				12.33
(b)	75	100	175	17.50
	270	315	585	6.50
				11.00
(c)	120	40	160	16.00
	240	330	570	6.33
				9.67

Note that the difference between row means changes from 12.33 (*a*) to 9.67 (*c*),
despite the constancy in the ratio of column frequencies, 32:68. This change
in the difference between row means is attributable to the change in disproportionality, which causes main effects and interaction to become entangled to a greater or lesser degree. If we give relatively more weight to the
upper class among blacks, we cause the difference between row means to
decrease; if we give relatively more weight to the lower class among blacks,
we cause the difference between row means to increase. In general, when
frequencies are disproportional, differences among marginal means are a
mixture of row, column, and row × column effects; consequently, these
differences will vary as this mixture changes its composition. In the absence
of interaction, we have only to free *A* from the effect of *B* and vice-versa;
when interaction is present, we must free *A* of this compound effect, as well
as the effect of *B*.

It is thus the presence of interaction that dictates our choice of procedure.
When there is no interaction, the *method of fitting constants* will do; otherwise
it is used in conjunction with the *method of weighted squares of means*.
Since the method of fitted constants is employed in both situations, we deal
with it first. This method was devised by the British statistician Yates (1934),
and became readily available to research workers in the United States through
Snedecor's writings (1946) on statistical methods. Although it would seem
to have considerable utility in social research, it has been used only in-
frequently by sociologists, probably because of their limited exposure to it.

PART 3
Method of Fitting Constants

Unsorted Values. To unfold the method of fitting constants, we take as our point of departure an illustrative 2×2 table consisting of four subsamples of three values each. These values are given in Table 4.3.1. Our first step,

Table 4.3.1   *Four Subsamples, Three Values Each*

	B_1	B_2
A_1	2	4
	4	6
	6	8
A_2	6	8
	8	10
	10	12

seemingly backward, is to merge these subsamples into a single set of un-sorted measures, arranging them arbitrarily without reference to either A or B. For example: 2, 4, 4, 6, 6, 6, 8, 8, 8, 10, 10, 12. With A and B thus disregarded, it is possible for us to conceive of each value (Y_i) as the sum of two parts: a common part, μ, which reflects an influence to which all measures are uniformly subject, and a variable part, e_i, which is attributable to random factors whose influence varies from one measure to another. As a model:

$$Y_i = \mu + e_i,$$

or

$$e_i = Y_i - \mu.$$

Since μ is constant, e_i and Y_i will have the same distribution, and

$$\sigma_y^2 = \sigma_e^2.$$

Our problem is to find that value of m which best fits all 12 measures in the sample and which will serve as our estimate of μ. If we choose m conventionally so as to minimize the sum of the squared deviations around it, m will necessarily be equal to the mean of the values, because the sum of the squared deviations around the mean is least.

If all values were alike, each value would necessarily be equal to m; hence, m is the value of Y expected in the absence of variation among values. To underline the conditional character of this expected value and expressly to avoid confusion in subsequent discussion, we give it a special symbol, $\hat{Y}$.

Since, for unsorted values, $\hat{Y}$ is identical for all cases, the sum of squares for constants will necessarily equal zero:

$$\hat{Y}SS = \sum \left(\hat{Y}_i - \frac{1}{n} \sum \hat{Y}_i \right)^2$$
$$= \sum (m - m)^2$$
$$= 0,$$

where n is the total frequency. Whenever the squared deviations are based on values composed of constants alone, we refer to their sum as the "sum of squares for constants."

When the sum of squares for constants is zero, the sum of squares for individual deviations, which we designate ESS (read "error sum of squares"), will equal the total sum of squares. Our conclusion is that with unclassified measures TSS = ESS. An implication is that TSS is not subject to decomposition unless measures are classified in at least one way, and that the analysis of variance (in its conventional meaning) is inapplicable to unsorted measures. Before continuing, the student should verify that in our problem

$$TSS = \sum (Y_i - \bar{Y})^2$$
$$= 92$$

and

$$ESS = \sum (Y_i - m)^2$$
$$= 92.$$

Computation of $\hat{Y}SS$. Looking ahead to a useful computing formula, we express the sum of squares for constants ($\hat{Y}SS$) as the product of the fitted constant (m) and the sum of all values of which it is a part (T), minus the standard correction term (C) for a given set of values. In symbols:

(4.3.1) $$\hat{Y}SS = mT - C,$$

where

$$C = (\sum Y_i)^2/n,$$

and

$$T = \sum Y_i.$$

Formula (4.3.1) is a special case of a more general formula (4.3.7) which will be regularly used in obtaining the sum of squares for constants. For our unsorted measures:

$$\hat{Y}SS = 7(84) - \frac{(84)^2}{12}$$
$$= 588 - 588$$
$$= 0.$$

Although the sum of squares for constants is necessarily zero for unsorted measures, it is rarely zero for measures sorted into rows and/or columns, as in a one-way table.

One-Way Table. Moving ahead, our next step is to reinstate the classification of measures by A, thereby dividing the 12 values into two groups of six each. With values thus arranged in a one-way table,

A_1	2, 4, 4, 6, 6, 8
A_2	6, 8, 8, 10, 10, 12

we may regard each value as being made up of three parts instead of two: one part ($\mu.$) common to all measures; one part (α_i) common to all members of A_i; and a variable part (e_{ij}), which we attribute to factors causing measures within classes to differ among themselves. We take this as our model. As an equation:

(4.3.2) $$Y_{ij} = \mu. + \alpha_i + e_{ij}.$$

In the absence of random variation within classes, Equation (4.3.2) reduces to

(4.3.3) $$Y_{ij} = \mu. + \alpha_i.$$

Our expected measures will now take two values instead of one, corresponding to the difference between fitted constants a_1 and a_2, respectively.

Where, in the case of unsorted measures, we had to fit only a single constant (m) to the values, we must now fit three constants, m, a_1, and a_2, which we take as estimates of $\mu.$, α_1, and α_2, respectively. Again, we have recourse to the principle of least squares and choose the a_i's and m to satisfy the requirement that $\sum e_{ij}^2$ be a minimum. It may be shown by mathematical methods that the least squares criterion will be satisfied when $m = \bar{Y}.$, and $a_i = \bar{Y}_i - \bar{Y}.$. In other words, the best-fitting constant (m) for all values in a one-way table is the overall mean, and the best-fitting constant (a_i) for values in the ith class is the deviation of the mean of that class from the overall mean. Substituting these sample estimates in (4.3.3), we obtain the simple result:

$$\hat{Y}_{ij} = (\bar{Y}_i - \bar{Y}.) + \bar{Y}.$$
$$= \bar{Y}_i.$$

Thus, the expected value for each measure in a one-way classification is simply the mean of its class: $\hat{Y}_{ij} = \bar{Y}_i$. Since fitted constants minimize the sum of the squared residuals, they may be interpreted as regression coefficients on binary variables with dummy values. When our qualitative variable has two categories, we require only one dummy variable; when our qualitative variable has three categories, we require two dummy variables. In general, we require as many dummy variables as there are categories less one. Dummy variables permit us to incorporate one or more nominal scales into a regression equation. For a discussion, consult Draper and Smith (1966: 134–141).

To get the sum of squares for constants, we take the mean of all n. expected values from each of them, square these deviations, and find their sum. But the mean of the expected values is equal to the mean of the observed measures;* hence, to get the sum of squares for expected values, we take the mean of all n. observed values from each of the n. expected values, square, and find the sum of the squares. In symbols,

(4.3.4) $$\hat{Y}SS = n_1(\bar{Y}_1 - \bar{Y}.)^2 + n_2(\bar{Y}_2 - \bar{Y}.)^2.$$

For our problem,

$$\hat{Y}SS = 6(5 - 7)^2 + 6(9 - 7)^2$$
$$= 24 + 24$$
$$= 48.$$

But Formula (4.3.4), it will be noticed, is the familiar between sum of squares for a one-way AOV table. Putting results together, we get this general conclusion: for a one-way AOV table, the sum of squares for constants is equal to the sum of squares for sample means (i.e., between sum of squares). In symbols:
$$\hat{Y}SS = BSS.$$

From this identity, we deduce that the sum of squares for individual deviations (errors), is equal to the conventional within sum of squares,

$$ESS = WSS,$$

and

$$TSS = \hat{Y}SS + ESS.$$

It is now an easy step to our main point: in a one-way classification, the mean square for constants provides an estimate of the hypothesized common variance and may be used against the mean square for error to test the

---

*
$$\sum \hat{Y}_{ij} = n_1(\bar{Y}_1 - \bar{Y}.) + n_2(\bar{Y}_2 - \bar{Y}.) + n.(\bar{Y}.)$$
$$= n_1\bar{Y}_1 + n_2\bar{Y}_2$$
$$= \sum Y_{ij}.$$

significance of the difference among r sample means (r is number of rows). Under the null hypothesis that $\alpha_1 = \alpha_2 = \cdots = \alpha_r = 0$,

$$\frac{\dfrac{\hat{Y}SS}{r-1}}{\dfrac{ESS}{r(n-1)}} = F, \quad df_1 = r - 1, \quad df_2 = r(n-1).$$

When α_i is a random variable, we use the same F to test the hypothesis that $\sigma_\alpha^2 = 0$.

Computation of $\hat{Y}SS$, One-Way Table. Although we may obtain the sum of squares for constants by squaring deviations and summing in the aforesaid way, we may find that sum more readily by the formula:

(4.3.5) $$\hat{Y}SS = \sum a_i T_i + mT_. - C,$$

where

$$T_i = \text{sum of values in } i^{\text{th}} \text{ class}$$

$$T_. = \text{sum of all values}$$

$$C = \text{correction factor.}$$

For two classes, the formula reduces to

(4.3.6) $$\hat{Y}SS = (a_1 T_1 + a_2 T_2) + mT_. - C.$$

Substituting values from our one-way table (p. 162) in (4.3.6), we get

$$\hat{Y}SS = -2(30) + 2(54) + 7(84) - 588$$
$$= 48,$$

and

$$ESS = 92 - 48$$
$$= 44.$$

To test the null hypothesis that A_1 and A_2 have identical means, we compute

$$\frac{1}{r-1}(\hat{Y}SS) = \frac{1}{2-1}(48)$$
$$= 48,$$

and

$$\frac{1}{r(n-1)}ESS = \frac{1}{2(6-1)}(44)$$
$$= 4.4.$$

Dividing the mean square for constants by the mean square for error, we get

$$F = 48/4.4$$
$$= 10.9,$$

with $p < .05$ on $df_1 = 1$, $df_2 = 10$. Our conclusion is that A_1 and A_2 probably have different means.

Two-Way Table. We are now ready to reinstate the B classification and thereby restore the two-way table with which we started our analysis. By this procedure, we recover the four subsamples representing all possible combinations of the dichotomies A and B. With measures thus grouped by both A and B, we may regard each value as the sum of four parts, rather than three as in preceding analysis: one part $(\mu_{..})$ common to all measures; one part (α_i) common to all members of A_i; one part (β_j) common to all members of B_j; and finally a variable part (e_{ijk}), which registers the effect of those factors producing random variation within subclasses. Each value may then be written as the sum of four components:

$$Y_{ijk} = \mu_{..} + \alpha_i + \beta_j + e_{ijk},$$

where Y_{ijk} is the kth measure in the ith row, j^{th} column. Because α_i and β_j are simply added together, as if there were no interaction between them, we refer to this representation of Y_{ijk} as an additive model. For two factors, A and B, the process of fitting constants is more complicated than for one factor alone, as we now require $r + c + 1$ constants (c is number of columns) where before we required only $r + 1$. Since the process is less tedious for proportionate than disproportionate frequencies, we begin with the simpler case of proportionate frequencies.

Proportionate Frequencies. As before, we find constants which best fit the observed values in the sense of minimizing the quantity:

$$\sum_{1}^{nrc} [Y_{ijk} - (a_i + b_j + m)]^2.$$

When proportionality prevails, we have these simple results

$$m = \bar{Y}_{..},$$

$$a_i = \bar{Y}_{i.} - \bar{Y}_{..},$$

and

$$b_j = \bar{Y}_{.j} - \bar{Y}_{..},$$

which we take as estimates of $\mu_{..}$, α_i and β_j, respectively. Equally simple is the form of each value expected in the absence of variation within sub-samples. This is:

$$
\begin{aligned}
\hat{Y}_{ijk} &= a_i + b_j + m \\
&= (\bar{Y}_{i.} - \bar{Y}_{..}) + (\bar{Y}_{.j} - \bar{Y}_{..}) + \bar{Y}_{..} \\
&= \bar{Y}_{i.} + \bar{Y}_{.j} - \bar{Y}_{...}
\end{aligned}
$$

Thus, to find the expected value of a measure in the ith row and j^{th} column, we simply add corresponding marginal means and subtract the overall mean.

On manipulating expected values and substituting, we get these pertinent results:

(1) The mean of the expected values is equal to the mean of the observed values:

$$
\frac{1}{n_{..}} \sum \hat{Y}_{ijk} = \bar{Y}_{...}
$$

(2) The sum of squares for constants is equal to the sum of the sums of squares for row and column means, respectively:

$$
\hat{Y}SS = RSS + CSS.
$$

(3) The sum of squares for subsample means minus the sum of squares for constants (which is a measure of additive effects alone) is equal to the sum of squares for interaction:

$$
ISS = BSS - \hat{Y}SS.
$$

Note of caution: although the sum of squares for interaction may always be obtained by deducting $\hat{Y}SS$ from BSS, whether frequencies are dispropor-tionate or not, the equality $\hat{Y}SS = RSS + CSS$ holds only for proportional frequencies. Consequently, with disproportionate data, we are warned *not* to subtract the quantity RSS + CSS from BSS for the interaction sum of squares.

Computing $\hat{Y}SS$, Two-Way Table. If the sum of squares for constants is our object, without reference to row and column sums of squares, we need only substitute in the expression

(4.3.7) $\hat{Y}SS = \sum a_i T_{i.} + \sum b_j T_{.j} + mT_{..} - C,$

which is an extension of the simpler expression for a one-way classification. (Formula (4.3.7) specializes to (4.3.5) when there is only one column.) To get the sum of squares for constants for our 2 × 2 table, we need only solve for those terms having b_i as a coefficient and add them to the previous result of 48 for the one-way table. This addendum will be:

$$b_1 T_{.1} + b_2 T_{.2} = (-1)(36) + (+1)(48)$$
$$= 12.$$

Hence,

$$\hat{Y}\text{SS} = \text{RSS} + \text{CSS}$$
$$= 48 + 12$$
$$= 60,$$

and

$$\text{ESS} = 32.$$

Case of Disproportionality. The student may legitimately ask: "Why go to the bother of fitting constants and setting up expected values if simpler methods will do?" The answer is that we do not trouble ourselves with constants with proportionate frequencies, since routine methods yield identical sums of squares as follows:

$$\hat{Y}\text{SS} = \text{RSS} + \text{CSS},$$

and

$$\text{BSS} - \hat{Y}\text{SS} = \text{BSS} - (\text{RSS} + \text{CSS})$$
$$= \text{ISS}.$$

With disproportionality, the situation is more complicated: the best-fitting constant m is no longer equal to the overall mean $\bar{Y}_{..}$, and the constants a_i and b_j are no longer equal to the differences between marginal means and the overall mean. And in consequence, the sum of squares for constants ($\hat{Y}\text{SS}$) is no longer equal to the sum of sums of squares for row and column means, respectively. Under these practically less convenient circumstances, we must find the best-fitting constants by direct methods, and from these constants get the sum of the squares for A free of the effects of B, and the sum of the squares for B free of the effects of A.

General Procedure. The general procedure (Kempthorne 1952: 79–83) for fitting constants a_i, b_j, and m to disproportionate data leads to a set of linear equations which may be written by rule and solved by standard methods. Such a set will include $r + c + 1$ equations, each having a specified total on the one side and the composition of that total in terms of weighted constants on the other side. Thus, for a 2 × 2 table, there will be $2 + 2 + 1 = 5$ equations, corresponding to the four marginal totals and the grand total:

$$T_{..} = n_{..}m + n_{1.}a_1 + n_{2.}a_2 + n_{.1}b_1 + n_{.2}b_2,$$

$$T_{1.} = n_{1.}m + n_{1.}a_1 \qquad\qquad + n_{11}b_1 + n_{12}b_2,$$

$$T_{2.} = n_{2.}m + \qquad\quad n_{2.}a_2 + n_{21}b_1 + n_{22}b_2,$$

$$T_{.1} = n_{.1}m + n_{11}a_1 + n_{21}a_2 + n_{.1}b_1,$$

$$T_{.2} = n_{.2}m + n_{12}a_1 + n_{22}a_2 + \qquad\quad n_{.2}b_2.$$

These equations may be expressed generally as follows:

$$T_{..} = n_{..}m + \sum n_{i.}a_i + \sum n_{.j}b_j,$$

$$T_{i.} = n_{i.}m + n_{i.}a_i + \sum n_{ij}b_j,$$

and

$$T_{.j} = n_{.j}m + \sum n_{ij}a_i + n_{.j}b_j.$$

Once we have solved the unknown constants, we set up expected values according to the formula $\hat{Y}_{ijk} = a_i + b_j + m$, as in the following table:

	B_1	B_2
A_1	$a_1 + b_1 + m$	$a_1 + b_2 + m$
A_2	$a_2 + b_1 + m$	$a_2 + b_2 + m$

Since these expected values are calculated from an additive model, they yield that sum of squares expected in the absence of interaction. Hence, to obtain the sum of squares for interaction, we need only deduct the sum of squares for constants ($\hat{Y}$SS) from the sum of squares for subsample means, BSS:

$$\text{ISS} = \text{BSS} - \hat{Y}\text{SS}.$$

To complete the analysis, we obtain sums of squares for row and column effects, each free of the effect of the other. To get these corrected sums of squares, we perform this simple operation: subtract the quantity (RSS + CSS) from $\hat{Y}$SS and attach this result as a correction for disproportionality to both row and column sums of squares. For an intuitive understanding of this adjustment, recall that given proportional frequencies, $\hat{Y}$SS − (RSS + CSS) = 0; otherwise, this quantity is larger or smaller than zero, according to the specific degree of disproportionality. Hence, by removing that excess (or deficiency) from the row and column sum of squares, we obtain those sums of squares occurring in the absence of disproportionality. In symbols:

$$R'SS = RSS + [\hat{Y}SS - (RSS + CSS)]$$

and

$$C'SS = CSS + [\hat{Y}SS - (RSS + CSS)],$$

which simplify to

(4.3.8) $$R'SS = \hat{Y}SS - CSS$$

and

$$C'SS = \hat{Y}SS - RSS,$$

where $R'SS$ is the adjusted sum of squares for rows; $C'SS$, for columns. These latter expressions (4.3.8) lead to the easily remembered rule: to get the adjusted row sum of squares ($R'SS$), subtract the sum of squares for columns (CSS) from the sum of squares for constants ($\hat{Y}SS$); to get the adjusted column sum of squares ($C'SS$), subtract the row sum of squares (RSS) from the sum of squares for constants ($\hat{Y}SS$).

From this overview, it is evident that the analysis of disproportionate data by the method of fitting constants falls naturally into two stages: first, a preliminary analysis by standard procedures; and, second, the fitting of constants, a_i, b_j, and m, to the observed measures and the manipulation of these constants to get required mean squares and significance ratios. As an outline:

I. Preliminary Analysis:
   (1) compute TSS and BSS,
   (2) subtract BSS from TSS for WSS, and
   (3) compute RSS and CSS.

II. Analysis by Constants:
   (1) find constants m, a_i, b_j,
   (2) get $\hat{Y}SS$ by computing formula,
   (3) subtract $\hat{Y}SS$ from BSS for ISS,
   (4) subtract RSS from $\hat{Y}SS$ for $C'SS$ and CSS from $\hat{Y}SS$ for $R'SS$,
   (5) test hypothesis of no interaction; if not rejected, test significance of adjusted mean squares, $C'SS$ and $R'SS$; otherwise
   (6) go to the alternative procedure of *weighted squares of means* (p. 182).

The $r \times 2$ Table. Let us now consider in some detail the procedure for fitting constants to the $r \times 2$ table, and the results to which such an analysis gives rise. These materials will serve both to exemplify this type of analysis and to suggest the general process of fitting constants to any $r \times c$ table. For tables having r rows and two columns, there will be one equation for the total,

$$T_{..} = n_{..}m + n_{.1}b_1 + n_{.2}b_2 + n_{1.}a_1 + \cdots + n_{r.}a_r,$$

two for column totals,

$$T_{.1} = n_{.1}m + n_{.1}b_1 + n_{11}a_1 + \cdots + n_{r1}a_r,$$

$$T_{.2} = n_{.2}m + n_{.2}b_2 + n_{12}a_1 + \cdots + n_{r2}a_r,$$

and r equations of the general form,

$$T_{i.} = n_{i.}m + \sum n_{ij}b_j + n_{i.}a_i$$

for the r row totals. It may be shown (Goulden 1952: 336–337) that

(4.3.9)
$$b_1 = \frac{T_{.1} - C_1}{2C_{12}},$$

and

(4.3.10)
$$a_i + m = \frac{T_{i.} - b_1(n_{i1} - n_{i2})}{n_{i.}},$$

where

(4.3.11)
$$C_1 = \sum_1^r \left(\frac{n_{i1}}{n_{i.}} T_{i.} \right),$$

$$C_{12} = \sum_1^r \frac{n_{i1}n_{i2}}{n_{i.}}.$$

Then, since $\sum a_i = \sum b_i = 0$, simplifying conditions not in conflict with the least-squares criterion,

$$b_2 = -b_1,$$

and

$$m = \frac{1}{r} \sum_1^r \left[\frac{T_{i.} - b_1(n_{i1} - n_{i2})}{n_{i.}} \right].$$

Subtracting m from the right side of (4.3.10), we get a_i. (As with the one-way table, we may construe fitted constants as regression coefficients on dummy binary variables since they are chosen to satisfy the least squares criterion.)

2 × 2 Table. To illustrate these formulas and the results which they yield, let us apply them to a 2 × 2 table whose cell frequencies are disproportional. We give the measures in Table 4.3.2. Our preliminary concern is with the

Table 4.3.2 *Four Subsamples, Disproportionate Data*

	B_1	B_2	$T_{i.}$
A_1	2 4	4, 6 8, 8	32
A_2	6, 8 6, 10	10 12	52
$T_{.j}$	36	48	84

subsample means and the possibility that the differences among them are statistically significant. Accordingly, we compute

$$\text{TSS} = 92,$$
$$\text{BSS} = 66,$$

and

$$\text{WSS} = 92 - 66$$
$$= 26.$$

For later use, we also compute

$$\text{RSS} = 33.33$$

and

$$\text{CSS} = 12.00.$$

To test differences among subsample means, and assuming that all conditions for testing have been met, we set up the *F*-ratio:

$$_1F_{10} = \frac{s_b^2}{s_w^2}$$
$$= \frac{22.00}{3.25}$$
$$= 6.78, \quad p < .05.$$

When these differences are judged significant, we proceed with the fitting of constants; otherwise, we would discontinue our analysis at this juncture.

Treating differences as significant, we move to the fitting of constants. We first get

$$C_1 = \tfrac{2}{6}(32) + \tfrac{4}{6}(52)$$
$$= 45.33,$$

and

$$C_{12} = \frac{(2)(4)}{6} + \frac{(4)(2)}{6}$$
$$= 2\ 67.$$

Substituting these results in (4.3.9), we get

$$b_1 = \frac{36 - 45.33}{2(2.67)}$$
$$= -1.75$$

and

$$b_2 = (-1.75)$$
$$= +1.75.$$

Substituting in (4.3.10), we get

$$a_1 + m = \frac{32 - (-1.75)(2 - 4)}{6}$$
$$= \frac{28.50}{6}$$
$$= 4.75.$$

$$a_2 + m = \frac{52 - (1.75)(4 - 2)}{6}$$
$$= \frac{55.50}{6}$$
$$= 9.25.$$

Continuing the analysis, we get

$$\sum(a_i + m) = 4.75 + 9.25$$
$$= 14$$

and

$$m = \tfrac{14}{2}$$
$$= 7.$$

Finally, subtracting m from $a_1 + m$ and $a_2 + m$, we get

$$a_1 = \left(\frac{28.5}{6}\right) - 7$$
$$= -2\,25$$
$$a_2 = \left(\frac{55.5}{6}\right) - 7$$
$$= +2.25.$$

With these results in hand, it is possible to get the sum of the squares for constants by substituting in (4.3.7), repeated here for easy reference:

$$\hat{Y}SS = \sum a_i T_{i.} + \sum b_i T_{.i} + mT_{..} - C.$$

Substituting calculated quantities, we get

$$\hat{Y}SS = -2.25(32) + 2.25(52) - 1.75(36) + 1.75(48) + 7(84) - 588$$
$$= 45 + 21 + 588 - 588$$
$$= 66.$$

Since $\hat{Y}SS$ is the sum of squares for subsample means on the assumption of no interaction between A and B, the difference between this result and BSS is the sum of squares for interaction. Applying this rule, we find

$$ISS = BSS - \hat{Y}SS$$
$$= 66 - 66$$
$$= 0.$$

Generally, $\hat{Y}SS$ will fall short of BSS, owing either to the accidents of random sampling or to the presence of interaction in the population. It is purely coincidental that ISS = 0 in our problem.

Next, we obtain sums of squares for main effects, A and B, respectively, adjusting row and column sums of squares in the aforesaid manner to eliminate the effect of disproportionality:

$$R'SS = \hat{Y}SS - CSS$$
$$= 66 - 12$$
$$= 54.$$
$$C'SS = \hat{Y}SS - RSS$$
$$= 66 - 33.33$$
$$= 32.67.$$

Alternately, we get the correction for disproportionality,

$$\hat{Y}SS - (RSS + CSS) = 66 - (33.33 + 12.00)$$
$$= 20.67,$$

and add this to the respective unadjusted sums of squares:

$$R'SS = 33.33 + 20.67$$
$$= 54.00.$$

$$C'SS = 12.00 + 20.67$$
$$= 32.67.$$

We may now complete the analysis of variance, listing results in conventional manner, as in Table 4.3.3.

Table 4.3.3   *Two-Way Analysis of Variance, Disproportionate Data*

	Source	df	Sum of squares	Mean squares	F
	Total	11	92.00		
	Within	8	26.00	3.25	
Stage I	Subsamples	3	66.00	22.00	6.77
	Rows		33.33		
	Columns		12.00		
	Constants	3*	66.00		
Stage II	Interaction	1	0.00	0	
	Rows	1	54.00	54.00	16.62
	Columns	1	32.67	32.67	10.05

*Constants in Stage II will have as many degrees of freedom as subsamples in Stage I.

When we examine these results, we observe that RSS and CSS taken together do not equal BSS. This is a consequence of the disproportionality of our cell frequencies. We take this finding as a demonstration of nonorthogonality between A and B and of the corresponding need to establish orthogonality by an appropriate adjustment. It is pertinent, too, that together the adjusted sums of squares (R'SS + C'SS) do not equal the sum of squares for constants, $86.7 \neq 66$, as one might have anticipated. This apparent discrepancy will resolve itself, if we remember that the correction for disproportionality is included twice in the quantity R'SS + C'SS, whereas it is included, and properly so, only once in the sum of squares for constants. Accordingly, by subtracting the quantity (R'SS + C'SS) from $\hat{Y}SS$, we get the numerical correction for disproportionality.

3 × 2 Table. As a second example, we apply Formulas (4.3.9) and (4.3.10) to a 3 × 2 grouping of measures. Table 4.3.4 gives this grouping. Our

Table 4.3.4 3 × 2 Table with Disproportionate Data

	B_1	B_2	$T_{i.}$
A_1	2 4	4 6 8 8	32
A_2	6 6 8 10	10 12	52
A_3	3 5 6 8	5 8 9 12	56
$T_{.i}$	58	82	140

3 × 2 table of values, it may be noticed, is the 2 × 2 table of the previous example, augmented by a third row of two subsamples, each with four values.

As with the 2 × 2 table, we first obtain the sum of squares for subsample means and the sum of squares for values within subsamples. If differences among subsamples means are not significant, we would probably discontinue the analysis; otherwise, we would proceed to the fitting of constants in order to test for the significance of main effects. The results of our preliminary analysis occupy the upper tier of Table 4.3.5.

Table 4.3.5 Two-Way AOV, Disproportionate Data

Source	df	Sum of squares	Mean square	F
Total	19	148		
Between	5	84	16.80	3.68
Within	14	64	4.57	
Rows		33.30		
Columns		68.80		
Constants	5	83.72		
A Factor	2	54.92	27.46	6.01
B Factor	1	50.39	50.38	11.02
Interaction	2	.28	.14	

Moving to the analysis by constants, we compute in routine manner:

$$C_1 = \tfrac{2}{6}(32) + \tfrac{4}{6}(52) + \tfrac{4}{8}(56)$$
$$= 10.67 + 34.67 + 28.00$$
$$= 73.33,$$

and

$$C_{12} = \tfrac{8}{6} + \tfrac{8}{6} + \tfrac{16}{8}$$
$$= 4.67.$$

Substituting in (4.3.9), we get

$$b_1 = \frac{58 - 73.33}{2(4.67)}$$
$$= \frac{-15.33}{9.33}$$
$$= -1.64,$$

and

$$b_2 = +1.64.$$

Substituting in (4.3.10), we get

$$a_1 + m = \frac{32 - (-1\,64)(2 - 4)}{6}$$
$$= 4.79,$$
$$a_2 + m = \frac{52 - (-1.64)(4 - 2)}{6}$$
$$= 9.21,$$

and

$$a_3 + m = \frac{56 - (-1.64)(4 - 4)}{8}$$
$$= 7.00.$$

We may now solve

$$m = \frac{4.79 + 9.21 + 7.00}{3}$$
$$= 7.00.$$

Lastly,

$$a_1 = 4.79 - 7.00$$
$$= -2.21,$$
$$a_2 = 9.21 - 7.00$$
$$= +2.21,$$

and

$$a_3 = 7.00 - 7.00$$
$$= 0.$$

Substituting obtained values for literal constants in (4.3.7), we get

$$\hat{Y}SS = (-2.21)(32) + (2.21)(52) + (7.00)(56) + (-1.64)(58 - 82)$$
$$+ 7.00(140) - 980$$
$$= -70.85 + 115.13 + 39.44 + 980 - 980$$
$$= 83.72$$

Checking $\hat{Y}SS$. As a check on our answer and to highlight the nature of $\hat{Y}SS$, we (1) set up expected values,

Subsample	$a_i + b_j + m$	$\hat{Y}_{ij}$
A_1B_1	$-2.21 - 1.64 + 7.00$	3.14
A_1B_2	$-2.21 + 1.64 + 7.00$	6.43
A_2B_1	$2.21 - 1.64 + 7.00$	7.57
A_2B_2	$2.21 + 1.64 + 7.00$	10.86
A_3B_1	$- 1.64 + 7.00$	5.36
A_3B_2	$+ 1.64 + 7.00$	8.64

(2) calculate squared deviations between these values and their mean of 7.00,

Subsample	$\hat{Y}_{ij} - 7.00 = \hat{y}_{ij}$	$\hat{y}_{ij}^2$
A_1B_1	$3.14 - 7.00 = -3.86$	14.88
A_1B_2	$6.43 - 7.00 = -.57$	.33
A_2B_1	$7.57 - 7.00 = .57$	.33
A_2B_2	$10.86 - 7.00 = 3.86$	14.88
A_3B_1	$5.36 - 7.00 = -1.64$	2.70
A_3B_2	$8.64 - 7.00 = 1.64$	2.70

and (3) weight these squared deviations by corresponding cell frequencies, and sum these weighted squared deviations:

Subsample	$n_{ij}\hat{y}_{ij}^2$
A_1B_1	(2)(14.88) = 29.76
A_1B_2	(4)(0.33) = 1.30
A_2B_1	(4)(0.33) = 1.30
A_2B_2	(2)(14.88) = 29.76
A_3B_1	(4)(2.70) = 10.80
A_3B_2	(4)(2.70) = 10.80
	83.72

After $\hat{Y}$SS has been calculated, we complete the analysis by computing the correction term for disproportionality and adding that quantity to the unadjusted row and column sums of squares, respectively:

$$\text{Correction for Disproportionality} = \hat{Y}\text{SS} - (\text{RSS} + \text{CSS})$$
$$= 83.72 - (33.33 + 28.80)$$
$$= 21.59.$$

Then

$$\text{R'SS} = 33.33 + 21.59 = 54.92$$
$$\text{C'SS} = 28.80 + 21.59 = 50.39.$$

Checking:

$$\text{R'SS} = \hat{Y}\text{SS} - \text{CSS}$$
$$= 83.72 - 28.80 = 54.92$$
$$\text{C'SS} = 83.72 - 33.33 = 50.39.$$

These results, together with mean squares, occupy the lower tier of Table 4.3.5.

$r \times 3$ Table. As the student will have surmised, the procedure for the $r \times 3$ table is identical in its essentials to the procedure for the $r \times 2$ table. (Computations are more numerous, but this will be no problem unless a digital computer is not available.) Where before there were $r + 2 + 1$ equations to be solved, there will now be $r + 3 + 1$ equations, corresponding to r levels of A, three levels of B and the general factor, m. The sum of all values is expressible as:

$$T_{..} = n_{..}m + n_{.1}b_1 + n_{.2}b_2 + n_{.3}b_3 + n_{1.}a_1 + \cdots + n_{r.}a_r,$$

the total for the ith column as

$$T_{.i} = n_{.i}m + n_{.i}b_i + n_{1i}a_1 + \cdots + n_{ri}a_r,$$

and the total for the ith row as

$$T_{i.} = n_{i.}m + n_{i1}b_1 + n_{i2}b_2 + n_{i3}b_3 + n_{i.}a_i.$$

Solving for b_1 and b_2, we get after extensive manipulation (Goulden 1952: 339–340),

(4.3.12) $\quad b_1 = \dfrac{C_1(C_{22} - C_{23}) - C_2(C_{12} - C_{13})}{(C_{11} - C_{13})(C_{22} - C_{23}) - (C_{12} - C_{13})(C_{12} - C_{23})}$

and

$$b_2 = \dfrac{C_1(C_{12} - C_{23}) - C_2(C_{11} - C_{13})}{(C_{12} - C_{13})(C_{12} - C_{23}) - (C_{11} - C_{13})(C_{22} - C_{23})},$$

where

(4.3.13)

$$C_1 = \sum \frac{n_{i1}T_{i.}}{n_{i.}} - T_{.1} \quad C_2 = \sum \frac{n_{i2}T_{i.}}{n_{i.}} - T_{.2} \quad C_3 = \sum \frac{n_{i3}T_{i.}}{n_{i.}} - T_{.3}$$

$$C_{11} = \sum \frac{(n_{i1})^2}{n_{i.}} - n_{.1} \quad C_{22} = \sum \frac{(n_{i2})^2}{n_{i.}} - n_{.2} \quad C_{33} = \sum \frac{(n_{i3})^2}{n_{i.}} - n_{.3}$$

$$C_{12} = \sum \frac{n_{i1}n_{i2}}{n_{i.}} \quad\quad C_{13} = \sum \frac{n_{i1}n_{i3}}{n_{i.}} \quad\quad C_{23} = \sum \frac{n_{i2}n_{i3}}{n_{i.}}$$

Then, since $\sum b_i = 0$, $b_3 = -(b_1 + b_2)$.

Solving next for $a_i + m$, we find after substitution and elimination,

(4.3.14) $\quad\quad\quad\quad a_i + m = \left(\dfrac{T_{i.}}{n_{i.}} - \sum \dfrac{n_{ij}b_j}{n_{i.}}\right).$

Summing all such quantities, we get

$$\sum_1^r (a_i + m) = \sum a_i + \sum m,$$

and

$$m = \frac{1}{r} \sum (a_i + m).$$

To obtain a_i, we take m from the right side of (4.3.14).

Taken together, the above formulas constitute a general method for finding constants for the $r \times 3$ table. By eliminating one column and dropping corresponding terms, we revert to the general formula for the $r \times 2$ table, as the student may verify. From this, we may infer that the procedure for the $r \times 3$ table is a reduction of the procedure for the $r \times 4$ and that generally the procedure for the $r \times (c - 1)$ table is a reduction of that for the $r \times c$ table.

3 × 3 Table. Let us now utilize the above formulas to find constants for numerical data in a 3 × 3 classification (Table 4.3.6), performing calculations as required to complete the analysis of variance. Our 3 × 3 table, be it noted, is the previously given 3 × 2 table, extended by a third column of three subsamples. We first run a preliminary analysis to determine whether subpopulations are alike. If they are, we stop the analysis, otherwise we go ahead with it. The results of our preliminary analysis are shown in the upper tier of Table 4.3.7.

Table 4.3.6 *3 × 3 Table, Disproportionate Data*

	B_1	B_2	B_3	$T_i.$
A_1	2	4	1	
	4	6	5	74
			7	
		8	8	
			9	
		8	12	
A_2	6	10	6	
	6	12	6	82
	8		10	
	10		8	
A_3	3	5	5	
	5	8	6	75
	6	9	8	
	8	12		
$T.i$	58	82	91	231

With the preliminary analysis performed, we proceed to the fitting of constants and thence to sums of squares and required variance ratios. To calculate our C values, it will be convenient first to express cell frequencies as proportions of row frequencies as these quantities are used repeatedly in our computations.

$n_{i1}/n_{i.}$	$n_{i2}/n_{i.}$	$n_{i3}/n_{i.}$
.167	.333	.500
.400	.200	.400
.364	.364	.272

Substituting known quantities in (4.3.13), we get:

$$C_1 = 14.46 \qquad C_2 = -13.66 \qquad C_3 = -.73$$
$$C_{11} = -6.61 \qquad C_{22} = -6.81 \qquad C_{33} = -7.58$$
$$C_{12} = 2.92 \qquad C_{13} = 3.69 \qquad C_{23} = 3.89$$

Then, $b_1 = -1.51$, $b_2 = 1.41$, and $b_3 = -.10$, as the student should verify.

We next obtain

$$a_1 + m = 5.90,$$
$$a_2 + m = 8.48,$$
$$a_3 + m = 6.83.$$

Summing these results and dividing by $r = 3$, we get

$$m = \tfrac{1}{3}(21.21)$$
$$= 7.07.$$

We now get:

$$a_1 = -1.17,$$
$$a_2 = 1.41,$$
$$a_3 = -.24.$$

Table 4.3.7 *Two-Way AOV, Disproportionate Data*

Source	df	Sums of squares	Mean square	F
Total	32	236.00		
Between	8	86.33	10.79	1.73
Within	24	149.67	6.24	
Rows		23.10		
Columns		28.80		
Constants	8	64.32		
Interaction	4	22.01	5.50	
A-factor	2	35.52	17.76	2.85
B-factor	2	41.22	20.61	3.31

For the sum of squares for constants, we substitute in Formula (4.3.7),

$$\hat{Y}SS = \sum a_i T_{i.} + \sum b_j T_{.j} + mT_{..} - C,$$

getting

$$\hat{Y}SS = 64.32.$$

Then

$$ISS = 86.33 - 64.32$$
$$= 22.01.$$

The correction for disproportionality is:

$$\hat{Y}SS - (RSS + CSS) = 64.32 - (23.10 + 28.80)$$
$$= 12.42.$$

Then

$$R'SS = 23.10 + 12.42 = 35.52$$
$$C'SS = 28.80 + 12.42 = 41.22.$$

These results, together with mean squares and the F-ratios in which they culminate, are shown in the lower tier of Table 4.3.7. Since our analysis rests on the assumption of no interaction, we may use the same F-ratios, whether we are sampling from fixed classes (Model I) or from classes subject to random variation (Model II).

When main effects are additive, we estimate them by fitted constants, as in the examples of this section; when main effects are not additive, we estimate them by the method of weighted squares of means. For an appreciation of this rule and as background for the method of weighted squares of means, we begin Part 4 with a consideration of the complications produced by interaction. The utility of the concept of statistical interaction in sociological theory construction has been considered by Blalock (1965); situational factors giving rise to interaction effects are discussed in Sonquist (1970).

PART 4
Weighted Squares of Means

Problem of Interaction. Let us suppose that we are required to assess the effect of religion (A) and sex (B) on tolerance (Y) from a 2 × 2 table of subsample means as follows:

		B	
		Men	Women
A	Protestant	12	20
	Catholic	2	10

The mean score for women is greater by 8 than the mean score for men within each religious grouping; the mean score for Protestants is greater by 10 than the mean score for Catholics within each sex grouping. Statistically speaking, main effects are additive. Under these circumstances, we fit a function of the form $a + b + m$ to our data and represent the effects of religion and sex by the constants a and b. We would take the difference between a_1 and a_2 as a measure of the effect of religion; we would take the difference between b_1 and b_2 as a measure of the effect of sex.

Let us now suppose that men are more tolerant than women among Protestants, and women more tolerant than men among Catholics, as in the following table of subsample means:

	Men	Women
Protestant	20	12
Catholic	2	10

Main effects are now interactive in the sense that the effect of religion on tolerance is contingent on sex. In this situation we are advised to abandon additive constants, which ignore the interaction actually present in our data, and instead use the unweighted marginal means as unbiased estimates of main effects. The mean of the cell means in the ith row serves to estimate the effect of A_i; the mean of the cell means in the ith column serves to estimate the effect of B_i. Since unweighted means (by definition) are uniformly responsive to the component means on which they rest, each will be higher or lower according to the degree of interaction between A and B, as reflected in the pattern of cell means. The overall average for men is higher, and the average of all women is lower by reason of the differential effects of religion on tolerance by sex. By employing unweighted marginal means as estimators, we take into account the interaction of A on B which our additive model disregards. Implicit in our choice of such means as estimators of main effects is the assumption that subpopulations are equal in size, or that categories of B are equally frequent for each category of A, and vice versa. Of course, we may reject this assumption as unrealistic and adopt some scheme which conforms more closely to known circumstances in the sampled population, or our conception of those circumstances. As Kempthorne (p. 91) observes: ". . . we can consider the effects of the i classification averaged over the set of conditions given by the j classification, assuming these conditions occur equally frequently, or alternately as they occurred in our data, or again according to some preassigned frequencies." Our choice of unweighted means of cell means for rows and columns as estimators of main effects reflects our judgment that categories of B are equally frequent for each category of A, or at least that it is reasonable to regard them as equally frequent for purposes of analysis.

But before mindlessly applying the method of weighted squares of means, as this method has come to be known, we should, paraphrasing Snedecor

(1946: 300), ask ourselves this question: "Since subgroups do not respond in the same way to treatments, is anything to be gained by estimates and tests of overall averages?" For our example: "Is it meaningful to compare all Protestants and all Catholics if the effect of religion on tolerance is contingent on one's sex?" If our considered answer to that question is "Yes," we may use the difference between means of cell means for rows to gauge the effect of religion on tolerance, and the difference between means of cell means for columns to gauge the effect of sex on tolerance. In other words, our test of the hypothesis that religious groups are identical will be based on the difference between unweighted means of subsample means for rows; our test of the hypothesis that men and women are identical (in tolerance) will rest on the difference between unweighted means of subsample means for columns.

To introduce this method, we present a resumé of its underlying theory as given by Yates (1934).

Consider first the variance of any subsample mean $\bar{Y}_{ij}$:

$$\sigma^2_{\bar{Y}_{ij}} = \frac{\sigma^2}{n_{ij}},$$

where $\sigma^2 =$ population variance, $n_{ij} =$ sample size.

Consider next the variance of the sum of c subsample means in the ith row. On the assumption that subsample means are independent and that subpopulations have equal variances, this will be the sum of subsample variances:

$$\sigma^2_{\Sigma \bar{Y}_{ij}} = \left[\frac{\sigma^2}{n_{i1}} + \frac{\sigma^2}{n_{i2}} + \cdots + \frac{\sigma^2}{n_{ic}} \right]$$

$$= \sigma^2 \sum \frac{1}{n_{ij}},$$

where

$$c = \text{number of columns in the } r \times c \text{ table.}$$

Now, the mean of the subsample means in the ith row is the sum of the subsample means divided by the number of columns c,

$$\bar{Y}_{i.} = \frac{1}{c} \sum \bar{Y}_{ij},$$

where $\bar{Y}_{i.}$ is the unweighted mean of the ith row. But the variance of a sum divided by a constant is the sum of the variances divided by the square of that constant. Therefore the variance of $\bar{Y}_{i.}$ is

$$\sigma^2_{\bar{Y}_{i.}} = \frac{\sigma^2}{c^2} \sum \frac{1}{n_{ij}}.$$

As a notational convenience, we write (after Yates)

$$\frac{1}{w_{i.}} = \sum_1^c \frac{1}{n_{ij}},$$

so that

$$\sigma^2_{\bar{Y}_{i.}} = \frac{\sigma^2}{c^2 w_{i.}}.$$

Transposing terms, we get the population variance as a multiple of the variance of the mean of subsample means, with $c^2 w_{i.}$ as the multiplier:

$$\sigma^2 = (c^2 w_{i.})\sigma^2_{\bar{Y}_{i.}}.$$

If we have r sample terms of the form $w_{i.}(\bar{Y}_{i.} - \bar{Y})^2$, where $\bar{Y} = \sum w_{i.}\bar{Y}_{i.}/\sum w_{i.}$ (or the weighted mean of the unweighted means), and r = number of rows in the $r \times c$ table, then by statistical theory (given in Yates):

$$c^2 E \sum_1^r w_{i.}(\bar{Y}_{i.} - \bar{Y})^2 = (r - 1)\sigma^2.$$

Rearranging terms, we get the population variance,

$$\sigma^2 = \frac{c^2 E \sum^r w_{i.}(\bar{Y}_{i.} - \bar{Y})^2}{r - 1}.$$

We thus see that the sum of the weighted squared deviations of unweighted row means from their weighted means leads to an estimate of the population variance, σ^2. This quantity will be an unbiased estimator of that variance in the absence of differences among population means; otherwise it will tend to be too large. Therefore, its magnitude relative to the mean square for error provides a test of the null hypothesis that populations represented by rows (or columns) have identical means.

Computing Weighted Squares of Means. The computing formulas for finding sums of squares based on the means of subsample means for rows and columns, respectively, in the $r \times c$ table are:

(4.4.1) $$c^2\sum w_{i.}(\bar{Y}_{i.} - \bar{Y})^2 = c^2\left[\sum w_{i.}\bar{Y}^2_{i.} - \frac{(\sum w_{i.}\bar{Y}_{i.})^2}{\sum w_{i.}}\right].$$

(4.4.2) $$r^2\sum w_{.i}(\bar{Y}_{.i} - \bar{Y})^2 = r^2\left[\sum w_{.i}\bar{Y}^2_{.i} - \frac{(\sum w_{.i}\bar{Y}_{.i})^2}{\sum w_{.i}}\right].$$

To illustrate these formulas, we first apply them to the literal values of a 2×2 table, our application taking the form of a set of directions.

(1) Set up table of subclass means and its companion table of subclass frequencies:

Subclass Means

B

A	$\bar{Y}_{11}$	$\bar{Y}_{12}$
	$\bar{Y}_{21}$	$\bar{Y}_{22}$

Subclass Frequencies

B

A	n_{11}	n_{12}
	n_{21}	n_{22}

(2) Take the reciprocals of subclass frequencies and record these in a 2×2 table:

B

A	$\dfrac{1}{n_{11}}$	$\dfrac{1}{n_{12}}$
	$\dfrac{1}{n_{21}}$	$\dfrac{1}{n_{22}}$

(3) Sum reciprocals by rows and columns:

Rows

$$\frac{1}{w_{1.}} = \frac{1}{n_{11}} + \frac{1}{n_{12}}$$

$$\frac{1}{w_{2.}} = \frac{1}{n_{21}} + \frac{1}{n_{22}}$$

Columns

$$\frac{1}{w_{.1}} = \frac{1}{n_{11}} + \frac{1}{n_{21}}$$

$$\frac{1}{w_{.2}} = \frac{1}{n_{12}} + \frac{1}{n_{22}}$$

(4) Take reciprocals of sums obtained in (3) above and record these below "$w_{i.}$" and alongside "$w_{.i}$" in the margins of a table set up for that purpose:

B

A	$\bar{Y}_{11}$	$\bar{Y}_{12}$
	$\bar{Y}_{21}$	$\bar{Y}_{22}$
$w_{.i}$	$w_{.1}$	$w_{.2}$	$\sum w_{.i}$
$\bar{Y}_{.i}$	$\bar{Y}_{.1}$	$\bar{Y}_{.2}$
$w_{.i}\bar{Y}_{.i}$	$w_{.1}\bar{Y}_{.1}$	$w_{.2}\bar{Y}_{.2}$	$\sum w_{.i}\bar{Y}_{.i}$
$w_{.i}\bar{Y}_{.i}^2$	$w_{.1}\bar{Y}_{.1}^2$	$w_{.2}\bar{Y}_{.2}^2$	$\sum w_{.i}\bar{Y}_{.i}^2$

$w_{i.}$	$\bar{Y}_{i.}$	$w_{i.}\bar{Y}_{.i.}$	$w_{i.}\bar{Y}^2$
$w_{1.}$	$\bar{Y}_{1.}$	$w_{1.}\bar{Y}_{1.}$	$w_{1.}\bar{Y}_{1.}^2$
$w_{2.}$	$\bar{Y}_{2.}$	$w_{2}\bar{Y}_{.2.}$	$w_{2.}\bar{Y}_{2.}^2$
$\sum w_{i.}$		$\sum w_{i.}\bar{Y}_{i.}$	$\sum w_{i.}\bar{Y}_{i.}^2$

(5) Get the means of the cell means for rows and columns and enter these under $\bar{Y}_{i.}$ and alongside $\bar{Y}_{.i}$ in the margins of our table of cell means.

(6) Multiply each mean of cell means for rows and columns by its corresponding weight and record these results under and alongside the headings "$w_{i.}\bar{Y}_{i.}$" and "$w_{.i}\bar{Y}_{.i}$", respectively.

(7) Multiply each product of the form $w_{i.}\bar{Y}_{i.}$ by $\bar{Y}_{i.}$ and each product of the form $w_{.i}\bar{Y}_{.i}$ by $\bar{Y}_{.i}$ and enter results in the appropriate cell in the above table.

(8) Sum for columns "$w_{i.}$", "$w_{i.}\bar{Y}_{i.}$" and "$w_{i.}\bar{Y}_{i.}^2$"; likewise, sum for rows "$w_{.i}$", "$w_{.i}\bar{Y}_{.i}$" and "$w_{.i}\bar{Y}_{.i}^2$".

(9) Substitute sums obtained in (8) above in (4.4.1) and (4.4.2) for sums of squares for rows and columns.

(10) To convert sums of squares to means squares, divide by $r - 1$ and $c - 1$, respectively.

(11) To test the significance of row and column means, express each mean square as a multiple of the mean square for error (which will have been obtained in the preliminary analysis) and refer to an F-table.

Numerical Example. To become better acquainted with the method of weighted squares of means, we apply (4.4.1) and (4.4.2) to a 2×2 table of numerical values. As before, we (1) set up subsample means and subsample frequencies:

Subsample Means   *Subsample Frequencies*

	B	
A	20	12
	2	10

	B	
A	5	10
	10	5

(2) Find reciprocals of subsample frequencies:

	B	
A	.20	.10
	.10	.20

(3) Get sums of reciprocals for rows *A* and columns *B*:

Rows   *Columns*

$$\frac{1}{w_{1.}} = .30 \qquad \frac{1}{w_{.1}} = .30$$

$$\frac{1}{w_{2.}} = .30 \qquad \frac{1}{w_{.2}} = .30$$

(4) Get reciprocals of sums of reciprocals:

Rows	Columns
$w_{1.} = 3.33$	$w_{.1} = 3.33$
$w_{2.} = 3.33$	$w_{.2} = 3.33$

(5) Find means of subsample means for rows A and columns B:

Rows	Columns
$\bar{\bar{Y}}_{1.} = 16$	$\bar{\bar{Y}}_{.1} = 11$
$\bar{\bar{Y}}_{2.} = 6$	$\bar{\bar{Y}}_{.2} = 11$

(6) Multiply means of subsample means by corresponding w's:

Rows	Columns
$w_{1.}\bar{\bar{Y}}_{1.} = 53.33$	$w_{.1}\bar{\bar{Y}}_{.1} = 36.66$
$w_{2.}\bar{\bar{Y}}_{2.} = 20.00$	$w_{.2}\bar{\bar{Y}}_{.2} = 36.66$

(7) Multiply each product of the form $w_{i.}\bar{\bar{Y}}_{i.}$ by $\bar{\bar{Y}}_{i.}$ to get

Rows	Columns
$w_{1.}\bar{\bar{Y}}_{1.}^2 = 853.24$	$w_{.1}\bar{\bar{Y}}_{.1}^2 = 403.29$
$w_{2.}\bar{\bar{Y}}_{2.}^2 = 120.00$	$w_{.2}\bar{\bar{Y}}_{.2}^2 = 403.29$

(8) Get sums of weights, weighted means of subsample means, and weighted squares of weighted means of subsample means:

Rows

$$\sum w_{i.} = 3.33 + 3.33$$
$$= 6.67$$

$$\sum w_{i.}\bar{\bar{Y}}_{i.} = 53.33 + 20.00$$
$$= 73.33$$

$$\sum w_{i.}\bar{\bar{Y}}_{i.}^2 = 853.24 + 120.00$$
$$= 973.24$$

Columns

$$\sum w_{.i} = 3.33 + 3.33$$
$$= 6.67$$

$$\sum w_{.i}\bar{\bar{Y}}_{.i} = 36.66 + 36.66$$
$$= 73.33$$

$$\sum w_{.i}\bar{\bar{Y}}_{.i}^2 = 403.29 + 403.29$$
$$= 806.59$$

(9) Substitute in formulas for RSS and CSS:

$$\text{CSS} = 2^2\left[806.59 - \frac{(73.33)^2}{6.67}\right]$$

$$= 4[0]$$

$$= 0,$$

$$\text{RSS} = 2^2\left[973.24 - \frac{(73.33)^2}{6.67}\right]$$

$$= 4[166.65]$$

$$= 666.60.$$

(10) Estimate population variance from means of cell means:

$$\frac{\text{RSS}}{r-1} = \frac{666.60}{2-1}$$

$$= 666.60.$$

(11) Express this mean square as a multiple of the mean square for error and refer that result to the F-table. Given that $s_w^2 = 100$ with 96 degrees of freedom,

$$_1F_{96} = 6.67, \quad p < .05,$$

which completes the analysis.

As a convenience, we put successive results together in a single tabular display:

	B_1	B_2		$w_{i.}$	$\bar{Y}_{i.}$	$w_{i.}\bar{Y}_{i.}$	$w_{i.}\bar{Y}_{i.}^2$
A_1	20	12		3.33	16	53.33	853.24
A_2	2	10		3.33	6	20.00	120.00
$w_{.i}$	3.33	3.33	6.67	6.67		73.33	973.24
$\bar{Y}_{.i}$	11	11					
$w_{.i}\bar{Y}_{.i}$	36.66	36.66	73.33				
$w_{.i}\bar{Y}_{.i}^2$	403.29	403.29	806.59				

Summary and Concluding Remarks. When frequencies in a two-way table are disproportional, simple routine procedures will not do, and more general methods (of which routine procedures are a special case) must be employed.

When main effects are additive, the method of constants will suffice; when interaction is present, we complete our analysis by the method of weighted squares of means. In the absence of interaction, we take fitted constants as estimates of main effects and mean squares based on these estimates as estimates of the common variance. In the presence of interaction, we take unweighted marginal means as estimates of main effects and weighted mean squares based on these unweighted means as estimates of the common variance. If we mistakenly assume interaction in the population when there is none, the method of weighted squares leads to estimates which are unbiased but less efficient than those supplied by the method of fitting constants. If we mistakenly assume no interaction in the population when it actually exists, the method of fitted constants will give biased estimates of main effects. The latter mistake has bias as its consequence; the former has inefficiency as its consequence.

Neither method is restricted in its application to the two-way table with two or more measures in each subclass (as in our examples). The procedure for a two-way table may be adapted to tables with only one measure in each cell (as in a randomized block design) and to multiple classifications, or to n-way tables, $n > 2$. When we have only one entry in each cell, and when one or more entries are missing, main effects will be entangled and we will have to fit constants in order to free one effect from the other. The procedure for fitting constants to single entries is no different in principle from those given above, but does differ in its detail. These matters are usually discussed under the heading of "the problem of missing data in AOV."

When measures are classified by three or more criteria and so give rise to a multiple classification, procedures must be extended to cover the greater complexities inherent in such multiple tables. Thus, if we classify measures of prejudice by education, income, and occupation, we will have to fit as many constants as there are categories for education, income, and occupation, respectively, plus a constant to represent the factor (m) common to all measures. Our assessment of interaction will likewise be more complicated, owing to the possible presence of three two-way interactions, and one three-way interaction. Despite such intricacies, the fitting of constants to an n-way table $(n > 2)$ is identical in its essentials to fitting in a two-way table, as in our illustrations.

The research worker may draw some consolation from the availability of simple approximate methods which may be employed under appropriate circumstances. When cell frequencies are virtually equal, but still disproportional, we may with confidence employ the *method of unweighted means*, which proceeds as if subclass frequencies were equal. If cell frequencies are very nearly proportional, we may suppose that subpopulations frequencies are proportional. On that supposition, we may calculate subclass frequencies on the assumption of proportionality in the population and apply routine procedures to those expected frequencies. We base our analysis on a set of hypothetical frequencies. Both the method of unweighted means and the method of hypothetical frequencies are described in Bancroft (1968: 35–41).

But however the problem of disproportionate data is resolved, it behooves the social researcher to take disproportionate data as the norm and proportional frequencies as the exception. The data of large-scale surveys, when subclassified, will not have the neat proportionality we have come to associate with the agricultural experiment, and the social investigator should not anticipate such tidy symmetry, unless he has deliberately designed his study to yield it. It is the norm of disproportionate data that dictates a greater familarity among sociologists with the method of fitted constants and its companion, the method of weighted squares of means.

EXERCISES

1. Given a two-way table of cell means with no interaction as follows:

6	8
8	10

Calculate the difference between weighted row means for each of the following tables of proportionate frequencies:

10	10
10	10

12	12
8	8

14	14
6	6

15	10
9	6

Are differences between means affected by the changing frequencies? What generalization is suggested by this exercise?

2. Given a two-way table of cell means with interaction as follows:

8	6
6	12

Calculate the difference between weighted row means for each of the frequency tables in Exercise 1. What qualification on your generalization from Exercise 1 is suggested by this result? Are differences affected by the changing cell frequencies?

3. Given cell means without interaction as follows:

6	8
8	12

Calculate the difference between weighted row means for each of the following tables of disproportionate frequencies:

10	10		10	10		10	10
8	12		6	14		2	18

Compare this result with Exercise 1 and discuss.

4. Given cell means with interaction as follows:

8	6
6	12

Calculate difference between weighted row means for each of the frequency tables from Exercise 3. Compare with Exercise 2 and comment.

5. Given disproportionate cell frequencies as follows:

10	10
6	14

Calculate the difference between weighted row means for each of the following sets of cell means with interaction:

8	6		10	4		12	2
6	12		4	14		2	16

Compare with Exercises 4 and 3.

6. Formulate a general rule from the results of Exercises 1–5 and express each separate result as a special case of this generalization.

7. Given one-way classifications (*a*) and (*b*). For each verify that $\hat{Y}SS = (a_1 T_{1.} + a_2 T_{2.} + mT) - C$ gives the same result as Formula (4.3.4).

	A_1	0, 4, 5			A_1	0, 6
(a)			(b)			
	A_2	3, 5, 7			A_2	3, 5, 7, 5

8. If measures in Tables (a) and (b) were samples from populations B_1 and B_2, respectively, they could arrange themselves in a two-way table as follows:

	B_1	B_2
	0	0
A_1	4	
	5	6
	3	3
A_2	5	5
	7	7
		5

Since this table contains no interaction, the method of fitting of constants is appropriate. Find the value to be added to RSS and CSS to correct for disproportionality. Form the appropriate ratios for testing the null hypotheses that row and column effects, respectively, are zero.

9. Find the expected values ($\hat{Y}_{ij}$) for the two-way table in Exercise 8, and show that the sum of the weighted squared deviations of these values from their weighted mean gives (within rounding error) $\hat{Y}$SS. Verify that the mean of the weighted expected values is equal to the mean of the observed values, i.e., $\sum n_{ij}\hat{Y}_{ij}/\sum n_{ij} = \bar{Y}$.

10. Consider the effect of income (A) and education (B) on attitude toward free public college education (Y), as measured on a 10-point scale. Fit constants and present the results with appropriate tests in an AOV table. Assume that TSS = 800.

		$\bar{Y}_{ij}$ Education (B)		
		Lo	M	Hi
	Hi	6	4	2
Income (A)	M	7	5	3
	Lo	8	6	4

		n_{ij} Education (B)		
		Lo	M	Hi
	Hi	4	6	10
Income (A)	M	20	60	20
	Lo	30	40	10

11. In Exercise 10, we use m as an estimate of the overall population mean μ. Compare this value with the value $\bar{Y}_{..}$. These values generally differ. Why? Under what circumstances would $\bar{Y}_{..}$ be used to estimate μ?

12. Verify numerically that the method of fitting constants, the method of weighted squares of means, and ordinary routine yield identical mean squares when applied to the following measures:

	B_1	B_2
A_1	6	2
	3	5
	5	9
A_2	3	7
	8	3
	1	3

13. Repeat calculations of Exercise 12 on these measures.

	B_1	B_2
A_1	1	9
	5	7
	6	7
	9	2
	6	0
A_2	1	7
	1	1
	6	6

REFERENCES

Bancroft, T. A.
   1968   Topics in Intermediate Statistical Methods. Ames, Iowa: Iowa State University Press.

Blalock, Hubert M., Jr.
   1965   "Theory building and the statistical concept of interaction." American Sociological Review 30: 374–380.

Cochran, W. G.
   1947   "Some consequences when the assumptions for the analysis of variance are not satisfied." Biometrics 3: 22–38.

Coleman, James S., Ernest Q. Campbell, *et al.*
   1966   Equality of Educational Opportunity. U.S. Department of Health, Education and Welfare, Office of Education. Washington, D.C.: U.S. Government Printing Office.

Draper, Norman and Harry Smith
   1966   Applied Regression Analysis. Chapter 6: "Selecting the 'best' regression equation." New York: John Wiley and Sons.

Edwards, Allen L.
   1964   Expected Values of Discrete Random Variable and Elementary Statistics. New York: John Wiley and Sons.

Eisenhart, C.
   1947   "The assumptions underlying the analysis of variance." Biometrics 3: 1–21.

Goulden, Cyril H.
   1952   Methods of Statistical Analysis. Second Edition. New York: John Wiley and Sons.

Kempthorne, Oscar
   1952   The Design and Analysis of Experiments. New York: John Wiley and Sons.

Keyfitz, Nathan
   1964   "Analysis of variance procedures in the study of ecological phenomena." Pp. 148–162 in E.W. Burgess and Donald J. Bogue (eds.), Contributions to Urban Sociology. Chicago: The University of Chicago Press.

Nair, K. R.
   1940–1941   "A note on the method of fitting constants for analysis of nonorthogonal data arranged in a double classification." Sankhya 5: 317–328.

Snedecor, George W.
   1946   Statistical Methods. Fourth Edition. Ames, Iowa: Iowa State University Press.

Sonquist, John A.
   1970   Multivariate Model Building. Ann Arbor: Institute for Social Research, University of Michigan.

Stevens, W. L.
   1948   "Statistical analysis of a nonorthogonal tri-factorial experiment." Biometrika 35: 346–347.

Wilk, M. B. and O. Kempthorne
   1955   "Fixed, mixed and random models." Journal of the American Statistical Association 50: 1144–1167.

Yates, Frank
   1934   "The analysis of multiple classifications with unequal numbers in the different classes." Journal of the American Statistical Association 29: 51–66.

5

Analysis of Covariance*

PART 1
General Purpose

Many questions which sociologists are called upon to answer empirically are similar in form to those underlying the analysis of covariance (AOCOV). Furthermore, diverse techniques which sociologists commonly employ to answer those questions are closely similar to the techniques of covariance analysis. Because of these considerations, sociologists may find the study of covariance analysis profitable to pursue, as a line of general inquiry or as a statistical method, or both. With this justification in mind, we (1) state the general purpose of AOCOV, (2) summarize its rudiments as an elementary statistical method, (3) consider its relationship to the process of elaboration, ecological correlation, and contextual analysis, and (4) discuss its application to correlations ordered by both time and place. Altogether, these materials lend weight to the argument that the covariance model may serve as a convenient framework for unifying various techniques of data analysis, as well as findings based on the application of those techniques. Moreover, the covariance model is a specialization of the general linear model which provides an even wider basis for unifying many seemingly disparate techniques of data analysis (Fennessey, 1969).

In covariance analysis (AOCOV), we compare two or more samples on the dependent variable (Y) after measures within samples have been corrected for regression on a control variable, or covariable (X). We do this

---

* Some of the contents of this chapter have been taken from the author's article (1969).

to guard against falsely ascribing an effect to the factor of classification (A) that rightly belongs to the covariable (X). An illustration may clarify these points.

If pupils from desegregated schools surpass pupils from segregated schools in scholastic achievement (as measured by a standard test), we may be tempted to regard that superiority as an effect of desegregation. But before drawing that conclusion, we would probably ask whether the two groups of pupils are approximately equal in intelligence (as measured by a standard intelligence test). For, if achievement is highly correlated with intelligence, and if our two groupings of pupils differ in average intelligence, the difference in achievement could be due to a difference in intelligence rather than to a difference in degree of desegregation. To determine whether this alternative hypothesis is credible, we would standardize achievement scores (by regression methods) on intelligence, and make comparisons between averages based on these adjusted scores. We do this to guard against mistakenly ascribing to desegregation what should be attributed to group differences in intelligence. To avoid such mistakes, we have recourse to AOCOV when the requisite data are available and its use is otherwise justified. (Since the analysis of covariance reduces to the analysis of variance after correction for regression, its use as a significance test is subject to the same restrictions as the analysis of variance. Its use for significance testing is also subject to the requirement that the covariable not be confounded with the classification factor.)

In the course of getting adjusted averages for groups, we routinely obtain results which permit us to determine (1) whether the relationship between X and Y is uniform for all groups, (2) whether the average relationship of X and Y within groups differs from the relationship based on group means, $\overline{X}_i$ and $\overline{Y}_i$, and (3) whether the relationship based on group means differs from the relationship between X and Y for all groups combined. For example, in studying delinquent behavior (Y) and family income (X) within and between local areas for a single large city, we may (by AOCOV) ascertain whether the relationship between these variables differs from one area to another, whether the average relationship within areas differs from the relationship between areal means, and whether the relationship between areal means differs from the relationship for all areas combined (Slatin 1969). Such results may reconcile superficial discrepancies among "findings" based on different aggregations of the same data and provide clues to aspects of social structure of the city that might otherwise be overlooked. The capacity of AOCOV to disentangle such relationships and perhaps to dispel some of the confusion produced by such entanglements supplies a major justification for its study in sociology.

As an arithmetical operation, the analysis of covariance may be applied whenever cases within two or more samples have values on both X and Y. Naturally, we use AOCOV not because such bivariate data are available, but rather because it permits us to test the effect of our main classification (A) on the dependent variable (Y) after controlling for the covariable (X). Of course, such testing, however essential to our research design, will be impossible to conduct unless values on X and Y are available within all groups. But, whenever our data take this form, we may use the AOCOV to determine whether we have assigned to our main classification (A) an influence that probably belongs to X. Thus, we seek to determine whether we have assigned an effect to desegregation that is due to intelligence, or whether we have imputed an effect to local area that should be attributed to family income.

The analysis of covariance is restricted neither to a single covariable (X) nor to a single classification (A). It may be applied to multivariate data classified by two or more criteria. For example, if we have reason to believe that physical fitness is, no less than intelligence, a factor in scholastic achievement, we might adjust scholastic achievement scores by both physical fitness and intelligence before comparing pupils from segregated and desegregated schools. Similarly, if we have reason to believe that achievement is affected by race as well as segregation, and that the effect of segregation is contingent on race, we would subclassify pupils as black or white before comparing pupils from segregated and desegregated schools. Although there is no limit on the intricacy of our classification, most of the relatively few applications of AOCOV in sociology are limited to quite simple designs. For that reason and for the sake of a simplified presentation, we restrict ourselves to the one-way table. For the same reason, we limit ourselves to procedures for bivariate data, or a single covariable. Higher-order, or n-way $(n > 2)$, classifications, and multivariate data (two or more covariables) involve more extensive computations, but no new principles.

Historical Note. The analysis of covariance as a systematic procedure was developed by R. A. Fisher during the 1920s. Like all new schemes, this one was the product of both earlier and contemporary scholarship. Nevertheless, Fisher's contribution was probably sufficiently distinctive to warrant applying the sociological term "invention" to it, although this may be debatable. It is of historical interest that a section on covariance analysis appeared first in the fourth edition of *Statistical Methods for Research Workers*, published in 1932.

The method became available to researchers in the United States with the publication of Snedecor's monograph (1934), the object of which was to present "in simple fashion a group of successful applications in the analysis of variance and covariance." Shortly afterward, Jackson (1940) and Lindquist (1940), respectively, sought to do for research students of education and psychology what Snedecor had done for experimentally-minded agriculturists. Hagood's (1941) presentation of the analysis of covariance was framed with sociologists in mind, and the stated purpose of Taves' article (1951) was to acquaint sociologists with some of the potentialities of this method in social research. Bogue and Harris's (1954) study of factors in the suburbanization of metropolitan areas was undertaken in part to demonstrate the utility of covariance analysis in population and urban research.

In spite of these and related efforts (Blau and Duncan 1967: 147–152), few sociologists have used the technique of covariance analysis in their research, notwithstanding its general promise. Both a lack of familiarity on the part of sociologists and the uncertain applicability of covariance analysis to many bodies of nonexperimental social data probably account for its infrequent use.

PART 2
Statistical Procedures

Arithmetic of Covariance. Where in the analysis of variance (AOV) we decompose the sum of squares for Y alone, in the analysis of covariance we decompose the sums of squares for both X and Y, and, in addition, we decompose the sum of the products of X and Y. Since in AOCOV we resolve the sum of the products as well as the sums of squares, we quite literally add the analysis of covariation to the analysis of variation to get covariance analysis, as the term itself suggests. This statement will be clarified by a consideration of the arithmetic of AOCOV which combines elements of both regression and variance analysis. In this demonstration, we take as our point of departure a total of N pairs of values for X and Y which have been grouped into k different classes according to a given criterion (A). We denote the number of pairs in the ith class by the symbol n_i, unless numbers in classes are equal, in which case we drop the subscript. The sum of the numbers is equal to $\sum_1^k n_i = N$.

When bivariate data are grouped into k classes, the deviations of X and Y from their respective overall means are expressible as

$$X_{ij} - \overline{X}_{.} = (X_{ij} - \overline{X}_i) + (\overline{X}_i - \overline{X}_{.}),$$

and

$$Y_{ij} - \overline{Y}_{.} = (Y_{ij} - \overline{Y}_i) + (\overline{Y}_i - \overline{Y}_{.}),$$

where X_{ij} is the jth value in the ith sample, $\overline{X}_i$ is the mean of the ith sample, and $X_{.}$ is mean of all N measures. Upon forming products and summing over all pairs of values, we get, after simplification,

(5.2.1)

$$\sum_1^k \sum_1^{n_i} (X_{ij} - \overline{X}_{.})(Y_{ij} - \overline{Y}_{.})$$

$$= \sum_1^k \sum_1^{n_i} (X_{ij} - \overline{X}_i)(Y_{ij} - \overline{Y}_i) + \sum_1^k n_i(\overline{X}_i - \overline{X}_{.})(Y_i - \overline{Y}_{.}),$$

or the total sum of products on the left of (5.2.1) as the algebraic sum of its component product sums on the right side. Since a product sum may be positive or negative in sign, the component sums on the right may differ in sign.

In order to simplify cumbersome expressions, it is customary to denote sums of squares and products by the letter C, with an appropriate subscript. In this notation, the total sum of products as the sum of its parts takes the simple form,

$$C_{xyT} = C_{xyw} + C_{xyb},$$

with the letter after "xy" in the subscript giving the source of the product sum as the *total* sample, values *within* samples, or differences *between* sample means. To express the sum of the products within groups in decomposed form, we denote the sum of the products within the ith group by C_{xyw_i}:

$$C_{xyw} = C_{xyw_1} + C_{xyw_2} + \cdots + C_{xyw_k}.$$

The expression on the right is a reminder that the sum of products within groups (C_{xyw}) is itself an amalgamation of k sums which may vary among themselves, and which may differ in sign.

The economy of this notation is apparent in the conventional table of sums of squares and products, and their corresponding degrees of freedom:

Source	df	Sum of squares		Sum of products
Between	$k - 1$	C_{xxb}	C_{yyb}	C_{xyb}
Within	$N - k$	C_{xxw}	C_{yyw}	C_{xyw}
Total	$N - 1$	C_{xxT}	C_{yyT}	C_{xyT}

To illustrate these formulas, we apply them to 30 (N) paired measures, grouped into six (k) classes of five (n_i) values each. These measures are given in Table 5.2.1. Although n_i is uniform in this problem, in general it will

Table 5.2.1

A_1		A_2		A_3		A_4		A_5		A_6	
X	Y	X	Y	X	Y	X	Y	X	Y	X	Y
13	35	10	47	16	28	9	45	12	38	15	47
11	40	9	53	13	30	12	36	17	22	11	51
18	25	8	56	15	28	10	40	19	20	9	60
14	37	12	40	10	42	13	34	11	46	14	43
12	43	11	44	12	32	8	55	14	34	17	39

differ from one class to another. Substituting paired values of X and Y in the formulas represented by the C's, we get these results:

Source of Variation	df	C_{xx}	C_{yy}	C_{xy}
Between	5	86.30	1376.67	−227.00
Within	24	165.20	1516.00	−466.00
Total	29	251.50	2892.67	−693.00

Relationship between X and Y, Cases Unsorted. Each row of the table of squares and products gives rise to coefficients expressing the relationship between X and Y under different restrictions. Dividing the total sum of products by the total sum of squares for X, we get the slope of the regression line of Y on X for all cases:

$$b_T = \frac{C_{xyT}}{C_{xxT}}.$$

The direction of the relationship as positive or negative is given by the sign of the sum of products. For the correlation coefficient of all N cases, we divide the total sum of products by the geometric mean of the corresponding sums of squares for X and Y. In symbols:

(5.2.2) $$r_T = \frac{C_{xyT}}{\sqrt{C_{xxT}C_{yyT}}}.$$

Applying these formulas to our numerical data, we calculate:

$$b_T = \frac{-693.00}{251.50}$$
$$= -2.76,$$

and

$$r_T = \frac{-693.00}{\sqrt{(251.50)(2892.67)}}$$
$$= \frac{-693.00}{852.93}$$
$$= -.81.$$

Relationship between Group Means, $\bar{X}_i$ and $\bar{Y}_i$. Continuing our analysis, we next inquire into the relationship between paired means, $\bar{X}_i$ and $\bar{Y}_i$, as if there were no differences among values within classes on either X or Y, only differences between class means. For the slope of $\bar{Y}_i$ on $\bar{X}_i$, we divide the product sum between groups by the sum of squares between groups for X:

$$b_b = \frac{C_{xyb}}{C_{xxb}}.$$

For the correlation coefficient between paired means, we divide the product sum between groups by the geometric mean of the respective sums of squares between groups for X and Y:

$$r_b = \frac{C_{xyb}}{\sqrt{C_{xxb}C_{yyb}}}.$$

Substituting our numerical data in these formulas, we obtain

$$b_b = \frac{-227.00}{86.30}$$
$$= -2.63,$$

and

$$r_b = \frac{-227.00}{\sqrt{(86.30)(1376.67)}}$$
$$= \frac{-227.00}{344.50}$$
$$= -.66.$$

Although r_b is numerically smaller than r_T in this problem, one should not conclude that it is necessarily smaller; it will be larger or smaller according to the degree of homogeneity in both X and Y within classes (p. 216).

Relationship between X and Y, Cases Sorted. Our next question has to do with relationship between X and Y as determined by the pooled sums of squares and sums of products within the respective samples. For the composite slope within groups, we divide the sum of products within groups by the sum of squares within groups for X:

$$b_w = \frac{C_{xyw}}{C_{xxw}}.$$

The composite correlation within samples is obtained by dividing the product sum within groups by the geometric mean of the respective sums of squares within groups:

$$r_w = \frac{C_{xyw}}{\sqrt{C_{xxw}C_{yyw}}}.$$

Applying these formulas to our numerical data, we get:

$$b_w = \frac{-466.00}{165.20}$$
$$= -2.82,$$

and

$$r_w = \frac{-466}{\sqrt{(165.20)(1516.00)}}$$
$$= \frac{-466.00}{500.44}$$
$$= -.93.$$

These composite coefficients, be it noted, are not arithmetic means: the correlation coefficient for pooled sums is not the mean of as many correlations as there are groups; rather, it is a ratio based on sums of sums for k separate groups. Likewise, the slope for pooled sums is not the mean of as many slopes as groups; it too is a ratio based on sums of sums for k groups.

Since the total sum of products is determined when component sums are given, it is possible to write the total correlation in terms of component product sums, each expressed as a multiple of the geometric mean of the total sums of squares, which is the denominator in (5.2.2). In symbols:

(5.2.3) $$r_T = \frac{C_{xyw}}{\sqrt{C_{xxT}C_{yyT}}} + \frac{C_{xyb}}{\sqrt{C_{xxT}C_{yyT}}}.$$

For our problem,

$$r_T = \frac{-466.00}{852.93} + \frac{-277.00}{852.93}$$
$$= (-.54) + (-.27)$$
$$= -.81.$$

By means of this identity (5.2.3), we may assess the relative contribution of component product sums to the total correlation. Warning: we cannot add r_w and r_b together to get r_T. For example, $-.67$ plus $-.93$ does not equal $-.81$. However, from any two of these coefficients it is possible to get the third—provided that each of the two given coefficients is properly weighted— a procedure we shall consider in a subsequent discussion.

Hypothesis of Common Slope. Although it is a natural step from sums of squares and products to correlation coefficients, as in the foregoing analysis, this step is somewhat incidental to the main business of the AOCOV. The main business, as noted at the outset, is to assess the effect of the factor (A) on the dependent variable (Y) after taking into account the covariable (X).

In that assessment, we must first determine whether it is reasonable to assume that our k populations have a common slope. An affirmative answer to that question will be our justification for pooling sums of squares and products for a more stable estimate of the common slope; if our answer is negative, we must forego such pooling and, of course, the significance testing in which our operations would otherwise culminate. The reason is this: we cannot apply a uniform correction factor (b_w) to sample means on Y, unless the change of Y on X is uniform from one population to another, i.e., unless $\beta_1 = \beta_2 = \cdots = \beta$.

To test the hypothesis that populations have identical slopes, we compare the mean square based on differences between sample slopes with the mean square based on deviations from regression lines within samples. When the null hypothesis of a common slope is true, both mean squares provide unbiased estimates of the residual variance, $\sigma_{y\cdot x}^2$; when the hypothesis is false and population slopes actually differ, the mean square based on differences among slopes will tend to be excessive and at odds with the hypothesis of a common slope.

To get the aforesaid mean squares, we partition the sum of the squared deviations around the composite slope (b_w) into its component sums: (1) the sum of the squared deviations of values from individual regression lines within groups, and (2) the sum of the squared deviations of sample slopes from the composite slope. In doing this by hand, it will expedite matters to set up a worksheet with columns for squares and products, and rows for samples, as in Table 5.2.2. As our first step, we transcribe entries from Row 1, Table 5.2.1, to Row 1 of the worksheet (Table 5.2.2). The square of the sum of the products within groups divided by the sum of the squares within groups for X gives us the sum of the squares attributable to the composite slope, b_w, or the variation explained by the composite slope.

Table 5.2.2   *Worksheet for Computing Sum of Squared Deviations from Regressions Within Groups and Sum of Squared Deviations of Group Slopes from Composite Slope*

(1) Sample No.	(2) C_{xxw}	(3) C_{yyw}	(4) C_{xyw}	(5) $C_{\hat{y}\cdot x}$	(6) $C_{y\cdot x}$
	165.20	1,516.00	−466.00	1,314.50	$201.50 = C_{y\cdot xw}$
1	29.20	188.00	− 69.00	163.05	24.95
2	10.00	170.00	− 41.00	168.10	1.90
3	22.80	136.00	− 50.00	109.65	26.35
4	17.20	282.00	− 65.00	245.64	36.36
5	45.20	480.00	−144.00	458.76	21.24
6	40.80	260.00	− 97.00	230.61	29.39
Sum	165.20	1,516.00	−466.00	1,375.81	$140.19 = C'_{y\cdot xw}$ $61.31 = C''_{y\cdot xw}$

In symbols,

$$C_{\hat{y}.xw} = \frac{(C_{yxw})^2}{C_{xxw}}.$$

For our problem,

$$C_{\hat{y}.xw} = \frac{(-466.00)^2}{165.20}$$
$$= 1,314.50.$$

Subtracting the sum of squares for regression within groups from the sum of the squares within groups for Y, we obtain the sum of the squares around regression within groups. In symbols,

$$C_{y.xw} = C_{yyw} - C_{\hat{y}.xw}.$$

Subtracting the entry in Column 5 from the entry in Column 3, we obtain in the first row,

$$C_{y.xw} = 1,516.00 - 1,314.50$$
$$= 201.50.$$

We enter this result in the first row, last column of the worksheet.

As our second main step, we calculate the sum of the squared deviations from the individual regression line of each group. As a necessary preliminary, we get sums of squares and products within each group, recording these results in Columns 2–4, in rows corresponding to samples. For the first sample and by way of illustration, we have

$$C_{xxw_1} = 29.20,$$
$$C_{yyw_1} = 188.00,$$
$$C_{xyw_1} = -69.00.$$

Manipulating sums of squares and products row by row, we obtain for each group the squares due to regression, and the squares around regression, which results are entered in Columns 5–6. By way of example, for the first sample, we get,

$$C_{\hat{y}.xw_1} = \frac{(-69.00)^2}{29.20}$$
$$= 163.05.$$
$$C_{y.xw_1} = 188.00 - 163.05$$
$$= 24.95.$$

Our third major step entails adding up entries in Column 6, excluding the entry in Row 1 ($C_{y.xw}$). In symbols,

$$C'_{y.xw} = \sum C'_{y.xw_i}.$$

This is the sum of the sums of the squared deviations around fitted regressions within groups. For our example,

$$C'_{y.xw} = 24.95 + 1.90 + 26.35 + 36.36 + 21.24 + 29.39$$
$$= 140.19.$$

Note that the sums of Columns 5 and 6, excluding Row 1, together equal the sum of squares within groups for Y.

As our final step in this sequence of operations, we get the sum of the squares for differences among slopes. We may obtain this sum either by straightforward methods or by subtracting $C'_{y.xw}$ from $C_{y.xw}$. Since the latter method is more convenient, particularly when computations are performed manually, we employ it here. In symbols,

$$C''_{y.xw} = C_{y.xw} - C'_{y.xw}.$$

For our problem,

$$C''_{y.xw} = 201.50 - 140.19$$
$$= 61.31,$$

which result is entered on the worksheet immediately below $C'_{y.xw} = 140.19$.

At this juncture, we divide component sums of squares by corresponding degrees of freedom to get mean squares which are unbiased estimators of the residual variance $\sigma^2_{y.x}$ when the null hypothesis of a common slope is true. To simplify subscripts, we abbreviate "*y.xw*" to "*w*".

$$s^2_{w'} = \frac{C'_{y.xw}}{N - 2k},$$

and

$$s^2_{w''} = \frac{C''_{.xw}}{k - 1}.$$

Substituting numerical results, we calculate

$$s^2_{w'} = \frac{140.19}{18}$$
$$= 7.79,$$

and

$$s_{w''}^2 = \frac{61.31}{5}$$

$$= 12.26.$$

We will rest our decision to reject the hypothesis of homogeneity of regression on the probability of an F as large or larger than $s_{w''}^2/s_{w'}^2$. In our problem,

$$F = \frac{12.26}{7.79}$$

$$= 1.57,$$

on 5, 18 degrees of freedom. Since this result is not improbably large, we would probably not reject the hypothesis of a common slope. To summarize results, we assemble them in conventional form as follows:

Source	df	Sum of Squares	Mean Square	F
$(y_{ij} - b_w x_{ij})$	23	201.50		
$(y_{ij} - b_{w_i} x_{ij})$	18	140.19	7.79	
$(b_{w_i} - b_w)x_{ij}$	5	61.31	12.26	1.57

where $y_{ij} = Y_{ij} - \bar{Y}_i$, and $x_{ij} = X_{ij} - \bar{X}_i$.

For a summary of literal results, we replace numerical values by their corresponding literal expressions as follows:

Source	df	Sum of Squares	Mean Square	F
$(y_{ij} - b_w x_{ij})$	$(N - k) - 1$	$C_{y.xw}$	s_w^2	
$(y_{ij} - b_{w_i} x_{ij})$	$N - 2k$	$C'_{y.xw}$	$s_{w'}^2$	
$(b_{w_i} - b_w)x_{ij}$	$k - 1$	$C''_{y.xw}$	$s_{w''}^2$	$s_{w''}^2/s_{w'}^2$

Significance of Regression. On the assumption that all k populations have the same slope, we next inquire into significance of the sum of the squares explained by the regression of Y on X. Fitted slopes within samples may be consistent with the null hypothesis that populations have identical slopes, but the variation explained by regression may be insufficiently large to contradict the hypothesis that the common slope is zero ($H:\beta = 0$). To test this possibility, we partition the pooled sum of squares for samples C_{yyw} into its two component sums: one sum attributable to the regression of

Y on X, the other sum to factors disturbing that regression. In tabular form:

Element	df	Sum of Squares	Mean Square	F
y_{ij}	$N - k$	C_{yyw}		
$(y_{ij} - b_w x_{ij})$	$(N - k) - 1$	$C_{y.xw}$	s_w^2	
$b_w x_{ij}$	1	$C_{\hat{y}.xw}$	$s_{\hat{w}}^2$	$\dfrac{s_{\hat{w}}^2}{s_w^2}$

Dividing both component sums by their corresponding degrees of freedom, we get mean squares which are independent estimates of the same population variance, σ_y^2, provided that the slope of Y on X is equal to zero. Of the $N - k$ degrees of freedom available for assignment, 1 goes to the explained sum of squares, $N - k - 1$ to the unexplained sum of squares. Putting mean squares together in ratio form, we test the null hypothesis that the common slope β is equal to 0. For our example:

Name	Source	df	Sum of Squares	Mean Square	F
Within Groups	y_{ij}	24	1,516.00		
Unexplained	$(y_{ij} - b_w x_{ij})$	23	210.50	8.76	
Explained	$b_w x_{ij}$	1	1,314.50	1,314.50	150.60

The large value of F dictates that we reject the hypothesis that $\beta = 0$ and continue with our analysis. If the value of F had been small, we would terminate our analysis at this stage. If Y does not regress on X, the "correction" for regression is pointless, since that "adjustment" will leave group means unchanged.

Testing Significance of Adjusted Means. The stage is now set to test the possibility which prompted the inquiry in the first place: namely, that the regression of Y on the covariable (X) accounts for the observed differences among sample means on the dependent variable (Y). In running this test, we set up the hypothesis that all populations have the same line of regression $Y = \alpha + \beta X$, where α is Y-intercept and β is the common slope, in accordance with this logic: if all populations do in fact have the same line of regression (i.e., same intercept, as well as same slope), differences among population means on Y will vanish if we adjust each to the same value of X; if populations have the same slope (as we assume at this stage in our analysis) but different intercepts, differences among population means will nòt vanish if we adjust each to the same value of X, although the magnitudes of these differences may change. Therefore, rejection of the hypothesis that all populations have the same intercept ($H{:}\sigma_{\alpha_i}^2 = 0$) implies acceptance of the alternative hypothesis that populations have different intercepts ($H{:}\sigma_{\alpha_i}^2 > 0$).

If we accept the alternative, our conclusion would be that the covariable (X) does not account for the differences among unadjusted means.

In running our test, we simply divide the mean square based on the unexplained sum of squares between groups by the mean square based on the unexplained sum of squares within groups, and refer that result to the F distribution. A rare value of F would be against the null hypothesis and for the statistical significance of means adjusted for regression. These operations, together with results for our problem, may be arranged in tabular form as follows:

Literal Values

Source	df	Unexplained Sum of Squares	Mean Square	F
Total	$N-2$	$C_{y.xT}$		
Within	$N-k-1$	$C_{y.xw}$	s_w^2	
Between	$k-1$	$C_{y.xb}$	s_b^2	$\dfrac{s_b^2}{s_w^2}$

Numerical Values

Source	df	Unexplained Sum of Squares	Mean Square	F
Total	28	983.13		
Within	23	201.50	8.76	
Between	5	781.63	156.33	17.85

From these results it is clear that our test of adjusted means rests on the decomposition of the total sums of squares and products into the between-sample and within-sample sums of squares and products, respectively. No other partitioning is required. For that reason, when it is safe to assume that slopes are identical within populations, we may proceed immediately to test the hypothesis that the regression of Y on X accounts for the observed differences among sample means on Y. In our example, as noted, regression does not account for the differences among the adjusted means, and we conclude that the effect of A on Y is statistically significant after correction for regression.

Computing Adjusted Means. Although it is unnecessary to calculate adjusted means to test their significance, these means may be required for some specific purpose, and the F-ratio alone tells us nothing about their magnitudes. It may be necessary to compare observed and adjusted means, to compare adjusted means two at a time, to identify deviant cases (outliers), and so on. It is a simple matter to get the adjusted means: compute the predicted value of $\overline{Y}_i - \overline{Y}_.$ on the assumption that the change of Y on X is uniformly b_w (our best estimate of the common slope, β), and subtract this correction from the observed mean, $\overline{Y}_i$. As a formula:

$$(5.2.4) \qquad\qquad \overline{Y}'_i = \overline{Y}_i - b_w(\overline{X}_i - \overline{X}_.),$$

where $\overline{Y}'_i$ = adjusted mean of ith group, given that $\overline{Y}_i$ changes b_w for each unit change in $\overline{X}_i$. By this formula, we in effect standardize all sample means on Y to the same value of X. To apply Formula (5.2.4), we set up columns as in Table 5.2.3 and perform the required operations.

Table 5.2.3   *Calculation of Adjusted Means,* $\overline{Y}'_i$
$\overline{X}_. = 12.5, \overline{Y}_. = 39.67, b_w = 2.82$

(1) Sample No.	(2) $\overline{X}_i$	(3) $\overline{X}_i - \overline{X}_.$	(4) $b_w(\overline{X}_i - \overline{X}_.)$	(5) $\overline{Y}_i$	(6) $\overline{Y}_i - b_w(\overline{X}_i - \overline{X}_.)$
1	13.6	1.1	−3.102	36.00	39.10
2	10.0	−2.5	7.050	48.00	40.95
3	13.2	.7	−1.974	32.00	33.97
4	10.4	−2.1	5.922	42.00	36.08
5	14.6	2.1	−5.922	32.00	37.92
6	13.2	.7	−1.974	48.00	49.98
Sum	75.00	0.0	0.000	238.00	238.00

By comparing observed and adjusted means (Columns 5 and 6) our attention may be directed to empirical relationships of theoretical importance. For example, Samples 2 and 6 have the same observed means (48.00) but very different adjusted means (40.95 and 49.98). In this case, the correction for regression of Y on X uncovered a difference between means which the covariable was suppressing. Such changes in the difference between means may throw light on factors of significance that otherwise might be overlooked. It seems fair to say that the information supplied by the adjusted means justifies the effort in obtaining them.

Regression of Group Means. In none of the foregoing tests were we called upon to investigate either the linearity of the trend of population means or the possibility that the trend for population means, although linear, is different in its slope from the trend for measures within populations. However, such matters may be deserving of study. For it is quite possible that the relationship between population means is not linear, notwithstanding a pronounced linear trend between X and Y within populations. On the other hand, the scatter of population means may match the scatter of X and Y within populations in the degree of its linearity, even though its slope is quite different.

$H:\overline{Y}_i = \alpha' + \beta'\overline{X}_i$. The hypothesis to be tested is that the regression of population means is linear with intercept $= \alpha'$ and slope $= \beta'$. To test this hypothesis, we partition the between-sample sum of squares on Y (C_{yyb}) into explained and unexplained (by regression) sums as follows:

$$C_{yyb} = \frac{(C_{xyb})^2}{C_{xxb}} + \left[C_{yyb} - \frac{(C_{xyb})^2}{C_{xxb}} \right]$$
$$= C'_{\hat{y}.xb} + C'_{y.xb}.$$

Note that $C'_{y.xb}$ is not equal to $C_{y.xb} = C_{y.xT} - C_{y.xw}$. For an explanation, consult Cochran (1957). The unexplained sum of squares divided by its $k - 2$ degrees of freedom,

$$s^2_{b'} = \frac{C'_{y.xb}}{k - 2},$$

is an unbiased estimate of $\sigma^2_{y.x}$ when the regression of population means is actually linear. Therefore, the ratio,

$$F = \frac{s^2_{b'}}{s^2_{w'}},$$

on $k - 2$, $N - 2k$ df, serves as a test of the hypothesis that the regression among group means is linear. The results of the foregoing procedures are assembled in Table 5.2.4. When the regression of population means is linear, this ratio will have an F-distribution, whether or not slopes within populations are identical (Mood 1950: 356). An ordinary value of F is for the hypothesis of linearity, a rare value is against that hypothesis. Since $F = 25.00$ in our problem (Table 5.2.5) is relatively rare ($p < .01$), we reject the hypothesis that the regression among population means is linear and we tacitly accept the alternative that the regression among population means is nonlinear.

$H:\beta = \beta'$. If our F had dictated acceptance of the hypothesis of linearity for population means, we would probably have extended our investigation to consider the possibility that the slope of the regression line for means differs from the slope of the regression line of Y on X within populations. In short, we would test $H:\beta = \beta'$. To run this test, we perform these operations in sequence:

(1) Subtract the sum of squares unexplained by the regression of sample means from the unexplained (adjusted) sum of squares between samples. In symbols:

$$C''_{y.xb} = C_{y.xb} - C'_{y.xb}.$$

(2) Divide this remainder sum of squares by its one degree of freedom for the mean square:

$$s_{b''}^2 = \frac{C''_{y.xb}}{1}.$$

(3) Form the ratio of this mean square to the mean square derived from the unexplained sum of squares within samples ($C_{y.xw}$). In symbols:

$$F = \frac{s_{b''}^2}{s_n^2}.$$

When the slopes β and β' are identical, this ratio will have an F-distribution; consequently, it may be employed to test the null hypothesis of identical slopes. This process is represented in Table 5.2.4; calculations for our problem are given in Table 5.2.5. It should be emphasized that this procedure is valid only if populations have the same slope and the regression of population means is linear. It would be misleading to compare b_b and b_w, if the sample evidence were against the hypothesis of linear regression for population means. As Snedecor (1946: 329) states: "... where there is no pronounced trend of means, it is idle to bother about the difference between this (trend) and any other trend."

Table 5.2.4 *Partition of Adjusted Sum of Squares ($C_{y.xb}$)*

Between Groups	df	Sum of Squares	Mean Square	F
Adjusted	$k-1$	$C_{y.xb}$	s_b^2	
b_b	$k-2$	$C'_{y.xb}$	$s_{b'}^2$	$s_{b'}^2/s_{w'}^2$
$(b_b - b_w)$	1	$C''_{y.xb}$	$s_{b''}^2$	$s_{b''}^2/s_w^2$

$$s_w^2 = \frac{C_{y.xw}}{N-k-1} \qquad s_{w'}^2 = \frac{C'_{y.xw}}{N-2k}$$

Table 5.2.5 *Partition of Adjusted Sum of Squares ($C_{y.xb}$)*

Between Groups	df	Sum of Squares	Mean Square	F
Adjusted	5	781.63		
b_b	4	779.58	194.90	25.00
$(b_b - b_w)$	1	2.05	2.05	.24

$$s_w^2 = 8.76 \qquad s_{w'}^2 = 7.79$$

Summary. As a convenience, we present a summary of hypotheses subject to test in the one-way AOCOV, together with corresponding test statistics. We use the Greek letter "ν" to designate degrees of freedom.

Hypothesis	Test Statistic	ν_1	ν_2
1. Sampled populations have common slope $(\beta_1 = \cdots = \beta_i = \cdots = \beta)$	$\dfrac{s_{w''}^2}{s_{w'}^2}$	$k - 1$	$N - 2k$
2. Common slope not zero $(|\beta| > 0)$	$\dfrac{s_{\tilde{w}}^2}{s_w^2}$	1	$N - k - 1$
3. Sampled populations have common intercept $(\alpha_1 = \cdots = \alpha_i = \cdots = \alpha)$	$\dfrac{s_b^2}{s_w^2}$	$k - 1$	$N - k - 1$
4. Regression of population means is linear $(\overline{Y}_i = \alpha' + \beta'\overline{X}_i)$	$\dfrac{s_{b'}^2}{s_{w'}^2}$	$k - 2$	$N - 2k$
5. Population means and measures within populations have same slope $(\beta = \beta')$	$\dfrac{s_{b''}^2}{s_w^2}$	1	$N - k - 1$

One does not run these tests because they are available, but because they answer to some specific research question. If there is good reason to believe that populations have the same slope, one may test immediately the hypothesis of a common intercept. And, as noted, if there is evidence against the hypothesis that the regression of means is linear, one would not test for the significance of the difference between b_w and b_b.

Covariance Model. The hypothesis that population means on Y are equal after correction for regression is tested by expressing the adjusted mean square between samples as a multiple of the adjusted mean square within samples and referring that result to the F-table. However, that procedure will be strictly justified only if (1) sampled populations are identically normal for each level of X, and (2) slopes are identical within populations. This latter assumption is explicit in the linear model for the analysis of covariance, usually written as follows (Cochran 1957: 261):

$$Y_{ij} = \mu_. + \alpha_i + \beta(X_{ij} - \overline{X}_.) + e_{ij}.$$

This equation expresses our conception of each value (Y_{ij}) as consisting of one part ($\mu_.$) common to all values, one part (α_i) common to all values in the ith population, one part, $\beta(X_{ij} - \overline{X}_.)$, which determines the elevation of the jth value in the ith population, and finally, a component (e_{ij}) having its source in random factors. Subtracting the correction for regression from Y_{ij}, we get

$$Y_{ij} - \beta(X_{ij} - \overline{X}.) = \mu. + \alpha_i + e_{ij},$$

which is the population model for the one-way analysis of variance. We would obtain the same result by setting $X_{ij} = \overline{X}.$, as if the covariable were a constant:

$$
\begin{aligned}
Y_{ij} &= \mu. + \alpha_i + \beta(\overline{X}. - \overline{X}.) + e_{ij} \\
&= \mu. + \alpha_i + \beta(0) \qquad\quad + e_{ij} \\
&= \mu. + \alpha_i + e_{ij}.
\end{aligned}
$$

As in the analysis of variance, the assumption that populations have a common variance is routinely checked; if that assumption is accepted, the assumption of a common slope $(\beta_1 = \cdots = \beta_i = \cdots = \beta)$ is tested in the manner described above; if that assumption is accepted in turn, the hypothesis that population intercepts are identical $(\alpha_1 = \cdots = \alpha_2 = \cdots = \alpha)$ may be tested as the last step in the analysis.

Although the finding that sample slopes differ would preclude a test of the hypothesis that intercepts are equal (i.e., that adjusted population means are equal), that finding may be instrumental in reconciling superficially incompatible conclusions based on the total correlation (r_T) and the correlation between groups (r_b), respectively. But whatever the degree of correspondence between r_b and r_T, their relationship will be clarified when we examine the pattern of correlations within samples. That clarification will be aided if we express both r_T and r_b as functions of r_w. The following paragraphs explain this procedure.

Correlation Ratio. This term is used to designate the ratio of the sum of squares between groups to the total sum of squares. It is usually symbolized η^2 with subscript. Since the sum of squares between groups reflects the effect of the factor of classification (A), the correlation ratio (η^2) serves to gauge the strength of the relationship between A and the dependent variable (Y) under study. For present purposes, we set up these correlation ratios:

$$\eta_{yA}^2 = \frac{C_{yyb}}{C_{yyT}},$$

and

$$\eta_{xA}^2 = \frac{C_{xxb}}{C_{xxT}}.$$

To express the variation in Y explained by A after correction for regression on X, we set up the ratio,

$$\eta_{yA.x}^2 = \frac{C_{y.xb}}{C_{y.xT}}.$$

In subsequent examples, we will calculate these ratios and consider the interpretation to which they are subject; at this juncture we use them to clarify the relations among the total, within-group and between-group correlations.

Relations Among r_T, r_w, and r_b. We begin with our basic formula for r_T:

$$r_T = \frac{C_{xyT}}{\sqrt{C_{xxT}C_{yyT}}}.$$

Rewriting the numerator and separating terms, we get

$$r_T = \frac{C_{xyw}}{\sqrt{C_{xxT}C_{yyT}}} + \frac{C_{xyb}}{\sqrt{C_{xxT}C_{yyT}}}.$$

Multiplying the first term on the right by $\sqrt{\dfrac{C_{xxw}C_{yyw}}{C_{xxw}C_{yyw}}}$ and the second term by $\sqrt{\dfrac{C_{xxb}C_{yyb}}{C_{xxb}C_{yyb}}}$, and rearranging, we get

$$r_T = \frac{C_{xyw}}{\sqrt{C_{xxw}C_{yyw}}} \sqrt{\frac{C_{xxw}}{C_{xxT}} \frac{C_{yyw}}{C_{yyT}}} + \frac{C_{xyb}}{\sqrt{C_{xxb}C_{yyb}}} \sqrt{\frac{C_{xxb}}{C_{xxT}} \frac{C_{yyb}}{C_{yyT}}}.$$

Substituting, we get

$$r_T = r_w \sqrt{1 - \eta_{xA}^2} \sqrt{1 - \eta_{yA}^2} + r_b(\eta_{xA}\eta_{yA}),$$

or the total correlation as a function of its component correlations, each weighted by a quantity whose magnitude depends on the correlation ratios. Transposing, we can solve for r_w and r_b as follows:

$$r_w = \frac{r_T - r_b\eta_{yA}\eta_{xA}}{\sqrt{1 - \eta_{yA}^2} \sqrt{1 - \eta_{xA}^2}}.$$

$$r_b = \frac{r_T - r_w\sqrt{1 - \eta_{yA}^2} \sqrt{1 - \eta_{xA}^2}}{\eta_{yA}\eta_{xA}}.$$

Applying these formulas to our data (Table 5.2.1), we obtain:

$$\eta^2_{yA} = \frac{1376.67}{2892.67} = .48.$$

$$\eta^2_{xA} = \frac{86.30}{251.50} = .34.$$

$$
\begin{aligned}
r_T &= (-.93)\sqrt{1 - .48}\sqrt{1 - .34} + (-.66)\sqrt{.48}\sqrt{.34} \\
&= -.93(.72)(.81) \qquad\qquad + (-.66)(.69)(.59) \\
&= (-.54) \qquad\qquad\qquad + (-.27) \\
&= -.81.
\end{aligned}
$$

$$
\begin{aligned}
r_w &= [-.81 - (-.66\sqrt{.48}\sqrt{.34})]/\sqrt{1 - .48}\sqrt{1 - .34} \\
&= [-.81 + .66(.69)(.59)]/(.72)(.81) \\
&= -.54/.58 \\
&= -.93.
\end{aligned}
$$

$$
\begin{aligned}
r_b &= [-.81 - (-.93\sqrt{1 - .48}\sqrt{1 - .34})]/\sqrt{.48}\sqrt{.34} \\
&= [-.81 + .93(.72)(.81)]/(.69)(.59) \\
&= -.26/.40 \\
&= -.65.
\end{aligned}
$$

By permitting correlation ratios to vary from 0 to 1, we may judge their effect on r_T, r_b, and r_w, respectively. If both ratios tend to 0, we get

$$r_T = r_w.$$

If both ratios tend to 1, we get

$$r_T = r_b.$$

When both ratios take values close to .5, we obtain

$$r_T \doteq \tfrac{1}{2}(r_w + r_b),$$

as the student should verify. By thus permitting η^2_{xA} and η^2_{yA} to vary on their range, we may discern the effect of homogeneity in X or Y within groups on the respective correlation coefficients, r_T, r_b, and r_w. When measures are very nearly alike within groups but quite different between groups, as in some ecological studies, we may find a high correlation for group means, a low correlation within groups, and a total correlation which is intermediate in value. In such cases, the total correlation represents a resolution of opposing forces, the one tending to 1, the other to 0. The point of resolution will depend not only on the component correlation coefficients, but on the correlation ratios as well.

PART 3
Group Effects

In social research we are often required to sort out individual and group effects, to measure their relative strength, and perhaps to test their statistical significance. Sociologists have employed a wide variety of methods to deal with this problem, ranging from very informal schemes to quite systematic procedures. Some purpose would be served by an analysis of the similarity of these procedures and by a representation of that similarity in somewhat abstract terms. With this objective in mind, we note the similarity between the analysis of covariance and (1) elaboration, (2) ecological correlation, and (3) contextual, structural, and compositional analysis, respectively, and thereby suggest the potentialities of this model as a way of subtending different techniques of data analysis and findings based on those techniques. We start with the process of elaboration, due to Kendall and Lazarsfeld (1950).

Elaboration. In elaboration, we study the dependence of Y on X, with the test factor, A, under control. In the analysis of covariance, we study the dependence of Y on A with the covariable, X, under control. Although this distinction is inessential, we find it useful in comparing the results of one method with the results of the other. In elaboration, we investigate the possibility that the observed relation between X and Y will vanish with A constant; in the analysis of covariance, we investigate the possibility that the relation between Y and A will vanish with X constant. In elaboration, we compute the *partial relation* (defined below) between X and Y for each level of A, as well as the *marginal relations* (defined below) between X and A and Y and A. When the partial relations vanish, we ascribe to A what was originally ascribed to X; when the marginal relations tend to zero, we retain our initial conclusion about the relationship between Y and X. In the analysis of covariance, we get the sum of the products within groups and the sum of the products between groups, which correspond to the partial relations and the marginal relations of elaboration, respectively. When the sum of products between groups is small relative to the sum of products within groups, we ascribe to X what we had originally ascribed to A; otherwise we retain our original conclusion in respect to the effect of A.

When both X and Y are restricted to values of 0 or 1, and A is a dichotomy, the arithmetic of elaboration, as given by Lazarsfeld, is equivalent to the arithmetic of covariance analysis; thus, conclusions about the relative influence of X and A on Y must be identical. To verify this, we set up the arithmetic of elaboration and translate it into the arithmetic of covariance analysis. From these results, together with numerical examples, we conclude that the dependence of Y on X is proportional to the weighted correlation within groups, and its dependence on A is proportional to the weighted correlation between groups, in agreement with previous results.

As a statistical procedure, elaboration entails the decomposition of the total relationship between X and Y, as represented by the crossproduct, into component parts which reflect the relationship between X and Y with A constant; and the relationships, respectively, between X and A, and Y and A—the so-called *marginal relations*. To substantiate that the arithmetic of this decomposition, as given by Lazarsfeld (1958: 119), is equivalent to the arithmetic of the analysis of covariance, consider a 2×2 table of proportions, each based on the total frequency n.

	X	$\bar{X}$	
Y	p_{xy}	$p_{\bar{x}y}$	p_y
$\bar{Y}$	$p_{x\bar{y}}$	$p_{\bar{x}\bar{y}}$	$p_{\bar{y}}$
	p_x	$p_{\bar{x}}$	1.00

where $p_{xy} = n_{xy}/n$, $p_y = n_y/n$, etc. Note especially that in this treatment $\bar{X}$ and $\bar{Y}$ represent values in dichotomies and not arithmetic means. Following Lazarsfeld (1958), the crossproduct for this table is by definition:

(5.3.1) $$[xy] = p_{xy}p_{\bar{x}\bar{y}} - p_{\bar{x}y}p_{x\bar{y}}.$$

Rewriting proportions on the right side in terms of frequencies and multiplying both sides by n, we get

$$n[xy] = n_{xy} - \frac{n_x n_y}{n},$$

which result will be the link between elaboration and the analysis of covariance.

If we treat X and Y as point variables, taking arbitrary values of 1 or 0, we may get their product sum by formula:

$$\sum xy = \sum XY - \frac{\sum X \sum Y}{n},$$

where $X = Y = 1$, and $\bar{X} = \bar{Y} = 0$. But,

$$\sum X = n_x(1) + n_{\bar{x}}(0)$$
$$= n_x,$$

$$\sum Y = n_y(1) + n_{\bar{y}}(0)$$
$$= n_y,$$

and

$$\sum XY = n_{xy}(1)(1) + n_{\bar{x}y}(0)(1) + n_{x\bar{y}}(1)(0) + n_{\bar{x}\bar{y}}(0)(0)$$
$$= n_{xy}.$$

Hence,

(5.3.2)
$$\sum xy = n_{xy} - \frac{n_x n_y}{n}$$
$$= n[xy],$$

and

$$[xy] = \frac{1}{n} \sum xy,$$

which serves to demonstrate that the crossproduct for a 2×2 table is proportional to the product sum for the same table, with $1/n$ as the constant of proportionality.

Given two partial tabulations whose frequencies sum to total frequencies (as in the example below), it is possible, as Lazarsfeld (1958: 119) has shown, to write the total crossproduct in expanded form as follows:

(5.3.3)
$$[xy] = p_a[xy.a] + p_{\bar{a}}[xy.\bar{a}] + \frac{[xa][ay]}{p_a p_{\bar{a}}},$$

where $[xy.a]$ is the crossproduct for all a's, and $[xy.\bar{a}]$ is the crossproduct for all $\bar{a}$'s. To convert this crossproduct to its corresponding product sum, we multiply both sides by n and obtain after simplification,

(5.3.4)
$$n[xy] = n_a[xy.a] + n_{\bar{a}}[xy.\bar{a}] + \frac{n^3[xa][ay]}{n_a n_{\bar{a}}},$$

where $[xa] = p_{xa}p_{\bar{x}\bar{a}} - p_{\bar{x}a}p_{x\bar{a}}$, and $[ya] = p_{ya}p_{\bar{y}\bar{a}} - p_{\bar{y}a}p_{y\bar{a}}$.

From the foregoing rule that product sum for a 2×2 table is equal to the crossproduct multiplied by the frequency for that table, we have for the partial tables,

$$\sum xy.a = n_a[xy.a],$$
$$\sum xy.\bar{a} = n_{\bar{a}}[xy.\bar{a}].$$

But,

$$C_{xyw_a} = \sum xy.a,$$

and

$$C_{xyw\bar{a}} = \sum xy.\bar{a}.$$

Hence,

$$(5.3.5) \qquad C_{xyw} = n_a[xy.a] + n_{\bar{a}}[xy.\bar{a}].$$

Our conclusion is that the product sum within classes is equal to the sum of the weighted partial crossproducts. Subtracting the product sum within classes from the total product sum, we get the product sum between classes:

$$\begin{aligned} C_{xyb} &= n[xy] - n_a[xy.a] - n_{\bar{a}}[xy.\bar{a}] \\ &= \frac{n[xa][ay]}{p_a p_{\bar{a}}} . \end{aligned}$$

In words: the sum of the products between classes is equal to the product of the marginal crossproducts [xa] and [ay], weighted by factor $n/p_a p_{\bar{a}}$. When C_{xyw} is negligible relative to C_{xyb}, we assign relatively more importance to the marginal relations, as in M-type analysis (p. 225), and correspondingly more importance to A than to X; when C_{xyb} is negligible relative to C_{xyw}, we assign relatively more importance to the partial relations, as in P-type analysis, and correspondingly more importance to X than to A.

Because product sums may be mechanically transformed into cross-products, we may employ the analysis of covariance to get partial relations and marginal relations, as required in elaboration. To illustrate these operations, consider the joint distribution of X and Y for two groups, A and $\bar{A}$:

	A				$\bar{A}$		
	1	0			1	0	
1	25	5	30	1	15	5	20
0	5	15	20	0	5	25	30
	30	20	50		20	30	50

Combining tables, we get the joint distribution of X and Y for the total sample:

	1	0	
1	40	10	50
0	10	40	50
	50	50	100

Computing sums of squares and sums of products for combined groups, within and between groups, we obtain in succession:

$$C_{xxT} = \frac{(50)(50)}{100}$$
$$= 25.$$

$$C_{yyT} = \frac{(50)(50)}{100}$$
$$= 25.$$

$$C_{xyT} = 40 - \frac{(50)(50)}{100}$$
$$= 15.$$

$$C_{xxw} = \frac{(30)(20)}{50} + \frac{(20)(30)}{50}$$
$$= 24.$$

$$C_{yyw} = \frac{(30)(20)}{50} + \frac{(20)(30)}{50}$$
$$= 24.$$

$$C_{xyw} = \left[25 - \frac{(30)(30)}{50}\right] + \left[15 - \frac{(20)(20)}{50}\right]$$
$$= 14.$$

$$C_{xxb} = 25 - 24 = 1.$$

$$C_{yyb} = 25 - 24 = 1.$$

$$C_{xyb} = 15 - 14 = 1.$$

To assess the effect of A on Y, disregarding X, we compute the correlation ratio,

$$\eta^2_{ya} = \tfrac{1}{25}$$
$$= .04.$$

For the effect of A on Y after correction for regression, we get the partial correlation ratio

$$\eta^2_{ya.x} = \frac{\left[25 - \frac{(15)^2}{25}\right] - \left[24 - \frac{(14)^2}{24}\right]}{\left[25 - \frac{(15)^2}{25}\right]}$$
$$= \frac{16 - 15.833}{16}$$
$$= .01.$$

To assess the effect of X on Y disregarding A, we calculate

$$r_T = \sqrt{\frac{(15)^2}{(25)(25)}}$$
$$= \sqrt{.36}$$
$$= .60.$$

For an assessment of the effect of X on Y with A constant, we get

$$r_w = \sqrt{\frac{(14)^2}{(24)(24)}}$$
$$= \sqrt{.34}$$
$$= .58.$$

We note in passing that r_b is necessarily 1.00, when $k = 2$, since there can be no deviations from a line fitted to only two points.

From these results, assembled here for ready reference, we conclude that the

Source	C_{xx}	C_{yy}	C_{xy}	r	$C_{y.x}$
Total	25	25	15	.60	16.00
Within	24	24	14	.58	15.83
A	12	12	7		
$\overline{A}$	12	12	7		
Between	1	1	1		.17

difference between groups on Y is attributable to X rather than to A. Before correction, A accounts for 4 percent of the variance in Y; after correction it accounts for only 1 percent of the variance. This reduction in the explained variance may be clarified by comparing group means before and after correction by $b_w = 14/24 = .58$ as follows:

Group	$\overline{X}_i$	$\overline{X}_i - \overline{X}.$	$b_w(\overline{X}_i - \overline{X}.)$	$\overline{Y}_i$	$\overline{Y}_i - b_w(\overline{X}_i - \overline{X}.)$
A	.60	.10	.058	.60	.542
$\overline{A}$	.40	−.10	−.058	.40	.458

The difference between group means before adjustment is $.60 - .40 = .20$; the difference after adjustment is $.542 - .458 = .084$.

The foregoing conclusion is consistent with the stability of the correlation between X and Y when A is introduced as a control: the total correlation between X and Y is .60; controlling for A, the correlation is .58. Since the dependence of Y on X as reflected by r_T is not affected by A, we ascribe the original difference between groups to the covariable, X.

To render an elaboration of the relationship between X and Y, we divide both sides of $C_{xyT} = C_{xyw} + C_{xyb}$ by $n = 100$ to get the crossproduct for combined groups on the left side, the sum of the weighted partial crossproducts and the weighted product of the marginal crossproducts on the right side. Substituting results from p. 222, we calculate

$$[xy] = \tfrac{15}{100}$$
$$= .15,$$

$$p_a[xy.a] = \tfrac{7}{100}$$
$$= .07,$$

$$p_{\bar{a}}[xy.\bar{a}] = \tfrac{7}{100}$$
$$= .07,$$

and

$$\frac{[xa][ya]}{p_a p_{\bar{a}}} = \frac{1}{100}$$
$$= .01.$$

To calculate partial crossproducts, if required, we divide the product sum for each group by its own frequency.

$$[xy.a] = \tfrac{7}{50}$$
$$= .14,$$

and

$$[xy.\bar{a}] = \tfrac{7}{50}$$
$$= .14.$$

To get marginal crossproducts, it is helpful to set up 2×2 tables for both X and A, and Y and A as follows:

	A	$\bar{A}$	
Y	30	20	50
$\bar{Y}$	20	30	50
	50	50	100

	A	$\bar{A}$	
X	30	20	50
$\bar{X}$	20	30	50
	50	50	100

Solving for marginal relations, we get

$$[xa] = (.3)(.3) - (.2)(.2)$$
$$= .09 - .04$$
$$= .05,$$

and

$$[ya] = (.3)(.3) - (.2)(.2)$$
$$= .09 - .04$$
$$= .05.$$

Substituting these results in (5.3.3), we obtain

$$\frac{[xa][ya]}{p_a p_{\bar{a}}} = \frac{(.05)(.05)}{(.50)(.50)}$$
$$= \frac{.0025}{.2500}$$
$$= .01,$$

which serves as a check. Assembling results, we have

$$[xy] = .15,$$
$$[xa] = .05,$$
$$[ya] = .05,$$
$$[xy.a] = .14,$$
$$[xy.\bar{a}] = .14,$$
$$p_a[xy.a] = .07,$$
$$p_{\bar{a}}[xy.\bar{a}] = .07,$$
$$\frac{[xa][ya]}{p_a p_{\bar{a}}} = .01,$$

and

$$[xy] = .07 + .07 + .01$$
$$= .14 + .01.$$

Our interpretation of these numerical results, as dictated by the goals of elaboration, would run something like this: the relationship between X and Y is not explained by the test factor (A), since that relationship maintains itself with A held constant. Under these circumstances, we may ignore A, since it "causes" the partial relations neither to vanish nor to differ in direction or in magnitude. If the partials had been large and different, i.e., if there had been a significant interaction of $[xy]$ on A, we would have been required to specify the conditions under which a given partial relation occurs, as in P-type analysis. For reference purposes and to distinguish P-type from M-type analysis, we classify the outcomes to which the process of elaboration may give rise and supply an example. For a detailed account consult Hyman (1955).

Elaboration by Partial Relations and Antecedent Variable

Antecedent Variable	P-Type $\sum[xy.a_i] \lessgtr [xy]$	M-Type $\sum[xy.a_i] \rightarrow 0$
A	Specification	Explanation
X	Prediction	Interpretation

Let us suppose that we are interested in the dependence of academic achievement (*AA*) on educational aspiration (*EA*) with and without intelligence (*IQ*) under control. In this problem, intelligence is our test factor. To simplify matters, we assume that persons are scored high (1) or low (0) on all three variables. At the start, we find a positive correlation between *AA* and *EA*, suggesting that one's achievement may be affected by one's aspiration. Before introducing *IQ* as a control, we note two possible outcomes: (1) the relationship between *AA* and *EA* may vanish at both levels of intelligence, and (2) the relationship may become stronger at one level, weaker at the other. First, let us suppose that both partial relations vanish. In this case, we may hypothesize either that the effect of *EA* on *AA* is transmitted through *IQ* which has little or none itself, or that *IQ* has an effect on both *AA* and *EA* which causes them to be spuriously correlated. In either event, if we remove the effect of *IQ*, however regarded, the correlation between *AA* and *EA* tends to zero. If aspiration and achievement are affected equally by *IQ* but are otherwise independent, we state that the test factor (*IQ*) *explains* the relationship between *EA* and *AA*; if *IQ* does no more than transmit the effect of aspiration, we state that the test factor *interprets* the relationship between *AA* and *EA*. Explanation and interpretation fall under the heading of M-type analysis.

Second, let us suppose that the partial relations between *AA* and *EA* differ by level of intelligence, and that both are significantly different from zero. In particular, let us suppose that the correlation between achievement and aspiration is stronger for persons of high intelligence, weaker for persons of low intelligence. In the former case, we may surmise that *IQ* has a negative effect on aspiration and that its statistical removal causes the correlation between aspiration and achievement to become stronger. In the latter case, we surmise that *IQ* has a positive effect on *EA* and that its statistical removal causes the correlation between *AA* and *EA* to become weaker. Our conclusion is that bright persons would have higher aspirations if they were less bright, dull persons would have weaker aspirations if they were less dull. Since such tendencies could occur with intelligence antecedent in time to aspiration or the reverse, as a final step we must settle on the temporal sequence of these variables. If *IQ* is antecedent, we *specify* the conditions that must prevail if *EA* is to have a given effect on *AA*. For example, the effect of *EA* on *AA* will be relatively strong, given persons of high intelligence; the effect of *EA* on *AA* will be relatively weak, given persons of low intelligence. If aspiration precedes intelligence, we give the intervening condition that must materialize if a specific *prediction* is to hold. For example, the prediction of high achievement from high aspiration will be more accurate for persons of high intelligence than for persons of low intelligence. The terminology of elaboration thus directs our attention to some of the ways in which the test factor (*A*) may affect the relationship between the dependent variable (*Y*) and the independent variable (*X*). It also introduces us to the difficulties in drawing causal inferences from nonexperimental data.

Ecological Relationships. It is common practice in social research to arrange the population of a specified territory into *k* districts in order to discern the differences among them in their social and economic characteristics. These *k* districts may be subdivided into *mk* smaller districts or combined into *k/m* larger districts, if we wish to examine the differences among larger or smaller groupings. Thus, we may find it necessary to combine states into regions, or, reversing ourselves, to divide states into counties. Similarly, we may divide the inhabitants of a city into either relatively broad census tracts or relatively small neighborhoods, according to the purposes of our research. In analyzing geographical relationships, it is well to bear in mind that group averages and correlations based on them are affected by our grouping procedure. If this principle is forgotten, we may credit our findings with a "universality" which may be nullified by either combining groups into larger amalgamations or subdividing them into smaller segments.

When the elements in a one-way analysis of covariance are persons and the primary classification is composed of areal units, the total correlation will be the individual correlation, and the correlation for subgroup means will be the ecological correlation. Hence, the relationship between the ecological and the individual correlation may be studied within the framework of the analysis of covariance. This point is mentioned by Robinson (1950) in his well-known article on the ecological fallacy, and noted by Duncan, Cuzzort, and Duncan (1961: 64–67) in their discussion of the relationship between the respective characteristics of subpopulations by areas and the corresponding characteristics of the total population for all areas combined. In studying the relationship between the individual and the ecological correlation, it may be desirable to examine the correlations within districts, since that relationship is a function of these correlations. And since correlations within districts are routinely obtained in the analysis of covariance, this method has the advantage of providing information which might otherwise remain concealed. Moreover, correlations within districts, particularly when they differ in direction or magnitude, or both, may be sociologically more interesting than the total correlation which may be unamenable to interpretation because of its composite make-up.

To illustrate the correspondence between ecological correlation and the correlations for group means, and the correspondence between individual and total correlations, and to exemplify the prominence which the analysis of covariance gives to correlations within districts, we have recourse to hypothetical figures on color and education for each of nine census districts and for the United States as a whole. The actual figures for 1960 have been deliberately distorted in order to sharpen differences among districts and thereby to display more advantageously the utility of covariance analysis in ecological research.

Table 5.3.1 *Years of Schooling by Color and District*

District		Years of Schooling *(frequencies in tens of thousands)*		
		9+	*0–8*	*Total*
United States	White	5589	3351	8940
	Nonwhite	378	584	962
	Total	5967	3935	9902
New England	White	380	215	595
	Nonwhite	12	1	13
	Total	392	216	608
Middle Atlantic	White	1072	805	1877
	Nonwhite	155	1	156
	Total	1227	806	2033
South Atlantic	White	754	354	1108
	Nonwhite	1	269	270
	Total	755	623	1378
East South Central	White	282	221	503
	Nonwhite	12	111	123
	Total	294	332	626
East North Central	White	1162	701	1863
	Nonwhite	76	74	150
	Total	1238	775	2013

(continued on page 228)

West North Central	White	474	351	825
	Nonwhite	31	1	32
	Total	505	352	857
West South Central	White	457	303	760
	Nonwhite	42	91	133
	Total	499	394	893
Mountain	White	235	101	336
	Nonwhite	6	8	14
	Total	241	109	350
Pacific	White	773	300	1073
	Nonwhite	43	28	71
	Total	816	328	1144

From Table 5.3.1, we calculate the correlation between color and years of schooling for the entire population; the correlation between color and education for each of the nine districts; and the correlation between district means (proportions). These correlations, together with the sums of squares and sums of products on which they are based, are assembled in Table 5.3.2.

Table 5.3.2 *Sums of Squares and Products, Correlation Coefficients, and Slopes*

Source	C_{xx}	C_{yy}	C_{xy}	r	b	$C_{y.x}$
Total	2371.3	868.5	201.7	.14	.08	851.34
NE	139.3	12.7	− 3.6	−.09	−.03	
MA	486.5	144.0	−60.8	−.23	−.12	
SA	341.3	217.1	146.9	.54	.43	
ESC	155.9	98.8	45.8	.37	.29	
ENC	476.6	138.8	16.3	.06	.03	
WNC	207.4	30.8	−12.1	−.15	−.06	
WSC	220.2	113.2	32.3	.20	.15	
Mt.	75.1	13.4	3.6	.11	.05	
Pac.	234.0	66.6	7.6	.06	.03	
Within	2336.3	835.4	176.0	.13	.08	822.14
Between	35.0	33.1	25.7	.76	.73	29.20

$$\eta^2_{ya} = .04 \qquad \eta^2_{ya.x} = .03$$

In analyzing these results, we note that correlations within districts differ among themselves, ranging in numerical value from $-.23$ to $.54$; the positive correlation between color and years of schooling is relatively large in the southern districts, and relatively small in the northern districts, becoming negative in three districts. Given such differences among correlations within districts, the total correlation for all districts could be misleading, since it masks the effect of region on the correlation between color and education within districts. By the same token, a preoccupation with the ecological correlation as a basis for estimating the total correlation may be misguided, unless the total correlation is specifically required. From the ecological correlation of $.76$, we could undertake to estimate by Goodman's (1959) method the magnitude of the total correlation, but that estimate would not disclose the interesting differences among districts. Although the concern in sociology with the drawing of false inferences from ecological correlations is justified, that concern may lead in specific instances to the neglect of the correlations within areas; for this reason, ecological and individual correlations should, whenever possible, be studied within the framework of covariance analysis. Furthermore, the analysis of covariance permits areal effects to be assessed, after controlling for the influence of the independent covariable. In the foregoing problem, the correlation ratio between education and area after correction for color is $.03$.

The comparison of regression coefficients, or slopes, is also facilitated by the covariance model, and the importance of such comparisons provides another compelling reason for studying ecological correlations within the framework of covariance analysis. Regression coefficients are less subject to the effect of arbitrary grouping, and for that reason are probably preferred to correlations in testing theory. This point, which has been cogently made by Blalock (1964: 97–114), applies with equal force to all manipulations of aggregated data by correlational and regression methods.

Contextual, Structural, and Compositional Analysis. Generally speaking, contextual analysis (Sills 1961: 572) answers to the question of whether the effect of an individual trait is contingent on the specific context in which a person finds himself. "Does a kind person act more kindly in the company of kind men and women?" Turning the question around, we ask whether the context has an effect on one's behavior after the effect of one's predisposition to act in a specific way has been taken into account. Thus phrased, the problem of contextual analysis is similar to the general problem of AOCOV and in consequence lends itself to resolution by that method.

To illustrate this possibility, we apply the AOCOV to contrived data on factors in college planning, taking plans for attending college as the dependent variable (Y), with values of 1 (yes) and 0 (no); student's own family income as the covariable (X); and proportion in student body from well-to-do families as the factor of classification (A). Each student may thus be characterized in three ways: (1) by his plans for attending college (yes or no), (2) by his family's income, and (3) by the proportion of students from well-to-do families in his school. For example, a given individual may plan to attend college, come from a poor family, and attend a school where the majority come from poor homes. Our general question is whether an individual's plans for college are dependent on the make-up of his student body, as well as on his own economic background. Put as a homely question: are poor boys and girls more likely to plan for college in the company of boys and girls from more favorable economic circumstances?

We begin our analysis with all students ($N = 37,000$) crossclassified by family income and college plans:

	Income Level of Student's Family (frequencies in hundreds)		
Plan to Attend College	High	Low	
Yes	43	66	109
No	34	227	261
	77	293	370

Here, we ignore the possibility that the effect of family income on college income may be attenuated by treating it as a dichotomy instead of permitting it to vary continuously on its range. For the limitations of the dichotomy as a control variable, see Cochran (1968).

Inspecting this tabulation, we discern a moderate association between family income and college planning ($r = .33$). From this finding, we might conclude that family income affects college plans. Next, as required by our design, we divide the total sample into five subgroups, each composed of students from schools relatively similar in their economic make-up. These results are given in Table 5.3.3. The first subgroup includes all students ($N_1 = 11,000$) from schools where the proportion of students from well-to-do families is less than .10; the second subgroup includes students ($N_2 = 10,000$) from schools where the proportion is between .10 and .20, etc. We wish to assess the importance of group context (as defined) relative to that of individual economic background (as defined).

For a preliminary assessment of the effect of context, we consolidate the subtables of Table 5.3.3 into a single table, giving the proportion of students planning to attend college by family income and by proportion of student body from well-to-do families:

		Proportion High Income in School				
Income Level of Student's Family		.00–.09	.10–.19	.20–.29	.30–.39	.40–.49
	High	.30	.40	.50	.67	.86
	Low	.10	.18	.33	.41	.50

Table 5.3.3 College Plans by Family Income and
Proportion High Income in School

Proportion High Income in School	Plan to Attend College	Family Income		
.00–.09		High	Low	Total
	Yes	3	10	13
	No	7	90	97
	Total	10	100	110
.10–.19	Yes	6	15	21
	No	9	70	79
	Total	15	85	100
.20–.29	Yes	10	20	30
	No	10	40	50
	Total	20	60	80
.30–.39	Yes	12	13	25
	No	6	19	25
	Total	18	32	50
.40–.49	Yes	12	8	20
	No	2	8	10
	Total	14	16	30

There are marked differences from one group (context) to another within
income classes, and we would probably conclude there is a contextual effect.

To weigh the relative importance of this effect, we have recourse to the
AOCOV, taking the partial correlation ratio as a measure of context after
correction for individual inputs, and the composite correlation within groups
as a reflection of the influence of the individual effect with context under
control. The results of this analysis are given in Table 5.3.4.

In interpreting these results, we may focus on either the correlation
between X and Y within subgroups, or the correlation between Y and A
after correction for regression. The coefficient of determination (r^2) for
X and Y disregarding A is .088; controlling for A, this coefficient drops to
.045. Of the approximately 9 percent of the variance in Y explained by X,
we must ascribe approximately one-half to A. This result is evidence in favor
of a contextual effect. Shifting to the relationship between Y and A, we find
a correlation ratio of .14; controlling for X, this ratio drops to .10. Our

Table 5.3.4 *Sums of Squares and Products,*
Correlation Coefficients, and Slopes

Source	C_{xx}	C_{yy}	C_{xy}	r	b_{yx}	$C_{y.x}$
Total	60.976	76.889	20.316	.297	.333	70.120
.00–.09	9.091	11.464	1.818	.178	.200	
.10–.19	12.750	16.590	2.850	.196	.224	
.20–.29	15.000	18.750	2.500	.149	.167	
.30–.39	11.520	12.500	3.000	.250	.260	
.40–.49	7.467	6.667	2.667	.378	.357	
Within	55.828	65.970	12.835	.211	.230	63.020
Between	5.148	10.919	7.481	.998	1.453	7.100

$$\eta_{ya}^2 = .142 \qquad\qquad \eta_{ya.x}^2 = .101$$

conclusion is that of the 14 percent of the variance in Y attributable to A, roughly 30 percent of that part must be credited to the covariable, X. Our final judgment, taking into account both sets of results, is in favor of a contextual effect. The correlation (r^2) between X and Y is reduced by roughly 50 percent with A under control and the correlation ratio between Y and A maintains itself at 70 percent of its initial level with X under control. Both findings point to the existence of a contextual effect.

Blau's "Structural Effects." A common question in sociological research is whether a person's behavior is affected not only by his own attitude but also by the prevalence of that attitude in his group. In his study of structural effects, Blau (1960) put that question in this way: "In dealing with clients, are social workers affected by the value pattern of their work group, as well as by their own values?" To answer that question, Blau compared workers in groups whose members were mostly service-oriented with workers in groups whose members were mostly rule-oriented. His comparison thus called for three pieces of information on each social worker: his method of dealing with clients, his own orientation toward clients, and the prevalence of that orientation in his work group. The general notion was that an individual's practice would be affected by the value pattern of the work group, as well as by individual values. Since the analysis of covariance was devised to answer the question of whether subgroup differences would persist after correcting for the dependence of Y on X, it is natural to consider its applicability to Blau's data.

   In this analysis, we first set up the total relationship between worker's method of dealing with clients (Y) and worker's own orientation toward clients (X) as follows:

	Worker Orientation (X)		
	Service	Rule	
Worker Method (Y) Service	16	10	26
Rule	13	21	34
	29	31	60

Next, we partition this table into partial tables, according to whether a person's co-workers are mostly service-oriented or mostly rule-oriented:

	Group Orientation					
	Service			Rule		
Method	Worker Orientation			Worker Orientation		
	S	R		S	R	
Service	12	4	16	4	6	10
Rule	8	5	13	5	16	21
	20	9	29	9	22	31

As our next step, we express cell numbers in the first row of each partial table as proportions of corresponding column totals and arrange these results in a single table:

Worker Orientation	Group Orientation	
	S	R
Service	.60	.44
Rule	.44	.27

From this table it is possible to judge whether subclasses differ for social workers having the same attitude. For example, the difference between entries in the first row (.60 − .44 = .16) may be taken as evidence of a group effect free of individual effects; likewise, the difference between entries in the second row (.44 − .27 = .17) may be taken as evidence of group effects. A loose and perhaps jocular interpretation of this table might run something like this: social workers are more likely to practice what they preach when surrounded by workers who preach the same thing.

Lastly, treating X and Y as point variables, we partition the total sum of squares and the total sum of products and eventually get an adjusted sum of squares based on the difference between subgroups in worker method (Y) after correction for the effect of worker orientation (X). That result could provide some basis for judging the relative importance of individual and structural effects.

Running the analysis, we obtain results as follows:

Source	Sum of Squares		Sum of Products	r^2	Unexplained Sum of Squares
Total	15.0	14.7	3.4	.05	14.0
Within	12.6	13.9	2.1	.03	13.5
Service	6.2	7.1	1.0		
Rule	6.4	6.8	1.1		
Between	2.4	.8	1.4		.5

$$\eta_{ya}^2 = .8/14.7 \qquad \eta_{ya.x}^2 = .5/14.0$$
$$= .05 \qquad\qquad = .04$$

In making an interpretation of these results, we would note that worker orientation (X) accounts for only a negligible proportion (.05) of the variation in worker procedure (Y) for all cases in the sample, and a somewhat smaller proportion (.03) of that variation for cases within subgroups. Similarly, group orientation (A) explains only five percent of the variation in worker method (Y) for all cases, and an even smaller percentage for persons having the same attitude toward clients. Our general conclusion would be that a worker's method of handling cases is affected by his own attitudes and by the attitudes of his co-workers but not to an appreciable extent.

One might take exception to the application of covariance analysis to data such as these. However, it was applied here more as a technique for describing the strength of individual and structural effects, rather than for making statistical estimates of parameters. In the foregoing demonstration no significance tests were run, and the interpretation was based solely on descriptive measures of correlation. If both X and Y had been interval scales, and if the assumptions of normality and homogeneity had been met, tests of significance for both statistical interaction and differences among intercepts might have been run. Such testing is required to meet the objection posed by Tannenbaum and Bachman (1964) that the presence of structural effects in sample data does not prove their presence in the population, and that sample data should therefore be examined for statistical significance.

The applicability of AOCOV to arbitrarily scaled data aside, one might argue that a structural effect is only indirectly reflected by a correlation coefficient and would be more directly measured by the difference between subgroup proportions for a given value of the covariable (X). In line with this argument, we would take the difference between subgroup proportions for workers having the same work orientation as a measure of the effect of social structure on worker method, unconfounded by the effect of individual attitudes. Thus, in our problem, we would take $.44 - .27 = .17$ and $.60 - .44 = .16$ as measures of structural effects. Since these results may be construed as differences between arithmetic means, they perhaps lend themselves more readily to interpretation than does the more complex correlation coefficient.

Davis' "Compositional Effects." Davis and his associates (1961), like Blau, have been concerned with disentangling individual and group effects in the social behavior of persons. In their writing, they acknowledge the potential utility of the analysis of covariance in assessing compositional effects, but they supply no numerical examples. To exemplify its possible utility, we apply it to Davis' data on 1,730 members of 172 Great Books discussion clubs. In that study Davis (1961) sought to determine whether a member's tendency to remain in his club—the dependent variable (Y)—was affected by both the rate of his own participation at club meetings—the covariable (X)—and the average rate of participation for his club—the factor of classification (A). Informally expressed: are droppers more likely to drop out of inactive clubs, less likely to drop out of active clubs? To compare the importance of club participation and individual participation on dropping out, Davis arranged the 1,730 persons in his sample into seven subgroups by magnitude of club participation score. The first subgroup consisted of persons whose club scores ranged from .20 to .29, etc. Within each of these seven subgroups, droppers and stayers were subclassified as actives or inactives, as in Table 5.3.5.

To evaluate the relative importance of club activity on individual dropping out, Davis computed the proportion of droppers within subgroups at level of individual activity, as follows:

Club Level of Activity

Individual Level	0–.19	.20–.29	.30–.39	.40–.49	.50–.59	.60–.69	.70–1.00
Active	.34	.32	.30	.29	.19	.18	.22
Inactive	.53	.45	.40	.41	.31	.37	.32

The differences among column proportions within rows may be taken as evidence of club effect, free of individual tendency to participate. In clubs where 70 percent or more of the members are active, only one in five of the actives drops out; in clubs where fewer than 30 percent are active, one in three actives drops out. The finding for inactives is similar in its essentials:

Table 5.3.5 *Droppers and Stayers by Individual
Level of Participation and Club Level of Activity*

Club Level		Active	Inactive	Total
.00– .19	Drop	16	241	257
	Stay	31	214	245
	Total	47	455	502
.20– .29	Drop	14	56	70
	Stay	30	69	99
	Total	44	125	169
.30– .39	Drop	31	72	103
	Stay	74	108	182
	Total	105	180	285
.40– .49	Drop	31	56	87
	Stay	77	80	157
	Total	108	136	244
.50– .59	Drop	25	35	60
	Stay	108	78	186
	Total	133	113	246
.60– .69	Drop	18	21	39
	Stay	82	36	118
	Total	100	57	157
.70–1.00	Drop	22	8	30
	Stay	80	17	97
	Total	102	25	127

in clubs where 70 percent or more are active, one in three of the inactive members drops out; in clubs where fewer than 30 percent are active, roughly four in seven of the inactives drop out.

Such comparisons may suffice to indicate the presence of a compositional effect. However, if a single index is required, we may have recourse to the analysis of covariance which supplies a single measure of group effect corrected for the effect of individual differences on the covariable. Carrying out the necessary calculations, we get results as follows:

	C_{xx}	C_{yy}	C_{xy}	r^2	$C_{y.x}$
Total	403.0	404.8	81.6	.04	388.3
Within	319.1	385.8	43.1	.02	380.0
Between	83.9	19.0	38.5		8.3

$$\eta_{ya}^2 = 19.0/404.8 \qquad \eta_{ya.x}^2 = 8.3/388.3$$
$$= .05 \qquad\qquad = .02$$

In interpreting these results, we note that subgroup means (club levels) account for only a negligible proportion of the total variation in dropping out or staying ($\eta_{ya}^2 = .05$), and for an even smaller proportion after correction for regression on individual participation ($\eta_{ya.x}^2 = .02$); we also note that level of individual participation accounts for only a small proportion of the variation in dropping out for all subgroups combined ($r_{xy}^2 = .04$), and that within subgroups the proportion is even smaller ($r_{xy.a}^2 = .02$). On the basis of these results, we would probably conclude that level of group participation does not affect the tendency to drop out to any considerable degree, since the effect of that factor is relatively small after the effect of individual activity has been neutralized. As in the case of Blau's data, one might question the applicability of algebraic methods to data that are at best ordinal. To such questioning there is no single answer, except that "it all depends." If the purpose of such an application is merely to obtain a rough indicator of group effect, the application may be justified, even though that index cannot be tested for significance. Furthermore, we may always consider the merits of alternative methods for analyzing compositional effects. It may be appropriate to test the significance of differences among percentages by the χ^2 method (Costner and Wager 1965; Goodman 1965). Or in some circumstances we may find it appropriate to transform proportions to arcsins and to run an analysis of variance on the transformed values. In the latter case, we would take the covariable (X) and the factor of classification (A) as main factors and test them separately and in interaction for significance.

For some purposes, a regression model may do better than the covariance model for representing compositional effects, even though they are alike in their essentials. This possibility is considered in a recent paper by Werts and Linn (1969) as follows: Characterize each case by the covariable X_{ij} and the mean value of the covariable for its group $\overline{X}_i$. Now set up regression equation,

(5.3.6) $$Y_{ij} = b_1 X_{ij} + b_2 \overline{X}_i + e_{ij}.$$

Subtract $b_1X_{ij} + b_2\overline{X}_i$ from both sides, and find b_1 and b_2 by the method of least squares. This gives:

$$b_1 = C_{yxw}/C_{xxw},$$
$$b_2 = (C_{yxb}/C_{xxb}) - b_1$$
$$= b_3 - b_1$$

where $b_3 = C_{yxb}/C_{xxb}$. When $b_3 - b_1 = 0$, Eq. (5.3.6) reduces to

$$Y_{ij} = b_1X_{ij} + e_{ij},$$

signifying that $\overline{X}_i$ has no effect on Y_{ij}.

In covariance analysis, our model is

(5.3.7) $$Y_{ij} = A_i + b_1X_{ij} + e_{ij},$$

where

$$A_i = \overline{Y}_i - b_w\overline{X}_i.$$

Substituting the right side of (5.3.7) for the left side of (5.3.6), we get

$$A_i + b_1X_{ij} + e_{ij} = b_1X_{ij} + b_2\overline{X}_i + e_{ij}.$$

Subtracting $b_1X_{ij} + e_{ij}$ from both sides, we obtain

$$b_2\overline{X}_i = A_i$$
$$= \overline{Y}_i - b_1\overline{X}_i.$$

When $b_2 = 0$, $\overline{Y}_i = b_1\overline{X}_i$, which finding is against the existence of a compositional effect; when $b_2 \neq 0$, $\overline{Y}_i \neq b_1\overline{X}$, which finding is for the existence of a compositional effect.

PART 4

Covariance Analysis of Trends and Areas

Time and place correlations (or slopes) bearing on the same research issue are not always consistent in direction or magnitude; the consequence is that the research question is either left open or settled by debate. For example, correlations based on trends in crime and economic conditions generally admit to greater equivocation than those based on areal distributions of crime and economic conditions (Vold 1958). Criminologists who favor an economic interpretation of crime are prone to give greater weight to the geographic correlations, whereas the opponents of a strict economic interpretation are likely to give greater emphasis to the time studies. Since neither set of findings can be disregarded, it is essential to establish the link between them by appropriate methods of data analysis. In establishing that link, the analysis of covariance may be of some utility.

To be more concrete: in Seattle the number of major property crimes rose from 23 per thousand population in 1940 to 33 per thousand in 1960 (Uniform Crime Reports, 1940–60). During the same period, there was an improvement in economic conditions for the population as gauged by conventional economic indicators, and presumably the standard of living rose to a higher level. From such trend data, one might conclude that the incidence of crime varies directly as the standard of living, or at least that a rising standard of living does not depress the crime rate. But that conclusion is contradicted by Schmid's finding (1960) that crime is most prevalent in the poorest districts of Seattle. The Pearsonian product-moment correlations between median income and eleven property crimes for 93 census tracts in Seattle for the period 1949–51 were negative with one exception, and ranged in numerical value from .08 to .55. The correlations between property crime and such economic indicators as home ownership and employment were likewise generally negative. A similar pattern of findings holds for 1959–61 data (Schmid and Tagashira 1967). However, as noted above, this recurrent finding of a negative areal correlation between crime and economic conditions is inconsistent with the trend data which suggest a positive relationship.

Some clarification of this discrepancy might be achieved by the method of covariance, provided that the requisite data were available. At least the analysis of covariance might be used for heuristic purposes. In working out this discrepancy, we would draw a sample of n districts from each of k selected years for a total of nk districts. To run the analysis, a measure of the standard of living (X) and the incidence of crime (Y) for each of these nk districts would be required. The data would thus consist of as many pairs of values as districts per year, multiplied by the number (k) of sampled years. In processing these data, we would get the correlation (slope) between X and Y for all sampled years (r_T); the correlation between X and Y within each sampled year (r_{w_i}), and the composite value of those relations (r_w); and the correlation between the mean crime rate and the mean standard of living for the k sampled years (r_b).

Judging from the pattern of recent events in American cities, we would expect the scatter diagram of such data to display cross trends as in Figure 5.4.1. In that figure, trend lines for separate years slope downward, left to right, conforming to the inverse relation between crime and the standard of living within years. On the other hand, the trend line for sample (column) means has an upward slope, reflecting the tendency of the crime rate for the city to increase as the standard of living increases. From the

Figure 5.4.1 *Trend of Crime on Standard of Living Within and Between Years*

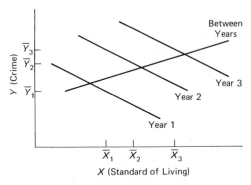

plotted lines, it is not possible to determine the magnitudes of respective correlation coefficients, r_T, r_b, and r_w; however, it is possible to order them on their range from -1 to $+1$, as follows: r_w, r_T, r_b. The graph shows that $r_w < 0$, and $r_b > 0$, but it does not give us the sign of r_T.

Upon extrapolating regression lines within years by sight, so that all have the same mean value on X, we find that the adjusted differences between means on Y are larger than the observed differences. We conclude that differences in the rate of crime between years cannot be laid to the regression of crime on the standard of living within years, for the aforesaid reason that differences are larger after correction for regression. Similarly, the relationship between crime and the standard of living within years (r_w) cannot be laid to the regression of crime on the standard of living between years, since that relationship maintains its strength after correction for the tendency of both crime and the standard of living to rise together over time. There is no tendency for X and Y to achieve statistical independence when time stands still.

To corroborate these points numerically, we apply the AOCOV to measures selected to yield results similar to those based on the scatter diagram. These measures are given in Table 5.4.1. They are taken to represent five

Table 5.4.1 *Crime (Y) and Income (X) by Year and District*

Year

District	0		10		20		30		40		Sum	
	X	Y	X	Y	X	Y	X	Y	X	Y	X	Y
1	2	7	1	9	2	10	4	11	4	15	13	52
2	1	3	2	6	2	9	2	10	3	12	10	40
3	0	16	3	15	4	16	3	19	3	20	13	86
4	4	0	4	5	4	7	7	10	7	10	26	32
5	3	4	2	6	3	8	4	12	5	13	17	43
Σ	10	30	12	41	15	50	20	62	22	70	79	253

samples of five measures each, with adjacent samples separated by ten-year intervals. The first X-Y column in Table 5.4.1 depicts the situation at the start of the time series; the second X-Y column depicts matters after ten years; the fifth X-Y column reflects the state of affairs at the end of the series.

In applying the analysis of covariance to these measures, we intend to determine whether differences among mean crime rates will maintain themselves, after we adjust these rates for the regression of crime on income within years. Although the graph (Figure 5.4.1) gives us an answer to this question, we carry out the calculations anyway in order to verify more precisely that (a) differences among mean (column) crime rates will increase after correction for regression, and (b) the correlation between crime and income for districts will increase when we control for the correlation between mean crime and mean income.

The sums of squares and products required to check these points are given in Table 5.4.2. To register the effect of differences among mean crime

Table 5.4.2　Sums of Squares and Products for Crime and Income.

Source	df	C_{xx}	C_{yy}	C_{xy}	$C_{y.x}$
Total	24	65.36	586.64	11.52	584.61
Within	20	44.40	382.00	−53.40	305.23
Between	4	20.96	204.64	64.92	279.38

rates on the total variation, we calculate the correlation ratio:

$$\eta^2_{ya} = \frac{204.64}{586.64}$$

$$= .35.$$

We interpret this to mean that 35 percent of the total variation in district crime rates may be ascribed to differences among mean rates.

To register the relative effect of differences among mean crime rates after correction for regression, we get the partial correlation ratio:

$$\eta^2_{ya.x} = \frac{279.38}{584.61}$$

$$= .48.$$

As anticipated, the "corrected" means explain more of the total variation (corrected for regression) than the observed means; $\eta^2_{y.ax} = .48$ is one-third larger than $\eta^2_{ya} = .35$. Evidently, differences among mean crime rates would have been larger if they had "obeyed" the law of regression as determined by the cross-sectional data.

To establish the degree of association between areal measures of crime and income, unsorted by years, we compute the total correlation:

$$r_T = \frac{11.52}{\sqrt{[(65.36)(586.64)]}}$$
$$= .06.$$

For an estimate of the degree of association between crime and income within years, we calculate the correlation within years:

$$r_w = \frac{-53.40}{\sqrt{[(44.40)(382.00)]}}$$
$$= -.41.$$

Comparing r_w with r_T, we conclude that the negative correlation between income and crime as observed within years is severely attenuated by the tendency for mean crime and mean income to increase together over time.

In making an interpretation of these results, one might be tempted to speculate along these lines: the stability of differences in crime by economic level in the face of increasing affluence of the general population may be attributed to the persistent imbalance between social means and ends and the personal deprivations to which such imbalance gives rise; whereas the upward trend in crime over time may be attributed to the changing pattern of social organization for and against crime, which a changing standard of living produces. In weighing the validity of that speculation, one would have to keep in mind the way in which the data were collected and aggregated, and the possibility that statistical results reflect specific procedures as well as social circumstance. In particular, one would have to bear in mind the limitations of an analysis which (1) takes subpopulations as elements and (2) employs different districts each year instead of the same districts year after year.

Subpopulations as Elements. We encounter at least two complications when subpopulations are taken as elements: (1) the ecological correlation for any given year is itself a function of the total correlation for individuals and the average correlation for individuals within subgroups; (2) the magnitude of our ecological correlations may be dependent on our grouping procedure.

We may solve the first problem by extending our analysis to individual measures, the manipulation of which would enable us to express our ecological correlation as the weighted difference between the total correlation and the average correlation within subgroups (p. 215). In doing this, we would require no new methods, but measures on individuals would have to be available.

In respect to grouping effects, we can do no more than echo the warning of Yule and Kendall (1950) to the effect that correlations will usually increase if we group measures into larger and larger categories. This problem may also be attacked within the framework of covariance analysis; it merely entails decomposing our original measures into a larger number of components, each corresponding to a given grouping, and analyzing the relative contribution of each component to the total sum of squares and the total sum of products. For example, after splitting each of m districts into quarters for a total of $4m$ subdistrict measures, we may express the deviation of each measure from the overall mean as the sum of three components as follows:

$$Y_{ijk} - \bar{Y} = (Y_{ijk} - \bar{Y}_{ij}) + (\bar{Y}_{ij} - \bar{Y}_i) + (\bar{Y}_i - \bar{Y}),$$

$$X_{ijk} - \bar{X} = (X_{ijk} - \bar{X}_{ij}) + (\bar{X}_{ij} - \bar{X}_i) + (\bar{X}_i - \bar{X}),$$

where X_{ijk} is the kth value in the jth subdistrict, i^{th} district; $\bar{X}_{ij}$ is the mean of the jth subdistrict, i^{th} district: $\bar{X}_i$ is the mean of the ith district; $\bar{X}$ is the mean of all values.

Upon forming products, summing and simplifying, we get:

(5.4.1)

$$
\sum\sum\sum (X_{ijk} - \bar{X})(Y_{ijk} - \bar{Y}) = \sum\sum\sum (X_{ijk} - \bar{X}_{ij})(Y_{ijk} - \bar{Y}) \\
+ \sum\sum n_{ij}(\bar{X}_{ij} - \bar{X}_i)(\bar{Y}_{ij} - \bar{Y}_i) \\
+ \sum n_i(\bar{X}_i - \bar{X})(\bar{Y}_i - \bar{Y}),
$$

where n_{ij} is the number in the jth subdistrict, i^{th} district, and n_i is the number in the ith district. The first term on the right of (5.4.1) represents the covariation between X and Y expressed as deviations from means of subdistricts; the middle term represents the covariation between means of subdistricts expressed as deviations from district means; the third term represents the covariation between district means expressed as deviations from the overall mean. When the middle term is negligible in value, separate analyses based on $4m$ and m units, respectively, will yield closely similar results; otherwise, they will produce different results, with results for $4m$ units (subdistricts) more closely similar than m units (districts) to the correlation of individual measures within groups. This is, of course, in accord with common sense that the finer the grouping, the smaller the divergence between results for ungrouped and grouped data. Differences between results for finer and coarser groupings are of no methodological importance, except as a caution against crediting our ecological correlations with a stability 'hey do not possess.

Correlated Samples. The one-way analysis of covariance, as in the example above, requires that samples (years) be independent in order to run significance tests. When that requirement is waived, and we have correlated samples instead of independent samples, we may have recourse to the two-way analysis of covariance, performing what the statistically-minded agriculturist calls a "correction for stand." To make that correction, we deduct the sums of squares and products for districts from the total sums of squares and products. After total sums have been thus reduced, we carry out our calculations as in the one-way AOCOV.

To illustrate the procedure for getting a reduced table, we apply it to Table 5.4.1, using computations from Table 5.4.2 whenever possible. We construe the data as consisting of five sets of repeated measures, corresponding to as many years. Calculating sums of squares and products for rows and columns and adding up these sums, we get these quantities:

	C_{xx}	C_{yy}	C_{xy}
Rows	30.96	354.24	-48.08
Columns	20.96	204.64	64.92
Rows + Columns	51.92	558.88	16.84

Subtracting sums of squares and products for columns and rows from the total sums of squares, we obtain these remainder sums:

	C_{xx}	C_{yy}	C_{xy}
Total	65.36	586.64	11.52
Rows + Columns	51.92	558.88	16.84
Remainder	13.44	27.76	-5.32

Adding remainder and column sums, we obtain what will be the totals in our reduced table:

Source	C_{xx}	C_{yy}	C_{xy}
Remainder	13.44	27.76	-5.32
Columns	20.96	204.64	64.92
Total	34.40	232.40	59.60

Running the one-way AOCOV on this reduced table, we get explained and unexplained (by regression) sums of squares, as follows:

Source	df	$C_{\hat{y}.x}$	$C_{y.x}$	Mean Square
Total		103.27	129.14	
Within	15	2.11	25.65	1.71
Between	4	101.16	103.49	25.65

$$\eta_{ya.x}^2 = \frac{103.49}{129.14}$$

$$= .80.$$

$$_4F_{15} = \frac{25.65}{1.71}$$

$$= 15.59.$$

Dividing the unexplained sum of squares between years by the total unexplained sum of squares, we obtain the correlation ratio, or the proportion of variance attributable to years, after correcting for both row effects and regression. The between-years mean square with 4 df expressed as a multiple of the within-years (remainder) mean square with 15 df may be used to test the significance of the differences between years, when that test is warranted. The correlation ratio may be interpreted to mean that differences among years explain 80 percent of the variation in crime rates, after both differences among districts and the regression of Y on X have been eliminated. Our "as if" substantive conclusion is that differences between years would be larger if districts were equal in average income and if the trend over time had conformed to the trend for cross-sectional data (i.e., if $\beta' = \beta$).

Epilogue. The burden of the foregoing was to demonstrate that techniques for analyzing the effects of a given classification A on a dependent variable Y, after controlling for the covariable X, may be brought within the framework of covariance analysis. Thus, the attempt to measure the effect of a specific social structure after controlling for individual inputs may be regarded as a particular instance of covariance analysis.

An implication is that the analysis of covariance, at least as a set of questions, might be applied as a matter of course whenever such group effects are being investigated. The standard questions of covariance analysis deal with (1) the relation between X and Y for all populations combined, (2) the relation between X and Y within populations, and the differences among these relations, (3) the differences between populations on Y after controlling for X. These guiding questions should be distinguished from arithmetical techniques that are applied to the data themselves. In its usual sense, the term "analysis of covariance" refers not only to a set of questions to be answered, but also to specific linear methods for adjusting the differences between sample means. But for a given set of data, linear methods may be inadequate and curvilinear methods may be required. In other instances, it may be necessary to forego the calculation of squares and products and rely on methods more appropriate to ordinal measures or attributes (Coleman 1964: 189–240; Bross 1964). In such cases, there need be no departure from the standard line of questioning, rather a replacement of one set of techniques by another set that is more suitable to ordinal or nominal data.

Since modifications of technique do not modify the questions to be answered, the basic covariance design would be maintained in such studies.

In drawing attention to the covariance model, with the implication that its capabilities have been overlooked, there is danger of exaggerating and over-selling its potential usefulness of sociology. It is, after all, a technique for analyzing data and not a machine for making sociology.

EXERCISES

1. Given three samples of seven cases each, test the following hypotheses:

$$H: \beta_1 = \beta_2 = \beta_3,$$

$$H: \beta = 0,$$

$$H: \alpha_1 = \alpha_2 = \alpha_3.$$

A_1		A_2		A_3	
X	Y	X	Y	X	Y
3	6	4	8	3	6
1	4	5	9	2	7
3	5	5	7	2	7
1	3	4	9	3	7
2	4	3	8	4	8
1	3	1	5	1	5
4	6	2	7	4	7
15	31	24	53	19	47

2. Given four samples of five cases each, test the following hypotheses:

$$H: \beta_1 = \beta_2 = \beta_2 = \beta_4,$$

$$H: \beta = 0,$$

$$H: \alpha_1 = \alpha_2 = \alpha_3 = \alpha_4.$$

A_1		A_2		A_3		A_4	
X	Y	X	Y	X	Y	X	Y
10	65	0	55	20	60	20	70
5	50	10	70	10	55	0	65
10	65	15	55	10	60	5	65
20	75	10	60	0	50	15	80
15	70	10	60	10	10	0	60
60	325	45	300	50	235	40	340

3. Given a sample of boys and a sample of girls as follows:

	Boys (1)		Girls (2)	
	X	Y	X	Y
	4	3	4	3
	3	1	3	3
	2	2	5	4
	4	3	3	2
	2	1	5	3

Test these hypotheses:

$$\beta_1 = \beta_2,$$

$$\beta = 0,$$

$$\alpha_1 = \alpha_2.$$

4. Test significance of difference between private school mean height and rural school mean height after correction for regression of height on age.

Height and Age of Private and Rural School Children in a Study in North Carolina in 1948*

	Private School		Rural School	
Students	Age (x) (months)	Height (y) (cm.)	Age (x) (months)	Height (y) (cm.)
1	109	137.6	121	139.0
2	113	147.8	121	140.9
3	115	136.8	128	134.9
4	116	140.7	129	149.5
5	119	132.7	131	148.7
6	120	145.4	132	131.0
7	121	135.0	133	142.3
8	124	133.0	134	139.9
9	126	148.5	138	142.9
10	129	148.3	138	147.7
11	130	147.5	138	147.7
12	133	148.8	140	134.6
13	134	133.2	140	135.8
14	135	148.7	140	148.5
15	137	152.0	—	—
16	139	150.6	—	—
17	141	165.3	—	—
18	142	149.9	—	—
Total	2,283	2,601.8	1,863	1,983.4
Mean	126.8	144.5	133.1	141.7

* Source: Bernard G. Greenberg, "The Use of Analysis of Covariance and Balancing in Analytical Surveys," *American Journal of Public Health*, 43 (June, 1953), p. 694. Reprinted with permission.

REFERENCES

Blalock, Hubert M., Jr.
  1964 Causal Inferences in Nonexperimental Research. Chapel Hill:
         University of North Carolina Press.

  1967 "Status inconsistency, social mobility, status integration and
         structural effects." American Sociological Review 32: 790–801.

Blau, Peter M.
  1960 "Structural effects." American Sociological Review 25: 178–193.

Blau, P. M. and O. D. Duncan
  1967 The American Occupational Structure. New York: John Wiley
         and Sons.

Bogue, R. J. and D. L. Harris
  1954 Comparative Population and Urban Research via Multiple
         Regression and Covariance Analysis. Scripps Foundation for
         Research in Population Problems, Miami University, Oxford,
         Ohio.

Boyle, Richard P.
  1966 "Causal theory and statistical measures of effect." American
         Sociological Review 31: 843–851.

Bross, I. D. J.
  1964 "Taking a covariable into account." Journal of American
         Statistical Association 57: 725–736.

Cochran, William G.
  1957 "Analysis of covariance: Its nature and uses." Biometrics 13:
         261–281.

  1965 "The planning of observational studies of human populations."
         The Journal of the Royal Statistical Society, Series A, 128,
         Part 2: 234–265.

  1968 "The effectiveness of adjustment by subclassification in removing
         bias in observational studies." Biometrics 24: 295–313.

  1969 "The use of covariance in observational studies." The Journal of
         the Royal Statistical Society, Series C, 18: 270–275.

Cohen, Jacob
  1968 "Multiple regression as a general data-analytic system." Psy-
         chological Bulletin 70: 426–443.

Coleman, J. S.
  1964 Introduction to Mathematical Sociology. New York: Free Press.

Costner, Herbert L. and L. Wesley Wager
  1965 "The multivariate analysis of dichotomized variables." American
         Journal of Sociology 70: 455–466.

Davis, J. A.
  1961 "Compositional effects, role systems, and the survival of small
         discussion groups." Public Opinion Quarterly 25: 574–584.

Davis, J. A., J. L. Spaeth, and C. Huson
    1961   "A technique for analyzing the effects of group composition." American Sociological Review 26: 215–225.

Dogan, Mattei
    1969   "A covariance analysis of French electoral data." Pp. 285–298 in Mattei Dogan and Stein Rokkan (eds.), Quantitative Ecological Analysis in the Social Sciences. Cambridge: The M.I.T. Press.

Duncan, Otis Dudley, R. Cuzzort, and Beverly Duncan
    1961   Statistical Geography. Glencoe, Illinois: Free Press.

Duncan, Otis Dudley and Beverly Davis
    1953   "An alternative to ecological correlation." American Sociological Review 18: 665–666.

Evans, S. H. and E. J. Anastasio
    1968   "Misuse of analysis of covariance when treatment effect and covariate are confounded." Psychological Bulletin 69: 225–234.

Fennessey, James
    1968   "The general linear model: A new perspective on some familiar topics." American Journal of Sociology 74: 1–27.

Fisher, R. A.
    1932   Statistical Methods for Research Workers. Fourth Edition. London: Oliver and Boyd.

Goodman, L. A.
    1959   "Some alternatives to ecological correlation." The American Journal of Sociology 64: 610–625.

    1965   "On the multivariate analysis of three dichotomous variables." The American Journal of Sociology 71: 290–301.

    1970   "The multivariate analysis of qualitative data: Interactions among multiple classifications." Journal of the American Statistical Association 65: 226–256.

Greenberg, Bernard G.
    1953   "The use of analysis of covariance and balancing in analytical surveys." American Journal of Public Health 43: 692–699.

Hagood, M. J.
    1941   Statistics for Sociologists. New York: Reynal and Hitchcock.

Hauser, Robert M.
    1970   "Context and consex: A cautionary tale." The American Journal of Sociology 75: 645–664.

Hyman, Herbert
    1955   Survey Design and Analysis. Chapter 7: "The introduction of additional variables and the elaboration of the analysis." Glencoe, Illinois: Free Press.

Jackson, R. W. B.
    1940   "Application of the analysis of variance and covariance method to educational problems." Bulletin No. 11, Dept. of Educational Research: University of Toronto.

Kalton, Graham
    1968   "Standardization: A technique to control for extraneous variables." Applied Statistics 17: 118–136.

Kendall, P. L. and P. F. Lazarsfeld
    1950   "Problems of survey analysis." Pp. 133–196 in R. K. Merton and P. F. Lazarsfeld (eds.), Continuities in Social Research: Studies in the Scope and Method of 'The American Soldier.' Glencoe, Illinois: Free Press.

Lazarsfeld, P. F.
    1958   "Evidence and inference in social research." Daedalus 87: 99–130.

Lindquist, E. F.
    1940   Statistical Analysis in Educational Research. Boston: Houghton Mifflin.

Lord, F. M.
    1960   "Large-sample covariance analysis when the control variable is fallible." Journal of the American Statistical Association 55: 307–321.

    1967   "A paradox in the interpretations of group comparisons." Psychological Bulletin 68: 304–305.

Mood, Alexander M.
    1950   Introduction to the Theory of Statistics. New York: McGraw-Hill.

Robinson, William S.
    1950   "Ecological correlations and the behavior of individuals." American Sociological Review 15: 351–357.

Schmid, C. F.
    1960   "Urban crime areas: Part I." American Sociological Review 25: 527–542.

Schmid, C. F. and K. Tagashira
    1967   "Urban crime areas: A replication and extension of an earlier study." Paper presented to the American Sociological Association, San Francisco.

Schuessler, Karl
    1969   "Covariance analysis in sociological research." Pp. 219–245 in Edgar Borgatta (ed.) Sociological Methodology 1969. San Francisco: Jossey-Bass.

Selvin, H. C.
    1965   "Durkheim's suicide: Further thoughts on a methodological classic." Pp. 113–136 in Robert A. Nisbet (ed.), Emile Durkheim. Englewood Cliffs: Prentice-Hall.

Sills, D. L.
    1961   "Three climate of opinion studies." Public Opinion Quarterly 25: 571–573.

Slatin, Gerald T.
    1969   "Ecological analysis of delinquency: Aggregation effects." American Sociological Review 34: 894–907.

Snedecor, G. W.
　1934　Calculations and Interpretation of Analysis of Variance and Covariance. Ames, Iowa: Collegiate Press.

　1946　Statistical Methods. Fourth Edition. Ames, Iowa: Iowa State University Press.

Street, David
　1965　"The inmate group in custodial and treatment settings." American Sociological Review 30: 40–55.

Tannenbaum, A. S. and J. G. Bachman
　1964　"Structural versus individual effects." The American Journal of Sociology 69: 585–595.

Taves, M. J.
　1951　"The application of analysis of covariance in social science research." American Sociological Review 16: 373–381.

Theil, Henri
　1954　Linear Aggregation of Economic Relations. Amsterdam: North Holland Publishing Co.

Vold, G. B.
　1958　Theoretical Criminology. New York: Oxford University Press.

Werts, C. E. and R. L. Linn
　1969　"Considerations when making inferences within the analysis of covariance model." Research Bulletin 69-28. Princeton: Educational Testing Service.

　1969　"A regression model for compositional effects." Unpublished paper.

Yule, G. Udny and M. G. Kendall
　1950　An Introduction to the Theory of Statistics. Fourteenth Edition. London: Charles Griffin.

6

Multi-stage Sampling

PART 1
Introduction

This chapter is a brief introduction to the subject of multi-stage sampling. It sets forth with little detail the essential characteristics of this method and considers its precision relative to simple random sampling. Because it is sometimes the only feasible technique for sampling a human population, it is of special interest to the sociologist. Its inclusion here reflects this circumstance. However, little more than a glimpse of its rudiments and potentialities are provided by the contents of this chapter. These materials do not intend to provide proficiency in multi-stage sampling; that will come only through extensive practical experience, accompanied by intensive study of such treatises as Cochran's (1963) or Kish's (1965b). On the other hand, this chapter does intend to supply an answer to the specific question "Why is the mean of a multi-stage sample generally less precise than the mean of a simple random sample of the same size?" The answer to that question lies in the somewhat complex way in which multi-stage samples are drawn and analyzed. Our presentation has been framed to provide some understanding of these complexities which sometimes perplex the student, and to demonstrate that formulas for simple random sampling are inapplicable to multi-stage samples, although they are sometimes mistakenly applied to them.

Multi-stage Sampling: The General Idea. If, in drawing for a door prize, a person is required to choose between two boxes before drawing a slip, he is, in effect, sampling in two stages. At the first stage, he selects a box; at the second, a numbered slip. Since two drawings are required, we refer to this procedure as two-stage sampling. If there were only one box, our sampling procedure would encompass but one stage.

The number of stages in multi-stage sampling is theoretically unlimited, although usually it will be governed by practical circumstances. In sampling the inhabitants of a small city, it may be sufficient to select blocks at the first stage, and persons within blocks at the second stage. In a large city, it may be necessary to sample in sequence as follows: census tracts, blocks within census tracts, and people within blocks for a three-stage sample. There is no hard and fast rule which holds for all problems, excepting the principle of parsimony that the number of stages be held to the minimum consistent with our objectives.

Generally speaking, multi-stage sampling consists of two or more independent drawings, where the units at each stage are groupings of units from the next higher stage, excepting that ultimate units, however defined, are not subject to decomposition into smaller units.

Object. The object of multi-stage sampling is to reduce the cost of the sample by increasing the accessibility of the population whose characteristics are to be described. It thus may be regarded as a device for procuring sample data of acceptable accuracy more cheaply than would be possible under alternative sampling schemes. In this respect, it is similar to stratified and systematic sampling which likewise seek to lower the cost of sample information with no loss in precision. In stratified sampling, we sample from each of M strata into which the total population has been divided, with a view to generalizing about the characteristics of that population. The technique of systematic sampling consists of drawing every k^{th} case from a list of all cases in the population or stratum. Quite possibly, the different forms of restricted sampling would not have evolved at all, had not simple direct sampling been prohibitively costly in so many of its projected applications.

Among samplers, it is a rule that, whenever more than one sampling design is available, we select whichever does the work most cheaply. Multi-stage sampling, of course, will be chosen whenever it yields the required precision, as measured by the standard error, at the lowest cost; or yields greater precision for a fixed expenditure than any other plan. This criterion of choice obviously embodies the principle that we purchase our required information as economically as possible, or—putting it another way—that we "get the most for our money."

Of course, if a given sampling plan has intangible assets, the cost criterion of "best plan" may be waived. We may decide to interview students in every school for reasons of public policy, although such a complete canvass of schools may be quite uneconomical. We would want no school principal to feel left out. The criterion of least cost will also require modification if the best plan "on paper" is impossible to carry out by reason of practical obstacles. We may have to forego simple random sampling if a list of elements is not available, notwithstanding its general promise in other respects. But, all other things equal, we choose that plan requiring the least outlay of effort to achieve a fixed standard of precision. When multi-stage sampling is cheapest, we carry out the sampling in that manner.

Advantages. The advantages of multi-stage sampling correspond to its objectives when those are actually realized. Its main objective, to reiterate briefly, is to lower costs by reducing the spread of the sampling units which ultimately must be reached. By utilizing neighborhoods as clusters, it may be possible to restrict the sampling to a relatively small number of compact geographical areas and thereby to lower substantially travel time and sampling costs. The cost of reaching an equal number of persons by simple random sampling will be greater because of the greater average distance between interviews.

Secondly, multi-stage sampling requires that elements be listed only for those subpopulations from which elements are drawn. The cost of such lists may be low relative to the complete list necessary for simple random sampling. Multi-stage sampling thus becomes feasible, where simple random sampling would be prohibitive because of the cost of preparing a complete list of elementary units.

The potentiality for reducing costs through partial listing and concentrated field work appears to be the greatest practical asset of multi-stage sampling.

Concept of Cost. The concept of cost, when figured in dollars and cents, may seem to hold no more than academic interest for the graduate student who often conducts his research with little or no financial support. Granting this, he would still wish to design his sample to maximize information for time spent, or to minimize time spent in obtaining the required information. Even where the student himself makes all of his field observations, he would still want to get as much precision as possible for effort expended, or to expend as little effort as necessary to secure the requisite data. He will thus be guided by the principle of least cost, even though his costs cannot be exactly translated into dollars and cents. By thus extending the concept of cost to cover time and effort, and thereby becoming more cost-conscious, the student will have cultivated a mentality that is appropriate when substantial funds become available for more extensive research.

Terminology. The terminology of multi-stage sampling is subject to some variety, and in consequence may be troublesome to the inexperienced user. While strict definitions could be given, that procedure might discourage contact with the many sources in which discussions of multi-stage sampling are embedded. Hence, insofar as possible, we have elected to proceed informally by examples rather than formally by definitions, which are often subject to rapid obsolescence in a growing science.

The term multi-stage sampling is a natural extension of two-stage sampling, which term appears to be due to Mahalanobis (Cochran 1963: 270). The term two-stage sampling was suggested as an alternative to subsampling, a term sometimes used to designate sampling within randomly selected subpopulations. Subsampling is exemplified by the sampling of households within randomly selected blocks, rather than over the entire city without restriction.

When our sampling units at any stage are well-defined clusters of units from the next higher stage, we sometimes speak of our stagewise selection procedure as *cluster sampling*. The term is especially appropriate when our primary sampling units consist of natural social clusters—communities, neighborhoods, and households. Because such groupings may be quite accessible, we may find them economical to use in the sampling of human populations. Thus, we may find it efficient to sample churches before sampling church members; similarly, we may find it efficient to sample colleges before we sample college students. When clusters correspond to separate territorial units, we may use the special term "area sampling." In some writing, cluster sampling has come to mean a complete canvass of every unit within each selected cluster; however, such 100 percent sampling within clusters is not essential to the method and subsampling may be employed.

In two-stage sampling, we apply the label "primary sampling units" to subpopulations, and the label "secondary sampling units" to the elements within subpopulations, corresponding to the drawing of subpopulations before the drawing of elements. However, this form of labeling has its difficulties for the general case of k-stage ($k > 2$) sampling and might therefore be discarded in favor of the more general expression "i^{th}-stage sampling units," where i takes all values 1 through k. Nevertheless, for the sake of convenience and because our discussion is limited largely to two-stage sampling, we regularly refer to first-stage units as psu's and second-stage units as ssu's, or elements.

Notation. As with its terminology, the notation of multi-stage sampling is somewhat unstandardized. While this diversity may be an inconvenience to the student using several references, it does not bespeak disagreement over the fundamentals of multi-stage sampling theory. The variety of notational usage is more a sign of vitality than a symptom of confusion. Nevertheless, for purposes of presentation, some notation must be adopted.

In conformity with recent writing on sampling statistics, and unless circumstances dictate otherwise, we employ capital Roman letters to designate population parameters and lower case Roman letters to designate their sample estimates. However, this rule cannot be strictly maintained; like other rules which encounter difficulties in practice, this one too has its exceptions.

Varieties of Multi-stage Sampling. Multi-stage sampling takes a variety of forms, each best suited to a distinct combination of circumstances. Inasmuch as there is no restriction on the selection procedure at each stage, except that the drawing be random, we may employ whichever technique is best for the units being sampled. We may, for example, stratify first-stage units, leave second-stage units unstratified, and revert to stratified sampling in the final stage of three-stage sampling. We may select units in any manner at all, so long as the drawing is affected by random factors alone, as required by probabilistic sampling.

It is possible not only to alternate between selection techniques from stage to stage, but also to vary the sampling fraction, or the proportion of units selected at each stage. In two-stage sampling, we may take one in ten units at the first stage, but only one in fifty at the second. Our sampling fractions are naturally chosen so that together they yield a more precise sample of cases than any other combination whose total cost is the same.

Here we restrict ourselves to the simplest forms of multi-stage sampling, since our purpose is to lay down general ideas, rather than provide an exhaustive list of alternative sample designs. Accordingly, we restrict ourselves to two-stage sampling, with first and second-stage units chosen by simple random sampling, and the number of secondary units proportional to the size of the primary units. In other words, primary and secondary units will be selected by simple random sampling, with a constant second-stage sampling fraction. We consider four cases, corresponding to different restrictions on the number of psu's (M) and the number of ssu's (N) within psu's:

(1) $M = 1$, N infinite

(2) M and N infinite

(3) M finite, N's finite and equal

(4) M finite, N's finite and unequal

Although the requirement that M and/or N be infinite (Cases 1 and 2) can never be empirically satisfied, it is a reasonable restriction to impose for purposes of abstract analysis. The relatively complicated results for finite populations (Cases 3 and 4) are a natural extension of the relatively uncomplicated results for infinite populations. This progression from simple to complex theory is the justification for taking up the unrealistic but analytically useful case of infinite populations. For each case, our general procedure will be to give:

(1) the estimator whose variance is sought,

(2) a description of that variance, and

(3) a formula which will enable us to estimate the value of that variance from our sample data.

To simplify matters, we restrict the discussion to simple estimates of the population mean and, when it exists, to the population total from which that mean was derived. Also, for the sake of simplicity, we limit ourselves to the variance of the mean and extend the discussion to the standard error (square root of the variance) only when that statistic is specifically required. Furthermore, we do not consider the complications which may arise in testing the significance of a difference when samples are drawn in two or more stages.

PART 2
M = 1, N Infinite

We begin with the familiar case of random sampling from an infinite population. When $M = 1$, sampling at the first stage is impossible, and sampling occurs at only the second stage. Sampling from a single population thus may be regarded as a degenerate form of two-stage sampling. Since statistical results are unaffected by the disposition of a case once drawn from an infinite population, we may or may not replace it in the population according to our convenience. For this reason, we need not distinguish here between unrestricted random sampling (with replacement) and simple random sampling (without replacement) as we would in discussing sampling from a finite population. Strictly speaking, sampling from an infinite population falls outside the realm of practicable sample survey theory (Kendall and Stuart 1966: 166), since a population cannot be surveyed if it is infinite. However, results for sampling from an infinite population are exceedingly simple and provide a convenient base against which results for other sampling schemes may be compared.

The statistic whose variance is sought is the simple mean of the sample values; it is an unbiased estimate* of the population mean. In symbols:

$$E(\bar{y}) = \mu.$$

Our interest in this statistic is somewhat incidental; our main interest is in its variance, which is a measure of its precision. For example, that variance will permit us to assess the precision of n cases drawn from an infinite population with variance σ^2, relative to the precision of as many cases drawn from a finite population with the same variance σ^2.

---

* A biased estimator will be preferred to an unbiased estimator if it is much more precise and not very biased.

Symbolism and Terminology. The symbols and terms required for this case are as follows:

Symbol	Term
	Population
μ	population mean
σ^2	population variance
$\sigma_{\bar{y}}^2 = \dfrac{\sigma^2}{n}$	variance of mean
	Sample
n	sample size
y_i	value of ith sample unit
$y = \sum y_i$	sum of sample values
$\bar{y} = \dfrac{y}{n}$	sample mean
$s^2 = \dfrac{1}{n-1} \sum (y_i - \bar{y})^2$	estimate (unbiased) of population variance
$s_{\bar{y}}^2 = \dfrac{s^2}{n}$	estimate of variance of mean

Variance of the Sample Mean. For purpose of analysis, we regard a randomly selected value as the sum of two parts: the population mean and the deviation of that value from the population mean. In notation:

$$y_i = \mu + (y_i - \mu).$$

Given a sample of n such values, their mean is:

(6.2.1)
$$\bar{y} = \frac{y}{n}$$
$$= \frac{1}{n} \sum [\mu + (y_i - \mu)]$$
$$= \mu + \frac{1}{n} \sum (y_i - \mu).$$

The conclusion to be drawn from the right side is that the mean of n randomly selected values is equal to the population mean and the mean amount by which these values deviate from the population mean. It is the variance of this quantity (6.2.1) that we wish to establish.

To write that variance, we need only transpose $\mu = E(\bar{y})$ from right to left, square and take the expectation of both sides:

(6.2.2) $$E[\bar{y} - E(\bar{y})]^2 = E\left[\frac{1}{n}\sum(y_i - \mu)\right]^2.$$

The expectation on the left side is the variance of the sample mean $(\sigma_{\bar{y}}^2)$ by definition, while the expectation on the right side works out to the population variance (σ^2) divided by sample size (n) (Mood 1950: 133). Substituting this latter result in (6.2.2), we get

(6.2.3) $$\sigma_{\bar{y}}^2 = \frac{\sigma^2}{n}.$$

This formula (6.2.3), which holds for any population with a finite variance, is the basis of the familiar statement that the variance of the mean varies inversely as sample size, given random sampling from an infinite population. An implication is that, with this particular design, a reduction in the variance of the mean may be produced only by an increase in the size of the sample. In other words, to increase precision, we must increase n.

Estimate of Variance of Mean. For an unbiased estimate of $\sigma_{\bar{y}}^2$, we substitute s^2, as defined above, for σ^2 in (6.2.3), a procedure with which the student is probably familiar from his study of elementary sampling theory:

(6.2.4) $$s_{\bar{y}}^2 = \frac{s^2}{n}.$$

Taking the square root of (6.2.4), we get the familiar standard error of the mean (not an unbiased estimator):

(6.2.5) $$s_{\bar{y}} = \frac{s}{\sqrt{n}},$$

which is generally used either to set up a confidence interval for the population mean or to test an exact hypothesis about that mean. When n is large, the sampling error of the mean divided by the estimated standard error distributes as a normal deviate, z. That is,

$$z = \frac{\bar{y} - \mu}{s_{\bar{y}}}.$$

By virtue of this result, we may readily determine whether our sample mean is rare under a given hypothesis or set up a confidence interval which probably includes the true mean.

Example. To illustrate the calculation of $s_{\bar{y}}^2$ and a 95 percent confidence interval, we perform the necessary operations on the following series of 10 values:

y_i
9
13
11
19
3
4
17
1
7
16
$\Sigma = \overline{100}$

$$\bar{y} = 10$$

$$\sum(y_i - \bar{y})^2 = 352$$

$$s^2 = 39.11$$

$$s_{\bar{y}}^2 = \frac{39.11}{10} = 3.91$$

$$s_{\bar{y}} = 1.98$$

$$10 \pm 1.96(1.98) = 95 \text{ percent confidence interval.}$$

EXERCISES

1. Given the following sample of measures:

4	0	5	4	9
6	10	4	5	8
3	3	7	4	7
7	3	0	3	5

   (a) Compute the variance of the mean, $\dfrac{\sum(y_i - \bar{y})^2}{n(n-1)} = \dfrac{s^2}{n}$, and the standard error of the mean, $s_{\bar{y}}$.

   (b) Explain the meaning of this result: $E\left(\dfrac{s}{\sqrt{n}}\right) \neq \dfrac{\sigma}{\sqrt{n}}$.

2. Plot $\sigma_{\bar{x}}^2$ on n for $n = 1, 2, 3, \ldots, 10$, given that $\sigma^2 = 10$.

3. Set up a numerical series to illustrate that the standard error of the mean varies inversely as the square root of n.

4. Show that $E\left[\dfrac{1}{n}\sum(y_i - \mu)\right]^2 = \dfrac{\sigma^2}{n}$.

PART 3
M and N Infinite

In the preceding section, we approached the variance of the mean by formulating each value as the sum of the population mean and its deviation around that mean. This approach will serve equally well as we move to the variance of the sample mean for values of M greater than 1. We begin with M and N infinite, since results for two-stage sampling under these conditions are simpler than those for two-stage sampling with both M and N finite. Since M cannot exceed infinity, sampling from infinitely many psu's may be regarded as the upper limit of two-stage sampling, just as we construed sampling from one psu as its lower limit. As in the preceding case ($M = 1$, N infinite), it is unnecessary to specify that sampling be with or without replacement, since results are identical for both procedures. An infinite population is unaffected by either the removal or the restoration of units.

Symbolism and Terminology. Our symbolism will be somewhat more intricate (and cumbersome) owing to the more complex character of results based on cluster sampling in two stages:

Symbol	Term
	Population
Y_{ij}	j^{th} value, i^{th} psu
μ_i	mean of ith psu
σ_i^2	variance of ith psu
μ	population mean
σ^2	population variance
σ_w^2	within psu variance (mean psu variance)
σ_b^2	between psu variance (variance of psu means)
$\sigma_{\bar{y}}^2$	variance of sample mean
	Sample
m	number of psu's selected
n	subsample size

mn	total sample size
y_{ij}	j^{th} value, i^{th} subsample
$y_i = \sum_1^n y_{ij}$	sum of values, i^{th} subsample
$y = \sum_1^m \sum_1^n y_{ij}$	sum of values, all subsamples
$\bar{y} = \dfrac{y}{m}$	mean sum
$\bar{y}_i = \dfrac{y_i}{n}$	mean value, i^{th} subsample
$\bar{\bar{y}} = \dfrac{y}{mn}$	mean value, all subsamples
$s_w^2 = \sum_1^m \sum_1^n \dfrac{(y_{ij} - \bar{y}_i)^2}{m(n-1)}$	within-subsample mean square
$s_b^2 = \dfrac{n\sum(\bar{y}_i - \bar{\bar{y}})^2}{m-1}$	between-subsample mean square
$s_{\bar{\bar{y}}}^2 = \dfrac{s_b^2}{mn}$	estimate of variance of sample mean

Note that we place a single bar over y to represent the mean sum for primary sampling units (psu's), and two bars over y to represent the mean of the values attached to secondary sampling units (ssu's). When necessary, we attach subscripts to variances to signify their basis as variation within or between subsamples.

Variance of Mean, $\sigma_{\bar{\bar{y}}}^2$. Our problem revolves around the quantity,

$$\bar{\bar{y}} = \frac{y}{mn},$$

which is both an unbiased and simple estimate of the population mean:

(6.3.1) $E(\bar{\bar{y}}) = \mu.$

It is unbiased in the sense that its expectation is equal to the population mean; it is simple in its calculation: sum all values and divide by their number. Our limited object is to establish the variance of this mean, and to set forth a procedure for estimating that variance. From these results, we may gauge the effect of subsampling on the precision of the sample mean. In this analysis, we again take as our point of departure any randomly selected value (y_{ij}) in decomposed form:

$$y_{ij} = \mu + (\mu_i - \mu) + (y_{ij} - \mu_i).$$

Where before we regarded each value as consisting of two parts, we now regard each value (y_{ij}) as the sum of three parts: (1) the population mean (μ), (2) the deviation of its psu mean (μ_i) from the population mean (μ), and (3) its deviation from the mean of its psu $(y_{ij} - \mu_i)$. The mean of mn such measures, where m is the number of randomly selected primary sampling units and n is the number of elements drawn from each of the m psu's, is

$$\bar{y} = \mu + \frac{1}{m} \sum (\mu_i - \mu) + \frac{1}{mn} \sum\sum (y_{ij} - \mu_i),$$

as the student should verify. To express the variance of this quantity, we transpose μ from right to left, square and take the expectation of both sides:

$$E(\bar{y} - \mu)^2 = E\left[\frac{1}{m} \sum (\mu_i - \mu) + \frac{1}{mn} \sum\sum (y_{ij} - \mu_i)\right]^2.$$

The left side is the variance of the sample mean by virtue of (6.3.1), while the right side reduces to the sum of the between and within subpopulation variances, weighted respectively by $\frac{1}{m}$ and $\frac{1}{mn}$ (Cochran 1953: 217). In symbols:

(6.3.2)
$$\sigma_{\bar{y}}^2 = \frac{\sigma_b^2}{m} + \frac{\sigma_w^2}{mn}.$$

Estimate of $\sigma_{\bar{y}}^2$. The procedure for estimating $\sigma_{\bar{y}}^2$ is remarkable for its simplicity. To provide some understanding of that procedure, we start with the expectation of s_b^2, given m independent samples of n cases each from subpopulations (psu's) having identical means. This is:

$$E(s_b^2) = \frac{1}{m-1} E\sum n(\bar{y}_i - \bar{y})^2$$
$$= \sigma_w^2,$$

in agreement with theory for the analysis of variance (p. 141). However, in sampling from subpopulations whose means differ, the expectation of s_b^2 is larger than σ_w^2 by the quantity $n\sigma_b^2$, reflecting the differences among subpopulation means (p. 141). In symbols:

$$E(s_b^2) = \sigma_w^2 + n\sigma_b^2.$$

But by Formula (6.3.2) the variance of the mean for subsampling is:

$$\sigma_{\bar{y}}^2 = \frac{\sigma_w^2}{mn} + \frac{\sigma_b^2}{m}.$$

Hence, we need only to divide s_b^2 by mn to obtain an unbiased estimate of the variance of the mean, given m subsamples, n cases each. In notation:

(6.3.3)
$$s_{\bar{y}}^2 = \frac{s_b^2}{mn}.$$

We thus arrive at the final rule: to estimate the variance of the mean of mn elements, given that both M and N are infinite, divide the mean square for subsamples by mn. This mean square reflects variation within samples and variation between samples and hence covers the total sampling variation.

Estimate of σ_b^2. Although the foregoing procedure has the merit of simplicity, it does not supply an estimate of σ_b^2 which would serve to gauge the degree to which the variability of $\bar{y}$ is affected by differences among psu means. We would expect that variability to increase as the differences among the means of the psu's increase.

To estimate σ_b^2 and to judge its contribution of $\sigma_{\bar{y}}^2$, we return to the expectation of s_b^2:

$$E(s_b^2) = \sigma_w^2 + n\sigma_b^2.$$

Transposing σ_w^2 from right to left and dividing both sides by n, we get

$$\sigma_b^2 = \frac{E(s_b^2) - \sigma_w^2}{n},$$

but $E(s_w^2) = \sigma_w^2$, hence $[E(s_b^2) - E(s_w^2)]/n = \sigma_b^2$. From this result we get the rule: to estimate the variance of subpopulation means (σ_b^2), subtract the within-subsample mean square from the between-subsample mean square and divide by subsample size: $\hat{\sigma}_b^2 = (s_b^2 - s_w^2)/n$. Replacing σ_b^2 and σ_w^2 in (6.3.2) by their estimates, we obtain,

(6.3.4)
$$s_{\bar{y}}^2 = \frac{s_b^2 - s_w^2}{mn} + \frac{s_w^2}{mn}.$$

Two-Stage Sampling as Form of Analysis of Variance. To throw more light on multi-stage sampling and to give it perspective, we present the foregoing results in a conventional AOV table:

Analysis of Variance of Sample Measures.

Source	df	Sum of Squares	Mean Square	Expectation
Between subsamples	$m-1$	$n\sum(\bar{y}_i - \bar{\bar{y}})^2$	s_b^2	$\sigma_w^2 + n\sigma_b^2$
Within subsamples	$m(n-1)$	$\sum\sum(y_{ij} - \bar{y}_i)^2$	s_w^2	σ_w^2

This is not to suggest that multi-stage sampling is merely a special case of the analysis of variance; rather it is to take advantage of a convenient format, and to call attention to the close similarity between multi-stage sampling and AOV.

When numerical results are arranged in this way, we may readily judge whether the sample mean is affected more by variation within psu's or by variation between them. Consider a sample of 400 observations, consisting of 40 subsamples of 10 cases each, with mean squares as follows:

Source	df	Mean square	Expectation
Between subsamples	39	800	$\sigma_w^2 + n\sigma_b^2$
Within subsamples	360	600	σ_w^2

To estimate $\sigma_{\bar{y}}^2$, we divide s_b^2 by mn:

$$s_{\bar{y}}^2 = 800/400$$
$$= 2.00,$$

which in turn provides an estimate of the standard error, $s_{\bar{y}} = \sqrt{2.00} = 1.41$. If it is reasonable to suppose that the ratio of the sample mean to its estimated standard error has a z distribution, we may use that distribution to set up a confidence interval. If we require 99 percent confidence, our interval would have $\bar{y} \pm z_{.995}s_{\bar{y}}$ as its upper and lower limits.

That procedure will suffice if our sole object is to set up a confidence interval for the population mean; however, it will not disclose the respective contributions of σ_b^2 and σ_w^2 to $\sigma_{\bar{y}}^2$, which information may be pertinent to our analysis. When such an assessment is required, we take s_w^2 from s_b^2 and divide by n for an estimate of σ_b^2. For our figures:

$$\hat{\sigma}_b^2 = \frac{800 - 600}{10}$$
$$= 20.$$

Substituting this result together with $s_w^2 = 600$ in (6.3.4), we obtain the variance of the sample mean as the sum of its components:

$$s_{\bar{\bar{y}}}^2 = \frac{20}{40} + \frac{600}{400}$$

$$= 0.5 + 1.5$$

$$= 2.0,$$

as before. Our conclusion is that differences among subsample means account for 25 percent of the estimated variability of the mean, since the value of estimate would be only 75 percent as large in the absence of such differences. Alternatively, we may state that the variance of the mean is 33 percent greater because of differences among subpopulation means, assuming that the degree of internal variation (σ_w^2) is independent of such differences.

Analysis of Theory. The foregoing method will strike some sociologists as unrealistic for purposes of social research in that its validity depends on the assumption of M and N infinite. Human populations are not infinite in number, nor do they have infinitely many members. But notwithstanding its limited practical utility, we may profitably manipulate Formula (6.3.2) to discern the conditions under which the variance of the sample mean will be least, or the precision of the mean greatest. The conclusions growing out of this analysis, while more in the nature of abstract principles than working rules, may sometimes help us to avoid gross mistakes in formulating our sample designs.

When the total number (mn) of ssu's is fixed, the contribution of σ_w^2/mn to the variance of the mean will necessarily be constant; however, the contribution of σ_b^2/m will vary as m, the number of psu's. Evidently, to get the smallest possible variance $\sigma_{\bar{\bar{y}}}^2$ under these conditions, we must maximize m, or equivalently minimize n. Since the theoretically smallest possible value of n is 1, we maximize m by letting $n = 1$, so that $mn = m$. Thus, in theory at least, we obtain the maximum degree of precision by drawing as many psu's as there are elements in the sample. If there are 100 elements in the sample, we would select one element from as many different psu's.

When $\sigma_w^2 = 0$, the variance of the mean reduces to σ_b^2/m. In this case, whatever the value of m, $\sigma_{\bar{\bar{y}}}^2$ is the same for all values of n; hence, all drawings beyond the first within each sampled psu are superfluous. Since $\sigma_w^2 = 0$ implies that elements within each psu have the same value, it follows that one element will represent a psu as well as two or more elements, and that the optimum value of n is 1. This is merely a special case of the general rule that we get the greatest precision by setting $mn = m$, when mn cases are to be drawn.

An exception occurs when $\sigma_b^2 = 0$. In this case, $\sigma_{\bar{\bar{y}}}^2$ reduces to σ_w^2/mn, and therefore is the same for all values of m. Since $\sigma_{\bar{\bar{y}}}^2$ is unaffected by the number of psu's, we choose whichever number is cheapest. Since it is cheaper to draw a smaller than larger number of psu's, and since one is the smallest possible number, we set $m = 1$, when $\sigma_b^2 = 0$. This rule is the basis of the suggestion that, when the opportunity to do so exists, psu means be made to resemble one another as nearly as possible, so that a few psu's, or even one psu, will serve as well as many, with a consequent lowering of the cost of the survey. This suggestion has no practical value unless psu's are arbitrary in their composition and subject to manipulation by the sampler.

Optimum Allocation. From the foregoing, one should not conclude that we either draw as many clusters as there are elements in the sample $(mn=m)$ or draw all of our elements from one psu $(mn = n)$. It all depends on the cost of one psu relative to the cost of one element (ssu). Let us suppose that the cost of our sample is not to exceed $1,200 and that the cost (C_1) of a psu is $20 and the cost (C_2) of an element is $4. We are given that $s_w^2 = 600$, $\hat{\sigma}_b^2 = 20$. Our question is: how many psu's should we draw in order to obtain the smallest possible standard error (greatest precision), given an outlay of $1,200 for the sample? We could draw as many as 50 psu's and still stay within our budget. However we would be limited to only one element from each psu, as may be shown by solving for n in the simple cost equation:

(6.3.5)
$$mC_1 + mnC_2 = C,$$
$$50(20) + 50n(4) = 1,200,$$
$$n = 1,$$

where C is the total cost. If we draw one element from each of 50 psu's, the estimated variance of the mean would be

$$s_{\bar{y}}^2 = \frac{20}{50} + \frac{600}{50}$$
$$= 12.4.$$

It is natural to wonder whether there is a more efficient way to allocate our $1,200 between psu's and elements. As a trial possibility, let us set m equal to 30 and solve for n:

$$30(20) + 30n(4) = 1200,$$
$$n = 5.$$

Substituting $m = 30$ and $n = 5$ in (6.3.5), we get

$$s_{\bar{y}}^2 = \frac{20}{30} + \frac{600}{150}$$
$$= 4.67,$$

which is substantially smaller than the result obtained by setting $m = 50$.

Although we may "purchase" 50 psu's and 50 elements for the same price as 30 psu's and 150 elements, the sample of 150 elements evenly distributed among 30 psu's produces a smaller standard error than the sample of 50 elements drawn from as many psu's. A sample of 20 psu's produces an even smaller variance of the mean, as the student should verify. From this example we surmise that the optimum number of psu's will depend on their average cost relative to the average cost of an element. There are standard methods for determining the optimum allocation of fixed resources. However, it is not necessary to approach the problem of sample size from the standpoint of getting the most for a fixed sum of money. In fact, the preferred procedure is to determine the optimum number of psu's to obtain a prescribed level of precision. In this latter case, we first decide how much precision is required by the nature of our work and then proceed to design our sample to get that precision at the lowest possible cost. This is a more rational procedure in that we first fix our requirements and then determine the cheapest way to meet them.

Relative Precision of Two-stage Sampling. It is instructive to compare the precision of the sample mean in two-stage sampling with its precision in sampling from the total population. In brief, what is the relation of $\sigma_{\bar{y}}^2$ to $\sigma_{\bar{y}}^2$? We ask in particular: is the variance of the mean for m subsamples of n cases each generally larger or smaller than the variance of the mean of a random sample of mn cases from the total population? In answering that question, we take the total variance as the sum of its component variances as our point of departure. This is:

(6.3.6) $$\sigma^2 = \sigma_b^2 + \sigma_w^2.$$

Transposing σ_b^2 from right to left, we get

$$\sigma_w^2 = \sigma^2 - \sigma_b^2.$$

Substituting $(\sigma^2 - \sigma_b^2)$ for σ_w^2 in (6.3.2), we get

$$\sigma_{\bar{y}}^2 = \frac{\sigma_b^2}{m} + \frac{\sigma^2 - \sigma_b^2}{mn}.$$

Collecting terms on the right and factoring, we obtain

$$\frac{\sigma^2}{mn}\left[1 + \frac{\sigma_b^2}{\sigma^2}(n-1)\right].$$

But σ^2/mn is the variance of the sample mean for a random sample of mn cases from the total, undivided population; hence:

$$\sigma_{\bar{\bar{y}}}^2 = \sigma_{\bar{y}}^2 \left[1 + \frac{\sigma_b^2}{\sigma^2} (n - 1) \right],$$

and

(6.3.7) $$\sigma_{\bar{\bar{y}}}^2 / \sigma_{\bar{y}}^2 = 1 + \frac{\sigma_b^2}{\sigma^2} (n - 1).$$

Focusing on the right side of (6.3.7), we note that the magnitude of $\sigma_{\bar{\bar{y}}}^2$ relative to $\sigma_{\bar{y}}^2$ will vary as the ratio of σ_b^2 to σ^2. Since σ_b^2 can be neither smaller than zero nor larger than σ^2, the ratio of σ_b^2 to σ^2 is necessarily limited to values between 0 and 1. When $\sigma_b^2 = 0$, the ratio is zero; when $\sigma_b^2 = \sigma^2$, the ratio is equal to 1. Amplifying this point: when there are differences among psu means but items within psu's are identical, σ_b^2 will be equal to σ^2 and σ_b^2 / σ^2 will be equal to 1. At the other extreme, where there are no differences between psu means, but where items differ among themselves within psu's, then $\sigma_b^2 = 0$, and σ_b^2 / σ^2 is likewise equal to zero.

Intraclass Correlation, ρ. The ratio σ_b^2 / σ^2 is thus a measure of the homogeneity of values within subpopulations. Because it varies directly as the degree of similarity among values within psu's, it has come to be known as the coefficient of intraclass correlation, usually symbolized by the Greek letter "ρ" with subscript when needed. Substituting ρ for σ_b^2 / σ^2 in (6.3.7), we get the simpler expression:

(6.3.8) $$\sigma_{\bar{\bar{y}}}^2 / \sigma_{\bar{y}}^2 = 1 + \rho(n - 1).$$

From this linear equation we see that ρ, together with n, determines the excess of $\sigma_{\bar{\bar{y}}}^2$ over $\sigma_{\bar{y}}^2$. In the extreme but unrealistic situation where $\sigma_b^2 = \sigma^2$, the ratio of $\sigma_{\bar{\bar{y}}}^2$ to $\sigma_{\bar{y}}^2$ will be equal to $1 + (n - 1) = n$, the number of cases in each subsample. In this case, when $n = 2$, $\sigma_{\bar{\bar{y}}}^2$ will be twice as large as $\sigma_{\bar{y}}^2$; when $n = 5$, $\sigma_{\bar{\bar{y}}}^2$ will be five times as large as $\sigma_{\bar{y}}^2$; etc.

To verify that the relative precision of two-stage sampling falls as ρ rises, other things being equal, let us assign an arbitrary value to n, and permit ρ to vary between 0 and 1.00. Taking $n = 5$ and selected values of ρ, we get

ρ	$\sigma_{\bar{\bar{y}}}^2 / \sigma_{\bar{y}}^2$
.00	1.00
.25	2.00
.50	3.00
.75	4.00
1.00	5.00

Inspecting this series, we see that when $\rho = .25$, and given that $n = 5$, the variance of the mean for two-stage sampling is twice as large as the variance of the mean for random sampling from the total population. In other words, two-stage sampling will be only one-half as precise as simple sampling when $\rho = .25$. Continuing along these lines, we see that when $\rho = .50$, two-stage sampling will be only one-third as precise as simple sampling; when $\rho = .75$, sampling in two stages will be only one-fourth as precise. In the extreme cases, as previously noted, when $\rho = 1.00$, the variance of the mean for two-stage sampling will be exactly n times as large as the variance of the mean for random sampling from the total population, or only $1/n^{\text{th}}$ as precise. From these examples, it is clear that the precision of cluster sampling declines as clusters become more homogeneous, on the assumption that the total variance (σ^2) is fixed.

It is of interest that the precision of two-stage sampling is identical for $\rho = .60$ and $n = 5$, and $\rho = .10$ and $n = 25$. From this we deduce that precision may be depressed by either a large n or a large ρ.

Estimate of ρ. To estimate $\rho = \dfrac{\sigma_b^2}{\sigma^2}$ from sample data, we avail ourselves of previously established results. We combine estimates of σ_b^2 and σ_w^2 for an estimate of σ^2 as follows:

$$(6.3.9) \qquad \begin{aligned} s_t^2 &= \left(\frac{s_b^2 - s_w^2}{n}\right) + s_w^2 \\ &= \frac{s_b^2 + s_w^2(n-1)}{n}, \end{aligned}$$

where s_t^2 is an estimate of σ^2. To estimate ρ, we divide our estimate of σ_b^2 by our estimate of σ^2. This works out as follows:

$$(6.3.10) \qquad \hat{\rho} = \frac{s_b^2 - s_w^2}{s_b^2 + s_w^2(n-1)},$$

where $\hat{\rho}$ is the estimate of ρ. For the numerical example given above (p. 265), we have

$$\hat{\rho} = \frac{800 - 600}{800 + (600)(10 - 1)}$$
$$= .03.$$

Substituting $\hat{\rho} = .03$ and $n = 10$ in (6.3.8), we get

$$1 + .03(10 - 1) = 1.27,$$

which result serves to gauge the precision of two-stage sampling, relative to sampling from the total population. Our conclusion is that the variance of the mean for 400 cases spread evenly among 40 psu's is 27 percent larger (within the limits of sampling error) than the variance of mean for 400 cases drawn without restriction from the total population.

Variance of Sample Proportion, σ_p^2. In studying the variance of the sample proportion (p), it is convenient to treat that proportion as the arithmetic mean of a discrete variable taking dummy values of 0 and 1, and to rewrite the variance formula under this restriction. If we assign a value of 1 to every case in category A_1 and a value of 0 to every case in A_0, the population will have P, the proportion of cases in A_1, as its arithmetic mean, and $P(1 - P)$, the proportion of cases in A_1 multiplied by the proportion in A_2, as its variance.

For a simple confirmation of these results, let

$$N = \text{number in population}$$
$$N_1 = \text{number in } A_1$$
$$N_0 = \text{number in } A_0.$$

Then for the dummy binary variable Y,

$$\sum Y = N_1,$$
$$\bar{Y} = \frac{1}{N}(N_1) = P,$$

and

$$\sigma^2 = \frac{1}{N}[N_1(1 - P)^2 + N_0(0 - P)^2],$$

which simplifies after expansion and collection to

$$\sigma^2 = \frac{NP(1 - P)}{N}$$
$$= PQ,$$

where $Q = 1 - P$.

In two-stage sampling with M and N infinite, the mean value of $(P_i - P)^2$ is the psu variance (σ_b^2), and the mean value of $(Y_{ij} - P_i)^2$ is the within psu variance (σ_w^2), where P_i = proportion in i^{th} subpopulation, $Y_{ij} = j^{th}$ value in i^{th} subpopulation. From a sample of m psu's of n cases each, we get these mean squares:

(6.3.11) $$s_b^2 = \frac{n}{m-1}\sum_1^m (p_i - p)^2, \text{ and}$$

(6.3.12) $$s_w^2 = \frac{n}{m(n-1)}\sum_1^m p_i(1 - p_i),$$

where p_i = proportion in i^{th} subsample. A word or two on s_w^2 by way of explanation: to get the sum of the squares for the ith subsample, we multiply its variance $p_i q_i$ by its sample size n. Summing all such quantities and dividing that sum by its degrees of freedom $m(n - 1)$ gives s_w^2, the estimate of σ_w^2.

To estimate σ_p^2 without regard to its component parts, we simply divide s_b^2 by mn (6.3.3). For an estimate of σ_b^2, when required, we take s_w^2 from s_b^2 and divide by n. This result gauges the contribution of differences among subpopulations to the variance of the proportion. To get the intraclass correlation coefficient ρ, we substitute s_w^2 and s_b^2 in (6.3.10). Although ρ cannot be less than zero, given N infinite, we may obtain, owing to the accidents of random sampling, a negative sample estimate. We probably would consider that result as evidence that ρ tends to 0 in the population.

Numerical Example. Let us suppose that we have five subsamples of 40 cases each and that we are required to estimate the variance of the sample proportion. Our calculations are given in this worksheet:

Subsample	p_i	$p_i q_i$	$n p_i q_i$	$p_i - p$	$(p_i - p)^2$
1	.30	.21	8.40	−.30	.09
2	.90	.09	3.60	.30	.09
3	.60	.24	9.60	.00	.00
4	.40	.24	9.60	−.20	.04
5	.80	.16	6.40	.20	.04
Sum	3.00		37.60	.00	.26

$$s_w^2 = \frac{37.60}{5(39)} = .19 \qquad s_b^2 = \frac{40}{4}(.26) = 2.60, \qquad s_p^2 = \frac{2.60}{200} = .013$$

$$\hat{\sigma}_b^2 = \frac{2.60 - .19}{40} \qquad\qquad \hat{\rho} = \frac{2.60 - .19}{2.60 + .19(39)}$$

$$= \frac{2.41}{40} \qquad\qquad\qquad = \frac{2.41}{10.12}$$

$$= .06 \qquad\qquad\qquad\qquad = .24$$

Multi-stage Sampling. Before proceeding to finite populations, we note that the theory for infinite populations may be readily extended to sampling in three or more stages. To illustrate this point, we make the extension to three stages, taking as our point of departure any sample value in its decomposed form:

$$y_{ijk} = \mu + (\mu_i - \mu) + (\mu_{ij} - \mu_i) + (y_{ijk} - \mu_{ij}).$$

The mean of kmn such measures would be:

$$\bar{\bar{y}} = \mu + \frac{1}{k}\sum(\mu_i - \mu) + \frac{1}{km}\sum(\mu_{ij} - \mu) + \frac{1}{kmn}\sum(y_{ijk} - \mu_{ij}),$$

where k = the number of first-stage units,

m = the number of second-stage units drawn from each of the k first-stage units, and

n = the number of third-stage units (elements).

Transposing $\mu = E(\bar{\bar{y}})$ and taking the expectation, we get the variance of the mean (Cochran 1953: 229),

(6.3.13) $$E(\bar{\bar{y}} - \mu)^2 = \frac{\sigma_{b_1}^2}{k} + \frac{\sigma_b^2}{km} + \frac{\sigma_w^2}{kmn}$$

where $\sigma_{b_1}^2$ is the mean value of $(\mu_i - \mu)^2$ and $\sigma_{b_2}^2$ is the mean value of $(\mu_{ij} - \mu_i)^2$. To estimate this variance, we divide $s_b^2 = mn\sum(\bar{y}_i - \bar{\bar{y}})^2/k - 1$ by kmn in accordance with the following argument:

$$E(s_b^2) = \frac{mn}{k-1}E\sum(\bar{y}_i - \bar{\bar{y}})^2$$

(6.3.14) $$= mn\sigma_{b_1}^2 + n\sigma_{b_2}^2 + \sigma_w^2,$$

where

$$\bar{\bar{y}} = \frac{y}{kmn}$$

and

$$\bar{y}_i = \frac{y_i}{mn}.$$

Dividing both sides of (6.3.14) by kmn, we obtain

$$\frac{1}{kmn}E(s_b^2) = \frac{\sigma_{b_1}^2}{k} + \frac{\sigma_{b_2}^2}{km} + \frac{\sigma_w^2}{kmn},$$

which serves to demonstrate that s_b^2/kmn is an unbiased estimate of $\sigma_{\bar{\bar{y}}}^2$.

From (6.3.13) we see that the variance of the mean will consist of three terms when we sample in three stages. Putting this result together with previous results, we infer that the variance of the mean will consist of as many terms as there are sampling stages. In one-stage sampling, the variance of the mean will consist of a single term; in two-stage sampling, the variance of the mean will consist of two terms, etc. Since each stage in the sampling process contributes one term to the variance of the mean, the precision of multi-stage sampling relative to sampling from the total population decreases as the number of stages increases. However, our choice of design depends not on relative precision, but rather on the cost per case. Because of the sharp reduction in the cost per interview, we may draw a two-stage sample even though its precision relative to a simple random sample is quite low.

EXERCISES

1. Given the following five subsamples of four measures each, M and N infinite:

(1)	(2)	(3)	(4)	(5)
4	0	0	4	9
6	10	4	5	8
3	3	7	4	7
7	3	1	3	4

   (a) Compute s_w^2, s_b^2, $\hat{\sigma}_b^2$, and $s_{\bar{y}}^2$ and interpret.
   (b) Determine the 95 percent confidence interval for the true mean on the assumption that the ratio of $\bar{y}$ to $s_{\bar{y}}$ is approximately normal.
2. Fill in the missing information in the following AOV presentation of sample data:

	SS	df	MS
Total		99	
Between-subsample means	960		240
Within-subsamples			10

   What proportion of $\sigma_{\bar{y}}^2$ is attributable to differences between psu means?

3. Given that \$1,750 is available to draw a sample of $mn = 100$ cases, that $C_1 = \$20$ and $C_2 = \$10$, and that $\sigma_w^2 = 10$, $\sigma_b^2 = 12$,
   (a) which of the following combinations of m and n is best? Explain your reasoning.

m	n
50	2
25	4
20	5
10	10
5	20
4	25
2	50

   (b) What is the numerical value of the intraclass correlation coefficient for this problem?

(c) For the different values of n in (a), show by calculation that the precision of cluster sampling relative to simple random sampling decreases as n increases.

4. Calculate the intraclass correlation coefficient ($\hat{\rho}$) for the data given in Exercise 1 (p. 274). What is the relative precision of two-stage sampling for that problem?

5. Given that $m = 5$, $n = 40$, find the appropriate estimates and run an AOV for the following cluster sample of proportions. Compute an estimate of ρ, and evaluate the relative precision of cluster sampling against simple random sampling.

Subsample	p_i	$p_i q_i$	$n p_i q_i$	$p_i - p$	$(p_i - p)^2$
1	.50				
2	.93				
3	.67				
4	.80				
5	.90				

6. Given these ten subsamples of five cases each, calculate s_w^2, s_b^2, $\hat{\sigma}_b^2$, and $s_{\bar{y}}^2$.

					Subsamples					
	1	2	3	4	5	6	7	8	9	10
	4	10	11	2	14	17	13	7	3	9
	6	15	9	19	4	9	18	2	18	12
	1	9	13	11	8	12	4	10	5	16
	7	20	4	8	16	7	14	15	8	18
	12	6	18	5	3	5	6	11	1	20
y_i	30	60	55	45	45	50	55	45	35	75
$\bar{y}_i$	6	12	11	9	9	10	11	9	7	15

$$y = 495 \qquad \bar{y} = 49.5$$

$$\bar{\bar{y}} = \frac{495}{50} = 9.9.$$

PART 4
M Finite, N's Finite and Equal

We now lift the restriction that M and N be infinite and permit both to take any finite number. The composition of the variance of the sample mean in its essentials is unaffected by the removal of this restriction, although the formulas are somewhat more complex. At least, they appear more complex, perhaps because of the presence of finite multipliers which vanish under the assumption of M and N infinite. These additional terms reflect the principle that a sample drawn without replacement from a finite population (simple random sample) will yield greater precision than a comparable sample drawn with replacement (unrestricted random sampling) from the same population. This principle is embodied in the equation linking the variances of the mean for sampling with and without replacement from a single population of N units (Deming 1950: 102). This is:

$$S_{\bar{y}}^2 = S^2 \left(\frac{1}{n} - \frac{1}{N} \right)$$

$$= \frac{S^2}{n} \left(1 - \frac{n}{N} \right)$$

(6.4.1)
$$= \tilde{S}_{\bar{y}}^2 \left(1 - \frac{n}{N} \right),$$

where $S^2 = \dfrac{1}{N-1} \sum\limits_{1}^{N} (Y_i - \bar{Y})^2$,

$S_{\bar{y}}^2 = $ variance of mean, sampling without replacement,

and $\quad \tilde{S}_{\bar{y}}^2 = $ variance of mean, sampling with replacement (as if population were infinite).

From this result (6.4.1), it is clear that $S_{\bar{y}}^2$ will always be smaller than $\tilde{S}_{\bar{y}}^2$, the extent depending on the sampling fraction, n/N. Our conclusion is that the mean of n units drawn without replacement from a finite population of size N will have a smaller standard error than the mean of as many units drawn with replacement from the same population. Likewise, the mean of mn units drawn without replacement at both stages will have a smaller standard error than the mean of as many units drawn with replacement at both stages, as if both M and N were infinite.

To verify this general principle, we deal first with the case of equal N_i's: $N_1 = N_2 = \cdots = N_i = \cdots = N$, since results for this case are quite similar to those for M and N infinite, as given in Part 3. In this treatment, we require that both psu's (subpopulations) and ssu's (elements) be selected by simple random sampling (without replacement) and, further, that the sampling fraction within psu's be uniform. This is in keeping with our general purpose to exemplify general principles by simple procedures, rather than to give alternative designs for special purposes. Since the population sum is measurable for a finite population, we consider a procedure for estimating that sum, as well as a procedure for estimating the population mean. Although the population sum may be needed for its own sake, we utilize it primarily to simplify the analysis of unequal N_i's, considered in Part 5.

Notation. As we progress, our symbolism will necessarily become more complex and unwieldy, owing principally to the sampling fractions which now appear as terms in the formulas, where before they were absent.

Symbol	Term

Population

M	number of psu's
N	elements in each psu
Y_{ij}	j^{th} value, i^{th} psu
$Y_i = \sum_1^N Y_{ij}$	sum, i^{th} psu
$\bar{Y}_i = \dfrac{Y_i}{N}$	mean, i^{th} psu
$Y = \sum Y_i$	population sum
$\bar{Y} = \dfrac{Y}{M}$	sum per psu
$\bar{\bar{Y}} = \dfrac{Y}{MN}$	population mean
$S_t^2 = \dfrac{1}{MN - 1} \sum\sum(Y_{ij} - \bar{\bar{Y}})^2$	population variance
$S_{1Y}^2 = \dfrac{1}{M - 1} \sum(Y_i - \bar{Y})^2$	first-stage variance
$S_b^2 = \dfrac{\sum(\bar{Y}_i - \bar{\bar{Y}})^2}{M - 1} = \dfrac{S_{1Y}^2}{N^2}$	between psu variance
$S_w^2 = \dfrac{1}{M(N - 1)} \sum\sum(Y_{ij} - \bar{Y}_i)^2$	within psu variance
$S_{\bar{\bar{y}}}^2 = E(\bar{\bar{y}} - \bar{\bar{Y}})^2$	variance of mean
$\dfrac{S_{\bar{\bar{y}}}^2}{\bar{\bar{Y}}^2}$	rel-variance of mean

Sample

m	number of psu's selected
n	subsample size
$f_1 = \dfrac{m}{M}$	sampling fraction, first stage
$f_2 = \dfrac{n}{N}$	sampling fraction, second stage
$f = f_1 f_2$	overall sampling fraction
y_{ij}	j^{th} value, i^{th} subsample

$$y_i = \sum_{1}^{n} y_{ij} \qquad\qquad\qquad \text{sum of values, } i^{\text{th}} \text{ subsample}$$

$$\bar{y}_i = \frac{y_i}{n} \qquad\qquad\qquad\qquad \text{mean value, } i^{\text{th}} \text{ subsample}$$

$$y = \sum y_i \qquad\qquad\qquad\qquad \text{sample sum}$$

$$\bar{y} = \frac{y}{m} \qquad\qquad\qquad\qquad \text{sum per psu}$$

$$\bar{\bar{y}} = \frac{y}{mn} \qquad\qquad\qquad\qquad \text{sample mean}$$

$$s_b^2 = \frac{n}{m-1} \sum (\bar{y}_i - \bar{\bar{y}})^2 \qquad\qquad \text{between sample variance}$$

$$s_w^2 = \frac{1}{m(n-1)} \sum\sum (y_{ij} - \bar{y}_i)^2 \qquad \text{within sample variance}$$

$$s_{\bar{\bar{y}}}^2 = (1 - f_1) \frac{s_b^2}{mn} + f_1(1 - f_2) \frac{s_w^2}{mn} \qquad \text{estimate of variance of mean}$$

Sample Estimates. The sample estimates whose respective variances we wish to determine are

$$\bar{\bar{y}} = \frac{y}{mn},$$

which is an unbiased estimate of the population mean,

$$E(\bar{\bar{y}}) = \bar{Y},$$

and

$$y' = MN\bar{\bar{y}},$$

which is an unbiased estimate of Y, the population total,

$$E(y') = Y$$

To estimate $\bar{Y}$, be it noted, we divide the sum of all sample values by the number of values; to estimate the population sum (Y), we divide the sum of all sample values (y) by the overall sampling fraction, $f = f_1 f_2$. Because of their simple form, these estimates have come to be known as simple estimates; they are also called self-weighting estimates, as no weights need be attached to the y_i's before they are summed and averaged.

Variance of $\bar{\bar{y}} = y/mn$. In getting the variance of $\bar{\bar{y}}$, our first step is to put that average in decomposed form as follows:

$$\bar{\bar{y}} = \bar{Y} + \frac{1}{m} \sum (\bar{Y}_i - \bar{Y}) + \frac{1}{mn} \sum \sum (y_{ij} - \bar{Y}_i).$$

On transposing $\bar{Y} = E(\bar{\bar{y}})$ from right to left, squaring and taking the expectation of both sides, we obtain the variance of the mean $(S_{\bar{\bar{y}}}^2)$:

(6.4.2) $\qquad E(\bar{\bar{y}} - \bar{Y})^2 = (1 - f_1) \dfrac{S_b^2}{m} + (1 - f_2) \dfrac{S_w^2}{mn}.$

A proof is given by Cochran (1953: 222). Formulas (6.3.2) and (6.4.2) are essentially alike, except for $(1 - f_1)$ and $(1 - f_2)$, which are attached as coefficients to S_b^2 and S_w^2, respectively. Since a finite multiplier will decrease in magnitude as the sampling fraction increases, the variance of the mean of a two-stage sample will decrease as the overall sampling fraction increases. An increase in either f_1 or f_2 will reduce the value of $S_{\bar{\bar{y}}}^2$. We may ignore the finite population corrections if sampling fractions are negligible, otherwise we must take them into account. If we neglect the finite population corrections when they are substantial, we overestimate the true variance of the mean. This will make the sample mean seem less precise than is actually the case.

Variance of Estimated Population Sum (y'). At this juncture, as ground work for subsequent developments, we give the variance of the estimated population sum, $y' = MN\bar{\bar{y}}$. In approaching that variance, we have recourse to the principle that the variance of $Y = kX$, where k is a constant, is equal to the variance X multiplied by k^2. That is,

$$\sigma_y^2 = k^2 \sigma_x^2.$$

By this principle, the variance of $y' = MN\bar{\bar{y}}$ is

$$S_{y'}^2 = (MN)^2 S_{\bar{\bar{y}}}^2$$

(6.4.3) $\qquad = (MN)^2 (1 - f_1) \dfrac{S_b^2}{m} + (MN)^2 (1 - f_2) \dfrac{S_w^2}{mn}.$

Substituting S_{1Y}^2/N^2 for S_b^2, we get the simpler expression:

(6.4.4) $\qquad S_{y'}^2 = M^2 (1 - f_1) \dfrac{S_{1Y}^2}{m} + (MN)^2 (1 - f_2) \dfrac{S_w^2}{mn}.$

To the degree that the variance of psu sums is more readily calculated than the variance of psu means, Formula (6.4.4) is more convenient than (6.4.3). It is employed regularly in standard works on sampling theory (Hansen, Hurwitz, and Madow I 1953: 253).

Rel-Variance. We digress here to introduce the rel-variance of the sample mean ($\bar{y}$) and the rel-variance of the estimated population sum (y'). Aside from its descriptive utility, the rel-variance of y' is especially useful in analyzing the variance of the mean when psu's are not equal in size (see Part 5).

If we divide a variance by the square of the mean on which that variance is based, the result is termed the *rel-variance*. In notation:

$$V_x^2 = \frac{S_x^2}{\bar{X}^2}.$$

The square root of this result is the familiar *coefficient of variation*, or the ratio of the standard deviation to the mean. To get the rel-variance of $\bar{y}$, we divide its variance by the square of its mean (expected) value as follows:

(6.4.5)
$$V_{\bar{y}}^2 = \frac{S_{\bar{y}}^2}{\bar{Y}^2}$$

Similarly, to get the rel-variance of y', we divide its variance by the square of its mean value $(MN\bar{Y})^2$. Carrying out this operation, we obtain

(6.4.6)
$$V_{y'}^2 = \frac{(MN)^2 S_{\bar{y}}^2}{(MN\bar{Y})^2}$$
$$= \frac{S_{\bar{y}}^2}{\bar{Y}^2}.$$

Comparing the rel-variance of $\bar{y}$ and y', we find that

$$V_{\bar{y}}^2 = V_{y'}^2.$$

The student should be cautioned that this equality does not hold for unequal N_i's (Hansen, Hurwitz, and Madow I 1953: 253–254); nevertheless, it is of interest that for the case of equal N_i's, the estimated mean and the estimated sum have the same relative variability.

Estimating $S_{\bar{y}}^2$. To estimate $S_{\bar{y}}^2$ from a sample of mn elements, we replace S_b^2 and S_w^2 in (6.4.2) by their corresponding sample estimates. The within-sample mean square is an unbiased estimate of S_w^2:

$$E(s_w^2) = S_w^2,$$

and we may substitute s_w^2 for S_w^2 without further ado. However, the estimation of S_b^2 is a trifle more complicated. We start with the expectation of s_b^2. This is:

(6.4.7)
$$E(s_b^2) = nS_b^2 + S_w^2\left(1 - \frac{n}{N}\right).$$

This result in different notation is proved in Cochran (1953:223). Transposing terms and substituting $E(s_w^2)$ for S_w^2, we obtain

$$S_b^2 = \frac{1}{n} E(s_b^2) - \left(\frac{1}{n} - \frac{1}{N}\right) E(s_w^2),$$

which is a demonstration that the quantity,

(6.4.8)
$$\hat{S}_b^2 = \frac{s_b^2}{n} - s_w^2 \left(\frac{1}{n} - \frac{1}{N}\right),$$

is an unbiased estimate of S_b^2. Substituting this estimate (6.4.8) for S_b^2 in (6.4.2), we get after simplification,

(6.4.9)
$$s_{\bar{\bar{y}}}^2 = (1 - f_1) \frac{s_b^2}{mn} + f_1(1 - f_2) \frac{s_w^2}{mn}.$$

We may use this formula to estimate the variance of the mean when subpopulations are equal in size.

Effect of Sampling Fractions on $S_{\bar{\bar{y}}}^2$ and $s_{\bar{\bar{y}}}^2$. By permitting f_1 and f_2 to vary from 0 to 1, we may observe the effect of changing sampling fractions on $S_{\bar{\bar{y}}}^2$ (6.4.2) and $s_{\bar{\bar{y}}}^2$ (6.4.9). We restrict ourselves to values of 0 and 1, since these limits represent points of correspondence between multi-stage sampling and other sampling techniques. When the sample is as large as the population, the sampling fraction is 1; when the sample is infinitesimal in relation to the population, the sampling fraction is 0.

We first deal with the true variance of the mean (6.4.2) with constants S_b^2 and S_w^2. When both m/M and n/N are negligible, the variance of the mean simplifies to

$$S_{\bar{\bar{y}}}^2 = \frac{S_b^2}{m} + \frac{S_w^2}{mn},$$

which is the same as the variance of the mean with M and N infinite, except that S_b^2 and S_w^2 appear in place of σ_b^2 and σ_w^2.

As m approaches M, the variance of the mean reduces to

$$\frac{S_w^2}{Mn} (1 - f),$$

which is identical with the variance of the mean for proportional stratified sampling (Cochran 1953). Since we select cases from every stratum in stratified sampling, results based on proportional stratified sampling will necessarily be identical to those produced by uniform subsampling from every primary sampling unit. Our conclusion is that two-stage sampling corresponds to stratified sampling when $m = M$. And, as with stratified sampling, it will usually be more precise than simple random sampling, since S_w^2 is generally smaller than S_t^2.

Thirdly, consider the situation in which n approaches N or 100% sampling within psu's. Under this restriction, which is sometimes regarded as the distinguishing feature of cluster sampling, (6.4.2) reduces to

$$S_{\bar{\bar{y}}}^2 = (1 - f) \frac{S_b^2}{m},$$

which is the same as the variance of the mean of m elements drawn without replacement from a population of M elements. Since the quantity $\sum_1^N (Y_{ij} - \mu_i)$ will be constantly zero for each sample mean when $n = N$, the variation in $\bar{\bar{y}}$ will be affected only by variation in the quantity $\sum_1^m (\mu_i - \mu)$.

Consider now the effect of changing sampling fractions on $s_{\bar{\bar{y}}}^2$ (6.4.9) which has s_w^2 and s_b^2 as its principal terms. If m/M is negligible, (6.4.9) reduces to s_b^2/mn, which corresponds to the previous result for both M and N infinite. On the other hand, if n/N is negligible, (6.4.9) maintains itself with practically no change,

$$s_{\bar{\bar{y}}}^2 = (1 - f_1) \frac{s_b^2}{mn} + (f_1) \frac{s_w^2}{mn},$$

and entails the calculation of both s_b^2 and s_w^2.

If $m = M$, the formula (6.4.9) becomes identical to that for proportional stratified sampling with M psu's as strata:

$$s_{\bar{\bar{y}}}^2 = (1 - f) \frac{s_w^2}{Mn}.$$

In this case, we ignore s_b^2.

If $n = N$, the formula reduces to that appropriate for simple random sampling of elements with psu means as elements:

$$s_{\bar{\bar{y}}}^2 = (1 - f) \frac{s_b^2}{mN}.$$

In this case, we ignore s_w^2.

The foregoing results are quoted not because of their possible practical value, but rather to exemplify an approach to the precision of the mean. By manipulating sampling fractions, or equivalently the finite multipliers, it is possible to study their bearing on sample precision.

Subsampling as Analysis of Variance. To link subsampling to the analysis of variance, we arrange the foregoing results in a conventional AOV table:

Analysis of Variance for Population

Source	df	Sum of Squares	Mean Square
Between psu's	$M - 1$	$\sum(\bar{Y}_i - \bar{\bar{Y}})^2$	$\dfrac{\sum(\bar{Y}_i - \bar{\bar{Y}})^2}{M - 1} = S_b^2$
Within psu's	$M(N - 1)$	$\sum\sum(Y_{ij} - \bar{Y}_i)^2$	$\dfrac{\sum\sum(Y_{ij} - \bar{Y}_i)^2}{M(N - 1)} = S_w^2$

Analysis of Variance for Sample

Source	df	Sum of Squares	Mean Square	Expectation
Between	$m - 1$	$n\sum(\bar{y}_i - \bar{y})^2$	$\dfrac{n\sum(\bar{y}_i - \bar{y})^2}{m - 1}$	$nS_b^2 + S_w^2\left(\dfrac{N - n}{N}\right)$
Within	$m(n - 1)$	$\sum\sum(y_{ij} - \bar{y}_i)^2$	$\dfrac{\sum\sum(y_{ij} - \bar{y}_i)^2}{m(n - 1)}$	S_w^2

Numerical Example. An example of between-sample and within-sample sums of squares, and the results in which they culminate is given in Table 6.4.1. The analysis of variance for the same data is also given in that table.

Table 6.4.1 Five Subsamples, Ten Values Each, $f_1 = 5/100$, $f_2 = 10/1{,}000$, $f = 50/10{,}000$.

	(1)	(2)	(3)	(4)	(5)
	16	20	15	30	16
	24	25	28	10	33
	18	31	21	27	23
	19	17	10	24	34
	13	27	16	19	9
	15	19	11	18	10
	17	24	14	23	35
	13	30	22	29	21
	20	26	27	12	32
	25	21	16	28	17
$y_i = $	180	240	180	220	230
$\bar{y}_i = $	18	24	18	22	23

$$y = 1{,}050$$

$$\bar{y} = 210$$

$$\bar{\bar{y}} = 21$$

$$s_w^2 = 45.6$$

$$s_b^2 = 80.0$$

$$s_{\bar{y}}^2 = (1 - .05)\frac{80}{50} + .05(1 - .01)\frac{45.6}{50}$$

$$= 1.52 + .05$$

$$= 1.57$$

Analysis of Variance

Source	df	SS	Mean Square	Expectation
Within subsamples	45	2052	45.6	S_w^2
Between subsamples	4	320	80.0	$nS_b^2 + S_w^2\left(n - \dfrac{n}{N}\right)$

Intraclass Correlation Coefficient, ρ_I. To measure the inflation in $S_{\bar{y}}^2$ due to subsampling, we again have recourse to the intraclass correlation coefficient ρ_I. To distinguish this coefficient from the product-moment correlation coefficient (ρ_{xy}), we attach the subscript "I" to "ρ". By appropriate operations it may be shown that

(6.4.10) $$S_{\bar{y}}^2/S_{\bar{y}}^2 \doteq 1 + \rho_I(n - 1),$$

which expresses the tendency of precision to decrease as ρ_I increases, other things being equal. Note that the right side of (6.4.10) is an approximation of the left side rather than an equal; it approaches full equality as the sampling fractions, m/M and n/N, tend to zero.

The core of the intraclass correlation coefficient continues to be the ratio of S_b^2 to S_t^2, as in sampling from infinite populations; however, with M and N finite, its form is somewhat more complex, owing to the presence of terms which vanish when M and N become very large. To aid our understanding of these alterations, we start with the total sum of squares in expanded form as follows:

$$\sum\sum(Y_{ij} - \bar{\bar{Y}})^2 = N\sum(\bar{Y}_i - \bar{\bar{Y}})^2 + \sum\sum(Y_{ij} - \bar{Y}_i)^2.$$

Dividing both sides by MN, we get

$$\frac{MN - 1}{MN} S_t^2 = \frac{M - 1}{M} S_b^2 + \frac{N - 1}{N} S_w^2$$

$$= \left[\frac{M - 1}{M} S_b^2 - \frac{S_w^2}{N} \right] + S_w^2.$$

Dividing the first term on the right (in brackets) by the left side, we get

(6.4.11)
$$\rho_I = \frac{\dfrac{M - 1}{M} S_b^2 - \dfrac{S_w^2}{N}}{\dfrac{MN - 1}{MN} S_t^2}.$$

With M and N large, as is often the case, Formula (6.4.11) reduces to

$$\rho_I = \frac{S_b^2}{S_t^2}$$

in agreement with previous theory (p. 269).

When $S_w^2 = 0$, $\dfrac{MN - 1}{MN} S_t^2 = \dfrac{M - 1}{M} S_b^2$, and

$$\rho_I = 1.00.$$

When $S_b^2 = 0$, $\dfrac{MN - 1}{MN} S_t^2 = \dfrac{N - 1}{N} S_w^2$, and

$$\rho_I = \frac{-1}{N - 1}.$$

We thus see that with M and N finite, ρ_I has $-1/N - 1$ as its lower limit, and the intraclass correlation will be negative when psu means are identical in value.

Intraclass Correlation (ρ_I) and Product-Moment Correlation (ρ_{xy}). From the foregoing, the student will have anticipated the procedure for estimating ρ_I from sample data; however, before setting forth that procedure, we consider an alternative approach to ρ_I to demonstrate its relationship to the product-moment correlation coefficient (ρ_{xy}). In this analysis we take the product-moment correlation coefficient (ρ_{xy}) as our point of departure. This coefficient is appropriate as a measure of correlation between M paired values, when each pair contains one X and one Y, so that there are as many X and Y values, respectively, as there are pairs of values. In short, ρ_{xy} is appropriate as a measure of relationship between two different variables. To obtain the product-moment ρ_{xy}, we get the covariance for X and Y and divide that result by the product of the respective standard deviations:

$$\rho_{xy} = \frac{\sum xy}{M\sigma_x\sigma_y},$$

where $x = X - \bar{X}$, $y = Y - \bar{Y}$, and M represents the number of pairs. A simple numerical example of this well-known procedure is supplied at this point.

X	Y	x	y	x^2	y^2	xy
1	3	-2	-2	4	4	4
2	4	-1	-1	1	1	1
3	5	0	0	0	0	0
4	6	1	1	1	1	1
5	7	2	2	4	4	4
15	25			10	10	10

$$\sum xy = 10 \qquad\qquad \rho_{xy} = \frac{\sum xy}{M\sigma_x\sigma_y}$$

$$\sigma_x = \sqrt{2} \qquad\qquad\qquad = \frac{10}{5\sqrt{2}\sqrt{2}}$$

$$\sigma_y = \sqrt{2}$$

$$M = 5 \qquad\qquad\qquad\quad = 1.00$$

Continuing our analysis, we ask: what is the appropriate measure of correlation between M pairs of values when values within pairs carry no identification as X or Y and are regarded as mere replicates? Such paired replicates, like bivariate data, may be arranged in two columns, except that the order of values within rows is immaterial; it makes no difference whether a given replicate appears in the first column or in the second column.

The problem of measuring the degree of similarity between such paired replicates finds its solution in the intraclass correlation coefficient, ρ_I. As expounded by R. A. Fisher (1946), the solution requires that each pair of replicates be listed twice instead of once, and that the order of replicates within pairs differ between entries. In consequence of this requirement, each series (column) will have $2M$ instead of M entries, and both series will necessarily have the same mean and variance (standard deviation) since they are identically composed. From this set-up of $2M$ pairs, we calculate the product-moment coefficient ρ_{xy}, which is taken as an index of homogeneity of values within pairs. As a reminder that each pair has been recorded twice, and that both series have the same mean and standard deviation, the result was named by Fisher the intraclass correlation coefficient.

In Table 6.4.2, we double list the entries of the foregoing table (p. 286) and calculate ρ_I. Note that $\rho_I = .33$ is appreciably smaller than $\rho_{xy} = 1.00$, consistent with the principle that paired measures standardized on the mean and standard deviation of the combined series will generally show less similarity than measures standardized on their own means and standard deviations, respectively. The student should satisfy himself as to the validity of this principle.

Table 6.4.2 Calculation of ρ_I

X_1	X_2	x_1	x_2	x_1^2	x_2^2	$x_1 x_2$
1	3	-3	-1	9	1	3
2	4	-2	0	4	0	0
3	5	-1	1	1	1	-1
4	6	0	2	0	4	0
5	7	1	3	1	9	3
3	1	-1	-3	1	9	3
4	2	0	-2	0	4	0
5	3	1	-1	1	1	-1
6	4	2	0	4	0	0
7	5	3	1	9	1	3
Sum 40	40			30	30	10
Mean 4	4			3	3	1

$$\sum x_1 x_2 = 10$$

$$\sigma_1 = \sqrt{3}$$

$$\sigma_2 = \sqrt{3}$$

$$2M = 10$$

$$\rho_{12} = \frac{\sum x_1 x_2}{2M\sigma_1\sigma_2}$$

$$= \frac{10}{10\sqrt{3}\,\sqrt{3}}$$

$$= .33.$$

N > 2. The foregoing procedure is immediately applicable to pairs of values, but what is to be done when each grouping consists of three or more values? In response to this question, it was proposed that all combinations of values two at a time be formed from each group of *N* values and that replicates within each *different* pair be recorded twice, but in reverse order. In other words, each value for each of $\binom{N}{2}$ pairs would appear once in the first series and once in the second series.

By way of example, let us suppose that we have $N = 3$ replicates within each of $M = 5$ groups as follows:

Grouping No.	Replicate No.		
	1	2	3
1	1	3	2
2	2	4	3
3	3	5	4
4	4	6	5
5	5	7	6

From each grouping of three replicates, we get $\binom{3}{2} = 3$ pairs. Since we record each pair twice in reverse order, each grouping gives rise to six entries in the double table. Manipulating each grouping in this way, we get a total of $5 \times 6 = 30$ pairs, as in Table 6.4.3. From this example, we see that ρ_I is the product-moment correlation coefficient for permutations of values two at a time formed from M groupings of N values each. The entire procedure may be summarized compactly as follows:

$$(6.4.12) \qquad \rho_I = \frac{\sum (X_1 - \overline{X})(X_2 - \overline{X})}{2M\binom{N}{2}\sigma_1\sigma_2}$$

$$= \frac{\sum x_1 x_2}{MN(N-1)\sigma_x^2},$$

where $\quad \overline{X}_1 = \overline{X}_2 = \overline{X},$

$\qquad \sigma_1 = \sigma_2 = \sigma_x,$

$MN(N-1) = 2M\binom{N}{2}$ = number of pairs in the double table.

Now, it may be shown (Hansen, Hurwitz, and Madow II 1953: 164; Kish 1965b: 170) that Formula (6.4.12), the covariance of the double table divided by the variance of that table, is identical with

$$\rho_I = \frac{\dfrac{M-1}{M}S_b^2 - \dfrac{S_w^2}{N}}{\dfrac{MN-1}{MN}S_t^2}.$$

Our conclusion from all this is that the intraclass correlation coefficient may be interpreted (with caution) as the proportion of the total variance attributable to the variance of psu means. This interpretation requires no qualifications when both M and N are infinitely large.

Table 6.4.3   Calculation of ρ_I, $M = 5$, $N = 3$.

Entry No.	X_1	X_2	x_1	x_2	x_1^2	x_2^2	$x_1 x_2$
1	1	3	-3	-1	9	1	3
2	2	4	-2	0	4	0	0
3	3	5	-1	1	1	1	-1
4	4	6	0	2	0	4	0
5	5	7	1	3	1	9	3
6	3	1	-1	-3	1	9	3
7	4	2	0	-2	0	4	0
8	5	3	1	-1	1	1	-1
9	6	4	2	0	4	0	0
10	7	5	3	1	9	1	3
11	1	2	-3	-2	9	4	6
12	2	3	-2	-1	4	1	4
13	3	4	-1	0	1	0	1
14	4	5	0	1	0	1	0
15	5	6	1	2	1	4	2
16	2	1	-2	-3	4	9	6
17	3	2	-1	-2	1	4	2
18	4	3	0	-1	0	1	0
19	5	4	1	0	1	0	0
20	6	5	2	1	4	1	2
21	3	2	-1	-2	1	4	2
22	4	3	0	-1	0	1	0
23	5	4	1	0	1	0	0
24	6	5	2	1	4	1	2
25	7	6	3	2	9	4	6
26	2	3	-2	-1	4	1	2
27	3	4	-1	0	1	0	0
28	4	5	0	1	0	1	0
29	5	6	1	2	1	4	2
30	6	7	2	3	4	9	6
Sum	120	120	0	0	80	80	50
Mean	4	4			2.67	2.67	1.67

$$\rho_I = \frac{1.67}{2.67}$$

$$= .63$$

Estimating ρ_I. From sample data, we may obtain results whose expectations are, respectively, S_b^2, S_w^2, and S_t^2, and which upon substitution provide an unbiased estimate of ρ_I, as defined in (6.4.11). We substitute s_w^2 for S_w^2 and $\dfrac{s_b^2}{n} - s_w^2\left(\dfrac{1}{n} - \dfrac{1}{N}\right)$ for S_b^2. For an estimate of S_t^2, we substitute previously obtained estimates of S_b^2 and S_w^2 in the right side of this expression:

$$S_t^2 = \left(\frac{MN}{MN-1}\right)\left[\left(\frac{M-1}{M}\right)(S_b^2) + \left(\frac{N-1}{N}\right)(S_w^2)\right].$$

When $\dfrac{M-1}{M}$ and $\dfrac{N-1}{N}$ can be approximated by 1, as is often the case,
the estimate of S_t^2 reduces to

$$s_t^2 = \frac{s_b^2 + (n-1)s_w^2}{n},$$

and the estimate of ρ_I reduces to

$$\hat{\rho}_I = \frac{s_b^2 - s_w^2}{s_b^2 + (n-1)s_w^2},$$

as in the case of M and N infinite. An example of this procedure is given in the Exercises.

EXERCISES

1. Assume the following finite population:

counties (psu's)

		A	B	C
towns (ssu's)	1	3	4	0
	2	2	3	7
	3	1	5	2

Y_{ij} = number of banks in jth town, ith county

	A	B	C
Y_i	6	12	9
$\bar{Y}_i$	2	4	3

$Y = 27,$ $\bar{Y} = 9,$ $\bar{\bar{Y}} = 3$

With sampling fractions $f_1 = f_2 = 2/3$ there are $\binom{M}{m}\binom{N}{n}$ $M = 27$ possible samples as follow:

No.	A	B	No.	A	C	No.	B	C
1	3,2	4,3	10	3,2	0,7	19	4,3	0,7
2		4,5	11		0,2	20		0,2
3		3,5	12		7,2	21		7,2
4	3,1	4,3	13	3,1	0,7	22	4,5	0,7
5		4,5	14		0,2	23		0,2
6		3,5	15		7,2	24		7,2
7	2,1	4,3	16	2,1	0,7	25	3,5	0,7
8		4,5	17		0,2	26		0,2
9		3,5	18		7,2	27		7,2

(a) For the population, compute S_t^2, S_b^2, S_w^2, and $S_{\bar{y}}^2$.

(b) For each possible sample, compute the values of $\bar{\bar{y}}$, s_w^2, and s_b^2.

(c) Calculate $s_{\bar{\bar{y}}}^2$ for each sample.

(d) A statistic $\hat{\theta}$ is an unbiased estimator of the parameter θ if $E(\hat{\theta}) = \theta$. For finite sampling distributions, $E(\hat{\theta}) = \sum_i \hat{\theta}_i p_i$. For the sampling distribution given above $p_i = 1/27$ for $1 \leq i \leq 27$; hence, to get $E(s_{\bar{\bar{y}}}^2)$ we calculate the mean of the estimates obtained in (c) above. Verify that $s_{\bar{\bar{y}}}^2$ is an unbiased estimate of $S_{\bar{y}}^2$.

(e) Find $V_{y'}^2$.

2. The ratio of $S_{\bar{\bar{y}}}^2$ to $S_{\bar{y}}^2$ is approximated by the following expression: $1 + \rho(n - 1)$. Calculate $S_{\bar{y}}^2$ and $S_{\bar{\bar{y}}}^2$. Solve for ρ. Next, calculate ρ by Formula (6.4.11). Finally, calculate ρ by Formula (6.4.12). Note that the approximation of ρ by (6.4.10) is not very good when M and N are small.

3. Consider the following population:

Block No.	Store No.	Daily Payroll (hundreds of dollars)
1	1	100
	2	50
2	1	100
	2	150
3	1	80
	2	60
4	1	150
	2	140
5	1	100
	2	40
6	1	50
	2	180

(a) Determine the variance of the sample mean under each of the following conditions:

   (i) simple random sampling with $n = 4$

   (ii) $m = 3$, $n = 1$

   (iii) $m = 6$, $n = 1$

   (iv) $m = 1$, $n = 2$

(b) Compute ρ by the direct method. Verify that

$$\rho = \frac{\dfrac{M-1}{M} S_b^2 - S_w^2/N}{\dfrac{MN-1}{MN} S_t^2} .$$

PART 5
M Finite, N's Finite and Unequal

We now lift the restriction that N_i's be equal and consider the more general case of sampling from subpopulations with unequal N_i's. This is the more realistic model for sociologists, since natural clusters rarely have the same number of persons: no two neighborhoods have exactly the same number of residents; no two schools have the same enrollment; no two congregations the same number of members. Thus, the researcher may anticipate that whenever he uses natural social clusters as primary sampling units, the number of elements within psu's will differ. The theory for sampling from subpopulations with unequal N_i's is thus more likely to be applicable in actual social surveys than that for sampling from psu's with equal N_i's. And we might very well have begun with the more general case of unequal N_i's, except that its theory does not lend itself so readily to simple expression as the theory for equal N_i's.

Although there are other ways of selecting psu's besides simple random sampling, we restrict ourselves to that procedure in keeping with our quite limited objectives. Actually, with unequal N_i's, there are decided advantages in requiring that the probability of selecting every psu be proportional to its size (PPS). When N_i's are equal, that requirement (PPS) is automatically fulfilled by simple random sampling. However, when N_i's are unequal, PPS will not be met by simple random sampling, and different techniques must be used. Sampling with probabilities proportional to size recommends itself especially when our population consists of large organizations (e.g., schools, business firms, churches) and we wish to characterize not only those organizations *per se*, but also their individual members (Kish 1965a). Students interested in sampling with probabilities proportional to size should consult Kish (1965b: 217–246) or Yamane (1967: 237–271).

Statement of the Problem. If N_i's are equal, n_i's will necessarily be equal for a uniform sampling fraction of elements within psu's. Hence, for a given m, mn will be constant for repeated samples. No matter which psu's are selected at the first stage, the sample will always contain mn elements. If $f_2 = 1$ (100 percent sampling within psu's), each sample will have mN cases; if $f_2 = \frac{1}{2}$, each sample will have $\frac{1}{2}mN$ cases, and so forth. Of necessity, mn will be constant in repeated samples given equal N_i's and proportional subsampling.

On the other hand, when N_i's are unequal, proportional subsampling will give rise to unequal n_i's and in consequence for a fixed m, the number of elements in each sample, $\sum n_i = m\bar{n}$, will vary on repeated trials. By way of example, let us suppose that we have four psu's with 6, 8, 12, 14 elements, respectively. For $f_1 = 1/4$ (or $m = 1$) and $f_2 = 1$, our samples on repeated trials would have 6, 8, 12, 14 units, respectively. If we keep $f_1 = 1/4$ and set $f_2 = 1/2$, we would obtain samples of 3, 4, 6, and 7 elements. In the first example, the mean (expected) number of elements ($\bar{n}$) is 10; in the second example, the mean number is 5. Thus, for a uniform sampling fraction, differences among N_i's will be matched by differences among $m\bar{n}$'s, or the number of elements in the sample.

Such variability in $m\bar{n}$ cannot be disregarded, since it affects the variability of estimates based on $m\bar{n}$ observations. It is a familiar principle that larger samples are more reliable than smaller samples, other things being equal; hence, we would expect the average reliability of estimates based on a succession of larger or smaller samples to conform to this generalization: less than the reliability provided by the largest $m\bar{n}$, more than the reliability provided by the smallest $m\bar{n}$. The truth of this conjecture is borne out by sampling theory as it pertains to $\bar{y}$, relevant parts of which follow. In pursuing this matter, we shall require some additional notation as follows:

Symbol	*Term*

Population

Symbol	Term
N_i	number of elements, i^{th} psu
$\sum N_i = X$	number of elements, population
$\dfrac{1}{M} \sum N_i = \bar{N}$	number of elements per psu
$X/M = \bar{X}$	number of elements per psu
$\bar{X} = \bar{N}$	number of elements per psu
$R = Y/X$	population mean (ratio)
$f_2 = \bar{n}/\bar{N}$	sampling fraction, second stage
$f = m\bar{n}/M\bar{N}$	overall sampling fraction
$S_w^2 = \dfrac{1}{M\bar{N}} \sum \dfrac{N_i}{N_i - 1} \sum\sum (Y_{ij} - \bar{Y}_i)^2$	within-psu variance
$S_{xyb} = \dfrac{\sum (X_i - \bar{X})(Y_i - \bar{Y})}{M - 1}$	between-psu covariance
$S_{xyw} = \dfrac{1}{MN} \sum \dfrac{N_i}{N_i - 1} \sum (X_{ij} - \bar{X}_i)(Y_{ij} - \bar{Y}_i)$	within-psu covariance

$$S_r^2 \doteq R^2(V_{y'}^2 + V_{x'}^2 - 2V_{y'x'})$$
variance of sample ratio (r)

$$V_{y'x'} = \rho_{yx}V_{y'}V_{x'}$$
$$= (1 - f_1)\frac{S_{xyb}}{m\bar{X}\bar{Y}} + (1 - f_2)\frac{S_{xyw}}{m\bar{n}\bar{X}\bar{Y}}$$
rel-covariance of x' and y'

Sample

n_i — number of elements from i^{th} psu

$x = \sum n_i$ — number drawn from m psu's

$\frac{1}{m}\sum n_i = \bar{n}$ — elements per psu

$\frac{x}{m} = \bar{x}$ — elements per psu

$\bar{x} = \bar{n}$ — elements per psu

$x' = \frac{x}{f}$ — estimated number of elements in population

$y' = \frac{y}{f}$ — estimated sum of all Y values

$r = \frac{x}{y}$ — estimated population mean (ratio)

$v_{y'}^2 = (1 - f)\frac{\sum(y_i - \bar{y})^2}{m(m - 1)\bar{y}^2}$ — estimated rel-variance of y'

$v_{x'}^2 = (1 - f)\frac{\sum(x_i - \bar{x})^2}{m(m - 1)\bar{x}^2}$ — estimated rel-variance of x'

$v_{x'y'} = (1 - f)\frac{\sum(x_i - \bar{x})(y_i - \bar{y})}{m(m - 1)\bar{x}\bar{y}}$ — estimated rel-covariance of x' and y'

Variance of Mean (y/mn). When mn is constant in repeated sampling, the sample mean takes the form of a random variable (y) divided by a constant (mn). For equal N's, the variance of that mean is the variance of the sample sum (y) divided by the constant, $(mn)^2$:

$$S_{\bar{y}}^2 = \frac{S_y^2}{(mn)^2}$$
$$= \frac{mn[(1 - f_1)nS_b^2 + (1 - f_2)S_w^2]}{(mn)^2}$$

$$= (1 - f_1) \frac{S_b^2}{m} + (1 - f_2) \frac{S_w^2}{mn},$$

in agreement with previous theory (6.4.2). When the number of elements (mn) varies from sample to sample, as in the case of unequal N_i's and proportional sampling at the second stage, this simple result no longer holds. In such cases, the variance of the mean will be affected by the sampling variation of both y and $m\bar{n}$, or by both terms in the ratio, y/x. This is true whenever an estimator is the ratio of two random variables.

Variance of Ratio, $R = U/W$. To demonstrate this point, we take an approximation to the variance of the ratio between two random variables, U and W, as our point of departure (Hansen, Hurwitz, and Madow I 1953: 166):

(6.5.1) $\sigma_{u/w}^2 \doteq (R)^2 (V_u^2 + V_w^2 - 2\rho_{uw} V_u V_w),$

where

$$\rho_{uw} = \frac{\sigma_{uw}}{\sigma_u \sigma_w},$$

and

$$R = U/W.$$

The derivation of this approximation is quite technical and outside the scope of this book. Interested students should consult Hansen, Hurwitz, and Madow II (1953: 107–109). From the right side of (6.5.1), we deduce that (1) the larger the rel-variances of U and W, respectively, the larger the variance of the ratio, U/W; and (2) the larger the algebraic value of ρ_{uw} on its range from -1 to $+1$, the smaller that variance. Putting conclusions together, we get this single generalization: the variance of the ratio, U/W, varies directly as the difference between the sum of the rel-variances of U and W and the rel-covariance of U and W.

Variance of $r = y/x$. With these props in place, the stage is set for the variance of the sample ratio, $r = y'/x' = y/x$. Substituting the random variables y' and x' for U and W in (6.5.1), we get

(6.5.2) $S_r^2 \doteq R^2 (V_{y'}^2 + V_{x'}^2 - 2\rho_{y'x'} V_{y'} V_{x'}),$

which is a good approximation, provided that $V_{x'}$ is smaller than .05 (Hansen, Hurwitz, and Madow I 1953: 164). The rel-variance of y' is a simple modification of (6.4.4), with $\bar{n}$ and $\bar{N}$ replacing n and N respectively:

(6.5.3) $V_{y'}^2 = (1 - f_1) \frac{S_{1Y}^2}{m \bar{Y}^2} + \left(1 - \frac{\bar{n}}{\bar{N}}\right) \frac{S_w^2}{m\bar{n} \bar{Y}^2}.$

In like manner, the rel-variance of x' may be written:

$$V_{x'}^2 = (1 - f_1)\frac{S_{1X}^2}{m\overline{X}^2} + \left(1 - \frac{\bar{n}}{\overline{N}}\right)\frac{S_w^2}{m\bar{n}\overline{\overline{X}}^2},$$

with the understanding that S_w^2 is based on X_{ij} rather than Y_{ij}. Since the value of X_{ij} is 1 for every element, the second term on the right will be zero and the rel-variance for x' reduces to

$$V_{x'}^2 = (1 - f_1)\frac{S_{1X}^2}{m\overline{X}^2}.$$

By way of explanation: there can be no variation within psu's if every element has the same value; however, there may be variation between psu sums, since the number of elements may vary from one psu to another.

As one might have anticipated, the rel-covariance of y' and x' for two-stage sampling is identical in form to the rel-variance of y' (or x'), except that we substitute between and within-sample covariances for between and within-sample variances, and products between means for squared means as follows:

(6.5.4) $$\rho_{y'x'}V_{y'}V_{x'} = (1 - f_1)\frac{S_{xyb}}{m\overline{X}\,\overline{Y}} + (1 - f_2)\frac{S_{xyw}^2}{m\bar{n}\,\overline{\overline{X}}\,\overline{\overline{Y}}}.$$

With these formulas in hand, except for their estimation, we have come to the end of our task of distinguishing the variance of the mean for two-stage sampling from the variance of the mean for simple random sampling from the total population. From (6.5.2) we see that the variance of the mean is inflated by the variation in the estimated sum of all values (y') and the estimated number of all elements (x'), and deflated by a positive correlation ($\rho_{y'x'}$) between these estimates. From (6.5.3) and (6.5.4) we see that the rel-variances for y' and x', respectively, and the rel-covariance between them, are affected by variation both between and within psu's. By collecting like terms, we may assess the importance of variation between psu's relative to variation within psu's, and by such results assess the precision of cluster sampling relative to simple random sampling. Such extensions are given in advanced texts (Hansen, Hurwitz, and Madow I 1953: 258).

Estimate of S_r^2. Our procedure for estimating S_r^2 entails getting separate estimates of $V_{y'}^2$, $V_{x'}^2$, and $\rho_{yx}V_yV_x$, and amalgamating these into a single sum. If the ratio of m/M is negligible, these estimates are quite simple in form, otherwise they are more complex. We restrict ourselves to these simple estimates, given at this point.

Formulas for Estimating Rel-variance and Rel-covariance, Two-stage Sampling

Estimate	Parameter
$r = y/x$	$R = Y/X$
$v_{y'}^2 = (1 - f) \dfrac{\sum(y_i - \bar{y})^2}{m(m - 1)\bar{y}^2}$	$V_{y'}^2$
$v_{x'}^2 = (1 - f) \dfrac{\sum(x_i - \bar{x})^2}{m(m - 1)\bar{x}^2}$	$V_{x'}^2$
$v_{x'y'} = (1 - f) \dfrac{\sum(x_i - \bar{x})(y_i - \bar{y})}{m(m - 1)\bar{x}\bar{y}}$	$\rho_{xy}V_{x'}V_{y'} = V_{x'y'}$

Although these estimates together yield an estimate of S_r^2, they do not provide estimates of component variances. When such detail is required, more elaborate procedures must be used.

Numerical Example. Let us suppose that we drew 5 psu's from a total of 25, and that we selected 1 in 20 ssu's from each of the 5 psu's for subsamples as follows:

1	2	3	4	5
1	9	8	16	3
3	12	18	4	11
6	3	19	13	17
9	2	1	1	2
10	10	10	12	1
20	17	14	9	6
16	14		14	
15	13		8	
2			3	
3				
85	80	70	80	40

We wish to estimate the variance of the ratio S_r^2. As a first step, we calculate:

$$r = 9.103$$

$$v_{y'}^2 = 0.01296$$

$$v_{x'}^2 = 0.01041$$

$$v_{x'y'} = 0.00903.$$

Merging these results, we obtain

$$s_r^2 = (9.10)^2[.013 + .010 - .018]$$
$$= (82.81)(.005)$$
$$= .41.$$

For an interval carrying roughly 95 percent confidence, we double the standard error of .64 and attach that product of 1.28 to 9.10 in both directions.

Precision of Two-Stage Sampling. The precision of cluster sampling relative to simple random sampling generally decreases as the value of ρ_I increases, and this is true whether psu's are equal or unequal in size. However, the theory for unequal psu's has complications not present when psu's are equal. We must (a) broaden our definition of ρ_I to cover the case of unequal classes, and (b) replace variances for a single variable (y) by variances for ratios between two variables (y/x). Although these steps are not difficult to take, they increase materially the complexity of our formulas and for that reason are not given here. Interested students should consult Hansen, Hurwitz, and Madow I 1953: 266.

Epilogue. In this chapter we sought to demonstrate that multi-stage sampling generally yields less precision than simple random sampling. But we should not leap to the conclusion that simple random sampling is always preferred to multi-stage sampling. It all depends. It all depends on relative costs and benefits. The cost of many cases which are quite accessible may be appreciably less than the same number of cases which are somewhat inaccessible. If a sample of 200 cases selected in two stages is as precise as a simple random sample of 100 cases but we can get the 200 cases for less money, we would choose the larger two-stage sample over the smaller simple random sample. In general, it is not the relative precision of a design that determines our choice, but rather the "price tags" on alternative procedures of equal precision. We choose the cheapest, *ceteris paribus*. Accordingly, we may find ourselves in the paradoxical position of discarding a quite simple procedure in favor of a highly complex one.

Now, we have merely broached the subject of the complex sample survey. Complex surveys have their own problems which may prohibit their use, notwithstanding their relatively favorable price. These problems multiply and become critical when the objective of the survey is to draw comparisons between different populations, in order to determine whether differences exist, and to draw inferences concerning the causal forces producing those differences. Whenever the sociologist uses a complex survey for analytical rather than purely descriptive purposes—a quite conventional distinction in survey theory—he should anticipate problems in drawing inferences which do not arise with simple random samples. While a complex design may have the lowest price, it may not be subject to the very statistical analysis which will answer the questions for which the research was conducted. The student who wishes to pursue this matter should consult McCarthy's (1966) monograph for a discussion of the essential issues.

EXERCISES

1. Given five psu's with N_i's as follows: 100, 200, 300, 100, 200. What are the ten possible values of $\bar{n}$, given $f_1 = 2/5$ and $f_2 = 1/20$? Verify that the mean of these ten values is equal to $f_2 \bar{N}$.

2. Given a population of three blocks (psu's) and 12 households as follows:

Block	Household	Household Size
1	1	2
	2	4
	3	6
	4	3
	5	1
	6	2
2	1	3
	2	8
	3	4
	4	5
3	1	4
	2	2

Compute R, S_w^2, S_{xyb}^2, and S_{xyw}^2.

3. Let us suppose that we have drawn $m = 5$ psu's from a total of $M = 25$, and that we have selected a 1 in 20 subsample from each of them with the following results.

		psu		
1	2	3	4	5
3	8	1	6	10
0	2	3	2	7
7	5	9	0	8
9	5	2	1	2
2	3	0	3	5
11	7	4	1	0
4	9	10		2
5		12		3
3				1
1				

Carry out computations as needed to get s_r^2.

4. How is the variance of the ratio, $r = y/x$, affected by correlation between the estimate of the population total (y') and the estimate of the size of the population (x')? Demonstrate by numerical examples.

REFERENCES

Cochran, William G.
  1953 Sampling Techniques. New York: John Wiley and Sons.

  1963 Sampling Techniques. Second Edition. New York: John Wiley and Sons.

Deming, William E.
  1950 Some Theory of Sampling. New York: John Wiley and Sons.

Fisher, Ronald A.
  1946 Statistical Methods for Research Workers. Tenth Edition. Edinburgh: Oliver and Boyd.

Hansen, M. H., W. N. Hurwitz, and W. G. Madow
  1953 Sample Survey Methods and Theory. Vols. 1 and 2. New York: John Wiley and Sons.

Kendall, Maurice G. and Alan Stuart
  1966 The Advanced Theory of Statistics. Vol. 3. New York: Hafner.

Kish, Leslie
  1952 "A two-stage sample of a city." American Sociological Review 17: 761–769.

  1957 "Confidence intervals for clustered samples." American Sociological Review 22: 154–165.

  1964 "Generalizations for complex probability sampling." Proceedings of the Social Statistics Section, American Statistical Association.

  1965a "Sampling organizations and groups of unequal sizes." American Sociological Review 30: 564–572.

  1965b Survey Sampling. New York: John Wiley and Sons.

  1968 "Standard errors for indexes from complex samples." Journal of the American Statistical Association 63: 512–529.

Lazerwitz, Bernard
  1964 "A sample of a scattered group." Journal of Marketing Research. 1: 68–72.

  1968 "Sampling theory and procedures." Pp. 278–328 in Hubert M. Blalock, Jr. and Ann B. Blalock (eds.), Methodology in Social Research. New York: McGraw-Hill.

McCarthy, Philip J.
  1966 "Replication: An approach to the analysis of data from complex surveys." Public Health Service Publication No. 1000, Series 2, No. 14. Washington: U.S. Government Printing Office.

Mood, Alexander M.
   1950   Introduction to the Theory of Statistics. New York: McGraw-Hill.

Sharp, Harry and Allan Feldt
   1959   "Some factors in a probability sample survey of a metropolitan community." American Sociological Review 24: 650–661.

Stephan, Frederick F. and Philip J. McCarthy
   1958   Sampling Opinions: An Analysis of Survey Procedure. New York: John Wiley and Sons.

Sudman, Seymour
   1967   Reducing the Cost of Surveys. Chicago: Aldine.

   1970   "The multiple uses of primary sampling areas of national probability samples." Journal of the American Statistical Association 65: 61–70.

Yamane, Taro
   1967   Elementary Sampling Theory. Englewood Cliffs: Prentice-Hall.

Yates, Frank
   1960   Sampling Methods for Censuses and Surveys. Third Edition. New York: Hafner.

7

Attitude Measurement

PART 1
Introduction

The variety of attitude scales provokes some concern about their relative merits. Why does such a variety exist? What are the merits of each relative to the others? Why use paired comparisons instead of equal-appearing intervals? When might one use latent structure analysis rather than scale analysis?

This chapter seeks to answer some of these questions by comparing some of the major techniques of scale construction: *paired comparisons, equal-appearing intervals, summated ratings, scalogram analysis,* and *latent structure analysis.* Not a comprehensive discussion of attitude measurement, it makes only scant reference to such substantive issues as: What is an attitude? How is an attitude revealed? Does our final scale have validity? Is our scale applicable across several or more cultures? Will it be equally useful ten years hence? Nor does it consider techniques for constructing multidimensional scales and the potential of such scales in social research. All of these are quite legitimate problems which would be pursued as a matter of course in a self-contained and well-rounded discussion of attitude measurement. However, our special concern is with the statistical side of attitude measurement: the assumptions which comprise a given model and the procedures to which those assumptions give rise. Only incidentally are we concerned with the tenability of these models as idealized descriptions of human behavior, although that tenability must ultimately be judged. But whatever the credibility of our model, we can neither competently fit it to the data nor competently interpret the results of that fitting without a firm grasp of its statistical characteristics.

Terminology. It may be helpful to review briefly the notion of attitude measurement and some of the specialized vocabulary which has developed around it, before we consider the methods cited above. We begin with the idea of a *population of persons*, each holding a more or less favorable attitude toward a specified object. We imagine their being arranged in serial order along a single continuum from least to most favorable, with each person as high or higher (except the lowest person) than a certain fraction of the total population. Further, we imagine that it is possible to characterize each person according to his distance from an arbitrary origin on an interval scale, or alternatively, by the rank of his position in the series. To distinguish these values, which are conceptual, from those we obtain by actual measurement, we shall refer to the former as *true scores* and the latter as *test scores*. Eventually we shall compare the distribution of test scores with the hypothesized distribution of true scores to test by goodness of fit the credibility of our model.

The materials that give rise to a set of test scores will consist of one or more *test items* which, respectively, produce different item responses in the population of persons. Since attitudes may be aroused in almost any human situation, there is no limit in principle to the variety of test items that might be constructed. However, in order to simplify this discussion, we shall restrict ourselves to verbal statements which reflect a more or less favorable attitude on a given topic; for example, "It is necessary to win the war in Vietnam, whatever the cost," "America's role in the Vietnam war will live in infamy," etc. Likewise, as an expedient, we shall limit ourselves to verbal responses which are presented to subjects as fixed alternatives for checking: e.g., agree or disagree, accept or reject, etc. It is to be understood that this restriction to verbal responses is for the sake of simplicity, and that a person's attitude may be revealed in many different ways: by facial expression, by body postures, etc.

Because attitude statements are phrased so as to express varying degrees of favorableness, we may regard them, like persons, as ordered along a single continuum from least to most favorable. And like the persons whose attitudes are to be measured, each item may be represented by its scale distance from an arbitrary origin, or by the rank of its position in the complete serial progression of all items. And as with people, we find it useful to distinguish between the observed values of the items and their corresponding true scale values. Because observed and true values differ, the intervals between observed values will differ from the intervals between true values. True values may be evenly spaced along the scale, but the observed values may be irregularly spaced, and even out of order. Continuing, we find it useful to distinguish the totality of items that might be constructed and the particular subset of items that comprises our test. We refer to the latter as the *sample of items*. In the interest of clarity, we sometimes refer to the population of all possible items as the *universe of content*. Although somewhat wanting in precision, this term does serve as a reminder that our decision to accept a given model is always subject to some uncertainty because we test the credibility of that model by a sample of items.

In concluding this short review of terminology, it will be useful to introduce one last distinction: in a given testing, we may require that a respondent estimate the value of an item, or that he indicate the degree to which the item expresses his own attitude. In the former case, he judges the location of an item on the scale; in the latter case, he judges his own attitude by stating whether he is in accord with the sentiment expressed by the statement. We may thus differentiate between responses about items and responses about oneself. Usually it will be clear from the context whether we mean a judgment about the item or a judgment of self.

This distinction between judging items and judging self roughly corresponds to the chronology of scaling techniques, and is therefore a natural link between our short introduction on terminology and a description of the methods themselves. In paired comparisons, which came first chronologically, items are judged before they are used as a test; whereas in summated ratings and scale analysis, which came later, a subject is instructed to indicate the extent to which an item represents his own attitude, without the preliminary step of scaling items. In commenting on the history of scaling techniques, it is fair to say that the development of equal-appearing intervals (Thurstone and Chave 1929) represented a reaction to the complexities of paired comparisons (Thurstone 1927); summated ratings (Likert 1932) sought to eliminate the process of obtaining item values before they were used for testing; whereas scale analysis (Guttman 1941) sought to avoid the difficulty, inherent in previous methods, whereby two or more persons could get the same score by more than one combination of responses. In this sense, there has been an evolution of technique, with each innovation being an attempt to correct a limitation of the immediately preceding device.

The methods by which attitudes are scaled are quite general and may be applied to other traits as well. They may be employed to measure such traits as anxiety, empathy, maturity, identification, alienation, and the like. Nor are they limited in their application to individuals; they may be applied to groups and organizations as well. Families may be scaled on cohesion, universities on creativity, cities on degree of violence. They may be applied to any unit whatsoever, when the requisite data are available and where these data do not contradict the assumptions underlying our model.

That being the case, the student may wonder why our discussion is limited to attitude measurement. Why not give the methods on a more abstract level and invite the reader to supply his own examples? The answer is this: methods are more readily grasped when seen as a solution to a familiar problem, and diverse methods may be more readily compared and assessed when applied to the same problem. For that reason, we consider scaling techniques within the framework of attitude measurement, which may be familiar to many readers. With equal profit they might be considered within the framework of organizational measurement (Barton 1961). Their potential for producing more discriminating social indicators (Biderman 1966) would also be worthwhile to pursue.

PART 2
Paired Comparisons

The Scale of Items. In the method of paired comparisons (Thurstone 1927) we assume that two statements, Nos. 1 and 2, will differ in the attitude they express on a given topic: one statement will express a more favorable attitude than the other. For example, the statement "Our winning the war in Vietnam is absolutely necessary, whatever the cost" expresses a more favorable attitude toward our involvement in that war than the statement "Withdrawing our army from Vietnam at this time might make matters worse." Generalizing from this case of two statements, we conceive of several or more statements which differ in the attitudes they express. We assume that these statements are located along an interval scale and we take the distance between any two of them as a measure of the degree to which one statement is more favorable than another. We may put these ideas in a drawing:

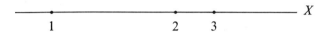

The straight line (X) is a graph of the hypothetical item scale and the dots mark the location of Items 1, 2, and 3. We represent the scale value of Item 1 by X_1, the scale value of Item 2 by X_2, the scale value of Item 3 by X_3. The distance from Item 1 to Item 2 is a measure of the degree to which Item 2 expresses a more favorable attitude than Item 1, the distance from Item 2 to Item 3 of the degree to which Item 3 expresses a more favorable attitude than Item 2, etc.

The aim of the method of paired comparisons is to locate n statements along an interval scale, or, equivalently, to determine the scale distance between each item and every other item. Once items have been scaled in this way, we instruct persons whose attitudes we wish to measure to check those items which express their own attitudes. Subsequently, we arrange these persons from low to high according to the average scale value of their checked items. For example, a person checking statements in the vicinity of Item 2 would stand higher in the group than a person checking statements in the vicinity of Item 1, etc. The statements thus serve to discriminate among persons holding varying attitudes, which is the express purpose of attitude measurement.

General Procedure. The procedure for scaling items by paired comparisons rests on the very general assumption that the estimated value of a given item will vary on repeated trials. The actual procedure for obtaining scale values is greatly simplified if, more restrictively, we assume that repeated estimates of a given item will be normally distributed, and that the distributions of repeated estimates for all items will have a common variance (discriminal dispersion). In brief, we assume normal distributions with a common variance but different means, as in Figure 7.2.1.

Figure 7.2.1   *Normal Curves for Estimates with Common Variance but Different Means*

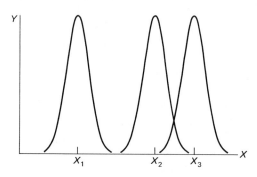

In the process of locating items along the continuum, a judge is required, not to estimate the scale value of a single item, as the foregoing theory might suggest, but rather to judge which one of two statements expresses the more favorable attitude. On a single trial, he designates one item as more favorable than the other; on a succession of trials, he will give a majority of his votes to one of the two items, unless it is impossible to discriminate between them. The strength of that majority, as may be inferred from Figure 7.2.1, will vary as the scale distance between the two items. Thus, the tendency to judge Item 3 as more favorable than Item 1 on repeated trials will be greater than the tendency to judge Item 2 as more favorable than Item 1, and so on. Conversely, the scale distance between items will vary as the strength of the tendency to regard one item as more favorable than the other—the wider the majority for one item over the other, the greater the scale separation between them. An implication is that from the strength of the tendency to perceive one item as more favorable than the other in a paired comparison, as measured by the proportion of such favorable judgments on many trials, we may obtain the scale distance between them. In its essentials, this is the procedure for finding the interval between two items: we determine the proportion of instances in which Item 1 is considered as more favorable than Item 2 in an "experiment" consisting of N trials, and from this empirical proportion we calculate the hypothetical difference between their scale values. (In an "experiment," we may secure a single judgment from each of N persons, or N judgments from a single person.)

Statistical Model. The foundation of the rule for obtaining the magnitude of that difference may be unfolded in this way: in judging which of two items, No. 1 or No. 2, is more favorable, given that $X_1 < X_2$, we assume that the judge tacitly estimates the scale values of Nos. 1 and 2, and mentally calculates the difference (*D*) between these two estimates before giving his decision. To these mental operations, Thurstone (1927) gave the name "discriminal process." It is further assumed that the distribution of such differences on repeated trials will be normal, with mean equal to the difference between the true scale values, $X_2 - X_1$, and variance equal to the variance of the difference. We may express that variance as follows:

$$\sigma_D^2 = \sigma_1^2 + \sigma_2^2 - 2r_{12}\sigma_1\sigma_2,$$

where σ_1^2 is the variance of the estimates of No. 1, σ_2^2 is the variance of the estimates of No. 2, and r_{12} is the product-moment correlation between estimates of Nos. 1 and 2 on repeated trials. But

$$\sigma_1^2 = \sigma_2^2 = \sigma^2,$$

by assumption, so that

(7.2.1) $$\sigma_D^2 = 2\sigma^2(1 - r_{12}).$$

Equation (7.2.1) may be rendered as follows: the variance of the difference between X_1 and X_2 is the sum of the individual variances reduced by the factor $(1 - r_{12})$. If we divide the square root of that variance into the difference between X_1 and X_2, we get a simple version of the "law of comparative judgment" (Torgerson 1958: 161).

The proportion of decisions for Item 2 higher than Item 1 will be the proportion of differences above zero on the sigma scale, since all differences less than zero require an estimate of X_1 greater than X_2. The problem of determining the proportion of judgments in favor of Item 2, given such a distribution of differences, is solved by expressing zero as a normal deviate (standard measure) and referring that result to a table of normal areas for the required answer. To convert zero into a normal deviate, we express it as a deviation from its mean, $[0 - (X_2 - X_1)]$, and divide that deviation by the standard error of the difference, σ_D. With zero in standard form, we may readily establish the expected proportion of differences larger or smaller than zero on repeated trials. For example, if $[0 - (X_2 - X_1)]/\sigma_D = -1$, Item 1 will be rated as more favorable than Item 2 on approximately 16% of all trials, and Item 2 will be rated as more favorable than Item 1 on 84% of all trials. If $[0 - (X_2 - X_1)]/\sigma_D = -1.96$, Item 1 will be judged as more favorable than Item 2 on 2.5% of all trials, Item 2 more favorable than Item 1 on 97.5% of all trials. Thus, given the scale distance between two items in sigma units, we may readily obtain the expected proportion of judgments for Item 1 or 2 by referring to the table of normal areas.

In applying the method of paired comparisons, we invert this procedure: we start with the observed proportion of judgments for Item 2 (or 1) and convert that proportion to the difference between scale values, expressed as a normal deviate. For example, if Item 2 is judged higher than Item 1, 84 times in 100, we take the scale distance between Items 1 and 2 to be $|1|$ in sigma units: Item 1 is one sigma below Item 2, Item 2 is one sigma above Item 1. If Item 2 is judged higher than Item 1, 99 times in 100, we take the scale distance between Items 1 and 2 to be $|2.33|$, and so on. The proportion of times one item is judged higher than another thus enables us to establish the directed distance between them.

A Simplifying Assumption. Corresponding to a test of n items, there will be as many hypothetical difference distributions as there are paired comparisons, namely, $\frac{n(n-1)}{2}$. The formula for the variance of any one of these distributions is:

$$(7.2.2) \qquad \sigma_D^2 = 2\sigma^2(1 - r_{ij}),$$

on condition that $\sigma_i^2 = \sigma_j^2 = \sigma^2$. Formula (7.2.2) is simply a general version of (7.2.1). If we impose the additional requirement that all correlations between paired estimates be equal, i.e., $r_{12} = r_{13} = \cdots = r_{(n-1)n}$, all difference distributions will have the same variance,

$$(7.2.3) \qquad \sigma_D^2 = 2\sigma^2(1 - r),$$

(where r is the constant correlation between paired estimates), and differences between item values in sigma units will be proportional to raw differences, with $1/\sigma_D$ as the constant of proportionality.* This result may be expressed as follows:

$$z_{ij} = \frac{1}{\sigma_D}(X_i - X_j).$$

This proportionality of standardized to absolute differences conveniently permits us to carry out the entire analysis with all differences in standard form. This is common practice among research workers and entails, as noted, the simplifying assumption that all correlations between paired estimates are equal, as well as the assumption that distributions of estimates for individual items are normal with a common variance. These assumptions permit us to treat σ_D and r as constants.

Finding Scale Values. When applied to concrete data, the method of paired comparisons produces a set of n measures which serve to locate as many items on the attitude scale. These n items constitute our attitude test. To

---

* By assuming that all correlations are zero, we obtain Thurstone's Case V.

explain the process of scaling items, we apply it to the fictitious responses of 342 judges to seven statements on the war in Vietnam*:

1. I suppose the United States has no choice but to continue the war in Vietnam.
2. We should be willing to give our allies in Vietnam more money if they need it.
3. Withdrawing our army from Vietnam at this time would only make matters worse.
4. The war in Vietnam might not be the best way to stop communism, but it is the only thing we can do.
5. Winning the war in Vietnam is absolutely necessary whatever the cost.
6. We are protecting the United States by fighting in Vietnam.
7. The reason we are in Vietnam is to preserve the American way of life.

(1) Our first step is to confront each of the 342 judges with every possible pair of items, directing them to indicate which item in each pair expresses the more favorable attitude toward the war. In general, our first step entails the presentation of n items two at a time to N judges for a total of $\left[\frac{N}{2}(n)(n-1)\right]$ decisions. These decisions constitute our raw data.

(2) After each judge has given his 21 responses, we count the number of times each item is judged more favorable than every other item, entering the resulting frequencies in a table set up for that purpose. In Table 7.2.1,

Table 7.2.1 *Number of Times Row Item Judged More Favorable than Column Item*

No.	1	2	3	4	5	6	7
1	171	96	75	58	44	34	20
2	246	171	150	147	123	106	68
3	267	192	171	161	150	147	106
4	284	195	181	171	154	150	120
5	298	219	192	188	171	168	137
6	309	236	195	192	174	171	147
7	321	274	236	222	205	195	171

which is a record for the 342 judges, each entry is the number of times the row item was judged more favorable than the column item. For example, No. 1 was judged more favorable than No. 2 by 96 judges; more favorable than No. 4 by 58 judges; more favorable than No. 7 by 20 judges; and so

---

* Paraphrase of Hill's (1953) questionnaire on the Korean War, reproduced in Edwards (1957).

forth. In judging an item against itself, we assume that it will be judged one way as frequently as the other way (no discrimination possible); hence, we enter $N/2$ along the major diagonal.

(3) We divide each cell frequency by $N = 342$ and thereby convert raw cell frequencies into proportions of the total N. In recording these results (Table 7.2.2), it is expeditious to arrange items according to the magnitude of their row sums, since this arrangement will correspond to the ultimate order of items on the scale (X) from the least to the most favorable.

Table 7.2.2 *Proportion of Times Row Item Judged More Favorable than Column Item*

No.	1	2	3	4	5	6	7
1	.50	.28	.22	.17	.13	.10	.06
2	.72	.50	.44	.43	.36	.31	.20
3	.78	.56	.50	.47	.44	.43	.31
4	.83	.57	.53	.50	.45	.44	.35
5	.87	.64	.56	.55	.50	.49	.40
6	.90	.69	.57	.56	.51	.50	.43
7	.94	.80	.69	.65	.60	.57	.50

(4) Continuing, we now convert each p_{ij} to its corresponding z_{ij} value, using a standard table of normal areas or a more specialized table (Edwards 1957: 246–247) if one is available. By this step, we calculate the scale distance between items in sigma units. Our problem is to locate that point on the base line of the unit normal curve such that p_{ij} of all values are smaller. For example, the point on the base line of the normal curve such that .22 of all values are smaller is $-.77$, which is the directed scale distance in units of σ_D from Item 3 to Item 1; the point on the base line such that $1.00 - .22 = .78$ of all values are smaller is $+.77$, which is the directed distance from Item 1 to Item 3. Corresponding to proportions smaller than .50, normal deviates z_{ij} above the diagonal will take the minus ($-$) sign; corresponding to proportions larger than .50, entries below the diagonal

Table 7.2.3 *Directed Distance between Items, z_{ij}*

No.	1	2	3	4	5	6	7	Σz_{ij}	$\bar{z}_i$	$\bar{z}_i + c$
1	00	−.58	−.77	−.95	−1.13	−1.28	−1.56	−6.27	−.90	00
2	.58	00	−.15	−.18	−.36	−.50	−.84	−1.45	−.21	.69
3	.77	.15	00	−.08	−.15	−.18	−.50	.01	.00	.90
4	.95	.18	.08	00	−.13	−.15	−.38	.55	.08	.98
5	1.13	.36	.15	.13	00	−.03	−.25	1.49	.21	1.11
6	1.28	.50	.18	.15	.03	00	−.18	1.96	.28	1.18
7	1.56	.84	.50	.38	.25	.18	00	3.71	.53	1.43

$c = .90$

will take the plus (+) sign. Since p_{ij} and p_{ji} take the same absolute z-value, it will suffice to find the z-value for each p_{ij} above the diagonal and record these with opposite sign (+) below the diagonal. This pattern is shown in Table 7.2.3, where we give z-values corresponding to the p-values of Table 7.2.2.

(5) The procedure producing the table of z-values gives us the directed distance (in sigma units) between any two items, but leaves us without scale values for the items themselves. To obtain values for the items, we sum all entries in the ith row, 1 through n:

$$\sum z_{ij} = \frac{1}{\sigma_D} \sum_{1}^{n} (X_i - X_j)$$

$$= \frac{1}{\sigma_D} \left(n X_i - \sum_{i}^{n} X_j \right),$$

and divide both sides by n, to obtain

$$\frac{1}{n} \sum z_{ij} = \frac{1}{n\sigma_D} \left(n X_i - \sum X_j \right),$$

$$\bar{z}_{i.} = \frac{(X_i - \bar{X})}{\sigma_D},$$

where $\bar{X} = \frac{1}{n} \sum X_j$.

Our conclusion is that the mean of the entries in the ith row ($\bar{z}_{i.}$) is equal to the deviation of the ith item from the mean of all items (expressed in sigma units). Consequently, we may take row means (Table 7.2.3) as our n scale values and employ them to locate our items along the attitude scale, with this refinement: since our interval scale has an arbitrary origin, we add a constant (c) to each row mean, so all will be conveniently positive in sign. Changing the sign of the largest negative value and adding this value to each row mean, we make all values positive (last column in Table 7.2.3), and assign a value of zero to the most unfavorable item in the set.

(6) Finally, as a check on the assumptions of our model, we compare our observed proportions with those expected from our derived scale values. Put as a question: do the proportions to which our derived scale values give rise closely fit the observed proportions with which we began the analysis? To test the fit between our observed and expected proportions, we may proceed in this way:

First, subtract each larger scale value from every smaller value for a total of $[n(n - 1)/2]$ differences, all carrying the minus sign. In doing this, it will be convenient to subtract every larger value in the stub column ($\bar{z}_i$) from every smaller value, as in Table 7.2.4.

Table 7.2.4 *Differences among n Scale Values*

No.	$\bar{z}_i$	2	3	4	5	6	7
1	.00	−.69	−.90	−.98	−1.11	−1.18	−1.43
2	.69		−.21	−.29	−.42	−.49	−.74
3	.90			−.08	−.21	−.28	−.53
4	.98				−.13	−.20	−.45
5	1.11					−.07	−.32
6	1.18						−.25
7	1.43						

Second, locate each of these values (z_{ij}) in the stub of a table of normal areas and subtract its corresponding entry in the body of the table from .50 to get the proportion (p'_{ij}) of times the row item would be judged more favorable than the column item. These expected proportions are recorded to the right of the diagonal in an $n \times n$ table set up for that purpose (Table 7.2.5).

Table 7.2.5 *Expected Proportions, p'_{ij}*

No.	2	3	4	5	6	7
1	.24	.18	.16	.13	.12	.08
2		.42	.39	.34	.31	.23
3			.47	.42	.39	.30
4				.45	.42	.33
5					.47	.37
6						.40

Third, to gauge the fit between observed and expected proportions, we obtain the mean numerical difference between them, as in Table 7.2.6.

Table 7.2.6 *Mean Absolute Difference between Observed and Expected Proportions.*

No.	2	3	4	5	6	7
1	.04	.04	.01	.00	−.02	−.02
2		.02	.04	.02	.00	−.03
3			.00	.02	.04	.01
4				.00	.02	.02
5					.02	.03
6						.03

$$\text{Mean} = \frac{\sum |p_{ij} - p'_{ij}|}{\dfrac{n(n-1)}{2}} = \frac{.43}{21} = .02$$

Although this arithmetic mean provides an indication of goodness of fit, it will not permit us to test probabilistically the credibility of our model. To run a significance test (Mosteller 1951), we calculate from our data a statistic that distributes as x^2 when our assumptions hold. We take square roots of both observed and expected proportions, convert these square roots to arcsins, find differences between corresponding observed and expected arcsins, square all such differences, and sum these squares. The ratio of this sum to the constant $821/N$ has a x^2-distribution with $[(n-1)(n-2)]/2$ degrees of freedom, when the conditions of our model hold; otherwise its value will be excessively large. Hence, the quantity,

$$(7.2.4) \qquad x^2 = \frac{N\sum(\theta_{ij} - \theta'_{ij})^2}{821},$$

$(\theta_{ij} = \sin^{-1}\sqrt{p_{ij}}, \theta'_{ij} = \sin^{-1}\sqrt{p'_{ij}})$, may be used to test the tenability of our model. Computing that ratio (7.2.4) for our data (Table 7.2.7), we get a value of 22.54. Since values larger than 22.54 with 15 degrees of freedom will occur at least five times in 100, we do not reject our model which specifies that repeated estimates for each item are normally distributed with a common variance, and that the correlation between paired estimates is constant.

Table 7.2.7 *Computation of* $X^2 = \dfrac{N\sum(\theta_{ij} - \theta'_{ij})^2}{821}$

Arcsins (θ_{ij}) for $\sqrt{p_{ij}}$

No.	2	3	4	5	6	7
1	31.95	27.97	24.35	21.13	18.44	14.18
2		41.55	40.98	36.87	33.83	26.56
3			43.28	41.55	40.98	33.83
4				42.13	41.55	36.27
5					44.43	39.23
6						40.98

Arcsins (θ'_{ij}) for $\sqrt{p'_{ij}}$

No.	2	3	4	5	6	7
1	29.33	25.10	23.58	21.13	20.27	16.43
2		40.40	38.65	35.67	33.83	28.66
3			43.28	40.40	38.65	33.21
4				42.13	40.40	35.06
5					43.28	37.47
6						39.23

$$(\theta_{ij} - \theta'_{ij})$$

No.	2	3	4	5	6	7
1	2.62	2.87	.77	0.00	−1.83	−2.25
2		1.15	2.33	1.20	0.00	−2.10
3			0.00	1.15	2.33	.62
4				0.00	1.15	1.21
5					1.15	1.76
6						1.75

$$(\theta_{ij} - \theta'_{ij})^2$$

No.	2	3	4	5	6	7
1	6.86	8.24	.59	0.00	3.35	5.06
2		1.33	5.43	1.44	0.00	4.41
3			0.00	1.32	5.43	.38
4				0.00	1.32	1.46
5					1.32	3.10
6						3.06

$$\sum(\theta_{ij} - \theta'_{ij})^2 = 54.10$$

$$\sigma_\theta^2 = 821/342 = 2.40$$

$$\chi^2 = \frac{\sum(\theta_{ij} - \theta'_{ij})^2}{821/N}$$

$$= \frac{54.10}{2.40}$$

$$= 22.54, \text{ on } 15 \; df, \; p < .10.$$

PART 3

Equal-Appearing Intervals

The method of equal-appearing intervals (Thurstone and Chave 1929) may be regarded as a device for obtaining results equivalent to those produced by paired comparisons but with less effort. Both have the same immediate objective of locating *n* items along a hypothetical continuum; both have the same ultimate objective of arranging persons from high to low according to their responses to the scaled items. They are also alike in their general theory. However, they differ in their raw data and in the methods by which those data are processed. In paired comparisons, the individual judge is required to compare each of n items with every other item, whereas in the method of equal-appearing intervals the judge is required to sort n items into equal-appearing intervals along a continuum. The plot of these intervals, A through K, is a straight line (X) with equally spaced boundaries as follows:

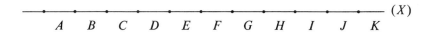

Since the method of equal-appearing intervals requires only n responses from each judge, it is more economical to apply than the method of paired comparisons, which required $[n(n-1)]/2$ responses from each judge. Presumably, the scaling of items is accomplished with less effort.

In the method of paired comparisons, scale values are obtained indirectly from comparisons between items two at a time; in equal intervals they are based on multiple estimates of the location of items one at a time. In this sense, equal-appearing intervals is a more direct technique than paired comparisons for scaling items. But it is nonetheless comparative in that the judge is required to estimate the distance (in equal-appearing intervals) between each item and an actual or imaginary item at the midpoint of the scale. Both techniques thus entail comparative responses on the part of the judges.

Statistical Model. Notwithstanding their differences in technique, both paired comparisons and equal-appearing intervals start with the same general postulate, namely: the estimate of the scale value of an item will vary on repeated trials around the hypothetical true value. To simplify the method of paired comparisons, we assume that all such distributions are normal and have the same variance, even though this assumption may later prove to be inconsistent with the data. In the method of equal intervals, we assume only that the estimate of an item will vary on repeated trials, without specifying the distribution of that estimate. The models could be made identical by either lifting the requirement of normal distributions with a common variance in paired comparisons, or imposing that requirement in the case of equal-appearing intervals. The difference between the two models may be depicted by adjacent graphs, each consisting of several or more ogives spread along the base line. Figures 7.3.1 and 7.3.2 are such a visual aid. In the simplified model of paired comparisons, ogives are identically normal; in the less restrictive model of equal intervals, no two ogives need be alike, although they may be.

Figure 7.3.1 *Cumulative Curves (Ogives) for Normally Distributed Estimates*

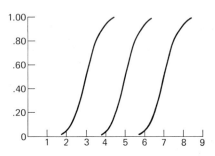

Figure 7.3.2 *Cumulative Curves (Ogives) for Unspecified Distributions of Estimates*

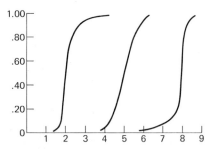

General Procedure. The procedure for scaling items and eliminating those which do not belong on the continuum entails only the simplest statistical operations. Before giving these operations, and as a useful preliminary, we cite typical directions to judges for sorting *n* items into equal-appearing intervals. The following statement is a paraphrase of Thurstone and Chave (1929: 31).

> You are given eleven cards with letters on them, *A, B, C, D, E, F, G, H, I, J, K*. Please arrange these before you in alphabetical order. On card *A* put those statements which you believe express the most favorable attitude. On card *F* put those statements expressing a neutral position. On card *K* put those statements expressing the most unfavorable attitude. On the rest of the cards, sort statements in such manner that the intervals in attitude appear equal from one pile of slips to the next.

Note that there is no claim that intervals are actually equal, merely that they appear equal to the rater.

Item Distribution. After all *n* statements have been sorted by all *N* judges, we construct the frequency distribution of responses for each item, as in the following example:

Category	Interval Midpoint	Frequency	Cumulated Frequency
A	.5	1	1
B	1.5	1	2
C	2.5	3	5
D	3.5	5	10
E	4.5	7	17
F	5.5	18	35
G	6.5	33	68
H	7.5	17	85
I	8.5	9	94
J	9.5	4	98
K	10.5	2	100
		100	

For each such distribution, we get the median and the quartile range $(Q_3 - Q_1)$. For our example:

$$\text{Median} = 6.00 + \frac{50 - 35}{33} \qquad Q_1 = 5.00 + \frac{25 - 17}{18} \qquad Q_3 = 7.00 + \frac{75 - 68}{17}$$

$$= 6.45 \qquad\qquad\qquad = 5.44 \qquad\qquad\qquad = 7.41$$

$$Q_3 - Q_1 = 7.41 - 5.44$$

$$= 1.97$$

We take the median as the scale value of the item, and the quartile range as a measure of the extent to which the judges agree on the location of that item. In constructing our scale, we discard items on which judges tend to disagree, and retain those items on which there is agreement. We keep items with relatively small quartile ranges, reject those with relatively large quartile ranges.

As a statistical procedure, the method of equal-appearing intervals merely consists of finding the quartile range for each item, together with the median. When performed manually, the calculation of these values may be expedited by plotting each distribution as an ogive (see Figure 7.3.2) from which the median and quartiles may be readily obtained by graphic interpolation. Not all statements having a relatively small dispersion will be included in the final questionnaire which will be our attitude test; rather that questionnaire will be composed of roughly two or three times as many statements as there are intervals, with items evenly spaced along the scale from low to high. For example, if we discard 100 of 200 initial statements, we would probably utilize no more than 25 to 35 of the usable statements in our final form.

Procedure Illustrated. To describe the process of scale construction by equal-appearing intervals, we attach a selection of materials from the experiments of Thurstone and Chave (1929: 23–29) on a scale for measuring the attitude of individuals toward the church. We first quote some of the statements themselves, chosen not because of their particular content, but rather because of the appreciable differences among their respective medians and quartile ranges.

No.	*Statement*
8	I believe the church has good influence on the lower and uneducated classes but has no value for the upper, educated classes.
9	I don't believe church-going will do anyone any harm.
28	I believe in what the church teaches but with mental reservations.
39	I believe the church is absolutely needed to overcome the tendency to individualism and selfishness. It practices the golden rule fairly well.
48	The church represents shallowness, hypocrisy, and prejudice.
51	I feel I can worship God better out of doors than in the church, and I get more inspiration there.
113	I feel the church perpetuates the values which man puts highest in his philosophy of life.

In Table 7.3.1, we give both the simple and cumulative frequency distribution of responses for $N = 300$ judges for each of the above items; in Figure 7.3.3, we have plotted the cumulative distributions of Items 8, 28, and 51. By graphic interpolation, we may locate quartiles (including the median) on the base line. We may "read off" their scale values, once they are located. For example, the median value of No. 8 is 6.7 and its quartile

Figure 7.3.3   *Cumulative Curves for Nos. 28, 8, 51*

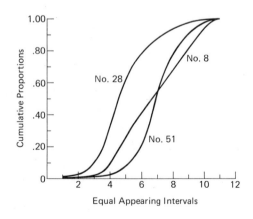

Table 7.3.1 *Proportion* of*
Responses in Categories, Selected Items

Item No.		Category										Median	Quartile Range
		A	B	C	D	E	F	G	H	I	J	K		
8	p	00	01	01	07	18	14	13	13	14	12	7		
	cp	00	01	02	09	27	41	54	67	81	93	100	6.7	3.6
9	p	01	01	01	03	19	62	06	03	02	02	00		
	cp	01	02	03	06	25	87	93	96	98	100	100	5.3	0.7
28	p	01	01	08	21	34	12	09	09	03	01	01		
	cp	01	02	10	31	65	77	86	95	98	99	100	4.5	2.0
39	p	16	41	28	10	04	00	00	01	00	00	00		
	cp	16	57	85	95	99	99	99	100	100	100	100	1.8	1.3
48	p	00	00	00	00	01	00	01	02	06	24	66		
	cp	00	00	00	00	01	01	02	04	10	34	100	10.4	1.4
51	p	00	01	00	02	05	13	33	22	15	07	02		
	cp	00	01	01	03	08	21	54	76	91	98	100	6.9	1.7
113	p	56	28	11	03	01	00	01	00	00	00	00		
	cp	56	84	95	98	99	99	100	100	100	100	100	1.6	0.8

* p is proportion, cp is cumulative proportion; decimals omitted for p's and cp's.
Source: L. L. Thurstone and E. J. Chave, *The Measurement of Attitude*. Chicago: University of Chicago Press, 1929. Copyright by the University of Chicago. All rights reserved. Reprinted with permission.

range is 3.6. Although this item is centrally located, there is some difference of opinion about that location, with the middle 50 percent of the judges spread over an interval of approximately three and one-half scale units.

Remark. The distribution of responses for items that appear to be located at either extreme (Nos. 48 and 113) will necessarily be one-tailed to the right or to the left. We could reconstruct the missing tail by extrapolation and base our quartile range on that segment. However, it will usually suffice for practical purposes to double the difference between the median and the quartile in the plotted tail for an estimate of the quartile range. The justification for this doubling is the assumption that, in the absence of arbitrary limits on the equal-appearing interval scale, the distribution of responses would be symmetrical around the median; hence, the distance from the median to either quartile multiplied by two will give the quartile range.

Ambiguous Items. If an item means the same thing to all judges, its quartile range will be relatively small; if that item means different things to different judges, its quartile range will be relatively large. In the latter case, when an item is ambiguous, it will be useless as a scale item, since it will be equally acceptable to persons holding opposite attitudes. Persons having a strongly negative attitude may regard it as consistent with their position; persons with a strongly positive attitude may likewise regard it as consistent with their position. Consequently, we eliminate those items which fail to elicit a more or less uniform response from the N persons judging them. But how do we distinguish between a high and a low quartile range? There is no categorical answer to this question, except the general rule that "a statement with a high-Q value should be eliminated from the scale" (Thurstone and Chave 1929: 44). For the sake of a standard procedure, it would be possible to take the mean quartile range for all items as the upper limit of acceptability, rejecting all items whose quartile ranges are higher than that mean value. Alternatively, it would be possible to group items according to their medians and to select from each class interval (category) the two or three items with the smallest quartile ranges. The resulting attitude test would then consist of the least ambiguous items from each interval, with perhaps twice as many items as intervals, spread evenly along the continuum from high to low. For example, if we select two or three items from each of the 11 intervals, our battery would have between 25 and 35 statements.

Attitude Scores. The distinctive feature of these evenly spaced items on the scale of equal-appearing intervals lies not in their outward appearance, which is the same as that of items processed by the method of paired comparisons, but rather in the procedure by which scale values were determined. That procedure requires many judges to sort many items into equal-appearing intervals along the attitude scale. When these items, after culling, are given as a test to persons whose attitudes are to be measured, they carry instructions similar to those attached to items whose scale values were determined by the method of paired comparisons. For example: "This is a study of attitudes toward the church. Check ($\checkmark$) those items that express your attitude toward the church." In brief, the individual is required to endorse those items expressing his attitude.

For a person's attitude score, we simply take the mean value of his endorsed items. If he checked items whose respective values were 3.6, 3.2, and 3.4, we would take the mean value of 3.4 as his attitude score. Since a person's response to a given statement is expected to vary on repeated trials, as in our theoretical model, we expect that the average of several or more responses will be a more stable indicator of his position in the group than his response to a single item. With the calculation of these scores for all persons in the sample, the investigator will face new problems having to do with reliability and validity, or the application of parametric statistics to measures which do not qualify as interval scales. However, these matters are not peculiar to the method of equal-appearing intervals, and generally arise in the manipulation of scores based on questionnaire responses.

PART 4

Likert's Summated Ratings

General Comment. Presumably, a person who agrees that the war against North Vietnam is a national necessity has a more favorable attitude toward that war than a person who disagrees; by the same token, a person "strongly agreeing" has a more favorable attitude than a person merely "agreeing" with that idea. It would thus appear possible to group persons from least to most favorable, according to the strength of their agreement with a statement expressing a specified attitude. This is the principle of Likert's (1932) method: persons are ranked from high to low according to the strength of their agreement with one or more items, which express attitudes of varying degrees of favorableness.

To put persons into a fixed number of ordered classes by this general method, we could obtain either finely differentiated measures of agreement to a small number of items, or coarsely differentiated measures to many items. Thus, we could obtain 100 different scores by the employment of either a single item and a 100-point scale, or by 20 items and a 5-point scale. Although fewer items and a finer scale would seem to be more economical to use than many items and a coarser scale, the latter device is usually employed, owing in part to the human difficulty of choosing between tiny adjacent intervals. A person has less difficulty in making a broad "interval estimate" of his attitude than a narrow "point estimate."

Economy of Likert's Method. When persons are scored according to the strength of their agreement with each of n items, it becomes unnecessary to scale the items themselves, as in the method of equal-appearing intervals or in the method of paired comparisons. To the extent that the dispensing with this step is a saving of effort, Likert's method is more economical to apply than either the method of equal-appearing intervals or paired comparisons. This possible economy, coupled with the finding of a high correlation between attitude test scores based on equal-appearing intervals and those based on degree of agreement, probably accounts for the wide currency of Likert's technique in social research.

Statistical Model. Likert's model may be conveniently put in the form of three propositions about the manner in which measures of agreement distribute themselves and the relation of such measures to a person's attitude on a given subject. Although these propositions are implicit in the writing of Likert, he did not formulate them as a statistical model, probably because the concept "model" was not in vogue at that time (circa 1930).

First, we assume that individuals differ in the strength of their agreement with a given item, and that hypothetically continuous measures of that strength will be normally distributed in the population. In brief, the variable "strength of agreement" is assumed to be normally distributed.

Secondly, we assume that two or more such distributions will differ in their mean values, corresponding to differences among the items in degree of favorableness. A mild item will elicit stronger agreement on the average than a severe one, and its mean therefore will stand higher on the strength of agreement scale.

Thirdly, we postulate that strength of agreement is directly proportional to a person's attitude: a person with a relatively favorable attitude will agree more strongly with an item expressing a favorable attitude than a person with a relatively negative attitude.* Hence, if we plot strength of agreement on degree of favorableness, we would get an upwardly sloping straight line, as in Figure 7.4.1. If we plot another graph of the same coordinate axes, we would get a graph parallel to the graph of the first, except that it would intercept the vertical axis at a higher or lower point, depending on the average amount of agreement for that item. According to Figure 7.4.1, agreement is higher on No. 3 than on No. 2, higher on No. 2 than on No. 1. Persons are less likely to agree with a highly favorable item (No. 1) than a moderately favorable item (No. 2).

Figure 7.4.1 *Plot of Strength of Agreement on Degree of Favorableness*

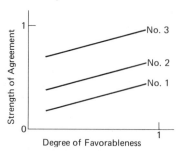

* Or, equivalently, that a person with a relatively favorable attitude will disagree more strongly with an item expressing an unfavorable attitude than a person with a relatively unfavorable attitude. So that agreement will always have the same meaning, and to keep the discussion manageable, we shall restrict our discussion to favorable items. In practice, however, we must decide for each item whether agreement reflects a favorable or unfavorable attitude and assign our weights accordingly. For example, if the category "strongly agree" to a positive item carries a weight of "5," the same response to a negative item would carry a weight of "1."

Measuring Strength of Agreement. Now, if we are to use strength of agreement as an indicator of degree of favorableness, we must have a technique for measuring that variable. Likert's solution was: (1) to divide the range of agreement for each item into five successive intervals, which he labeled *strongly agree, agree, neutral, disagree,* and *strongly disagree;* (2) to treat the width of each of these five intervals (in sigma units) as if the cumulative distribution of agreement were a normal ogive; and (3) to take as a measure of agreement for persons in each category the normal deviate such that one-half of the cases were on either side of it. For example, we would assign the value of C_{20} (as a normal deviate) to all persons answering "strongly disagree," if 40 percent of the total sample gave that response; we would assign the value of C_{50} (as a normal deviate) to all answering "disagree," if 20 percent gave that response for a cumulative total of 60 percent; we would continue in this manner until all persons had been scored. Since test items ordinarily will differ in their distributions, no two will carry the same set of weights, with the spread between adjacent weights being greatest for items with relatively small frequencies in the extreme categories, the spread being least for items having a uniform distribution of frequencies. By weighting many items in this way, and by taking the sum of a person's weights as his test score, we may differentiate among persons according to the sum of their scores on a large battery of items. It is reasonable to suppose that such a broadly based sum will be a more stable indicator of a person's attitude than an index based on only one or two items.

Procedure in Detail. Let us consider the procedure in detail. We start with a set of n items which will be given to N persons whose attitudes are to be measured. These items will be chosen to represent all shades of opinion from least to most favorable. It is essential to include some extreme items, otherwise it will be impossible to sort out persons whose scores fall in the tails of the distribution. As originally formulated by Likert, each item is to be accompanied by five ordered categories of agreement: *strongly agree, agree, neutral, disagree,* and *strongly disagree.** A person taking the attitude test is instructed to select one of these five options as his response to each item; a person is thus required to supply as many responses as there are items in the battery.

Finding Category Weights. After the items have been administered to all persons in the group, we find the distribution of cases by categories for each item. Since no two attitude statements are exactly alike, it is anticipated that no two frequency distributions will be exactly alike. Practically all persons might agree with a barely positive statement, while almost none might agree with a radically positive statement. Once we have the frequency

---

* An item could be accompanied by a larger or smaller number of categories.

distribution for each item in hand, we are ready to find the weights to be assigned to the respective categories, item by item. To illustrate the procedure of getting weights, let us suppose that the responses of N persons to the item "We are protecting the U.S. by fighting in Vietnam" had the following distribution:

Category	Proportion
Strongly disagree	.10
Disagree	.40
Neutral	.25
Agree	.15
Strongly agree	.10

Our problem is to find the class limits (as normal deviates) of these intervals on the base line of a unit normal distribution, and the points in each of these intervals such that one-half the frequency is on either side of that point. To find these points, which we shall employ as weights for that item, we proceed as follows:

(1) Cumulate class frequencies (reduced to proportions):

SD	D	N	A	SA
.100	.500	.750	.900	1.000

(2) Divide simple class frequencies by 2:

.050	.200	.125	.075	.050

(3) Subtract these halved class frequencies from the cumulated frequencies obtained in (1) above:

.050	.300	.625	.825	.950

(4) Convert the cumulative proportions obtained in (3) above to normal deviates by referring to a table with cumulative proportions in the stub (Walker and Lev 1953: 455):

-1.645	$-.524$	.319	.935	1.645

(5) Make all values zero or positive by adding an appropriate constant:

.000	1.121	1.964	2.580	3.290

These five values are then assigned to persons within the respective categories for the item "We are protecting the U.S. by fighting in Vietnam." For example, persons responding "neutral" would receive a score of 1.964, or 2.0, rounded to nearest tenth.

Dual Meaning of Agreement. As a mere routine, the weighting procedure involves no more than finding normal deviates for observed proportions in a normal probability table. The application of this procedure is complicated somewhat by the dual meaning of agreement: agreement may reflect a favorable or an unfavorable attitude depending on the wording of the item. If agreement with a positively worded item carries the highest weight, then agreement with a negatively worded item must carry the lowest weight, or vice versa. Accordingly, before giving the items, we must classify them as positive or negative, according to whether agreement reflects a favorable or unfavorable attitude. If we give "strongly agree" the highest weight for positive items, we would give "strongly disagree" the highest weight for negative items. Although an item may be misclassified at the start, such a mistake will come to light in the process of checking items for internal consistency and may be corrected at that time.

Simplified Scoring. Since no two items have exactly the same distribution of responses, no two items have the same sigma weights. For practical reasons, it would be convenient if a given category had the same weight for every item. It was Likert's (1932) finding that scores based on sigma weights were closely correlated (.99) with scores based on arbitrary weights consisting of as many consecutive integers as categories, e.g., 1, 2, 3, 4, 5. Scores based on sigma weights and arbitrary weights may be regarded as interchangeable indices in the sense that their correlation with an outside criterion will have approximately the same value. It is this result which supplies a justification for replacing weights in the form of normal deviates by consecutive integers, or ranks.

Internal Consistency. The sum of a person's weights for all items is taken as a measure of his attitude.* But the validity of that sum as a measure of attitude may be impaired by the presence of "foreign" items which evoke a pattern of agreement which diverges from that produced by the majority of the items. Contrary to the dominant trend, persons with low total scores may score as high or higher on a given item than persons with high total scores. This is most likely to occur with neutral items which are equally disagreeable to both extremes. To eliminate such items, which blur the very differences we seek to establish, we may have recourse to one of the following alternative but not strictly equivalent techniques of *item analysis:*

(1) *Comparison of Extreme Quartiles.* If an item is consistent with the total score, persons with high scores will tend to score higher on that item than persons with low scores. To check whether an item is consistent in this sense, we may proceed as follows: (a) arrange persons into quartiles according to their total scores; (b) compute the mean item score for persons in the highest quartile and the mean score for persons in the lowest quartile; (c) test the significance of the difference between these means by the *t*-ratio.

---

* Since attitude scores are obtained by summing weights, the method has come to be known as "summated ratings."

If the difference is significant at, for instance, the 5 percent level, we may retain the item for inclusion in the final questionnaire; otherwise, we discard it as worthless for discriminating among persons. By way of example, let us suppose three patterns:

	Mean Value	
Item No.	Lowest Quartile	Highest Quartile
1	.3	1.7
2	1.0	1.0
3	1.7	.3

Persons in the highest quartile score high on No. 1, while persons in the lowest quartile score low. No. 1 is a consistent item. Persons in the highest and lowest quartiles react identically to No. 2; it is independent of total score. In the case of No. 3, persons with high total scores score low; persons with low total scores score high. It is an inconsistent item but may be made consistent by reversing weights. By this technique of comparing extreme groups, we judge which items are consistent among themselves, which are independent and useless, and which are inconsistent and misclassified.

(2) *Correlation Between Item Score and Total Score.* As an alternative to comparing extreme groups, we may compute the product-moment correlation between item score and total score. Since item and total scores are presumably measures of the same thing, they should be closely correlated. This procedure will produce results closely similar to those based on a comparison of extreme groups, except that a correlation which is based on all persons may be low when the difference between the means of extreme quartiles is statistically significant. On the other hand, if the correlation is high, the difference between extreme groups will be significant. Since the correlation coefficient is more discriminating, it is preferred to a comparison between means.

(3) *Factor Analysis.* As a third procedure, we may subject the intercorrelations among the n items to a standard factor analysis, retaining those k items with suitably high loadings on the general factor, discarding the $n - k$ others. Alternatively, we may retain all n items and weight them according to their contribution to the prediction of the general factor score. The procedure for predicting a factor score from n variables is given in Harman (1967: 350).

PART 5
Guttman's Method

Guttman's model (1941; 1944) differs from those constructed by Thurstone and Likert in that it is free of assumptions about the distribution of comparative judgments and the distribution of individuals along the hypothetical attitude scale. Its foundation is the assertion that a specific attitude is completely contained in a single dimension. We may represent this dimension by a straight line as follows:

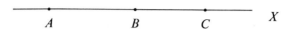

Let us suppose that persons are scattered along this axis and that we cut it at several points, say, *A, B,* and *C,* as in the diagram. When the axis has been partitioned in this way, we may characterize each person according to the number of points above (or below) him. All points may be above him, in which case he will be located in the lowest interval on the axis. Or two, one, or no points may be above him, as the case may be. In its essentials, this is the Guttman model: a partitioned dimension which permits us to classify each person according to the rank of his last partition, or the number of partitions below him. If there are three partitions, it will be possible to arrange persons serially in four ordered classes: 3, 2, 1, 0. Corresponding to this notion, a set of attitude statements may be regarded as a scale if a positive response to any given statement requires a no less positive response to all statements standing lower on the scale. If a person gives a positive response to the highest item, he must give a positive response to every other item; if he gives a negative response to the lowest item, he must give a negative response to every other item. We employ what has come to be known as *scale analysis* to determine whether a set of items conforms to this model. Broadly speaking, we fit the pattern of responses to *n* items, as observed in a sample of *N* persons, to the ideal pattern to which the scale model gives rise. Let us consider this ideal pattern briefly before discussing the criteria of goodness of fit, restricting ourselves throughout (for the sake of simplicity) to dichotomous items (e.g., yes-no, true-false, etc.).

Consequences of the Model. If the items are a Guttman scale, and we rank scores from high to low in rows, and items from high to low in columns (by either of the response categories), we necessarily obtain a triangular figuration of entries. For example, in the case of five dichotomous items, we would get an arrangement as follows:

Item (+)

Score	5	4	3	2	1
5	×	×	×	×	×
4		×	×	×	×
3			×	×	×
2				×	×
1					×
0					

There is one less entry in each successive row, top to bottom; one more entry in each successive column, left to right; accordingly, the triangle of entries is identical to the triangle of empty cells. Since each score in the margin on the left corresponds to one and only one combination of responses, the responses for each person may be perfectly reproduced from his test score. Likewise, since each item in the margin at the top corresponds to one and only one combination of responses, we may reproduce the pattern of acceptances (or rejections) for each item in the set. For example, we would predict that persons scoring 5 would endorse Item 5, but no one else. At the other extreme, we would predict that no one would reject Item 1, except persons scoring 0. In general, from an entry in the margin, side, or top, we may reproduce the pattern of entries in the row (or column) corresponding to that marginal entry.

Scalogram. If we extend the table to include negative responses, we get a pattern of entries in the right hand of the chart which corresponds to the triangle of empty cells in the left half of the same chart, as follows:

						Item						
		(+)						(−)				
Score	5	4	3	2	1		5	4	3	2	1	
5	×	×	×	×	×							
4		×	×	×	×		×					
3			×	×	×		×	×				
2				×	×		×	×	×			
1					×		×	×	×	×		
0							×	×	×	×	×	

Since the complete pattern of "×'s" resembles a parallelogram, it was named a scalogram by Guttman. A scalogram is thus the pattern of responses to which the *n* items forming a scale give rise, when we record them in the aforesaid manner.

Cornell Chart. If we arrange categories within items (instead of items within categories), the pattern of entries with one cut for each item will resemble a staircase (as shown on p. 329). This arrangement was devised by Guttman (1947) when he was a professor at Cornell University. The Cornell chart, it will be observed, is equivalent to the scalogram, except that we display the pattern of responses for each item together, rather than in separate columns as in the scalogram.

Testing the Model. To test the model, we subject our raw data to scale analysis and from our findings draw inferences about its credibility. Since the model requires that responses be reproducible from scale scores, our

Item

Score	5 +	5 −	4 +	4 −	3 +	3 −	2 +	2 −	1 +	1 −
5	×		×		×		×		×	
4		×	×		×		×		×	
3		×		×	×		×		×	
2		×		×		×	×		×	
1		×		×		×		×	×	
0		×		×		×		×		×

principal task will be to determine the degree of reproducibility in our sample. To calculate reproducibility, we arrange scores in rank order, recording alongside each score the pattern of responses on which it is based. The resulting configuration may take the form of either a scalogram or a Cornell chart, according to the arrangement of response categories in columns. From the resulting display, we may judge visually but roughly the degree to which the responses conform to the model. We might characterize the fit as good or poor. For a more precise measure of fit, we count by rule the number of responses (E) which are not reproducible from the N scale scores, express that number as a proportion of the total number of responses (Nn), and subtract the resulting proportion from 1. This index, named the "coefficient of reproducibility" by Guttman, is the proportion of responses that may be reproduced without error from scale scores. In symbols:

$$(7.5.1) \qquad R = 1 - \frac{E}{Nn},$$

where N = number of persons, n = number of items, E = number of errors, and R = coefficient of reproducibility. Although it would appear to be a simple matter to count the number of errors, the results for a given set of Nn responses will differ according to the number of restrictions we impose on our counting procedure. Since different procedures produce different values of E, and, hence, R, it is good practice to specify our prediction rule, or our rule for counting errors, in our research report.

One Score, One Prediction. If we restrict ourselves to one prediction for each score, we will minimize the number of errors by predicting the modal pattern for each score. This restriction is based on the scale requirement that there be no more scale patterns than scale scores. In predicting by this rule, we identify the modal pattern for each score and predict that pattern for all persons with that score. The modal patterns in Table 7.5.1 are (+++), (−++), (−−+) and (−−−), corresponding to frequencies of

Table 7.5.1 *Frequency Distribution of Response Patterns, n = 3, N = 100*

No. of Positive Responses	Response Pattern			Frequency
	1	*2*	*3*	
3	+	+	+	30
2	−	+	+	25
2	+	−	+	3
2	+	+	−	1
1	−	−	+	22
1	−	+	−	4
1	+	−	−	1
0	−	−	−	14
				N = 100

30, 25, 22, and 14, respectively. Upon predicting these patterns for scores of 3, 2, 1, 0, and counting errors, we get these results: no prediction errors for scores of 3 and 0 (by reason that extreme scores may arise in one and only one way); two errors apiece for scores of 2 based on combinations other than (−++), for a total 4 × 2 = 8 errors in the subset of all 2's; two errors apiece for scores of 1 based on combinations other than (−−+), for a total 5 × 2 = 10 errors in the subset of all 1's. The total of all errors is therefore 8 + 10 = 18. Expressing this count as a proportion of all *nN* responses and subtracting that proportion from 1, we get the coefficient of reproducibility:

$$R = 1 - \frac{18}{300}$$
$$= .94.$$

This result may be interpreted as a proportion of responses that will be reproduced without error, given that we predict the modal pattern for each case. In general, this rule yields the largest number of errors, and, in that sense, is the most conservative.

Guttman's Rule. We may lift the restriction of only one prediction for each score and predict for each case whichever pattern will minimize the number of prediction errors. This is Guttman's rule, and its application yields the coefficient of reproducibility in the original meaning of that term. The sense of this rule is that a person's true score may be more reliably estimated by the pattern of his responses than by the composite score based on that pattern. Applying this rule to our example, we would predict (+++) for all 2's except the modal group; similarly, we would predict (−−−) for all 1's except the modal group. The total number of prediction errors will now be 9 instead of 18, as the student should verify, and the coefficient of reproducibility will be

$$R = 1 - \frac{9}{300}$$
$$= .97.$$

This result may be interpreted as the proportion of responses that may be reproduced by predicting the best-fitting scale pattern for each case. It rests on this operating rule: find the minimum number of observed responses that must be changed in order that all Nn of them are reproducible without error.

Green's (1956) Method of Counting Errors. Instead of finding the minimum number of responses that must be changed to produce a perfect scale, we may count the number of persons positive on Item i and negative on Item $i + 1$ (given that Item i is more favorable than Item $i + 1$), and sum these counts for all possible comparisons. If responses in error (out of order) are removed in succession until no more errors remain, this procedure yields the number of responses breaking the scale pattern, or Guttman's minimum error; if the process is not carried to the limit, it generally gives fewer errors than that minimum number. This method does not modify Guttman's rule of predicting the best-fitting pattern for each case, rather it defines error so as to be readily sorted out by the computer.

As an example, consider the number of errors (adjacent entries out of order) for each combination in Table 7.5.1: we find no errors for $(+++)$, $(-++)$, $(--+)$ and $(---)$, but one error apiece for $(+-+)$, $(++-)$, $(-+-)$ and $(+--)$. Multiplying these errors by their corresponding frequencies, we get the total error for our sample:

$$
\begin{aligned}
3 \times 1 &= 3 \\
1 \times 1 &= 1 \\
4 \times 1 &= 4 \\
1 \times 1 &= \underline{1} \\
& \;\, 9
\end{aligned}
$$

Substituting the total error of 9 in the reproducibility formula, we get a coefficient of .97, which is exactly equal to the value produced by Guttman's rule. But this equality is the exception. When $n = 3$, this method will give rise to the same total error as Guttman's rule; however, when $n > 3$, and when restricted to the first stage alone, this method will produce a smaller total error, and therefore an overestimate of Guttman's reproducibility.

Ninety Percent Rule. Question: To what level of reproducibility, however obtained, must the sample data attain in order for the investigator to accept the hypothesis that the attitude is unidimensional in Guttman's sense? Guttman suggested that responses be at least 90 percent reproducible from test scores, and this criterion is generally adopted by most research workers. The justification for this standard is that human responses fluctuate from one trial to another in purely random fashion; hence, it is not unreasonable to accept the hypothesis that the attitude is unidimensional, notwithstanding that as many as 10 out of 100 responses break the perfect scale pattern. To provide further assurance that the errors in reproducibility are not caused by determining factors or biases, Guttman suggested that two supplementary criteria be met: (1) no response category to have more than 50 percent error in reproducibility, and (2) no clustering of error by test scores. The principle underlying these suggestions is that any concentration of error by either item or score is evidence that the items do not form a scale in the population under study. The limitations of Guttman's criteria have been noted intermittently and various proposals (Loevinger 1948; Menzel 1953; Green 1956) have been advanced to alleviate their alleged effects. Although these alternative procedures differ in their detail, all purport to provide a more valid inference concerning the unidimensionality of a set of items.

Recently, the suggestion has been advanced that reproducibility in the sample be computed on the assumption that items are statistically independent, and that expectation be compared with the value based on the observed responses in the sample. The sense of this procedure is to guard against the ascription of significance to a reproducibility which could readily occur when the items themselves are statistically independent. All such techniques are motivated by the methodological principle that we guard against the possibility of rejecting the null hypothesis that items are statistically independent when true, or accepting that hypothesis when false. Students wishing to pursue this topic should consult the article by Chilton (1969), which reviews and evaluates this line of work.

PART 6
Latent Structure Analysis

This method, due to Lazarsfeld (1950: 454–472), begins with the idea of a latent attitude (X) which N persons have in varying degree and which has a frequency distribution in the population. There are no restrictions on the distribution of X which may be symmetrical or skewed. It may be graphically represented in the usual way:

where X is the latent variable, and $f(X)$ is the population density.

It is the aim of latent structure analysis to order N persons along the latent continuum (X) on the basis of their responses to k^* test items. It is thus a technique for processing observed data in order to draw inferences about latent parameters which are hypothetical. In its postulate of an underlying continuum and its manipulation of conventional test items, it is similar to other methods; its distinctiveness lies in its conceptualization of (1) the relation of each item to the latent variable (X); (2) the relation of each item to every other item in the entire population; and (3) the statistical interrelations among items for persons having the same value of X.

For present purposes, that conceptualization may be expressed in the form of three assumptions: (1) the probability of a given response (A) to a given item is a function of the latent variable (X); (2) items may be correlated in the population; (3) items will be mutually independent of one another for all persons having the same value of X.

The first assumption imposes no restriction on the form of the relationship between the probability of a given response and the latent variable, and merely asserts that such a relationship exists; hence, the plot of that relationship, or *trace line*, may be a straight line or curve, as in these examples:

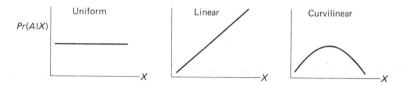

where A is the response in question. When the probability of a given response is constant for all values of X, the trace line will be parallel to the X-axis, as in the first drawing; when the probability is proportional to X, the trace line will be a sloping straight line; when the probability first increases and then decreases, the trace line will be a curve, as in the third drawing.

The second assumption expresses the expectation that items related to the same attitude will be related to one another. Although we assume that items will be correlated in the population, we place no restriction on the degree of correlation between any two items. That correlation may be weak or strong as in these examples:

		Item 2		Item 3		Item 4	
		+	−	+	−	+	−
Item 1	+	32	18	40	10	48	2
	−	16	14	8	22	0	30

---

* In this discussion, we use "k" to represent the number of test items, because we require "n" for another purpose.

In the first example, items are nearly independent; in the second, items are moderately correlated; in the third, the correlation between items is complete (given the marginal frequencies). There is no constraint on the degree of correlation between items in the population. This is our second assumption.

However, a restriction is imposed on the relations among items for a given value of X, and this restriction constitutes the third assumption of latent structure analysis. This assumption answers to the question: "Is the probability of an individual's response to the ith item affected by his response to any other item?" A negative reply to this question is required by the third assumption which holds that items are mutually independent for a given value of X. An implication is that the responses for each person to all n items may be regarded as an *independent trials process* (Kemeny, Snell, and Thompson 1956: 146). To illustrate this, consider someone who has given $k - 1$ positive responses to as many items and has one more response to make. Will his response to the last (k^{th}) item be affected by his run of $k - 1$ positive replies? The negative answer is the assumption of *local independence*, as it has been named: a person's response to any given item is statistically independent of his responses to each and every other item. Technically speaking, the probability of a set combination of responses is equal to the product of the probabilities of the constituent responses.

Deductions from the Model. Consider now some of the implications of these assumptions. When our empirical data do not contradict these implications, we will not reject the assumptions which constitute our model. In this analysis, it will be practicable (to free ourselves of the notation of calculus) to divide the latent variable into m successive intervals with the understanding that the probability of a given response will be identical for all persons in the same interval. (Since these probabilities will jump from one interval to another, we refer to latent structure analysis under this restriction as *latent class analysis*.) Further, for the sake of simplicity, we shall limit the discussion to dichotomous items which permit only a positive $(+)$ or negative $(-)$ response. The ensuing discussion thus pertains to latent class models for dichotomous items, and not to latent structures in general.

We begin with the distribution of a population of N persons who have been grouped into m intervals along the latent continuum. We take N_i as the number of persons in the ith class interval, and p_{ij} as the proportion of persons in the ith class interval giving a positive response to the jth item. For m class intervals and k items, we have m class frequencies and km proportions which may be set forth as follows:

		Item		
Class Interval	*Frequency*	$1 \cdots$	$j \cdots$	k
1	N_1	$p_{11} \cdots$	$p_{1j} \cdots$	p_{1k}
i	N_i	$p_{i1} \cdots$	$p_{ij} \cdots$	p_{ik}
m	N_m	$p_{m1} \cdots$	$p_{mj} \cdots$	p_{mk}

From these entries, we may obtain (after manipulation) these subtotals:

$$n_j \quad = \text{total number positive on item } j$$
$$n_{jk} \quad = \text{total number positive on items } j \text{ and } k$$
$$n_{jkl} \quad = \text{total number positive on items } j, k, \text{ and } l$$
$$n_{12\ldots m} = \text{total number positive on all } k \text{ items}$$

To get n_j, we multiply each class frequency by the proportion (in that interval) responding positively to the jth item. The sum of all such products is the subtotal responding positively to the jth item. In symbols:

$$n_j = N_1 p_{1j} + \cdots + N_m p_{mj}.$$

In closely similar fashion, we get n_{jk}. If we multiply p_{ij} by p_{ik}, we get (by the assumption of independence) the proportion of cases in the ith interval responding positively to both items, j and k. Multiplying this compound proportion by N_i, we get the number of persons in the ith interval responding positively to both Item j and Item k. Summing all such frequencies, we get the number of persons in the population responding positively to both items, j and k.

$$n_{jk} = N_1 p_{1j} p_{1k} + \cdots + N_m p_{mj} p_{mk}.$$

Continuing, if we multiply p_{il} by $p_{ij} p_{ik}$, we get the compound proportion of persons in the ith interval responding positively to items j, k, and l. Multiplying this result by N_i, we obtain the number of persons in the ith class answering positively to items j, k, and l. Summing all such products, we get:

$$n_{jkl} = N_1 p_{1j} p_{1k} p_{1l} + \cdots + N_m p_{mj} p_{mk} p_{ml}.$$

By natural extension, we may write the number of persons responding positively to all k items, given the assumption of local independence as defined above. This will be:

$$n_{12\ldots k} = N_1 p_{11} p_{12} \ldots p_{1k} + \cdots + N_m p_{m1} p_{m2} \ldots p_{mk}.$$

The problem of latent class analysis may now be stated as follows: given observed frequencies in the form n_j, n_{jk}, $\ldots$, $n_{12\ldots k}$, find m latent parameters of the form N_i and mk parameters of the form p_{ij} such that all equations of the general form,

(7.6.1)
$$n_{12\ldots k} = \sum_{1}^{m} N_i p_{i1} p_{i2} \ldots p_{ik},$$

are satisfied (within the limits of sampling error). Because the frequency on the left side is accounted for by the weighted compound probabilities on the right side, Equation (7.6.1), or a specialization of it. is called "the accounting equation."

Fitting Constants. The procedure for getting estimates of latent parameters is a rather intricate procedure which does not lend itself to easy description. For that reason, we limit ourselves to a presentation of results which could arise when we apply the least complicated forms of that procedure. For the simplest case of two unordered classes, our goal is to segregate the sample into two subgroups, such that n items are independent of one another within each subgroup, but correlated with one another for both subgroups combined. If we are able to partition the sample in this manner, we will have met the general criterion of latent structure analysis. Since we are dealing with unordered classes, we sometimes refer to this particular procedure as *latent attribute analysis*.

To be more concrete, consider three yes-no items on student opinion about university affairs:

Item	*Statement*
1	The undergraduate major should be abolished.
2	In their personal lives, students should be subject to no university control.
3	Students should vote on the firing of teachers.

Let us suppose that 50 out of 100 persons have responded positively to each of these items and that items are moderately associated in the population as follows:

		Item 2 yes	Item 2 no			Item 3 yes	Item 3 no			Item 3 yes	Item 3 no	
Item 1	yes	31	19	50	1	27	23	50	2	22	28	50
	no	19	31	50		23	27	50		28	22	50
		50	50			50	50			50	50	

We note in passing that Items 1 and 2, and Items 1 and 3 are positively associated, whereas Items 2 and 3 are negatively associated.

Imagine now that we have solved all equations of the general form (7.6.1) and that these solutions give rise to joint distributions within subgroups as follows:

Subgroup			Item 2 yes	Item 2 no			Item 3 yes	Item 3 no			Item 3 yes	Item 3 no	
I	yes	1	28	7	35	1	21	14	35	2	6	4	10
	no		12	3	15		9	6	15		24	16	40

		yes	no	
II	yes 1	3	12	15
	no	7	28	35
		10	40	

	yes	no	
1	6	9	15
	14	21	35
	20	30	

	yes	no	
2	16	24	40
	4	6	10
	20	30	

Since the row proportions within columns are equal to marginal proportions in each table, which is the earmark of statistical independence, we accept the possibility of a latent structure composed of $m = 2$ classes. Accordingly, we might argue that the latent variable, whatever its nature, explains the interrelations among items in the total sample, since the partial relations vanish when we control on this variable. It is plausible that the first group is composed of persons who are identified with the New Left and that the second group is composed of persons who are affiliated with the Old Right. But whatever our substantive interpretation, our results provide a demonstration that the sample may be divided into two groups which differ externally, but which are internally homogeneous. In short, our data are consistent with a latent structure composed of two classes.

From this simple example, we may discern the similarity between a structure composed of a single latent variable and Spearman's one-factor theory (p. 58). According to that theory, when four or more variables are held together by a single common factor, all first-order residuals, or tetrads, will be equal to zero. Since these tetrads are the equivalent of the partial correlations between variables with the common factor held constant, we may say that the interrelationships among variables are attributable to the common factor. In an analogous manner, the manifest interrelationships among items vanish when the influence of the latent factor is removed. However, when that latent factor is reintroduced, the intercorrelations among items reestablish themselves. It is thus fair to say that latent structure analysis and factor analysis are alike in their conception of observed relationships as being accounted for by a hypothetical underlying factor(s).

Latent Distance Analysis. Let us now impose the requirement that classes be ordered from low to high along the latent continuum, and impose the additional restriction that the probability of a given response change at one and only one class boundary. The plot of such a changing probability on the latent axis will always consist of a single step as in Figure 7.6.1:

Figure 7.6.1

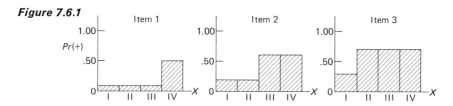

By "reading" these graphs (Figure 7.6.1), we may restore the tabulations from which the figures were drawn:

Item

Latent Class	1	2	3
IV	.50	.60	.70
III	.10	.60	.70
II	.10	.20	.70
I	.10	.20	.30

Because such a hierarchy of probabilities could result from the social distance separating the members of one group from those of another, it was named by Lazarsfeld "the social distance model." In scaling social distance by several or more items, we usually obtain such a pattern of frequencies, with the intergroup distance being least for those in the highest category, and greatest for persons in the lowest category. By way of example, consider these items:

(1) Would you be willing to marry a Protestant?

(2) Would you be willing to live next door to a Protestant?

(3) Would you be willing to work with a Protestant?

Persons answering "yes" to the first question would probably answer "yes" to the second and third items with no less certainty; persons answering "yes" to the second, but "no" to the first item, would probably answer "yes" to the third item; persons responding positively to the third, but negatively to the second, would probably answer negatively to the first. If these predictions are correct, we could arrange persons into four classes, according to their tendency to respond positively to one or more items, with results such as these:

Item

Latent Class	1	2	3
IV	.60	.80	.90
III	.30	.80	.90
II	.30	.40	.90
I	.30	.40	.50

Since the requirement that the probability of a given response change at one and only one point gives rise to just such a pattern of probabilities, this requirement may be regarded as the essential condition of the latent distance model.

Let us now impose the additional requirement that the "probability" of a given response be either 0 or 1. In this limiting case, the height of a plotted step will always be one, but its width will vary according to the location of the point at which the probability jumps from zero to one, as in Figure 7.6.2:

Figure 7.6.2

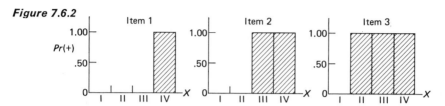

If we reconstruct the tabulations from which these graphs (Figure 7.6.2) were drawn, we get the following pattern of conditional probabilities:

	Item		
Latent Class	1	2	3
IV	1.00	1.00	1.00
III	0.00	1.00	1.00
II	0.00	0.00	1.00
I	0.00	0.00	0.00

But this pattern conforms to the requirements of the Guttman scale. We thus come to the conclusion that the scalogram may be regarded as a special case of the latent distance model. However, the classification of the scalogram as a latent structure is not to disparage the scalogram, which is important in its own right and which may be studied without reference to latent structure theory. In applying scale analysis we are at liberty to ignore its theoretical link with latent structure analysis when that link has no practical relevance.

Concluding Opinion. By and large, the method of latent structure analysis is the most intricate of the processes for measuring attitudes that we have encountered in this chapter. And its complexities have undoubtedly been a deterrent to its regular use in applied research. Before persons are ever put in classes, we must find m class frequencies and mk probabilities which could produce the observed frequencies, and which together constitute the latent model. As of this writing, a general solution to this problem has not been formulated (Lazarsfeld and Henry 1968), and the research worker is therefore restricted to a few special cases for which working procedures have been devised. Furthermore, latent structure analysis finds itself in the same quandary as factor analysis: we both derive and interpret the latent variable from the same manifest data. For these and related reasons, the method of latent structure analysis is probably the least practicable of the alternatives presently available to the research worker, although it may be theoretically most germinal, a point which has been made by several commentators.

Concluding Remarks on Attitude Measurement. From the foregoing presentation, we conclude that the researcher has some leeway in the choice of an attitude scale. Of the five techniques considered, paired comparisons and latent structure analysis are used less frequently than the other three. This reflects their relative impracticability more than their theoretical inferiority. Equal intervals, summated ratings, and scalogram analysis all do an adequate job with relatively less effort.

Although we have exemplified the process of attitude measurement, we have by no means done justice to the variety of techniques that have been devised and refined. No mention was made of the semantic differential (Osgood, Suci, and Tannenbaum 1957), Stephenson's (1953) Q-technique, Stevens's (1959) ratio method, or Coombs's (1964) unfolding technique. Multidimensional scaling was also excluded (Shephard 1962). All of these, as well as others, would be included in a comprehensive account of techniques for measuring attitudes.

Nor did we give consideration to such problems as the reliability and validity of observed scores, and the capacity of the test to detect individual differences within different subpopulations. In the next chapter, we deal with the problem of reliability and broach the problem of validity. However, we do not attack the problem of a test's universality. That problem may be phrased as a question: "Does the test perform identically in all subpopulations?" This question takes on critical importance in comparative research. If an attitude test is not equally discriminating in all subpopulations, we cannot use readings from that test to compare two or more populations on that attitude. This is a recurring problem in scaling—"Does the intelligence test measure equally well in the North and the South?" "Does the ink-blot test work for nonliterate populations?" Paraphrasing these questions: Will a test of political liberalism, pretested on American college students, serve to discriminate among individuals in Western Europe, Southeast Asia, or the Middle East? As sociologists extend their research efforts to non-American populations, such questions will become more pressing.

EXERCISES

1. Seven items on urban violence were given two at a time to 500 judges; row items were judged more favorable than column items as follows:

Item	1	2	3	4	5	6	7
1	250	217	159	91	47	35	18
2	283	250	203	140	82	63	28
3	341	297	250	218	133	87	58
4	409	360	282	250	174	138	99
5	453	418	367	326	250	228	147
6	465	327	413	362	272	250	210
7	482	472	442	401	353	290	250

(a) By the method of paired comparisons, determine scale values of seven items.
(b) Use Mosteller's X^2 test to check the tenability of the assumption of equal variances and a constant correlation (p. 313).

2. One hundred (100) judges sorted six (6) attitude statements into 11 equal-appearing intervals as follows:

Item	A	B	C	D	E	F	G	H	I	J	K
1	0	12	48	38	2	0	0	0	0	0	0
2	0	2	1	8	16	15	17	11	15	10	5
3	35	37	14	13	0	0	1	0	0	0	0
4	0	0	1	0	11	59	18	8	3	0	0
5	0	0	0	0	0	0	5	5	26	22	42
6	24	23	20	14	9	7	2	1	0	0	0

(a) Which items would be discarded as ambiguous?
(b) Compute scale values (medians) for all six items.

3. The marginals (as percentages) for five items on an anomie scale were as follows:

Item	SD	D	N	A	SA
1. These days a person doesn't really know who he can count on.	5	15	25	35	20
2. Nowadays a person has to live pretty much for today and let tomorrow take care of itself.	10	15	30	30	15
3. It's hardly fair to bring children into the world with the way things look for the future.	2	30	30	30	8

4. In spite of what some people say, the lot   20   40   10   25   5
of the average man is getting worse.
5. There's little use writing to public officials   25   30   20   20   5
because they really aren't interested in
the problems of the average man.

On the assumption that strength of agreement is normally distributed, find the
category weights for each of the five items (Srole 1956).

4. Using weights from (3), find anomie scores of persons responding as indicated:

			Item		
Person	1	2	3	4	5
A	A	D	A	D	A
B	SA	SD	A	A	D
C	N	A	SD	SA	D
D	A	D	SA	N	SD

5. A set of four dichotomous items was given to 200 persons. The frequency for
each of the 16 possible response patterns was as follows:

	Response Pattern				
No. of Positive Responses	I	II	III	IV	f
4	+	+	+	+	28
3	−	+	+	+	34
3	+	−	+	+	12
3	+	+	−	+	3
3	+	+	+	−	1
2	−	−	+	+	35
2	−	+	−	+	2
2	−	+	+	−	0
2	+	−	−	+	4
2	+	−	+	−	3
2	+	+	−	−	2
1	−	−	−	+	43
1	−	−	+	−	10
1	−	+	−	−	2
1	+	−	−	−	2
0	−	−	−	−	19

(a) Calculate the coefficient of reproducibility by predicting the modal response
pattern for each score.
(b) Calculate the coefficient of reproducibility by predicting the best-fitting
pattern for each case (i.e., predict such that errors are minimized).
(c) Do the results of (a) and (b) justify the conclusion that the items form a
Guttman scale?

6. Scale values (prestige) for ten occupations by the method of paired comparisons are given by Reiss (1961: 102) as follows:

Occupation	Scale Value
Garbage collector	0.000
Truck driver	1.046
Machine operator	1.401
Clerk in a store	1.888
Electrician	2.899
Bookkeeper	2.919
Foreman in a factory	3.126
Manager in a store	4.102
Minister	5.096
Physician	5.894

From the differences among these values, find the proportion of judges rating each occupation as higher or lower than every other occupation.

REFERENCES

Barton, Allan H.
  1961 Organizational Measurement. New York: College Entrance Board.

Biderman, Albert D.
  1966 "Social indicators." Pp. 68–153 in Raymond A. Bauer (ed.), Social Indicators and Goals. Cambridge: M.I.T. Press.

Bonjean, Charles M., Richard J. Hill, and S. Dale McLemore
  1967 Sociological Measurements: An Inventory of Scales and Indices. San Francisco: Chandler.

Chilton, Roland J.
  1969 "A review and comparison of simple statistical tests for scalogram analysis." American Sociological Review 34: 237–245.

Coombs, Clyde H.
  1964 A Theory of Data. New York: John Wiley and Sons.

Coombs, Clyde H., Robyn M. Dawes, and Amos Tversky
  1970 Mathematical Psychology: An Elementary Introduction. Chapter 3: "Scaling and data theory." Englewood Cliffs, New Jersey: Prentice-Hall.

Cotton, J. W.
  1969 "The sensitivity of coefficients of reproducibility to intercorrelation among items, dispersion of pass-fail proportions, and multiple factor structure." Multivariate Behavioral Research 4: 347–362.

Duncan, Otis Dudley and Beverly Duncan
　　1955　"A methodological analysis of segregation indexes." American
　　　　　Sociological Review 20: 210–217.

Edwards, Allen L.
　　1957　Techniques of Attitude Scale Construction. New York: Appleton-
　　　　　Century-Crofts.

Freeman, Linton C. and Robert F. Winch
　　1957　"Social complexity: An empirical test of a typology of societies."
　　　　　American Journal of Sociology 62: 461–466.

Goodenough, Ward H.
　　1944　"A technique for scale analysis."--Educational and Psychological
　　　　　Measurement 4: 179–190.

　　1963　"Some applications of Guttman scale analysis to ethnography
　　　　　and culture theory." Southwestern Journal of Anthropology 19:
　　　　　235–250.

Goodman, L. A.
　　1959　"Simple statistical methods for scalogram analysis." Psycho-
　　　　　metrika 24: 29–43.

Green, Bert F., Jr.
　　1956　"A method of scalogram analysis using summary statistics."
　　　　　Psychometrika 21: 79–89.

Guttman, Louis
　　1941　"The quantification of a class of attributes." Pp. 321–348 in
　　　　　Paul Horst et al., The Prediction of Personal Adjustment. New
　　　　　York: Social Science Research Council.

　　1944　"A basis for scaling qualitative data." American Sociological
　　　　　Review 9: 139–150.

　　1947　"The Cornell technique for scale and intensity analysis." Educa-
　　　　　tional and Psychological Measurement 7: 247–280.

　　1950　"The relation of scalogram analysis to other techniques." Pp.
　　　　　172–212 in S. A. Stouffer et al., Measurement and Prediction.
　　　　　Princeton: Princeton University Press.

Harman, Harry H.
　　1967　Modern Factor Analysis. Second Edition. Chicago: University
　　　　　of Chicago Press.

Hill, Richard J.
　　1953　"A note on inconsistency in paired judgments." American
　　　　　Sociological Review 18: 564–566.

Kemeny, J. G., J. L. Snell, and G. L. Thompson
　　1956　Introduction to Finite Mathematics. Englewood Cliffs: Prentice-
　　　　　Hall.

Lazarsfeld, P. F.
　　1950　"The logical and mathematical foundation of latent structure
　　　　　analysis." Pp. 454–472 in S. A. Stouffer et al., Measurement and
　　　　　Prediction. Princeton: Princeton University Press.

1959 "Latent structure analysis." Pp. 476–543 in Sigmund Koch (ed.), Psychology: A Study of a Science, Conceptual and Systematic. Vol. 4. New York: McGraw-Hill.

1960 "Latent structure analysis and test theory." Pp. 83–95 in H. Gulliksen and S. Messick (eds.), Psychological Scaling: Theory and Applications. New York: John Wiley and Sons.

Lazarsfeld, P. F. and Neil W. Henry
1968 Latent Structure Analysis. Boston: Houghton Mifflin.

Likert, Rensis
1932 "A technique for the measurement of attitudes." Archives of Psychology, No. 140.

Lingoes, James C.
1963 "Multiple scalogram analysis: A set-theoretic model for analyzing dichotomous items." Educational and Psychological Measurement 23: 501–523.

Loevinger, Jane
1948 "The technic of homogeneous tests compared with some aspects of 'scale analysis' and factor analysis." Psychological Bulletin 45: 507–529.

MacRae, Duncan, Jr.
1970 Issues and Parties in Legislative Voting: Methods of Statistical Analysis. Chapter 2: "Scale analysis." New York: Harper and Row.

Menzel, Herbert
1953 "A new coefficient for scalogram analysis." Public Opinion Quarterly 17: 268–280.

Miller, Delbert C.
1970 Handbook of Research Design and Social Measurement. Second Edition. New York: McKay.

Moses, Lincoln E., *et al.*
1967 "Scaling data on inter-nation action." Science 156: 1054–1059.

Mosteller, Frederick
1951 "Remarks on the method of paired comparisons III." Psychometrika 16: 207–218.

Ofshe, Richard and Ronald E. Anderson
1969 "Testing a measurement model." Pp. 263–275 in Edgar F. Borgatta (ed.), Sociological Methodology 1969. San Francisco: Jossey-Bass.

Osgood, Charles E., George E. Suci, and Percy H. Tannenbaum
1957 The Measurement of Meaning. Urbana: University of Illinois Press.

Reiss, Albert J., Jr.
1961 Occupations and Social Status. Chapter 5: "Scaling operations." Glencoe, Illinois: Free Press.

Riley, Matilda White, John W. Riley, Jr., and Jackson Toby
    1954   Sociological Studies in Scale Analysis. New Brunswick: Rutgers University Press.

Robinson, John, and Philip R. Shaver
    1970   Measures of Social Psychological Attitudes. Ann Arbor, Michigan: Institute for Social Research.

Sagi, Philip C.
    1959   "A statistical test for the significance of a coefficient of reproducibility." Psychometrika 24: 19–27.

Schuessler, Karl
    1961   "A note on statistical significance of scalogram." Sociometry 24: 312–318.

    1966   "A note on scale analysis and factor analysis." Sociometry 29: 461–467.

Sellin, Thorsten, and Marvin E. Wolfgang
    1964   The Measurement of Delinquency. New York: John Wiley and Sons.

Shepard, R. N.
    1962   "The analysis of proximities: Multidimensional scaling with an unknown distance function I." Psychometrika 27: 125–154.

    1962   "The analysis of proximities: Multidimensional scaling with an unknown distance function II." Psychometrika 27: 219–245.

Srole, Leo
    1956   "Social integration and certain corollaries: An exploratory study." American Sociological Review 21: 709–716.

Stephenson, William
    1953   The Study of Behavior. Chicago: The University of Chicago Press.

Stevens, S. S.
    1959   "Measurement, psychophysics and utility." Pp. 18–63 in C. West Churchman and Philburn Ratoosh (eds.), Measurement: Definition and Theories. New York: John Wiley and Sons.

    1966   "A metric for the social consensus." Science 151: 530–541.

    1968   "Ratio scales of opinion." Pp. 171–199 in D. K. Whitlo (ed.), Handbook of Measurement and Assessment in Behavioral Science. Reading, Massachusetts: Addison-Wesley.

Suppes, P., and J. L. Zinnes
    1963   "Basic measurement theory." Pp. 1–76 in R. D. Luce, R. R. Bush, and E. Galanter (eds.), Handbook of Mathematical Psychology. New York: John Wiley and Sons.

Thurstone, Louis L.
    1927   "A law of comparative judgment." Psychological Review 34: 273–286.

Thurstone, Louis L., and E. J. Chave
  1929   The Measurement of Attitude. Chicago: The University of Chicago Press.

Torgerson, Warren S.
  1958   Theory and Methods of Scaling. New York: John Wiley and Sons.

Upshaw, Harry S.
  1968   "Attitude measurement." Pp. 60–111 in Hubert M. Blalock, Jr. and Ann B. Blalock (eds.), Methodology in Social Research. New York: McGraw-Hill.

Walker, Helen M., and Joseph Lev
  1953   Statistical Inference. New York: Henry Holt.

8

The Reliability of Observations

PART 1
Some Error Theory

No body of empirical data is free of error; hence, no conclusion may be drawn without due regard for observational error. For purposes of assessing the reliability of observed measures, statisticians have devised an assortment of techniques, each corresponding to a specific process of measurement. Although these methods are commonplace in scientific work, sociologists have been somewhat neglectful of them. Reasons for the neglect lie in the relative paucity of sociological data which lend themselves to statistical manipulation and in the relative inaccessibility of these methods which have developed outside the field of sociology. But with an increasing emphasis on measurement and quantitative analysis in the social sciences, we may expect that sociologists will employ these techniques more routinely and perhaps even assist in their elaboration and refinement.

Problem of Reliability. Reduced to its lowest terms and expressed as a question, the general problem of reliability is this: "May we rely on our observed measures, whether it be for purposes of testing theory or for purposes of practical enterprise?" If our measures are inaccurate, we may mistakenly accept a false hypothesis and thereby be led into a blind alley. If our information is unreliable, we may adopt a less desirable social policy with costly consequences for the general public. Because of an inaccurate census, a city may fail to receive its fair share of public money and, as a result, be forced to curtail its welfare programs.

Another facet of this problem, common in social research, faces the interviewer who must assure himself of the dependability of the information which he solicits from his respondents; otherwise he cannot generalize with confidence about their characteristics. And his difficulties will be multiplied whenever he seeks information about subjective traits such as opinions and attitudes which are not amenable to direct observation and which must be inferred from words or deeds.

In criminological studies, we must have a reliable record of crime if we wish to determine the deterrent effect of punishment on crime; similarly, in population studies, we must have a reliable measure of the birth rate if we wish to determine the effect of family planning on fertility.

In order to cultivate a sensitivity to such issues, we present in this chapter a selection of common techniques for the assessment of error in systematic observations. These techniques may be divided, but not without some overlap, according to whether they apply to errors of measurement or to errors of classification. A measurement error, as the term is used here, is itself a magnitude on an interval scale which may be relatively small or large; whereas a classification error is an attribute which is either present or absent on a given trial. For example, if we misclassify a Republican as a Democrat, a classification error is present; otherwise it is absent. We consider measurement errors first, not because they are more (or less) important than errors of classification, but rather because the methodology for dealing with them is more extensively developed.

Measurement Error. By definition, measurement error is the difference between an object's true value, which is hypothetical, and its measured value, which is observed. In symbols:*

$$E = X - \hat{X},$$

where $\hat{X}$ is the hypothetical true value, X is the observed measure. Thus, the difference between an individual's true attitude score and his observed attitude score is the amount by which the latter is in error. In analyzing measurement error, it is expedient to separate random error and constant error. On a conceptual level we do this by writing the total error as the sum of its component errors:

$$E = e + c,$$

where e is random error, c is constant error.

Random errors arise from the operation of chance factors, whereas constant errors arise from the operation of biases which cause the observed

---

* In some writing, the true value is symbolized by the Greek letter "τ" and error, by the Greek letter "ϵ."

measures to deviate from the true value by a constant amount. Because constant errors are not subject to analysis by routine statistical methods, they are disregarded in this discussion. But this is not to discount their importance; in their way they are as consequential as random errors. It is simply that they are categorically different in character and their adjustment requires different procedures. If their presence is suspected, an effort should be made to assess their magnitude and to supply appropriate corrections. In making such corrections, an intimate familiarity with the empirical events under study is required; statistical prowess alone will not suffice. The apparent excess of U.S. females age 39 years is perfectly intelligible to the trained demographer who correctly attributes this distortion to the tendency of many respondents to misrepresent their age in order to remain "under forty." He corrects this distortion by "smoothing the age curve," confident that this adjustment is consistent with the true facts.

In the absence of constant error (c), a condition we shall hereafter take as given, the difference (E) between the observed measure (X) and the true value $(\hat{X})$ reduces to random error (e). Although random errors arise from the operation of chance factors, they do not behave collectively in a capricious way, but rather conform to specific statistical laws. These laws, some of which are set forth below, permit us to judge probabilistically the reliability of our obtained measures.

Many Measures of the Same Thing. We first take up many measures of the same thing or, more specifically, the lawful behavior of errors attached to many measures of the same thing. For purposes of abstract analysis, we postulate a true value $(\hat{X})$ which is stationary, and a succession of observed measures (X) whose variability may be ascribed to the operation of random factors. In brief, our model is an unchanging object, characterized by mutually independent measures whose fluctuations correspond to random errors of measurement. Some of the characteristics of such errors in infinite number are given here. The proof of these results is beyond the scope of this book.

Mean Error. Random errors tend to compensate one another in the long run so that the mean of infinitely many random errors will be zero. In statistical notation:

$$E(e) = 0$$

From this result, we deduce that the mean value of repeated measures of the same thing will be equal to the hypothetical true value of that thing $(\hat{X})$. In symbols:

$$E(X) = E(\hat{X}) + E(e)$$
$$= \hat{X} + 0$$
$$= \hat{X}.$$

Turning this around, the true value of an object is the mean of infinitely many measures of that object, on condition that each is affected by random error alone.

Standard Error of Measurement (SEM). If repeated measures of the same thing are relatively accurate, they will be tightly bunched about the true value which they represent, whereas relatively inaccurate measures will be widely dispersed about their true value. To register the degree of that dispersion, we could employ the mean deviation, the simplest of all measures of average variation. However, it is the standard deviation that is conventionally employed, primarily because of its greater utility in analytic statistics. When used to summarize the dispersion of random errors in repeated measures, it is designated the *standard error of measurement*. By reason that $E(X) = \hat{X}$, and $e = X - \hat{X}$, it may be represented in the following alternative ways:

$$\begin{aligned} \text{SEM} &= \sqrt{E[X - E(X)]^2} \\ &= \sqrt{E(X - \hat{X})^2} \\ &= \sqrt{E(e^2)}. \end{aligned}$$

We may interpret the SEM like any other standard deviation, since that is what it is. And like any standard deviation, its interpretation is facilitated if we assume, as we usually do, that our repeated measures, or errors, have a normal distribution. It is of parenthetic interest that the concept of a normal distribution had its origin in the finding of astronomers that repeated measures of the same celestial phenomenon tend to form a smooth bell-shaped curve. The tendency for the binomial distribution to converge on the normal distribution as N increases without limit was discovered by mathematicians over 200 years ago (Walker 1929). On the assumption that errors are normally distributed, two-thirds of our measures will lie within one SEM of the true value; 95 percent will fall within two SEMs, and approximately 99 percent will lie within two-and-one-half SEMs of the true value. By virtue of such relationships, we may readily set up a confidence interval with a specified probability of including the hypothetical true value. For example, if we are given an SEM of 2.5 and an observed score of 100, we may be 95 percent confident that the interval extending from 95 to 105 will include the true score.* The general assumption that random errors are normally distributed around a mean of zero permits us to judge the degree to which our observed measure is in error, provided that the SEM is given or can be estimated.

---

* On condition that the observed score is an unbiased estimate of the true score; otherwise, the confidence interval will not be centered on the observed score. See Nunnally (1967: 220) for a discussion.

Single Measures of Many Things. In the foregoing discussion, we analyzed infinitely many measures of the same object. We shift now to infinitely many measures of as many different objects, with the understanding that the objects collectively comprise a statistical population. In this analysis, we will be concerned with the relationship between averages based on infinitely many observed measures and the same averages based on the corresponding true values. A symbolism convenient for present purposes is as follows:

Average	Observed Measures	True Values
Mean	$\overline{X}$	μ
Variance	σ_x^2	$\sigma_{\hat{x}}^2$
Covariance	σ_{xy}	$\sigma_{\hat{x}\hat{y}}$
Correlation	ρ_{xy}	$\rho_{\hat{x}\hat{y}}$

Mean of Observed Measures. As before, we begin by expressing an observed measure as the sum of its target (true) value and the margin of its miss (error):

(8.1.1)
$$X_i = \hat{X}_i + e_i,$$

where $\hat{X}_i$ is the true value for the ith unit, X_i is the observed measure for the ith unit. By the rule that the mean of the sum is the sum of the means, we get

$$E(X_i) = E(\hat{X}_i) + E(e_i).$$

But the mean of infinitely many random errors is zero; hence,

(8.1.2)
$$E(X_i) = \mu.$$

Our conclusion is that random errors do not affect the mean of the observed measures, since that mean ($\overline{X}$) is equal to the mean of the true values (μ).

A word of caution: Formula (8.1.2) holds for the infinite population and not for a finite population of N measures. The mean of N measures will not necessarily equal the mean of the corresponding true values, since the mean of N random errors may be larger or smaller than zero. And since the mean of the errors tends to 0 as N increases, the larger the value of N, the smaller the discrepancy between the observed mean and the true mean. This complication arises in sampling, where the mean of n observed measures may be some distance from the mean of the corresponding n true values (Cochran 1963: 377–380), and possibly more distant from the population mean than implied by the standard error of the mean or some multiple of that standard error (confidence interval).

Variance of Observed Values. Having ascertained that the mean of the observed measures is equal to the mean of the true values (provided that assumptions are fulfilled), we next determine the effect of random errors on the variance of the observed measures. Stated as a question: will the variance of the observed measures coincide with the variance of the true values? Subtracting μ from both sides of (8.1.1), we get

$$X_i - \mu = \hat{X}_i - \mu + e_i,$$

or

$$x_i = \hat{x}_i + e_i,$$

where $x_i = X - \mu$, $\hat{x}_i = \hat{X}_i - \mu$. Squaring both sides and summing for all values in the population, and reducing sums to means, we obtain

$$\sigma_x^2 = \sigma_{\hat{x}}^2 + \sigma_e^2 + 2\sigma_{\hat{x}e}.$$

But random errors in observed measures are statistically independent of true values; hence, the covariance of X_i and e_i is 0. (The independence of errors and their true values may be regarded as an inherent characteristic of random errors.) Upon dropping that covariance on the right side, we get the variance of the observed measures as the sum of the variance of the true values and the variance of the errors:

$$\sigma_x^2 = \sigma_{\hat{x}}^2 + \sigma_e^2,$$

where σ_x^2 is the observed variance, $\sigma_{\hat{x}}^2$ is the true variance and σ_e^2 is the error variance. Our conclusion is that the observed variance exceeds the true variance by the quantity σ_e^2, on condition that $\hat{X}_i$ and e_i are statistically independent. Transposing the true variance $\sigma_{\hat{x}}^2$, we get the error variance as the difference between the observed variance and the true variance:

$$\sigma_e^2 = \sigma_x^2 - \sigma_{\hat{x}}^2.$$

Remark. The error variance for the total population (σ_e^2) should be distinguished from the squared standard error of measurement (SSEM) for a given unit in that population. The former gauges the degree of error for all units in the population; the latter, the degree of error in repeated measures for a given unit. These variances will be equal if, and only if, all units have the same SSEM; otherwise, the error variance for the population will be an average of the respective SSEMs for individual units, larger than some, smaller than others. If it is reasonable to suppose that SSEMs for units are identical, we may use the population error variance to fix the probable degree of error in the individual measure.

Covariance of *X* and *Y*. Continuing our analysis, let us consider next the effect of random errors on the covariance of *X* and *Y*. We ask: will the covariance of the observed measures be larger or smaller than the covariance of the true values? We begin by writing each deviation in the crossproduct as the sum of the true deviation and error:

$$
\begin{aligned}
xy &= (\hat{X} + e_x - \mu_x)(\hat{Y} + e_y - \mu_y) \\
&= (\hat{x} + e_x)(\hat{y} + e_y) \\
&= \hat{x}\hat{y} + e_x\hat{y} + e_y\hat{x} + e_x e_y.
\end{aligned}
$$

Summing for all values in the population and reducing sums to means, we get

$$
\sigma_{xy} = \sigma_{\hat{x}\hat{y}} + \sigma_{e_x\hat{y}} + \sigma_{e_y\hat{x}} + \sigma_{e_x e_y},
$$

which is the covariance of X and Y, by definition. Since error terms are independent both of one another and of the true values, all terms on the right tend to zero except the first. Dropping these vanishing terms, we get

$$
\sigma_{xy} = \sigma_{\hat{x}\hat{y}}.
$$

Our conclusion from these procedures is that random errors do not cause the covariance of the observed measures to diverge from the covariance of the true values, given that errors are uncorrelated both with one another and with the true values.

Correlation of X and Y. Since the product-moment correlation coefficient of X and Y,

$$
\rho_{xy} = \frac{\sigma_{xy}}{\sigma_x \sigma_y},
$$

is the covariance in standard form, we might suppose that it too would be unaffected by random errors of measurement. On the contrary, random errors will cause that coefficient to deviate from the same coefficient based on the true values. The reasoning is as follows: the covariance of observed measures is equal to the covariance of true values, but the standard deviations of X and Y, respectively, are larger than the standard deviations of $\hat{X}$ and $\hat{Y}$, unless there is no measurement error. Consequently, observed measures will have a smaller correlation coefficient than true values:

$$
\frac{\sigma_{xy}}{\sigma_x \sigma_y} < \frac{\sigma_{\hat{x}\hat{y}}}{\sigma_{\hat{x}} \sigma_{\hat{y}}},
$$

or

(8.1.3) $$\rho_{xy} < \rho_{\hat{x}\hat{y}}.$$

Generally speaking, the observed correlation coefficient tends to have a lower value than the true correlation coefficient.

Theory for Duplicate Measures. None of the foregoing theories is of immediate practical utility. The error variance for the individual unit (SSEM) is based on infinitely many replications which are never available. In social research we usually measure a thing once, not twice and rarely, if ever, several times. The error variance for the population is based on errors which cannot be directly observed. Our data yield only the observed measures, neither the true measures nor the errors. Indeed, if it were possible to obtain true values directly, there would be no need for a theory of error. It is this predicament which led to what may be termed the theory of duplicate measures. This theory gets its impetus from the idea that it may be practicable to obtain two measures for many units, when it is impracticable or impossible to measure each unit many times. For example, we might test many persons two times, although it would be prohibitive to test each person many times.

Duplicate Measures Defined. If we measure all objects in the population twice instead of once, we get duplicate measures. Since the second set of measures is based on the same population as the first, both sets of measures will have the same mean value. For example, in the case of duplicate measures, X and X',

$$\mu_x = \mu_{x'}.$$

Furthermore, if both sets of errors have the same variance, as in this analysis, both sets of observed measures will necessarily have the same variance:

$$\sigma_x^2 = \sigma_{x'}^2.$$

Reliability as Correlation between Duplicate Measures. We avail ourselves of this result (or definition) to demonstrate that the true variance, expressed as a fraction of the observed variance, is equal to the product-moment coefficient between duplicate measures for the same population.

For this purpose, let us suppose that we have a set of duplicate measures, X and X', ignoring for the moment the procedure by which these measures were produced, except to note that our procedure is subject to no change between trials. We would not expect a perfect correlation between such paired measures, owing to random error which is present in every observation. Two measures of the same thing will never be identical unless our rounding is relatively coarse. Moreover, we would expect larger errors more than smaller errors to weaken the correlation between paired measures. If this reasoning is sound, we might plausibly employ the product-moment correlation between paired measures as an index of the accuracy of those measures: the higher the correlation coefficient, the greater the accuracy of the observed measures.

To evaluate this possibility, we begin with the product-moment correlation between duplicate measures, X and X':

(8.1.4)
$$\rho_{xx'} = \frac{\sigma_{xx'}}{\sigma_x \sigma_{x'}},$$

where $\sigma_{xx'}$ is the covariance between the observed measures. But the covariance of the observed measures is equal to the variance of the true values. To verify this proposition, we first set up the product between paired duplicates for any unit in the population:

$$xx' = (\hat{x} + e)(\hat{x} + e')$$
$$= \hat{x}\hat{x} + e\hat{x} + e'\hat{x} + ee'.$$

Summing products for all units in the population and reducing sums to means, we get

$$\sigma_{xx'} = \sigma_{\hat{x}}^2 + \sigma_{e\hat{x}} + \sigma_{e'\hat{x}} + \sigma_{ee'}.$$

On the assumption that errors are independent of one another and of true values, we get the reduced expression,

$$\sigma_{xx'} = \sigma_{\hat{x}}^2,$$

which is the identity we sought to confirm. Now, by reason of the aforesaid assumption that duplicate measures have the same variance,

$$\sigma_x \sigma_{x'} = \sigma_x^2.$$

Substituting $\sigma_{\hat{x}}^2$ for $\sigma_{xx'}$, and σ_x^2 for $\sigma_x \sigma_{x'}$ in (8.1.4), we finally obtain

(8.1.5)
$$\rho_{xx'} = \sigma_{\hat{x}}^2 / \sigma_x^2,$$

which is the culmination of our argument. The product-moment correlation between duplicate measures for a population may thus be construed as the proportion of variance in the observed measures which is attributable to the variance in true values. Accordingly, it goes by the title of the *reliability coefficient*. When the true variance is large relative to the observed variance, the reliability coefficient will be high; when the true variance is small relative to the observed variance, the reliability coefficient will be low. The reliability coefficient thus gauges the relative magnitude of errors in measurement for a population.

Relationship of Error Variance to Reliability Coefficient. If the true variance as a proportion of the observed variance is equal to $\rho_{xx'}$, the error variance as a proportion of the observed variance must equal $1 - \rho_{xx'}$. To satisfy ourselves that this is the case, we return to the observed variance as the sum of its component variances:

$$\sigma_x^2 = \sigma_{\hat{x}}^2 + \sigma_c^2.$$

Dividing both sides by the observed variance, we get

$$1 = \frac{\sigma_{\hat{x}}^2}{\sigma_x^2} + \frac{\sigma_e^2}{\sigma_x^2},$$

or

$$1 = \rho_{xx'} + \frac{\sigma_e^2}{\sigma_x^2}.$$

Transposing $\rho_{xx'}$ from left to right, we get

(8.1.6)
$$1 - \rho_{xx'} = \frac{\sigma_e^2}{\sigma_x^2},$$

which is the proposition we sought to verify.

Sample Estimates. Upon multiplying both sides of (8.1.6) by the observed variance σ_x^2, we get the error variance in terms which may be estimated from our sample data:

(8.1.7)
$$\sigma_e^2 = \sigma_x^2(1 - \rho_{xx'}).$$

The sample reliability coefficient, $r_{xx'}$, provides an estimate of reliability coefficient for the population, $\rho_{xx'}$, and the quantity, $\frac{1}{2}(s_b^2 + s_w^2)$*, provides an estimate of the variance of the observed measures, σ_x^2, where s_b^2 is the mean square based on differences between units in the sample, and s_w^2 is the mean square based on differences within units. Upon substituting in Equation (8.1.7), we get

$$\hat{\sigma}_e^2 = \frac{1}{2}(s_b^2 + s_w^2)(1 - r_{xx'})$$

where $\hat{\sigma}_e^2$ is the estimator of σ_e^2. Although the use of this estimator cannot always be justified, it will serve for many practical purposes, especially when

---

* Obtained by substituting $n = 2$ in the general formula (p. 290),

$$\frac{s_b^2 + (n - 1)s_w^2}{n},$$

which yields an unbiased estimate of the total variance of a population consisting of infinitely many replicates for infinitely many persons (units).

the number of units in the sample is large. With small samples, it will be necessary to use estimates "obtained by a commonly accepted rationale that is known to produce minimum-variance unbiased quadratic estimates ..." (Lord and Novick 1968: 192).

PART 2
Reliability of Test Scores

Foreword. In determining the reliability of scores based on attitude tests and the like, sociologists regularly apply the theory of duplicate measures, even though they do not make that theory explicit. In this evaluation, it is necessary to treat test scores as interval measures, since our basic theory takes such measures as given. Although somewhat gratuitous, this assumption usually finds pragmatic justification in the utility of the results to which it leads.

At first glance, it would seem a simple matter to obtain a set of duplicate test scores (i.e., scores whose errors are independent) by administering the same test twice to a given sample of individuals. However, that procedure is not without its practical difficulties as follows: first, social traits such as attitudes and values are subject to continual change; hence, the variation in scores between trials may reflect not only random disturbances, but substantive change in attitude as well (Heise 1969). In a particular study, we may judge our measures to be unreliable when, in fact, they are reliably registering a change in the trait being measured. Second, when the results of the second testing are dependent on the results of the first, contrary to the conditions of our model, errors will be correlated with one another and with true values, and our formulas will give faulty results. By recall, a person may respond identically on consecutive trials, although his initial response was wholly arbitrary. He may appear to have a favorable attitude because of his tendency to repeat his first answer. Third, two administrations of the same test are often difficult to arrange, unless respondents are institutionally required to submit to testing as in the case of members of the armed forces or school children.

To surmount these difficulties and still obtain a reliability coefficient, various procedures have been invented, each with its own special features. Of the major alternatives, we focus on split halves and mention the other techniques only in passing. This is a practical restriction and does not carry the connotation that other procedures might not serve as well or better under specific circumstances.

Split Halves. It is a relatively simple matter to split the items of a single test into halves by some random procedure and to correlate scores for these halves. For example, if a test consists of 50 items, we would correlate scores based on 25 items each. The result of that operation is sometimes labeled the *split-half reliability coefficient,* to distinguish it from the same coefficient based on the test as originally constituted, or the *unit test,* as it has been named. By this technique of splitting, we are enabled to judge the reliability of our measures from a single administration of one test.

Although easier to get than retest unit scores, scores based on random halves will generally yield a smaller reliability coefficient than scores for the unit test. As a rule: the longer the test, the higher the reliability; the shorter the test, the lower the reliability. It is natural, therefore, to inquire into the loss of reliability we incur for having used half-tests instead of the unit test. In a more practical vein, we ask whether it is possible to reconstruct the reliability coefficient for the unit test from the reliability coefficient based on split halves.

Brown-Spearman Prophecy Formula. This problem was solved independently by Brown and Spearman whose respective studies were published in the same issue of the British Journal of Psychology (1910). That solution, which carries the names of both men, answers to the question "What is the effect on $\rho_{xx'}$ if we increase the number of test items by a factor k?" By this method, it is possible to calculate the reliability of a test with k times as many items as the test that was actually administered. In particular, it provides a solution to this problem: "Find the reliability of a test which is twice as long as the test whose reliability was calculated."

In unraveling the method of Brown and Spearman, it is conventional to postulate four sets of replicates*, produced by as many equivalent tests. By virtue of their equivalence, these four tests necessarily have the same mean (μ) and the same variance (σ^2), and equal covariances and correlations:

$$\sigma_{12} = \sigma_{13} = \cdots = \sigma_{34} = \sigma^2\rho,$$

where ρ is the common correlation between tests.

By appropriately combining tests two at a time, we get composite tests, Y and Y', both twice as long as each of the original tests. Thus:

$$Y = X_1 + X_2$$
$$Y' = X_3 + X_4.$$

To verify that such composite variables have the same mean and same variance, we have recourse to quite standard methods. By the rule that the mean of the sum is the sum of the means, we obtain

$$\mu_y = 2\mu$$

---

* Sometimes referred to as "parallel measures."

and

$$\mu_{y'} = 2\mu;$$

hence,

$$\mu_y = \mu_{y'}.$$

By the analogous rule that the variance of the sum is the sum of the variances and the sum of the covariances, we get

$$\sigma_y^2 = [\sigma_1^2 + \sigma_2^2] + [\sigma_{12} + \sigma_{21}]$$
$$\sigma_{y'}^2 = [\sigma_3^2 + \sigma_4^2] + [\sigma_{34} + \sigma_{43}].$$

But the original tests have the same variance and, taken two at a time, the same covariance, hence,

$$\sigma_y^2 = \sigma_{y'}^2 = 2\sigma^2(1 + \rho).$$

With these results, we are ready to move, via the covariance, to the correlation between composite scores, which will be their reliability coefficient. Finally, we shall note the difference between that result and the reliability coefficient for component scores. To get the covariance of Y and Y', we write the cross-product between deviations in expanded form:

$$yy' = x_1x_3 + x_1x_4 + x_2x_3 + x_2x_4.$$

Summing products for all units in the population, and reducing sums to means, we obtain

$$\sigma_{yy'} = \sigma_{13} + \sigma_{14} + \sigma_{23} + \sigma_{24}.$$

But the covariances of equivalent tests are equal; hence,

$$\sigma_{yy'} = 4\rho\sigma^2$$

where $\rho\sigma^2$ is the common covariance.

To convert the covariance to the correlation, we divide it by the product of the standard deviations of the composite variables. In this case:

$$\rho_{yy'} = \frac{4\rho\sigma^2}{\sqrt{2\sigma^2(1 - \rho)}\sqrt{2\sigma^2(1 - \rho)}}$$

$$(8.2.1) \qquad = \frac{2\rho}{1 + \rho},$$

where $2\sigma^2(1 - \rho)$ is the common variance. This is the well-known Brown-Spearman "prophecy formula" for a test of double length. It is a "what if" formula. By applying it to sample data, we may estimate what the reliability coefficient would be if we used a test twice as long as that based on "split halves." It is the appropriate procedure whenever the reliability of a test is computed by correlating odd and even items, or halves of a unit test obtained by some other random procedure. For example, from a sample $r_{xx'}$ of .50 for 25 items, we infer that

$$\rho_{yy'} = \frac{2(.50)}{1 + .50}$$

$$= .67$$

for a test of 50 items. When our reliability is lowered by the method of split halves, we use the Brown-Spearman method to prophesy its unit strength.

By an identical procedure, we arrive at the reliability coefficient of a test k times the length of the test that was administered. The resulting formula is similar to (8.2.1) except that the numerical constants 2 and 1 are replaced by k and $(k - 1)$, respectively,

$$\rho_{yy'} = \frac{k\rho}{1 + (k - 1)\rho} .$$

For example, if the reliability coefficient for a test of 25 items is .70, the reliability for a test of 75 items would be

$$\rho_{yy'} = \frac{3(.70)}{1 + 2(.70)}$$

$$= \frac{2.10}{2.40}$$

$$= .88.$$

This formula is the basis of the commonplace statement that the reliability of a test increases as the number of test items, other things being equal. Reliability is perfect for infinitely many items, as the student may wish to demonstrate.

Attenuation Formula. It is of theoretical interest that the correlation of X and Y is smaller than the correlation of $\hat{X}$ and $\hat{Y}$ (8.1.3), but the method for correcting that deficiency has more practical value. In approaching this method, we start with the reliability coefficient as the ratio of variances:

$$\rho_{xx'} = \sigma_{\hat{x}}^2 / \sigma_x^2.$$

Multiplying both sides by σ_x^2, we get the true variance as the product of the reliability coefficient and the observed variance:

$$\sigma_{\hat{x}}^2 = \rho_{xx'}\sigma_x^2.$$

Substituting $\rho_{xx'}\sigma_x^2$ for $\sigma_{\hat{x}}^2$ in the product-moment coefficient of $\hat{X}$ and $\hat{Y}$, we obtain

$$\rho_{\hat{x}\hat{y}} = \frac{\sigma_{\hat{x}\hat{y}}}{\sqrt{\rho_{xx'}\sigma_x^2}\sqrt{\rho_{yy'}\sigma_y^2}}.$$

Rearranging terms and substituting σ_{xy} for $\sigma_{\hat{x}\hat{y}}$, we get

$$\rho_{\hat{x}\hat{y}} = \frac{1}{\sqrt{\rho_{xx'}\rho_{yy'}}}\frac{\sigma_{xy}}{\sqrt{\sigma_x^2\sigma_y^2}}.$$

Relabelling terms, we get the simpler expression,

$$(8.2.2) \qquad\qquad \rho_{\hat{x}\hat{y}} = \frac{\rho_{xy}}{\sqrt{\rho_{xx'}\rho_{yy'}}},$$

which is the result we sought to establish.

By (8.2.2) we may restore ρ_{xy} to full strength, as if it had not been weakened by random errors of measurement; hence, this procedure goes by the name "correction for attenuation." Formula (8.2.2) provides a measure of what would have been obtained had there been no errors of measurement. It is to be understood that the "correction for attenuation" is for the infinite population of measures, and its respective terms must be estimated from sample data. Students interested in the detailed composition of this estimator should consult Lord and Novick (1968: 211–213).

Validity Coefficient. To establish the validity of prejudice scores, we correlate them with the actual conduct of persons in the community; to validate intelligence test scores, we correlate them with scholastic performance. For the same purpose, we correlate delinquency ratings with police records, alienation scores with social participation, prestige scores with income. Such correlations are called *validity coefficients*. Validity in this sense is the measured correlation between a variable (Y) whose validity is in question, and a criterion variable (X) whose validity is taken for granted. The employment of a given variable as criterion is always for present purposes; in the next study the validity of that criterion variable may be in question. We are thereby reminded that validity is not intrinsic to an observed variable; rather it is a matter of definition. Statistical validity, as conventionally measured, is a mutual affair between two variables; each is validated by the other to exactly the same degree. The validity of Y, as gauged by its correlation with X, is exactly the same as the validity of X, as gauged by its correlation with Y. Nevertheless, as between two variables, we often regard one as more intimately related to the characteristic of ultimate interest and therefore more deserving of the title "criterion." But we should not forget that actual validity coefficients are based on observed data that may be suffused with error and that a particular "validity coefficient" may be undeserving of that title.

There is nothing complicated about the validity coefficient as a statistical average; in fact, it is the familiar product-moment correlation coefficient with a fancy name. Notwithstanding its simplicity and utility, it seldom appears in reports on sociological research. The probable reason is the relative paucity of acceptable criterion variables. A validity coefficient has no "validity" and is useless unless the validity of the criterion variable has been substantiated. Although these matters are of the utmost importance in social science, except for this scant reference they are ignored in this discussion, since our concern is with statistical procedures rather than general methodological problems.

To discern the effect of random errors in measurement on the validity coefficient ρ_{xy}, we need only to rearrange terms in (8.2.2) as follows:

(8.2.3)
$$\rho_{xy} = \rho_{\hat{x}\hat{y}}\sqrt{\rho_{xx'}\rho_{yy'}}$$
$$= \rho_{\hat{x}\hat{y}} \cdot \frac{\sigma_{\hat{x}}}{\sigma_x} \cdot \frac{\sigma_{\hat{y}}}{\sigma_y}.$$

The right side of (8.2.3) may be viewed as the product of three terms: the true correlation, the square root of the reliability coefficient for X, and the square root of the reliability coefficient for Y.* (In some writing, the square root of the reliability coefficient is referred to as the *reliability index*, a terminology we shall adopt whenever convenient.) For a given true correlation, the magnitude of the validity coefficient will depend on the size of the respective reliabilities. When $\rho_{xx'}$ and $\rho_{yy'}$ both equal 1, their product is equal to 1, and the validity coefficient will be equal to the correlation between $\hat{X}$ and $\hat{Y}$. Continuing this line of thought: the lower the reliabilities, the smaller their product, and correspondingly the lower the value of the validity coefficient. In the extreme but unlikely case, where either $\rho_{xx'}$ or $\rho_{yy'}$ is equal to zero, the validity coefficient will be zero no matter how high the correlation between $\hat{X}$ and $\hat{Y}$.

Generalizing, the validity coefficient of a variable Y on a criterion variable X can be no greater than its *index of reliability*, $\sigma_{\hat{y}}/\sigma_y$. To satisfy ourselves on this point, we need only to recall that the validity coefficient is the product of three decimal fractions: $\sqrt{\rho_{yy'}}$, $\sqrt{\rho_{xx'}}$ and $\rho_{\hat{x}\hat{y}}$. But the product of any three fractions is always smaller than any one of them taken individually. By this argument from elementary arithmetic, we may claim that the validity coefficient for Y cannot exceed the reliability index of Y. It is

---

* It may be shown (Lord and Novick 1968: 57) that the correlation between true values and observed measures is equal to the square root of the reliability coefficient.

this result that is the basis of the familiar statement that the validity of a measure cannot exceed its own reliability.

It is noteworthy that a low validity coefficient does not preclude a high reliability for Y. The true correlation between X and Y may be low, while the reliability for Y is relatively high. A low reliability is sure to depress the validity coefficient, but a high reliability will not necessarily raise it. High reliability is needed but not enough for high validity.

Analysis of Variance Model. In his standard work on test theory, Gulliksen (1950) devotes only several pages to the analysis of variance as a procedure for measuring test reliability. However this approach is gaining on classical theory, as it were, owing possibly to the greater range and versatility of its theory and possibly to its greater emphasis on problems of estimation. The student may thus anticipate that test reliability will be more regularly posed as a problem in variance analysis, with probably less attention to the so-called classical theory. This is not to suggest that the classical theory of reliability as developed by Spearman has been repudiated. Rather, our intention is to note the tendency among specialists on reliability to place that theory within the framework of the analysis of variance. This tendency is noticeable, if not dominant, in the writing of Lord and Novick (1968: 160–171).

In line with these recent trends, we introduce the analysis of variance as an approach to test reliability, taking as our point of departure the intraclass correlation coefficient, ρ_I, to which the analysis of variance gives rise. Since this coefficient tends to be neglected in social statistics, it may not be amiss to compare it with the product-moment correlation coefficient, and to specify the conditions under which these two coefficients converge. With this background, it will be readily possible to construe the so-called classical method as a special form of the analysis of variance. The writings of R. A. Fisher (1946: 211–241) are a primary source of information on the intraclass correlation coefficient, and the student is advised to read his lucid discussion of that statistic. In what follows, we assume a familiarity with the elementary analysis of variance.

Product-Moment Coefficient of X_1 and X_2, ρ_{12}. In determining the correlation between X_1 and X_2, our fundamental procedure is to compare paired values on the relative distance of each from its own mean. For a summary measure of covariation, we multiply paired deviations and get the mean of those products:

$$\sigma_{12} = \frac{1}{N} \sum (X_{1i} - \overline{X}_1)(X_{2i} - \overline{X}_2).$$

This is the covariance of X_1 and X_2. Putting all deviations in standard form, we get the familiar product-moment correlation coefficient:

$$\rho_{12} = \frac{\sum (X_{1i} - \overline{X}_1)(X_{2i} - \overline{X}_2)}{N\sigma_1\sigma_2}.$$

Intraclass Correlation Coefficient, ρ_I. When our concern is with the relation between two different variables, we cannot arbitrarily shuffle values within pairs of values before computing the correlation coefficient. If we did, the result would be meaningless and useless. We cannot shift height and weight and still get a meaningful correlation between these two variables. However, such reshuffling would be permitted if paired values were independent measures (replicates) of the same thing. In that event, it would be immaterial whether we put a value in the one series or the other. Further, we would be justified in using the mean and the standard deviation of the combined series to convert all values into standard form, since both series are based on the same population. When conversion of all $2N$ values is according to this rule, the mean of the standardized crossproducts is by definition the intraclass correlation ρ_I. Its symbolization is closely similar to the product-movement coefficient:

$$\rho_I = \frac{\sum (X_{1i} - \overline{X})(X_{2i} - \overline{X})}{N\sigma^2},$$

where X_{1i} and X_{2i} are replicates for the ith unit, $\overline{X}$ is the mean of the combined series, and σ^2 is the variance of the combined series.

Intraclass Correlation for k-tuplets. For bivariate data, ρ_{12} will be equal to ρ_I, given that $\overline{X}_1 = \overline{X}_2$, and $\sigma_1 = \sigma_2$; otherwise ρ_I will be smaller than ρ_{12} (see exercises). But how is ρ_I linked to ρ_{ij} ($i \neq j$) in the case of multivariate data? Strictly speaking, there is no link, since the product-moment coefficient is restricted to bivariate data, whereas ρ_I is applicable to multivariate data (k-tuplets) of any order. Nevertheless, there is a similarity between the mean of all possible ρ_{ij}'s ($i \neq j$) among k variables two at a time, and the intraclass correlation ρ_I applied to the same data. The mean product-moment coefficient is the sum of the $\dfrac{k(k-1)}{2}$ individual ρ_{ij}'s, divided by that number:

$$\bar{\rho}_{ij} = \frac{2}{k(k-1)} \sum \rho_{ij}.$$

The intraclass coefficient is analogously the mean of $\dfrac{k(k-1)}{2}$ mean products, except that all replicates are measured from the mean of the combined series ($\overline{X}$) in units of the standard deviation of the combined series (σ). In symbols:

$$\rho_I = \frac{2}{k(k-1)} \sum \left\{ \frac{\sum x_i x_j}{N\sigma^2} \right\},$$

where

$$\bar{X} = \sum_{1}^{k}\sum_{1}^{N} X_{ij}/kN,$$

$$\sigma^2 = \sum_{1}^{k}\sum_{1}^{N} (X_{ij} - \bar{X})^2/kN,$$

$$\sum x_i x_j = \sum (X_{ij} - \bar{X})(X_{jj} - \bar{X}).$$

Thus, the intraclass correlation may be construed as the mean of a set of mean products; and in that respect it is exactly like $\bar{p}_{ij}$. But there is this important difference: the constituent terms in $\bar{p}_{ij}$ are themselves product-moment coefficients, each having the properties of that statistic; whereas, the constituent terms (in brackets) in ρ_I are not intraclass coefficients for replicates two at a time, since they are all standardized to the same mean and the same standard deviation. They are intraclass coefficients in appearance only.

ρ_I *for* $k = 3$. To clarify these matters, consider the case of three ($k = 3$) values for each of N units, i.e., N sets of triplets. Our problem is to measure the average degree of homogeneity (intraclass correlation) among triplicates for N sets of them. For triplets, our formula for ρ_I must be extended as follows:

$$\rho_I = \frac{1}{3}\left\{\frac{\sum x_1 x_2}{N\sigma^2} + \frac{\sum x_1 x_3}{N\sigma^2} + \frac{\sum x_2 x_3}{N\sigma^2}\right\}$$

$$= \frac{1}{3}\sum_{1}^{3}\left\{\frac{\sum x_i x_j}{N\sigma^2}\right\}.$$

Note that the sum on the right consists of three mean products, corresponding to the number of ways of combining triplets two at a time. To get the mean of these three mean products, we divide the sum of these means by that number. For duplicates, the sum consists of a single term; hence, division by the number of ways of combining 2-tuplets two at a time is suppressed.

ρ_I *for* $k = 4$. Consider now the case of quadruplets. Our problem is to measure the average degree of homogeneity among quadruplets for N sets of them. Our sum will now consist of $\{4(4 - 1)\}/2 = 6$ mean products, and the intraclass correlation is that sum divided by 6:

$$\rho_I = \frac{1}{6}\left\{\frac{\sum x_1 x_2}{N\sigma^2} + \frac{\sum x_1 x_3}{N\sigma^2} + \frac{\sum x_1 x_4}{N\sigma^2} + \frac{\sum x_2 x_3}{N\sigma^2} + \frac{\sum x_2 x_4}{N\sigma^2} + \frac{\sum x_3 x_4}{N\sigma^2}\right\}$$

$$= \frac{1}{6}\sum_{1}^{6}\left\{\frac{\sum x_i x_j}{N\sigma^2}\right\}.$$

Clearly, as the number of replicates increases, the number of mean products likewise increases, and the calculation of ρ_I by this procedure becomes increasingly intricate. For example, when there are 10 replicates in each set, the intraclass correlation will be an average of 45 mean products. It is practically convenient that an alternative and more compact procedure for calculating ρ_I is available. It is based on this identity due to Harris (Fisher 1946: 214):

$$k \sum_{1}^{N} (\bar{X}_i - \bar{X})^2 = N\sigma^2[(k-1)\rho_I].$$

Rearranging terms, we obtain

(8.2.4)
$$\rho_I = \frac{k \sum_{1}^{N} (\bar{X}_i - \bar{X})^2 - N\sigma^2}{(k-1)N\sigma^2}.$$

From (8.2.4), we see that it is possible to obtain ρ_I from two distributions: (1) the distribution of all kN observations from which we obtain the overall mean $\bar{X}$ and the total variance σ^2, and (2) the distribution of the respective means $\bar{X}_i$ of the N groups of replicates from which we calculate the sum of squares for group means. This expression for ρ_I may be put in terms which arise as a matter of course in the analysis of variance and which correspond to the true score variance and the observed score variance, respectively. In showing this, we first set up a one-way classification of observed scores, with k scores for each of N persons.

Score

	1	j	k
1			
i		X_{ij}	
N			

Person i

where X_{ij} is j^{th} score of ith person. We sometimes refer to this as a person-by-score matrix, with persons in rows and scores in columns.

Our aim is to demonstrate that the correlation among scores within persons may be construed as the ratio of the true score variance to the observed score variance, or simply as a reliability coefficient, $\rho_{xx'}$. In pursuing this matter, we first verify that ρ_I is the ratio of the variance of group means to the total variance, taking as our point of departure the total sum of squares in decomposed form:

$$\sum\sum(X_{ij} - \overline{X})^2 = \sum\sum(X_{ij} - \overline{X}_i)^2 + k\sum(\overline{X}_i - \overline{X})^2,$$

or,

$$\text{TSS} = \text{WSS} + \text{BSS}.$$

Substituting TSS/k for $N\sigma^2$ and $\text{TSS} - \text{WSS}$ for $k\sum(\overline{X}_i - \overline{X})^2$ in (8.2.4), we get, after some algebra:

$$\rho_I = 1 - \frac{\text{WSS}}{k-1} \cdot \frac{k}{\text{TSS}}.$$

When both the ratio of $k - 1$ to k and $N - 1$ to N can be approximated by 1 (i.e., when both k and N tend to infinity), we get the simpler expression

$$\rho_I = \frac{\text{TSS} - \text{WSS}}{\text{TSS}}$$

$$= \frac{\text{BSS}}{\text{TSS}},$$

which in turn may be reduced to the ratio of variances:

(8.2.5)
$$\rho_I = \frac{\sigma_{\bar{x}}^2}{\sigma_{\bar{x}}^2 + \sigma_w^2},$$

given that $\sigma^2 = \sigma_{\bar{x}}^2 + \sigma_w^2$. Taken as a directive, Formula (8.2.5) requires that we divide the variance of the group means by the total variance to get the intraclass correlation.

To interpret ρ_I as a reliability coefficient, we need only link (1) the true score variance to the variance of group means, and (2) the error variance to the within-group variance. In this matching of terms, we take as our point of departure the standard identity:

(8.2.6)
$$X_{ij} - \mu = (X_{ij} - \mu_i) + (\mu_i - \mu),$$

where μ is the population mean, μ_i is the mean of ith subpopulation, and X_{ij} is the jth value in i^{th} subpopulation. Corresponding to μ, μ_i, and X_{ij} respectively, we have

$$\hat{X} = \text{true mean, all scores,}$$

$$\hat{X}_i = \text{true score, } i^{\text{th}} \text{ person,}$$

$$X_{ij} = j^{\text{th}} \text{ score, } i^{\text{th}} \text{ person.}$$

Substituting these terms in the foregoing identity (8.2.6), squaring both sides and summing, and reducing sums to means, we obtain

$$\sigma_x^2 = \sigma_{\hat{x}}^2 + \sigma_e^2,$$

or the observed score variance as the sum of the true score variance and the error variance. To estimate these variances and ρ_I from a sample of kn measures, we use

$$s_w^2 = \frac{\text{WSS}}{n(k-1)}$$

as an estimator of the error variance, σ_e^2, and

$$\frac{s_b^2 - s_w^2}{k}$$

as an estimator of the true score variance, $\sigma_{\hat{x}}^2$ ($s_b^2 = \text{BSS}/[n-1]$). Substituting these expressions in (8.2.5) and simplifying, we obtain

(8.2.7)
$$r_I = \frac{s_b^2 - s_w^2}{s_b^2 + s_w^2(k-1)},$$

which is the sample estimate of the reliability coefficient.

By way of example, let us suppose we have three ($k = 3$) scores on the same attitude test for each of ten ($n = 10$) persons, as in Table 8.2.1, and that we are required to get the reliability coefficient r_I. We first calculate

Table 8.2.1 *Person-By-Score Matrix*

Person	Score			Sum
1	61	60	60	181
2	65	62	64	191
3	57	59	57	173
4	71	69	68	208
5	50	54	55	159
6	49	48	51	148
7	62	65	65	192
8	64	64	61	189
9	53	50	51	154
10	61	63	61	185

Table 8.2.2 *One-Way AOV For Table 8.2.1.*

Source	Sum of Squares	df	Mean Square
Between persons	1,102	9	122.44
Within persons	51	20	2.55

between- and within-person mean squares and record these in the usual way (Table 8.2.2). Substituting mean squares in Formula 8.2.7, we obtain

$$r_I = \frac{122.44 - 2.55}{122.44 + 2(2.55)}$$

$$= \frac{119.89}{127.54}$$

$$= .94.$$

From this result, we draw the inference that the variance in true scores accounts for 94 percent of the variance in observed scores, or that measurement error accounts for 6 percent of that observed variance.

Remark. In using (8.2.7) to estimate ρ_I, we may disregard the distribution of X_{ij} within subpopulations; however, in using r_I to test the null hypothesis that $\rho_I = 0$ by the F-statistic, we must satisfy ourselves that the distribution of X_{ij} is identically normal within subpopulations. When this condition is met, we may employ the F-ratio to test the significance of r_I; in fact, we may, with caution, employ the F-ratio when this condition is only approximately satisfied, owing to the robustness of the F-statistic (Kendall and Stuart, Vol. 3, 1966: 97–108). In studies of reliability, we would ordinarily have no interest in the hypothesis that all true scores are identical; rather our interest lies in the possibility that replicates for each person are very nearly identical, or carry very little measurement error.

Two-Way Analysis of Variance. At this juncture, it is natural to ask whether we must restrict ourselves to the one-way analysis of variance in the assessment of test reliability. As the student might expect from our question, there is no such restriction; we may use whichever design yields the best estimate of the reliability coefficient. We may use a randomized-block design, a factorial design, or any design whatever, provided that it is appropriate to our problem.

As an exemplification of such more complex schemes, let us suppose that the order of columns in Table 8.2.1 corresponds to the order in which the scores were obtained. The scores in the second column were obtained after the scores in the first column, but before the scores in the third column. When scores are thus sequentially arranged and we treat sequence as a main effect, we are no longer free to shift scores within rows arbitrarily, since their position in the table is fixed according to the order in which they were secured. Given such a two-way classification of data, it is natural to seek an estimate of the reliability coefficient which is free of the effect of sequence. To obtain such a corrected measure, we decompose the total sums of squares into three parts, as in a *randomized-block design*, and manipulate these results by standard operations to obtain an estimate of ρ_I. To simplify the symbolization of such results, we employ the capital letters A and B to represent person (row) and order (column) effects, respectively; and R (for residual) to represent whatever variation cannot be assigned to persons or sequence. To simplify matters further, we use "a" to represent the number of persons in our sample, and "b" the number of trials (terms) in the sequence, as in Table 8.2.3. Running a two-way analysis of variance on Table 8.2.1, we get Table 8.2.4. Since the residual mean square ($s_R^2 = 2.83$) is presumably free of the effect of sequence (which happens to equal zero in our problem),

Table 8.2.3 *Two-Way AOV of Person-By-Sequence Matrix*

Source of Variation	Mean Square	Expectation
Persons (A)	$s_A^2 = \dfrac{\text{ASS}}{a-1}$	$\sigma^2 + b\sigma_A^2$
Sequence (B)	$s_B^2 = \dfrac{\text{BSS}}{b-1}$	$\sigma^2 + a\sigma_B^2$
Residual (R)	$s_R^2 = \dfrac{\text{RSS}}{(a-1)(b-1)}$	σ^2

Table 8.2.4 *Two-Way AOV of Table 8.2.1.*

Source	Sum of Squares	df	Mean Square
Persons	1,102	9	122.44
Sequence	0	2	0.00
Residual	51	18	2.83

we substitute that mean square for s_w^2 in Formula (8.2.7). Making this change, we get (Lindquist 1953: 368):

$$(8.2.8) \qquad r_I = \frac{s_A^2 - s_R^2}{s_A^2 + (b-1)s_R^2}.$$

Substituting numerical values from Table 8.2.4 in Formula (8.2.8), we calculate

$$r_I = \frac{122.44 - 2.83}{122.44 + 2(2.83)}$$

$$= \frac{119.61}{128.10}$$

$$= .93.$$

Our conclusion is that 93 percent of the variance in observed scores is attributable to the variance in true scores, with the effect of order statistically removed. Since the uncorrected (.94) and corrected (.93) coefficients have approximately the same value, we conclude that our reliability is not depressed by an order effect.

Kuder-Richardson Method. At this juncture, we introduce a method for determining the reliability of a total score by analyzing the variance of the item scores of which it is composed. This method, which has its origin in the work of Kuder and Richardson (1937), obviates the need to split the items in a test given once, or to administer the same test on separate occasions. Therefore, it has considerable practical value for the research worker. We analyze the internal consistency of all items rather than the degree of correspondence between split halves or between test-retest scores. As a procedure, it entails calculating the mean square for persons, and the mean square for person-by-items, and manipulating these by formula to get a reliability coefficient.

In unfolding this method, it is convenient to begin with the hypothetical product-moment correlation between sums X and X'

$$r_{xx'} = \frac{\sum (x_1 + x_2 + \cdots + x_b)(x_1' + x_2' + \cdots + x_b')}{a s_x s_{x'}},$$

where a is the number of persons and b is the number of elements (items). The numerator consists of b^2 sums of products; it reduces to b^2 covariances, or $b^2 \bar{s}_{ij}$, upon dropping a from the denominator. On the assumption that both composite measures have the same variance, we may substitute s_x for $s_{x'}$ in the denominator, so that the entire expression reduces to

$$r_{xx'} = \frac{b^2 \bar{s}_{ij}}{s_x^2}.$$

Upon substituting component sums of squares and sums of products, we get after simplification

(8.2.9) $$r_{xx'} = \alpha = \frac{b^2 \bar{s}_{ij}}{s_x^2} = \frac{s_A^2 - s_R^2}{s_A^2},$$

where s_A^2 is the mean square for persons and s_R^2 is the residual mean square. As a reminder that the reliability of sums is derived from an analysis of the item scores of which the sums consist, it has been suggested (Cronbach 1951) that the Greek letter α be used instead of r. If we require the reliability of row sums rather than cell elements in Table 8.2.1, we would substitute mean squares from Table 8.2.4 in Formula (8.2.9) and calculate the answer. Performing these operations, we get

$$\alpha = \frac{122.44 - 2.83}{122.44}$$

$$= .98.$$

An alternative computing procedure requires that we calculate the variance for each item (column) and the sum of these variances, and the variance of composite scores (row sums). These quantities we substitute in Formula (8.2.10), which is algebraically equivalent to (8.2.9):

$$(8.2.10) \qquad \alpha = \frac{b}{b-1}\left(1 - \frac{\sum s_i^2}{s_t^2}\right),$$

where $s_i^2 = \dfrac{1}{a-1}\sum(X_{ij} - \bar{X}_{.i})^2$ and $s_t^2 = \dfrac{1}{a-1}(T_{i.} - \bar{T})^2$, where $T_{i.}$ is the sum of the item scores in the ith row, and $\bar{T}$ is the mean sum. To verify that equivalence, both procedures are applied to Table 8.2.5. The calculations required by Formula (8.2.9) are given in Table 8.2.6.

Table 8.2.5 *Person-By-Item Score Matrix*

Person	1	2	3	4	5	Σ
			Item			
1	6	2	1	0	0	9
2	8	6	5	2	4	25
3	10	12	7	7	7	43
4	5	11	11	9	8	44
5	6	3	0	0	1	10
6	11	7	9	6	1	34
7	7	7	2	5	5	26
8	4	7	4	4	1	20
9	6	3	3	2	4	18
10	6	5	1	3	1	16
Σ	69	63	43	38	32	245
Mean	6.9	6.3	4.3	3.8	3.2	24.5
Variance	4.29	9.81	12.21	7.96	7.16	140.05

$$\alpha = \frac{5}{4}\left(1 - \frac{41.43}{140.05}\right)$$
$$= .88$$

Table 8.2.6 *AOV of Table 8.2.5.*

Source	df	Sum of Squares	Mean Square
Total	49	513.50	
Person (A)	9	280.00	31.1
Items (B)	4	100.00	
Residual (R)	36	136.50	3.7

$$\alpha = \frac{31.1 - 3.7}{31.1}$$
$$= .88$$

From the brevity of our discussion, one should not conclude that the Kuder-Richardson method is of little practical value in applied social research. On the contrary, it has considerable utility, especially when the number of items is small. Further, the value of alpha for n items is equal to the mean values of every possible alpha for two composite measures, each formed from a random split of the n items (Lord and Novick 1968: 93). A recent article (Bohrnstedt 1969), addressed to sociologists, gives an abbreviated method for calculating coefficient alpha and supplies some bibliography. In a related article, Werts and Linn (1970) note some of the theoretical difficulties of judging validity from multi-item scales.

Two-Way Table, $n \geq 2$. The $ab = 10 \times 3$ measures of Table 8.2.1 will yield a reliability coefficient if both persons and trials are random variables; otherwise—if both are fixed factors—we must assume no interaction between them. If the assumption of no interaction is risky, it will be necessary to obtain n ($n \geq 2$) replicates for each cell by appropriate observational methods. Our summary table (Table 8.2.7) will now consist of four parts instead of three, and our mean squares and their corresponding expectations will reflect the greater complexity of our analysis. In this table we employ n to denote the number of replicates in each cell, retaining a and b to represent the number of persons and trials, respectively. We denote interaction by AB.

Table 8.2.7   *AOV for Two-Way Score Matrix, n > 1.*

Source	Mean Square	Expectation Fixed Effects	Expectation Random Effects
Persons	$s_A^2 = \dfrac{\text{ASS}}{a-1}$	$\sigma^2 + nb\sigma_A^2$	$\sigma^2 + n\sigma_{AB}^2 + nb\sigma_A^2$
Sequence	$s_B^2 = \dfrac{\text{BSS}}{b-1}$	$\sigma^2 + na\sigma_B^2$	$\sigma^2 + n\sigma_{AB}^2 + na\sigma_B^2$
Interaction	$s_{AB}^2 = \dfrac{\text{ISS}}{(a-1)(b-1)}$	$\sigma^2 + n\sigma_{AB}^2$	$\sigma^2 + n\sigma_{AB}^2$
Random Factors	$s_w^2 = \dfrac{\text{WSS}}{ab(n-1)}$	σ^2	σ^2

To illustrate the uses to which Table 8.2.7 may be put in measuring reliability, we apply it to 60 subscores based on split halves for 10 persons on three consecutive trials. We arrange these 60 subscores in a 10×3 matrix, with persons in rows and order of testing in columns (Table 8.2.8). Applying the analysis of variance to this matrix, we obtain mean squares which may be manipulated to yield various reliability coefficients, each valid under a given set of conditions. The formulas for three sets of conditions and their values for our illustrative data (Table 8.2.9) follow.

Table 8.2.8 Duplicate Scores for 10 Persons on
Three Consecutive Trials

Person	1		2		3		Sum
1	30	31	29	31	29	31	181
2	32	33	31	31	31	33	191
3	28	29	28	31	28	29	173
4	36	35	34	35	33	35	208
5	25	25	27	27	26	29	159
6	25	24	23	25	25	26	148
7	29	33	32	33	31	34	192
8	31	33	31	33	32	31	189
9	27	26	25	25	24	27	154
10	30	31	30	33	29	32	185

Table 8.2.9 Two-Way AOV of Numbers in Table 8.2.8.

Source	Sum of Squares	df	Mean Square
Total	631.3	59	
Within	55.0	30	1.8
Between subclasses	576.3	29	
Between persons	551.0	9	61.2
Between trials	0.0	2	
Interaction	25.3	18	1.4

Conditions	Formula	Value	
A and B Fixed	$r_I = \dfrac{s_A^2 - s_w^2}{s_A^2 + (b-1)s_w^2}$	$r_I = \dfrac{61.2 - 1.8}{61.2 + 2(1.8)}$	(8.2.11)
		$= \dfrac{59.4}{64.8}$	
		$= .92$	
A and B Random	$r_I = \dfrac{s_A^2 - s_{AB}^2}{s_A^2 + (b-1)s_{AB}^2}$	$r_I = \dfrac{61.2 - 1.4}{61.2 + 2(1.4)}$	(8.2.12)
		$= \dfrac{59.8}{64.0}$	
		$= .93$	
A Random, B Fixed	$r_I = \dfrac{s_A^2 - s_w^2}{s_A^2 + (b-1)s_w^2}$	$r_I = \dfrac{61.2 - 1.8}{61.2 + 2(1.8)}$	(8.2.13)
		$= \dfrac{59.4}{64.8}$	
		$= .92$	

Remark. The student may wonder about the derivation of Formulas 8.2.7–
8.2.13. These are too technical to be given here; however, we do give this
general formula (Haggard 1958: 19) for converting a sample F to a sample r_I.
This is:

(8.2.14)
$$r_I = \frac{F - 1}{F + (k - 1)},$$

where k is the number of main classes, or levels. To obtain the proper expression for the intraclass correlation, one merely sets up the proper F-ratio and
substitutes this ratio in (8.2.14). For example, on the assumption that both
effects in a two-classification are random, we use the interaction mean square
as the error term in the F-ratio.

$$F = \frac{61.2}{1.4}$$
$$= 43.71.$$

Substituting 43.71 in (8.2.14) gives

$$r_I = \frac{43.71 - 1.00}{43.71 + (3 - 1)}$$
$$= .93,$$

as required by Formula (8.2.12). Of course, if one mistakenly sets up the
wrong F-ratio (uses the wrong error term), the intraclass correlation will be
incorrectly calculated.

The foregoing analysis is primarily to hint at the potentiality of the analysis
of variance for purposes of obtaining an estimate of the error variance
uninflated by extraneous factors. When the total variance has its source in
such factors as time and place of testing, or in such variables as social class
and ethnic background, we may use the analysis of variance to get a more
precise estimate of the error variance.

PART 3
Errors in Classification

In social research, we classify as well as measure; we have recourse to
nominal scales as well as to interval scales. In this process of classifying,
we expect to be in error intermittently as a matter of chance: we will per-
chance misclassify a Republican as a Communist, a Jew as a Catholic, a
teacher as a student. Although such errors have no magnitude, we can still
count them. And such a count, relative to the total number of observations,

may be taken as a gauge of the reliability of those observations. We will rely on our observations if errors are relatively infrequent; we will not depend on those observations if errors are frequent. An error rate of 50% will give us less confidence than an error rate of 5%. That reliability would vary inversely as the probability of error is quite consistent with common sense.

In any empirical study, the magnitude of that probability is unknown; hence, we must estimate it from our sample of observations. Although procedures for making such an estimate have been tentatively proposed, none has been widely adopted (partly because of their recency) and all reflect the undeveloped state of a reliability theory for qualitative data. To exemplify this line of thought, we cite Harper's recent proposal (1964) and some work by Goodman and Kruskal (1954). For additional examples, the student should consult Kendall's (1948) coefficient of concordance, Robinson's (1957) measure of agreement, and Cohen's (1960) coefficient of agreement for nominal scales. A probability model for errors of classification has been formulated by Sutcliffe (1965).

Harper begins with the notion that each A in the population has a probability $1 - q$ of being classified correctly, and each $\overline{A}$, a probability q of being misclassified as A. If X is the proportion of A's in the population and $1 - X$ the proportion of $\overline{A}$'s, the expected proportion of A's on any trial i will be

(8.3.1)
$$\begin{aligned} Y_i &= (1 - q)X + q(1 - X) \\ &= X - 2qX + q. \end{aligned}$$

Expressing X in terms of Y_i and q, we get

(8.3.2)
$$X = \frac{Y_i - q}{1 - 2q}.$$

If the population is classified twice, and given that trials are independent, the expected proportion of persons classified as A on both trials, i and j, will be

(8.3.3)
$$\begin{aligned} Y_{ij} &= (1 - q)^2 X + q^2(1 - X) \\ &= X - 2qX + q^2. \end{aligned}$$

Subtracting (8.3.1) from (8.3.3), we get a standard quadratic:

$$Y_{ij} - Y_i = q^2 - q,$$

or

(8.3.4)
$$q^2 - q + Y_i - Y_{ij} = 0.$$

Solving this quadratic, subject to the condition (imposed by Harper) that $q < .5$, we get

(8.3.5) $$q = \frac{1 - \sqrt{1 - 4(Y_i - Y_{ij})}}{2},$$

which is the probability that $\bar{A}$ will be misclassified as A, expressed in terms of Y_i and Y_{ij}.

As an example of this method, Harper cites market research in which the same people were asked in two different interviews whether they owned a car. The results are given in Table 8.3.1.

Table 8.3.1 *Responses of 288 Persons to Question on Car Ownership*

		2nd Interview		
		Car	*No Car*	*Total*
1st Interview	*Car*	158	23	181
	No car	18	89	107
	Total	176	112	288

From these data, we compute Y_1, Y_2, and Y_{12}:

$$Y_1 = \frac{181}{288} = .628,$$

$$Y_2 = \frac{176}{288} = .611,$$

$$Y_{12} = \frac{158}{288} = .549.$$

Substituting these quantities in (8.3.5) and (8.3.2), we obtain two values for q and X, corresponding to Y_1 and Y_2, respectively.

$$q_1 = \frac{1 - \sqrt{1 - 4(.628 - .549)}}{2},$$
$$= .086,$$

$$X_1 = \frac{.628 - .086}{1 - 2(.086)},$$
$$= .655,$$

$$q_2 = \frac{1 - \sqrt{1 - 4(.611 - .549)}}{2},$$
$$= .067,$$

$$X_2 = \frac{.611 - .067}{1 - 2(.069)},$$
$$= .627.$$

Following Harper, we take the mean of q_1 and q_2 as our best estimate of q,

$$q = \tfrac{1}{2}(.086 + .067) = .076,$$

and the mean of X_1 and X_2 as our best estimate of X,

$$X = \tfrac{1}{2}(.655 + .627) = .641.$$

Our conclusion is that 64 percent of the population are A's and that each has a 92 percent chance of correct classification in a particular survey.

Goodman and Kruskal's Lambda. Since duplicate observations may be arranged in a two-way table, their consistency might be represented by an index akin to the reliability coefficient. Goodman and Kruskal have proposed such an index, which we quote not as a pat formula but rather as a stimulus to further study.

They take as their point of departure a set of duplicate observations for a given population; for example, the responses to the same question in separate interviews (Table 8.3.1). In developing their index, they first ask: "If we classify a randomly selected person on the basis of the first or second interview, and if both interviews are equally probable, what is the maximum rate of success (or minimum rate of error) in the long run?" To maximize the rate of success, we predict on every trial whichever attribute has the higher probability of occurrence. For our numerical example, we always predict ownership, since ownership has the larger probability of occurrence on both interviews. We thereby minimize our errors in the long run. Since interviews are equally likely by definition, the probability of success will be

$$Pr(\text{Success}) = \tfrac{1}{2}(p_{m.} + p_{.m}),$$

where $p_{m.}$ is the largest row marginal, and $p_{.m}$ is the largest column marginal. For our example, the probability of success is

$$Pr(\text{Success}) = \tfrac{1}{2}(.63 + .61) = .62.$$

Continuing their development, Goodman and Kruskal now ask whether the odds would be bettered if we always knew how the other interview had classified a randomly selected case, and followed without exception the rule of always guessing that classification. For instance, if, upon drawing a case, we were informed that our subject was a non-owner on the other interview, we would automatically classify that case as non-owner. In adhering to that procedure, the probability of success would be the sum of the diagonal probabilities $\sum p_{ii}$. For our example, $.55 + .31 = .86$. To reflect the possible improvement (or deterioration) in prediction attributable to information about the other interview, we set up the difference,

$$\sum p_{ii} - \tfrac{1}{2}(p_{m.} + p_{.m}).$$

In our illustration, $.86 - .62 = .24$. Since this quantity varies from $\tfrac{1}{2}$ to $-\tfrac{1}{2}$, rather than from $+1$ to -1 as would a conventional correlation coefficient, Goodman and Kruskal suggest that it be normed on the probability of error, given no information about the other interview, i.e., on the quantity $1 - \tfrac{1}{2}(p_{m.} + p_{.m})$. This leads to the measure,

(8.3.6)
$$\lambda_r = \frac{\sum p_{ii} - \tfrac{1}{2}(p_{m.} + p_{.m})}{1 - \tfrac{1}{2}(p_{m.} + p_{.m})},$$

which is a special case of the more general formula for lambda,

$$\lambda_{yx} = \frac{E_1 - E_2}{E_1},$$

where E_1 is error based on marginal distribution of Y, and E_2 is error based on the joint distribution of X and Y. An elementary exposition of Goodman and Kruskal's lambda is given by Mueller, Schuessler, and Costner (1970: 249–254).

Applying (8.3.6) to our example, we get

$$\lambda_r = \frac{.86 - .62}{1.00 - .62}$$

$$= \frac{.24}{.38}$$

$$= .63.$$

In concluding their discussion of this measure of reliability, Goodman and Kruskal comment as follows:

> The measure λ_r can take values from -1 to 1. It takes the value -1 when all the diagonal p_{aa}'s are zero and the modal probability $p_{m.} + p_{.m}$ is 1. It takes the value 1 when the two methods always agree. λ_r is indeterminate only when both methods always give only one and the same class. In the case of independence λ_r assumes no particular value. This characteristic might be considered a disadvantage, but it seems to us that an index of this kind would only be used where there is known to be dependence between the methods, so that misbehavior of the index for independence is not important.

Recent Trends. Since empirical generalizations rest on observations, and all observations have error, it is necessary to determine how such generalizations may be affected by errors of observation. In attacking this problem, sociologists have relied heavily on techniques devised in biology and psychology. Recently they have explored on a limited basis the possible use of path analysis for estimating reliability. Representative of this line of work is Heise's (1969) study of reliability when the true values themselves are changing, and Costner's (1969) study of the correlation between true values when each variable is measured by multiple indicators. In commenting on these studies, Blalock (1970) notes that both may be regarded as specializations of a more general method. These advanced studies are related to the more elementary materials of this chapter in their conception of an observed measure as a sum of a true value and an error. They differ in their more complicated assumptions about the relationships among errors and the relation of errors to true values. Since the assumptions of the simpler models given in this chapter may be unrealistic, these more complex models eventually may have more practical value for research. It is to be anticipated that the utility of this approach will be examined in the present decade, and its relevant features for sociology will be identified. For an introduction to this line of inquiry, a student should read Siegel and Hodge's (1967) discussion, which contains bibliography.

EXERCISES

1. Calculate $\rho_{xx'}$ and ρ_I, and $r_{xx'}$ and r_I for following duplicate measures:

X	X'
45	40
43	42
100	80
70	70
70	65
75	65
40	35
40	35

Account for the difference between ρ_I and $\rho_{xx'}$; between r_I and $r_{xx'}$.

2. Calculate r_I on the assumption of no column effect (one-way AOV).

Person	Replicate				
1	1	2	3	4	5
1	25	20	23	22	20
2	60	40	30	30	20
3	70	65	75	75	67
4	60	45	30	25	30

3. Calculate r_I for the same numbers (Exercise 2) on the assumption of a column effect (two-way AOV).

4. Calculate coefficient α for the same numbers (Exercise 2) and interpret.

5. Calculate α for the following person-by-item matrix:

Person	\multicolumn{6}{c}{Item}
	1	2	3	4	5	6
1	1	1	1	1	0	1
2	1	1	1	1	1	1
3	1	1	1	1	1	0
4	1	1	1	1	1	1
5	1	0	1	1	0	1
6	1	1	0	1	1	0

6. Calculate α for the following person-by-item matrix:

Person	Item				
	1	2	3	4	5
1	1	1	1	1	1
2	1	1	1	1	0
3	1	1	1	0	0
4	1	1	0	1	0
5	1	1	0	0	0
6	0	1	0	0	1
7	1	0	1	0	0
8	1	0	1	1	0
9	0	0	0	0	1
10	0	0	0	0	0

7. Calculate Harper's q and Goodman and Kruskal's λ_r for the following 2×2 tables:

92	8
8	92

92	8
28	72

92	8
58	42

REFERENCES

American Psychological Association
1966 Standards for Educational and Psychological Tests and Manuals. Washington, D.C.: American Psychological Association.

Blalock, Hubert M., Jr.
1965 "Some implications of random measurement error for causal inferences." American Journal of Sociology 71: 37–47.

1970 "Estimating measurement error using multiple indicators and several points in time." American Sociological Review 35: 101–111.

Bogue, Donald J., and Edmund M. Murphy
1964 "The effect of classification errors upon statistical inference: A case analysis with census data." Demography 1: 42–55.

Bohrnstedt, George
1969 "A quick method for determining the reliability and validity of multiple-item scales." American Sociological Review 34: 542–548.

Brown, William
1910 "Some experimental results in the correlation of mental abilities." British Journal of Psychology 3: 296–332.

Campbell, Donald T., and Donald W. Fiske
1959 "Convergent and discriminant validation by the multitrait-multimethod matrix." Psychological Bulletin 56: 81–105.

Cochran, William
1963 Sampling Techniques. Second Edition. Chapter 13: "Sources of errors in surveys." New York: John Wiley and Sons.

1970 "Some effects of errors of measurement on multiple correlation." Journal of the American Statistical Association 65: 22–34.

Cohen, Jacob
1960 "A coefficient of agreement for nominal scales." Educational and Psychological Measurement 20: 37–46.

Costner, Herbert
1969 "Theory, deduction and rules of correspondence." American Journal of Sociology 75: 245–263.

Cronbach, L. J.
1951 "Coefficient alpha and the internal structure of tests." Psychometrika 16: 297–334.

Cronbach, L. J., Nageswari Rajaratnam, and Goldine C. Gleser
1963 "A liberalization of reliability theory." British Journal of Statistical Psychology 16: 137–163.

Cureton, E. E.
1965 "Reliability and validity: Basic assumptions and experimental designs." Educational and Psychological Measurement 25: 327–346.

Fisher, Ronald A.
    1946 Statistical Methods for Research Workers. Tenth Edition.
          Edinburgh: Oliver and Boyd.

Goodman, L. A., and William Kruskal
    1954 "Measures of association for cross classification." Journal of the
          American Statistical Association 49: 732–763.

Gulliksen, Harold
    1950 Theory of Mental Tests. New York: John Wiley and Sons.

Haggard, E. A.
    1958 Intraclass Correlation and the Analysis of Variance. New York:
          Dryden.

Harper, Dean
    1964 "Misclassification in epidemiological surveys." American Journal
          of Public Health 54: 1882–1886.

Heise, David
    1969 "Separating reliability and stability in test-retest correlation."
          American Journal of Sociology 34: 93–101.

Hoyt, Cyril
    1941 "Test reliability estimated by analysis of variance." Psychomet-
          rika 6: 153–160.

Kendall, Maurice G.
    1948 Rank Correlation Methods. London: Griffin.

Kendall, Maurice G., and Alan Stuart
    1966 The Advanced Theory of Statistics. Volume 3. New York:
          Hafner.

Kuder, G. F., and M. W. Richardson
    1937 "The theory of the estimation of test reliability." Psychometrika
          2: 151–160.

Lindquist, E. F.
    1953 Design and Analysis of Experiments in Psychology and Educa-
          tion. Boston: Houghton Mifflin.

Lord, Frederic M., and Melvin R. Novick
    1968 Statistical Theories of Mental Test Scores. Reading, Massachu-
          setts: Addison-Wesley.

Morgenstern, Oskar
    1963 On the Accuracy of Economic Observations. Princeton, N.J.:
          Princeton University Press.

Mueller, John H., Karl Schuessler, and Herbert Costner
    1970 Statistical Reasoning in Sociology. Second Edition. Pp. 249–254.
          Boston: Houghton Mifflin.

Nunnally, Jum C.
    1967 Psychometric Theory. New York: McGraw-Hill.

Rajaratnam, Nageswari, L. J. Cronbach, and Goldine C. Gleser
    1965 "Generalizability of stratified-parallel tests." Psychometrika 30:
          39–56.

Robinson, W. S.
 1957 "The statistical measure of agreement." American Sociological Review 22: 17–25.

Scott, W. A.
 1955 "Reliability of content analysis: The case of nominal scale coding." Public Opinion Quarterly 19: 321–325.

Siegel, Paul M., and Robert W. Hodge
 1968 "A causal approach to study of measurement." Pp. 28–59 in Hubert M. Blalock, Jr. and Ann B. Blalock (eds.), Methodology in Social Research. New York: McGraw-Hill.

Spearman, Charles
 1910 "Correlation calculated from faulty data." British Journal of Psychology 3: 271–295.

Spiegelman, Mortimer
 1968 Introduction to Demography. Chapter 3: "Errors in census statistics and vital statistics and their adjustment." Cambridge: Harvard University Press.

Sutcliffe, J. P.
 1965 "A probability model for errors of classification: I. General considerations." Psychometrika 30: 73–96.

Tryon, R. C.
 1957 "Reliability and behavior domain validity: Reformulation and historical critique." Psychological Bulletin 54: 229–249.

Walker, Helen M.
 1929 Studies in the History of Statistical Method. Baltimore: Williams and Wilkins.

Werts, Charles E., and Robert L. Linn
 1970 "Cautions in applying various procedures for determining the reliability and validity of multiple-item scales." American Sociological Review 35: 757–759.

Wiley, David E., and James A. Wiley
 1970 "The estimation of measurement error in panel data." American Sociological Review 35: 112–117.

9

Transformation of Statistical Data

PART 1
Common Practices

Events and Measures. We cannot increase our wealth by exchanging American dollars for English pounds; nor change the temperature by substituting a Fahrenheit for a Centigrade reading; nor raise a student's test performance by expressing it as a centile rank instead of a raw score; nor reduce the distance from London to Edinburgh by expressing it in miles rather than kilometers. Actual events have a quality which is independent of the way in which they are numerically represented.

Why, then, so many ways of expressing the same underlying magnitude? The answer is that measures, like words, may be arbitrarily put in any form so long as they effectively serve their purpose, namely: to register differences in magnitude. Sociologically, it is not extraordinary that different metrical systems have evolved in different settings, much as different languages have developed in different places. Correspondingly, much as one language may be translated into another, we may transform by prescribed operations one set of values into another without changing their essential meaning. The user of social statistics should therefore accustom himself to the possibility of expressing a given measure in more than one way, with a view to selecting whichever alternative is best suited to his stated purpose.

To illustrate briefly: we often find it expeditious to subtract a suitable constant from each value in a set before computing the variance of that set—the variance will not be affected by such a shift in origin, and smaller numbers are usually easier to manipulate than larger ones. On the other hand, we convert absolute frequencies to percentages, not to make them more manageable, but rather to establish greater comparability among the items and to facilitate their interpretation: the sex ratio permits us to compare easily two or more populations in respect to sex composition; the birth rate permits the demographer to compare vastly different countries in respect to fertility.

Thus, for the sake of mere convenience or more discriminating analysis, or both, the research worker will often have recourse to an appropriate transformation. Because transformations permeate all statistical analysis, it may be profitable to consider them collectively as a group, rather than separately, without regard for their common properties. By such an alignment of diverse techniques, we may be able to discern their similarities and differences, and also to appreciate more fully the potentialities of transformations in applied statistics. Consistent with these goals, we first present a selection of techniques with which the student is probably familiar to a certain degree: norming by ratios and percentages, substitution of ranks for raw values, replacement of raw values by normal deviates, classification of scales according to their transformations, coding for computation. From these familiar examples, we move to a selection of elementary mathematical transformations regularly employed in statistical research—the logarithmic, the square root, and the arcsin transformation. These are discussed as techniques for simplifying data that depart from some standard model such as the straight line or normal curve. Finally, we briefly consider the rotation of Cartesian axes as a technique for simplifying results derived from factoring a correlation matrix. This subject is also discussed in Chapter 3 (119–127).

Measures to Ranks. A very simple but common transformation involves the substitution of a set of consecutive integers, 1 through N, for the N measures comprising our series. We may discard measures and replace them by integers when the additivity of our scale is in question; when we cannot justify the use of parametric significance tests; when our interest is in comparing rank orders, rather than the measures themselves. Although we customarily refer to the exchange of measures for integers as a rank-order transformation, it is not a transformation in the strict sense of that term; rather it is the arbitrary substitution of whole numbers for interval measures.

This operation consists of arranging the observed values from low to high and, beginning with the lowest value, substituting integers for consecutive values in the array. For example:

Array	Rank
67	1
68	2
71	3
72	4
75	5

In case of tied values, we take the mean of the integers corresponding to the tied values and assign this mean value to the two or more tied values. Since integers give only the rank order of the items and not their respective magnitudes, we call them ranks.

Mean and Variance. In some problems, particularly in the correlation of rank orders, it may be necessary, at least implicitly, to obtain the mean and the variance of a full set of ranks. These results, together with the sums on which they rest, may be readily obtained by simple formulas, given here without proof. These formulas are as follows: The sum of the set of integers 1 through N is

(9.1.1) $$\sum X = \frac{N}{2}(N+1).$$

Dividing (9.1.1) by N, we get the mean of the ranks,

(9.1.2) $$\overline{X} = \tfrac{1}{2}(N+1).$$

The sum of squared ranks is

(9.1.3) $$\sum X^2 = \frac{N(N+1)(2N+1)}{6},$$

and the variance is the difference between the mean of the squared ranks and the square of the mean rank:

(9.1.4) $$\sigma^2 = \frac{N(N+1)(2N+1)}{6N} - \frac{(N+1)^2}{4}$$

$$= \frac{(N^2-1)}{12}.$$

By way of example: The sum of the ranks 1 through 20 is

$$\sum X = \frac{(20)(21)}{2}$$

$$= 210,$$

and the mean,

$$\overline{X} = \frac{210}{20}$$

$$= 10.5.$$

The sum of the squared ranks is

$$\sum X^2 = \frac{20(21)(41)}{6}$$

$$= 2{,}870,$$

and the variance,

$$\sigma^2 = \frac{400 - 1}{12}$$

$$= 33.25.$$

Although the student of social statistics need not be able to derive these formulas, a familiarity with their composition will often permit an easy grasp of important statistical relations which otherwise might be quite unintelligible. Thus, by means of (9.1.4) it may be readily shown that Spearman's formula for rank-order correlation is a special case of the product-moment coefficient of correlation. In this demonstration, we begin with the standard identity:

(9.1.5)
$$\frac{\sum xy}{N\sigma_x\sigma_y} = \frac{\sigma_x^2 + \sigma_y^2 - \sigma_D^2}{2\sigma_x\sigma_y},$$

where $\sigma_D^2 = \dfrac{\sum(X - Y)^2}{N}$. The left side, it will be recognized, is the co-variance of X and Y in standard form, while the right side is the same result expressed in terms of mean squares. When both series have the same mean and variance, i.e., when $\bar{X} = \bar{Y}$, and $\sigma_x^2 = \sigma_y^2 = \sigma^2$, the right side of (9.1.5) simplifies to

$$1 - \frac{\sum(X - Y)^2}{2N\sigma^2}.$$

Continuing, when both X and Y comprise rank orders, we may substitute $\dfrac{(N^2 - 1)}{12}$ for σ^2 to get,

(9.1.6)
$$\frac{\sum xy}{N\sigma_x\sigma_y} = 1 - \frac{\sum(X - Y)^2}{\dfrac{2N(N^2 - 1)}{12}}$$

$$= 1 - \frac{6\sum(X - Y)^2}{N(N^2 - 1)}$$

$$= 1 - \frac{6\sum D^2}{N(N^2 - 1)},$$

where $\sum D^2 = \sum(X - Y)^2$. This is Spearman's well-known rank correlation formula, to be used when both X and Y are in the form of ranks. That it (9.1.6) yields the same numerical value as the standard product-moment formula may be confirmed by applying both to a set of arbitrarily paired ranks:

X	Y	x	y	xy	D	D^2
1	2	−2	−1	2	−1	1
2	1	−1	−2	2	1	1
3	4	0	1	0	−1	1
4	5	1	2	2	−1	1
5	3	2	0	0	2	4
				$\overline{6}$		$\overline{8}$

$$\sigma_x^2 = 24/12 \qquad \sigma_y^2 = 24/12 \qquad \sum xy = 6 \qquad \sum D^2 = 8$$

$$= 2 \qquad\qquad\quad = 2$$

$$\frac{\sum xy}{N\sigma_x\sigma_y} = \frac{6}{5\sqrt{2}\,\sqrt{2}} \qquad\qquad 1 - \frac{6\sum D^2}{N(N^2 - 1)} = 1 - \frac{6(8)}{5(24)}$$

$$= 6/10 \qquad\qquad\qquad\qquad\qquad = 1 - .40$$

$$= .60 \qquad\qquad\qquad\qquad\qquad\quad = .60$$

Values to Centiles. Instead of replacing N measures by as many ranks, we may replace them by 100 centile ranks. To effect this change, we divide the array of N measures into 100 equal groups and fix the boundary values of these groups. These boundaries are designated as *centile points*. The first centile point corresponds to the upper boundary of the first interval and is interpreted as the point below which one percent of the items fall; the second centile point is interpreted as the point below which two percent of the items fall, etc. The 50th centile, or the point below which fifty percent of the cases fall, is of course the median; likewise, the 25th and 75th centiles correspond to the first and third quartiles, respectively.

To convert centile points to centile ranks, we simply exchange them for consecutive integers, 1, 2, 3, . . . , 100. For example, we would replace the obtained scale value of the median by 50. With this shift, we may characterize each case by the upper boundary of its class interval, expressed as a centile rank. A centile rank of 60 would signify that at least 40 percent of all cases are larger in value, and 59 percent, smaller. The employment of a limited number of ranks instead of N ranks will represent a convenient simplification of the rank order when N is large. Furthermore, centile ranks are more amenable to interpretation than raw ranks, since they are normed ranks. Knowledge that a person stands 30th in his group is relatively useless unless we know the total number in that group. But a centile rank of 80 immediately establishes that approximately 80 percent of the population is below that person, whatever its size, and 20 percent is above him.

In discarding centile points for centile ranks, we necessarily obtain a rectangular frequency distribution of cases, since differences between adjacent boundaries are equal by definition. For this reason, the substitution of ranks for point values is referred to as a *rectangular transformation*. In general, whenever we discard interval measures for *quantile* ranks we obtain a rectangular frequency distribution.

Coding Measures. It is usually possible to simplify our hand calculations by adding a constant to each value, multiplying each value by a constant, or both. Since we encode values at the start of our operations and decode them at the end, this process has come to be known as coding for computation. In its essentials, such coding represents the application of rules expressing the relationship between the original series (X) and the transformed series (Y). To exemplify the application of such rules, we cite the more common of them and the ways in which they may be invoked for more economical computation. We consider first the mean and the variance of the variable Y formed by the addition of a constant value a to the variable X. Rule 1: The mean of $Y = X + a$ is the sum of mean X and the constant a. In statistical notation,

$$\bar{Y} = \frac{1}{N} \sum (X + a)$$

$$= \bar{X} + a.$$

Rule 2: The variance of $Y = X + a$ is equal to the variance of X,

$$\sigma_y^2 = \sigma_x^2.$$

Second, consider the mean and the variance of the variable Y, formed by multiplying the variable X by a constant value b. Rule 3: The mean of Y is the product of b and mean X,

$$\bar{Y} = \frac{1}{N} \sum (bX)$$

$$= b\bar{X}.$$

Rule 4: The variance of Y is equal to the product of the squared constant and the variance of X,

$$\sigma_y^2 = b^2 \sigma_x^2.$$

By combining rules, we get rules which cover transformations by both addition and multiplication. Rule 5: The mean of $Y = bX + a$ is the sum of mean bX and the constant a:

$$\bar{Y} = b\bar{X} + a.$$

Rule 6: The variance of $Y = bX + a$ is the product of the squared constant (b^2) and the variance of X:

$$\sigma_y^2 = b^2\sigma_x^2.$$

To demonstrate the manner in which transformations by addition and multiplication may be applied to simplify the computation of simple averages, let us subtract a constant a from each value X and divide that result by a constant c. In symbols:

$$x' = \frac{X - a}{c},$$

where x' equals the twice-coded value. The mean of the twice-coded values according to Rules 5 and 6 will be

$$\bar{x}' = \frac{\bar{X} - a}{c},$$

and the variance,

$$\sigma_{x'}^2 = \frac{\sigma_x^2}{c^2}.$$

By transposition, we may easily obtain the mean and the variance of the original measures:

$$\bar{X} = c\bar{x}' + a,$$
$$\sigma_x^2 = c^2\sigma_{x'}^2$$

When values have been grouped into equal class intervals, and calculations are to be performed by hand, it is usually economical to employ an appropriate class midpoint m as the constant of subtraction, and the class width w as the constant of division. With these constants, the formulas for the mean and the variance become:

$$\bar{X} = w\bar{x}' + m,$$

and

$$\sigma_x^2 = w^2\sigma_{x'}^2.$$

The application of these formulas is shown in Table 9.1.1.

Table 9.1.1 *Forty Persons Grouped by Body Weight (in Pounds)**

Class Limits	Midpoint X	Frequency f	$x' = \dfrac{X-170}{10}$	fx'	fx'²
135–145	140	2	−3	−6	18
145–155	150	5	−2	−10	20
155–165	160	5	−1	−5	5
165–175	170	7	0	0	0
175–185	180	9	1	9	9
185–195	190	5	2	10	20
195–205	200	4	3	12	36
205–215	210	1	4	4	16
215–225	220	1	5	5	25
225–235	230	0	6	0	0
235–245	240	1	7	7	49
		40		26	198

$$\bar{x}' = \tfrac{26}{40}$$
$$= .65$$

$$\bar{X} = 10(.65) + 170$$
$$= 176.5$$

$$\sigma^2_{x'} = \tfrac{198}{40} - \left(\tfrac{26}{40}\right)^2$$
$$= 4.950 - 4.225$$
$$= .725$$

$$\sigma^2_x = 10^2(.725)$$
$$= 72.5$$

* Hypothetical data.

Standard Form. For many purposes, it is convenient to transform our values so that the mean of coded values will be zero and the standard deviation will be equal to 1. To obtain these values, we set $a = \bar{X}$, and $c = \sigma$. We employ $\bar{X}$ as our scale origin and σ as our scale unit. In symbols:

$$x' = \frac{X - \bar{X}}{\sigma}.$$

This is the well-known transformation into standard form (p. 6). To put measures into standard form, we get the deviation of each value from the mean and divide by the standard deviation of the series. Such twice-coded values have come to be known as *standard measures*, probably because they are normed on the standard deviation. When a given theoretical distribution has been tabulated in standard form, we may use that table as a model against which to compare our observed data, likewise reduced to standard form. We regularly employ the normal distribution in standard form to assess the normality of our observed measures, after those measures have been expressed in standard form.

Rates and Ratios. Practically every sociologist has had occasion to compute a sex ratio, or the number of males per 100 females in a given aggregate of persons. Such an average is sometimes more useful than a statement giving the absolute number of men and women, respectively. Equally familiar to every social analyst is the crude birth rate, or the number of births per 1,000 population at a given time and place. It is as if we divided the total population into lots of 1,000 individuals each, and then calculated the mean number of births per group.

The employment of 10, or a multiple thereof, as a base in all such calculations is a consequence, be it noted, of our decimal system in which the result of any division is necessarily expressed in multiples of 10. For example, 360 divided by 15 is equal to two tens and four ones; 1 divided by 20 is equal to no tenths and five hundredths. Were we to employ a base other than ten, as two in the binary system, then correspondingly our products and quotients would be expressed as multiples of the chosen base, although their essential meaning would be unaffected.

By reducing successive frequencies of the same category to a common base (e.g., 10), we render them more comparable and thereby more meaningful. A birth rate of 24 in the United States and in the Netherlands has the same meaning, irrespective of the actual number of births in each country. Similarly, the respective percentages of married men in the U.S. in 1900 and 1970 are readily comparable, but not the actual numbers themselves. However, percentages are subject to misinterpretation and should not be recklessly quoted. When we discard the totals on which a derived figure is based, we lose the basis for judging the reliability of that percentage. We do not accord the same degree of dependability to percentages based on five cases as to percentages based on 5,000 cases. For that reason, it is considered essential that the base of a percentage always be given in a scientific report (Davis and Jacobs 1968). Furthermore, the statistical manipulation of rates and indexes is fraught with complications and may give rise to quite misleading results. For example, the correlation between indexes may be spuriously high by reason of their common base, or common deflating variable.

Scales and Their Transformations. We may classify variables by the operations producing them—ranking, counting, or measuring—or by the relations into which scale values may enter—inequalities, differences, and ratios. This latter criterion of permissible relations is the principle of Stevens' (1946) fourfold classification of scales as *ratio, interval, ordinal,* and *nominal.**
When we classify scales in this way, we may ask: "On condition that no permissible relation be lost, to what transformations is a given scale subject?"

---

* Since the nominal scale is not subject to transformation in the usual sense of the term, we omit it from this discussion.

Ratio scales are less restricted than interval scales, in that scale values may be expressed as multiples of one another. Interval scales in turn are less restricted than ordinal scales, in that values may be subtracted from one another to find the scale distance between them. Ordinal scales are therefore the most restricted of all scales, since relations between values may be expressed as inequalities alone. Nevertheless, ordinal scales are subject to a more general class of transformations than interval scales, and interval scales to a more general class than ratio scales. Hence, the generalization: ratio scales, whose elements are least restricted in their relations *inter se*, are subject to a more limited class of transformations than interval scales. On the other hand, ordinal scales, whose elements are most restricted, are subject to a wider class of transformations than interval scales, as the ensuing discussion will attempt to make clear.

A ratio scale consists of additive units extending from a fixed zero. If we are given such a scale, we may change only the scale unit, or multiply each value X by a constant b,

$$Y = bX.$$

Otherwise, we would disturb the ratios between values which must remain constant in a ratio scale (unless we are willing to sacrifice that constancy for some other advantage). In transforming a ratio scale by multiplication, we in effect replace our initial scale unit by one that is b^{-1} times as large. For example, in converting feet into inches, we multiply X by 12, or replace our original scale unit by one that is $12^{-1} = 1/12$ as large. In converting inches to feet, we multiply by $1/12$ or replace our initial scale unit by one that is $(\frac{1}{12})^{-1} = 12$ times as large.

An interval scale consists of additive intervals around an arbitrary zero. If we are given such a scale, we may change not only our scale unit; we also may add a constant to each value (i.e., change our scale origin) and still leave unchanged the distances between values. In symbols:

$$Y = a + bX.$$

But we may do no more; otherwise we would alter the differences among scale values which must remain constant in an interval scale (unless we are willing to forego that constancy). In scaling attitude items by the method of paired comparisons (Chapter 7), we may add a constant to each of our initially obtained scale values in order that all scale values be greater than zero. Our justification is based on the assumption that our scale consists of additive units around an arbitrary origin, i.e., it is an interval scale.

An ordinal scale is an ordering of objects from high to low by means of an arbitrary series of numbers. If we are given a set of ordinal numbers, we may perform any operation on them whatsoever, provided that we preserve their rank order. In other words, any transformation of ordinal values (X), linear or otherwise, into ordinal values (Y) is permissible, provided that the rank-order correlation between Y and X is equal to 1.

The conclusion to be drawn from the above discussion is that scales may be differentiated according to the transformations to which each is subject, on condition that relations intrinsic to the elements composing them be preserved. Ratio scales are subject to the restricted linear transformation of the form $Y = bX$; interval scales to the general linear transformation of the form $Y = a + bX$; ordinal scales to all monotonic transformations, since such transformations by definition preserve the order of elements. But one should not conclude that ratio and interval scales are never subjected to nonlinear transformations. It is common practice to disturb the ratios among observed values in order to obtain a distribution which is statistically more tractable. If our observed measures on a ratio scale are badly skewed, we may take the logarithm of each (p. 417) in order to produce a more nearly symmetrical distribution. We deliberately change our ratios in order to get a distribution more amenable to statistical analysis.

Normalizing a Frequency Distribution. We may force any distribution of observed measures into the normal mold by the prccess of expanding and contracting successive intervals along the scale of values. In this process of stretching and shrinking, we (1) find the cumulated percentage of cases below each class midpoint, and (2) express each such cumulated percentage as a normal deviate, using a table of normal areas or a special table if available. For example, from the cumulated percentages on the left, we get the normal deviates on the right:

Cumulated Percentage	Normal Deviate (z)
.10	−1.282
.25	−0.674
.40	−0.253
.50	0.000
.70	+0.524
.80	+0.824

We interpret this tabulation as follows: 10 percent of the cases in a normal distribution are below a point -1.282σ from the mean; 25 percent of the cases are below a point -0.674σ from the mean; etc. To convert these normal deviates to deviations having the same scale unit and origin as our observed measures, we (3) multiply each standardized deviate by the standard deviation of our observed measures, and (4) add this product to the mean of our observed measures. In symbols:

$$Y = \overline{X} + \sigma z.$$

For example, if $\overline{X} = 50$, $\sigma = 10$, and $z = -1.282$,

$$Y = 50 + 10(-1.282)$$
$$= 50 - 12.82$$
$$= 37.18,$$

or the value required, together with the other adjusted midpoints, to normalize the distribution along the original scale. As an example of this procedure, we convert the frequency distribution of triplets born in Switzerland, 1871–1900, into the normal form (Table 9.1.2).

Table 9.1.2 *Frequency Distribution of Triplets Born in Switzerland, 1871–1900.*

Deliveries	Years Observed	Percentage to Midpoint	Normal Deviate (z)	$Y = 10 + 3.07 \, (z)$
3	1	1.67	−2.13	3.46
4	0	3.33	−1.83	4.38
5	1	5.00	−1.65	4.93
6	1	8.33	−1.38	5.76
7	5	18.33	−0.90	7.54
8	1	28.33	−0.57	8.25
9	4	36.67	−0.34	8.96
10	4	50.00	0.00	10.00
11	4	63.33	+0.34	11.04
12	3	75.00	+0.67	12.06
13	2	83.33	+0.97	12.98
14	1	88.33	+1.19	13.65
15	2	93.33	+1.50	14.65
16	0	96.67	+1.83	15.62
17	1	98.33	+2.13	16.54
	30			

$$\overline{X} = \frac{300}{30}$$
$$= 10$$

$$\sigma = \sqrt{\frac{3283}{30} - 10^2}$$
$$= \sqrt{9.43}$$
$$= 3.07$$

Source: *Mathematics and Plausible Reasoning*, by G. Polya, Vol. 2, *Patterns of Plausible Inference* (Second Edition, copyright © 1968 by Princeton University Press): Table II, p. 69. Reprinted with permission.

To satisfy ourselves that the distribution of converted midvalues is indeed normal, we may plot it on normal probability paper. This paper is ruled so that the graph of the cumulative normal distribution is a straight line.

Accordingly, when our plotted ogive is a straight line on normal probability paper, we may be confident that our frequency distribution is normal. To illustrate this procedure, we have plotted both the observed and "normalized" distributions of Table 9.1.2 on normal probability graph paper. The degree of curvature in the plot of the observed distribution (Figure 9.1.1) serves to indicate the extent to which that distribution departs from normality. The absence of curvature in the plot of the normalized distribution (Figure 9.1.2) is a check on the accuracy of our arithmetical calculations.

Figure 9.1.1 *Cumulated Frequencies Plotted on Normal Deviates (Normal Probability Graph Paper)*

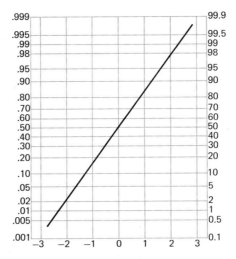

Figure 9.1.2 *Cumulated Frequencies Plotted on Observed Standard Measures (Normal Probability Graph Paper)*

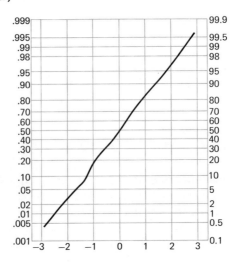

PART 2

Simple Mathematical Transformations

In the foregoing examples, we made the point that transformations are widely prevalent in elementary statistical analysis, even though users may be unaware of them. Reflecting on these materials, the student may discern two essentially different procedures: (1) performing the same mathematical operation on all values in the series, and (2) changing each value in the series as required in order to obtain a specified distribution. The first operation is exemplified by the addition of a constant value to each member in the set, the second operation by the substitution of normal deviates for percentages corresponding to cumulative class frequencies. It is perhaps questionable whether the latter procedure should be named a transformation at all, since we do not convert one series into another, rather we literally discard it and substitute something else.

A strict mathematical transformation has the obvious advantage of permitting us to recover the original measures from transformed values, provided that we are given the conversion formula. From $Y = 1/X$, we get $X = 1/Y$. On the other hand, when we "adjust" values arbitrarily, we can never restore the original measures unless we know the exact amount by which each measure was adjusted. From a set of integers, 1 through N, we cannot reproduce the interval measures which they replaced; from a full set of normal deviates, we cannot reconstruct the original measures which they replaced (unless these measures were normally distributed in the first place, and we know the mean and standard deviation of the observed measures).

From this point onward, we shall restrict ourselves to mathematical transformations in which all measures are subjected to the same algebraic operation. We consider first the process of reforming a statistical distribution to take advantage of a standard model which would otherwise be inapplicable. For example, we straighten out a curvilinear pattern before fitting a straight line. Secondly, we consider the process of rotating the coordinate axes of a rectilinear graph to bring these axes into closer proximity to a scatter of N points. We rotate axes so that all point coordinates will have values close to 0 or 1. This procedure is regularly employed in factor analysis to simplify factor loadings and render them more amenable to interpretation.

Time Series. In the study of social change, we may encounter complex trends which do not adhere to the linear pattern. To represent such patterns statistically (without specifying the process giving rise to that model), we may either fit a higher-order curve or transform one or both variables so that their plotted relationship will be linear. We refer to this latter process as *rectification*: we straighten out our scatter by transforming our variable(s). We do not rectify merely to rectify, rather to take advantage of simple linear methods which would otherwise give a poor fit.

In our first example, we take as our point of departure the Malthusian doctrine that the human population will grow at the same rate over time unless checked by social or physical circumstances. For present purposes, the Malthusian law of growth may be simply written:

$$P_t = P_0^t,$$

where P_0 = size of population at time zero, t = the number of intervals past zero, and P_t = the size of the population at time t. Since the size of the population is governed by the value of the exponent t, we refer to relation between P_t and t as an exponential relation, and the curve of P on t as an exponential curve. Because the exponential law finds so many applications in scientific work, it has been referred to as the "inexorable exponential." Obviously the larger the value of t, the larger the value of P_t, which is the dependent variable in this problem. By fixing the base value P_0 and permitting t to vary on its range, we obtain a set of values for P_t that exemplifies this pattern of growth. Setting $P_0 = 2$, we get:

t	P_t
1	2
2	4
3	8
4	16
5	32
6	64
7	128
8	256
9	512
10	1024

With such a simple series, it is possible to determine by sight whether P is increasing at a constant rate, or whether the rate itself is changing. We would probably notice that the population doubled in size during each interval of time and quadrupled during each period of two intervals, and that in general the percentage increase for equal periods of time was constant. But such generalizations will be difficult if not impossible to derive by inspection from extended series of substantive sociological significance. In such realistic cases, how may we judge whether the growth rate is constant, short of fitting the exponential curve?

A brief answer is: by recourse to logarithms.* As a procedural rule: to determine whether the rate of growth in a given series is constant, take the

---

* Examples are given in terms of both common and natural logarithms. To distinguish between common and natural logarithms and to eliminate the basal index, we designate

log of each P value and plot these logs on the given t values. If the plot of $\log P$ on t is linear, we may infer that the growth of the population is constant. The reasoning is this: if the relation of $\log P$ on t is linear, the relation between P and t must be exponential. Expressing this argument mathematically: if $\log P = t$, $P = 10^t$. Inverting this: if population increases exponentially over time—as Malthus suggested—the logarithm of population size will necessarily change arithmetically on time, as in a simple linear equation of the form, $Y = bX$.

To demonstrate such linearity, if it exists, we could plot $\log P$ and t on arithmetic graph paper. However, it is more convenient to plot P and t on semilog graph paper which automatically *transforms* one of the variables to logarithms. Semilog graph paper "takes" the logs for us and relieves us of the necessity of using a table of logarithms, which may be confusing for a person inexperienced in its use. If the plot of P and t on semilog paper conforms to the path of a straight line with only negligible residuals (in some well-defined sense), we may infer that the population is changing at a constant rate over the observed range of t. On the other hand, if the plotted line is marked by a significant curvature, we correctly infer that the rate of growth is not constant, although we may not detect the way in which the rate itself is changing.

When the plot of two variables on semilog paper is linear, we may state that we have rectified the data by the semilog transformation and that linear methods are now applicable. Examples of exponential curves before and after rectification are shown in Figures 9.2.1 and 9.2.2.

Figure 9.2.1 *Plot of Exponential Curves on Arithmetic Graph Paper*

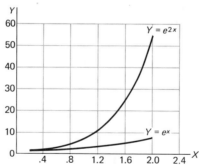

---

common logarithms by the abbreviation "log" and natural logarithms by the abbreviation "ln." The expression "log X" should be understood to mean the logarithm of X to the base 10; the expression "ln X" should be understood to mean the logarithm of X to the base $e = 2.71828\ldots$. To convert common to natural logarithms, we use the conversion formula:

$$\ln X = (2.3026)(\log X).$$

Students with little or no familiarity with logarithms should consult Walker (1951).

Figure 9.2.2 *Plot of Exponential Curves on Semi-Logarithmic Graph Paper*

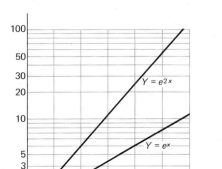

As intimated above, the exponential is not limited in its application to the growth of a population. It happens that many different phenomena change over time according to the general law:

(9.2.1) $y = ae^{kt},$

where a and k are constants. For example, McRae (1969) has fitted the exponential curve to the age distribution of scientific citations in several disciplines in an attempt to sort out the effects of selection favoring recent literature and the growth of the literature itself. His findings, plotted in Figure 9.2.3, suggest that both effects are present, and that citations in sociology refer to older articles than those in the natural sciences. Whenever a variable changes over time according to the exponential law, and if we have solved for a and k, we may forecast the expected magnitude of our variable after n intervals of time have elapsed. For example, populations increasing at the rate of 3 percent each year will double every 23 years; populations increasing at the rate of 2 percent each year will double every 35 years. Such statements are based on manipulations of the exponential equation (9.2.1).

Declining Rate of Growth. If a population were to grow at the same rate indefinitely, it would get out of hand sooner or later, as Malthus recognized explicitly in his doctrine of physical and social checks. Likewise, if social institutions, or the components of which they consist, were to increase indefinitely at the same rate, they would in time reach unmanageable proportions. But societies and cultures do not grow forever at the same rate. For whatever reason, civilizations level off after so long a time, as if nature had set an upper limit on their ultimate size. As is often true in sociology, our recognition of manifest tendencies has preceded our understanding of the natural forces behind them.

Figure 9.2.3 *Proportion of Articles Cited that are Older than T_e Years for Three Disciplines*

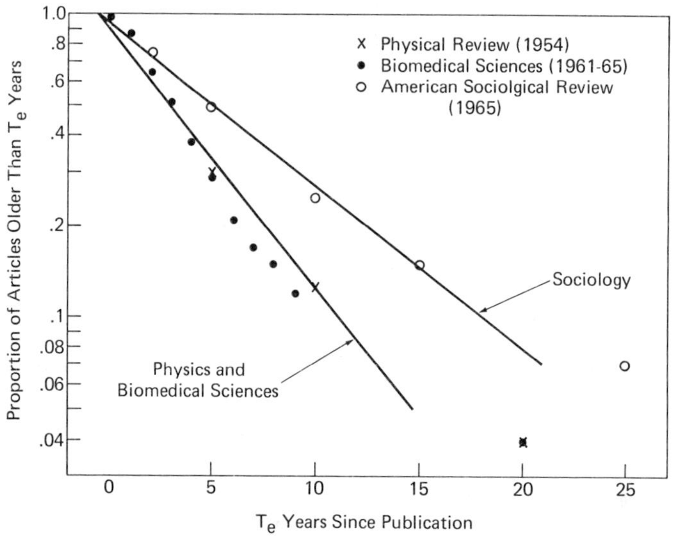

Based on figures kindly supplied by Professor Duncan McRae. Following McRae's suggestion, proportions are plotted on rounded class limits, but the lines of best fit are made to pass through the point $(-\frac{1}{2}, 1.00)$ so that the horizontal distance to n years will equal $(n + \frac{1}{2})$ years. A similar graph appears in McRae, 1969.

Be that as it may, when the growth of an entity is at a declining rate, the relation of its size to duration of time may sometimes be represented by the logarithmic curve:

$$Y = \log t,$$

where Y = the dependent variable, t = time past zero. Although Y continually increases as t (as in the exponential case), it increases at a decreasing rate. The dependent variable (Y) grows more slowly with the passage of time (t). Solving Y for selected values of t, we get paired values that conform to the logarithmic law of growth.

t	Y
1	0.0000
2	0.3010
3	0.4771
4	0.6021
5	0.6990
10	1.0000
25	1.3979
50	1.6990
100	2.0000

By inspection, one might identify the logarithmic relation of Y to t; however, with a longer, more realistic series, such identification would be difficult if not impossible by sight alone. In such instances, where we wish to test the hypothesis that our empirical relation is of the form, $Y = \log t$, we again have recourse to logs. For if the plot of Y on t is logarithmic, the plot of Y on $\log t$ must be linear. Hence, we need only to plot Y on $\log t$ to verify that the data conform to the log curve. And as in the case of the exponential series, we may avail ourselves of semilog paper, except that we now plot t on the log scale, and Y on the arithmetic scale. If the resulting plot is linear, we will have demonstrated that Y increases as $\log t$, or that Y is growing at a diminishing rate. Examples of logarithmic curves before and after transformation are shown in Figures 9.2.4 and 9.2.5.

Figure 9.2.4   *Plot of Logarithmic Curves on Arithmetic Graph Paper*

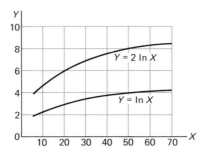

Figure 9.2.5   *Plot of Logarithmic Curves on Semi-Logarithmic Graph Paper*

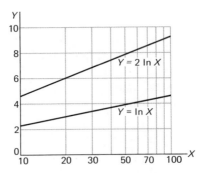

Remark. The inclusion of the logarithmic curve should not be taken to mean that it has been widely used in sociology. On the contrary, sociologists have made relatively little use of it. However, its applications may be more numerous in the future, as sociological theory becomes more quantitative in form. Blau (1970), for example, has adduced evidence in support of the proposition that structural differentiation within an organization increases at a decreasing rate as the size of that organization increases. Such generalizations lend themselves to representation by the logarithmic equation. A general discussion of fitting logarithmic curves to empirical data is contained in Ezekiel and Fox (1959).

Logistic Curve. From the foregoing examples, one should not conclude that change over time is expressible by a simple law such as the logarithmic. Opposing tendencies may be present in the same series of empirical observations. With some phenomena, a period of waning growth seems to be the inevitable sequel to a period of waxing growth. From a variety of evidence, the biologist Raymond Pearl concluded that under stated conditions the growth of the human population falls naturally into two stages: growth at an increasing rate up to a point, beyond which there is growth at a declining rate. In Pearl's (1924: 569) words:

> At first the population grows slowly, but the rate constantly increases to a certain point where it, the rate of growth, reaches a maximum. This point may presumably be taken to present the optimum relation between numbers of people and the subsistence resources of the defined area. The point of maximum rate of growth is the point of inflection of the population growth curve. After that point is passed, the rate of growth becomes progressively slower, till finally the curve stretches along nearly horizontally, in close approach to the upper asymptote which belongs to the particular cultural epoch and area involved.

Such a curve has the form of a stretched out "S," and accordingly has come to be known as the S-curve, as in Figure 9.2.6.

Figure 9.2.6 *Logistic Curve of Growth Fitted to Partial Data for Puerto Rico*

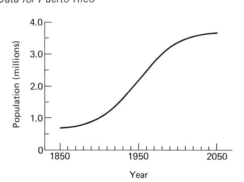

Reprinted from "Population Growth in Puerto Rico and Its Relation to Time Changes in Vital Statistics," *Human Biology*, Volume 17, December 1945 by J. Janer; by permission of the Wayne State University Press.

Its equation in simplified form is:

$$(9.2.2) \qquad y = \frac{k}{1 + e^{at}},$$

where a and k are constants. It is also known as the *logistic* curve, a label which is attributed to Verhulst, a Belgian mathematician who studied its properties. Although the notion that human populations grow logistically is sometimes at odds with the facts, it appears to hold in a number of cases. Furthermore, the logistic seems to have considerable utility for describing the flow and diffusion of information in specified human populations. Studies by Dodd (1955), DeFleur and Larsen (1958), and Coleman, Katz, and Menzel (1957) are illustrative of its use in such cases. Its principal utility thus appears to lie in the study of social change and process, and research workers in this field might be expected to be familiar with its distinctive features. Students who wish to pursue this subject will find it profitable to consult Pearl's (1924) original writings, together with more current writing on the subject (Nair 1954). Students who are interested in mathematical models of social change and growth will find a statement of the problem in Coleman (1968).

Remark on Reconversion. In fitting a straight line to a rectified scatter, our constants are chosen to minimize the sum of the squared residuals. The slope of Y on X and the Y-intercept are chosen to satisfy that requirement. Now, we may invert these constants and enter these inverted values in the equation linking Y to X before transformation. But these reconverted constants will not necessarily minimize the sum of the squared residuals between the observed and the predicted values.

By way of example, let us suppose that Y tends to increase as X to some power b increases. Our empirical equation would take the form:

$$Y = aX^b.$$

Taking the logarithm, we get the rectified model:

$$\log Y = \log a + b \log X.$$

Fitting this equation to the plot of $\log Y$ and $\log X$ by least squares, we get the value of $\log a$ (Y-intercept) and the value of b (slope of $\log Y$ on $\log X$). But the antilog of $\log a$, together with b, will not necessarily minimize the sum of the squared deviations between Y and $\hat{Y} = aX^b$.

To make matters more concrete: consider the following set of coordinates (Sterling and Pollack 1968: 360):

X	Y
2.0	2.4
2.5	3.8
4.0	5.0
5.3	5.6
7.2	7.4
9.1	9.9

By the proper method (plotting on logarithmic paper), it may be shown that Y is linked to X as follows:

$$Y = aX^b.$$

Taking logs and fitting the straight line by least squares, we get

$$b = 0.824$$
$$\log a = 0.173.$$

Taking the antilog of $\log a$, we get

$$a = 1.49,$$

which value, together with $b = 0.824$, we substitute in our equation before transformation to get:

$$Y = 1.49 X^{0.824}.$$

Calculating predicted values and the sum of the squared residuals, we obtain

$$\Sigma(Y - \hat{Y})^2 = 1.11.$$

However, it may be shown by trial-and-error methods that the constants $a = 1.66$ and $b = 0.780$ give a better fit. Our conclusion is that, if least squares constants for unrectified data are required, we may have to obtain them by operating directly on the untransformed data.

Linear Correlation. In measuring the degree of correlation between two variables, it is convenient to employ the product-moment method which automatically fits a straight line to the data (pp. 5–8). But a straight line will be a poor fit when the observed relationship is curvilinear. If $Y = \log X$, one should not fit $Y = X$. When confronted by curvilinearity, we may consider whether the observed relationship between X and Y could be rectified by a suitable transformation of one or both variables. If so, and after that transformation has been performed, we may employ the simpler linear methods. In principle, our procedure in this case does not differ from that employed to rectify the plot of a curvilinear time series: we transform X or Y, or both, to straighten out the trend line. There is this difference: the value of time past zero can occur only once; hence, the "distribution of time"—if that is not a contradiction in terms—is necessarily uniform (rectangular); whereas, the distribution of a statistical variable may take any form whatsoever. Nor can the measures in a time series be grouped by magnitude (except heuristically), since they constitute a sequence over time rather than a statistical population which by definition is "time-free." At this point in our discussion, we are concerned with the linear relationship between two variables whose respective marginal distributions are subject to no restrictions. Since a linear relationship between X and Y is most likely to materialize when both marginal distributions are normal, we choose for each variable whichever transformation will render it most nearly normal in form.

To exemplify this approach, we cite Butt's (1967) Master's thesis on the effect of transformations on the correlations (r's) among selected social characteristics of large American cities for 1950. In that study, he sought to determine, among other matters, whether the intercorrelations among seven major crimes, shown in Table 9.2.1, could be raised significantly by suitable transformations. Since r_{yx}^2 may be construed as the proportion of variance in Y attributable to X and vice-versa, the study sought in effect to ascertain whether the proportion of explained variance might be raised appreciably by suitable transformations.

Table 9.2.1 *Intercorrelations among Seven Crime Rates, U.S. Cities 100,000 or More, 1950.*

	R	A	B	GL	PL	AT	Sum	Avg.	Rank
Murder	.33	.54	.38	.35	.10	.43	2.13	.36	6
Robbery		.42	.61	.55	.39	.58	2.88	.48	3
Assault			.42	.24	.15	.33	2.10	.35	7
Burglary				.55	.59	.59	3.14	.52	1
Grand Larceny					.44	.58	2.71	.45	4
Petty Larceny						.51	2.18	.36	5
Auto Theft							3.02	.50	2
							Sum	3.02	
							Average .43		

To answer that question, Butt proceeded by successive approximations as follows: (1) plotted the frequency curve for each of the seven crime rates; (2) judged from the plot of each crime rate which transformation would make it most nearly normal; (3) transformed each rate according to the formula which seemed best; (4) determined the degree of normality for each transformed distribution by standard methods; and (5) eliminated transformed rates which were approximately normal and required no further correction.

Those rates standing in need of further adjustment were put through a second cycle, consisting of essentially the same steps as the first: an examination of the once-transformed frequency curve for each rate; selection and application of a modified transformation formula; a check on the degree of normality for each twice-transformed rate; a decision as to which rates were sufficiently normal in their distribution to require no further adjustment. This cyclical process was repeated until all rates were approximately normal by a preestablished criterion of goodness of fit and produced transformation formulas as follows:

Offense	Transformation
Murder	$\sqrt{X/10}$
Robbery	$\sqrt{X/100}$
Assault	$\log(X+3)$
Burglary	$\sqrt{X/6}$
Grand Larceny	$\log X$
Petty Larceny	$\sqrt{X/20}$
Auto Theft	$\sqrt{X/60}$

Note that five of the seven formulas call for square roots—but not the roots of the raw values, rather the roots of raw values divided by a larger or smaller numerical constant. In these five cases, it was deemed expedient to change the unit of measure before taking square roots. For example, robbery rates were divided by 100, burglary rates by 6, before roots were taken. It should be noted that division by a constant has no effect on the form of a distribution, although by changing its scale location it may render that distribution more comparable with others. Two of the seven formulas called for logarithms. In one case, the logs of the given values were taken; in the other case, it was necessary to shift the scale origin by adding a constant value of 3 before taking logs. (Since it is impossible to take the logarithm of a negative number, the logarithmic transformation is inapplicable to series containing negative measures.) An implication of Butt's analysis is that transformations consisting of a single arithmetical operation may be wanting in one or more respects, and that compound operations may be required in order to obtain the required normal distribution. In Butt's study, it was necessary in one of the seven cases to move the scale origin before converting raw values to logs.

As the last step in his analysis, Butt computed the intercorrelations among the seven transformed rates, given in Table 9.2.2, and compared these with the coefficients based on the original rates.

Table 9.2.2   *Intercorrelations among Transformed Crime Rates,*
U.S. Cities 100,000 or More, 1950.

	R	A	B	GL	PL	AT	Sum	Avg.	Rank
M	.47	.73	.44	.41	.18	.51	2.74	.46	6
R		.60	.66	.57	.41	.62	3.33	.56	2
A			.53	.35	.22	.48	2.91	.49	5
B				.54	.60	.59	3.36	.56	1
GL					.48	.58	2.93	.49	4
PL						.49	2.38	.40	7
AT							3.27	.55	3
							Sum	3.51	
							Average	.50	

The student may wonder whether these somewhat intricate transformations served their purpose. Our answer will depend on the purpose we had
in mind. If our sole object was to obtain a better fit between observed
relationship and linear model, we would judge the transformation a moderate
success. The correlations based on transformed data had an average value
of .50, somewhat higher than the average value of .43 for correlations based
on untransformed data. The transformed data thus fit the linear model
better than the untransformed data. On the other hand, if our object was to
discriminate more sharply between groupings of variables, as in factor
analysis, we would probably judge the transformation to be relatively useless.
The pattern of 21 intercorrelations was affected only slightly by the transformation, as reflected by the rank-order correlation $(\rho = .86)$ between
coefficients based on original and transformed rates. Inasmuch as correlation
patterns generally tend to maintain themselves in the face of order-preserving
transformations, results derived from transformed patterns will necessarily
be closely similar to those derived from the original pattern. Butt's results
were generally consistent with this generalization which is sometimes cited
in writing on factor analysis (see Thurstone 1947: 368). However, it should
not be concluded that the transformation served no purpose. It did reduce
the unexplained variance and by that criterion could be justified. Whenever
our object is to reduce the residual variance as much as possible, as in
prediction, we should entertain the possibility of a transformation.

Transformations in Significance Testing. It is the theoretical distribution of
a sample statistic that permits us to test the credibility of a statistical hypothesis by means of a single sample value. In such analysis, we are usually
warned against using a given sampling distribution (t, F, z, etc.) unless the
conditions under which it materializes have been met approximately. If a
specified sampling distribution will realize itself only on condition that the
sampled population has a normal distribution, we must assure ourselves

that the sampled population has a normal distribution before using that sampling distribution. If there is evidence to the contrary, we will either forego the use of that particular sampling distribution, or transform our sample measures to justify the assumption that the population of transformed measures is normally distributed.

To exemplify this approach, and to orient the student to its possibilities, we consider some simple transformations of data to render them more compatible with the requirement that our sampled populations be normally distributed with a common variance. These conditions, together with the requirement that observations be independent, must be satisfied if we are to use the F-distribution to test the hypothesis that two or more populations have identical means, as in the analysis of variance. The requirement that observations be independent can be met only by proper experimental or sampling design. When our observations are lacking in independence, for whatever reason, we must adapt our procedures to that circumstance. On the other hand, it is sometimes possible, by an appropriate but simple transformation, to render our original measures more consistent with the requirement that sampled populations be normally distributed with a common variance. Further, in many instances the same transformation will serve both to stabilize the sample variances and to yield more nearly normal distributions within samples. On this point Kendall and Stewart (1966: 93) comment as follows: "Variance-stabilizing transformations commonly normalize as a byproduct, but they do not produce the optimum normalization." Nevertheless, for present purposes it will suffice to examine the stability of sample variances under a given transformation. In this analysis it is assumed that the sample variances vary systematically as the sample means, or that identically skewed measures within samples have approximately equal means.

Square Root Transformation. When our statistical data consist of whole numbers (e.g., counts) and our sample variances are roughly equal to sample means, we may suppose that our samples were drawn from populations having a Poisson distribution. Under these circumstances, the appropriate procedure is to convert all measures to their square roots before performing the analysis of variance. The reason is that if we take the square root of values in Poisson distributions whose means differ, we get distributions of values whose means will differ but whose variances will now be nearly equal. Hence, the rule: when sample variances are approximately equal to sample means, convert all measures to their square roots and run the analysis of variance on these converted values. When sample means range from 2 to 10, and in the presence of zeros in the data, we add $\frac{1}{2}$ to each value and take the square root of these adjusted values. The effect of the square root transformation on the variance of a Poisson distribution for selected values of the mean from 0 to 15 has been tabulated by Bartlett (1947) as follows:

Variance of Poisson Variate on Transformed Scale

Mean (on original scale)	$\sqrt{x}$	$\sqrt{(x + \frac{1}{2})}$
0.0	0.000	0.000
0.5	0.310	0.102
1.0	0.402	0.160
2.0	0.390	0.214
3.0	0.340	0.232
4.0	0.306	0.240
6.0	0.276	0.245
9.0	0.263	0.247
12.0	0.259	0.248
15.0	0.256	0.248

Source: M. S. Bartlett, "The Use of Transformations," *Biometrics*, 3(1947), pp. 39–52. Reprinted with permission.

The student may wonder about the circumstances giving rise to the Poisson distribution. The pat answer to this question is the occurrence of a rare event in time or space.* If a given event may occur at any instant of time but rarely does (i.e., if it is most improbable), the number of instances within some arbitrary interval of time will have a Poisson distribution. The distribution of yearly number of deaths by horsekick in ten Prussian army corps for twenty years provides an entertaining example:

Number of Deaths (X)	Frequency
0	109
1	65
2	22
3	3
4	1
5	. . .
6	. . .

This table is taken from Fisher: *Statistical Methods for Research Workers*, Tenth Edition, 1946, published by Oliver and Boyd, Edinburgh, and by permission of the author and publishers.

---

* See Coleman (1964: 288–311) for an extended discussion of the Poisson distribution and its potential uses in sociology. The possibility that racial disturbances have a Poisson distribution has recently been evaluated by Spilerman (1970).

Likewise, if a given event may occur at any point in space but rarely does, the number of instances within some appropriate space will have a Poisson distribution. A commonplace example is the distribution of the number of organisms actually counted in one square of a haemocytometer:

Number of Cells (X)	Frequency
0	0
1	20
2	43
3	53
4	86
5	70
6	54
7	37
8	18
9	10
10	5
11	2
12	2
13	0
	400

This table is taken from Fisher: *Statistical Methods for Research Workers*, Tenth Edition, 1946, published by Oliver and Boyd, Edinburgh, and by permission of the author and publishers.

An analysis of these distributions (number of deaths and number of cells) will demonstrate that both conform to the general Poisson law:

$$(9.2.3) \qquad Y = \frac{m^X e^{-m}}{X!},$$

where m is the mean value of X, and Y is the expected frequency (as a proportion) for a given value of X. The student may wish to verify that in each distribution the mean is approximately equal to the variance. To get the values expected by the Poisson law, we substitute the obtained value of the mean for m in Equation (9.2.3) and solve for the observed values of X in the series. By comparing observed and expected values, we may judge whether the Poisson curve is a good fit.

Before leaving the square root transformation, we note that it is not necessary to demonstrate that the sampled population has a Poisson distribution in order to employ that transformation in the analysis of variance. If the square root transformation stabilizes our sample variances, we may use it, even though we may be somewhat uncertain about the form of our sampled populations.

Arcsin Transformation. When measures in each sample are proportions p, each based on N independent observations, and when the sample variance is approximately proportional to the sample mean,

$$k = s_i^2/\overline{X}_i,$$

or

$$s_i^2 = k\overline{X}_i,$$

where k is the constant of proportionality, we may suppose samples were drawn from binomial populations, with P_i and $[P_i(1 - P_i)]/N$ as the mean and variance for the ith population. On that assumption, and for the purpose of stabilizing sample variances, we may take (1) the square root of each proportion p, and (2) the arcsin of that square root. The arcsin transformation may thus be regarded as an extension of the square root transformation, except that we operate on proportions rather than absolute numbers. In symbols:

$$Y = \arcsin \sqrt{p},$$

where p is the proportion of N cases in a given category. The arcsin transformation stands in relation to the binomial distribution as the square root transformation stands in relation to the Poisson distribution. And it carries an identical justification: when we apply the arcsin transformation to measures comprising two or more binomial distributions whose means and variances are different, we get transformed distributions whose variances are more nearly equal but whose means maintain their separation. A table of angles corresponding to percentages is included in the appendix, a brief excerpt from which is presented here:

Percentage	Arcsin	
	0	5
0	0	12.9
10	18.4	22.8
20	26.6	30.0
30	33.2	36.3
40	39.2	42.1
50	45.0	47.9
60	50.8	53.7
70	56.8	60.0
80	63.4	67.2
90	71.6	77.1

With $N < 50$, we add $1/4N$ to values close to zero before entering the table, very much as we add the quantity $\frac{1}{2}$ to small values in the Poisson series before taking square roots.

An improvement of the simple arcsin transformation has been devised by Freeman and Tukey (1950) as follows:

$$Y = \frac{1}{2}\left(\arcsin\sqrt{\frac{x}{N+1}} + \arcsin\sqrt{\frac{x+1}{N+1}}\right),$$

where $x/N = p$. Instead of taking the arcsin of $\sqrt{p}$, we (1) take the arcsin of quantities slightly smaller and larger than $\sqrt{p}$, respectively, and (2) sum these two arcsins and divide that sum by 2. Substituting v_1 for $\arcsin\sqrt{\frac{x}{N+1}}$ and v_2 for $\arcsin\sqrt{\frac{x+1}{N+1}}$, we get the more compact expression:

$$Y = \frac{1}{2}(v_1 + v_2).$$

We have computed the mean and the variance for p, $\arcsin\sqrt{p}$, and $\frac{1}{2}(v_1 + v_2)$ for selected values of N and P, where P is the population proportion. From these results, given in Table 9.2.3, it is clear that the Freeman-Tukey formula generally gives the more dependable results, but that it makes very little difference for values of N larger than 50. Our conclusion is that we may use the simple arcsin transformation with $N > 50$.

Table 9.2.3 *Mean and Variance of $p = x/N$, arcsin $\sqrt{p}$, and $\frac{1}{2}(v_1 + v_2)$, Selected Values of N and P.*

		p		arcsin $\sqrt{p}$		$\frac{1}{2}(v_1 + v_2)$	
N	P	Mean	Variance	Mean	Variance	Mean	Variance
	.10	0.100	0.009	14.706	135.966	19.327	74.909
	.20	0.200	0.016	24.631	125.833	27.167	81.897
10	.30	0.300	0.021	32.257	106.427	33.639	78.822
	.40	0.400	0.024	38.832	96.517	39.453	76.653
	.50	0.500	0.025	45.000	93.830	45.000	76.043
	.10	0.100	0.005	16.805	63.432	19.041	42.195
	.20	0.200	0.008	25.883	48.709	27.015	39.953
20	.30	0.300	0.010	32.855	44.555	33.491	39.239
	.40	0.400	0.012	39.070	43.556	39.365	39.187
	.50	0.500	0.013	45.000	43.339	45.000	39.195
	.10	0.100	0.003	17.529	36.537	18.931	27.725
	.20	0.200	0.005	26.162	29.756	26.893	26.494
30	.30	0.300	0.007	32.987	28.706	33.406	26.461
	.40	0.400	0.008	39.128	28.413	39.324	26.495
	.50	0.500	0.008	45.000	28.338	45.000	26.506

Table 9.2.3 (continued)

N	P	p Mean	p Variance	$arcsin \sqrt{p}$ Mean	$arcsin \sqrt{p}$ Variance	$\frac{1}{2}(v_1 + v_2)$ Mean	$\frac{1}{2}(v_1 + v_2)$ Variance
40	.10	0.100	0.002	17.836	24.688	18.847	20.396
	.20	0.200	0.004	26.275	21.677	26.818	19.956
	.30	0.300	0.005	33.046	21.243	33.360	19.996
	.40	0.400	0.006	39.155	21.098	39.302	20.023
	.50	0.500	0.006	45.000	21.059	45.000	20.030
50	.10	0.100	0.002	17.990	18.575	18.782	16.153
	.20	0.200	0.003	26.337	17.112	26.771	16.036
	.30	0.300	0.004	33.081	16.869	33.331	16.075
	.40	0.400	0.005	39.171	16.780	39.288	16.094
	.50	0.500	0.005	45.000	16.756	45.000	16.099
60	.10	0.100	0.002	18.079	14.954	18.732	13.413
	.20	0.200	0.003	26.377	14.148	26.738	13.409
	.30	0.300	0.004	33.103	13.990	33.312	13.440
	.40	0.400	0.004	39.181	13.931	39.279	13.454
	.50	0.500	0.004	45.000	13.914	45.000	13.458
70	.10	0.100	0.001	18.137	12.563	18.694	11.492
	.20	0.200	0.002	26.405	12.063	26.714	11.524
	.30	0.300	0.003	33.119	11.951	33.298	11.548
	.40	0.400	0.003	39.189	11.908	39.272	11.559
	.50	0.500	0.004	45.000	11.897	45.000	11.562
80	.10	0.100	0.001	18.178	10.857	18.663	10.064
	.20	0.200	0.002	26.426	10.515	26.696	10.104
	.30	0.300	0.003	33.131	10.431	33.287	10.123
	.40	0.400	0.003	39.194	10.399	39.267	10.131
	.50	0.500	0.003	45.000	10.390	45.000	10.134
90	.10	0.100	0.001	18.209	9.571	18.639	8.957
	.20	0.200	0.002	26.442	9.319	26.682	8.996
	.30	0.300	0.002	33.140	9.254	33.279	9.011
	.40	0.400	0.003	39.198	9.229	39.263	9.018
	.50	0.500	0.003	45.000	9.223	45.000	9.020
100	.10	0.100	0.001	18.233	8.562	18.620	8.072
	.20	0.200	0.002	26.455	8.368	26.670	8.106
	.30	0.300	0.002	33.147	8.316	33.272	8.120
	.40	0.400	0.002	39.202	8.296	39.260	8.125
	.50	0.500	0.002	45.000	8.291	45.000	8.127

Logarithmic Transformation. When sample standard deviations are proportional to sample means,

$$k = \frac{s_i}{\overline{X}_i},$$

or

$$s_i = kX_i,$$

we may suppose that sampled populations are skewed to the right, and that the greater the mean, the greater the skew. A mean of 100 would signify greater skew than a mean of 50. In this situation, we may have recourse to the logarithmic transformation,

$$Y = \log X,$$

which tends to equalize the sample variances without affecting the differences among the means.

To understand this process, consider the reverse procedure of upsetting the equality among variances by an exponential transformation of values. Start with several approximately normal distributions whose means range from low to high but whose variances are equal. Now transform each value (Y) in each series according to the rule:

$$X = e^Y.$$

The numerical difference between X and Y will increase as the value of Y, and frequency distributions whose locations are higher on the scale of Y-values will have larger standard deviations than distributions whose locations are lower on that scale.

The materials presented in Table 9.2.4 are corroborative of these tendencies. We begin with bell-shaped distributions for Y_i with equal standard deviations but different means and necessarily different coefficients of variation. Now we convert each value in each Y series into its antilog ($X_i = e^{Y_i}$) and get means, standard deviations, and coefficients of variation for these transformed values. Standard deviations now differ where before they were equal. On the other hand, the coefficients of variation are now equal where before they were different.

Clearly, to equalize the different variances of X_i, we must reverse ourselves and take the log of each value in each X series. By this reverse operation, we restore our original values and thereby the equal variances. It should not be concluded (from our demonstration) that we must "prove" that log X has an approximately normal distribution for the population before applying the log transformation to our sample measures. Whenever the coefficient of variation, $s_i/\overline{X}_i$, is roughly constant, we may pragmatically resort to this technique. If the log transformation performs as required, we will use it, provided the other assumptions for the F-test are met satisfactorily.

Table 9.2.4   *Mean and Standard Deviation of Y_i and e^{Y_i}.*

Frequency	Y_1	Y_2	Y_3	$X_1 = e^{Y_1}$	$X_2 = e^{Y_2}$	$X_3 = e^{Y_3}$
1	0.0	2.0	4.0	1.0	7.4	54.6
10	1.0	3.0	5.0	2.7	20.1	148.4
45	2.0	4.0	6.0	7.4	54.6	403.4
120	3.0	5.0	7.0	20.1	148.4	1,096.6
210	4.0	6.0	8.0	54.6	403.4	2,981.0
252	5.0	7.0	9.0	148.4	1,096.6	8,103.1
210	6.0	8.0	10.0	403.4	2,981.0	22,026.5
120	7.0	9.0	11.0	1,096.6	8,103.1	59,874.1
45	8.0	10.0	12.0	2,981.0	22,026.5	162,754.8
10	9.0	11.0	13.0	8,103.1	59,874.1	442,413.4
1	10.0	12.0	14.0	22,026.5	162,754.8	1,202,604.3
Mean	5.0	7.0	9.0	493.3	3,645.1	26,934.0
Standard Deviation	1.6	1.6	1.6	1,201.1	8,874.7	65,575.5
Coefficient of Variation	0.32	0.23	0.18	2.43	2.43	2.43

We note that when small numbers and zeros are present in our samples, we add 1 to each value before taking the log:

$$Y = \log (1 + X).$$

Remark. Only minor complications result from the transformation of measures in a one-way analysis of variance table; however, major complications may come with the transforming of measures in a k-way table ($k > 1$). In these cases, interaction effects may disappear with the rescaling of the data, and conclusions about the presence of interaction may differ, depending on whether they are based on transformed or untransformed data. Students interested in pursuing this topic should consult the article by Box and Cox (1964) for an appreciation of the complexities of the problem.

Transforming the Sampling Distribution. Instead of transforming the observed measures so as to render plausible an assumption about the sampled population, we may transform the sample statistic so that its distribution will conform to a prescribed model. We cite two familiar instances.

Fisher's z. When the value of the product-moment correlation coefficient (ρ) in the population is zero, the sampling distribution of the sample coefficient (r) will be approximately normal around zero, with variance equal to $\frac{1}{\sqrt{n-1}}$ (where n is the number of cases in the sample). However, this distribution will depart from normality as the population value (ρ) tends to its limit of 1. Under these circumstances, instead of transforming individual measures—their distribution is not in question—we adjust the obtained sample statistic so that its distribution will be approximately normal in form. For that purpose, Fisher (1946) derived the following statistic:

$$z = \tfrac{1}{2}[\log_e (1 + r) - \log_e (1 - r)],$$

which is distributed almost normally with variance,

$$s_z^2 = \frac{1}{n - 3},$$

and which is "practically independent of the value of the correlation in the population from which the sample was drawn." As in many instances of this kind, the operations prescribed by this formula need not be actually carried out, since conversion tables are available for ready reference. We use z and s_z to handle the ordinary tasks of statistical inference, namely:
  (1) to set up a confidence interval with a given probability of including the population coefficient (ρ);
  (2) to test the hypothesis that ρ has a specific value; and
  (3) to test the hypothesis that two samples were drawn from the same bivariate population.

χ^2 to Normal Deviate (z). The χ^2 distribution (Appendix Table 5) finds many applications in social statistics, especially in the analysis of attributes. Unlike the normal distribution, which is not subject to change, the distribution of χ^2 changes as its degrees of freedom (df): the greater the df, the greater the degree of symmetry of the distribution. Obviously, it would be impracticable to prepare as many tables as there are degrees of freedom, since that number is indefinitely large. However, such a proliferation of detail is obviated by reason that, with $df > 30$, the distribution of $\sqrt{\chi^2}$ is approximately normal with mean equal to $\sqrt{df - .5}$ and variance equal to $\sqrt{.5}$. Accordingly, if df is relatively large, we need only express $\sqrt{\chi^2}$ as a standard measure and refer that result to a table of normal areas in order to evaluate the probability of its occurrence. To reduce $\sqrt{\chi^2}$ to standard form, we take out the mean and divide that remainder by the standard deviation:

$$z = \frac{\sqrt{\chi^2} - \sqrt{df - .5}}{\sqrt{.5}},$$

which simplifies to

$$z = \sqrt{2\chi^2} - \sqrt{2df - 1}.$$

By this procedure, we are permitted the convenience of a single table, where otherwise a multiplicity of tables would be required.

Transformation of Factor Loadings. As our last example of transformations regularly employed in sociological research, we consider the transformation of loadings, produced by factoring a correlation matrix, to rotated loadings that are more susceptible to interpretation. Upon factoring a matrix of inter-correlations among n variables, we obtain the loadings of these variables on m $(m < n)$ uncorrelated factors. We usually display the loadings for the ith variable in the ith row of an $n \times m$ table, and the loadings of the jth factor in the jth column, as follows:

		Factor			
		1	2	m	h_i^2
	1	a_{11}	a_{12}	a_{1m}	$\sum a_{1j}^2$
Variable	2	a_{21}	a_{22}	a_{2m}	
	$\vdots$				
	n	a_{n1}	a_{n2}	a_{nm}	$\sum a_{nj}^2$

From a table of such loadings, we may restore the correlation between the ith and j^{th} variables by rule:

$$r_{ij} = \sum_1^m a_{ik}a_{jk}.$$

This result, it will be noticed, entails multiplying the ith and j^{th} rows for all m columns and getting the sum of these products. In mathematical writing, this sum is known as the inner product, a terminology we shall use when convenient.

In similar manner, we may reconstruct the communality (proportion of variance attributable to the common factors) for each variable:

$$h_i^2 = \sum_1^m a_{ik}^2.$$

Thus, to obtain the communality for the ith variable, we square all loadings in the ith row and sum these squares. The communality of the ith variable (subject to the condition that factors are uncorrelated) may thus be construed as the inner product of the ith variable with itself.

It is rather remarkable, at least at first glance, that we may transform each loading in the $n \times m$ table by rule without disturbing intercorrelations and communalities. In factor analysis, the purpose of such a transformation is to render both factors and variables more amenable to interpretation. A factor running through many heterogenous variables is more difficult to interpret than one running through a few homogeneous variables. Similarly, a variable loaded by several or more common factors is less amenable to interpretation than one loaded by only one common factor. We thus seek a transformation which will decrease all loadings but one in each row, which single loading we wish to increase as much as possible. Our justification for this procedure is to obtain results which, colloquially speaking, make more theoretical sense.

To furnish a glimpse of this technique, consider the loadings of ten ($n = 10$) variables on two ($m = 2$) factors as follows:

Variable	Factor Loading	
	a_{i1}	a_{i2}
1	.70	.56
2	.72	.52
3	.69	.53
4	.63	.58
5	.58	.50
6	.74	−.53
7	.75	−.52
8	.69	−.63
9	.67	−.60
10	.66	−.59

By plotting each variable as a point on rectangular coordinates, taking loadings on the first factor as abscissas and loadings on the second factor as ordinates, we may discern the relationship of each variable to each factor. That plot is shown in Figure 9.2.7. By rotating axes F_1 and F_2 to a different

Figure 9.2.7 *Factors in Initial Position*

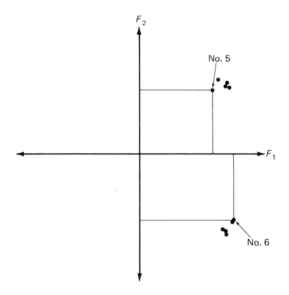

position, we may secure a better fit of axes to points, in the sense that each point will be relatively distant from one axis and relatively close to the other. To exemplify that possibility, we have rotated our axes 45° clockwise (Figure 9.2.8). In making this adjustment, we necessarily change the projections of points on axes, or the respective abscissas and ordinates for the ten points of the scatter. Since each variable (point) now lies close to the origin of one axis, and close to the extremity of the other, all coordinates tend to 0 or 1 in value, which was our goal.

Figure 9.2.8 *Factors Rotated 45° Clockwise*

At this juncture, it is natural to wonder whether intercorrelations and communalities will be disturbed by such a transformation of coordinates. The answer is contained in this theorem of geometry: a rotation of rectangular (orthogonal) axes will leave inner products unchanged. The implication is that, in principle, we may transform our factor loadings, as given by the factoring process, according to the criterion that each variable be negligibly loaded on all factors but one. To effect such a transformation, we need only to relocate axes by sight so that each point lies close to one axis, but quite distant from the other. To get the new loadings, we measure the lengths of the new abscissas and ordinates by means of appropriate measuring instruments. However, such manual work is quite unnecessary by reason of the following standard "formulas of rotation":

Clockwise	Counterclockwise
$a'_{i1} = \cos \theta (a_{i1}) - \sin \theta (a_{i2})$	$a'_{i1} = \cos \theta (a_{i1}) + \sin \theta (a_{i2})$
$a'_{i2} = \sin \theta (a_{i1}) + \cos \theta (a_{i2})$	$a'_{i2} = -\sin \theta (a_{i1}) + \cos \theta (a_{i2})$

where a_{ij} are the given loadings, and a'_{ij} are the transformed loadings.

To apply these formulas, we would proceed by these steps: (1) measure on a protractor the angle of rotation θ; (2) find the sine and cosine of that angle from a table of such values; (3) substitute these constant values in the foregoing formulas; (4) successively substitute each pair of coordinates (loadings) and calculate the rotated values. In our application of this procedure to our numerical example (p. 421), we substitute $\sin 45° = .707$ and $\cos 45° = .707$ in the formulas of rotation, successively substitute the ten pairs of given loadings, and calculate each pair of transformed loadings. These transformed loadings (two significant digits) are shown below. We observe that all values lie close to 0 or 1; this is in agreement with our graphic impression.

Variable	Rotated Loadings a'_{i1}	a'_{i2}
1	.10	.89
2	.14	.88
3	.11	.86
4	.04	.86
5	.06	.76
6	.90	.15
7	.90	.16
8	.98	−.01
9	.90	.05
10	.88	.05

For an alternative expression (common in writing on factor analysis), we may replace $\sin \theta$ by its cofunction, $\cos (1 - \theta)$, whereupon the coefficients in the formulas of rotation become the direction cosines of the rotated axes with respect to axes in their initial position. (The direction cosines of a given line are the cosines of the angles between that line and its coordinate axes. For a given line there will be as many direction cosines as there are coordinate axes. A line in 2-space will have two direction cosines; a line in 3-space will have three direction cosines; etc.) Denoting the direction cosine of j with respect to i by λ_{ij}, we may write the formulas for rotation in the following manner:

$$a'_{i1} = \lambda_{11}a_{i1} + \lambda_{21}a_{i2},$$

$$a'_{i2} = \lambda_{12}a_{i1} + \lambda_{22}a_{i2},$$

where λ_{11} is the cosine of the angle between the first factor in its rotated and initial position; λ_{12} is the cosine of the angle between the second factor in its rotated position and the first factor in its initial position; etc.

It is convenient and quite conventional to arrange direction cosines in a 2×2 table as follows:

	F'_1	F'_2
F_1	λ_{11}	λ_{12}
F_2	λ_{21}	λ_{22}

with the axes in their initial positions in rows and rotated axes in columns. It may be mentioned in passing that for this table the sum of the squares by columns will be 1, and the inner products ($i \neq j$) will be identically zero. These results serve to corroborate the theorem that in orthogonal rotation each factor remains perfectly correlated with itself but uncorrelated with all other factors. It is also anticipatory of a more general conclusion to the effect that inner products are identically zero and sums of squares for columns are identically 1 for an $m \times m$ table of direction cosines, subject to the restriction that axes remain orthogonal.

The procedure for transforming loadings on three factors is an easy extension of that for two factors, and from the case of three factors we may move readily to the general case of m factors. In principle, we rotate our m axes until each variable is relatively close to all axes but one of them. When axes have been rotated to satisfy this criterion, we determine the angular distance between each axis in its best position and each of the m axes in its initial position. We get the cosines of these angles, which become coefficients in a set of m equations, with each equation consisting of m terms. For example, when $m = 3$ we have

$$a'_{i1} = \lambda_{11}a_{i1} + \lambda_{21}a_{i2} + \lambda_{31}a_{i3},$$
$$a'_{i2} = \lambda_{12}a_{i1} + \lambda_{22}a_{i2} + \lambda_{32}a_{i3},$$
$$a'_{i3} = \lambda_{13}a_{i1} + \lambda_{23}a_{i2} + \lambda_{33}a_{i3}.$$

Substituting in these equations, we get the transformed loadings.

From this very sketchy account the student should not conclude that rotation is an uncomplicated process. On the contrary, it is a rather involved procedure consisting of numerous iterations before an acceptable solution may be obtained. It becomes more complicated when we lift the restriction that factors be mutually uncorrelated. On a large scale, it is impractical to carry out a rotation without the aid of a digital computer. Nevertheless, in its essentials, it does not differ from the procedure set forth above: rotating axes, getting direction cosines, applying these cosines by rule to get transformed loadings. Students interested in a detailed account of transformations in factor analysis should consult Harman (1967).

Epilogue. Like every other procedure, we have recourse to transformations when they serve some useful purpose. In statistical work, transformations are undertaken generally to produce a series which lends itself more readily to analysis than the untransformed series. By reforming the distribution, we render the data more amenable to procedures which would otherwise be inappropriate. Thus, after a suitable transformation, linear correlational methods may be justified where before they would have been unwarranted; with transformed data, we may run an analysis of variance where otherwise that procedure would have to be foregone.

However, transformations have their complexities and their mechanical application may create new problems. For example, a practical problem may arise when we have obtained averages for the transformed data and discover afterwards that we require these averages for the untransformed data. This would be no problem, except that averages for transformed measures may not be readily convertible into averages for the original series, if that is possible at all. We cannot convert the mean of the arcsins of proportions into the mean of the proportions by the inverse procedure of squaring the sine of that mean. If it is the mean of the raw proportions we want, and we have the mean of their arcsins, we must return to the original measures and compute their mean or employ a special method for removing bias (Kendall and Stewart 1966: 95). For this reason, we should always anticipate the results we require before we begin our data processing. But this principle holds for all statistical work.

Another problem has to do with the tendency to attribute to a transformation a power which it does not possess. A transformation cannot convert an interval scale into a ratio scale; yet a research worker may mistakenly proceed as if such a change had taken place. To quote the coefficient of variation for a transformed interval scale would be no more valid than would be that quotation for the untransformed scale.

On the other hand, the disruption of a ratio scale by a curvilinear transformation is permissible, provided we keep in mind that ratios between transformed values will not equal ratios between raw values. If Y is a ratio scale, and we go to common logs, the ratio of 1,000 to 100 will be represented by the ratio 3 to 2. This will create no confusion if we remember that equal intervals on the log scale correspond to equal percentage differences on the antilog scale.

As a caution, we reiterate that we have merely broached the subject of transformation and not entered into its mathematical complexities. Interested students are advised to begin with J. Kruskal's article (International Encyclopedia of Social Sciences, Vol. 15) and move from there to the more specialized references to be found in his bibliography.

EXERCISES

1. Compute the sex ratio for a population of 7,550 with 3,105 females.

2. Given a sex ratio of 98, how many females are there in a population of 9,900?

3. A population of 23,500 had 430 births last year.
    (a) What is the crude birth rate?
    (b) If the sex ratio is 135, how many women are there in the population?
    (c) If 80 percent of these women are of childbearing age, what is the refined birth rate on the population of childbearing women?

4. A population of 36,500 had a birth rate of 21 last year. Calculate the number of births.

5. In a population of 200,000, there are 95,000 women, and 340 births. What is the female-specific birth rate?

6. Compute the sum, mean, and variance for ranks 1 through 15, 10 through 20, 50 through 100.

7. Verify that

$$\frac{\sigma_x^2 + \sigma_y^2 - \sigma_D^2}{2\sigma_x\sigma_y} = 1 - \frac{6\sum D^2}{N(N^2 - 1)} = \frac{53}{60}$$

for the following numbers:

X	Y
1	3
2	1
3	2
4	6
5	4
6	5
7	8
8	7
9	9

8. Verify that the product-moment difference formula and the Spearman rank-order correlation formula yield the same coefficient for these numbers:

X	Y
1	4
2	2
3	7
4	1
5	6
6	3
7	5

9. Given that $X = Y - 2$, and $U = W - 3$,

X	U
1	15
3	14
6	22
7	9
5	21
4	7
10	18
12	20

verify that:

(a) $\sigma_x^2 = \sigma_y^2$
(b) $\sigma_{xu} = \sigma_{yw}$
(c) $\bar{Y} = \bar{X} + 2$

10. Given that $X = Y/3$, and $U = W/2$,

X	U
1	15
3	14
6	22
7	9
5	21
4	7
10	18
12	20

verify that

(a) $\sigma_y^2 = 3^2 \sigma_x^2$
(b) $\sigma_{yw} = (3)(2)\sigma_{xu}$
(c) $\bar{Y} = 3\bar{X}$

11. Given that $Y = 3X + 2$, $W = 2U + 3$,

X	Y	U	W
1	5	15	33
3	11	14	31
6	20	22	47
7	23	9	21
5	17	21	45
4	14	7	17
10	32	18	39
12	38	20	43

verify that

(a) $\sigma_y^2 = 3^2 \sigma_x^2$
(b) $\sigma_{yw} = (3)(2)\sigma_{xu}$

12. Using the values of X and Y, as given below, show that:

X	Y
15	12
27	8
31	7
82	13
9	4

(a) $\dfrac{1}{N}\sum(X+5) = \bar{X} + 5$

(b) $\sigma^2_{x+5} = \sigma^2_x$

(c) $\sigma_{(x+5)(y+7)} = \sigma_{xy}$

(d) $\dfrac{1}{N}\sum(3X) = 3\bar{X}$

(e) $\sigma^2_{3x} = 3^2\sigma^2_x$

(f) $\sigma_{(3x)(6y)} = (3)(6)\sigma_{xy}$

(g) $\dfrac{1}{N}\sum(3X+5) = 3(\bar{X}) + 5$

(h) $\sigma^2_{3x+5} = 3^2\sigma^2_x$

(i) $\sigma_{(3x+5)(6y+7)} = (3)(6)\sigma_{xy}$

13. Using the measures in Exercise 12, show by calculations that
when $y' = \dfrac{Y-4}{12}$ and $x' = \dfrac{X-2}{3}$:

(a) $\bar{y}' = \dfrac{\bar{Y}-4}{12}$ (b) $\sigma^2_{y'} = \dfrac{\sigma^2_y}{12^2}$ (c) $\sigma_{y'x'} = \dfrac{\sigma_{xy}}{(12)(3)}$

14. The coefficient of variation is the standard deviation of a distribution divided by the mean. Its value will change if we add a constant to each measure in the distribution. Comment on its applicability to interval measures.

15. Transform y into w, so that the plot of w on x is a straight line:

$$y = x^2$$
$$y = 10^x$$
$$y = \log x$$
$$y = x^{1/2}$$

16. Whittaker notes that in 1,000 consecutive issues of *The Utopian Seven-Daily Chronical* the deaths of centenarians were recorded as follows:

Number	0	1	2	3	4	5	6	7	8
Frequency	229	325	257	119	50	17	2	1	0

Calculate the frequencies in the Poisson distribution with the same mean and the same total frequency of 1,000. How well do the expected frequencies fit the observed frequencies? Does the fit substantiate the Poisson model? Explain.

17. To apply linear correlation, how might you transform one of the variables in each of the following pairs of variables?

X_0	X_1	X_0	X_1	X_0	X_1
2	3	10	1.0	1	2
3	10	25	1.4	2	5
7	50	40	1.6	3	9
8	62	60	1.8	4	16
10	104	100	2.0	5	30

18. Calculate the mean and the standard deviation for each group of measures.

I	II
2	6
4	12
3	10
2	6
0	6

Transform each measure by the formula, $Y' = \sqrt{Y + .5}$, and calculate means and standard deviations for transformed values. What do these revised averages suggest about the distribution of the untransformed measures?

19. Calculate the Poisson distribution of urban racial disorders with $N = 673$, mean $= .507$. Compare expected frequencies with actual frequencies given below (Spilerman 1970).

Number of Disorders	Number of Cities with k Disorders (actual)
0	504
1	93
2	36
3	19
4	10
5	4
6	2
7	1
8	0
9	1
10	2
11	1
	673

Calculate the variance of the observed distribution. Comment on the "goodness of fit" between observed and expected distributions.

REFERENCES

Anderson, Norman
    1961   "Scales and statistics: Parametric and nonparametric." Psychological Bulletin 58: 305–316.

Bartlett, M. S.
    1936   "The square root transformation in the analysis of variance." Journal of the Royal Statistical Society, Suppl. 3: 68–78.

    1947   "The use of transformations." Biometrics 3: 39–52.

Blau, Peter M.
    1970   "A formal theory of differentiation in organizations." American Sociological Review 35: 201–218.

Boulding, Kenneth E.
    1953   "Toward a general theory of growth." The Canadian Journal of Economics and Political Science 19: 326–340.

Box, G. E. P. and D. R. Cox
    1964   "An analysis of transformations." Journal of the Royal Statistical Society, Series B 26: 211–252.

Butt, Steve T.
    1967   The Effect of Transformations on the Factor Structure of Crime Data. Master's Thesis, Department of Sociology, Indiana University.

Coleman, James S.
    1964   Introduction to Mathematical Sociology. Glencoe, Illinois: Free Press.

    1968   "The mathematical study of change." Pp. 428–478 in Hubert M. Blalock, Jr. and Ann Blalock (eds.), Methodology in Social Research. New York: McGraw-Hill.

Coleman, James S., Elihu Katz, and Herbert Menzel
    1957   "The diffusion of an innovation among physicians." Sociometry 20: 253–270.

Davis, James A. and Ann M. Jacobs
    1968   "Tabular presentation." Pp. 497–509 in The International Encyclopedia of the Social Sciences, Vol. 15. New York: Macmillan and Free Press.

DeFleur, Melvin H. and Otto N. Larsen
    1958   The Flow of Information. New York: Harper and Row.

Dodd, Stuart C.
    1955   "Diffusion is predictable: Testing probability models for laws of interaction." American Sociological Review 20: 392–401.

Eisenhart, C.
    1947   "The assumptions underlying the analysis of variance." Biometrics 3: 1–21.

Ezekiel, Mordecai and Karl A. Fox
    1959   Methods of Correlation and Regression Analysis. Third Edition. New York: John Wiley and Sons.

Feller, William
   1940 "On the logistic law of growth and its empirical verifications in biology." Acta Biotheoretica 5: 51–65.

Fisher, Ronald A.
   1946 Statistical Methods for Research Workers. Tenth Edition. Edinburgh: Oliver and Boyd.

Freeman, M. F. and J. W. Tukey
   1950 "Transformations related to the angular and the square root." Annals of Mathematical Statistics 21: 607–611.

Harman, Harry H.
   1967 Modern Factor Analysis. Second Edition. Chicago: University of Chicago Press.

Hart, Hornell
   1945 "Logistic social trends." American Journal of Sociology 50: 337–352.

Janer, J.
   1945 "Population growth in Puerto Rico and its relation to time changes in vital statistics." Human Biology 17: 267–313.

Kadane, Joseph B. and Gordon H. Lewis
   1969 "The distribution of participation in group discussion: An empirical and theoretical appraisal." American Sociological Review 34: 710–723.

Kendall, M. G. and Alan Stuart
   1966 The Advanced Theory of Statistics. Chapter 37: "The assumptions of the analysis of variance." New York: Hafner.

Kimball, Bradford F.
   1960 "On the choice of plotting positions on probability paper." Journal of the American Statistical Association 55: 546–560.

Kruskal, Joseph B.
   1968 "Statistical analysis: Transformations of data." Pp. 182–193 in International Encyclopedia of the Social Sciences, Volume 15. New York: Macmillan and Free Press.

Labowitz, Sanford
   1967 "Some observations on measurement and statistics." Social Forces 46: 151–160.

MacRae, Duncan, Jr.
   1969 "Growth and decay curves in scientific citations." American Sociological Review 34: 631–636.

Mueller, Conrad G.
   1949 "Numerical transformations in the analysis of experimental data." Psychological Bulletin 46: 198–223.

Nair, K. R.
   1954 "The fitting of growth curves." Pp. 119–132 in Oscar Kempthorne et al. (eds.), Statistics and Mathematics in Biology. Ames, Iowa: Iowa State University Press.

Olds, Edwin G., Thomas B. Mattson, and Robert E. Odeh
1956   "Notes on the use of transformations in the analysis of variance." WADC Technical Report 56–308, ASTIA Document No. AD 97208. Wright-Patterson AFB: Wright Air Development Center.

Pearl, Raymond
1924   Studies in Human Biology. Baltimore: Williams and Wilkins.

Polya, G.
1954   Mathematics and Plausible Reasoning. Vol. 2. Chapter 14: "Chance, the ever-present rival conjecture." Princeton: Princeton University Press.

Rangarajan, C. and S. Chatterjee
1969   "A note on comparison between correlation coefficients of original and transformed variables." The American Statistician 23: 28–29.

Snedecor, G. W. and W. G. Cochran
1967   Statistical Methods. Sixth Edition. Ames, Iowa: Iowa State University Press.

Spilerman, Seymour
1970   "The causes of racial disturbances: A comparison of alternative explanations." American Sociological Review 35: 627–649.

Sterling, Theodor D. and Seymour Pollack
1968   Introduction to Statistical Data Processing. Chapter 10: "Automatic search techniques." Englewood Cliffs: Prentice Hall.

Stevens, S. S.
1946   "On the theory of scales of measurement." Science 103: 677–680.

1968   "Measurement, statistics, and the schemapiric view." Science 161: 848–856.

Theil, Henri
1970   "On the estimation of relationships involving qualitative variables." American Journal of Sociology 76: 103–154. (Considers advantages of logit transformation in analyzing qualitative data.)

Thurstone, Louis L.
1947   Multiple-Factor Analysis. Chicago: University of Chicago Press.

Tukey, John W.
1957   "On the comparative anatomy of transformations." Annals of Mathematical Statistics 28: 602–632.

Walker, Helen
1951   Mathematics Essential for Elementary Statistics. Revised Edition. Chapter 17: "Logarithms." New York: Holt.

Whittaker, Lucy
1914   "On the Poisson law of simple numbers." Biometrika 10: 36–71.

Appendix

Table 1 Areas of the Normal Curve*

$\dfrac{x}{\sigma}$	.00	.01	.02	.03	.04	.05	.06	.07	.08	.09
0.0	.0000	.0040	.0080	.0120	.0159	.0199	.0239	.0279	.0319	.0359
0.1	.0398	.0438	.0478	.0517	.0557	.0596	.0636	.0675	.0714	.0753
0.2	.0793	.0832	.0871	.0910	.0948	.0987	.1026	.1064	.1103	.1141
0.3	.1179	.1217	.1255	.1293	.1331	.1368	.1406	.1443	.1480	.1517
0.4	.1554	.1591	.1628	.1664	.1700	.1736	.1772	.1808	.1844	.1879
0.5	.1915	.1950	.1985	.2019	.2054	.2088	.2123	.2157	.2190	.2224
0.6	.2257	.2291	.2324	.2357	.2389	.2422	.2454	.2486	.2518	.2549
0.7	.2580	.2612	.2642	.2673	.2704	.2734	.2764	.2794	.2823	.2852
0.8	.2881	.2910	.2939	.2967	.2995	.3023	.3051	.3078	.3106	.3133
0.9	.3159	.3186	.3212	.3238	.3264	.3289	.3315	.3340	.3365	.3389
1.0	.3413	.3438	.3461	.3485	.3508	.3531	.3554	.3577	.3599	.3621
1.1	.3643	.3665	.3686	.3718	.3729	.3749	.3770	.3790	.3810	.3830
1.2	.3849	.3869	.3888	.3907	.3925	.3944	.3962	.3980	.3997	.4015
1.3	.4032	.4049	.4066	.4083	.4099	.4115	.4131	.4147	.4162	.4177
1.4	.4192	.4207	.4222	.4236	.4251	.4265	.4279	.4292	.4306	.4319
1.5	.4332	.4345	.4357	.4370	.4382	.4394	.4406	.4418	.4430	.4441
1.6	.4452	.4463	.4474	.4485	.4495	.4505	.4515	.4525	.4535	.4545
1.7	.4554	.4564	.4573	.4582	.4591	.4599	.4608	.4616	.4625	.4633
1.8	.4641	.4649	.4656	.4664	.4671	.4678	.4686	.4693	.4699	.4706
1.9	.4713	.4719	.4726	.4732	.4738	.4744	.4750	.4758	.4762	.4767
2.0	.4772	.4778	.4783	.4788	.4793	.4798	.4803	.4808	.4812	.4817
2.1	.4821	.4826	.4830	.4834	.4838	.4842	.4846	.4850	.4854	.4857
2.2	.4861	.4865	.4868	.4871	.4875	.4878	.4881	.4884	.4887	.4890
2.3	.4893	.4896	.4898	.4901	.4904	.4906	.4909	.4911	.4913	.4916
2.4	.4918	.4920	.4922	.4925	.4927	.4929	.4931	.4932	.4934	.4936
2.5	.4938	.4940	.4941	.4943	.4945	.4946	.4948	.4949	.4951	.4952
2.6	.4953	.4955	.4956	.4957	.4959	.4960	.4961	.4962	.4963	.4964
2.7	.4965	.4966	.4967	.4968	.4969	.4970	.4971	.4972	.4973	.4974
2.8	.4974	.4975	.4976	.4977	.4977	.4978	.4979	.4980	.4980	.4981
2.9	.4981	.4982	.4983	.4984	.4984	.4984	.4985	.4985	.4986	.4986
3.0	.49865	.4987	.4987	.4988	.4988	.4988	.4989	.4989	.4989	.4990
3.1	.49903	.4991	.4991	.4991	.4992	.4992	.4992	.4992	.4993	.4993
4.0	.49997									

* Source: Herbert Arkin and Raymond R. Colton, *Tables for Statisticians*. New York: Barnes and Noble, 1950, p. 114, Table 10. Reprinted by permission.

Table 2   *Ordinates of the Normal Curve**

$\dfrac{x}{\sigma}$	.00	.01	.02	.03	.04	.05	.06	.07	.08	.09
0.0	1.00000	.99995	.99980	.99955	.99920	.99875	.99820	.99755	.99685	.99596
0.1	.99501	.99396	.99283	.99158	.99025	.98881	.98728	.98565	.98393	.98211
0.2	.98020	.97819	.97609	.97390	.97161	.96923	.96676	.96420	.96156	.95882
0.3	.95600	.95309	.95010	.94702	.94387	.94055	.93723	.93382	.93024	.92677
0.4	.92312	.91799	.91558	.91169	.90774	.90371	.89961	.89543	.89119	.88688
0.5	.88250	.87805	.87353	.86896	.86432	.85962	.85488	.85006	.84519	.84060
0.6	.83527	.83023	.82514	.82010	.81481	.80957	.80429	.79896	.79459	.78817
0.7	.78270	.77721	.77167	.76610	.76048	.75484	.74916	.74342	.73769	.73193
0.8	.72615	.72033	.71448	.70861	.70272	.69681	.69087	.68493	.67896	.67298
0.9	.66689	.66097	.65494	.64891	.64287	.63683	.63077	.62472	.61865	.61259
1.0	.60653	.60047	.59440	.58834	.58228	.57623	.57017	.56414	.55810	.55209
1.1	.54607	.54007	.53409	.52812	.52214	.51620	.51027	.50437	.49848	.49260
1.2	.48675	.48092	.47511	.46933	.46357	.45793	.45212	.44644	.44078	.43516
1.3	.42956	.42399	.41845	.41294	.40747	.40202	.39661	.39123	.38569	.38058
1.4	.37531	.37007	.36487	.35971	.35459	.34950	.34445	.33944	.33447	.32954
1.5	.32465	.31980	.31500	.31023	.30550	.30082	.29618	.29158	.28702	.28251
1.6	.27804	.27361	.26923	.26489	.26059	.25634	.25213	.24797	.24385	.23978
1.7	.23575	.23176	.22782	.22392	.22008	.21627	.21251	.20879	.20511	.20148
1.8	.19790	.19436	.19086	.18741	.18400	.18064	.17732	.17404	.17081	.16762
1.9	.16448	.16137	.15831	.15530	.15232	.14939	.14650	.14364	.14083	.13806
2.0	.13534	.13265	.13000	.12740	.12483	.12230	.11981	.11737	.11496	.11259
2.1	.11025	.10795	.10570	.10347	.10129	.09914	.09702	.09495	.09290	.09090
2.2	.08892	.08698	.08507	.08320	.08136	.07956	.07778	.07604	.07433	.07265
2.3	.07100	.06939	.06780	.06624	.06471	.06321	.06174	.06029	.05888	.05750
2.4	.05614	.05481	.05350	.05222	.05096	.04973	.04852	.04737	.04618	.04505
2.5	.04394	.04285	.04179	.04074	.03972	.03873	.03775	.03680	.03586	.03494
2.6	.03405	.03317	.03232	.03148	.03066	.02986	.02908	.02831	.02757	.02684
2.7	.02612	.02542	.02474	.02408	.02343	.02280	.02218	.02157	.02098	.02040
2.8	.01984	.01929	.01876	.01823	.01772	.01723	.01674	.01627	.01581	.01536
2.9	.01492	.01449	.01408	.01367	.01328	.01288	.01252	.01215	.01179	.01145
3.0	.01111									
4.0	.00034									

* Source: Herbert Arkin and Raymond R. Colton, *Tables for Statisticians.* New York: Barnes and Noble, 1950, p. 115, Table 11. Reprinted by permission.

Table 3 *Percentile Values of the Unit Normal Curve**

p	0	1	2	3	4	5	6	7	8	9
.99	2.326	2.366	2.409	2.457	2.512	2.576	2.652	2.748	2.878	3.080
.98	2.054	2.075	2.097	2.120	2.144	2.170	2.197	2.226	2.257	2.290
.97	1.881	1.896	1.911	1.927	1.943	1.960	1.977	1.995	2.014	2.034
.96	1.751	1.762	1.774	1.787	1.799	1.812	1.825	1.838	1.852	1.866
.95	1.645	1.655	1.665	1.675	1.685	1.695	1.706	1.717	1.728	1.739
.94	1.555	1.563	1.572	1.580	1.589	1.598	1.607	1.616	1.626	1.635
.93	1.476	1.483	1.491	1.499	1.506	1.514	1.522	1.530	1.538	1.546
.92	1.405	1.412	1.419	1.426	1.433	1.440	1.447	1.454	1.461	1.468
.91	1.341	1.347	1.353	1.359	1.366	1.372	1.379	1.385	1.392	1.398
.90	1.282	1.287	1.293	1.299	1.305	1.311	1.317	1.323	1.329	1.335
.89	1.227	1.232	1.237	1.243	1.248	1.254	1.259	1.265	1.270	1.276
.88	1.175	1.180	1.185	1.190	1.195	1.200	1.206	1.211	1.216	1.221
.87	1.126	1.131	1.136	1.141	1.146	1.150	1.155	1.160	1.165	1.170
.86	1.080	1.085	1.089	1.094	1.098	1.103	1.108	1.112	1.117	1.122
.85	1.036	1.041	1.045	1.049	1.054	1.058	1.063	1.067	1.071	1.076
.84	.994	.999	1.003	1.007	1.011	1.015	1.019	1.024	1.028	1.032
.83	.954	.958	.962	.966	.970	.974	.978	.982	.986	.990
.82	.915	.919	.923	.927	.931	.935	.938	.942	.946	.950
.81	.878	.882	.885	.889	.893	.896	.900	.904	.908	.912
.80	.842	.845	.849	.852	.856	.860	.863	.867	.871	.874
.79	.806	.810	.813	.817	.820	.824	.827	.831	.834	.838
.78	.772	.776	.779	.782	.786	.789	.793	.796	.800	.803
.77	.739	.742	.745	.749	.752	.755	.759	.762	.765	.769
.76	.706	.710	.713	.716	.719	.722	.726	.729	.732	.736
.75	.674	.678	.681	.684	.687	.690	.693	.697	.700	.703
.74	.643	.646	.650	.653	.656	.659	.662	.665	.668	.671
.73	.613	.616	.619	.622	.625	.628	.631	.634	.637	.640
.72	.583	.586	.589	.592	.595	.598	.601	.604	.607	.610
.71	.553	.556	.559	.562	.565	.568	.571	.574	.577	.580
.70	.524	.527	.530	.533	.536	.539	.542	.545	.548	.550
.69	.496	.499	.502	.504	.507	.510	.513	.516	.519	.522
.68	.468	.470	.473	.476	.479	.482	.485	.487	.490	.493
.67	.440	.443	.445	.448	.451	.454	.457	.459	.462	.465
.66	.412	.415	.418	.421	.423	.426	.429	.432	.434	.437
.65	.385	.388	.391	.393	.396	.399	.420	.404	.407	.410
.64	.358	.361	.364	.366	.369	.372	.375	.377	.380	.383
.63	.332	.335	.337	.340	.342	.345	.348	.350	.353	.356
.62	.305	.308	.311	.313	.316	.319	.321	.324	.327	.329
.61	.279	.282	.285	.287	.290	.292	.295	.298	.300	.303
.60	.253	.256	.259	.261	.264	.266	.269	.272	.274	.277
.59	.228	.230	.233	.235	.238	.240	.243	.246	.248	.251
.58	.202	.204	.207	.210	.212	.215	.217	.220	.222	.225
.57	.176	.179	.181	.184	.187	.189	.192	.194	.197	.199
.56	.151	.154	.156	.159	.161	.164	.166	.169	.171	.174
.55	.126	.128	.131	.133	.136	.138	.141	.143	.146	.148
.54	.100	.103	.105	.108	.111	.113	.116	.118	.121	.123
.53	.075	.078	.080	.083	.085	.088	.090	.093	.095	.098
.52	.050	.053	.055	.058	.060	.063	.065	.068	.070	.073
.51	.025	.028	.030	.033	.035	.038	.040	.043	.045	.048
.50	.000	.003	.005	.008	.010	.013	.015	.018	.020	.023

*Source: *Techniques of Attitude Scale Construction* by Allen L. Edwards. Copyright © 1957. Reprinted by permission of Appleton-Century-Crofts, Educational Division, Meredith Corporation.

Table 3   *Percentile Values of the Unit Normal Curve (Continued)*

p	0	1	2	3	4	5	6	7	8	9
.49	− .025	− .023	− .020	− .018	− .015	− .013	− .010	− .008	− .005	− .003
.48	− .050	− .048	− .045	− .043	− .040	− .038	− .035	− .033	− .030	− .028
.47	− .075	− .073	− .070	− .068	− .065	− .063	− .060	− .058	− .055	− .053
.46	− .100	− .098	− .095	− .093	− .090	− .088	− .085	− .083	− .080	− .078
.45	− .126	− .123	− .121	− .118	− .116	− .113	− .111	− .108	− .105	− .103
.44	− .151	− .148	− .146	− .143	− .141	− .138	− .136	− .133	− .131	− .128
.43	− .176	− .174	− .171	− .169	− .166	− .164	− .161	− .159	− .156	− .154
.42	− .202	− .199	− .197	− .194	− .192	− .189	− .187	− .184	− .181	− .179
.41	− .228	− .225	− .222	− .220	− .217	− .215	− .212	− .210	− .207	− .204
.40	− .253	− .251	− .248	− .246	− .243	− .240	− .238	− .235	− .233	− .230
.39	− .279	− .277	− .274	− .272	− .269	− .266	− .264	− .261	− .259	− .256
.38	− .305	− .303	− .300	− .298	− .295	− .292	− .290	− .287	− .285	− .282
.37	− .332	− .329	− .327	− .324	− .321	− .319	− .316	− .313	− .311	− .308
.36	− .358	− .356	− .353	− .350	− .348	− .345	− .342	− .340	− .337	− .335
.35	− .385	− .383	− .380	− .377	− .375	− .372	− .369	− .366	− .364	− .361
.34	− .412	− .410	− .407	− .404	− .402	− .399	− .396	− .393	− .391	− .388
.33	− .440	− .437	− .434	− .432	− .429	− .426	− .423	− .421	− .418	− .415
.32	− .468	− .465	− .462	− .459	− .457	− .454	− .451	− .448	− .445	− .443
.31	− .496	− .493	− .490	− .487	− .485	− .482	− .479	− .476	− .473	− .470
.30	− .524	− .522	− .519	− .516	− .513	− .510	− .507	− .504	− .502	− .499
.29	− .553	− .550	− .548	− .545	− .542	− .539	− .536	− .533	− .530	− .527
.28	− .583	− .580	− .577	− .574	− .571	− .568	− .565	− .562	− .559	− .556
.27	− .613	− .610	− .607	− .604	− .601	− .598	− .595	− .592	− .589	− .586
.26	− .643	− .640	− .637	− .634	− .631	− .628	− .625	− .622	− .619	− .616
.25	− .674	− .671	− .668	− .665	− .662	− .659	− .656	− .653	− .650	− .646
.24	− .706	− .703	− .700	− .697	− .693	− .690	− .687	− .684	− .681	− .678
.23	− .739	− .736	− .732	− .729	− .726	− .722	− .719	− .716	− .713	− .710
.22	− .772	− .769	− .765	− .762	− .759	− .755	− .752	− .749	− .745	− .742
.21	− .806	− .803	− .800	− .796	− .793	− .789	− .786	− .782	− .779	− .776
.20	− .842	− .838	− .834	− .831	− .827	− .824	− .820	− .817	− .813	− .810
.19	− .878	− .874	− .871	− .867	− .863	− .860	− .856	− .852	− .849	− .845
.18	− .915	− .912	− .908	− .904	− .900	− .896	− .893	− .889	− .885	− .882
.17	− .954	− .950	− .946	− .942	− .938	− .935	− .931	− .927	− .923	− .919
.16	− .994	− .990	− .986	− .982	− .978	− .974	− .970	− .966	− .962	− .958
.15	−1.036	−1.032	−1.028	−1.024	−1.019	−1.015	−1.011	−1.007	−1.003	− .999
.14	−1.080	−1.076	−1.071	−1.067	−1.063	−1.058	−1.054	−1.049	−1.045	−1.041
.13	−1.126	−1.122	−1.117	−1.112	−1.108	−1.103	−1.098	−1.094	−1.089	−1.085
.12	−1.175	−1.170	−1.165	−1.160	−1.155	−1.150	−1.146	−1.141	−1.136	−1.131
.11	−1.227	−1.221	−1.216	−1.211	−1.206	−1.200	−1.195	−1.190	−1.185	−1.180
.10	−1.282	−1.276	−1.270	−1.265	−1.259	−1.254	−1.248	−1.243	−1.237	−1.232
.09	−1.341	−1.335	−1.329	−1.323	−1.317	−1.311	−1.305	−1.299	−1.293	−1.287
.08	−1.405	−1.398	−1.392	−1.385	−1.379	−1.372	−1.366	−1.359	−1.353	−1.347
.07	−1.476	−1.468	−1.461	−1.454	−1.447	−1.440	−1.433	−1.426	−1.419	−1.412
.06	−1.555	−1.546	−1.538	−1.530	−1.522	−1.514	−1.506	−1.499	−1.491	−1.483
.05	−1.645	−1.635	−1.626	−1.616	−1.607	−1.598	−1.589	−1.580	−1.572	−1.563
.04	−1.751	−1.739	−1.728	−1.717	−1.706	−1.695	−1.685	−1.675	−1.665	−1.655
.03	−1.881	−1.866	−1.852	−1.838	−1.825	−1.812	−1.799	−1.787	−1.774	−1.762
.02	−2.054	−2.034	−2.014	−1.995	−1.977	−1.960	−1.943	−1.927	−1.911	−1.896
.01	−2.326	−2.290	−2.257	−2.226	−2.197	−2.170	−2.144	−2.120	−2.097	−2.075
.00		−3.090	−2.878	−2.748	−2.652	−2.576	−2.512	−2.457	−2.409	−2.366

Table 4   *Distribution of t**

df	Level of significance for one-tailed test					
	.10	.05	.025	.01	.005	.0005
	Level of significance for two-tailed test					
	.20	.10	.05	.02	.01	.001
1	3.078	6.314	12.706	31.821	63.657	636.619
2	1.886	2.920	4.303	6.965	9.925	31.598
3	1.638	2.353	3.182	4.541	5.841	12.941
4	1.533	2.132	2.776	3.747	4.604	8.610
5	1.476	2.015	2.571	3.365	4.032	6.859
6	1.440	1.943	2.447	3.143	3.707	5.959
7	1.415	1.895	2.365	2.998	3.499	5.405
8	1.397	1.860	2.306	2.896	3.355	5.041
9	1.383	1.833	2.262	2.821	3.250	4.781
10	1.372	1.812	2.228	2.764	3.169	4.587
11	1.363	1.796	2.201	2.718	3.106	4.437
12	1.356	1.782	2.179	2.681	3.055	4.318
13	1.350	1.771	2.160	2.650	3.012	4.221
14	1.345	1.761	2.145	2.624	2.977	4.140
15	1.341	1.753	2.131	2.602	2.947	4.073
16	1.337	1.746	2.120	2.583	2.921	4.015
17	1.333	1.740	2.110	2.567	2.898	3.965
18	1.330	1.734	2.101	2.552	2.878	3.922
19	1.328	1.729	2.093	2.539	2.861	3.883
20	1.325	1.725	2.086	2.528	2.845	3.850
21	1.323	1.721	2.080	2.518	2.831	3.819
22	1.321	1.717	2.074	2.508	2.819	3.792
23	1.319	1.714	2.069	2.500	2.807	3.767
24	1.318	1.711	2.064	2.492	2.797	3.745
25	1.316	1.708	2.060	2.485	2.787	3.725
26	1.315	1.706	2.056	2.479	2.779	3.707
27	1.314	1.703	2.052	2.473	2.771	3.690
28	1.313	1.701	2.048	2.467	2.763	3.674
29	1.311	1.699	2.045	2.462	2.756	3.659
30	1.310	1.697	2.042	2.457	2.750	3.646
40	1.303	1.684	2.021	2.423	2.704	3.551
60	1.296	1.671	2.000	2.390	2.660	3.460
120	1.289	1.658	1.980	2.358	2.617	3.373
∞	1.282	1.645	1.960	2.326	2.576	3.291

* Source: Abridged from Table III of R. A. Fisher and F. Yates, *Statistical Tables for Biological, Agricultural and Medical Research* (1948 ed.). Edinburgh and London: Oliver & Boyd, Ltd., by permission of the authors and publishers.

Table 5   *Values of* χ^2*

df	$P = .99$	.98	.95	.90	.80	.70	.50
1	.000157	.000628	.00393	.0158	.0642	.148	.455
2	.0201	.0404	.103	.211	.446	.713	1.386
3	.115	.185	.352	.584	1.005	1.424	2.366
4	.297	.429	.711	1.064	1.649	2.195	3.357
5	.554	.752	1.145	1.610	2.343	3.000	4.351
6	.872	1.134	1.635	2.204	3.070	3.828	5.348
7	1.239	1.564	2.167	2.833	3.822	4.671	6.346
8	1.646	2.032	2.733	3.490	4.594	5.527	7.344
9	2.088	2.532	3.325	4.168	5.380	6.393	8.343
10	2.558	3.059	3.940	4.865	6.179	7.267	9.342
11	3.053	3.609	4.575	5.578	6.989	8.148	10.341
12	3.571	4.178	5.226	6.304	7.807	9.034	11.340
13	4.107	4.765	5.892	7.042	8.634	9.926	12.340
14	4.660	5.368	6.571	7.790	9.467	10.821	13.339
15	5.229	5.985	7.261	8.547	10.307	11.721	14.339
16	5.812	6.614	7.962	9.312	11.152	12.624	15.338
17	6.408	7.255	8.672	10.085	12.002	13.531	16.338
18	7.015	7.906	9.390	10.865	12.857	14.440	17.338
19	7.633	8.567	10.117	11.651	13.716	15.352	18.338
20	8.260	9.237	10.851	12.443	14.578	16.266	19.337
21	8.897	9.915	11.591	13.240	15.445	17.182	20.337
22	9.542	10.600	12.338	14.041	16.314	18.101	21.337
23	10.196	11.293	13.091	14.848	17.187	19.021	22.337
24	10.856	11.992	13.848	15.659	18.062	19.943	23.337
25	11.524	12.697	14.611	16.473	18.940	20.867	24.337
26	12.198	13.409	15.379	17.292	19.820	21.792	25.336
27	12.879	14.125	16.151	18.114	20.703	22.719	26.336
28	13.565	14.847	16.928	18.939	21.588	23.647	27.336
29	14.256	15.574	17.708	19.768	22.475	24.577	28.336
30	14.953	16.306	18.493	20.599	23.364	25.508	29.336

* Source: Reprinted from Table IV of R. A. Fisher and F. Yates, *Statistical Tables for Biological, Agricultural, and Medical Research*. Edinburgh: Oliver & Boyd Ltd., by permission of the authors and publishers.

Table 5 Values of χ^2 (Continued)

df	P = .30	.20	.10	.05	.02	.01	.001
1	1.074	1.642	2.706	3.841	5.412	6.635	10.827
2	2.408	3.219	4.605	5.991	7.824	9.210	13.815
3	3.665	4.642	6.251	7.815	9.837	11.345	16.268
4	4.878	5.989	7.779	9.488	11.668	13.277	18.465
5	6.064	7.289	9.236	11.070	13.388	15.086	20.517
6	7.231	8.558	10.645	12.592	15.033	16.812	22.457
7	8.383	9.803	12.017	14.067	16.622	18.475	24.322
8	9.524	11.030	13.362	15.507	18.168	20.090	26.125
9	10.656	12.242	14.684	16.919	19.679	21.666	27.877
10	11.781	13.442	15.987	18.307	21.161	23.209	29.588
11	12.899	14.631	17.275	19.675	22.618	24.725	31.264
12	14.011	15.812	18.549	21.026	24.054	26.217	32.909
13	15.119	16.985	19.812	22.362	25.472	27.688	34.528
14	16.222	18.151	21.064	23.685	26.873	29.141	36.123
15	17.322	19.311	22.307	24.996	28.259	30.578	37.697
16	18.418	20.465	23.542	26.296	29.633	32.000	39.252
17	19.511	21.615	24.769	27.587	30.995	33.409	40.790
18	20.601	22.760	25.989	28.869	32.346	34.805	42.312
19	21.689	23.900	27.204	30.144	33.687	36.191	43.820
20	22.775	25.038	28.412	31.410	35.020	37.566	45.315
21	23.858	26.171	29.615	32.671	36.343	38.932	46.797
22	24.939	27.301	30.813	33.924	37.659	40.289	48.268
23	26.018	28.429	32.007	35.172	38.968	41.638	49.728
24	27.096	29.553	33.196	36.415	40.270	42.980	51.179
25	28.172	30.675	34.382	37.652	41.566	44.314	52.620
26	29.246	31.795	35.563	38.885	42.856	45.642	54.052
27	30.319	32.912	36.741	40.113	44.140	46.963	55.476
28	31.391	34.027	37.916	41.337	45.419	48.278	56.893
29	32.461	35.139	39.087	42.557	46.693	49.588	58.302
30	33.530	36.250	40.256	43.773	47.962	50.892	59.703

For larger values of df, the expression $\sqrt{2\chi^2} - \sqrt{2df - 1}$ may be used as a normal deviate with unit variance, remembering that the probability of χ^2 corresponds with that of a single tail of the normal curve.

Table 6 *Variance Ratio**
10% Points

n_2	n_1									
	1	2	3	4	5	6	8	12	24	∞
1	39.86	49.50	53.59	55.83	57.24	58.20	59.44	60.70	62.00	63.33
2	8.53	9.00	9.16	9.24	9.29	9.33	9.37	9.41	9.45	9.49
3	5.54	5.46	5.39	5.34	5.31	5.28	5.25	5.22	5.18	5.13
4	4.54	4.32	4.19	4.11	4.05	4.01	3.95	3.90	3.83	3.76
5	4.06	3.78	3.62	3.52	3.45	3.40	3.34	3.27	3.19	3.10
6	3.78	3.46	3.29	3.18	3.11	3.05	2.98	2.90	2.82	2.72
7	3.59	3.26	3.07	2.96	2.88	2.83	2.75	2.67	2.58	2.47
8	3.46	3.11	2.92	2.81	2.73	2.67	2.59	2.50	2.40	2.29
9	3.36	3.01	2.18	2.69	2.61	2.55	2.47	2.38	2.28	2.16
10	3.28	2.92	2.73	2.61	2.52	2.46	2.38	2.28	2.18	2.06
11	3.23	2.86	2.66	2.54	2.45	2.39	2.30	2.21	2.10	1.97
12	3.18	2.81	2.61	2.48	2.39	2.33	2.24	2.15	2.04	1.90
13	3.14	2.76	2.56	2.43	2.35	2.28	2.20	2.10	1.98	1.85
14	3.10	2.73	2.52	2.39	2.31	2.24	2.15	2.05	1.94	1.80
15	3.07	2.70	2.49	2.36	2.27	2.21	2.12	2.02	1.90	1.76
16	3.05	2.67	2.46	2.33	2.24	2.18	2.09	1.99	1.87	1.72
17	3.03	2.64	2.44	2.31	2.22	2.15	2.06	1.96	1.84	1.69
18	3.01	2.62	2.42	2.29	2.20	2.13	2.04	1.93	1.81	1.66
19	2.99	2.61	2.40	2.27	2.18	2.11	2.02	1.91	1.79	1.63
20	2.97	2.59	2.38	2.25	2.16	2.09	2.00	1.89	1.77	1.61
21	2.96	2.57	2.36	2.23	2.14	2.08	1.98	1.88	1.75	1.59
22	2.95	2.56	2.35	2.22	2.13	2.06	1.97	1.86	1.73	1.57
23	2.94	2.55	2.34	2.21	2.11	2.05	1.95	1.84	1.72	1.55
24	2.93	2.54	2.33	2.19	2.10	2.04	1.94	1.83	1.70	1.53
25	2.92	2.53	2.32	2.18	2.09	2.02	1.93	1.82	1.69	1.52
26	2.91	2.52	2.31	2.17	2.08	2.01	1.92	1.81	1.68	1.50
27	2.90	2.51	2.30	2.17	2.07	2.00	1.91	1.80	1.67	1.49
28	2.89	2.50	2.29	2.16	2.06	2.00	1.90	1.79	1.66	1.48
29	2.89	2.50	2.28	2.15	2.06	1.99	1.89	1.78	1.65	1.47
30	2.88	2.49	2.28	2.14	2.05	1.98	1.88	1.77	1.64	1.46
40	2.84	2.44	2.23	2.09	2.00	1.93	1.83	1.71	1.57	1.38
60	2.79	2.39	2.18	2.04	1.95	1.87	1.77	1.66	1.51	1.29
120	2.75	2.35	2.13	1.99	1.90	1.82	1.72	1.60	1.45	1.19
∞	2.71	2.30	2.08	1.94	1.85	1.77	1.67	1.55	1.38	1.00

Lower 10% points are found by interchange of n_1 and n_2; i.e., n_1 must always correspond with the greater mean square.

*Table 6 is reprinted from Table V of Fisher and Yates: *Statistical Tables for Biological, Agricultural, and Medical Research*, Oliver and Boyd Ltd., Edinburgh, by permission of the authors and publishers.

Table 6 *Variance Ratio (Continued)*
5% Points

n_2	n_1									
	1	2	3	4	5	6	8	12	24	∞
1	161.4	199.5	215.7	224.6	230.2	234.0	238.9	243.9	249.0	254.3
2	18.51	19.00	19.16	19.25	19.30	19.33	19.37	19.41	19.45	19.50
3	10.13	9.55	9.28	9.12	9.01	8.94	8.84	8.74	8.64	8.53
4	7.71	6.94	6.59	6.39	6.26	6.16	6.04	5.91	5.77	5.63
5	6.61	5.79	5.41	5.19	5.05	4.95	4.82	4.68	4.53	4.36
6	5.99	5.14	4.76	4.53	4.39	4.28	4.15	4.00	3.84	3.67
7	5.59	4.74	4.35	4.12	3.97	3.87	3.73	3.57	3.41	3.23
8	5.32	4.46	4.07	3.84	3.69	3.58	3.44	3.28	3.12	2.93
9	5.12	4.26	3.86	3.63	3.48	3.37	3.23	3.07	2.90	2.71
10	4.96	4.10	3.71	3.48	3.33	3.22	3.07	2.91	2.74	2.54
11	4.84	3.98	3.59	3.36	3.20	3.09	2.95	2.79	2.61	2.40
12	4.75	3.88	3.49	3.26	3.11	3.00	2.85	2.69	2.50	2.30
13	4.67	3.80	3.41	3.18	3.02	2.92	2.77	2.60	2.42	2.21
14	4.60	3.74	3.34	3.11	2.96	2.85	2.70	2.53	2.35	2.13
15	4.54	3.68	3.29	3.06	2.90	2.79	2.64	2.48	2.29	2.07
16	4.49	3.63	3.24	3.01	2.85	2.74	2.59	2.42	2.24	2.01
17	4.45	3.59	3.20	2.96	2.81	2.70	2.55	2.38	2.19	1.96
18	4.41	3.55	3.16	2.93	2.77	2.66	2.51	2.34	2.15	1.92
19	4.38	3.52	3.13	2.90	2.74	2.63	2.48	2.31	2.11	1.88
20	4.35	3.49	3.10	2.87	2.71	2.60	2.45	2.28	2.08	1.84
21	4.32	3.47	3.07	2.84	2.68	2.57	2.42	2.25	2.05	1.81
22	4.30	3.44	3.05	2.82	2.66	2.55	2.40	2.23	2.03	1.78
23	4.28	3.42	3.03	2.80	2.64	2.53	2.38	2.20	2.00	1.76
24	4.26	3.40	3.01	2.78	2.62	2.51	2.36	2.18	1.98	1.73
25	4.24	3.38	2.99	2.76	2.60	2.49	2.34	2.16	1.96	1.71
26	4.22	3.37	2.98	2.74	2.59	2.47	2.32	2.15	1.95	1.69
27	4.21	3.35	2.96	2.73	2.57	2.46	2.30	2.13	1.93	1.67
28	4.20	3.34	2.95	2.71	2.56	2.44	2.29	2.12	1.91	1.65
29	4.18	3.33	2.93	2.70	2.54	2.43	2.28	2.10	1.90	1.64
30	4.17	3.32	2.92	2.69	2.53	2.42	2.27	2.09	1.89	1.62
40	4.08	3.23	2.84	2.61	2.45	2.34	2.18	2.00	1.79	1.51
60	4.00	3.15	2.76	2.52	2.37	2.25	2.10	1.92	1.70	1.39
120	3.92	3.07	2.68	2.45	2.29	2.17	2.02	1.83	1.61	1.25
∞	3.84	2.99	2.60	2.37	2.21	2.09	1.94	1.75	1.52	1.00

Lower 5% points are found by interchange of n_1 and n_2: i.e., n_1 must always correspond with the greater mean square.

Table 6 *Variance Ratio* (*Continued*)
1% Points

n_2	n_1									
	1	2	3	4	5	6	8	12	24	∞
1	4052	4999	5403	5625	5764	5859	5981	6106	6234	6366
2	98.49	99.01	99.17	99.25	99.30	99.33	99.36	99.42	99.46	99.50
3	34.12	30.81	29.46	28.71	28.24	27.91	27.49	27.05	26.60	26.12
4	21.20	18.00	16.69	15.98	15.52	15.21	14.80	14.37	13.93	13.46
5	16.26	13.27	12.06	11.39	10.97	10.67	10.27	9.89	9.47	9.02
6	13.74	10.92	9.78	9.15	8.75	8.47	8.10	7.72	7.31	6.88
7	12.25	9.55	8.45	7.85	7.46	7.19	6.84	6.47	6.07	5.65
8	11.26	8.65	7.59	7.01	6.63	6.37	6.03	5.67	5.28	4.86
9	10.56	8.02	6.99	6.42	6.06	5.80	5.47	5.11	4.73	4.31
10	10.04	7.56	6.55	5.99	5.64	5.39	5.06	4.71	4.33	3.91
11	9.65	7.20	6.22	5.67	5.32	5.07	4.74	4.40	4.02	3.60
12	9.33	6.93	5.95	5.41	5.06	4.82	4.50	4.16	3.78	3.36
13	9.07	6.70	5.74	5.20	4.86	4.62	4.30	3.96	3.59	3.16
14	8.86	6.51	5.56	5.03	4.69	4.46	4.14	3.80	3.43	3.00
15	8.68	6.36	5.42	4.89	4.56	4.32	4.00	3.67	3.29	2.87
16	8.53	6.23	5.29	4.77	4.44	4.20	3.89	3.55	3.18	2.75
17	8.40	6.11	5.18	4.67	4.34	4.10	3.79	3.45	3.08	2.65
18	8.28	6.01	5.09	4.58	4.25	4.01	3.71	3.37	3.00	2.57
19	8.18	5.93	5.01	4.50	4.17	3.94	3.63	3.30	2.92	2.49
20	8.10	5.85	4.94	4.43	4.10	3.87	3.56	3.23	2.86	2.42
21	8.02	5.78	4.87	4.37	4.04	3.81	3.51	3.17	2.80	2.36
22	7.94	5.72	4.82	4.31	3.99	3.76	3.45	3.12	2.75	2.31
23	7.88	5.66	4.76	4.26	3.94	3.71	3.41	3.07	2.70	2.26
24	7.82	5.61	4.72	4.22	3.90	3.67	3.36	3.03	2.66	2.21
25	7.77	5.57	4.68	4.18	3.86	3.63	3.32	2.99	2.62	2.17
26	7.72	5.53	4.64	4.14	3.82	3.59	3.29	2.96	2.58	2.13
27	7.68	5.49	4.60	4.11	3.78	3.56	3.26	2.93	2.55	2.10
28	7.64	5.45	4.57	4.07	3.75	3.53	3.23	2.90	2.52	2.06
29	7.60	5.42	4.54	4.04	3.73	3.50	3.20	2.87	2.49	2.03
30	7.56	5.39	4.51	4.02	3.70	3.47	3.17	2.84	2.47	2.01
40	7.31	5.18	4.31	3.83	3.51	3.29	2.99	2.66	2.29	1.80
60	7.08	4.98	4.13	3.65	3.34	3.12	2.82	2.50	2.12	1.60
120	6.85	4.79	3.95	3.48	3.17	2.96	2.66	2.34	1.95	1.38
∞	6.64	4.60	3.78	3.32	3.02	2.80	2.51	2.18	1.79	1.00

Lower 1% points are found by interchange of n_1 and n_2: i.e., n_1 must always correspond with the greater mean square.

Table 7 Table of 5% and 1% Points for r and R*

Degrees of Freedom	Number of Variables				Degrees of Freedom	Number of Variables			
	2	3	4	5		2	3	4	5
1	.997	.999	.999	.999	24	.388	.470	.523	.562
	1.000	**1.000**	**1.000**	**1.000**		**.496**	**.565**	**.609**	**.642**
2	.950	.975	.983	.987	25	.381	.462	.514	.553
	.990	**.995**	**.997**	**.998**		**.487**	**.555**	**.600**	**.633**
3	.878	.930	.950	.961	26	.374	.454	.506	.545
	.959	**.976**	**.983**	**.987**		**.478**	**.546**	**.590**	**.624**
4	.811	.881	.912	.930	27	.367	.446	.498	.536
	.917	**.949**	**.962**	**.970**		**.470**	**.538**	**.582**	**.615**
5	.754	.836	.874	.898	28	.361	.439	.490	.529
	.874	**.917**	**.937**	**.949**		**.463**	**.530**	**.573**	**.606**
6	.707	.795	.839	.867	29	.355	.432	.482	.521
	.834	**.886**	**.911**	**.927**		**.456**	**.522**	**.565**	**.598**
7	.666	.758	.807	.838	30	.349	.426	.476	.514
	.798	**.855**	**.885**	**.904**		**.449**	**.514**	**.558**	**.591**
8	.632	.726	.777	.811	35	.325	.397	.445	.482
	.765	**.827**	**.860**	**.882**		**.418**	**.481**	**.523**	**.556**
9	.602	.697	.750	.786	40	.304	.373	.419	.455
	.735	**.800**	**.836**	**.861**		**.393**	**.454**	**.494**	**.526**
10	.576	.671	.726	.763	45	.288	.353	.397	.432
	.708	**.776**	**.814**	**.840**		**.372**	**.430**	**.470**	**.501**
11	.553	.648	.703	.741	50	.273	.336	.379	.412
	.684	**.753**	**.793**	**.821**		**.354**	**.410**	**.449**	**.479**
12	.532	.627	.683	.722	60	.250	.308	.348	.380
	.661	**.732**	**.773**	**.802**		**.325**	**.377**	**.414**	**.442**
13	.514	.608	.664	.703	70	.232	.286	.324	.354
	.641	**.712**	**.755**	**.785**		**.302**	**.351**	**.386**	**.413**
14	.497	.590	.646	.686	80	.217	.269	.304	.332
	.623	**.694**	**.737**	**.768**		**.283**	**.330**	**.362**	**.389**
15	.482	.574	.630	.670	90	.205	.254	.288	.315
	.606	**.677**	**.721**	**.752**		**.267**	**.312**	**.343**	**.368**
16	.468	.559	.615	.655	100	.195	.241	.274	.300
	.590	**.662**	**.706**	**.738**		**.254**	**.297**	**.327**	**.351**
17	.456	.545	.601	.641	125	.174	.216	.246	.269
	.575	**.647**	**.691**	**.724**		**.228**	**.266**	**.294**	**.316**
18	.444	.532	.587	.628	150	.159	.198	.225	.247
	.561	**.633**	**.678**	**.710**		**.208**	**.244**	**.270**	**.290**
19	.433	.520	.575	.615	200	.138	.172	.196	.215
	.549	**.620**	**.665**	**.698**		**.181**	**.212**	**.234**	**.253**
20	.423	.509	.563	.604	300	.113	.141	.160	.176
	.537	**.608**	**.652**	**.685**		**.148**	**.174**	**.192**	**.208**
21	.413	.498	.552	.592	400	.098	.122	.139	.153
	.526	**.596**	**.641**	**.674**		**.128**	**.151**	**.167**	**.180**
22	.404	.488	.542	.582	500	.088	.109	.124	.137
	.515	**.585**	**.630**	**.663**		**.115**	**.135**	**.150**	**.162**
23	.396	.479	.532	.572	1000	.062	.077	.088	.097
	.505	**.574**	**.619**	**.652**		**.081**	**.096**	**.106**	**.115**

*Reprinted by permission from *Statistical Methods*, 4th edition, by George W. Snedecor, © 1946 by the Iowa State University Press, Ames, Iowa.

Table 8 *Angles Corresponding to Percentages**

%	0	1	2	3	4	5	6	7	8	9
0.0	0	0.57	0.81	0.99	1.15	1.28	1.40	1.52	1.62	1.72
0.1	1.81	1.90	1.99	2.07	2.14	2.22	2.29	2.36	2.43	2.50
0.2	2.56	2.63	2.69	2.75	2.81	2.87	2.92	2.98	3.03	3.09
0.3	3.14	3.19	3.24	3.29	3.34	3.39	3.44	3.49	3.53	3.58
0.4	3.63	3.67	3.72	3.76	3.80	3.85	3.89	3.93	3.97	4.01
0.5	4.05	4.09	4.13	4.17	4.21	4.25	4.29	4.33	4.37	4.40
0.6	4.44	4.48	4.52	4.55	4.59	4.62	4.66	4.69	4.73	4.76
0.7	4.80	4.83	4.87	4.90	4.93	4.97	5.00	5.03	5.07	5.10
0.8	5.13	5.16	5.20	5.23	5.26	5.29	5.32	5.35	5.38	5.41
0.9	5.44	5.47	5.50	5.53	5.56	5.59	5.62	5.65	5.68	5.71
1	5.74	6.02	6.29	6.55	6.80	7.04	7.27	7.49	7.71	7.92
2	8.13	8.33	8.53	8.72	8.91	9.10	9.28	9.46	9.63	9.81
3	9.98	10.14	10.31	10.47	10.63	10.78	10.94	11.09	11.24	11.39
4	11.54	11.68	11.83	11.97	12.11	12.25	12.39	12.52	12.66	12.79
5	12.92	13.05	13.18	13.31	13.44	13.56	13.69	13.81	13.94	14.06
6	14.18	14.30	14.42	14.54	14.65	14.77	14.89	15.00	15.12	15.23
7	15.34	15.45	15.56	15.68	15.79	15.89	16.00	16.11	16.22	16.32
8	16.43	16.54	16.64	16.74	16.85	16.95	17.05	17.16	17.26	17.36
9	17.46	17.56	17.66	17.76	17.85	17.95	18.05	18.15	18.24	18.34
10	18.44	18.53	18.63	18.72	18.81	18.91	19.00	19.09	19.19	19.28
11	19.37	19.46	19.55	19.64	19.73	19.82	19.91	20.00	20.09	20.18
12	20.27	20.36	20.44	20.53	20.62	20.70	20.79	20.88	20.96	21.05
13	21.13	21.22	21.30	21.39	21.47	21.56	21.64	21.72	21.81	21.89
14	21.97	22.06	22.14	22.22	22.30	22.38	22.46	22.55	22.63	22.71
15	22.79	22.87	22.95	23.03	23.11	23.19	23.26	23.34	23.42	23.50
16	23.58	23.66	23.73	23.81	23.89	23.97	24.04	24.12	24.20	24.27
17	24.35	24.43	24.50	24.58	24.65	24.73	24.80	24.88	24.95	25.03
18	25.10	25.18	25.25	25.33	25.40	25.48	25.55	25.62	25.70	25.77
19	25.84	25.92	25.99	26.06	26.13	26.21	26.28	26.35	26.42	26.49
20	26.56	26.64	26.71	26.78	26.85	26.92	26.99	27.06	27.13	27.20
21	27.28	27.35	27.42	27.49	27.56	27.63	27.69	27.76	27.83	27.90
22	27.97	28.04	28.11	28.18	28.25	28.32	28.38	28.45	28.52	28.59
23	28.66	28.73	28.79	28.86	28.93	29.00	29.06	29.13	29.20	29.27
24	29.33	29.40	29.47	29.53	29.60	29.67	29.73	29.80	29.87	29.93
25	30.00	30.07	30.13	30.20	30.26	30.33	30.40	30.46	30.53	30.59
26	30.66	30.72	30.79	30.85	30.92	30.98	31.05	31.11	31.18	31.24
27	31.31	31.37	31.44	31.50	31.56	31.63	31.69	31.76	31.82	31.88
28	31.95	32.01	32.08	32.14	32.20	32.27	32.33	32.39	32.46	32.52
29	32.58	32.65	32.71	32.77	32.83	32.90	32.96	33.02	33.09	33.15
30	33.21	33.27	33.34	33.40	33.46	33.52	33.58	33.65	33.71	33.77
31	33.83	33.89	33.96	34.02	34.08	34.14	34.20	34.27	34.33	34.39
32	34.45	34.51	34.57	34.63	34.70	34.76	34.82	34.88	34.94	35.00
33	35.06	35.12	35.18	35.24	35.30	35.37	35.43	35.49	35.55	35.61
34	35.67	35.73	35.79	35.85	35.91	35.97	36.03	36.09	36.15	36.21
35	36.27	36.33	36.39	36.45	36.51	36.57	36.63	36.69	36.75	36.81
36	36.87	36.93	36.99	37.05	37.11	37.17	37.23	37.29	37.35	37.41
37	37.47	37.52	37.58	37.64	37.70	37.76	37.82	37.88	37.94	38.00
38	38.06	38.12	38.17	38.23	38.29	38.35	38.41	38.47	38.53	38.59
39	38.65	38.70	38.76	38.82	38.88	38.94	39.00	39.06	39.11	39.17
40	39.23	39.29	39.35	39.41	39.47	39.52	39.58	39.64	39.70	39.76
41	39.82	39.87	39.93	39.99	40.05	40.11	40.16	40.22	40.28	40.34
42	40.40	40.46	40.51	40.57	40.63	40.69	40.74	40.80	40.86	40.92
43	40.98	41.03	41.09	41.15	41.21	41.27	41.32	41.38	41.44	41.50
44	41.55	41.61	41.67	41.73	41.78	41.84	41.90	41.96	42.02	42.07
45	42.13	42.19	42.25	42.30	42.36	42.42	42.48	42.53	42.59	42.65
46	42.71	42.76	42.82	42.88	42.94	42.99	43.05	43.11	43.17	43.22
47	43.28	43.34	43.39	43.45	43.51	43.57	43.62	43.68	43.74	43.80
48	43.85	43.91	43.97	44.03	44.08	44.14	44.20	44.25	44.31	44.37
49	44.43	44.48	44.54	44.60	44.66	44.71	44.77	44.83	44.89	44.94

*Reprinted by permission from *Statistical Methods*, 4th edition, by George W. Snedecor, © 1946 by the Iowa State University Press, Ames, Iowa.

Table 8 *Angles Corresponding to Percentages (Continued)*

%	0	1	2	3	4	5	6	7	8	9
50	45.00	45.06	45.11	45.17	45.23	45.29	45.34	45.40	45.46	45.52
51	45.57	45.63	45.69	45.75	45.80	45.86	45.92	45.97	46.03	46.09
52	46.15	46.20	46.26	46.32	46.38	46.43	46.49	46.55	46.61	46.66
53	46.72	46.78	46.83	46.89	46.95	47.01	47.06	47.12	47.18	47.24
54	47.29	47.35	47.41	47.47	47.52	47.58	47.64	47.70	47.75	47.81
55	47.87	47.93	47.98	48.04	48.10	48.16	48.22	48.27	48.33	48.39
56	48.45	48.50	48.56	48.62	48.68	48.73	48.79	48.85	48.91	48.97
57	49.02	49.08	49.14	49.20	49.26	49.31	49.37	49.43	49.49	49.54
58	49.60	49.66	49.72	49.78	49.84	49.89	49.95	50.01	50.07	50.13
59	50.18	50.24	50.30	50.36	50.42	50.48	50.53	50.59	50.65	50.71
60	50.77	50.83	50.89	50.94	51.00	51.06	51.12	51.18	51.24	51.30
61	51.35	51.41	51.47	51.53	51.59	51.65	51.71	51.77	51.83	51.88
62	51.94	52.00	52.06	52.12	52.18	52.24	52.30	52.36	52.42	52.48
63	52.53	52.59	52.65	52.71	52.77	52.83	52.89	52.95	53.01	53.07
64	53.13	53.19	53.25	53.31	53.37	53.43	53.49	53.55	53.61	53.67
65	53.73	53.79	53.85	53.91	53.97	54.03	54.09	54.15	54.21	54.27
66	54.33	54.39	54.45	54.51	54.57	54.63	54.70	54.76	54.82	54.88
67	54.94	55.00	55.06	55.12	55.18	55.24	55.30	55.37	55.43	55.49
68	55.55	55.61	55.67	55.73	55.80	55.86	55.92	55.98	56.04	56.11
69	56.17	56.23	56.29	56.35	56.42	56.48	56.54	56.60	56.66	56.73
70	56.79	56.85	56.91	56.98	57.04	57.10	57.17	57.23	57.29	57.35
71	57.42	57.48	57.54	57.61	57.67	57.73	57.80	57.86	57.92	57.99
72	58.05	58.12	58.18	58.24	58.31	58.37	58.44	58.50	58.56	58.63
73	58.69	58.76	58.82	58.89	58.95	59.02	59.08	59.15	59.21	59.28
74	59.34	59.41	59.47	59.54	59.60	59.67	59.74	59.80	59.87	59.93
75	60.00	60.07	60.13	60.20	60.27	60.33	60.40	60.47	60.53	60.60
76	60.67	60.73	60.80	60.87	60.94	61.00	61.07	61.14	61.21	61.27
77	61.34	61.41	61.48	61.55	61.62	61.68	61.75	61.82	61.89	61.96
78	62.03	62.10	62.17	62.24	62.31	62.37	62.44	62.51	62.58	62.65
79	62.72	62.80	62.87	62.94	63.01	63.08	63.15	63.22	63.29	63.36
80	63.44	63.51	63.58	63.65	63.72	63.79	63.87	63.94	64.01	64.08
81	64.16	64.23	64.30	64.38	64.45	64.52	64.60	64.67	64.75	64.82
82	64.90	64.97	65.05	65.12	65.20	65.27	65.35	65.42	65.50	65.57
83	65.65	65.73	65.80	65.88	65.96	66.03	66.11	66.19	66.27	66.34
84	66.42	66.50	66.58	66.66	66.74	66.81	66.89	66.97	67.05	67.13
85	67.21	67.29	67.37	67.45	67.54	67.62	67.70	67.78	67.86	67.94
86	68.03	68.11	68.19	68.28	68.36	68.44	68.53	68.61	68.70	68.78
87	68.87	68.95	69.04	69.12	69.21	69.30	69.38	69.47	69.56	69.64
88	69.73	69.82	69.91	70.00	70.09	70.18	70.27	70.36	70.45	70.54
89	70.63	70.72	70.81	70.91	71.00	71.09	71.19	71.28	71.37	71.47
90	71.56	71.66	71.76	71.85	71.95	72.05	72.15	72.24	72.34	72.44
91	72.54	72.64	72.74	72.84	72.95	73.05	73.15	73.26	73.36	73.46
92	73.57	73.68	73.78	73.89	74.00	74.11	74.21	74.32	74.44	74.55
93	74.66	74.77	74.88	75.00	75.11	75.23	75.35	75.46	75.58	75.70
94	75.82	75.94	76.06	76.19	76.31	76.44	76.56	76.69	76.82	76.95
95	77.08	77.21	77.34	77.48	77.61	77.75	77.89	78.03	78.17	78.32
96	78.46	78.61	78.76	78.91	79.06	79.22	79.37	79.53	79.69	79.86
97	80.02	80.19	80.37	80.54	80.72	80.90	81.09	81.28	81.47	81.67
98	81.87	82.08	82.29	82.51	82.73	82.96	83.20	83.45	83.71	83.98
99.0	84.26	84.29	84.32	84.35	84.38	84.41	84.44	84.47	84.50	84.53
99.1	84.56	84.59	84.62	65.65	84.68	84.71	84.74	84.77	84.80	84.84
99.2	84.87	84.90	84.93	84.97	85.00	85.03	85.07	85.10	85.13	85.17
99.3	85.20	85.24	85.27	85.31	85.34	85.38	85.41	85.45	85.48	85.52
99.4	85.56	85.60	85.63	85.67	85.71	85.75	85.79	85.83	85.87	85.91
99.5	85.95	85.99	86.03	86.07	86.11	86.15	86.20	86.24	86.28	86.33
99.6	86.37	86.42	86.47	86.51	86.56	86.61	86.66	86.71	86.76	86.81
99.7	86.86	86.91	86.97	87.02	87.08	87.13	87.19	87.25	87.31	87.37
99.8	87.44	87.50	87.57	87.64	87.71	87.78	87.86	87.93	88.01	88.10
99.9	88.19	88.28	88.38	88.48	88.60	88.72	88.85	89.01	89.19	89.43
100.0	90.00	—	—	—	—	—	—	—	—	—

Table 9 Poisson Distribution for Selected Values of m*

x	1	2	3	4	5
0	.367879	.135335	.049787	.018316	.006738
1	.367879	.270671	.149361	.073263	.033690
2	.183940	.270671	.224042	.146525	.084224
3	.061313	.180447	.224042	.195367	.140374
4	.015328	.090224	.168031	.195367	.175467
5	.003066	.036089	.100819	.156293	.175467
6	.000511	.012030	.050409	.104196	.146223
7	.000073	.003437	.021604	.059540	.104445
8	.000009	.000859	.008102	.029770	.065278
9	.000001	.000191	.002701	.013231	.036266
10		.000038	.000810	.005292	.018133
11		.000007	.000221	.001925	.008242
12		.000001	.000055	.000642	.003434
13			.000013	.000197	.001321
14			.000003	.000056	.000472
15			.000001	.000015	.000157
16				.000004	.000049
17				.000001	.000014
18					.000004
19					.000001
20					
21					
22					
23					
24					
25					
26					
27					
28					
29					
30					
31					
32					

*From *Poisson's Exponential Binomial Limit* by E. C. Molina, Copyright © 1942 by Litton Educational Publishing, Inc., by permission of Van Nostrand Reinhold Company.

Table 9 Poisson Distribution for Selected Values of m (Continued)

x	6	7	8	9	10
0	.002479	.000912	.000335	.000123	.000045
1	.014873	.006383	.002684	.001111	.000454
2	.044618	.022341	.010735	.004998	.002270
3	.089235	.052129	.028626	.014994	.007567
4	.133853	.091226	.057252	.033737	.018917
5	.160623	.127717	.091604	.060727	.037833
6	.160623	.149003	.122138	.091090	.063055
7	.137677	.149003	.139587	.117116	.090079
8	.103258	.130377	.139587	.131756	.112599
9	.068838	.101405	.124077	.131756	.125110
10	.041303	.070983	.099262	.118580	.125110
11	.022529	.045171	.072190	.097020	.113736
12	.011264	.026350	.048127	.072765	.094780
13	.005199	.014188	.029616	.050376	.072908
14	.002228	.007094	.016924	.032384	.052077
15	.000891	.003311	.009026	.019431	.034718
16	.000334	.001448	.004513	.010930	.021699
17	.000118	.000596	.002124	.005786	.012764
18	.000039	.000232	.000944	.002893	.007091
19	.000012	.000085	.000397	.001370	.003732
20	.000004	.000030	.000159	.000617	.001866
21	.000001	.000010	.000061	.000264	.000889
22		.000003	.000022	.000108	.000404
23		.000001	.000008	.000042	.000176
24			.000003	.000016	.000073
25			.000001	.000006	.000029
26				.000002	.000011
27				.000001	.000004
28					.000001
29					.000001
30					
31					
32					

Table 10   *Squares and Square Roots of the Numbers from 1 to 1,000*

Number	Square	Square Root	Number	Square	Square Root
1	1	1.000	41	16 81	6.403
2	4	1.414	42	17 64	6.481
3	9	1.732	43	18 49	6.557
4	16	2.000	44	19 36	6.633
5	25	2.236	45	20 25	6.708
6	36	2.449	46	21 16	6.782
7	49	2.646	47	22 09	6.856
8	64	2.828	48	23 04	6.928
9	81	3.000	49	24 01	7.000
10	1 00	3.162	50	25 00	7.071
11	1 21	3.317	51	26 01	7.141
12	1 44	3.464	52	27 04	7.211
13	1 69	3.606	53	28 09	7.280
14	1 96	3.742	54	29 16	7.348
15	2 25	3.873	55	30 25	7.416
16	2 56	4.000	56	31 36	7.483
17	2 89	4.123	57	32 49	7.550
18	3 24	4.243	58	33 64	7.616
19	3 61	4.359	59	34 81	7.681
20	4 00	4.472	60	36 00	7.746
21	4 41	4.583	61	37 21	7.810
22	4 84	4.690	62	38 44	7.874
23	5 29	4.796	63	39 69	7.937
24	5 76	4.899	64	40 96	8.000
25	6 25	5.000	65	42 25	8.062
26	6 76	5.099	66	43 56	8.124
27	7 29	5.196	67	44 89	8.185
28	7 84	5.292	68	46 24	8.246
29	8 41	5.385	69	47 61	8.307
30	9 00	5.477	70	49 00	8.367
31	9 61	5.568	71	50 41	8.426
32	10 24	5.657	72	51 84	8.485
33	10 89	5.745	73	53 29	8.544
34	11 56	5.831	74	54 76	8.602
35	12 25	5.916	75	56 25	8.660
36	12 96	6.000	76	57 76	8.718
37	13 69	6.083	77	59 29	8.775
38	14 44	6.164	78	60 84	8.832
39	15 21	6.245	79	62 41	8.888
40	16 00	6.325	80	64 00	8.944

Table 10 *Squares and Square Roots of the Numbers from 1 to 1,000 (Continued)*

Number	Square	Square Root	Number	Square	Square Root
81	65 61	9.000	121	1 46 41	11.000
82	67 24	9.055	122	1 48 84	11.045
83	68 89	9.110	123	1 51 29	11.091
84	70 56	9.165	124	1 53 76	11.136
85	72 25	9.220	125	1 56 25	11.180
86	73 96	9.274	126	1 58 76	11.225
87	75 69	9.327	127	1 61 29	11.269
88	77 44	9.381	128	1 63 84	11.314
89	79 21	9.434	129	1 66 41	11.358
90	81 00	9.487	130	1 69 00	11.402
91	82 81	9.539	131	1 71 61	11.446
92	84 64	9.592	132	1 74 24	11.489
93	86 49	9.644	133	1 76 89	11.533
94	88 36	9.695	134	1 79 56	11.576
95	90 25	9.747	135	1 82 25	11.619
96	92 16	9.798	136	1 84 96	11.662
97	94 09	9.849	137	1 87 69	11.705
98	96 04	9.899	138	1 90 44	11.747
99	98 01	9.950	139	1 93 21	11.790
100	1 00 00	10.000	140	1 96 00	11.832
101	1 02 01	10.050	141	1 98 81	11.874
102	1 04 04	10.100	142	2 01 64	11.916
103	1 06 09	10.149	143	2 04 49	11.958
104	1 08 16	10.198	144	2 07 36	12.000
105	1 10 25	10.247	145	2 10 25	12.042
106	1 12 36	10.296	146	2 13 16	12.083
107	1 14 49	10.344	147	2 16 09	12.124
108	1 16 64	10.392	148	2 19 04	12.166
109	1 18 81	10.440	149	2 22 01	12.207
110	1 21 00	10.488	150	2 25 00	12.247
111	1 23 21	10.536	151	2 28 01	12.288
112	1 25 44	10.583	152	2 31 04	12.329
113	1 27 69	10.630	153	2 34 09	12.369
114	1 29 96	10.677	154	2 37 16	12.410
115	1 32 25	10.724	155	2 40 25	12.450
116	1 34 56	10.770	156	2 43 36	12.490
117	1 36 89	10.817	157	2 46 49	12.530
118	1 39 24	10.863	158	2 49 64	12.570
119	1 41 61	10.909	159	2 52 81	12.610
120	1 44 00	10.954	160	2 56 00	12.649

Table 10   *Squares and Square Roots of the Numbers from 1 to 1,000 (Continued)*

Number	Square	Square Root	Number	Square	Square Root
161	2 59 21	12.689	201	4 04 01	14.177
162	2 62 44	12.728	202	4 08 04	14.213
163	2 65 69	12.767	203	4 12 09	14.248
164	2 68 96	12.806	204	4 16 16	14.283
165	2 72 25	12.845	205	4 20 25	14.318
166	2 75 56	12.884	206	4 24 36	14.353
167	2 78 89	12.923	207	4 28 49	14.387
168	2 82 24	12.961	208	4 32 64	14.422
169	2 85 61	13.000	209	4 36 81	14.457
170	2 89 00	13.038	210	4 41 00	14.491
171	2 92 41	13.077	211	4 45 21	14.526
172	2 95 84	13.115	212	4 49 44	14.560
173	2 99 29	13.153	213	4 53 69	14.595
174	3 02 76	13.191	214	4 57 96	14.629
175	3 06 25	13.229	215	4 62 25	14.663
176	3 09 76	13.266	216	4 66 56	14.697
177	3 13 29	13.304	217	4 70 89	14.731
178	3 16 84	13.342	218	4 75 24	14.765
179	3 20 41	13.379	219	4 79 61	14.799
180	3 24 00	13.416	220	4 84 00	14.832
181	3 27 61	13.454	221	4 88 41	14.866
182	3 31 24	13.491	222	4 92 84	14.900
183	3 34 89	13.528	223	4 97 29	14.933
184	3 38 56	13.565	224	5 01 76	14.967
185	3 42 25	13.601	225	5 06 25	15.000
186	3 45 96	13.638	226	5 10 76	15.033
187	3 49 69	13.675	227	5 15 29	15.067
188	3 53 44	13.711	228	5 19 84	15.100
189	3 57 21	13.748	229	5 24 41	15.133
190	3 61 00	13.784	230	5 29 00	15.166
191	3 64 81	13.820	231	5 33 61	15.199
192	3 68 64	13.856	232	5 38 24	15.232
193	3 72 49	13.892	233	5 42 89	15.264
194	3 76 36	13.928	234	5 47 56	15.297
195	3 80 25	13.964	235	5 52 25	15.330
196	3 84 16	14.000	236	5 56 96	15.362
197	3 88 09	14.036	237	5 61 69	15.395
198	3 92 04	14.071	238	5 66 44	15.427
199	3 96 01	14.107	239	5 71 21	15.460
200	4 00 00	14.142	240	5 76 00	15.492

Table 10 *Squares and Square Roots of the Numbers from 1 to 1,000 (Continued)*

Number	Square	Square Root	Number	Square	Square Root
241	5 80 81	15.524	281	7 89 61	16.763
242	5 85 64	15.556	282	7 95 24	16.793
243	5 90 49	15.588	283	8 00 89	16.823
244	5 95 36	15.620	284	8 06 56	16.852
245	6 00 25	15.652	285	8 12 25	16.882
246	6 05 16	15.684	286	8 17 96	16.912
247	6 10 09	15.716	287	8 23 69	16.941
248	6 15 04	15.748	288	8 29 44	16.971
249	6 20 01	15.780	289	8 35 21	17.000
250	6 25 00	15.811	290	8 41 00	17.029
251	6 30 01	15.843	291	8 46 81	17.059
252	6 35 04	15.875	292	8 52 64	17.088
253	6 40 09	15.906	293	8 58 49	17.117
254	6 45 16	15.937	294	8 64 36	17.146
255	6 50 25	15.969	295	8 70 25	17.176
256	6 55 36	16.000	296	8 76 16	17.205
257	6 60 49	16.031	297	8 82 09	17.234
258	6 65 64	16.062	298	8 88 04	17.263
259	6 70 81	16.093	299	8 94 01	17.292
260	6 76 00	16.125	300	9 00 00	17.321
261	6 81 21	16.155	301	9 06 01	17.349
262	6 86 44	16.186	302	9 12 04	17.378
263	6 91 69	16.217	303	9 18 09	17.407
264	6 96 96	16.248	304	9 24 16	17.436
265	7 02 25	16.279	305	9 30 25	17.464
266	7 07 56	16.310	306	9 36 36	17.493
267	7 12 89	16.340	307	9 42 49	17.521
268	7 18 24	16.371	308	9 48 64	17.550
269	7 23 61	16.401	309	9 54 81	17.578
270	7 29 00	16.432	310	9 61 00	17.607
271	7 34 41	16.462	311	9 67 21	17.635
272	7 39 84	16.492	312	9 73 44	17.664
273	7 45 29	16.523	313	9 79 69	17.692
274	7 50 76	16.553	314	9 85 96	17.720
275	7 56 25	16.583	315	9 92 25	17.748
276	7 61 76	16.613	316	9 98 56	17.776
277	7 67 29	16.643	317	10 04 89	17.804
278	7 72 84	16.673	318	10 11 24	17.833
279	7 78 41	16.703	319	10 17 61	17.861
280	7 84 00	16.733	320	10 24 00	17.889

Table 10   *Squares and Square Roots of the Numbers from 1 to 1,000 (Continued)*

Number	Square	Square Root	Number	Square	Square Root
321	10 30 41	17.916	361	13 03 21	19.000
322	10 36 84	17.944	362	13 10 44	19.026
323	10 43 29	17.972	363	13 17 69	19.053
324	10 49 76	18.000	364	13 24 96	19.079
325	10 56 25	18.028	365	13 32 25	19.105
326	10 62 76	18.055	366	13 39 56	19.131
327	10 69 29	18.083	367	13 46 89	19.157
328	10 75 84	18.111	368	13 54 24	19.183
329	10 82 41	18.138	369	13 61 61	19.209
330	10 89 00	181.66	370	13 69 00	19.235
331	10 95 61	18.193	371	13 76 41	19.261
332	11 02 24	18.221	372	13 83 84	19.287
333	11 08 89	18.248	373	13 91 29	19.313
334	11 15 56	18.276	374	13 98 76	19.339
335	11 22 25	18.303	375	14 06 25	19.363
336	11 28 96	18.330	376	14 13 76	19.391
337	11 35 69	18.358	377	14 21 29	19.416
338	11 42 44	18.385	378	14 28 84	19.442
339	11 49 21	18.412	379	14 36 41	19.468
340	11 56 00	18.439	380	14 44 00	19.494
341	11 62 81	18.466	381	14 51 61	19.519
342	11 69 64	18.493	382	14 59 24	19.545
343	11 76 49	18.520	383	14 66 89	19.570
344	11 83 36	18.547	384	14 74 56	19.596
345	11 90 25	18.574	385	14 82 25	19.621
346	11 97 16	18.601	386	14 89 96	19.647
347	12 04 09	18.628	387	14 97 69	19.672
348	12 11 04	18.655	388	15 05 44	19.698
349	12 18 01	18.682	389	15 13 21	19.723
350	12 25 00	18.708	390	15 21 00	19.748
351	12 32 01	18.735	391	15 28 81	19.774
352	12 39 04	18.762	392	15 36 64	19.799
353	12 46 09	18.788	393	15 44 49	19.824
354	12 53 16	18.815	394	15 52 36	19.849
355	12 60 25	18.841	395	15 60 25	19.875
356	12 67 36	18.868	396	15 68 16	19.900
357	12 74 49	18.894	397	15 76 09	19.925
358	12 81 64	18.921	398	15 84 04	19.950
359	12 88 81	18.947	399	15 92 01	19.975
360	12 96 00	18.974	400	16 00 00	20.000

Table 10   *Squares and Square Roots of the Numbers from 1 to 1,000 (Continued)*

Number	Square	Square Root	Number	Square	Square Root
401	16 08 01	20.025	441	19 44 81	21.000
402	16 16 04	20.050	442	19 53 64	21.024
403	16 24 09	20.075	443	19 62 49	21.048
404	16 32 16	20.100	444	19 71 36	21.071
405	16 40 25	20.125	445	19 80 25	21.095
406	16 48 36	20.149	446	19 89 16	21.119
407	16 56 49	20.174	447	19 98 09	21.142
408	16 64 64	20.199	448	20 07 04	21.166
409	16 72 81	20.224	449	20 16 01	21.190
410	16 81 00	20.248	450	20 25 00	21.213
411	16 89 21	20.273	451	20 34 01	21.237
412	16 97 44	20.298	452	20 43 04	21.260
413	17 05 69	20.322	453	20 52 09	21.284
414	17 13 96	20.347	454	20 61 16	21.307
415	17 22 25	20.372	455	20 70 25	21.331
416	17 30 56	20.396	456	20 79 36	21.354
417	17 38 89	20.421	457	20 88 49	21.378
418	17 47 24	20.445	458	20 97 64	21.401
419	17 55 61	20.469	459	21 06 81	21.424
420	17 64 00	20.494	460	21 16 00	21.448
421	17 72 41	20.518	461	21 25 21	21.471
422	17 80 84	20.543	462	21 34 44	21.494
423	17 89 29	20.567	463	21 43 69	21.517
424	17 97 76	20.591	464	21 52 96	21.541
425	18 06 25	20.616	465	21 62 25	21.564
426	18 14 76	20.640	466	21 71 56	21.587
427	18 23 29	20.664	467	21 80 89	21.610
428	18 31 84	20.688	468	21 90 24	21.633
429	18 40 41	20.712	469	21 99 61	21.656
430	18 49 00	20.736	470	22 09 00	21.679
431	18 57 61	20.761	471	22 18 41	21.703
432	18 66 24	20.785	472	22 27 84	21.726
433	18 74 89	20.809	473	22 37 29	21.749
434	18 83 56	20.833	474	22 46 76	21.772
435	18 92 25	20.857	475	22 56 25	21.794
436	19 00 96	20.881	476	22 65 76	21.817
437	19 09 69	20.905	477	22 75 29	21.840
438	19 18 44	20.928	478	22 84 84	21.863
439	19 27 21	20.952	479	22 94 41	21.886
440	19 36 00	20.976	480	23 04 00	21.909

Table 10   Squares and Square Roots of the Numbers from 1 to 1,000 (Continued)

Number	Square	Square Root	Number	Square	Square Root
481	23 13 61	21.932	521	27 14 41	22.825
482	23 23 24	21.954	522	27 24 84	22.847
483	23 32 89	21.977	523	27 35 29	22.869
484	23 42 56	22.000	524	27 45 76	22.891
485	23 52 25	22.023	525	27 56 25	22.913
486	23 61 96	22.045	526	27 66 76	22.935
487	23 71 69	22.068	527	27 77 29	22.956
488	23 81 44	22.091	528	27 87 84	22.978
489	23 91 21	22.113	529	27 98 41	23.000
490	24 01 00	22.136	530	28 09 00	23.022
491	24 10 81	22.159	531	28 19 61	23.043
492	24 20 64	22.181	532	28 30 24	23.065
493	24 30 49	22.204	533	28 40 89	23.087
494	24 40 36	22.226	534	28 51 56	23.108
495	24 50 25	22.249	535	28 62 25	23.130
496	24 60 16	22.271	536	28 72 96	23.152
497	24 70 09	22.293	537	28 83 69	23.173
498	24 80 04	22.316	538	28 94 44	23.195
499	24 90 01	22.338	539	29 05 21	23.216
500	25 00 00	22.361	540	29 16 00	23.238
501	25 10 01	22.383	541	29 26 81	23.259
502	25 20 04	22.405	542	29 37 64	23.281
503	25 30 09	22.428	543	29 48 49	23.302
504	25 40 16	22.450	544	29 59 36	23.324
505	25 50 25	22.472	545	29 70 25	23.345
506	25 60 36	22.494	546	29 81 16	23.367
507	25 70 49	22.517	547	29 92 09	23.388
508	25 80 64	22.539	548	30 03 04	23.409
509	25 90 81	22.561	549	30 14 01	23.431
510	26 01 00	22.583	550	30 25 00	23.452
511	26 11 21	22.605	551	30 36 01	23.473
512	26 21 44	22.627	552	30 47 04	23.495
513	26 31 69	22.650	553	30 58 09	23.516
514	26 41 96	22.672	554	30 69 16	23.537
515	26 52 25	22.694	555	30 80 25	23.558
516	26 62 56	22.716	556	30 91 36	23.580
517	26 72 89	22.738	557	31 02 49	23.601
518	26 83 24	22.760	558	31 13 64	23.622
519	26 93 61	22.782	559	31 24 81	23.643
520	27 04 00	22.804	560	31 36 00	23.664

Table 10 *Squares and Square Roots of the Numbers from 1 to 1,000 (Continued)*

Number	Square	Square Root	Number	Square	Square Root
561	31 47 21	23.685	601	36 12 01	24.515
562	31 58 44	23.707	602	36 24 04	24.536
563	31 69 69	23.728	603	36 36 09	24.556
564	31 80 96	23.749	604	36 48 16	24.576
565	31 92 25	23.770	605	36 60 25	24.597
566	32 03 56	23.791	606	36 72 36	24.617
567	32 14 89	23.812	607	36 84 49	24.637
568	32 26 24	23.833	608	36 96 64	24.658
569	32 37 61	23.854	609	37 08 81	24.678
570	32 49 00	23.875	610	37 21 00	24.698
571	32 60 41	23.896	611	37 33 21	24.718
572	32 71 84	23.917	612	37 45 44	24.739
573	32 83 29	23.937	613	37 57 69	24.759
574	32 94 76	23.958	614	37 69 96	24.779
575	33 06 25	23.979	615	37 82 25	24.799
576	33 17 76	24.000	616	37 94 56	24.819
577	33 29 29	24.021	617	38 06 89	24.839
578	33 40 84	24.042	618	38 19 24	24.860
579	33 52 41	24.062	619	38 31 61	24.880
580	33 64 00	24.083	620	38 44 00	24.900
581	33 75 61	24.104	621	38 56 41	24.920
582	33 87 24	24.125	622	38 68 84	24.940
583	33 98 89	24.145	623	38 81 29	24.960
584	34 10 56	24.166	624	38 93 76	24.980
585	34 22 25	24.187	625	39 06 25	25.000
586	34 33 96	24.207	626	39 18 76	25.020
587	34 45 69	24.228	627	39 31 29	25.040
588	34 57 44	24.249	628	39 43 84	25.060
589	34 69 21	24.269	629	39 56 41	25.080
590	34 81 00	24.290	630	39 69 00	25.100
591	34 92 81	24.310	631	39 81 61	25.120
592	35 04 64	24.331	632	39 94 24	25.140
593	35 16 49	24.352	633	40 06 89	25.159
594	35 28 36	24.372	634	40 19 56	25.179
595	35 40 25	24.393	635	40 32 25	25.199
596	35 52 16	24.413	636	40 44 96	25.219
597	35 64 09	24.434	637	40 57 69	25.239
598	35 76 04	24.454	638	40 70 44	25.259
599	35 88 01	24.474	639	40 83 21	25.278
600	36 00 00	24.495	640	40 96 00	25.298

Table 10   *Squares and Square Roots of the Numbers from 1 to 1,000* (*Continued*)

Number	Square	Square Root	Number	Square	Square Root
641	41 08 81	25.318	681	46 37 61	26.096
642	41 21 64	25.338	682	46 51 24	26.115
643	41 34 49	25.357	683	46 64 89	26.134
644	41 47 36	25.377	684	46 78 56	26.153
645	41 60 25	25.397	685	46 92 25	26.173
646	41 73 16	25.417	686	47 05 96	26.192
647	41 86 09	25.436	687	47 19 69	26.211
648	41 99 04	25.456	688	47 33 44	26.230
649	42 12 01	25.475	689	47 47 21	26.249
650	42 25 00	25.495	690	47 61 00	26.268
651	42 38 01	25.515	691	47 74 81	26.287
652	42 51 04	25.534	692	47 88 64	26.306
653	42 64 09	25.554	693	48 02 49	26.325
654	42 77 16	25.573	694	48 16 36	26.344
655	42 90 25	25.593	695	48 30 25	26.363
656	43 03 36	25.612	696	48 44 16	26.382
657	43 16 49	25.632	697	48 58 09	26.401
658	43 29 64	25.652	698	48 72 04	26.420
659	43 42 81	25.671	699	48 86 01	26.439
660	43 56 00	25.690	700	49 00 00	26.458
661	43 69 21	25.710	701	49 14 01	26.476
662	43 82 44	25.729	702	49 28 04	26.495
663	43 95 69	25.749	703	49 42 09	26.514
664	44 08 96	25.768	704	49 56 16	26.533
665	44 22 25	25.788	705	49 70 25	26.552
666	44 35 56	25.807	706	49 84 36	26.571
667	44 48 89	25.826	707	49 98 49	26.589
668	44 62 24	25.846	708	50 12 64	26.608
669	44 75 61	25.865	709	50 26 81	26.627
670	44 89 00	25.884	710	50 41 00	26.646
671	45 02 41	25.904	711	50 55 21	26.665
672	45 15 84	25.923	712	50 69 44	26.683
673	45 29 29	25.942	713	50 83 69	26.702
674	45 42 76	25.962	714	50 97 96	26.721
675	45 56 25	25.981	715	51 12 25	26.739
676	45 69 76	26.000	716	51 26 56	26.758
677	45 83 29	26.019	717	51 40 89	26.777
678	45 96 84	26.038	718	51 55 24	26.796
679	46 10 41	26.058	719	51 69 61	26.814
680	46 24 00	26.077	720	51 84 00	26.833

Table 10 *Squares and Square Roots of the Numbers from 1 to 1,000 (Continued)*

Number	Square	Square Root	Number	Square	Square Root
721	51 98 41	26.851	761	57 91 21	27.586
722	52 12 84	26.870	762	58 06 44	27.604
723	52 27 29	26.889	763	58 21 69	27.622
724	52 41 76	26.907	764	58 36 96	27.641
725	52 56 25	26.926	765	58 52 25	27.659
726	52 70 76	26.944	766	58 67 56	27.677
727	52 85 29	26.963	767	58 82 89	27.695
728	52 99 84	26.981	768	58 98 24	27.713
729	53 14 41	27.000	769	59 13 61	27.731
730	53 29 00	27.019	770	59 29 00	27.749
731	53 43 61	27.037	771	59 44 41	27.767
732	53 58 24	27.055	772	59 59 84	27.785
733	53 72 89	27.074	773	59 75 29	27.803
734	53 87 56	27.092	774	59 90 76	27.821
735	54 02 25	27.111	775	60 06 25	27.839
736	54 16 96	27.129	776	60 21 76	27.857
737	54 31 69	27.148	777	60 37 29	27.875
738	54 46 44	27.166	778	60 52 84	27.893
739	54 61 21	27.185	779	60 68 41	27.911
740	54 76 00	27.203	780	60 84 00	27.928
741	54 90 81	27.221	781	60 99 61	27.946
742	55 05 64	27.240	782	61 15 24	27.964
743	55 20 49	27.258	783	61 30 89	27.982
744	55 35 36	27.276	784	61 46 56	28.000
745	55 50 25	27.295	785	61 62 25	28.018
746	55 65 16	27.313	786	61 77 96	28.036
747	55 80 09	27.331	787	61 93 69	28.054
748	55 95 04	27.350	788	62 09 44	28.071
749	56 10 01	27.368	789	62 25 21	28.089
750	56 25 00	27.386	790	62 41 00	28.107
751	56 40 01	27.404	791	62 56 81	28.125
752	56 55 04	27.423	792	62 72 64	28.142
753	56 70 09	27.441	793	62 88 49	28.160
754	56 85 16	27.459	794	63 04 36	28.178
755	57 00 25	27.477	795	63 20 25	28.196
756	57 15 36	27.495	796	63 36 16	28.213
757	57 30 49	27.514	797	63 52 09	28.231
758	57 45 64	27.532	798	63 68 04	28.249
759	57 60 81	27.550	799	63 84 01	28.267
760	57 76 00	27.568	800	64 00 00	28.284

Table 10   *Squares and Square Roots of the Numbers from 1 to 1,000 (Continued)*

Number	Square	Square Root	Number	Square	Square Root
801	64 16 01	28.302	841	70 72 81	29.000
802	64 32 04	28.320	842	70 89 64	29.017
803	64 48 09	28.337	843	71 06 49	29.034
804	64 64 16	28.355	844	71 23 36	29.052
805	64 80 25	28.373	845	71 40 25	29.069
806	64 96 36	28.390	846	71 57 16	29.086
807	65 12 49	28.408	847	71 74 09	29.103
808	65 28 64	28.425	848	71 91 04	29.120
809	65 44 81	28.443	849	72 08 01	29.138
810	65 61 00	28.460	850	72 25 00	29.155
811	65 77 21	28.478	851	72 42 01	29.172
812	65 93 44	28.496	852	72 59 04	29.189
813	66 09 69	28.513	853	72 76 09	29.206
814	66 25 96	28.531	854	72 93 16	29.223
815	66 42 25	28.548	855	73 10 25	29.240
816	66 58 56	28.566	856	73 27 36	29.257
817	66 74 89	28.583	857	73 44 49	29.275
818	66 91 24	28.601	858	73 61 64	29.292
819	67 07 61	28.618	859	73 78 81	29.309
820	67 24 00	28.636	860	73 96 00	29.326
821	67 40 41	28.653	861	74 13 21	29.343
822	67 56 84	28.671	862	74 30 44	29.360
823	67 73 29	28.688	863	74 47 69	29.377
824	67 89 76	28.705	864	74 64 96	29.394
825	68 06 25	28.723	865	74 82 25	29.411
826	68 22 76	28.740	866	74 99 56	29.428
827	68 39 29	28.758	867	75 16 89	29.445
828	68 55 84	28.775	868	75 34 24	29.462
829	68 72 41	28.792	869	75 51 61	29.479
830	68 89 00	28.810	870	75 69 00	29.496
831	69 05 61	28.827	871	75 86 41	29.513
832	69 22 24	28.844	872	76 03 84	29.530
833	69 38 89	28.862	873	76 21 29	29.547
834	69 55 56	28.879	874	76 38 76	29.563
835	69 72 25	28.896	875	76 56 25	29.580
836	69 88 96	28.914	876	76 73 76	29.597
837	70 05 69	28.931	877	76 91 29	29.614
838	70 22 44	28.948	878	77 08 84	29.631
839	70 39 21	28.965	879	77 26 41	29.648
840	70 56 00	28.983	880	77 44 00	29.665

Table 10 *Squares and Square Roots of the Numbers from 1 to 1,000 (Continued)*

Number	Square	Square Root	Number	Square	Square Root
881	77 61 61	29.682	921	84 82 41	30.348
882	77 79 24	29.698	922	85 00 84	30.364
883	77 96 89	29.715	923	85 19 29	30.381
884	78 14 56	29.732	924	85 37 76	30.397
885	78 32 25	29.749	925	85 56 25	30.414
886	78 49 96	29.766	926	85 74 76	30.430
887	78 67 69	29.783	927	85 93 29	30.447
888	78 85 44	29.799	928	86 11 84	30.463
889	79 03 21	29.816	929	86 30 41	30.480
890	79 21 00	29.833	930	86 49 00	30.496
891	79 38 81	29.850	931	86 67 61	30.512
892	79 56 64	29.866	932	86 86 24	30.529
893	79 74 49	29.883	933	87 04 89	30.545
894	79 92 36	29.900	934	87 23 56	30.561
895	80 10 25	29.916	935	87 42 25	30.578
896	80 28 16	29.933	936	87 60 96	30.594
897	80 46 09	29.950	937	87 79 69	30.610
898	80 64 04	29.967	938	87 98 44	30.627
899	80 82 01	29.983	939	88 17 21	30.643
900	81 00 00	30.000	940	88 36 00	30.659
901	81 80 01	30.017	941	88 54 81	30.676
902	81 36 04	30.033	942	88 73 64	30.692
903	81 54 09	30.050	943	88 92 49	30.708
904	81 72 16	30.067	944	89 11 36	30.725
905	81 90 25	30.083	945	89 30 25	30.741
906	82 08 36	30.100	946	89 49 16	30.757
907	82 26 49	30.116	947	89 68 09	30.773
908	82 44 64	30.133	948	89 87 04	30.790
909	82 62 81	30.150	949	90 06 01	30.806
910	82 81 00	30.166	950	90 25 00	30.822
911	82 99 21	30.183	951	90 44 01	30.838
912	83 17 44	30.199	952	90 63 04	30.854
913	83 35 69	30.216	953	90 82 09	30.871
914	83 53 96	30.232	954	91 01 16	30.887
915	83 72 25	30.249	955	91 20 25	30.903
916	83 90 56	30.265	956	91 39 36	30.919
917	84 08 89	30.282	957	91 58 49	30.935
918	84 27 24	30.299	958	91 77 64	30.952
919	84 45 61	30.315	959	91 96 81	30.968
920	84 64 00	30.332	960	92 16 00	30.984

Table 10 Squares and Square Roots of the Numbers from 1 to 1,000 (Continued)

Number	Square	Square Root	Number	Square	Square Root
961	92 35 21	31.000	981	96 23 61	31.321
962	92 54 44	31.016	982	96 43 24	31.337
963	92 73 69	31.032	983	96 62 89	31.353
964	92 92 96	31.048	984	96 82 56	31.369
965	93 12 25	31.064	985	97 02 25	31.385
966	93 31 56	31.081	986	97 21 96	31.401
967	93 50 89	31.097	987	97 41 69	31.417
968	93 70 24	31.113	988	97 61 44	31.432
969	93 89 61	31.129	989	97 81 21	31.448
970	94 09 00	31.145	990	98 01 00	31.464
971	94 28 41	31.161	991	98 20 81	31.480
972	94 47 84	31.177	992	98 40 64	31.496
973	94 67 29	31.193	993	98 60 49	31.512
974	94 86 76	31.209	994	98 80 36	31.528
975	95 06 25	31.225	995	99 00 25	31.544
976	95 25 76	31.241	996	99 20 16	31.559
977	95 45 29	31.257	997	99 40 09	31.575
978	95 64 87	31.273	998	99 60 04	31.591
979	95 84 41	31.289	999	99 80 01	31.607
980	96 04 00	31.305	1000	100 00 00	31.623

Answers

Chapter 1, Part 1

1.

$$\text{Mean} = 10$$
$$\text{Standard deviation} = 4$$

Standard measures

$$-2.00$$
$$-.50$$
$$.25$$
$$.75$$
$$.75$$
$$.75$$

2. (a) $r_{01}^2 = .77$

3. (a) $r_{01} = -.86$

(c) $\hat{x}_{0.1} = .9565$
$$.9565$$
$$.6222$$
$$.5386$$
$$.5386$$
$$-1.1747$$
$$-1.2583$$
$$-.8404$$
$$-.3390$$

$x_{0.1} = 1.0435$
$$.0435$$
$$-.1222$$
$$-.5386$$
$$-.5386$$
$$-.3253$$
$$.7583$$
$$-.1596$$
$$-.1610$$

(f) $r_{01}^2 = .7313$

Chapter 1, Part 2

1. $R_{0.12}^2 = .74$

2. $R_{0.123}^2 = .43$

3. $R_{0.1234}^2 = .69$

4. $R_{5.4321}^2 = .45$

5. $R_{0.123}^2 = .47$

6. $\beta_{02.13} = .33$

$\beta_{03.12} = -.31$

Chapter 1, Part 3

1. (b) $r_{23.1} = 0.00$
$$r_{24.1} = 0.00$$
$$r_{25.1} = 0.00$$
$$r_{34.1} = 0.00$$
$$r_{35.1} = 0.00$$
$$r_{45.1} = 0.00$$

2. (a) $x_{0.2} = .29$
$$-.44$$
$$-.51$$
$$-.37$$
$$.22$$
$$.81$$

$x_{1.2} = .73$
$$-1.21$$
$$-1.01$$
$$-.09$$
$$1.08$$
$$.49$$

(b) $\dfrac{\sum x_{0.2}x_{1.2}}{N} = .32$

(c) $\dfrac{\sigma_{01.2}}{\sigma_{0.2}\sigma_{1.2}} = .78$

4. $r_{01.2} = .17$

5. $r_{01.2} = .70$
   $r_{01.3} = .67$
   $r_{01.23} = .64$

6. $r_{01.234} = .38$
   $r_{02.134} = -.36$

7. $r_{xz.y} = .04$
   $r_{wy.x} = .33$
   $r_{wz.xy} = -.08$

8. $r_{12.3} = .62$
   $r_{13.2} = .65$
   $r_{1.23}^2 = .83$
   $\beta_{12.3} = .47$
   $\beta_{13.2} = .51$

Chapter 2

1. $r_{1f}^2 = .16$ $r_{3f}^2 = .64$
   $r_{2f}^2 = .36$

2. $r_{13}r_{24} - r_{23}r_{14} = .15(.08) - .12(.1)$
   $= .000$
   $r_{12}r_{34} - r_{23}r_{14} = .2(.06) - (.12)(.1)$
   $= .000$
   $r_{12}r_{34} - r_{24}r_{13} = .2(.06) - .08(.15)$
   $= .000$

3. Number of r's = 45
   Number of tetrads = 630
   Number of linearly
   independent tetrads = 35

4.

	AT	GL	R	PL
B	.4332	.4256	.5016	.5472
AT		.3192	.3762	.4104
GL			.3696	.4032
R				.4752

5.

	2	3	4	5	6	7
1	.4850	.5325	.3550	.3625	.4000	.2750
2		.4250	.1900	.1250	.6400	.5100
3			.5050	.5625	.2800	.1450
4				.5125	.0500	-.0375
5					-.0500	-.1375
6						.5700

6. (c) f_1 34%
         f_2 10%
   (d) f_1 77%
         f_2 23%

8.

	a'_{i1}	a'_{i2}
1	.49	.55
2	.49	.53
3	.59	.65
4	.59	.33
5	.52	-.38
6	.33	-.45
7	.36	-.39

10.

	a'_{i1}	a'_{i2}
1	.66	-.34
2	.64	-.33
3	.78	-.41
4	.47	-.49
5	-.23	-.60
6	-.34	-.44
7	-.28	-.45

(f) 80%

11. (g) f_1 47.5%
         f_2 19.5%
         f_3 13.0%
   (h) f_1 59.4%
         f_2 24.4%
         f_3 16.3%

Chapter 3

4.

Y_i	a_{i1}	a_{i2}
1	.92	.00
2	.91	.15
3	.67	.49
4	.66	.62

5. (a)

Y_i	a_{i1}	a_{i2}	a_{i3}	a_{i4}
1	.66	.32	.00	.00
2	.88	-.25	-.25	.24
3	.77	.60	.51	.00
4	.91	.00	.00	.00

(b)

Y_i	a_{i1}	a_{i2}	a_{i3}	a_{i4}
1	.56	.64	−.40	.37
2	.89	.00	.00	.00
3	.45	.71	.00	.00
4	.89	.42	.42	.00

(c)

Y_i	a_{i1}	a_{i2}	a_{i3}	a_{i4}
1	1.00	.00	.00	.00
2	.50	.87	.00	.00
3	.70	.06	.71	.00
4	.60	.58	.35	.44

7.

Y_i	a_{i1}	a_{i2}	a_{i3}
1	.75	.18	.10
2	.61	.09	.08
3	.81	−.39	.00
4	.84	.10	−.21

	$\sum a_{ij}^2$ (centroid solution)	$\sum a_{ij}^2$ (diagonal solution)
1	.60	.61
2	.39	.39
3	.81	.81
4	.74	.74

8.

Y_i	a_{i1}	a_{i2}
1	.78	−.21
2	.75	.03
3	.69	.03
4	.73	.06
5	.54	.39
6	.59	−.46
7	.55	.25

Chapter 4

1. $\overline{Y}_{1.} - \overline{Y}_{2.}$

-2
-2
-2
-2

2. $\overline{Y}_{1.} - \overline{Y}_{2.}$

-2
-2
-2
-1.2

3. $\overline{Y}_{1.} - \overline{Y}_{2.}$

-3.4
-3.8
-4.6

4. $\overline{Y}_{1.} - \overline{Y}_{2.}$

-2.6
-3.2
-4.4

5. $\overline{Y}_{1.} - \overline{Y}_{2.}$

-3.2
-4.0
-4.8

8. (a) $-.33$
   (b) 11.33/6.00
       0.0/6.0

9. $\hat{Y}_{11} = 3$
   $\hat{Y}_{12} = 3$
   $\hat{Y}_{21} = 5$
   $\hat{Y}_{22} = 5$

	Source	SS	df	MS	F
10.	Total	800.00	199		
	Within	258.72	191	1.35	
	Subsamples	541.28	8	67.66	49.95
	Rows	192.48			
	Columns	464.40			
	Constants	541.28	8		
	Interaction	0.00	4		
	Rows	79.88	2	39.94	29.48
	Columns	348.80	2	174.40	128.75

	Source	SS	df	MS
12.	Total	68.92	11	
	Subsamples	2.92	3	
	Within	66.00	8	8.25
	Rows	2.08		
	Columns	.75		
	Constants	2.83	3	
	Interaction	.09	1	
	Rows	2.08	1	2.08
	Columns	.75	1	.75

	Source	SS	df
13.	Total	143.75	15
	Subsamples	15.22	3
	Within	128.53	12
	Rows	8.82	
	Columns	1.00	
	Constants	9.82	3
	Interaction	5.40	1
	Rows	8.82	1
	Columns	1.00	1

Chapter 5

1. (a) $H_0 : \beta_1 = \beta_2 = \beta_3$
   $F = .5193$
   (b) $H_0 : \beta = 0$
   $F = 27.3185$
   (c) $H_0 : \alpha_1 = \alpha_2 = \alpha_3$
   $F = 13.9702$

2. (a) $H_0 : \beta_1 = \beta_2 = \beta_3 = \beta_4$
   $F = .2577$
   (b) $H_0 : \beta = 0$
   $F = 2.5127$
   (c) $H_0 : \alpha_1 = \alpha_2 = \alpha_3 = \alpha_4$
   $F = 3.1319$

3. (a) $H_0 : \beta_1 = \beta_2$
   $F = .2727$
   (b) $H_0 : \beta = 0$
   $F = 7.6087$
   (c) $H_0 : \alpha_1 = \alpha_2$
   $F = .6522$

4. (a) $H_0 : \beta_1 = \beta_2$
   $F = 1.4893$
   (b) $H_0 : \beta = 0$
   $F = 8.7180$
   (c) $H_0 : \alpha_1 = \alpha_2$
   $F = 4.5067$

Chapter 6, Part 2

1. (a) $s_{\bar{y}}^2 = .35$
   $s_{\bar{y}} = .59$

Chapter 6, Part 3

1. (a) $s_w^2 = 7.3333$
   $s_b^2 = 9.2000$
   $\hat{\sigma}_b^2 = .4667$
   $s_{\bar{\bar{y}}}^2 = .4600$
   (b) lower limit $= 3.70$
   upper limit $= 5.50$

2.

	SS	df	MS
Total	1910	99	
Between psu's	960	4	240
Within psu's	950	95	10

.9583 is attributable to differences between psu means

3. (b) $\dfrac{\sigma_b^2}{\sigma^2} = .5455$

(c)

n	$\sigma_{\bar{y}}^2 / \sigma_{\bar{\bar{y}}}^2$
2	1.5455
4	2.6365
5	3.1820
10	5.9095
20	11.3645
25	14.0920
50	27.7295

4. $\rho = .0598$

$$\frac{\sigma_{\bar{\bar{y}}}^2}{\sigma_{\bar{y}}^2} = 1.1794$$

5.

	p_i	$p_i q_i$	$np_i q_i$	$p_i - p$	$(p_i - p)^2$
1	.50	.2500	10.000	−.26	.0676
2	.93	.6510	26.040	.17	.0289
3	.67	.2211	8.844	−.09	.0081
4	.80	.1600	6.400	.04	.0016
5	.90	.0900	3.600	.14	.0196
Σ	3.80		54.884	.00	.1258

$$\frac{\Sigma p_i}{n} = .76$$
$s_w^2 = .2815$
$s_b^2 = 1.2580$
$\hat{\sigma}_b^2 = .0244$
$s_p^2 = .0063$
$\rho = .0798$

6. $s_w^2 = 29.400$
   $s_b^2 = 32.720$
   $\hat{\sigma}_b^2 = .664$
   $s_{\bar{\bar{y}}}^2 = .654$

Chapter 6, Part 4

1. (a) $S_t^2 = 4.5,\ S_b^2 = 1.0$
   $S_w^2 = 5.0,\ S_{\bar{y}}^2 = .5833$
   (b)

	$\overline{\overline{Y}}$	s_w^2	s_b^2	(c) $s_{\bar{\bar{y}}}^2$
1	3.00	.50	1.00	.1111
2	3.50	.50	4.00	.3611
3	3.25	1.25	2.25	.2569

4	2.75	1.25	2.25	.2569	2.	$R = 3.6667$
5	3.25	1.25	6.25	.5902		$S_w^2 = 12.0896$
6	3.00	2.00	4.00	.4444		$S_{xyb} = 12.000$
7	2.50	.50	4.00	.3611		$S_{xyw} = 0.000$
8	3.00	.50	9.00	.7778		
9	2.75	1.25	6.25	.5902	3.	$S_r^2 = .8635$
10	3.00	12.50	1.00	.7777		
11	1.75	1.25	2.25	.2569		
12	3.50	6.50	4.00	.6389		*Chapter 7*
13	2.75	13.25	2.25	.9236		
14	1.50	2.00	1.00	.1944	1. (*a*)	.00 (*b*) $x^2 = 24.42$, 15 *df.*
15	3.25	7.25	6.25	.9236		.26
16	2.50	12.50	4.00	1.0277		.57
17	1.25	1.25	0.25	.0902		.85
18	3.00	6.50	9.00	1.0556		1.26
19	3.50	12.50	0.00	.5944		1.46
20	2.25	1.25	6.25	.5902		1.76
21	4.00	6.50	1.00	.3889	2. (*b*)	2.7917
22	4.00	12.50	1.00	.7777		6.4706
23	2.75	1.25	12.25	1.0902		1.4054
24	4.50	6.50	0.00	.3056		5.6441
25	3.75	13.25	0.25	.7569		9.6364
26	2.50	2.00	9.00	.8611		2.1500
27	4.25	7.25	0.25	.4236		

(*e*) $V_{y'}^2 = V_{\bar{y}}^2 = .0648$

		SD	*D*	*N*	*A*	*SA*
3.	(*i*)	0.00	0.81	1.51	2.28	3.24
	(*ii*)	0.00	0.72	1.40	2.17	3.09
	(*iii*)	0.00	1.38	2.25	3.07	4.08
	(*iv*)	0.00	1.03	1.67	2.21	3.24
	(*v*)	0.00	0.90	1.54	2.19	3.11

2. (*a*) $\rho = -.22$

       $-.25$ by Eq. (6.4.11)

       $-.25$ by Eq. (6.4.12)

4. (*A*) 9.29

  (*B*) 9.42

  (*C*) 7.82

  (*D*) 8.75

3. (*a*) (*i*) 357.5758

    (*ii*) 537.7778

    (*iii*) 180.5556

    (*iv*) 883.3333

  (*b*) $-.102$

5. (*a*) .8925

  (*b*) .945

6. Derived Proportions, p'_{ij}

Chapter 6, Part 5

1. psu's	$\bar{n}$
1, 2	7.5
1, 3	10.0
1, 4	5.0
1, 5	7.5
2, 3	12.5
2, 4	7.5
2, 5	10.0
3, 4	10.0
3, 5	12.5
4, 5	7.5

	2	3	4	5	6	7	8	9	10
1	.15	.08	.03	.00	.00	.00	.00	.00	.00
2		.36	.20	.03	.03	.02	.00	.00	.00
3			.31	.07	.06	.04	.00	.00	.00
4				.16	.15	.11	.01	.00	.00
5					.49	.41	.12	.01	.00
6						.42	.12	.01	.00
7							.16	.02	.00
8								.16	.04
9									.21

Chapter 8

1. $\alpha = -.1000$

2. $\alpha = .4729$

3. $r_I = .9077$
    $r_{xx'} = .9746$
    $\rho_I = .8952$
    $\rho_{xx'} = .9699$

4. $r_I = .7740$

5. $r_I = .8327$

6. $\alpha = .9614$

7. $q = .0417$ $\quad \lambda = .84$
    $.1050$ $\quad\quad .60$
    indeterminate $\quad .20$

Chapter 9

1. 143.1562

2. 5,000

3. 18.2979
   10,000
   53.75

4. 766.5

5. 3.5789

6. $\sum X = 120,\ \overline{X} = 8,\ \sigma^2 = 18.6667$
   $\sum X = 165,\ \overline{X} = 15,\ \sigma^2 = 10$
   $\sum X = 3825,\ \overline{X} = 75,\ \sigma^2 = 216.6667$

16. | Number | Expected Frequencies |
    |---|---|
    | 0 | 223 |
    | 1 | 335 |
    | 2 | 251 |
    | 3 | 126 |
    | 4 | 47 |
    | 5 | 14 |
    | 6 | 3 |
    | 7 | 1 |

17. | Number | Expected Frequencies |
    |---|---|
    | 0 | 405 |
    | 1 | 206 |
    | 2 | 52 |
    | 3 | 9 |
    | 4 | 1 |
    | 5 | 0 |
    | 6 | 0 |
    | 7 | 0 |
    | 8 | 0 |
    | 9 | 0 |
    | 10 | 0 |
    | 11 | 0 |

Index of Names

Index of Topics